W9-AHR-745

8.00

FARM JOURNAL'S COUNTRY COOKBOOK

revised, enlarged edition

FARM JOURNAL'S COUNTRY COOKBOOK

revised, enlarged edition

Edited by NELL B. NICHOLS
Farm Journal Field Food Editor
Photography supervised by Al J. Reagan
Farm Journal Art Staff

DOUBLEDAY & COMPANY, INC.
GARDEN CITY, NEW YORK

Copyright © 1959, 1972 by Farm Journal, Inc.
All Rights Reserved
Printed in the United States of America
Revised Edition

preface

Country Cooking at Its Best

YOU HOLD IN YOUR HANDS the new revised edition of *Farm Journal's Country Cookbook,* published as FARM JOURNAL approaches its 100th year. We are grateful for the warm reception women have given the original cookbook, pleased that it is much used in many thousands of homes, delighted with the continuing demand. You might ask: Why revise a cookbook with so many staunch friends?

We think of this cookbook as our Silver Jubilee edition. The original, published in 1959, included the best from recipes printed in FARM JOURNAL since 1947–twelve years. For the new edition we carefully weighed once more the merits of all recipes in the book–keeping and eliminating (difficult choices, sometimes). We especially wanted to share with you some exceptionally fine new recipes, more than 850, we have collected and perfected during the thirteen years since our book first came out; some of the new recipes in this book have appeared in FARM JOURNAL, but not all. And since thirteen plus twelve equals twenty-five years–Silver Jubilee!

Some recipes were developed in our Countryside Test Kitchens–exciting new ideas, taste adventures. All recipes in the book, old and new, have been carefully adapted to today's ingredients and style of living.

You'll find cherished old-time specials, like homemade country butter. Though the churn has disappeared, we make it with the electric mixer. We tell how to fix old-fashioned apple butter–not in a big iron kettle over a wood fire in the yard, but in the heat-controlled oven of your kitchen range. Because renewed interest in baking yeast breads is sweeping the countryside, we added a variety of recipes for sandwiches which nowadays rate as "main dishes."

There is a marvelous collection of meat and potato recipes to keep the meat-and-potato men and boys happy. You'll notice a change from 3½-inch steaks for broiling to 2-inch steaks, more widely available today.

To cover what's new in the *Country Cookbook* is like asking: What's new in food in the past quarter-century?

First, there have been new developments in cooking. The meringue method of making cakes with lard, which evolved in our Countryside Test Kitchens, is one excellent example. Many of you told us this method makes the best lard cakes ever baked; we simply had to include four recipes for this delicate, tender cake.

We have found new ways to make use of the home freezer. So many requests came to our food editors for ways to freeze potatoes when the crop is at its peak, that our home economists made this a project. We discovered in our Test Kitchens how to handle cooked potatoes so you can freeze them successfully for up to two months (see Heat-and-Eat Potato Treats from Your Freezer). Our home economists also developed a gorgeous lemon meringue pie you bake and freeze (see Lemon Meringue Pie Supreme).

Changes in food products required further updating of ingredients. For example, in the original *Country Cookbook,* a few recipes call for "thick sour milk" and "thick sour cream"–foods rarely available naturally today, even in the country. Widely distributed buttermilk replaces sour milk in this new cookbook. And dairy sour cream, which contains less fat than the thick sour cream our grandmothers skimmed from crocks of whole milk, is specified in many of our recipes. Top milk has also disappeared from our ingredient lists–homogenized milk is so extensively used–but dairy half-and-half or light cream takes its place.

Appetizers and snacks have become more important. Many a country hostess now serves a beverage as first course in the living room–often tomato or fruit juice, cocktails or wine, with crisp chips or vegetables and dips or dunks. This affords informal visiting for her husband and guests; meanwhile, the hostess puts final touches on the company meal. Smart country cooks tell us this sidetracks well-meaning friends who want to "help," but who often delay dinner instead. So in this edition full chapters are devoted to recipes for appetizers and snacks, and beverages.

Country hospitality continues to flourish and good food is an important part of it. The coffee break–halfway point between the day's meals is a country custom; family and visitors meet for friendly exchange of ideas and news. This calls for something good with coffee, tea or milk.

And women still take pride in toting delicious homemade food to church, club and other community suppers.

More recipes from faraway lands, adapted in our Countryside Test Kitchens to available ingredients and to American tastes, are to be found in this new version. Renewed interest in our heritages will help preserve some of the cherished favorites our ancestors brought from distant homelands. Farm people, like other Americans, also travel abroad more than they did a decade ago. They entertain students and visitors from all over the world. This promotes a lively concern with international cooking.

A major change in this new edition is the organization of recipes to make the book easier, more convenient for you to use. We group different food classifications separately—cakes, pies, breads, salads, vegetables and soups, for example—in their own chapters, mindful of the many country women who say they dislike using an index any more than necessary.

The original *Country Cookbook* grouped recipes according to situations or occasions for which the food was intended. For those who want such guidance, we include near the end of the book (in front of the Index) some important situations and ideal recipes for the occasions. You can still quickly find just the right dish to serve a crowd, or a de luxe bread for the coffee break. Even if you are a fan of the original book, we think you will be happy with the organization of our revised edition. We present the chapters according to the order in which most women plan a meal.

So our Silver Jubilee Country Cookbook comes to you with fond hopes that you will find many, many recipes you'll want to try right away. Borrowing from the introduction to our original cookbook: "If you enjoy using the recipes in this cookbook, we'll be happy. And if your friends use them, too, we know that country cooking will continue to rate first in good eating."

NELL B. NICHOLS
Field Food Editor
FARM JOURNAL

contents

COLOR ILLUSTRATIONS

Color Photographs by: Ken Bronstein/Mel Richman, Inc., Robert E. Coates, Peter Dant Studio, Faraghan Studio, Bob Hayman, William Hazzard/Faraghan Studios, William Hazzard/Hazzard Studios, William Hazzard/Mel Richman, Inc., Hoedt Studios, Ted Hoffman/Chas. P. Mills & Son, George Lazarnick, Chas. P. Mills & Son, Al Reagan, Mel Richman Studios, Paul Wing.

FARM JOURNAL'S COUNTRY COOKBOOK

revised, enlarged edition

chapter 1

Meats, the Menu Focus

COUNTRY MEN believe that some of the world's best eating comes with this trio—meat, potatoes and gravy; so meats take the spotlight in country kitchens. When a woman plans a meal, she thinks first about what kind of meat to have. Then she builds the rest of the menu with foods that complement her selection. Many women, catering to their husbands' likes, think next about the potato dish to accompany the meat.

If the meal planner has company coming to dinner, she considers such glamorous platter specialties as Standing Rib Roast of beef with its natural juices, glistening Glazed Pork Roast or Honey-glazed Ham. Then she remembers how tasty Barbecued Lamb Shanks and Company Corned Beef are. If it's a family dinner, she may rely on such winners as Veal Stew with Dumplings, Pork/Sauerkraut Pinwheel, broiled ground beef, lamb and pork patties, or Western Meat Balls and Franks—always the boys' choice.

In country kitchens, the first step in cooking meats often is toward the freezer. Some women prefer to let meats thaw in their original wrap at room temperature, while others like to defrost them in the refrigerator, which takes longer but is the safer way. If you thaw meats at room temperature, be sure to cook or refrigerate them while they are very cold. Here is a timetable that indicates how long it takes to defrost meats.

TIMETABLE FOR DEFROSTING FROZEN MEAT

Meat	*In Refrigerator*	*Room Temperature*
Large Roast	4 to 7 hrs. per lb.	2 to 3 hrs. per lb.
Small Roast	3 to 5 hrs. per lb.	1 to 2 hrs. per lb.
1" Steak	12 to 14 hrs.	2 to 4 hrs.

Some women skip the defrosting and cook frozen meats. This lengthens the cooking time; it takes at least one third to one half more time for a frozen than a thawed roast. The additional time for cooking frozen steaks and chops varies with thickness of the cut, surface area and the temperature in broiling. When broiling still frozen thick steaks, lamb and pork chops, and ground beef, lamb and pork patties, place them a little farther from the heat than thawed meats to prevent overbrowning on the outside.

One secret to the marvelous meat dishes served in country homes, in addition to the quality of the meat (farmers are good judges of this), is the wise choice of temperature used in cooking. Country women know that meats are more tender, juicy, tasty, and more evenly cooked if they are not hurried too much–if they are not cooked at too high temperatures. Follow temperatures that we give in this chapter for success. Rich, brown gravy has something to do with the reputation country meats enjoy for their fine flavors. It does not accompany all meat dishes, but enough of them to earn fame.

Beef at Its Best

All choice country collections of meat recipes start with roast beef. In most farm kitchens salt and pepper are the only seasonings added, but garlic is coming up in popularity. Some good cooks slice an onion and, with toothpicks, pin it on the ends and over the top of the meat. They discard the onion when the roast is cooked, but it leaves a faint flavor in the meat and brown gravy.

STANDING RIB ROAST

Follow this recipe and you'll have a masterpiece–the classic beef roast

1 (3-rib) standing rib roast, about 8 lbs.

• Stand roast, fat side up, on a rack in a shallow pan. Add no water. Insert roast-meat thermometer into center of roast, making sure point rests on meat, not in or on fat, gristle or bone.

• Roast uncovered in a slow oven (300 to 325°) until thermometer registers the doneness you like (140° for rare, 160° for medium and 170° for well-done meat), about 23 to 25 minutes per pound for rare, 27 to 30 minutes for medium and 32 to 35 minutes for well-done. Time estimates are not accurate, but are a guide. It takes from 3½ to 5 hours for an 8-lb., 3-rib roast that measures 6″ from tip of rib to backbone. (A longer cut roasts in less time.)

• When the thermometer registers 5 to 10 degrees lower than the desired temperature you want, remove the roast from the oven. Place it on a large warm platter with the broader cut surface down. The cooking will continue to the right temperature while you handle the last-minute details before dinner. The meat "sets" and carves easier.

• To serve, place the roast in front of the carver with the ribs to his left and the rib ends pointing toward him.

• Slice as desired. For big, king-size servings, cut so each rib makes 1 serving and the meat between two ribs makes 2 servings, or 7 servings in all; or slice thinly for 16 average servings.

Note: You can sprinkle the roast with salt and pepper before cooking, but the seasonings do not penetrate the meat.

HOW TO MAKE GRAVY

Roasting meat at the correct low temperature, 300 to 325°, results in a roasting pan almost free of browned meat extractives—flavor so necessary for making good gravy.

Country women, with their meat-potato-and-gravy husbands, have found a way out: Brown the flour in some of the fat from the roast. Then for flavor add canned meat broth instead of water for the liquid. Canned beef broth goes into gravy made with roast beef or lamb, and chicken broth for veal and pork.

Here's how to do it. Remove roast to hot platter. Pour fat from roaster and add broth to pan. Let stand a few minutes and scrape loose any browned particles. Measure 4 tblsp. of the fat into heavy skillet. Add 4 tblsp. flour and cook, stirring, until quite brown. Add 2 c. broth and cook, stirring until thickened. Season with salt and pepper. Makes about 2 cups.

TENDER SIRLOIN TIP ROAST

Tasty served warm and good cold in big crusty rolls for sandwiches

1 (4 lb.) sirloin tip roast
Seasoned instant meat tenderizer

• Sprinkle the roast with tenderizer as the label directs. Then roast it in slow oven (300 to 325°) like Standing Rib Roast. It takes about 2¼ hours for a 4-lb. sirloin tip to roast rare, 2¾ hours for medium and 3¼ hours for well-done meat. If you use a roast-meat thermometer, the temperatures are 140° for rare, 160° for medium and 170° for well-done.

• Serve warm or cold. If you wish to serve the roast cold in sandwiches, cook it a day ahead, cool and chill without slicing.

• When ready to make sandwiches, slice the cold meat very thin and place it in large buttered crusty rolls. The thinner you slice it, the tenderer the meat seems. Makes enough for eight generously filled sandwiches.

COUNTRY-STYLE BEEF WELLINGTON

You roast the beef one day, add the crust and bake the next

1 (6 to 8 lb.) whole tenderloin of beef (fold rib end under sirloin), or 5 lb. center cut of filet, or 6 lb. rib eye roast
1 (4 oz.) can mushrooms, drained and finely chopped
½ c. finely chopped onion
2 tblsp. melted butter
1 (8 oz.) pkg. liverwurst
3 c. sifted flour
1 tsp. salt
3 tblsp. chopped parsley
1½ tsp. celery seeds
⅔ c. shortening
½ c. plus 2 tblsp. cold water
1 egg, slightly beaten

• Tie meat securely if you use a folded filet. Insert meat thermometer into center of meat; roast uncovered in slow oven (300 to 325°) until thermometer reaches 140° (rare). Cool, wrap and refrigerate.

• Next day, sauté mushrooms and onion in butter until onion is tender. Combine with liverwurst, and mix. Chill.

• To make crust, mix flour, salt, parsley and celery seeds. Cut in shortening until mixture is consistency of tiny peas. Sprinkle on cold water, 1 tblsp. at a time, tossing mixture lightly with a fork.

• Shape dough into a ball and roll out in a rectangle about ⅛″ thick, measuring 2″ wider than the length of the roast, 2″ longer than its circumference. Save pastry scraps.

• Remove strings from cold roast. Pat liverwurst mixture on roast, covering top and sides only.

• Place roast, coated side down, on pastry rectangle. Fold up pastry to meet along center top and ends. Trim off extra pastry, moisten edges and press together firmly to seal well.

• Place pastry-covered roast, sealed edges down (liverwurst-coated side is now up), in a greased shallow pan.

• Roll pastry scraps and cut out 3 flowers, 3 leaves and 3 stems. Brush pieces with beaten egg and seal to top of roast in an attractive design. Brush entire surface with beaten egg; prick with a fork.

• Bake in moderate oven (375°) 1 hour, or until crust is golden brown. Remove roast from pan; let stand 15 minutes before carving. Makes about 12 servings.

HOW TO BROIL BEEF STEAKS AND GROUND BEEF PATTIES

• Set oven regulator for broiling. Place steak or pattie on rack of pan 2 to 3″ from heat for ground beef patties and steaks ¾ to 1″ thick, 3 to 5″ for steaks 1 to 2″ thick. (The heat output of broilers varies; you may need to alter the distance from heat.)

• Broil until top side of meat is brown. (Meat should be about half or slightly more than half-done). Season the brown top side, if you like, and turn meat. If salt is added before meat is brown, it draws moisture to the surface and delays browning.

• Use the Timetable for Broiling Beef as a guide to the minutes required in broiling. You can use a meat thermometer designed especially for broiling; with thick steaks it can be left in the meat throughout cooking. Or test the doneness with a roast beef thermometer shortly before broiling time is up.

Cooking Beef in Moist Heat

Among the all-time country beef favorites are pot roasts, Swiss steaks, short ribs, stews, corned beef and other treats that cook slowly in water or other liquid. Some of these beef dishes require little liquid—pot roasts and Swiss steaks, for instance. Other less tender meats, such as those for stews and corned beef, need to cook in liquid to cover. This provides even, no-watch cooking since the meat does not have to be turned.

Country women have a few pet rules for cooking beef in moist heat. One is to brown the meat on all sides before adding the liquid (corned beef is the exception to this rule). This gives it attractive color and en-

TIMETABLE FOR BROILING BEEF

CUT	WEIGHT	APPROXIMATE TOTAL COOKING TIME	
		Rare	*Medium*
BEEF	*Pounds*	*Minutes*	*Minutes*
Chuck Steak			
1″			
(high quality)	1½ to 2½	24	30
1½″	2 to 4	40	45
Rib Steak–1″	1 to 1½	15	20
1½″	1½ to 2	25	30
2″	2 to 2½	35	45
Rib Eye Steak–1″	8 to 10 ozs.	15	20
1½″	12 to 14 ozs.	25	30
2″	16 to 20 ozs.	35	45
Club Steak–1″	1 to 1½	15	20
1½″	1½ to 2	25	30
2″	2 to 2½	35	45
Sirloin Steak–1″	1½ to 3	20	25
1½″	2¼ to 4	30	35
2″	3 to 5	40	45
Porterhouse Steak			
1″	1¼ to 2	20	25
1½″	2 to 3	30	35
2″	2½ to 3½	40	45
Filet Mignon			
1″	4 to 6 ozs.	15	20
1½″	6 to 8 ozs.	18	22
Ground Beef Patties			
1″ thick by 3″	4 ozs.	15	25

hances flavors. They simmer the beef gently (do not boil) in a tightly covered utensil. A snug-fitting lid retains the steam, which softens the connective tissue.

BASIC POT ROAST

Seasonings contribute marvelous flavor to the rich brown gravy

2 tblsp. flour
2 tsp. salt
¼ tsp. pepper
1 (3 to 4 lb.) chuck or rump pot roast, cut 2″ thick
2 tblsp. fat or salad oil
1 medium onion, sliced
3 peppercorns
1 small bay leaf
1 c. water

• Combine flour, salt and pepper; rub mixture into surface of meat.

• Heat fat in Dutch oven or electric skillet. Brown meat well on one side; add onion, peppercorns and bay leaf. Turn meat; brown other side.

• Place meat on flat, low rack. Add water; cover; cook slowly 2½ to 3 hours, or until tender. Add water as needed to keep ½ to 1″ in pan. Remove meat to hot platter, discard bay leaf and make gravy. Makes 6 to 8 servings.

BASIC POT ROAST GRAVY: Skim most of fat from stock in Dutch oven or electric skillet. Add enough cold water to stock to make 1½ cups. Mix ¼ c. flour with ½ c. cold water to make a smooth paste. Remove Dutch oven from heat (turn off electricity in skillet). Slowly add flour mixture to stock. Return to heat (or turn on electricity) and cook, stirring constantly, until surface of gravy is covered with bubbles. Add bottled browning sauce if desired. Check salt. Cook and stir about 5 minutes longer.

CALIFORNIA POT ROAST

Browned beef simmers until tender in well-seasoned tomato sauce

- **1 (4 to 5 lb.) chuck or rump pot roast**
- **3 tblsp. fat or salad oil**
- **2 tsp. salt**
- **¼ tsp. pepper**
- **½ c. water**
- **1 (8 oz.) can tomato sauce**
- **3 medium onions, thinly sliced**
- **2 cloves garlic, minced**
- **2 tblsp. brown sugar**
- **½ tsp. dry mustard**
- **¼ c. lemon juice**
- **¼ c. vinegar**
- **¼ c. ketchup**
- **1 tblsp. Worcestershire sauce**
- **6 tblsp. flour**
- **½ c. water**

• Brown roast well on both sides in fat in heavy pan or Dutch oven. Add salt, pepper, ½ c. water, tomato sauce, onions and garlic. Cover tightly and simmer over low heat about 1½ hours.

• Combine brown sugar, mustard, lemon juice, vinegar, ketchup and Worcestershire sauce and pour over meat. Cover and continue cooking until meat is fork tender, about 1½ hours.

• Remove meat to warm platter; make gravy. Skim off most of the fat; measure the broth. Add enough water to make 3 c. Pour in cooking pan or Dutch oven. Mix flour with ½ c. water to make a smooth paste; stir into broth. Return to heat and cook over low heat, stirring constantly, until gravy bubbles all over. Check seasonings by tasting, adding more salt if needed. Cook and stir about 5 minutes longer. Makes about 3 cups.

• Serve roast cut in thin slices with the gravy, or shred the meat and mix it with the gravy to serve on halves of warm buns. Makes 8 to 10 servings.

SAVORY POT ROAST

Raisins are the big surprise in this garlic-seasoned pot roast

- **2 onions, sliced**
- **1 clove garlic, minced**
- **2 tblsp. fat**
- **1 (4 lb.) chuck or rump pot roast**
- **1 tblsp. salt**
- **¼ tsp. pepper**
- **2 large bay leaves**
- **½ c. raisins**
- **1 c. water**

• Brown onions and garlic lightly in hot fat in heavy skillet or Dutch oven. Remove onions and garlic.

• Add meat; brown slowly on all sides, about 20 minutes. Add remaining ingredients, including onions and garlic; cover tightly, and simmer slowly until tender, about 3 hours.

• Remove meat to warm platter. Discard bay leaves. Make gravy if desired. Makes 6 to 8 servings.

Note: For variety in pot roast seasonings, you can mix 1 tblsp. curry powder and 1 tsp. sugar with ½ c. water. Stir into broth around pot roast. Or, about ¾ hour before pot roast is done, add 2 medium onions, sliced, 1¼ c. chili sauce and ½ c. chopped dill pickles to broth. Don't thicken broth for gravy–skim off fat.

Carve-ahead Pot Roast

When you're having company, it's a big help to have the pot roast cooked, carved and ready to heat quickly before guests arrive. Our Braised Beef in Cream is such a roast–truly delicious! You can use light instead of heavy cream if you like a less rich sauce.

BRAISED BEEF IN CREAM

Use plenty of garlic to support beef flavor–two big cloves are just right

1 (4 lb.) boneless pot roast (sirloin tip, bottom round, rump or chuck)
2 tblsp. shortening (about)
Salt
Pepper
½ c. water
½ c. butter
2 c. heavy cream
2 large cloves garlic
¼ c. lemon juice
1½ tsp. salt (about)
¾ tsp. pepper (about)
Watercress or parsley (finely chopped and sprigs)

In Dutch oven or heavy casserole with cover, slowly brown meat on all sides in hot shortening. Season generously with salt and pepper. Add water; cover and simmer 2½ to 3 hours, or until meat is tender. Remove from kettle; allow to stand 20 minutes, then slice thinly.

• Pour off pan juices and save for another use. Heat butter in kettle until it bubbles and browns. Add cream, garlic, lemon juice, about 1½ tsp. salt and ¾ tsp. pepper. Cook over medium heat, stirring, about 3 minutes, or until sauce reduces slightly.

• Spoon half the sauce over bottom of a shallow heat-proof serving platter. Arrange meat slices, slightly overlapping, in sauce. Pour remaining sauce over top. Near serving time, bake in moderate oven (350°) 10 minutes, or until heated through. Spoon sauce over meat; sprinkle generously with watercress; garnish with watercress sprigs. Makes about 8 servings.

SWISS STEAK

Spicy chili sauce substitutes for tomatoes ordinarily used

6 tblsp. flour
2 tsp. salt
¼ tsp. pepper
2 lbs. round steak, cut 1" thick
4 medium onions
6 tblsp. shortening
½ c. chopped celery
1 clove garlic, minced
¾ c. chili sauce
¾ c. water
1 green pepper (optional)

• Combine flour, salt and pepper; rub into both sides of steak, or pound in with meat mallet or edge of heavy plate. Cut into 6 portions.

• Peel and slice onions. Preheat skillet; add half of shortening, then onions; brown lightly. Remove from skillet.

· Add remaining shortening. Brown steak on both sides. Reduce heat.

· Add celery, garlic, chili sauce and water. Cover; simmer 1 hour.

· Cut green pepper into slices. Add pepper and onions to meat. Continue cooking 30 minutes or until meat is tender. Makes 6 servings.

STEAK WITH TOMATO SAUCE

Good-tasting, easy-to-fix favorite

2 lbs. bottom round, chuck or rump steak, cut 1 to 1½″ thick
1½ tsp. salt
⅓ c. flour
¼ c. fat or salad oil
1 large onion, sliced
1 (8 oz.) can tomato sauce
½ c. water
1 (4 oz.) can mushrooms (stems and pieces)

· Cut meat in half or in serving-size pieces. Season with salt; rub with part of flour. Pound remaining flour into meat with meat mallet or edge of heavy plate. Continue to turn, flour and pound until all flour is used.

· Heat fat in heavy skillet; add meat; brown well on both sides. Add onion during browning.

· Pour tomato sauce, water and mushrooms over meat. Cover; bake in moderate oven (350°) 2 to 3 hours, or until tender. Makes 6 servings.

BROWN STEW

Take time to brown meat slowly for that gives stew extra-fine flavor

3 tblsp. fat
1 clove garlic, cut in half
2 lbs. beef chuck, cut in 1½″ cubes
2 tsp. salt
¼ tsp. pepper
1 tsp. Worcestershire sauce
1 tsp. lemon juice
1 small bay leaf
4 c. hot water
3 medium potatoes, peeled and cut in halves
4 carrots, peeled and cut in thirds
1 c. celery, cut in 1″ pieces
1 c. cooked lima beans
1 c. cooked peas
¼ c. flour
½ c. water

· Heat fat in Dutch oven, deep stew pan or large fryer. Add garlic and meat. Brown meat on all sides in hot fat.

· Add salt, pepper, Worcestershire sauce, lemon juice, bay leaf and 2 c. water. Cover. Simmer 2 hours; stir occasionally.

· Remove bay leaf. Add 2 c. water, potatoes, carrots and celery. Continue cooking 30 minutes or until vegetables are tender. Add beans and peas.

· Blend together until smooth ¼ c. flour and ½ c. water. Stir into liquid to thicken. Makes 8 servings.

CIDER STEW

Unusual in that meat cooks in cider instead of water—extra good

3 large onions, sliced
3 tblsp. drippings
2 lbs. beef (neck or shank), cut in chunks
3 tblsp. flour
2 tsp. salt
¼ tsp. pepper
¼ tsp. thyme leaves
1 c. apple cider
1 tblsp. ketchup
3 large potatoes, peeled
4 medium carrots, peeled

• Brown onions in hot drippings; push aside and brown meat.
• Combine flour, salt, pepper and thyme; add gradually to meat. Stir in cider and ketchup.
• Cover and cook slowly until meat is almost tender, about 2 hours.
• Cut potatoes and carrots into quarters; add to meat; simmer 30 minutes longer.
• Remove meat and vegetables to platter, and thicken drippings for gravy. Makes 6 servings.

BEEF AND RIGATONI STEW

Large macaroni and prunes help make this attractive company fare

1 c. dried prunes
¼ c. flour
1 tsp. salt
1½ lbs. lean chuck beef, cut in 1½″ cubes
2 tblsp. salad oil
1 medium onion, coarsely chopped
1 clove garlic, minced
2 tsp. salt
¼ tsp. pepper
½ tsp. orégano leaves
4 drops Tabasco sauce
1 (8 oz.) can tomato sauce
Hot water
½ (1 lb.) pkg. rigatoni, or other large macaroni

• To make pitting easier, stew prunes 5 minutes in 2 c. water. Drain and cool, then pit and set aside. (The pitted prunes now available do not require precooking.)
• In a plastic bag containing flour and 1 tsp. salt, shake beef cubes, a few at a time, until they are well coated.
• Brown beef in hot oil in deep 4-qt. Dutch oven. Add onion, garlic, 2 tsp. salt, pepper, orégano and Tabasco sauce.
• Add tomato sauce and enough hot water to keep liquid 1″ above meat (about 3 c.). Stir well.
• Cover tightly and bake in slow oven (300°) 2 hours.
• Add rigatoni and prunes. Add enough hot water to cover (about 2 c.). Bake 1 hour longer. Makes 6 servings.

SHORT RIBS

For rich flavor, brown ribs slowly and deeply before adding water

4 lbs. short ribs (2 × 2 × 4″ pieces)
1 tblsp. salt
¼ tsp. pepper
1 small bay leaf
4 c. water
6 carrots, peeled and cut in 1½″ pieces
2 c. small onions, peeled

• Brown meat on all sides in own fat; pour off excess. Add salt, pepper and bay leaf; cover with water. Simmer, covered, until tender, about 1½ to 2½ hours.
• Add carrots and onions the last 20 minutes. Remove ribs and vegetables to warm platter. Discard bay leaf.
• Measure broth; for every 2 cups, stir in 2 tblsp. flour mixed to a smooth paste with ¼ c. cold water. Cook, stirring, until thick. Serve separately in bowl or pour over meat and vegetables. Makes 6 to 8 servings.

Note: You can make Parsley Dumplings (see Index) and serve them with the Short Ribs.

BARBECUED SHORT RIBS

Subtle blending of seasonings does big things for ribs—favorite with ranchers

3 lbs. short ribs
1 c. tomato sauce, purée or ketchup

1 c. water
¼ c. vinegar
1 tblsp. sugar
1 tblsp. prepared horse-radish
1 tblsp. prepared mustard
1 tsp. salt
¼ tsp. pepper
2 onions, finely chopped
2 tblsp. chopped parsley

• Wipe meat with damp cloth; place in deep bowl.
• Combine remaining ingredients; pour over short ribs. Let stand in refrigerator 4 hours (overnight, for best flavor).
• Place in Dutch oven or shallow baking pan. Cover (use foil if pan is coverless) and cook until tender, about 2½ hours. Add more water as needed.
• Put meat in serving dish. Skim excess fat off sauce; then spoon sauce over ribs. Makes 6 servings.

Variation

DUTCH OVEN DINNER: An hour before end of cooking time, peel 12 medium-size whole onions and put alongside meat. Cut circle of aluminum foil, using lid for pattern, and fit into pan on top of meat. Put 6 scrubbed, medium potatoes on top of foil (out of barbecue sauce). Cover and continue cooking. Meat, onions and potatoes should be cooked in 1 hour. Makes 6 servings.

ROLLED STUFFED FLANK STEAK

Gives the family a happy surprise

1 (1½ to 2 lb.) flank steak
1 tsp. salt
⅛ tsp. pepper
1 tblsp. prepared mustard
1½ c. day-old bread, cut in ½″ cubes
1 tsp. poultry seasoning
1 medium onion, chopped
½ c. chopped celery
¼ c. melted shortening or salad oil
2 tblsp. flour
Fat for browning
1 c. water or beef broth

• Have steak scored (or do it yourself by crisscrossing shallow diamond-shaped cuts on both sides of meat to tenderize).
• Sprinkle both sides with salt and pepper; spread mustard over top.
• Toss bread, poultry seasoning, onion and celery with shortening.
• Spoon mixture evenly over top of steak. Roll up, beginning with narrow end; fasten with skewers, and lace with string, if necessary. Sprinkle with flour.
• Brown well on all sides in hot fat in Dutch oven over medium heat.
• Add water. Cover tightly; cook over low heat 1½ hours, or until tender. Or cover and bake in moderate oven (350°) 2 hours. Remove meat; make gravy. Makes 6 to 8 servings.

LEMON-BAKED BEEFSTEAK

Tantalizing aroma as chuck steak cooks steps up appetite appeal

3 lbs. chuck steak
2 tblsp. softened butter or regular margarine
2 tsp. salt
¼ tsp. pepper
1 large lemon, sliced
2 medium onions, sliced
1 c. ketchup
1 tblsp. Worcestershire sauce
¼ c. water

• Wipe steak with damp cloth; place in large baking dish. Rub with softened butter. Season with salt and pepper; cover with lemon and onion slices.

• Combine ketchup, Worcestershire sauce and water, and pour over steak. Cover tightly so meat will steam tender. (Aluminum foil makes a snug-fitting lid.) Bake in moderate oven (350°) 2 hours, or until tender. Makes 6 servings.

Variation

HERBED LEMON-BAKED STEAK: Combine equal amounts fresh minced chives, parsley and thyme. Sprinkle on steak.

SMOKY BEEF ROLLETTES

Much of seasoning comes from smoked sausage rolled in the beef

2 lbs. round steak, cut ½" thick
1 tsp. salt
¼ tsp. pepper
¾ c. finely chopped celery
6 smoked sausage links
¼ c. butter or regular margarine
1½ c. hot water
1 beef bouillon cube
3 c. carrots, split lengthwise and cut in 3 pieces
1 tblsp. cornstarch
¼ c. cold water
1 (1 lb.) can small whole boiled onions, drained
Salt
Pepper

• Cut steak into 6 equal pieces. Pound pieces to ¼" thickness with a mallet. Sprinkle each piece evenly with the 1 tsp. salt, ¼ tsp. pepper and chopped celery. Roll a sausage link into each one and secure roll with toothpicks or string.

• Brown rolls well in butter in a large skillet. Stir in hot water and bouillon cube. Reduce heat; cover and simmer 30 minutes. (If meal must wait, turn heat low; add carrots later and complete the cooking.)

• Add carrots; cover and simmer 20 minutes or until carrots are tender. Remove toothpicks or string.

• Stir cornstarch into cold water. Blend into meat juices; cook until thickened. Add onions and heat through. Salt and pepper to taste. Makes 6 servings.

COMPANY CORNED BEEF

Beef cooks in water, then bakes in a peppy sauce–serve warm or cold

4 to 5 lbs. corned beef
2 bay leaves
5 peppercorns
2 sprigs parsley
1 branch celery, cut in chunks
1 small onion, sliced
Whole cloves
2 tblsp. butter or regular margarine
1 tblsp. prepared mustard
⅓ c. brown sugar, firmly packed
⅓ c. ketchup
3 tblsp. vinegar
3 tblsp. water

• Wash corned beef thoroughly to remove brine. Place in a large kettle and cover with cold water. Add bay leaves, peppercorns, parsley, celery and onion. Cover and simmer 3 to 3¾ hours (about 45 minutes to a pound), or until tender.

• Remove hot beef to shallow baking dish. Insert whole cloves in it to decorate and season.

• Melt butter; add remaining ingredients and mix thoroughly. Cook over medium heat until ingredients are well blended.

• Pour sauce over corned beef and bake in moderate oven (350°) 30 minutes, basting with the sauce several times. Makes 8 to 10 servings.

CORNED BEEF CASSEROLE

Quick supper main dish for a busy day. Good served with coleslaw

¼ c. butter or regular margarine
¼ c. flour
2½ c. milk
2 tsp. salt
⅛ tsp. pepper
1 tblsp. prepared horse-radish
1 tsp. prepared mustard
1 (8 oz.) pkg. noodles, cooked
1 (12 oz.) can corned beef
1 (16 oz.) can peas, drained
1 tblsp. chopped pimiento

· Melt butter; add flour and stir until smooth. Gradually add milk and cook until thickened, stirring constantly. Add seasonings.

· Add half of sauce to drained noodles. Line bottom and sides of greased 2-qt. casserole with noodle mixture.

· To remaining sauce add cubed corned beef and peas. Fill center of casserole; sprinkle with chopped pimiento.

· Bake in moderate oven (350°) 20 minutes. Makes 6 to 8 servings.

CORNED BEEF PIE: Pat 1 (12 oz.) can corned beef hash into pie pan. Bake in moderate oven (350°) about 20 minutes. Loosen edges of hash, cut into 4 pie-shaped pieces. Serve topped with creamed peas. Makes 4 servings.

Old-fashioned Home-cured Corned Beef

Few farmers butcher meat at home in this freezer and locker era, but what country woman doesn't like once-in-a-blue-moon to cure and cook small quantities of old-time favorites? This recipe for home-cured corned beef is a classic example of a family treasure brought out occasionally. It's beef any hostess can be proud to serve. And what table talk it stimulates.

HOME-CURED CORNED BEEF

It makes superb sandwiches

1½ c. salt
1 c. sugar
¾ tsp. saltpeter
1 (8 to 10 lb.) beef brisket

· Mix together salt, sugar and saltpeter. Cut meat in 5″ chunks. Work on heavy brown paper; rub each piece of meat thoroughly with salt mixture.

· Pack meat tightly into 2-gal. crock or enamel pan. Spread remaining salt mixture over top of meat. Cover with plate that fits tightly and weight it down. (Tight packing and salt bring juices from meat, making a curing solution. Sugar improves flavor; saltpeter gives meat a reddish color.)

· Shift top pieces to bottom after 7 days. Keep crock in refrigerator or other cool place at least 24 days before using. Then use meat within 3 weeks, washing well in cold water before cooking. Leave unused meat in cure (dilute with half its volume of boiling water).

CORNED BEEF WITH CABBAGE

Please pass horse-radish and mustard

5 lbs. corned beef
Cold water
½ clove garlic
2 peppercorns

3 carrots, peeled and quartered
3 onions, peeled
1 head cabbage, cut in wedges

• Wash brine from corned beef, using 3 or 4 waters. Cover with cold water; add garlic and peppercorns. Simmer until meat is tender (1½ hours for young beef; up to 5 hours for older beef).
• Add carrots and onions for last hour of cooking, cabbage the last 20 minutes. Serve corned beef on platter, with vegetables around it. Makes 6 to 8 servings.

Beef Dishes–Quick

Country women take advantage of a leisurely day (frequently a stormy one when they must be indoors) to cook large quantities of such things as beef, or tomato sauce, or a big turkey for freezing. Later they use these foods as the basis for many tempting dishes that have no earmarks of leftovers. We give you a recipe for freezing beef cubes, then five quick recipes using the frozen cubes.

TENDER BROWN BEEF CUBES

4 tblsp. shortening
10 to 12 lbs. beef (cut as for stew)
Salt
Pepper

• Heat shortening in 2 heavy skillets; brown beef on all sides in hot fat.
• Place beef in large heavy kettle; add seasonings and water to the depth of 1″.
• Cover; simmer until just tender, 1 to 2 hours. Cool; package meat in 1 quart, 4 pint and 4 half-pint containers (to fit recipes). Package broth separately. Freeze. Makes 4 to 5 quarts.

QUICK STEW

Make this with frozen beef cubes

2 (10 oz.) pkgs. frozen mixed vegetables
2 c. beef broth
5 tblsp. flour
3 c. frozen Tender Brown Beef Cubes
Salt
Pepper
1 (7 oz.) pkg. instant mashed potatoes

• Cook vegetables as directed on package; drain.
• Heat 1½ c. broth; add flour blended with remaining ½ c. broth to make smooth paste. Heat, stirring frequently, until smooth and thickened.
• Add beef, vegetables, salt and pepper to taste; simmer about 20 minutes.
• While stew simmers, prepare instant mashed potatoes by package directions. Serve stew piping hot with potatoes around edge. Makes 6 servings.

Note: Omit potatoes and serve stew over quick-cooking rice, or top hot stew with packaged refrigerator biscuits; bake in hot oven (425°) 20 minutes.

HEARTY SHORTCAKE

A platter treat–hot biscuits and beef

3 c. frozen Tender Brown Beef Cubes
1 (10 oz.) pkg. frozen peas, cooked and drained

3 hard-cooked eggs, diced
1 onion, chopped
1 tblsp. prepared mustard
2 cans condensed cream of mushroom soup
½ c. beef broth or liquid drained from peas
3 c. all-purpose buttermilk biscuit mix

• Combine all ingredients except biscuit mix. Heat thoroughly, about 20 minutes.
• Make biscuits by package directions (may add ¾ c. shredded cheese).
• Split hot biscuits in halves; top with beef mixture. Makes 6 servings of 2 (3″) biscuits each.

DINNER BEEF PIE

Serve this plump meat pie oven hot

Pastry for 2-crust pie
2 tblsp. shortening
1½ c. chopped celery
1½ c. chopped onion
1½ c. chopped green pepper
3 c. frozen Tender Brown Beef Cubes
1 can condensed tomato soup
2 tblsp. prepared mustard
¼ c. ketchup
¾ tsp. salt

• Heat shortening in skillet; add celery, onion and green pepper; sauté until soft. Stir in beef, soup and seasonings.
• Place meat mixture in pastry-lined 9″ pie pan. Adjust top crust; flute edges and cut vents. Bake in hot oven (425°) 40 to 50 minutes. Makes 6 servings.

Note: Green pepper may be omitted; then use 2¼ c. each celery and onion.

BEEF WITH SOUR CREAM

Quick, unusual and tasty

2 tblsp. shortening
2 medium onions, thinly sliced
½ c. beef broth or water
3 c. frozen Tender Brown Beef Cubes
3 tblsp. shredded sharp cheese
½ tsp. salt
⅛ tsp. pepper
½ c. dairy sour cream

• Melt shortening in skillet. Add onions; sauté until soft and clear. Add broth, beef, cheese and seasonings. Cover, simmer gently to heat.
• Just before serving blend in sour cream. Makes 6 servings.

GOULASH WITH NOODLES

An eye-catcher—spicy red sauce trickles through buttery noodles

¾ block frozen Home-cooked Tomato Sauce (see Index)
3 onions, cut fine or minced
¾ tsp. salt
¼ tsp. pepper
4 c. Tender Brown Beef Cubes
1 (8 oz.) pkg. egg noodles
2 tblsp. butter or regular margarine
1 tblsp. caraway or poppy seeds

• Heat tomato sauce (3 c.) with onions and seasonings over medium heat to boiling. Stir in beef; simmer to heat.
• Cook noodles by package directions; drain. Toss with butter and seeds.
• Spread noodles on hot platter; pour meat mixture over them, leaving border of noodles. Serve hot. Makes 6 servings.

Note: Omit frozen Home-cooked Tomato Sauce and use 3 (8 oz.) cans tomato sauce.

Big Community Barbecues

Barbecues are a man's best chance to shine as a chef. Complete directions follow for serving a hungry crowd in this traditional western way, with pit-style cooking.

First dig your pit. Dig it deep, the size depending on the amount of meat you plan to barbecue. Here are some helpful figures: Make the pit 3½′ deep and 3′ wide for the large crowds; same depth, 1½′ wide by 3′ long for small groups. You can cook as little as 10 pounds of beef in it, enough for about 25 people. A trench, same depth, 3′ wide and 10′ long, will handle about 400 pounds of meat. For a general rule, allow about 3′ of length for each 100 pounds. For more than 800 pounds of meat, it's better to dig a second trench.

Clay in the soil helps hold the sides of a temporary pit. For a permanent one, wall up the sides with fire brick or concrete blocks; fit with sheet-metal cover.

Use dry, hard wood to make a 15 to 18″ bed of coals. Green wood takes longer to burn. Soft wood won't hold long enough. Hard wood about 4″ across will burn down to coals in 3 to 4 hours.

Throw out any half-burned chunks, and keep just the coals. Have plenty of wood on hand at the start—at least 1½ tons for a 10′ pit.

An iron rod with a hook on the end is handy for fire tending.

You'll need dry sand. If it's wet, you'll have too much smoke and no fire. So, while making coals, put the sand on a piece of sheet iron over part of the pit and dry it.

Beef is most often barbecued, but you can cook pork, lamb and chickens equally well this way. Allow a half-pound of best-quality, properly-aged boneless beef for one generous serving.

Bone the meat first—it takes less room in the pit and is easier to carve and serve. Tie the boned cuts into uniform rolls of not less than 4″ nor more than 8″ across. You may place pieces of fat in each roll to give extra flavor and juiciness. Season with salt and pepper, then wrap in cheesecloth, muslin or a double layer of stockinet. Cover with clean burlap. The forequarter has just the right amount of fat with lean to make it juicy. Divide the shoulder or chuck into an inside and outside roll, cut along the shoulder blade and arm bone. Bone and roll the rib and plate (navel end).

The hindquarter breaks down into excellent boned cuts. Divide the loin into the sirloin end and the short loin. In boning the sirloin end, cut it into two pieces and roll. Strip the tenderloin out of the short loin and roll with the boned short loin. Divide with round into the inside, outside and sirloin tip. Cut the inside and outside pieces into two rolls each. Bone the rump and trim off some of the excess fat.

Place the meat in the pit 10 to 12 hours before time to serve. For a noon meal, you'd start the fire after supper the previous evening. Allow 3 to 4 hours for it to burn down to coals. Level coals with a rake, and cover all with a 1 to 1½″ layer of the dry sand.

Working quickly, place the bundles of meat on the sand, leaving a little space between the bundles. Cover the pit at once with sheet iron or tight-fitting boards resting on pipe, steel posts or rods.

Throw 10 to 12″ of dirt on the cover to prevent loss of heat. If steam leaks develop, plug them with mud.

If there's danger of rain, put a temporary cover of some kind over the pit, and dig a trench around it for drainage. Now you can go off and sleep, if you want to—there's nothing more to do! The meat will be done in about 12 hours, but you can't overcook it, for the coals will die down after a time anyhow.

When ready to serve, uncover the pit and remove the meat bundles with a clean pitchfork. Take off the coverings. Have one man ready to slice the meat as fast as two can serve it. Work fast.

Your barbecue sauce should be hot and ready to pour over the sliced hot meat just before it is served.

A standby menu is served in this order from long tables: two barbecued sandwiches (meat on buns) for each person, potato chips, relishes, lettuce or cabbage salad, ice cream and cake. Serve coffee, sugar and cream at a separate table, and use paper plates, cups, spoons and forks.

Whether you serve 25 or 500, you'll need an orderly system to keep the lines moving fast so that everybody is served hot meat. Place your foods, buffet style, on long tables. Station your helpers at each food along the tables, to fill plates completely before they're handed to the guests. With four long tables and additional ones for slicing meat and reserve food, plus two meat slicers, you can serve 600 people in 28 minutes at such a barbecue!

BARBECUE SAUCE FOR A CROWD

Ingredients	For 25	For 100
Ketchup	2 c.	6 (14 oz.) bottles
Worcestershire sauce	½ c.	3 (5 oz.) bottles
Prepared mustard	¼ c.	1 (6 or 7 oz.) jar
Prepared barbecue sauce	½ c.	3 (7 oz.) bottles

- Combine all ingredients and mix well.
- Barbecue sauce should be hot and ready to pour over sliced hot meat just before serving.
- You can add other ingredients to the sauce to suit your taste—horse-radish, brown sugar, red pepper, salt or an oil.
- Lemon juice or vinegar will clean out bottles or measuring cups, and dilute the sauce to desired thickness.

Popular Ground Beef Specialties

Look in country-home freezers and you'll see neat packages of ground beef. This meat is a staple in today's meals, starting with hamburgers. Meat loaves and meat balls, casseroles and other baked dishes please people of all ages, but youngsters especially. Our recipes make unusual, interesting dishes that have won approval. Be sure to see the timetable for broiling beef when you want to broil ground beef patties.

JUMBO HAMBURGERS

Double-thick and doubly good cheese-stuffed burgers to grill

2 lbs. ground beef
Ketchup
Salt
Pepper
1 onion, thinly sliced
Hickory smoke flavored cheese
Butter or regular margarine
5 hamburger buns

• Divide beef into 10 equal portions, with ⅓ c. measure (if beef is lean, have 4 oz. suet ground with it). Place between sheets of waxed paper and flatten to form patties ½" thick, 4" across.

• Spread 5 patties with ketchup leaving ½" around edge for sealing. Season with salt and pepper and top each patty with onion slice and slice of cheese. Top with other beef patties and seal edges well. (This is important to prevent leaking.)

• Spread both sides of patties lightly with soft butter or margarine or grease the grill. Season top of hamburgers with salt and pepper, place on grill over embers and broil about 10 minutes; turn and broil 10 minutes longer, or until beef is cooked the way you prefer. (Or broil in broiling oven.) Slip hamburgers into split and toasted buns. Makes 5 servings.

Note: You can substitute prepared mustard for ketchup, pickle relish for onion. Or substitute ½" cubes sharp process American cheese for hickory smoke flavored cheese.

BARBECUED HAMBURGERS

These spicy sandwiches are great favorites with men at country sales

3 tblsp. shortening
3 lbs. ground beef
3 large onions, finely chopped
1 clove garlic, minced
1 tblsp. salt
1½ tsp. black pepper
½ tsp. ground red pepper
2 tsp. chili powder
2 tsp. Worcestershire sauce
¼ c. flour
1¼ c. canned tomatoes
¾ c. ketchup

• Melt shortening in heavy skillet. Combine ground beef, onions and garlic. Cook in skillet until lightly browned.

• Add seasonings. Stir in flour. Add tomatoes and ketchup, mixing well.

• Simmer 15 to 20 minutes until thickened. Spoon between split buns to make hot sandwiches. Makes 20 servings.

MIXY-BURGERS

You spoon seasoned meat mixture over hot buns—quick, easy and good

1 tblsp. shortening
½ c. chopped onion
¼ c. chopped green pepper
¼ c. chopped celery
1 lb. ground beef
¼ c. Cheddar cheese, diced
1 (8 oz.) can tomato sauce
1 tblsp. vinegar
1 tblsp. sugar
1½ tsp. Worcestershire sauce
⅛ tsp. pepper
1 tsp. salt
4 or 5 toasted hamburger buns, split in halves

· Melt shortening in top of chafing dish or heavy skillet directly over heat. Add onion, green pepper and celery; cook until lightly browned. Add beef; stir with fork or spoon while meat browns.
· Add remaining ingredients, except buns. Simmer 10 minutes, stirring occasionally. To serve, spoon onto warm buns. Eat with fork. Makes 8 to 10 servings.

EASY-BURGERS

Egg and milk help hold the meat together in these drop-patties

2 eggs
1 tsp. salt
1/8 tsp. pepper
1 tblsp. flour
1 tblsp. finely chopped onion
1 lb. ground beef
1/4 c. milk or cream
2 tblsp. fat

· Beat together eggs, seasonings and flour until smooth. Stir in onion, beef and milk; mix well.
· Drop 12 spoonfuls into hot fat in skillet; flatten to make small patties.
· Cook 2 to 3 minutes; turn and cook on other side. Serve between slices of buttered bread or in toasted buns. Makes about 12 thin patties.

CHEESE-STUFFED HAMBURGERS

Cheese hides between beef circles and glorifies the hamburgers

2 lbs. ground beef
1 tsp. salt
1/8 tsp. pepper
6 slices Cheddar or blue cheese

· Shape ground beef into roll, about 3" in diameter. Seal in plastic wrap; put in freezer.
· Cut roll of beef into 12 slices, 1/2" thick. Sprinkle with salt and pepper; lay slices of cheese on half of them. Top with remaining slices of beef, pinching sides together.
· Pan-fry or broil, about 10 minutes per side. Makes 6 servings.

BETTER BURGERS

Try this new version of spoon-on burgers—sauce adds zest

1 lb. ground beef
1 tblsp. fat
1/2 tsp. salt
1 c. Basic Red Sauce (see Index)

· Brown beef in hot fat. Add salt and sauce; cover and simmer 10 minutes. Serve on hamburger buns, split and toasted. Makes 4 to 6 servings.

BEEF LOAF

Seasonings are unusual. Scalloped potatoes are a perfect escort

2 lbs. ground beef
1 medium onion, sliced
2 eggs
1 1/2 tsp. dry mustard
1 tsp. chili powder
1 1/2 c. stewed tomatoes
2 slices bread, broken into pieces
2 tsp. salt
1/4 tsp. pepper
4 strips bacon

· Combine all ingredients, except bacon. Pack into 8 1/2 × 4 1/2 × 2 1/2" loaf pan. Place bacon strips across top. Bake in moderate oven (350°) 1 hour. Makes 8 to 10 servings.

SAVORY MEAT LOAF

Serve with buttered carrots and small whole potatoes, browned

1 c. milk
1 tsp. savory leaves
½ tsp. thyme leaves
2 tblsp. minced parsley
3 c. soft bread cubes
1 tblsp. prepared mustard
2¼ tsp. salt
2 eggs
2 lbs. ground beef

· Combine all ingredients, except meat.
· Add meat and mix well; shape into loaf in shallow pan, or pack into 8½ × 4½ × 2½″ loaf pan.
· Bake in moderate oven (350°) 1 hour. Makes 6 to 8 servings.

Variations

CHEESE MEAT LOAF: Place layer of meat loaf made from 2 lbs. meat mixture in loaf pan, gently press down and place 2 slices process cheese on top. Repeat until ½ lb. cheese is used. Have cheese slices on top. Bake as usual.

MEAT LOAF RING: Spread ½ c. ketchup in 6-c. ring mold. Turn meat mixture into mold and bake.

QUICK MEAT LOAF: Shape meat loaf mixture in 6 or 8 oval-shaped mounds; place in greased baking pan. Bake–cuts cooking time in half.

STUFFED MEAT LOAF

Keep loaves in freezer ready to bake. They'll come in handy

1 lb. lean ground beef
1 lb. ground pork
1 c. dry bread crumbs
½ c. grated carrot
¼ c. finely chopped onion
2 eggs, beaten
½ c. milk
2 tsp. salt
1 tsp. Worcestershire sauce
⅛ tsp. pepper
1 (4 oz.) can mushrooms, drained and chopped
1 tblsp. finely chopped onion
2 tblsp. butter
2 c. soft bread crumbs
1 tblsp. chopped parsley
½ tsp. poultry seasoning
¼ tsp. salt

· Mix together ground meat, bread crumbs, carrot, ¼ c. onion and eggs. Add milk, 2 tsp. salt, Worcestershire sauce and pepper. Mix lightly, but well.
· Place on a double-thick square of greased aluminum foil. Shape into a 14 × 8″ rectangle.
· Sauté mushrooms and 1 tblsp. onion in butter over medium heat. Combine with remaining ingredients.
· Spread stuffing over meat; roll up, starting with long side. Press overlapping edge into roll to seal. Bring foil edges together in a tight double fold on the top. Fold ends up, using tight double folds.
· Place wrapped meat loaf on rack in shallow pan. Bake in moderate oven (375°) 1 hour. Open foil; continue baking for 15 minutes or until loaf browns. Makes 4 to 5 servings.

Note: If you freeze meat loaf, bake it wrapped in very hot oven (450°) 1½ hours, then open foil and brown.

MEAT BALLS IN TOMATO SAUCE

You simmer browned meat balls in a tasty, easy-to-make sauce

2 tblsp. olive oil
1 clove garlic, minced
¾ c. chopped onion
2 (10 oz.) cans tomato puree (2½ c.)
1 tsp. salt
⅛ tsp. pepper
1 bay leaf
2 tsp. sugar
3 slices white bread
⅓ c. milk
1 lb. ground beef
2 eggs, unbeaten
1 tsp. salt
⅛ tsp. pepper
1 clove garlic, minced
2 tblsp. chopped parsley
2 tblsp. shortening

• Heat oil in saucepan. Add 1 clove garlic and onion; cook over low heat until golden brown.

• Add tomato purée, 1 tsp. salt, ⅛ tsp. pepper, bay leaf and sugar. Bring to boil; reduce heat; simmer 45 minutes. Meanwhile, prepare meat balls.

• Break bread into mixing bowl. Add milk and let stand about 5 minutes, or until milk is absorbed.

• Add meat, eggs, 1 tsp. salt, ⅛ tsp. pepper, 1 clove garlic and parsley. Mix until blended. Shape into 12 medium balls.

• Melt shortening in skillet; add meat and brown well.

• Add sauce; simmer with meat balls for 45 minutes more. Serve with ½ pound (8 oz.) spaghetti, cooked. Serves 6.

SWEET-SOUR MEAT BALLS

Let meat balls bake while you fix the unusual sauce—quick and easy

5 slices dry bread
2 lbs. ground beef
½ c. grated onion
½ tsp. garlic salt
¼ tsp. pepper
1 tsp. salt
2 eggs, slightly beaten
Sweet-Sour Sauce for Beef

• Cut bread in cubes. Soak in a little cold water until soft. Squeeze out water. Combine with remaining ingredients, except Sweet-Sour Sauce. Shape in balls the size of walnuts (1½″); place in 15½ × 10½ × 1″ jelly roll pan. (Or brown balls in skillet containing a little hot fat.)

• Bake in very hot oven (450°) 15 to 18 minutes.

• Place balls in Sweet-Sour Sauce and simmer 10 minutes. If balls are made ahead, add sauce to them and heat in the oven about 15 minutes. Makes about 36 meat balls, 8 to 9 servings.

SWEET-SOUR SAUCE FOR BEEF

A surprise ingredient—gingersnaps—makes this sauce different

1 (1 lb. 12 oz.) can tomatoes (about 3½ c.)
1 c. brown sugar, firmly packed
¼ c. vinegar
½ tsp. salt
1 tsp. grated onion
10 gingersnaps, crushed

• Combine all ingredients. Cook to boiling. Makes enough sauce for 36 (1½″) meat balls.

WESTERN MEAT BALLS AND FRANKS

Serve with green salad, crusty rolls and French fried potatoes

1 lb. ground beef
1 egg, slightly beaten
¼ c. dry bread crumbs
1 medium onion, grated
1 tsp. salt
¾ c. chili sauce
¼ c. grape jelly
2 tblsp. lemon juice
⅔ c. water
1 lb. frankfurters, cut diagonally in ½" slices

· Combine beef, egg, crumbs, onion and salt. Shape into small balls.
· Combine chili sauce, grape jelly, lemon juice and water in large skillet. Heat; add meat balls and simmer until meat cooks through.
· Just before serving, add frankfurters and heat through. Makes 6 servings.

MEAT BALL STEW

New use for ground beef—browned meat balls and vegetables in a stew

1½ lbs. ground beef
1½ tsp. salt
⅛ tsp. pepper
1 egg
1 tblsp. minced onion
½ c. soft bread crumbs
1 tblsp. salad oil
3 tblsp. flour
1 (1 lb.) can tomatoes
1 c. water
½ tsp. salt
2 tsp. sugar
1 tsp. crushed basil leaves
3 medium potatoes, peeled and diced
4 small carrots, peeled and diced
1 onion, coarsely chopped
1 branch celery, sliced

· Mix ground beef with 1½ tsp. salt, pepper, egg, minced onion and bread crumbs. Form into balls the size of walnuts. Brown in hot oil.
· Remove meat balls from skillet; pour off all fat except 3 tblsp. Blend in flour. Stir in remaining ingredients. Bring mixture to a boil; simmer over low heat 10 minutes, adding more water if necessary. Add to meat balls in a 2-qt. casserole.
· Bake, covered, in moderate oven (350°) 1 hour, or until vegetables are tender. Makes 6 servings.

MAZETTI

Serve this Southern favorite with coleslaw, lima beans and corn

2 lbs. ground beef
2½ c. finely chopped celery with leaves (about ½ bunch)
2 c. chopped onions
2 cloves garlic, finely chopped
1 tblsp. water
1 (8 oz.) pkg. medium-fine noodles
2 cans condensed tomato soup
1 (6 oz.) can mushrooms and liquid
2 tsp. salt
½ tsp. pepper
½ lb. grated sharp Cheddar cheese (2 c.)

· Brown meat in skillet. Add celery, onions, garlic and water. Cover and steam until vegetables are tender. Remove from heat.
· Cook noodles according to package directions; drain. Add noodles to beef mixture; mix in soup, undrained mushrooms, salt and pepper.
· Spread mixture in a 3-qt. casserole. Sprinkle cheese on top. (Dish may be refrigerated up to 24 hours, or frozen before cooking.)
· Place in cold oven; set at very slow (250°). Bake uncovered about 1 hour, until bubbly. Makes 10 to 12 servings.

ROUNDUP BEEF ROLLS

Herbed biscuit dough bakes around seasoned ground beef—tasty

Filling:
2 tblsp. shortening
1 lb. ground beef
¾ c. minced onion
½ c. finely diced celery
½ tsp. salt
¼ tsp. pepper
⅔ c. tomato sauce

Crust:
1½ c. sifted flour
2 tsp. baking powder
½ tsp. salt
⅛ tsp. marjoram leaves
¼ tsp. rubbed sage
3 tblsp. shortening
⅓ c. tomato sauce plus water to make ½ c. liquid

· Melt 2 tblsp. shortening in skillet; add ground beef, onion and celery. Cook over medium heat until beef is browned. Add salt, pepper and ⅔ c. tomato sauce. Cook until thickened. Set aside while making crust.
· Sift together flour, baking powder and salt. Add herbs and mix well. Cut in 3 tblsp. shortening until mixture resembles coarse cornmeal. Add tomato sauce mixture and mix just until flour is moistened. Knead dough gently about 4 times on lightly floured surface. Roll out to make a 13 × 9″ rectangle.
· Spread beef mixture on dough; roll like a jelly roll starting at the 9″ edge. Place on ungreased baking sheet. Bake in moderate oven (375°) 30 to 35 minutes. Cut in slices and serve with ketchup, chili sauce, Speedy or Fresh Mushroom Sauce or Mushroom/Cheese Sauce. Serves 6.

SPEEDY MUSHROOM SAUCE: Stir 1 c. milk or dairy sour cream into 1 can condensed cream of mushroom soup; heat. Do not let sauce containing sour cream come to a boil.

FRESH MUSHROOM SAUCE: Melt 5 tblsp. butter or regular margarine in skillet. Add ½ lb. fresh mushrooms, sliced. Sprinkle with 1 tblsp. flour. Toss and cook over medium heat, stirring occasionally, until tender, 8 to 10 minutes. Season with salt or stir in 1 tsp. soy sauce. Slowly stir in ¾ c. light cream. Cook and stir until mixture thickens.

MUSHROOM/CHEESE SAUCE: Stir ⅓ c. milk into 1 can condensed cream of mushroom soup. Add ½ c. shredded sharp Cheddar cheese. Heat and stir until cheese melts.

HAMBURGER/CHEESE BISCUIT RING

Savory meat mixture waits for tardy people. Add biscuits and bake when they arrive. Or fix meat a day ahead, chill and reheat at serving time

2 lbs. ground beef
⅓ c. chopped onion
1 can condensed cream of celery soup
½ c. tomato juice
¾ c. beef bouillon
¼ c. ketchup
1 tsp. chili powder
¼ c. sliced pimiento-stuffed olives
Cheese Biscuits
Sliced pimiento-stuffed olives (for top)

· Brown ground beef and onion in large skillet; pour off excess fat. Add all ingredients except biscuits; simmer until slightly thickened.

• To serve, spoon meat into center of platter and surround with hot Cheese Biscuits. Garnish with sliced pimiento-stuffed olives. Makes 6 servings.

CHEESE BISCUITS: Cut ¼ c. shortening and ⅓ c. shredded Cheddar cheese into 2 c. all-purpose buttermilk biscuit mix. Add ⅔ c. milk; stir with fork to make a soft dough; beat 15 strokes. Drop tablespoonfuls of dough onto greased baking sheet. Bake in very hot oven (425°) 12 to 15 minutes. Makes 12 large biscuits.

SPAGHETTI MEAT SAUCE

Ready for a spaghetti supper whenever you want to have one—keep it on hand

1 large onion, chopped
1 clove garlic, minced
¼ c. salad oil
1 lb. ground beef
2½ c. tomatoes, or 1 (1 lb.) can
1 (6 oz.) can tomato paste
1 c. water
1 tsp. salt
½ tsp. pepper
1 bay leaf

• Sauté onion and garlic in hot oil. Add meat and cook until browned.
• Add remaining ingredients; simmer slowly about 1 hour.
• Cool quickly; freeze in refrigerator trays (with dividers). Transfer cubes to freezer container.
• To serve, heat as many cubes as needed over low heat. Spoon sauce over freshly cooked spaghetti. Sprinkle with grated cheese. Makes 6 servings.

HOME-COOKED TOMATO SAUCE

Freeze this main dish starter

4 (1 lb. 12 oz.) or 8 (14 oz.) cans Italian-style peeled tomatoes
8 (6 oz.) cans tomato paste
1 qt. water
6 bay leaves
½ c. salad oil
4 cloves garlic
5 tsp. salt
½ tsp. pepper
¼ c. Parmesan cheese

• Combine all ingredients in 8-qt. kettle; bring to boil. Simmer uncovered over very low heat about 6½ hours, or until tomato pulp cooks down and flavors blend, stirring occasionally. Add more water, if necessary, to give sauce consistency of thick white sauce. Remove bay leaves. Divide into 1-qt. portions; cool.
• Freeze in glass loaf pans. When frozen, remove sauce from pans; wrap blocks separately in heavy-duty foil or place in plastic bags; store in freezer. Makes 4 (1 qt.) blocks. For recipe amounts, cut blocks with frozen food saw or heavy knife.

TAMALE PIE

Perfect accompaniments: Crisp green salad, cool pineapple or banana dessert

1 lb. ground beef
¾ block frozen Home-cooked Tomato Sauce (3 c.)
1 tsp. salt
4 tsp. chili powder
¼ tsp. garlic salt
1 qt. chilled cornmeal mush
Pitted ripe olives (optional)

• Brown beef in heavy skillet; drain

off fat. Add tomato sauce and seasonings; heat thoroughly.

• Pour into 2-qt. oblong baking dish lined with thin (⅛″) slices of mush; top with more mush slices. If desired, stud top with ripe olives.

• Bake in hot oven (425°) 25 to 30 minutes. Makes 6 servings.

Note: For a short cut, line baking dish with hot mush (following package directions for 3 c. cornmeal); reserve about ⅓ to spread over top of pie.

BEEFEATERS' KIDNEY BEANS

A dish to satisfy ravenous appetites

½ lb. ground beef
½ block frozen Home-cooked Tomato Sauce (2 c.)
½ c. water
2 (1 lb.) cans kidney beans
1 medium onion, chopped
1 tblsp. chili powder
¼ lb. process cheese, cut in ½″ cubes (¾ c.)

• Brown ground beef in large saucepan. Add tomato sauce, water, liquid from beans, onion and chili powder.

• Bring to boil, cover and simmer 10 minutes. Add beans; cover and simmer 10 to 15 minutes. Serve topped with cheese. Makes 6 servings.

Country-Kitchen Lamb Treats

Roast leg of lamb, broiled lamb chops and lamb stews are high on the list of country lamb dishes. But there are other ways to cook always-tender lamb, which is rich in protein and lower in fat than some meats. Our collection of recipes invites you to adventure into a variety of lamb dishes. Try Wyoming Lamb Kabobs, Lamb Chops with Jelly Gravy, broiled Lamb Patties with Lemon Butter, garnished with honeyed peach halves, and Lamb Balls in Red Sauce. Your excursion in cooking will be a pleasant surprise for your family and friends.

ROAST LEG OF LAMB

• Buy 7 to 8 lb. leg of lamb. Leave on the fell (thin parchment-like covering or skin which helps leg keep its shape and keeps meat moist and juicy while baking).

• Wipe meat with damp cloth or paper towel; rub surface with cut clove of garlic or an onion (optional). To add flavor to drippings, drop a few onion slices in pan during last half hour of roasting.

• Place roast on rack, skin side up, in shallow pan; add salt and pepper.

• Roast in slow oven (300 to 325°), about 30 to 35 minutes per pound. Do not cover or add water.

• If you use a meat thermometer, insert it into roast so that bulb reaches center of meatiest section. It should not touch bone or fat. The thermometer registers 175° for medium-well, 180° for well done.

• When roast is done, remove from pan; keep hot while making gravy. Makes 12 to 15 servings.

BROWN GRAVY: Drain fat and brown drippings from pan. Put ¼ c. fat back in pan; blend in ¼ c. flour; let bubble over low heat. Remove from heat. Pour or skim rest of fat off brown drippings; add drippings and 2 c. cold water to browned flour paste. Return to heat; cook until thick and smooth, stirring constantly. Season to taste with salt and pepper. Makes about 2 cups gravy.

MARINATED LAMB ROAST

This delicious roast comes from the oven sliced and ready to serve

1 (4 to 5 lb.) presliced square shoulder of lamb
1 medium onion, sliced
1 lemon, sliced
2 cloves garlic
1 tblsp. salt
½ tsp. pepper
½ tsp. orégano leaves
1 bay leaf, crushed
¼ c. salad oil
¼ c. water
½ c. vinegar
1 (8 oz.) can tomato sauce
2 drops Tabasco sauce

• Have meatman cut lamb shoulder into 1″ chops with hand saw; then tie together with cord into original shape.
• Tuck onion and lemon slices in between chops. Crush garlic into salt; add remaining ingredients; pour over lamb in large shallow bowl.
• Cover and marinate at least 6 hours, or overnight, in refrigerator, turning occasionally.
• Roast on rack in shallow pan in slow oven (300 to 325°), allowing 30 to 35 minutes per pound. Baste with marinade during last hour of roasting. Cut string to serve. Makes 8 servings.

Note: Try our marinade with a boned and rolled shoulder roast—perfect for rotisseries. Follow range manufacturer's directions. Insert meat thermometer to get correct degree of doneness: 175° for medium-well, 180° for well done.

LAMB SHOULDER CUSHION ROAST WITH STUFFING

The delightful stuffing is what makes this roast distinctive—try it

1 (3 to 4 lb.) square cut shoulder of lamb
2 tblsp. chopped onion
½ c. chopped celery
2 tblsp. butter or regular margarine
1 tsp. salt
¼ tsp. ground ginger
2 tblsp. brown sugar
1 tblsp. mint flakes (or 2 tblsp. chopped fresh mint)
2 c. chopped unpeeled apples
1 c. (¼″) bread cubes
¼ c. milk

• Have bones removed from roast to form a pocket.
• Sauté onion and celery in butter. Add remaining ingredients; toss lightly.
• Fill lamb cavity with stuffing; skewer or sew edges together.
• Place, fat side up, on rack in shallow pan. Roast uncovered in slow oven (300 to 325°) about 2½ hours, or 30 to 35 minutes per pound. Serves 6 to 8.

LAMB CHOP MARINADE

Chilling chops in marinade is the secret to their superb flavor

4 lamb chops (loin or rib, 1″ thick)
¼ c. salad oil
1 tblsp. lemon juice
1 tsp. salt
½ tsp. pepper
1 small bay leaf
1 tsp. chopped parsley
1 clove garlic
1 small onion, sliced

TIMETABLE FOR BROILING LAMB

Cut	*Weight Ounces*	*Approximate Total Cooking Time–Minutes*
Shoulder Chops		
1″	5 to 8 ozs.	12
1½″	8 to 10 ozs.	18
2″	10 to 16 ozs.	22
Rib Chops		
1″	3 to 5 ozs.	12
1½″	4 to 7 ozs.	18
2″	6 to 10 ozs.	22
Loin Chops		
1″	4 to 7 ozs.	12
1½″	6 to 10 ozs.	18
2″	8 to 14 ozs.	22
Ground Lamb Patties		
1″ by 3″	4 ozs.	18

Note: Lamb chops are not usually served rare. Broil lamb chops as directed for broiled steaks and lamb patties like beef patties. (See Index for "How to Broil Beef Steaks and Ground Beef Patties.")

· Place chops flat in glass baking dish or pan.
· Combine oil, lemon juice, salt, pepper, bay leaf and parsley.
· Mash garlic or put through press; add with onion to marinade.
· Pour marinade over chops; chill at least 3 hours. Turn once or twice.
· Set oven regulator for broil. Preheat broiler 10 minutes, or as range manufacturer directs. Arrange meat on oiled rack; place in broiler oven so top of meat is about 3″ from source of heat. (Or place as manufacturer directs.) Broil about 12 minutes, turning once during broiling. To test doneness, make slit with knife in one chop near bone. Note if color inside indicates the desired doneness. Makes 4 servings.

LAMB CHOPS WITH JELLY GRAVY

The jelly in the gravy makes these shoulder lamb chops extra-special

6 lamb shoulder chops (½″)
1 tblsp. fat
3 tblsp. flour
¾ tsp. salt
⅛ tsp. pepper
1½ c. water
3 tblsp. currant jelly

· Brown chops in hot fat in heavy skillet. Reduce heat and cook until done. Remove chops from skillet and keep hot while making gravy.
· If there are more than 4 tblsp. of fat in skillet, drain off surplus. Add flour and stir, loosening brown bits. Cook and stir until flour browns. Add salt, pepper and water and cook, stirring, until gravy is smooth. Add jelly and stir until it melts and blends in the gravy. Serve hot with chops. Makes 5 to 6 servings.

WYOMING LAMB KABOBS

Cook indoors in broiler or outdoors on grill after marinating the meat

1 (1½ lb.) lamb shoulder
¾ c. French dressing
1 clove garlic
4 slices bacon
½ lb. button mushrooms (optional)
1 tsp. salt
¼ tsp. pepper

· Cut lamb in 1″ cubes.
· Pour French dressing over meat; add cut clove of garlic unless dressing already contains garlic. Let stand at least 1 hour or overnight in refrigerator.
· Cut bacon into 1″ pieces.
· Alternate lamb, bacon and mushrooms on metal skewers. Allow space between for thorough cooking. Season with salt and pepper.
· Broil 3″ from source of heat, about 15 minutes, turning once. Makes 6 servings.

Variation

PINEAPPLE/LAMB KABOBS: Alternate cubes of lamb with canned pineapple chunks and 1″ pieces of bacon on skewers. Brush with melted butter and broil. Or, use small, whole cooked potatoes instead of the pineapple.

LAMB PATTIES WITH LEMON BUTTER

Hot drained, canned peaches add flavor and a touch of gold

2 lbs. ground lean lamb
2 tsp. salt
½ tsp. pepper
12 slices bacon
Lemon Butter
Chopped parsley
6 canned peach halves
Honey

· Combine lamb, salt and pepper. Shape into 12 patties 1″ thick. Wrap each with a slice of bacon. Arrange on broiler rack and broil 3 to 4″ from broiler for 8 minutes on one side and 6 to 8 minutes on the other (or place as range manufacturer suggests).
· Place lamb patties on a warm platter; spread with Lemon Butter. Sprinkle with chopped parsley.
· Drain peach halves; brush with honey and broil 10 minutes. Garnish platter with broiled peaches. Makes 6 servings.

LEMON BUTTER: Blend 6 tblsp. melted butter, 3 tblsp. lemon juice and a dash of garlic salt.

PERUVIAN LAMB STEW

Men really like this expertly seasoned stew hearty with lima beans

1 (2 lb.) lamb shoulder
Boiling broth
Juice of 1 lemon
2 tblsp. minced onion
1 clove garlic, crushed
⅛ tsp. ground allspice
½ tsp. pepper
3 tblsp. fat
¾ tsp. salt
4 c. cooked, seasoned lima beans (fresh, frozen or canned)

· Trim bones and skin from meat; cut in 2″ pieces. Prepare broth from bones and trimmings.
· Place meat in heavy pan with lemon juice, onion, garlic, allspice and pepper; let stand about 2 hours in this marinade.
· Remove meat, reserving marinade mixture. Drain; brown well in hot fat in heavy skillet.
· Place meat in stew pot; add mari-

nade, then boiling broth to cover ¾ of meat.

· Cover pot; bake in very slow oven (275°) until tender, adding salt at end of first hour.

· When meat is done, remove from broth; skim off all fat. Add limas; simmer on top of range about 15 minutes. If gravy is not thick enough, blend 1 tblsp. fat with 1 tblsp. flour; stir into gravy. Makes 6 to 8 servings.

BIG IRISH LAMB STEW

Somewhat tedious to make, but results justify the time and effort

- **3 lbs. lamb shoulder**
- **1 qt. cold water**
- **1 sliced medium onion**
- **1 celery top**
- **½ (10½ oz.) can consommé**
- **Fat**
- **1 small clove garlic, crushed**
- **1 tsp. brown sugar**
- **1 sprig parsley**
- **⅛ tsp. thyme leaves**
- **1 bay leaf**
- **¼ tsp. pepper**
- **2 finely shredded peeled raw potatoes**
- **12 small whole onions, parboiled**
- **6 potatoes, cut to walnut-size pieces**
- **1 tblsp. salt**
- **2 c. cooked peas (fresh, canned or frozen)**

· Trim bones and skin from meat; cut in 2″ pieces.

· Place all trimmings but skin in heavy saucepan with water, sliced onion and celery. Simmer slowly until all flavor is drawn from trimmings and bones, about 30 minutes if bones are small. Strain; reserve liquid for stew, adding comsommé.

· Brown meat in heavy skillet with fat. Place in stew pot; add garlic, brown sugar, parsley, thyme, bay leaf and pepper. Add shredded potatoes and boiling broth to cover.

· Cook slowly, uncovered, to reduce broth, about 1½ hours. (Liquid will be slightly thickened and shredded potatoes entirely dissolved.)

· Add whole onions, potato pieces and salt; cook 30 minutes. Serve in tureen with circle of peas around edge. Makes 9 to 12 servings.

LITTLE IRISH LAMB STEW

It's easy to double the recipe for this delicious meal-in-a-dish

- **2 tblsp. flour**
- **1 tsp. salt**
- **⅛ tsp. pepper**
- **1½ lbs. lamb, cut into 2″ pieces (shank, shoulder, breast or neck)**
- **2 tblsp. fat**
- **¼ tsp. dill seeds**
- **3 c. water**
- **8 small onions**
- **3 carrots, cut in 1″ slices**
- **2 cubed peeled potatoes**
- **½ c. light cream**
- **1 tblsp. flour**

· Mix 2 tblsp. flour, salt and pepper; roll meat in mixture; brown in hot fat. Add dill and water. Cover; simmer 1½ hours.

· Add onions, carrots and potatoes. Cover; cook 25 minutes, or until vegetables are tender.

· Combine cream and 1 tblsp. flour, stirring until smooth; blend into meat mixture; cook until thickened, stirring to avoid lumping. Makes 4 servings.

LAMB CURRY

Spoon it over hot, fluffy rice, fall to and enjoy some extra-good eating

2 lbs. boned lean lamb breast or shoulder
1 tsp. curry powder
1½ tsp. salt
⅛ tsp. pepper
⅛ tsp. ground ginger
¼ c. flour
3 tblsp. fat
1 c. hot water
1 sliced medium onion
1 sprig parsley
1 diced red apple
1 c. milk
3 c. hot cooked rice

• Wipe meat with damp paper towel; remove excess fat. Cut into small pieces.

• Combine curry, salt, pepper, ginger and 1 tblsp. flour; sprinkle over meat. Brown meat in hot fat over moderate heat (about 20 minutes). Add water, onion and parsley.

• Cover; cook over low heat 45 minutes or until meat is tender. Add apple.

• Blend remaining flour with milk; add slowly to meat, stirring constantly. Cook 3 minutes or until thickened. Serve with rice. Makes 6 servings.

Note: For a good menu, serve Lamb Curry, rice, tossed green salad, crusty rolls, peach chutney, fruit cup, tea, milk.

BARBECUED LAMB SHANKS

Have plenty of paper napkins on hand when you serve this treat

8 lamb shanks
½ c. flour
1 tsp. salt
½ c. salad oil or shortening
½ c. brown sugar, firmly packed
2 tsp. dry mustard
½ tsp. salt
½ tsp. pepper
1 c. ketchup
2 tblsp. vinegar
1 (1 lb.) can tomatoes

• Roll lamb shanks in mixture of flour and 1 tsp. salt. Brown several at a time in salad oil in large Dutch oven or kettle. When browned, remove from kettle and brown other shanks. Pour off all fat.

• Meanwhile combine brown sugar, dry mustard, ½ tsp. salt and pepper. Stir in ketchup and vinegar. Pour over lamb shanks in Dutch oven. Then pour tomatoes over.

• Cover and bake in moderate oven (350°) 1½ to 2 hours, until meat is tender. Or simmer gently on top of range. Makes 8 servings.

RICH BROWN LAMB DINNER

Ideal for summer—new-tasting lamb dish cooks on top of range

¼ c. salad oil
6 meaty lamb shanks, cracked, or 6 thick shoulder lamb chops
2 tblsp. bottled browning sauce
1 c. hot water
⅓ c. mint jelly or mint-flavored apple jelly
2 tsp. garlic salt
¼ tsp. pepper
10 to 12 small whole potatoes, frozen or fresh, peeled
2 tblsp. flour
½ c. cold water
½ c. evaporated milk
2 (1 lb.) cans small whole boiled onions, drained
Salt
Pepper

• Heat salad oil in large, deep skillet. Brush lamb shanks with bottled sauce; stir remaining sauce into oil. Brown lamb well on all sides.

· Combine hot water, jelly, garlic salt and pepper; add to browned shanks. Cover and simmer 1 hour or until meat is tender.

· Add potatoes and cook until tender (15 minutes for frozen, about 25 minutes for fresh).

· Remove shanks and potatoes to a heated platter; keep warm.

· Blend flour and ½ c. water together to make a smooth paste. Stir into drippings along with the milk; cook over medium heat, stirring until thick and smooth. Add onions; heat through. Salt and pepper to taste. Pour some gravy over meat and potatoes; serve remainder separately. Makes 6 servings.

LAMB AND SAUSAGE ROLL

Complete menu with peas, raisin-carrot salad and baked apples

3 lbs. boned breast of lamb
Salt
Pepper
½ lb. bulk pork sausage
2 tblsp. fat
½ c. ketchup
¾ c. water
½ c. chopped onion

· Rub lamb with salt and pepper. Spread with sausage meat. Roll lengthwise; tie or fasten with skewers.

· Brown in fat in heavy skillet.

· Combine ketchup, water and onion; pour over lamb. Cover; simmer about 1½ hours or until lamb is tender and sausage cooked through. (Add more water during cooking as needed.) Skim off fat. Slice; serve with the sauce. Makes 4 generous servings.

BASIC RED SAUCE

Keep in refrigerator or freezer—we give you ways to use it

1 c. finely chopped onion
⅓ c. salad oil
1½ c. ketchup
½ c. water
½ c. lemon juice
¼ c. sugar
¼ c. Worcestershire sauce
2½ tsp. salt
½ tsp. pepper
4 drops Tabasco sauce

· Cook onion in hot oil until soft and golden. Add remaining ingredients; simmer 15 minutes. Cool and store in refrigerator or freezer. Makes about 1 quart.

Note: For a more tart sauce, use an additional 2 tblsp. lemon juice. For a hotter sauce, add more Tabasco sauce to suit taste.

The following recipe used Basic Red Sauce as an ingredient. See Index for these other tempting recipes made with it: Better Burgers, Saucy Chicken Bake, Easy Shrimp Creole, Vegetables in Foil, Nippy Cheese Dip and Short-cut Salad Dressing.

LAMB BALLS IN RED SAUCE

Shape balls lightly, brown deeply and simmer tenderly in sauce

1 lb. ground lamb
½ c. fine bread crumbs
⅓ c. milk
1 egg yolk
1 tsp. salt

⅛ tsp. poultry seasoning
1 tblsp. fat
1 c. Basic Red Sauce

• Combine lamb, bread crumbs, milk, egg yolk, salt and poultry seasoning. Work together to blend ingredients. Form into 16 balls 1½″ in diameter.
• Brown meat balls on all sides in hot fat. Drain off fat. Add Red Sauce.
• Cover and simmer 10 to 15 minutes. Makes 4 servings.

Variation

BEEF BALLS IN RED SAUCE: Substitute ground beef for the lamb.

Wonderful Ways to Cook Pork

A pork loin or fresh pork leg roast, bright with glaze, is one of the tempting and rewarding dishes that comes to country dinner tables. The brown gravy especially makes appetites soar.

We give you also many other pleasing ways to cook pork. Be sure to try Fresh Pork Pot Roast with Dumplings. And look at our variety of pork chop recipes. Notice too, the Timetable for Broiling Pork. You can broil rib or loin chops, ¾ to 1″ thick, in 20 to 25 minutes, turning once during the cooking.

The Chinese excel in dishes made with strips or thin slices of pork. Our recipe collection contains some adaptations of oriental masterpieces—Chow Mein for instance. Ground pork makes quick Chop Suey and other dishes, such as Pork Cabbage Rolls.

GLAZED PORK ROAST

Pamper your guests with this regal roast that glistens with apricot glaze

4 to 5 lb. pork loin roast
Salt
Pepper
⅔ c. brown sugar, firmly packed
2½ tsp. dry mustard
2 tblsp. cornstarch
2 c. apricot nectar
4 tsp. cider vinegar

• Rub roast well with salt and pepper; score fat on roast in a diamond pattern.
• Place roast, fat side up, on a rack in an open roasting pan. Insert meat thermometer into the center of roast so it does not touch bone or rest in fat.
• Roast meat in a slow to moderate oven (325 to 350°) until meat thermometer indicates an internal temperature of 170°. Times vary with type of loin cut; center loin roast, roast about 30 to 35 minutes per pound; blade loin or sirloin roast, about 40 to 45 minutes per pound.
• About ½ hour before roast is done, mix brown sugar, mustard and cornstarch in a saucepan. Stir in apricot nectar and cider vinegar. Place over medium heat and cook, stirring constantly, until slightly thickened. Remove roast from oven and spoon about ½ c. glaze over it (reserve rest of glaze). Replace meat in oven until done. Remove roast from oven 20 minutes before serving for easier carving. Makes 8 servings.

APRICOT SAUCE: For a bonus make this sauce from extra glaze to spoon over the carved, tender pork. Mix about 3 tblsp. brown drippings from roasting pan with remaining apricot glaze. Heat and serve with the roast pork.

PORK ROAST WITH FLAVOR POCKETS

Spices and herbs tucked in roast's pockets season delightfully

1 (8 lb.) pork loin roast
1 tsp. fennel seeds, rubbed between palms of hands to bring out aroma
2 tsp. salt
¼ tsp. pepper
½ tsp. orégano leaves, crushed
½ bay leaf, crushed
⅛ tsp. ground nutmeg
⅛ tsp. ground cloves
2 tblsp. chopped parsley
1 tsp. minced onion
1 clove garlic, minced

· Place pork roast, fat side up, on rack in open roasting pan just large enough to hold roast. Mix remaining ingredients well with fingers.

· Make flavor pockets in roast—pierce meat with a knife to a depth of 1″. Move tip of knife from side to side to enlarge pocket. Make pockets at 2 to 3″ intervals over top side of roast.

· Place ½ tsp. flavor mixture in each pocket and press it deep into the pocket with fingers. Close pocket with fingers. Rub remaining flavor mixture over roast.

· Roast meat, uncovered, in slow to moderate oven (325 to 350°), allowing 30 to 35 minutes per pound, or until meat thermometer indicates internal temperature of 170°.

· Remove roast from oven about 20 minutes before serving. Make gravy with drippings in roasting pan. Makes about 8 servings.

ROAST FRESH HAM

Baked fresh ham basted with apple juice calls for sweet potatoes

1 (12 lb.) fresh ham
3 cloves garlic
1 tblsp. salt
½ tsp. pepper
1 tsp. caraway seeds, crushed
4 medium onions, sliced
2 medium carrots, sliced lengthwise
2 bay leaves
3 whole cloves
½ c. water
1 c. apple juice (about)
Spiced crab apples

· Score fat or skin of ham in diamond pattern. Rub well with one cut garlic clove, salt and pepper. Sprinkle with caraway seeds.

· Place roast, fat side down, on bed of onions, carrots, remaining garlic cloves, bay leaves and cloves. Add water.

· Roast, uncovered, 1 hour in slow to moderate oven (325 to 350°). Turn fat side up; insert meat thermometer. Roast to internal temperature of 170°, or about 22 to 26 minutes per pound. During last 2 hours, baste frequently with apple juice to make skin crisp and brown (cover loosely with foil if roast begins to get too brown). Remove meat and vegetables from pan and keep hot while making gravy. Serve garnished with crab apples. Makes 16 to 20 servings.

GRAVY: Strain meat juices in pan and skim off fat. Return ¼ c. drippings to pan. Stir in ¼ c. flour mixed with ¼ c. water; cook over direct heat until smooth. Add 1 c. apple juice, 1 tsp. salt and ¼ tsp. pepper. Just before serving, reduce heat, stir in

2 c. dairy sour cream; heat but do not boil. If too thick, thin with apple juice.

DEEP-PEPPERED PORK

You cook and carve meat ahead to reheat with potatoes at mealtime

1 (4 lb.) boneless rolled pork roast
Coarsely ground pepper
Salt
Fresh garlic (optional)
1 lemon
8 medium potatoes
Thin lemon slices

• With a sharp knife, pierce surface of pork about 1½″ deep in about ten places. With your forefinger, press into each hole about ⅛ tsp. pepper, about 1/16 tsp. salt, ¼ clove garlic and a thin strip of lemon peel (yellow part only). Rub surface of roast with lemon juice, salt and pepper.
• Place pork on rack in roasting pan; insert meat thermometer. Bake in slow to moderate oven (325 to 350°) until meat thermometer indicates internal temperature of 170°, or about 35 to 45 minutes per pound.
• Meanwhile, peel potatoes and cut in halves; cook until just tender; drain.
• Remove roast from oven, allow to stand at least 20 minutes, then slice, saving meat juices. Loosen crusty drippings from roasting pan. Arrange pork slices, slightly overlapping, in a deep platter or shallow casserole; spoon over meat juices and enough roast drippings to moisten (avoid excess fat) and remaining juice from lemon.
• Coat potatoes with roast drippings; arrange around pork slices. Bake in slow oven (300°) 20 to 30 minutes, or until pork is heated through, basting once or twice with pan juices. Garnish with lemon slices. Serve very hot. Makes about 8 servings.

Pig Roasts for Summer Entertaining

Pig roasts, called luaus, are traditional in Hawaii. Adapted versions of the feast are becoming popular on the mainland in farm communities. One reason is that country homes usually have the necessary makings —a young pig, space to dig a pit, the necessary rocks, wood and corn leaves—and room for many guests. The food is different and satisfies outdoor appetites.

WHOLE PIT-ROASTED PIG

You will need:

Whole young pig, dressed and shaved
Rock-lined pit dug ahead of time
Several rounded rocks from a stream, in 1 to 4 lb. weights. (Sun dry them for a week.)
3 bushels or more of dry hard wood
Green corn stalks and leaves
Big tongs for handling hot rocks
Chicken wire or fencing—enough to encircle pig
2 baling hooks to carry roasted pig
12 clean burlap sacks
Canvas large enough to cover pit

• Allow 1 lb. dressed meat per person.
• Dig hole about 2½′ deep at center, with diameter of 5½ to 8′ de-

pending on size of pig. Line with rocks.

· Stack wood on rocks, Indian-tepee style. Light fire. Place round rocks in fire where they will get most heat.

· While fire burns down, wet the burlap, and prepare pig. Rub inside of pig with salt and pepper, and garlic if desired. Place pig on chicken wire. Under legs, make slits big enough to insert round rocks. When fire has burned down and rocks are very hot, use tongs to fill abdominal cavity and slits in legs with hot rocks. Tie front legs together, then back legs. Wrap pig in wire, fastening well (so it can be lifted).

· Completely cover ashes and rocks with corn stalks and leaves. Lower pig right onto leaves. Cover it generously on top and sides with more leaves.

· Place wet burlap over leaves (this will hold heat and steam).

· Cover with large canvas; shovel gravel over canvas to keep steam in.

· Cooking time starts now. For 25 lb. pig, allow about 2 hours; for 50 lb. pig, 2½ hours; anything heavier, figure on at least 4 hours. If in doubt about doneness, leave pig in longer (because of steam, it won't burn).

· To uncover, remove gravel, canvas, burlap and covering leaves. Lift and carry wire-wrapped pig with hooks. Remove wire to serve.

· In Hawaii, the servers dip their hands frequently in cold water as they pull pork apart for individual servings. On the mainland, the servings of hot, juicy pork often are best liked when served in buttered buns, with barbecue sauce.

What to Cook with the Pig:

· About 1 hour before the pig is cooked, partly uncover pit and add apples, wrapped in foil, and corn on the cob. Either wrap corn ears individually in foil or peel back husks, remove silks, replace husks and soak in cold water about 15 minutes before adding to pit. (In Hawaii, whole sweet potatoes are roasted with the pig.) Cover the pit at once after adding apples and corn.

FRESH PORK POT ROAST WITH DUMPLINGS

Men especially like this hearty dish of dumplings, gravy and pork

½ fresh pork leg or shoulder (about 5 lb.)
2 tsp. salt
2 tsp. thyme leaves
1 large bay leaf, crushed
Dumplings

· Trim excess fat from meat. Rub meat with mixture of salt, thyme and bay leaf. Refrigerate 2 hours.

· Brown meat in fat trimmings in heavy deep pan or Dutch oven. Add water to depth of 2″. Cover, and simmer on top of range until well done (20 to 25 minutes per pound). Add more water if needed.

· Remove meat from pan; set aside, keeping it warm, while you make gravy and dumplings. Makes 6 to 8 servings.

GRAVY: Skim fat from drippings. Measure ¾ c. drippings into pan; stir in ½ c. flour; cook until bubbly. Stir in 4 c. water to make thin gravy; season with salt and pepper; simmer 5 minutes.

DUMPLINGS: Sift together 1½ c. sifted flour, 2 tsp. baking powder, ¾ tsp. salt and ⅛ tsp. rubbed sage. Cut in 3 tblsp. shortening. Combine 1 egg, slightly beaten, and ⅔ c.

TIMETABLE FOR BROILING PORK

Cut	*Approximate Total Cooking Time—Minutes*
PORK—SMOKED	
Ham slice—tendered	
½"	10–12
1"	16–20
Loin Chops	
¾ to 1"	15–20
Canadian style bacon	
¼" slices	6–8
½" slices	8–10
Bacon*	4–5
PORK—FRESH	
Rib or loin chops	
¾ to 1"	20–25
Shoulder steaks	
½ to ¾"	20–22

* Time required for broiling bacon depends on preferences for crispness. Broil pork chops and ground pork patties like steak and ground beef patties. (See Index for "How to Broil Beef Steaks and Ground Beef Patties.") Pork —smoked and fresh—should always be cooked well done for health reasons.

milk; stir in dry ingredients until all are moistened. Drop by spoonfuls into boiling gravy. Cook uncovered 10 minutes; cover and cook 10 minutes longer or until dumplings are fluffy. Serve with meat and gravy.

SWEET-SOUR PORK RIBS

You can use either regular spareribs or the more nearly uniform back ribs

3 lbs. pork ribs
1½ tsp. salt
¼ tsp. pepper
1 (1 lb. 4 oz.) can pineapple chunks
2 green peppers, cut in strips
2 tblsp. cornstarch
⅓ c. soy sauce
½ c. sugar
¼ c. vinegar

· Cover ribs with cold water; bring to boil and simmer 10 minutes. Drain; rinse ribs in cold water. Place in roasting pan; sprinkle with salt and pepper.

· Bake in very hot oven (450°) 15 minutes, until lightly browned. Pour off fat.

· Drain pineapple, reserving juice. Add pineapple chunks and peppers to ribs. Bake 10 minutes.

· Combine cornstarch, soy sauce, sugar, vinegar and reserved pineapple juice. Cook until clear, stirring constantly. Pour over ribs. Bake 10 minutes longer. Makes 6 servings.

Note: For crisper ribs, omit simmering step, and bake, uncovered, in shallow pan in hot oven (400°) 45 minutes; drain. Reduce heat to moderate (350°); add 1 c. sauce and pineapple chunks. Bake 30 minutes.

Turn meat and bake 10 minutes. Add peppers, mixed with remaining sauce, and bake 20 minutes.

PORK CHOPS WITH APPLES

Apple rings on top of chops have pretty cherry centers—extra good

9 loin pork chops, ¾″ thick
Salt
Pepper
3 unpeeled tart red apples
1½ tblsp. butter
9 maraschino cherries
6 tblsp. brown sugar
1 tsp. ground cinnamon
½ tsp. ground ginger

· Brown chops slowly in heavy skillet; place in shallow baking dish one layer deep. Sprinkle with salt and pepper.
· Core unpeeled apples and slice in ½″ thick rings. Add butter to skillet in which chops were browned, and sauté apple rings until slightly tender. Place one ring on top of each chop. Cover, and bake in slow oven (300°) 45 to 60 minutes.
· Remove from oven. Place cherry in center of each apple ring; sprinkle all with mixture of brown sugar, cinnamon and ginger. Baste with drippings to moisten sugar. Finish baking, uncovered, in moderate oven (350°) 15 to 20 minutes. Makes 9 servings.

MOCK FILET MIGNON

Perfect dish for special occasions. Point up menu with peach pickle

9 lean loin pork chops, boned, 1″ thick, or 9 pork tenderloin slices, 1″ thick
9 slices bacon
9 large whole mushrooms, stemmed
3 tblsp. butter

· Shape boned chops into rounds. Circle each with a strip of bacon and secure with toothpicks.
· Place in flat baking dish, cover. Bake in slow oven (300°) 1 hour. Uncover; brown under broiler.
· Sauté mushrooms in butter until brown and tender. Top each filet with a mushroom. Makes 9 servings.

CREOLE PORK CHOPS

You can brown the chops ahead and chill them for use later

4 loin or center cut pork chops 1½″ thick
Salt
Pepper
1 tblsp. fat or salad oil
⅓ c. ketchup
½ c. water
½ tsp. salt
½ tsp. celery seeds
3 tblsp. cider vinegar
¼ tsp. ground ginger
1 tsp. sugar
1 tsp. flour

· Sprinkle chops lightly with salt and pepper. Brown on both sides in fat in a heavy skillet. Remove chops to casserole or baking dish.
· Combine remaining ingredients; pour over chops.
· Bake uncovered in slow oven (325°) 1½ hours. Turn chops after first hour of baking. Makes 4 servings.

ZESTY PORK CHOPS

Tangy sauce makes this a company special—for looks and flavor

6 rib pork chops, ¾″ thick
2 tblsp. salad oil
1 tsp. salt
½ c. maple-blended syrup

½ c. hickory-flavor ketchup
2 tblsp. lemon juice
2 tsp. Worcestershire sauce
1 unpeeled large tart apple, cored and cut in 6 rings
1 tblsp. cornstarch
⅓ c. water

• Brown pork chops in salad oil; season with salt. Drain off oil.
• Combine syrup, ketchup, lemon juice and Worcestershire sauce. Reserve ½ c. mixture; pour remaining mixture over chops. Simmer, covered, over low heat for 25 minutes.
• Place an apple slice on each chop; top with remaining ½ c. sauce mixture. Cover and simmer 25 minutes longer.
• Remove chops to a hot platter. Blend cornstarch with water and stir into sauce in skillet. Cook, stirring, until sauce comes to a boil and thickens. Serve over pork chops. Makes 6 servings.

HONEYED PORK CHOPS

Adaptation of a fascinating old Chinese recipe. Good served with rice

6 pork chops, ¾″ thick
¼ c. soy sauce
1 tblsp. ketchup
½ c. water
3 tblsp. honey
1 small onion, finely chopped
¼ tsp. ground ginger
⅛ tsp. pepper
1 tblsp. Toasted Sesame Seeds (see **Index**)

• Brown chops in small amount of fat; place in 13 × 9 × 2″ baking pan. (Don't salt chops; soy sauce does the job.)
• Combine remaining ingredients, except sesame seeds. Pour over chops, sprinkle on sesame seeds.
• Cover baking pan and bake in slow oven (325°) about 1 hour, or until chops are tender. Makes 6 servings.

NIPPY PORK CHOP PLATTER

Mustard gives pork chops the tang

6 lean pork chops, ¾″ thick
Prepared mustard
¼ c. flour
1 tsp. salt
¼ tsp. pepper
2 tblsp. melted fat
1 can condensed chicken rice soup

• Spread pork chops with thin coating of mustard.
• Combine flour, salt and pepper in paper bag; shake chops in bag to coat with flour, then brown in melted fat in heavy skillet.
• Place chops in baking dish; cover with soup. Cover; bake in moderate oven (350°) 40 minutes. Makes 6 servings.

Note: Scalloped tomatoes and corn are a good accompaniment for these pork chops. Combine in casserole: Canned tomatoes, whole kernel corn, chopped onion, strips of green pepper and seasonings; top with crumbs. Bake in moderate oven (350°) 40 minutes. A relish tray of pickles and carrot sticks and a dessert of sherbet complete the meal.

STUFFED PORK CHOPS

Cut pockets as directed so they'll stay full of stuffing while baking

6 pork chops, at least 1″ thick for stuffing
2 tblsp. butter or regular margarine
2 tblsp. finely chopped onion
¼ tsp. rubbed sage

¼ tsp. crushed basil leaves
1 tblsp. parsley flakes or chopped fresh parsley
1½ c. small dry bread cubes
¼ c. onion soup mix
½ c. water

• Cut pork chops along the bone, about halfway through, then cut toward outside to make a pocket.
• Melt butter; add onion, sage, basil and parsley. Sauté until onion is golden. Toss with bread cubes. Stuff mixture into pork chop pockets.
• Brown chops in small amount of fat; place in 13 × 9 × 2″ baking pan or casserole. Sprinkle onion soup mix over chops. Pour on ½ c. water and cover.
• Bake in slow oven (325°) about 1 hour, or until chops are tender. Makes 6 servings.

SAVORY PORK ROLLS

Pork rolled around seasoned stuffing—"pork birds," children call them

6 pork shoulder steaks
1 tsp. salt
¼ tsp. pepper
1 egg, beaten
¼ c. milk
2 c. cubed soft bread (day old)
¼ c. chopped onion
½ lb. ground beef
1 tsp. prepared mustard
¼ tsp. poultry seasoning
½ tsp. salt
2 tblsp. flour
1 tblsp. fat or salad oil
½ c. water
1 can condensed cream of mushroom soup
½ c. milk

• Trim fat and remove any bone from steaks. Pound with mallet or meat hammer to flatten. Season with 1 tsp. salt and pepper.
• Combine egg, ¼ c. milk and bread cubes; add onion, ground beef, mustard, poultry seasoning and ½ tsp. salt; mix.
• Spoon stuffing on pork pieces. Roll up, jelly-roll fashion; fasten with wooden picks or string.
• Dust with flour; brown lightly in hot fat in skillet. Remove meat to 1½-qt. casserole.
• Pour off fat in skillet. Add water to brown drippings. Stir; pour over meat rolls in casserole; cover. Bake in moderate oven (350°) 1 hour.
• Serve with mushroom sauce made by combining mushroom soup and ½ c. milk; simmer 2 minutes. Serves 6.

PORK CABBAGE ROLLS

No one will guess this tasty dish is made with left-over pork

1 large head cabbage
2½ c. ground or finely chopped, cooked pork roast
½ c. fine bread crumbs
⅓ c. finely chopped onion
1 egg, slightly beaten
1 tblsp. chopped parsley
1 tsp. caraway seeds
1½ tsp. salt
¼ tsp. freshly ground pepper
1 (8 oz.) can tomato sauce
½ c. water
1 tsp. cornstarch
½ tsp. sugar
1 tblsp. lemon juice

• Discard wilted outer leaves of cabbage and remove core. Carefully remove 10 to 12 large whole leaves. Steam leaves 3 minutes in small amount of boiling, salted water, covered. Drain and cool.
• Mix pork, bread crumbs, onion,

egg, parsley, caraway seeds, salt and pepper. Put a heaping tablespoonful of pork mixture near the stem end of each cabbage leaf. Fold in the two sides, then roll leaf.

· Place cabbage rolls close together in a large skillet. Mix tomato sauce, water, cornstarch, sugar and lemon juice; pour over rolls. Cover tightly and simmer 30 minutes or until leaves are tender. Makes 10 to 12 rolls.

PORK/SAUERKRAUT PINWHEEL

Pork winds around sauerkraut—good served with scalloped potatoes

¾ c. dry bread crumbs
2 eggs, slightly beaten
⅓ c. milk
1½ tsp. salt
¼ tsp. pepper
1 tsp. thyme leaves
1 tblsp. Worcestershire sauce
2 lbs. ground lean pork
1 (1 lb.) can sauerkraut, drained and finely cut with scissors
¼ c. chopped onion
3 tblsp. chopped pimiento
1 tblsp. sugar
5 slices bacon

· Combine bread crumbs, eggs, milk, salt, pepper, thyme and Worcestershire sauce. Mix in pork.

· On waxed paper, pat pork mixture into a 12 × 9″ rectangle.

· Combine sauerkraut, onion, pimiento and sugar. Spread evenly over meat. Roll up from narrow end. Place loaf in greased, shallow baking dish; lay bacon over top.

· Bake in moderate oven (375°) 1 hour and 10 minutes. Makes 8 servings.

30-MINUTE CHOP SUEY

Cooks fast because pork is ground. Good served with pineapple salad

1½ lbs. ground pork
2 tblsp. butter or regular margarine
3 c. chopped onions
3 c. chopped celery
¾ c. chopped celery tops
2 (4 oz.) cans sliced mushrooms, undrained
2 green peppers, chopped
3 chicken bouillon cubes
3 c. hot water
½ c. flour
1 tblsp. soy sauce (optional)

· Brown pork in butter in large skillet. Add onions, celery and tops, mushrooms and green peppers.

· Dissolve bouillon cubes in hot water; add to pork mixture. Cook over low heat until meat is well done, about 15 minutes. (Vegetables should still be crisp.)

· Stir in flour, blended with small amount of water. Stir until mixture is thickened; add soy sauce. Makes 6 servings.

CHOW MEIN

Serve this Chinese-type main dish with canned crisp fried noodles

1½ lbs. lean pork, thinly sliced
¼ c. cornstarch
2 tsp. sugar
5 tblsp. soy sauce
2 tblsp. salad oil
2 tblsp. fat
2 c. water
1½ c. sliced celery
1 c. chopped or sliced onions
1 tblsp. molasses
1 (8 oz.) can water chestnuts, sliced
1 (1 lb. 4 oz.) can bean sprouts
1 (4 oz.) can sliced mushrooms, drained

Salt
Pepper
1 bunch small green onions
Toasted whole blanched almonds

· Cut meat into thin strips.

· Combine 2 tblsp. cornstarch and sugar; blend in 1 tblsp. soy sauce and oil. Let meat stand in this mixture 10 minutes. Brown lightly on all sides in hot fat; add remaining soy sauce and 1½ c. water; simmer 45 minutes. Add celery and onions; simmer 10 to 15 minutes.

· Blend remaining cornstarch and ½ c. water; stir into meat mixture. Add molasses, water chestnuts, bean sprouts and mushrooms; heat thoroughly. Season with salt and pepper.

· Garnish with green onions, cut in lengthwise strips, and toasted whole almonds. Makes 6 to 8 servings.

PORK CANTONESE

Ring fluffy rice on plates and fill with this oriental treat–a company dish

2 lbs. boneless lean pork, cut in 1" pieces
2 tblsp. salad oil
1 (14 oz.) can pineapple chunks
1 (4 oz.) can mushrooms
⅓ c. unsulphured molasses
¼ c. vinegar
2 green peppers, cut in strips
2 onions, sliced and separated in rings
1½ tblsp. cornstarch
2 tblsp. water

· Brown pork on all sides in hot oil in skillet.

· Drain pineapple and mushrooms, reserving liquids. Combine liquids and add enough water to make 2 c. Add liquid to pork; cover and simmer until tender, about 45 minutes.

· Stir in molasses and vinegar until blended. Add pineapple, mushrooms, green peppers and onions; cover and cook 10 minutes. (Vegetables retain a little crispness.)

· Blend together cornstarch and water. Stir into hot mixture and cook until slightly thickened. Serve over hot rice. Makes 8 servings.

PARSLIED TOMATO PORK

Chick-peas are the new note in this main dish bright with tomatoes

1½ lbs. lean boneless pork slices, cut about ¼" thick (use leg or loin)
3 tblsp. salad oil
1 medium onion, minced
1 (1 lb.) can chick-peas (garbanzos), drained
3 medium tomatoes, cut into wedges (sixths)
¼ c. chopped fresh parsley
¾ tsp. salt
¾ tsp. garlic salt
¾ tsp. pepper

· In a large skillet, sauté pork slices over medium heat in salad oil until browned and tender. Pour off any oil in excess of 1 tblsp. Add onion and sauté just until limp.

· Add chick-peas, tomatoes and parsley; season with salt, garlic salt and pepper. Cover and simmer 10 minutes; stir once or twice. Makes 6 servings.

Note: You may want to make two skilletfuls for 12 servings.

SWEET-SOUR PORK

Serve with fluffy rice, hot tea and pass cookies for dessert

3½ lbs. pork shoulder
½ tsp. salt

1 tblsp. fat or salad oil
¾ c. water
½ c. pineapple juice, drained from chunks
¾ c. water
3 tblsp. brown sugar
¼ tsp. ground ginger
3 tblsp. cornstarch
¼ c. cider vinegar
2 tblsp. soy sauce
1 green pepper
1 medium onion
1 c. drained pineapple chunks
Hot fluffy rice

• Trim excess fat from meat; remove bones to make 1½ lbs. lean pork. Cut lean meat into ½" slices. Cut slices into strips 2" long. Sprinkle with salt. Brown in fat in skillet. Add ¾ c. water. Cover; simmer 1 hour.

• Combine pineapple juice and ¾ c. water. Add brown sugar, ginger, cornstarch, vinegar and soy sauce. Pour over meat. Cook until slightly thickened.

• Cut green pepper into strips, lengthwise; the onion into thin crosswise slices. Add to meat. Add pineapple chunks. Bring to boil. Cook for 5 minutes. Serve with rice. Makes 4 servings.

Pork Sausage Country-style

If you long to return, at least for a few hours, to the simple pleasures of old-time country living, go to your kitchen and *make* pork sausage seasoned the way you like it. It's not too difficult, especially if you have an electric food chopper. Our recipe for Homemade Pork Sausage, which came to us from a Kentucky farmer, has won friends in many places. Serve some of it to guests—perhaps in our Crusty Sausage Cakes—with hot, brown-topped biscuits or waffles, plus butter, table syrup or honey and plenty of steaming coffee. This makes an ideal menu for a country-style Sunday evening supper. Good, too, for breakfast any old day.

HOMEMADE PORK SAUSAGE

Serve with fried apples for a treat

9 lbs. lean pork
¾ tsp. ground red pepper
3 tblsp. salt
½ tblsp. pepper
1½ tblsp. crushed fresh sage (1 tsp. dried sage)

• Cut raw meat into cubes; put through food chopper, using fine blade.

• Sprinkle seasonings over meat and mix well. Refrigerate or freeze. Makes about 9 lbs.

Note: Some good cooks shape and wrap sausage in rolls that resemble refrigerator cookie dough. It's easy to slice off circles the thickness you like.

GOLDEN SAUSAGE BOATS

This breakfast treat tempts everyone. Serve with warmed honey or syrup

12 pork sausage links
6 eggs
⅓ c. milk
Dash of salt
6 frankfurter buns

• Place links in an unheated skillet. Do not prick skins. Add 3 tblsp. water. Cook, covered, 5 minutes over low heat. Uncover; drain off liquid. Finish cooking links over low heat, turning until well browned on all sides.

· Meanwhile, beat together eggs, milk and salt. Dip buns in mixture. Grill on both sides until browned.

· Place sausages in buns. Serve with syrup. Makes 6 servings.

SKILLET SUPPER

Have this on a cold day, with corn muffins and pineapple salad

1 lb. bulk pork sausage
1 large onion, chopped
1 medium green pepper, chopped
1 (1 lb. 4 oz.) can tomatoes
½ c. water or tomato juice
2 c. uncooked elbow macaroni
1 tsp. salt
2 tblsp. sugar
2 tsp. chili powder
2 c. dairy sour cream

· Brown sausage in heavy skillet, breaking meat apart with a fork. Pour fat off as it collects (important).

· Stir in remaining ingredients, except sour cream.

· Bring to boil; cover pan. Simmer, stirring often to prevent sticking. Cook until macaroni is tender, 20 to 25 minutes.

· Blend in sour cream; reheat just to boiling. Makes 6 servings.

SAVORY SAUSAGE RICE

Hearty dish for hungry men—also have peas, apple salad and cookies

2 lbs. bulk pork sausage
1 c. finely chopped green pepper
¾ c. chopped onion
2½ c. coarsely chopped celery
2 (1¾ oz.) pkgs. chicken noodle soup mix
4½ c. boiling water
1 c. rice, uncooked
½ tsp. salt
1 c. slivered almonds (optional)

· Brown sausage in large skillet; pour off excess fat. Add green pepper, onion and celery; sauté.

· Combine soup mix and boiling water in large saucepan; stir in rice. Cover and simmer 20 minutes, or until rice is tender. Add sausage mixture, salt and almonds; stir well.

· Pour into greased 13 × 9 × 2" baking dish. Bake in moderate oven (375°) 20 minutes.

· To reheat, pour into a large saucepan, add ¼ c. water and warm over low heat. Makes 10 servings.

SWEET POTATO MAIN DISH

Sweet potatoes, apples, sausage and maple syrup blend deliciously

4 c. thinly sliced, unpeeled tart apples
4 c. thinly sliced, uncooked sweet potatoes
2 tsp. instant minced onion
2 tsp. salt
½ c. maple-blended syrup
½ c. apple juice
¼ c. melted butter
1 lb. bulk pork sausage
⅓ c. dry bread crumbs

· Arrange alternate layers of apple and sweet potato slices in greased 2-qt. casserole, sprinkling each layer with onion and salt.

· Combine syrup, apple juice and butter; blend and pour over all. Cover and bake in moderate oven (350°) 1 hour.

· Meanwhile, crumble sausage into skillet and brown. Drain; mix with crumbs.

· After an hour, uncover sweet potato-apple dish and spread with sausage mixture. Bake uncovered 20 minutes. Makes 6 servings.

CRUSTY SAUSAGE CAKES

Crisp coating adds a new note to country breakfast sausage cakes

1 lb. bulk pork sausage
2 eggs, slightly beaten
1 c. crushed corn flakes
1 tsp. fat

• Shape sausage into 8 patties, ½″ thick. Dip into egg, then roll in corn flakes. Pan-fry slowly in fat in heavy skillet to cook thoroughly. Turn to brown well on both sides. Serve with tart jelly or applesauce. Makes 4 to 6 servings.

Old-Time Farm Recipes

HEAD CHEESE

Hominy is a great escort for this

1 pig's or calf's head
1 large onion, quartered
4 whole cloves
6 celery tops
4 sprigs parsley
1 carrot
1 bay leaf
12 peppercorns
2 tsp. salt
Ground red pepper
Rubbed sage
Ground nutmeg (optional)

• Clean head, removing snout and reserving tongue and brains. Scrub well and place in large kettle. Cover with water; add onion, stuck with cloves, and tongue. Tie celery, parsley, carrot, bay leaf and peppercorns in cheesecloth and drop into kettle. Add salt.

• Bring to boil, skim carefully and simmer slowly about 4 hours, or until meat is tender and falls easily from bones. Remove tongue from water after it has cooked 1½ hours.

• Lift head onto a large platter. Strain and reserve liquid in kettle. Remove all rind from head; cut the meat and tongue, skin removed and excess tissue from root end, trimmed, into tiny pieces. (Some women like to put meat through food chopper.) Place in large bowl.

• Drop brains into a little of the cooking liquid; simmer, covered, 15 minutes. Remove, drain and add to meat and tongue. Season lightly with cayenne, sage and nutmeg. Toss to mix well.

• Pack mixture into 9 × 5 × 3″ loaf pan or mold, pressing firmly. Pour ½ c. cooking liquid, cooled until lukewarm, over mixture. Cover pan or mold and put weight on it. Chill at least 48 hours before using. Slice to serve. Makes 18 ½″ slices or 8 servings.

HOW TO RENDER LARD

Use the leaf fat, backfat and fat trimmings. Caul and ruffle fats from internal organs yield lard of darker color; if you use them, cook them separately.

Remove fat, wash and chill promptly.

Cut fat into small pieces or grind it to hasten the rendering. Place in a large, heavy kettle and *cook slowly,* starting with a small quantity to make stirring easier. When the fat begins to melt, add more pieces, but do not fill kettle or it might boil over. Stir frequently and cook slowly to avoid sticking and scorching.

As cooking begins, the temperature will stay at 212°. As the water evaporates from the fat, the temperature will rise slowly. Do not let it go beyond 255°.

During the cooking the brown cracklings will start to float. When the lard is almost rendered, they sink to the bottom of the kettle. *Be careful not to let them stick and scorch.* You can stop the cooking while the cracklings still float, but complete rendering removes more water and results in lard that keeps better. If moisture is eliminated by proper rendering, water souring should not develop during storage.

Let the lard cool slightly and settle before emptying the kettle. Dip the lard carefully into 5- or 10-lb. containers. Put the cracklings through a press. Then strain all the lard through three thicknesses of cheesecloth.

Store immediately in a cool place, at near freezing or freezing temperature. Quick cooling produces a fine-grain lard.

Keep lard in containers, sealed with a tight cover, and store in a dark cool place or in freezer or locker. Air and light often cause chemical changes that result in rancidity. If lard becomes rancid, you cannot improve it.

Note: You can greatly increase the storage life of lard by adding an antioxidant (available at most locker plants). Another way to prolong the fresh flavor is to stir 1 (3 lb.) can of hydrogenated vegetable shortening into every 50 pounds of lard while it is cooling.

Country Specials with Ham

Ham needs no introduction to country meal planners. They depend on beautiful baked hams for many special occasions, such as Christmas festivities, Easter dinner and year-round buffet suppers. Ham slices, fixed in many tempting ways, come to the table more frequently, as does ham shaped and baked in loaves and balls. Try lovely Rosy Ham Ring, our company version of ham loaf, on your friends. It's always a hit!

HONEY-GLAZED HAM

Especially delicious glazed with cider. Ham has a golden look

1 (10 to 12 lb.) fully cooked bone-in ham
2 c. apple juice or cider
¾ tsp. whole allspice
1 tsp. whole cloves
½ tsp. whole ginger
3 (2") cinnamon sticks
1 c. honey
Whole cloves
Paprika

• Place ham, fat side up, on rack in shallow pan. Insert meat thermometer into center so it does not touch bone.

• Heat apple juice with allspice, 1 tsp. whole cloves, ginger and stick cinnamon in saucepan, bringing to a boil. Cover and boil 5 minutes. Remove from heat and brush a little of this mixture over ham.

• Bake ham in slow oven (325°) 1½ to 2 hours, basting every 15 minutes with the spiced apple juice mixture.

• Drizzle ½ c. honey over ham. Bake 30 minutes longer. Remove from oven, and drizzle on remaining ½ c. honey. Bake 30 minutes, or until thermometer indicates internal temperature of 160°, about 15 minutes per pound.

· Remove from oven and cool 30 minutes. Score fat, stud with whole cloves and sprinkle lavishly with paprika. Place on platter. For the Christmas holidays, garnish platter with a few small holly sprays; at other seasons, garnish with pickled peaches, drained and tucked in nests of parsley. Serves 20 to 22.

CRANBERRY/ORANGE GLAZED HAM

If you want to dress up a ham for company, do try this beauty

1 (10 to 12 lb.) fully-cooked bone-in ham
2 unpeeled large oranges, sliced
3 maraschino cherries, halved
Whole cloves
1 tblsp. flour
⅓ c. brown sugar, firmly packed
2 tblsp. prepared mustard
1 c. cranberry juice cocktail
¼ c. cider vinegar
¼ c. honey
2 tblsp. butter

· Trim and score ham. Place fat side up on rack in shallow pan. Insert meat thermometer into center; do not let it touch bone. Bake in slow oven (325°) about 15 minutes per pound. Remove from oven. Cover top and sides with orange slices. Place a cherry half in center of each orange slice. Insert cloves around edge of each cherry.

· In 1½-qt. saucepan, combine flour, brown sugar and mustard; stir in remaining ingredients. Bring to a full boil; cook 1 minute. Pour over hot ham. Return to oven. Continue baking 30 minutes or until thermometer registers internal temperature of 160°, basting often with the glaze. Makes about 20 servings.

EASY-SERVE BAKED HAM

Just cut the string and presto—the big ham just falls apart in even slices!

1 (6 lb.) canned ham
1 (1 lb.) jar apricot preserves (about 1½ c.)
Whole cloves

· Slice ham and tie together with string. Your meat dealer may slice the ham on his slicer and tie it up for you.

· Place ham, fat side up, on rack in shallow baking pan. Spread apricot preserves over top. Stud with cloves.

· Heat in slow oven (325°) 15 minutes per pound. Baste with pan juices 3 or 4 times while baking.

· Place on platter to serve. Cut and remove string. Makes 15 to 20 servings.

HAM SLICE

Two-story treat with mincemeat spread between the ham slices

2 slices ham, cut 1" thick
1½ c. prepared mincemeat
½ c. pineapple juice

· Place one ham slice in shallow baking pan. Spread mincemeat over ham; cover with second ham slice. Pour pineapple juice over top.

· Bake in slow oven (325°) about 1 hour, basting frequently.

· Thicken liquid in pan for spicy gravy. Makes 6 servings.

HAM LOAF

Juicy, flavorful, brown-topped loaf —use the leftovers in sandwiches

- **2 lbs. ground smoked ham**
- **1 lb. ground veal**
- **2 c. soft bread cubes**
- **¼ c. chopped onion**
- **¼ c. chopped green pepper**
- **½ tsp. salt**
- **⅛ tsp. black pepper**
- **⅛ tsp. ground cloves**
- **½ tsp. Worcestershire sauce**
- **1 can condensed cream of celery soup**
- **2 eggs, beaten**

· Mix all ingredients; pack into 9 × 5 × 3″ loaf pan.

· Bake in moderate oven (350°) 1¼ hours. Makes 8 servings.

ROSY HAM RING

Country hostesses and their guests praise this pretty ham-pork loaf

- **3 lbs. ground smoked ham**
- **1 lb. ground pork**
- **2 eggs**
- **1¾ c. graham cracker crumbs**
- **1½ c. milk**
- **½ tsp. ground allspice**
- **Tomato Basting Sauce**

· Combine all ingredients except sauce; mix well. In a 15½ × 10½ × 1″ jelly roll baking pan, shape with hands to make a ring (or loaf) about 10″ across. Pour over half of sauce.

· Bake in moderate oven (350°) 45 minutes; pour over remaining sauce and bake 45 minutes longer, basting several times with sauce. Serves 12 to 14.

TOMATO BASTING SAUCE: Combine 1 can condensed tomato soup, ½ c. vinegar, ½ c. brown sugar, firmly packed, and 1½ tsp. prepared mustard.

Note: You can mix this loaf a few days early and freeze it. Allow a little longer cooking time. At serving time fill the center of the ring with buttered peas, corn or succotash.

MUSTARD HAM LOAF

Wreathe loaf with spiced crab apples when you take it to a party

- **1½ lbs. ground smoked ham**
- **½ lb. ground fresh pork**
- **1 c. milk**
- **1 c. bread cubes (2 slices)**
- **1 tblsp. dry mustard**
- **½ c. brown sugar, firmly packed**
- **¼ c. vinegar**
- **2 tblsp. water**

· Combine meat, milk and bread cubes. Mix lightly; form into loaf; place in shallow baking pan.

· Combine remaining ingredients for sauce; pour over meat.

· Bake in moderate oven (375°) 1½ hours, basting often with sauce in pan. Makes 8 to 10 servings.

PARTY HAM LOAF

The trick is to shape the loaf like a whole ham and to score it

- **5 c. ground cooked ham**
- **⅔ c. minced onion**
- **1 c. quick-cooking rolled oats**
- **½ tsp. pepper**
- **1 tsp. Worcestershire sauce**
- **¼ tsp. ground cloves**
- **2 eggs, slightly beaten**
- **⅓ c. milk**
- **¼ c. currant jelly**
- **1 tblsp. prepared horse-radish**

· Combine ham, onion, oats, seasonings, eggs and milk; mix thoroughly. Shape like a ham in shallow baking pan; score top in diamond designs.

• Bake in moderate oven (375°) 45 minutes. Remove; brush top with mixture of melted jelly and horseradish. Trim with pineapple and maraschino cherries if desired. Makes 8 servings.

HARVEST HAM BALLS

Crusty ham balls baked in golden peach halves please most guests

1 egg, beaten
½ c. soft bread crumbs
½ c. milk
1 tblsp. brown sugar
⅛ tsp. ground cloves
1 lb. ground cooked ham
8 canned peach halves, drained
Green celery tops or parsley

• Combine egg, crumbs, milk, sugar, cloves and ham; shape into 8 balls.

• Place peach halves, hollow sides up, in greased shallow baking dish. Nest a ham ball in each peach half. Bake in moderate oven (350°) 25 minutes.

• Garnish with celery. Makes 8 servings.

Delicately Flavored Veal

Since young beef has little time to put on fat, veal is lean. That's why country cooks add fat of some kind to prevent dry veal dishes; often they team pork with veal. Two excellent examples of this are recipes for roast veal in which bacon strips top the meat and baste it during the roasting, and the veal loaf which teams ground pork and veal.

Do try our gourmet special, Roast Veal with Sweet Onions, a hostess' prize. The meat tastes marvelous, it has eye appeal on the platter and you can cook and carve it ahead ready to reheat to perfection in 10 minutes at mealtime. Also try our hearty farmhouse meal-in-a-dish, Veal Stew with Dumplings. Really charms hungry men!

ROAST VEAL

• Select bone-in veal roast from leg, loin, rump or shoulder, or a boned and rolled roast from rump or shoulder. Place fat side up on rack in shallow pan. Lay strips of bacon over top to provide more fat. Insert thermometer in thickest part of meat, using care that the tip does not touch bone or fat.

• Roast in slow oven (300 to 325°) until thermometer registers 170°, about 25 to 35 minutes per pound for bone-in roasts, 40 to 50 minutes per pound for boned, rolled roasts. Makes about 2 servings per pound of bone-in roast, 3 servings per pound of rolled roast.

MUSHROOM GRAVY: Drain fat and brown drippings from pan. Put ¼ c. fat back in pan; blend in ¼ c. flour. Let bubble over low heat, stirring constantly, until mixture is light golden brown. Remove from heat. Pour remaining fat from drippings. Drain 1 (4 oz.) can mushrooms; add enough cold water to mushroom juice to make 2 c. Add drippings and mushroom liquid to browned flour and fat. Return to heat and cook, stirring constantly, until gravy thickens. Season with salt and pepper, and stir in mushrooms. (Mushroom stems and pieces may be used.) Let simmer 3 to 5 minutes. Makes about 2 cups gravy.

ROAST VEAL WITH SWEET ONIONS

Roast the carved veal or lamb ahead and reheat it at mealtime

1 (4 lb.) boneless veal roast (rolled shoulder or leg)
⅔ c. salad oil
6 tblsp. wine vinegar
1½ tsp. salt
½ tsp. pepper
1 sweet onion, very thinly sliced

· Place meat on rack in roasting pan; insert meat thermometer. Roast in slow oven (300 to 325°) until meat thermometer registers 170°, or about 40 to 45 minutes per pound. Remove from oven and allow to stand about 20 minutes, then slice, saving juices.

· Shake or beat together oil, vinegar, salt and pepper. Remove any excess fat and burned drippings from roasting pan; loosen drippings. Add meat juices and the oil-vinegar mixture; stir to blend.

· Arrange meat slices, slightly overlapping, in roasting pan; spoon on juices to moisten well. Cover with foil. Before serving, place in moderate oven (350°) 10 minutes, or until heated through. Arrange meat slices on a warm serving platter; top with onion slices separated into rings.

· Quickly heat remaining roasting pan juice mixture; pass as a sauce. Makes about 8 servings.

Variation

ROAST LAMB WITH SWEET ONIONS: Follow recipe for the roast veal, substituting 1 (4 lb.) boneless rolled leg of lamb (4 to 6 lbs. before boning) for the veal. Roast until meat thermometer registers 175 to 180°, about 30 to 35 minutes per pound. The lamb will make about 6 generous servings.

COMPANY-SPECIAL VEAL

Fine casserole for home meals or to tote to covered dish suppers

½ lb. fresh mushrooms, sliced
2 tblsp. butter or regular margarine
½ c. flour
1½ tsp. salt
¼ tsp. pepper
1 tsp. paprika
1½ lbs. boneless veal, cut in ½ × ½ × 1″ strips
¼ c. butter or regular margarine
1 clove garlic, minced
1 green pepper, cut in strips
1 onion, thinly sliced
1½ c. chicken broth
1½ c. processed rice, cooked (about 6 c.)
⅓ c. sliced pimiento-stuffed olives

· Brown mushrooms in 2 tblsp. butter. Remove from skillet and reserve.

· Combine flour, salt, pepper and paprika in paper bag. Shake veal in seasoned flour and brown in ¼ c. butter along with minced garlic. Add green pepper, onion and 1 c. chicken broth; cover and simmer 30 minutes, or until veal is tender.

· Blend remaining ½ c. chicken broth with 3 tblsp. flour from paper bag. (If not enough seasoned flour is left, add enough flour to make 3 tblsp.) Add to veal mixture and cook, stirring until thickened. Add mushrooms to veal. Serve over hot rice, cooked by package directions, with sliced pimiento-stuffed olives folded into the rice. Serves 8.

Note: If more convenient, cook rice, add olives and place in bottom of a 3-qt. greased casserole. Top with veal mixture, cover and bake in moderate oven (350°) 30 minutes. This makes a good and easy-to-serve company dish, but the rice is fluffier if veal mixture is spooned over it at serving time.

VEAL STEW WITH DUMPLINGS

Plump dumplings, vegetables and veal star in this good country dish

Stew:

2 lbs. veal, cut in 1″ cubes
¼ c. flour
¼ c. shortening
2½ c. hot water
1 c. diced potatoes
1 c. diced carrots
1 c. green lima beans or peas
½ c. chopped celery
½ c. chopped onion
2 bay leaves
1 tsp. Worcestershire sauce
2 tsp. salt
⅛ tsp. pepper
1 (8 oz.) can tomato sauce

Dumplings:

1½ c. sifted flour
2¼ tsp. baking powder
¾ tsp. salt
¾ c. milk
3 tblsp. melted shortening

• Roll meat in flour; brown in hot shortening. Add hot water; cover and cook slowly 1 hour, or until tender. Add vegetables and seasonings; continue cooking for 30 minutes.

• Meanwhile make dumplings. Sift together dry ingredients; stir in milk and shortening to make a soft dough.

• Add tomato sauce to stew; bring to a boil. Drop dumpling batter from spoon in 10 or 12 mounds on top of stew. Cook uncovered 10 minutes; cover and cook about 10 minutes longer, or until dumplings are fluffy. Makes 8 servings.

VEAL LOAF

Excellent served hot in cold weather, cold at summer suppers

1½ lbs. ground veal
¼ lb. ground lean pork
¼ tsp. garlic salt
½ c. finely chopped onion
2 c. bread cubes (4 slices)
¼ c. shredded Cheddar cheese
2 tsp. salt
½ tsp. pepper
2 eggs, beaten
¾ c. milk

• Combine all ingredients and mix well. Pack into 9 × 5 × 3″ loaf pan.

• Bake in moderate oven (375°) 1¼ hours. Makes 8 servings.

CHOPS BAKED IN SOUP

Requires no watching while it bakes. Good served with cranberry salad

6 rib chops, veal or pork
1 tsp. salt
¼ tsp. pepper
2 tblsp. butter or regular margarine
⅓ c. finely chopped onions
4 c. thinly sliced potatoes
1 can condensed cream of mushroom soup
1¼ c. milk

• Rub chops with salt and pepper.

• Melt butter in skillet; add chops; brown lightly on both sides. Remove chops, and add onions; brown lightly.

• Put sliced potatoes in buttered 2-qt. baking dish. Arrange chops over top.

• Add soup and milk to onions in

skillet. Blend until smooth. Pour over chops. Cover. Bake in moderate oven (350°) 30 minutes. Uncover; continue baking for 30 to 40 minutes, until potatoes are done. Makes 6 servings.

Recipes from Country Kitchen Files

GRILLED FRANKWICHES

Serve with potato salad on summery days–hot potato soup when it's cold

12 slices bread
2 c. ground frankfurters
1 c. chopped walnuts
2 tblsp. prepared mustard
1 c. mayonnaise or salad dressing

· Toast bread on one side.
· Combine remaining ingredients. Spread on untoasted side of bread.
· Broil about 2 minutes or until edges brown. Cut sandwiches in halves and serve hot. Makes 6 servings.

SAVORY FRANKFURTERS AND MACARONI

Sliced "franks" in a hot red sauce are the macaroni dress-up

1 (12 oz.) can frankfurters
3 tblsp. fat or salad oil
3 tblsp. flour
1 tsp. salt
⅛ tsp. dry mustard
Dash of rubbed sage
Dash of curry powder
⅛ tsp. chili powder
1 small bay leaf
1 (1 lb. 13 oz.) can tomatoes
1 (8 oz.) pkg. macaroni, cooked

· Cut frankfurters into 1″ pieces.
· Heat fat; add meat; brown lightly.
· Add flour and seasonings; blend with fat and frankfurters in pan.
· Force tomatoes through coarse sieve; add pulp to ingredients in pan. Bring to boil, stirring constantly. Reduce heat; continue to cook until thickened.
· Serve over hot, drained macaroni. Makes 6 servings.

SKILLET BARBECUED FRANKS

Serve on corn bread or toasted buns

¾ block frozen Home-cooked Tomato Sauce (see Index)
1 c. water
1 medium onion, finely chopped
½ tsp. salt
1 tsp. Worcestershire sauce
5 drops Tabasco sauce
1 lb. frankfurters

· Place tomato sauce (3 c.), water, onion and seasonings in skillet, heat to boiling. Add frankfurters, split and cut in 1″ lengths. Simmer uncovered 10 minutes. Makes 6 servings.

Note: Frankfurters are cooked when you buy them. They will keep two weeks or less in the freezer in original package. To store longer, rewrap in moisture-vapor-proof material.

LIVERBURGERS

Almost everyone goes for liver fixed with diced potatoes and onions

1 lb. liver
2 c. diced raw potatoes
1 c. chopped onions

1. COUNTRY-STYLE BEEF WELLINGTON—Roast the beef the day before you entertain. Next day pat on liverwurst, wrap in pastry and bake. Recipe, page 3.

2. ZESTY PORK CHOPS and PORK/SAUERKRAUT PINWHEELS–New, attractive and tasty ways to fix pork. Apple-topped chops cook gently in sauce. Recipe, pages 36, 39.

3. ROAST YOUNG CHICKENS–Try this two-step method. Precook chickens briefly, cool and freeze. To serve, complete cooking in hot oven. Recipe, page 55.

4. SHORT RIBS—Browned beef ribs, carrots and onions simmer tender in this dish. Add Parsley Dumplings for a hearty platter special. Recipes, pages 9, 66.

1½ tsp. salt
⅛ tsp. pepper
2 tblsp. fat
3 tblsp. tomato paste
1 tblsp. flour
1½ c. milk
½ c. light cream
1 tsp. salt
⅛ tsp. pepper

• Put liver, potatoes and onions through food chopper twice. Add 1½ tsp. salt and ⅛ tsp. pepper.
• Drop liver mixture by spoonfuls onto hot fat in skillet. Fry quickly. Remove burgers from pan.
• For gravy, blend tomato paste and flour into drippings in pan. Add milk, cream, 1 tsp. salt and ⅛ tsp. pepper. Bring to boil, stirring constantly.
• Add liverburgers; simmer, covered, 15 minutes. Makes 8 servings.

LIVER LYONNAISE

Have green beans, lettuce salad and hot biscuits with this main dish

1 lb. sliced liver
3 tblsp. flour
1 tsp. salt
⅛ tsp. pepper
3 tblsp. fat
3½ c. cubed potatoes
1 c. thinly sliced onions
1 can condensed cream of celery soup
½ c. milk
1 tsp. salt
⅛ tsp. pepper

• Cut liver in 1½" cubes.
• Blend flour, 1 tsp. salt and ⅛ tsp. pepper. Roll liver in flour mixture. Brown on all sides in hot fat in heavy skillet; remove liver from pan.
• Fry potatoes and onions in remaining fat until lightly browned and potatoes are tender.
• Alternate liver and potato-onion mixture in 1½-qt. baking dish. Combine soup, milk, 1 tsp. salt and ⅛ tsp. pepper and pour over top.
• Cover; bake in moderate oven (375°) 40 minutes. Makes 6 servings.

LIVER PUFFS

Serve the crisp-coated patties with ketchup, chili sauce or mustard

1½ lbs. liver
3 onions, peeled
1 egg
1 c. cracker crumbs
1 tsp. salt
1 c. hot water

• Simmer liver in water until firm, then grind it with onions.
• Add remaining ingredients. Blend; shape into 6 patties and pan-fry in hot bacon fat until brown on both sides. Makes 6 servings.

TONGUE WITH SPICY SAUCE

If you like tongue, try the canned kind fixed this interesting way

2 tblsp. fat or salad oil
1 small onion, minced
1 c. diced celery
1 (8 oz.) can tomato sauce
½ c. water
½ tsp. salt
1 tsp. Worcestershire sauce
⅛ tsp. pepper
Dash ground cloves
1 tblsp. vinegar
1 (6 oz.) can beef tongue

• Heat fat in saucepan. Add onion and celery; sauté until golden.
• Add remaining ingredients, ex-

cept the tongue; simmer 15 minutes.

• Cut tongue in ½" cubes; add to cooked sauce; heat through.

• Serve over cooked spaghetti, noodles or potatoes. Makes 4 servings.

DRIED BEEF WITH EGGS

Dried beef frizzled in butter gives scrambled eggs a new taste

1 (4 oz.) pkg. dried beef
Boiling water
3 tblsp. butter or regular margarine
8 eggs
½ c. milk

• Pour boiling water over dried beef. Drain. Melt butter in skillet. Cut dried beef in small pieces with scissors and pan-fry for a minute in the butter.

• Beat eggs and milk slightly. Pour over beef. Stir gently while cooking. Check for seasoning (beef may add enough salt). Serve at once while still moist. Makes 6 servings.

DRIED BEEF SANDWICHES

Serve tomato or fruit salad with these hot, open-face sandwiches

½ c. shredded dried beef
1 (5 oz.) jar pimiento cheese spread
⅓ c. pickle relish
⅓ c. mayonnaise or salad dressing
6 slices buttered bread

• Combine dried beef, cheese, relish and mayonnaise and spread equal portions on bread slices.

• Broil until bubbly and hot. Makes 6 servings.

DRIED BEEF SPRINKLES: Shape cream cheese in small balls (about 1" in diameter). Roll in finely shredded dried beef. Place on toothpicks and pass with crackers.

chapter 2

The Poultry Quartet

CHICKENS, TURKEYS, GEESE AND DUCKS contribute much to the prestige country meals enjoy. Who doesn't welcome an invitation to a Sunday chicken or Thanksgiving turkey dinner on the farm? And who doesn't experience pleasure at the sight of golden fried chicken heaped on the platter or of chicken fricassee wreathed with plump, light-as-air dumplings? Festive goose roast and ducklings appear less frequently, but for that reason plus their rich, moist meat these birds really create excitement when they show.

Not too long ago turkey belonged to Thanksgiving Day, fried chicken to summer and roast goose to the Christmas dinner; now the wide and easy availability of the poultry quartet is taken for granted. The poultry industry deserves credit for banishing seasons for these birds. And how much easier it is to go to the freezer than to the barnyard for your birds!

In this chapter you will find a collection of poultry recipes from country kitchens. Unless otherwise specified, ready-to-cook weights of birds are listed.

Chicken recipes come first and they're the most numerous because chicken is a basic staple for country menu planners. The types of birds commonly used and their dressed weights are: broiler-fryers, usually 1½ to 4 lbs.; roasters, a little older and heavier than broiler-fryers, 3½ to 6 lbs.; and hens, stewing chickens and fowl, 2½ to 8 lbs.

Our chicken recipes divide into five groups—(1) roasted, (2) broiled, (3) fried, (4) stewed (fricassee) and (5) those using cooked chicken.

Along with recipes for roast chicken, turkey, goose and duckling, you will find some excellent stuffings. An old farm rule that still holds is to allow about 1 cup stuffing to every pound of bird. Remember that the safe way is to stuff poultry just before you put it in the oven. Remove the stuffing from any leftover cooked poultry and refrigerate both at once, *separately*. You can freeze the meat, of course, but we do not recommend freezing the stuffing because it loses its fluffy texture and the seasonings usually change flavor. Use the refrigerated stuffing within a couple of days. If it is not convenient to stuff the bird just before putting it in the oven, you can spoon stuffing in a greased casserole and bake it in the oven with the poultry for the last hour. Moisten the stuffing a few times with chicken or giblet broth.

Cook giblets until tender in water to cover, with a small onion, celery branch and salt and pepper seasonings. Cooking time varies from 2 to 3 hours, depending on age of bird. Always remove the liver after cooking 20 minutes. Strain the broth to use in stuffing or gravy. Most cooks put the cooked giblets through the food chopper and add them to the hot, brown gravy to be ladled over fluffs of mashed potatoes and tempting stuffing.

ROAST CHICKEN

1 (4 lb.) broiler-fryer
Bread Stuffing

• Wash chicken inside with cold water, dry thoroughly with cloth or paper towels. Stuff with Bread Stuffing. Close opening with skewer. Fold neck skin over back; fasten with skewer. Fold wings across back and tie tips together with cord. Tie drumsticks to tail.

• Place breast side up in shallow roasting pan. Brush with melted butter or regular margarine. Do not cover. Roast in hot oven (400°) 1¾ to 2½ hours, or until tender, basting occasionally with pan drippings. When bird is two thirds done, cut cord between drumsticks and tail. Test for doneness by pressing thickest part of thigh meat (use paper towel to protect fingers from heat). If done, the meat will feel very soft and you can move the drumstick up and down easily. Place chicken on hot platter and let stand a few minutes before carving. Makes about 4 servings.

Variation

ROAST CHICKEN WITHOUT STUFFING: Rub 1 tsp. salt over inside of chicken and tuck in a few celery leaves and a little chopped onion. When chicken is two thirds done, cut cord that ties drumsticks to tail. Reduce roasting time about 20 minutes.

BREAD STUFFING

Double recipe for a 10-pound turkey

3 tblsp. chopped onion (optional)
⅓ c. melted butter or regular margarine
4 c. dry bread cubes
1 tsp. salt
¼ tsp. pepper
¼ tsp. poultry seasoning
Sage to taste (optional)
Hot chicken broth or water

• Cook onion in 2 tblsp. melted butter over low heat until it softens. Do not brown.

• Combine onion, bread cubes and seasonings. Add remaining butter and enough broth (canned broth may be used) to moisten. Toss to mix. Makes 4 cups.

Sunday-best Country Chicken

The recipe for Roast Young Chickens comes from a Santa Fe County, New Mexico, friend. You precook the chickens briefly, cool and freeze them. Then, when you want to have chicken for dinner, you hurry the birds into a hot oven or place them over glowing coals to thaw, finish cooking and brown. You can baste them with barbecue sauce or lemon juice while they cook. Either addition brings out interesting flavors.

ROAST YOUNG CHICKENS

Keep partially roasted chickens in the freezer ready to brown in the oven or over coals—saves time

2 (2½ to 3 lb.) broiler-fryers
1 tblsp. salt
¼ tsp. pepper
⅓ c. melted butter

• Rinse chickens in cold water; drain and pat dry with paper towels or a clean cloth. Rub the cavity in each bird with ½ tsp. salt. Fasten neck skin to back with skewers. Tie legs together.
• Rub outside of birds with remaining salt and pepper; brush with melted butter.
• Place chickens, breast side down, on rack in a shallow baking pan.
• Roast in a very hot oven (450°) 30 minutes; cool quickly. Wrap and freeze. Freeze pan drippings separately. Freezer storage time: up to 1 month.
• To serve, place frozen chickens on rack in shallow pan, breast side up. Roast in a hot oven (400°) about 1 hour, or until drumstick joints move easily. Baste with the thawed drippings (from freezer) several times during the roasting. Makes 6 to 8 servings.

Variations

ROAST CHICKEN WITHOUT FREEZING: Prepare broiler-fryers as in the preceding recipe. Roast in hot oven (400°) on rack in uncovered pan, 30 minutes per pound.

SOUTHERN BARBECUED CHICKEN: Instead of basting precooked, frozen broiler-fryers with pan drippings, baste them with this sauce: Mix and bring to a boil 2½ c. water, 1 tblsp. brown sugar, 2½ tsp. pepper, 2 tblsp. pan drippings or salad oil, ¼ c. vinegar, 2½ tsp. salt, 2 tblsp. Worcestershire sauce, 2 tblsp. finely chopped onion, 1 tsp. dry mustard, 2 tsp. chili powder, ½ tsp. Tabasco sauce and 1 clove garlic.

LEMON-BARBECUED CHICKEN: To the pan drippings (from the freezer) add ½ c. lemon juice for each broiler-fryer. Use to baste frozen precooked chickens while roasting, instead of plain pan drippings.

Barbecued Chicken for a Crowd

Along about first-frost time, lights go on week nights in churches as members gather in church basements or "parlors" for a truly

American style of Thanksgiving, a neighborhood supper. Southern Barbecued Chicken is a favorite for these occasions—it makes 50 servings.

SOUTHERN BARBECUED CHICKEN

Several women can cook the chicken at home and carry it to the supper

8 to 10 broiler-fryers (about 40 lbs.)
1 qt. water
2 lbs. sifted flour
5 tblsp. salt
1 tblsp. pepper
3 lbs. shortening
Southern Barbecue Sauce

· Cut chickens into serving pieces. Wash well and pat dry.
· Put giblets to stew in 1 qt. salted water. You'll use this broth in barbecue sauce.
· Put flour, salt and pepper into paper bag. Shake chicken in flour, a few pieces at a time.
· Sauté chicken pieces until golden brown on both sides in hot shortening in heavy skillets. Arrange pieces in uncovered pans. Add giblets, drained; pour Southern Barbecue Sauce over chicken.
· Bake in moderate oven (350°) 1½ hours, or until fork-tender, basting frequently. (No harm to bake chicken a little longer—flavor actually improves.) Makes 50 servings.

SOUTHERN BARBECUE SAUCE

The magic that gives the chicken a tangy taste and rich, appealing color

2 lbs. onions (about 8 medium)
2 c. salad oil
½ c. flour
1 c. prepared mustard
2½ tblsp. salt
2 tsp. pepper
¾ c. brown sugar, firmly packed
1 qt. vinegar
1 qt. chicken broth
2 (14 oz.) bottles ketchup
2 (1 lb. 13 oz.) cans tomato purée
1 c. Worcestershire sauce

· Chop onions; sauté lightly in oil in heavy skillet.
· Combine flour, mustard, salt, pepper and brown sugar. Stir into onions. Add remaining ingredients; heat to boiling, stirring constantly.
· Simmer 15 minutes to blend flavors. Makes enough sauce for 50 servings.

GOLDEN CHICKEN CASSEROLE

Its popularity shows up at buffets—guests keep coming back for helpings

1 (4 to 5 lb.) stewing chicken
1 large onion, quartered
1½ tsp. salt
½ c. chicken fat, butter or regular margarine
½ c. flour
2 (4 oz.) cans mushrooms, drained
1 c. evaporated milk
1 tsp. salt
⅛ tsp. pepper
½ tsp. ground turmeric
½ tsp. orégano leaves
1 c. rice
2½ c. boiling water
1½ tsp. salt
1 tblsp. butter
½ c. chopped green onions
½ c. shredded mild cheese

· Cook chicken until tender in water to cover with onion and 1½ tsp. salt added. Cool chicken (reserving broth); remove skin and cut chicken meat in small pieces with kitchen scissors.

• Melt chicken fat in saucepan. Stir in flour; add 4 c. liquid (juice drained from mushrooms and chicken broth) and evaporated milk. Cook and stir until sauce is thick and smooth. Add 1 tsp. salt, pepper, turmeric and orégano.

• Combine rice with boiling water; add 1½ tsp. salt and butter. Cover and bake in hot oven (400°) 30 minutes, or until tender.

• Spread rice in bottom of a large casserole or baking dish. Top with chicken, then with green onions, sauce and mushrooms; sprinkle cheese over top.

• Bake in moderate oven (350°) 30 minutes. Makes 10 to 12 servings.

CHICKEN-STUFFED PANCAKES

Serve with your favorite fruit salad

Pancakes:

2 eggs and 2 egg yolks, beaten
1 c. milk
1 c. flour
⅛ tsp. salt
2 tblsp. salad oil

Chicken Filling:

½ c. chopped onion
2 tblsp. butter
½ tsp. salt
¼ tsp. pepper
½ tsp. thyme leaves
¼ tsp. ground mace
¼ tsp. ground nutmeg
¼ c. flour
½ c. hot chicken stock (about)
1 (4 oz.) can chopped mushrooms
2 c. finely chopped cooked chicken

Coating:

¼ tsp. salt
¼ tsp. pepper
2 egg whites
½ c. fine dry bread crumbs

• Blend together all ingredients for pancakes until smooth. For each pancake, pour ¼ c. batter into preheated, lightly greased skillet. Tip pan so batter spreads evenly. When set, turn. Place baked pancakes on clean dish towels until ready to fill. You will have about 8 pancakes.

• To make filling, sauté onion in butter. Blend in seasonings and flour. Add enough chicken stock to liquid drained from mushrooms to make 1 c.; stir into onion mixture. Add mushrooms and chicken; cook until thick, stirring constantly. Cool.

• Spoon filling on one half of pancake; roll, tucking in ends.

• For coating, beat together salt, pepper and egg whites until foamy.

• Dip pancakes in seasoned egg whites, then roll in bread crumbs. Place in buttered 13 × 9 × 2″ pan. Bake in moderate oven (350°) about 45 minutes, or until golden brown; baste frequently with melted butter. Makes 8 servings.

TO FREEZE PANCAKES: After dipping rolled pancakes in egg white mixture and crumbs, place in a shallow pan lined with waxed paper. Cover tightly and freeze. To bake, place pancakes in buttered 13 × 9 × 2″ pan and bake in moderate oven (350°) about 60 minutes, or until golden brown. Baste frequently with melted butter while baking.

CHICKEN PIZZA

Youngsters say this is the best use for leftover chicken. Grownups agree

- 1 (6 oz.) can tomato paste
- 1 can condensed cream of mushroom soup
- 1 pkg. plain pizza mix
- ½ tsp. salt
- Pepper
- 5 c. chopped cooked chicken
- Grated Parmesan cheese

· Combine tomato paste, soup, sauce from pizza mix, salt and pepper. Simmer about 20 minutes.

· Prepare pizza crust by package directions and pat into a pizza pan. Add chicken to sauce; spread evenly on crust; sprinkle with cheese.

· Bake in a moderate oven (375°) 30 minutes, or until crust is browned. Makes 6 to 8 servings.

Note: If you do not have a pizza pan, pat the pizza crust into 3 (9″) pie pans.

CHICKEN ROLLS WITH SAUCE

Flaky pastry swirls around moist chicken filling—the sauce is unusual

- 2 c. sifted flour
- 2 tsp. baking powder
- 1 tsp. salt
- ½ c. plus 2 tblsp. shortening
- ¼ c. milk
- 1 egg, slightly beaten
- 2 c. chopped cooked chicken
- 2 tblsp. finely chopped parsley
- ¾ c. finely chopped celery
- ¼ c. chopped pimiento
- 1 can condensed cream of mushroom soup
- ½ c. dairy sour cream
- ½ c. milk

· Sift together dry ingredients. Cut in shortening. Add milk to egg; stir into dry mixture. Shape into two balls; wrap in waxed paper and refrigerate.

· Combine chicken, parsley, celery and pimiento. Stir in ½ can soup. Divide mixture in half.

· Roll half the dough into a 13 × 9″ rectangle. Spread with half the chicken mixture. Roll up like a jelly roll. Repeat with remaining dough and chicken mixture.

· Place the rolls on a greased baking sheet. Bake in moderate oven (375°) 30 minutes or until golden brown. Slice.

· Blend remaining soup and sour cream; stir in milk and heat over medium heat (do not boil). Serve hot over each chicken roll slice. Makes 8 servings.

CHICKEN BARBECUED IN FOIL

You can fix as many silvery packages of chicken as your oven will hold

- 3 tblsp. butter
- 1 tblsp. brown sugar
- ¾ c. chopped onion
- 1 tsp. vinegar
- 2 tblsp. Worcestershire sauce
- 1 tsp. prepared mustard
- ¼ c. lemon juice
- ½ c. ketchup
- 1 (2½ to 3 lb.) broiler-fryer, cut in half

· Combine all ingredients except the chicken. Bring to a boil; reduce heat and simmer, uncovered, 15 minutes.

· Meanwhile, rub chicken with salt

and pepper. Place each half on a piece of heavy aluminum foil, large enough for a drugstore wrap. Put half of the sauce on each chicken half. Wrap.

• Bake in moderate oven (350°) 1 hour, or a very slow oven (200°) for 2 hours. Carefully open packages to avoid burns from escaping steam; turn back the foil.

• Broil chicken until browned. Remove from foil and serve with sauce. Makes 2 generous servings.

CHICKEN BREASTS WITH SESAME

A happy discovery—this dish so easy to fix and serve, and so good to eat

- 6 large chicken breasts, boned
- 2 eggs, slightly beaten
- 1 tblsp. water
- 1 tblsp. soy sauce
- 1 tsp. salt
- ¼ tsp. pepper
- ¼ c. flour
- ½ c. sesame seeds
- ½ c. butter or regular margarine
- Creamy Mushroom Sauce

• Remove skin from chicken breasts. Blend together eggs, water, soy sauce, salt and pepper in a shallow dish. Dip chicken into flour, then into egg mixture and next in sesame seeds.

• Melt butter in 13 × 9 × 2″ pan. Add chicken and turn to coat with butter.

• Bake in hot oven (400°) 40 to 50 minutes, until golden brown and tender. Serve with Creamy Mushroom Sauce. Makes 6 servings.

CREAMY MUSHROOM SAUCE: Sauté 1 (4 oz.) can mushrooms, drained, in ¼ c. butter until golden. Cover and simmer 5 minutes. Blend in ¼ c. flour; slowly add 1 can condensed chicken broth, stirring until smooth. Stir in ½ c. light cream and 2 tblsp. chopped parsley. Season with ⅛ tsp. pepper. Heat just until mixture simmers.

Note: A half pound fresh mushrooms may be substituted for the canned mushrooms. Add ¼ tsp. salt.

Perfect Country Fried Chicken

Perfect fried chicken comes from heeding details. Here are steps country women, experts in this cooking, take to achieve success:

After coating chicken with seasoned flour, spread pieces on a wire rack to dry for a few minutes.

Heat from ¼ to ½″ salad oil or shortening in a heavy skillet until it sizzles when a drop of water is added.

For special occasions, cook only breasts, thighs and legs. Avoid crowding chicken. Use two skillets if necessary. Brown meaty pieces first (add liver the last 15 minutes of cooking). Brown lightly on one side, turn with tongs and brown on other side. It takes from 15 to 20 minutes to brown chicken.

Reduce heat, cover skillet tightly and cook until chicken is tender, 30 to 40 minutes. (If skillet's lid does not fit snugly, add 1 to 2 tblsp. water just before covering skillet.)

Remove cover the last 10 minutes of cooking to recrisp chicken.

PAN-FRIED CHICKEN

Traditional country fried chicken

2 (2 to 3 lb.) broiler-fryers, cut in serving pieces
6 tblsp. flour
1½ tsp. salt
1 tsp. paprika
⅛ tsp. pepper
Salad oil or shortening

· Toss chicken pieces in paper or plastic bag containing flour, salt, paprika and pepper. Spread on rack to dry coating.
· Heat oil (about ½″) in heavy skillet. Add chicken and brown lightly on all sides, about 20 minutes. Reduce heat; cover tightly and cook slowly until tender, about 30 to 40 minutes. Turn pieces for even browning.
· Uncover last 10 minutes to recrisp skin. Makes 4 servings.

To Make Gravy: Remove and save fat. Measure back into pan 3 tblsp. fat; add 3 tblsp. flour. Blend thoroughly. Add 2 c. liquid–milk, giblet broth or water. Season to taste. Simmer 5 minutes.

CRUSTY FRIED CHICKEN

A much praised recipe–chicken is moist within, brown outside

3 (3 lb.) broiler-fryers (use breasts, thighs and legs)
2 pkgs. garlic salad dressing mix
3 tblsp. flour
2 tsp. salt
¼ c. lemon juice
2 tblsp. soft butter or regular margarine
Fat or salad oil
1 c. milk
1½ c. pancake mix

· Wipe chicken pieces (use damp paper toweling).
· Combine salad dressing mix, flour and salt in small bowl. Add lemon juice and butter; mix to a smooth paste.
· Brush all sides of chicken pieces with paste. Stack in bowl; cover. Store in refrigerator overnight.
· About 1½ hours before mealtime, place ¼ to ½″ of fat in bottom of large skillet or Dutch oven; heat.
· Dip chicken parts in milk, then in pancake mix. Coat well. Dust off excess. Lightly brown in hot fat. Turn with tongs–not fork.
· Place browned chicken one layer deep, in shallow baking pan. Spoon about half the rest of dipping milk over pieces.
· Cover with lid or aluminum foil. Bake in moderate oven (375°) 30 minutes.
· Remove lid. Baste with remaining milk. Cook uncovered 20 to 30 minutes, or until tender. Makes 8 servings.

SAUCY CHICKEN BAKE

You just pour the bright sauce over chicken and vegetable–then bake

2 to 3 medium zucchini
1 (2½ to 3 lb.) broiler-fryer, cut in pieces
½ tsp. orégano leaves
1 c. Basic Red Sauce (see Index)
2 to 3 tblsp. grated Parmesan cheese

· Slice unpeeled squash in ½″ slices. Arrange in bottom of 3-qt. baking dish. Place chicken, skin side up, over zucchini.
· Add orégano to Basic Red Sauce; pour evenly over chicken and zucchini.
· Bake uncovered in hot oven (400°) 30 minutes. Baste chicken

and zucchini with drippings; bake another 30 minutes, or until chicken is tender. Sprinkle with cheese and return to oven for a few minutes. Makes 4 to 6 servings.

PAPRIKA CHICKEN

Serve with hot, buttered homemade noodles and a cranberry salad

2 (2¼ lb.) broiler-fryers, cut up
⅓ c. flour
¾ tsp. salt
1 tblsp. paprika
⅛ tsp. pepper
⅓ c. fat
½ c. chopped onion
2 to 3 chicken bouillon cubes
2½ to 3 c. hot water
1 c. dairy sour cream

• Thoroughly coat pieces of chicken with mixture of flour, salt, paprika and pepper. Dust any remaining flour over chicken pieces in pan.
• Brown chicken in fat in heavy skillet, about 15 minutes. Add onion.
• Dissolve bouillon cubes in hot water; add ½ c. to chicken in pan. (Add more as needed.) Cover and simmer over low heat 30 to 40 minutes, or until tender. Remove to serving platter.
• Add remaining bouillon and sour cream (add ½ c. more sour cream for extra lusciousness) to pan drippings. Stir well; heat, but do not boil. Pour over chicken. Makes 6 to 8 servings.

Variation

FRIED CHICKEN CREOLE STYLE: Coat chicken pieces with flour mixture and brown in fat as for Paprika Chicken. Add 1½ c. sliced onion, 1 tsp. salt, ¾ tsp. celery seeds, 1 green pepper, cut into strips, 2½ to 3 c. tomato juice and 2 tsp. Worcestershire sauce. Cover tightly and cook over moderate heat 25 minutes, or until tender. Makes 6 to 8 servings.

COMPANY CHICKEN

New color with frozen tomato sauce

2 (2½ to 3 lb.) broiler-fryers
½ c. shortening or salad oil
1⅓ c. chopped onion
1 qt. block frozen Home-cooked Tomato Sauce (see Index)
2 tsp. salt
2 tsp. garlic salt
1 c. apple juice
4 tsp. lemon juice
2 c. water

• Brown chicken pieces in hot shortening in skillet. Pour off fat. Add onion and cook over low heat until golden.
• Add chopped or thawed tomato sauce and remaining ingredients. Bring to boil; cover. Simmer 35 to 45 minutes or until chicken is tender. Makes 6 servings.

TEXAS BARBECUED CHICKEN

Chicken simmers in a lively sauce

1 (3 to 3½ lb.) broiler-fryer
¾ c. flour
1 tblsp. salt
1 tsp. paprika
3 tblsp. butter or regular margarine
Barbecue Sauce

• Shake chicken pieces in paper bag with flour and seasonings.
• Melt butter in skillet. Add chicken; fry until golden brown. Turn with tongs.
• Add Barbecue Sauce. Use ½ c. for each pound of chicken. Cook slowly for 40 to 45 minutes. Turn pieces frequently. Serve on platter with sauce. Makes 4 servings.

BARBECUE SAUCE: Combine in saucepan, 1 tsp. salt, ¼ tsp. pepper, 1 tsp. paprika, 1 tblsp. sugar, ½ clove garlic, minced, ½ c. chopped onion, ½ c. water and 1 c. ketchup. Heat to boiling; simmer, uncovered, 20 minutes. Remove from heat, add ¼ c. lemon juice and 2 tblsp. butter. Mix well. Makes 2½ cups sauce.

BARBECUE FRIED CHICKEN

A chicken-tomato skillet special

1 (4 lb.) broiler-fryer or 2 (2½ lb.) broiler-fryers
1 c. flour
Fat
¾ c. water
2 tblsp. vinegar
1 tsp. prepared mustard
1 tblsp. brown sugar
2 tsp. Worcestershire sauce
1 tblsp. chopped onion
2 c. canned tomatoes
1½ tsp. salt
½ tsp. pepper
¼ tsp. chopped garlic

· Wash chicken; pat dry with paper toweling. Cut into serving pieces.
· Flour, coating each piece thoroughly. Fry chicken in hot fat until golden brown.
· Blend together small amount of water with 2 tblsp. flour. Add remaining water. Mix well with remaining ingredients.
· Drain excess fat from chicken. Pour sauce over chicken, cover; simmer 1 hour, or until tender. Makes 4 servings.

OVEN-FRIED CHICKEN

Crisp and good—serve it to company

1 (2½ to 3 lb.) broiler-fryer, cut in serving pieces
⅓ c. melted butter or regular margarine
2 tsp. salt
¼ tsp. pepper
2 c. crushed corn flakes

· Dip chicken pieces in melted butter; sprinkle with salt and pepper, then roll in corn flakes. Place, skin side up and not touching, in greased 15½ × 10½ × 1″ jelly roll pan. Sprinkle with remaining butter and corn flake crumbs.
· Bake in moderate oven (375°) about 1 hour, or until done. Do not turn during cooking. Makes 4 to 6 servings.

Variation

GARLIC OVEN-FRIED CHICKEN. Use 2 c. crushed potato chips, sprinkled with ¼ tsp. garlic salt, for crushed corn flakes.

Starlight Chicken Barbecue

MENU

Barbecued Chicken Special
Hot Garlic Bread
Green Beans
Tomato Slices
Watermelon
Milk Coffee

The trick with the chicken is to brown it evenly. Watch it carefully and turn often if you don't have a revolving-type broiler. Buttered popped corn is an accompaniment that pleases. Slice man-size hunks of garlic bread. Serve big cuts of thumping-ripe melon. And have plenty of coffee—some hot, some iced. Folks like to sip until the stars come out.

BARBECUED CHICKEN SPECIAL

3 (2½ to 3 lb.) broiler-fryers
½ tsp. salt
¼ c. salad oil
½ c. lemon juice
2 tblsp. chopped onion
½ tsp. pepper
¼ tsp. paprika

• Wipe broilers with clean damp cloth.
• Mix remaining ingredients.
• Spoon this sauce inside and outside of chickens; let stand for 30 minutes.
• Place chickens on spit.
• Brush with sauce, turning so chickens brown evenly (if you don't have revolving-type broiler or spit).
• Cook about 1 hour—until leg pulls away easily. Makes 6 servings.

HOW TO BROIL CHICKEN

• Use broiler-fryers about 2½ lbs. in weight. Split lengthwise in halves with backbone and neck removed (freeze them and giblets to use later). If you want to serve quarter chickens, cut halves in two crosswise.
• Brush with salad oil. Sprinkle both sides of chicken with salt and pepper, 1 tsp. salt and ¼ tsp. (or less) pepper for each chicken.
• Arrange chicken, skin side down, in broiler pan. Do not use rack. Broil 5 to 7″ from heat (or follow range manufacturer's directions) about 30 minutes, or until lightly browned, brushing occasionally with salad oil. Turn and broil 15 to 20 minutes longer. When drumstick moves very easily and meat feels soft when you press it with fingers (protected with paper toweling) in thickest part, the chicken is done.

BROILED CHICKEN

Today and tomorrow recipe—fix the chicken one day, cook it the next

2 (2 to 2½ lb.) broiler-fryer chickens
Italian salad dressing
1½ tsp. salt
⅛ tsp. pepper

• Cut chickens in halves. Break wing, hip and drumstick joints so chicken will stay flat while cooking. Brush both sides generously with salad dressing. Cover and chill in refrigerator overnight (or 4 to 5 hours).
• Season chicken with salt and pepper. Place skin side down in broiling pan.
• Broil 5 to 7″ from heat 25 minutes, or until lightly browned, basting occasionally with Italian salad dressing. Turn, brush again with salad dressing and continue broiling 15 minutes longer, or until chicken is golden brown. (Chicken is cooked when drumstick cuts easily and no pink color shows.) Makes 4 servings.

Chicken Barbecue Supper

Take a lazy, summer evening, the family and a few friends and toss in the smoky aroma of chicken sizzling over charcoal as it turns a rich, golden brown—that's a recipe for happy times. All the food in this menu is kitchen-made except the chicken. Why don't you bring out a big, full-to-the-top cookie jar? That's an invitation to several helpings. Of course, there will be plenty of milk and coffee to drink.

Menu

Charcoal-broiled Chicken
Potato Salad Sliced Tomatoes
Watermelon Pickles
French Bread
Butter-Pecan Ice Cream
Bar Cookies
Hot Coffee Milk

CHARCOAL-BROILED CHICKEN

4 broiler-fryers (not over 2½ lbs. each)
Golden Ember Sauce

• Split chickens in halves lengthwise.

• Brush generously on both sides with Golden Ember Sauce. Store in refrigerator and let flavors penetrate for several hours or overnight.

• Place on grill, hollow side down, over coals white with ash (intense heat must have subsided). Cook for 20 to 25 minutes; brush with sauce and turn. Cook 20 or more minutes until chicken is tender. Another method is to brush with sauce often and turn chicken every 10 minutes. The exact time depends on size of the broiler and amount of heat. To test for doneness, grasp end of leg. If leg joint moves easily, meat is done. Too hot a fire will give a charred coating before the chicken is done. Each half should serve one adult or two children.

GOLDEN EMBER SAUCE: Combine in a jar or bottle ¾ c. salad oil, ¼ c. melted butter or regular margarine, ¼ c. lemon juice, 1 tblsp. prepared mustard, 2 tblsp. brown sugar, 1 tblsp. salt, 1 tsp. paprika, ¼ tsp. pepper, 2 tsp. grated onion, 2 cloves garlic cut in halves, ½ tsp. Worcestershire sauce, ¼ tsp. Tabasco sauce and ¼ c. ketchup. Shake thoroughly. Let stand several hours before using. Shake before brushing on chicken.

GLAZED BROILED CHICKEN

You can broil or bake this chicken in your oven or grill it over coals

3 (1½ to 3 lb.) broiler-fryers
Fruit Barbecue Sauce

• Split chicken in halves, lengthwise. Place in large bowl, skin side down. Pour heated Fruit Barbecue Sauce over chicken and rotate pieces in it to coat completely. Cover bowl and marinate in refrigerator overnight or for several hours. Turn the chicken occasionally.

• Remove chicken from sauce. Place, skin side down, in broiler pan without rack, or in large shallow pan. Brush top of chicken with heated sauce.

• Broil according to range manufacturer's directions. Chickens should be 7 to 9" from heat and will take 20 to 30 minutes for each side to brown completely. If broiler does not allow this distance, reduce heat to about 350°. After 10 minutes, chicken should begin to brown on one side. If it browns faster, reduce heat. Sauce browns quickly, so watch chicken carefully. Cover with foil if skin is completely brown before chicken is cooked thoroughly.

• Baste with remaining sauce every 10 minutes. Turn when top side is brown.

• Chicken is done when drumstick twists easily out of thigh joint, about 40 to 60 minutes, according to weight. Serve with any remaining sauce. Makes 6 to 10 servings, depending on size of chickens.

Variations

BAKED GLAZED CHICKEN: To cook chicken with Fruit Barbecue Sauce in oven, prepare and marinate as for broiling. Place chicken, skin side down, on rack in shallow pan. Line bottom of pan with foil to catch drippings. Baste chicken with heated sauce.

• Bake in hot oven (400°). After about 30 minutes, turn chicken; baste with heated sauce. Bake 30 minutes more or until done. If chicken browns too fast, cover with foil.

OUTDOOR GRILL BROILED CHICKEN: Prepare and marinate chicken as for cooking in range broiler. Wait until charcoal in grill has burned to white in daylight; if still red, heat will be too intense. Place chicken on grill, skin side up. Baste with heated sauce. Broil 10 minutes, baste again and turn. Repeat basting and turning every 10 minutes until done, about 30 to 40 minutes. If heat gets too intense, sprinkle water on coals.

FRUIT BARBECUE SAUCE

The secret of the chicken's tangy taste and its inviting glossy, browned look

1 (6 oz.) can frozen pineapple juice concentrate
1 tsp. salt
¼ tsp. ground ginger
3 tblsp. lemon juice
6 tblsp. butter or regular margarine

• Thaw juice concentrate and combine with salt, ginger and lemon juice. Heat to boiling.

• Before basting chicken, reheat glaze with butter. Makes 1⅓ cups.

Variations

DEVILED CHICKEN SAUCE: Brush chicken with blend of 1 tblsp. dry mustard and ¾ c. prepared mustard; cover and refrigerate for several hours or overnight. Baste while cooking with this mixture: ¾ c. melted butter or regular margarine, ¼ tsp. salt, 1½ tsp. onion salt, ½ tsp. pepper, ½ tsp. celery salt and 1½ tsp. dry mustard.

HERB CHICKEN SAUCE: Melt ⅓ c. butter or margarine; add ½ tsp. marjoram leaves, ½ tsp. thyme leaves, ⅛ tsp. pepper, ¼ c. snipped fresh parsley and 2 tblsp. minced onion. Heat slowly 5 minutes. Add 1 tblsp. lemon juice, 1 chicken bouillon cube and ¾ c. water. Heat to dissolve bouillon cube. Pour over chicken and marinate several hours. Reheat and use to baste chicken during broiling. Makes 1½ cups.

LEMON-BROILED CHICKEN

Everyone gets light and dark meat

2 broiler-fryers (not over 2½ lbs. each), split in halves
1 lemon, quartered
¼ c. melted butter or regular margarine
2 tsp. salt
¼ tsp. pepper
½ tsp. paprika
2 tblsp. sugar

• Rub chicken halves on both sides with lemon (squeeze lemon to bring out juice); brush with butter.

• Mix together salt, pepper, paprika and sugar; sprinkle lightly over chicken.

• Place in broiler pan, skin side down. Place pan in bottom of broiler. Turn chicken after 20 minutes and raise closer to heat. Baste occasionally to insure even browning. Broil 25 to 40 minutes, until pink color at bone disappears. Makes 4 servings.

CHICKEN WITH DUMPLINGS

Pass cranberry jelly or peach pickle

1 qt. water
2 tsp. salt
2 carrots, peeled and sliced
1 onion, sliced
1 branch celery
1 (4 to 5 lb.) stewing chicken, cut in pieces
1 c. milk
⅓ c. flour
Parsley Dumplings

• Heat water to boiling; add salt, carrots, onion, celery and chicken. Cover and simmer (do not boil) 2½ to 3 hours, or until chicken is tender.

• Remove chicken from broth and keep warm. Strain broth and measure; add enough water to make 3 cups.

• Return broth to saucepan and heat. Put milk and flour in jar with cover and shake until mixture is smooth. Add slowly to hot broth, beating with wire whisk to keep smooth. Cook about 5 minutes. Add chicken to gravy.

• Make Parsley Dumplings and add to simmering chicken about 20 minutes before serving. Makes 8 servings.

PARSLEY DUMPLINGS: Sift together 2 c. flour, 3 tsp. baking powder and 1 tsp. salt. Add ¼ c. finely chopped parsley (or 3 tblsp. chopped chives). Cut in ¼ c. shortening until mixture looks like coarse cornmeal. With fork mix in 1 c. milk to make a soft dough; stir as little as possible. Drop by spoonfuls onto chicken pieces. Simmer 10 minutes uncovered; cover and simmer 10 minutes longer. Serve at once. Makes 8 to 10 dumplings.

HOMEMADE NOODLES

Fascinate guests with these ribbons of egg dough cooked in chicken broth

3 egg yolks
1 egg
3 tblsp. cold water
1 tsp. salt
2 c. flour

• Beat egg yolks and egg until very light; beat in water and salt. Stir and work flour in with the hands to make a stiff dough.

• Divide into three parts. Roll each part out on a cloth-covered board as thinly as possible—paper thin. Place each piece of dough between towels until partially dry (it will look like a chamois skin).

• Roll each piece up like a jelly roll and cut with a sharp knife to make strips ⅛″ wide for fine noodles, ½″ for broad noodles. Shake out the strips and let them dry before cooking. Makes 6 cups.

Note: Noodles freeze successfully if packaged in airtight containers. To cook, break noodles into smaller pieces and add to 3 qts. boiling salted water (1 tblsp. salt) 12 to 15 minutes, or until tender. Drain well in sieve or colander. Makes about 6 cups. Here is a good serving suggestion: Mix 2 tsp. poppy seeds with hot, buttered noodles and serve with Paprika Chicken (see Index).

FAMILY-SIZE BRUNSWICK STEW

Recipe is big enough for a family meal with leftovers to freeze

2 (3 lb.) broiler-fryers, or 2 (4 lb.) stewing chickens
1 lb. salt pork, sliced thin or chopped
2 qts. freshly cut corn

5 qts. sliced peeled tomatoes
1 qt. diced peeled potatoes
2 qts. butter beans (lima beans)
2 medium onions, chopped
¼ tsp. ground red pepper or 1 medium pepper pod
Salt and pepper to taste

• Cut up chicken. Cover with water in heavy kettle; cook until meat falls away from bone, adding water if necessary.
• Add salt pork. Add vegetables and seasonings. Simmer slowly until tender, and mixture is thick and well blended. Remove pepper pod, if used. Serve hot. Makes 15 to 20 servings.

CHICKEN AND SWEET CREAM BISCUITS

A Sunday special—bring guests home from church to enjoy it

1 (5 lb.) stewing chicken
2 tsp. salt
1 branch celery
1 medium onion, quartered
5 carrots, cut in big pieces
¼ c. chicken fat
2 c. chicken broth
¾ c. flour
2 c. light cream
2 egg yolks, beaten
Parsley
Sweet Cream Biscuits

• Cut chicken in serving-size pieces; place in kettle. Add hot water to cover. Add salt, celery and onion. Simmer, covered, until tender, about 3 hours. Add carrots the last 30 minutes of cooking.
• Drain broth from chicken. Skim fat from broth, saving ¼ c. fat for gravy. Strain broth; save carrots. Measure 2 c. broth for gravy. Pour remaining broth back into kettle with chicken to keep hot.
• Measure chicken fat into saucepan; blend in flour. Gradually add broth and cream. Cook until thick and smooth, stirring constantly. Add a small amount of hot gravy to egg yolks; then add yolks to gravy. Cook 2 minutes more.
• Place hot chicken and carrots in serving dish or soup tureen; pour in gravy. Sprinkle with parsley and top with baked Sweet Cream Biscuits. Makes 10 to 12 servings.

SWEET CREAM BISCUITS: Sift together 4 c. sifted flour, 1 tsp. salt and 2 tblsp. baking powder. Stir in 1½ c. heavy cream with fork just until all flour is moistened; add water (about 4 tblsp.) if necessary.
• Knead on lightly floured surface, about 10 times. Roll ¾″ thick; cut with small floured cutter. Bake on ungreased baking sheet in very hot oven (450°) 12 minutes or until golden brown. Makes 36 small biscuits.

CHICKEN/RICE TETRAZZINI

Splendid casserole dish to tote to potlucks and to serve guests at home

1 qt. water
2 tsp. salt
1 (4 to 5 lb.) stewing chicken, cut in pieces
1¾ c. chicken broth
1 (2 to 4 oz.) can sliced mushrooms
2 tblsp. flour
½ tsp. garlic salt
⅛ tsp. pepper
½ c. light cream
1 c. grated Cheddar cheese
4 c. cooked rice
1 tblsp. chopped parsley
4 strips crisp-cooked bacon, crumbled
¼ c. cracker crumbs
¼ tsp. poultry seasoning

· Heat water in saucepan, add salt and chicken; cover. Simmer (do not boil) 2½ to 3 hours or until the thigh meat is tender. Take meat from bones and cut into chunks.

· Heat chicken broth with juice from mushrooms. Blend flour, garlic salt, pepper and cream. Stir into broth; cook, stirring constantly until thickened. Remove from heat. Stir in cheese.

· Combine rice, chicken, mushrooms and parsley in another container.

· Alternate layers of chicken mixture and sauce in buttered 3-qt. casserole.

· Combine bacon, crumbs and seasoning; sprinkle over casserole. Bake in very hot oven (450°) 30 minutes. Serves 10.

Note: Chicken casserole accompaniments are pickled peaches, jellied cranberry sauce, olives (green, pimiento-stuffed or ripe), pineapple slices topped with coleslaw or whole apricots, pickles (dill, sour, sweet), celery (cheese-stuffed), carrots (sticks or curls) and currant jelly.

CHICKEN SUPREME

Use cooked asparagus for broccoli

1 (5 lb.) stewing chicken
2 lbs. broccoli or 3 (10 oz.) pkgs. frozen
½ c. grated Parmesan cheese
Mock or Easy Hollandaise Sauce

· Simmer chicken until tender in boiling salted water about 3 hours, or pressure cook. Cool quickly in broth. Remove meat from bones in large pieces; slice.

· Cook broccoli in salted water until tender; place on heat-proof platter (or in shallow baking pan). Sprinkle with ¼ c. cheese. Arrange chicken slices on broccoli. Spoon Mock or Easy Hollandaise Sauce over top. Sprinkle with cheese.

· Broil, 5″ from source of heat until sauce browns. Makes 6 servings.

MOCK HOLLANDAISE SAUCE: Blend ½ c. mayonnaise or salad dressing, ½ c. heavy cream and 2 tblsp. lemon juice.

EASY HOLLANDAISE SAUCE: Cream thoroughly ½ c. butter or regular margarine; gradually beat in 3 egg yolks, 1½ tblsp. lemon juice, ½ tsp. salt, dash paprika and few grains ground red pepper; blend well. Slowly stir in ¼ c. boiling water. Place in top of double boiler. Cook over 1½″ boiling water (so water doesn't touch top part of double boiler) 5 minutes, stirring constantly. Remove from heat; beat 1 minute. Makes 1 cup.

CHICKEN TAMALES

Popular group-meal dish in Arkansas

1 (4 to 5 lb.) stewing chicken, cut up
1 large onion, chopped
1 clove garlic, minced or crushed
2 tblsp. salad oil
Paprika
Salt
Ground red pepper
Chili powder
Cumin powder
10 c. boiling chicken broth
2 c. cornmeal
1½ tsp. salt
Corn shucks
Salad oil (for greasing shucks)

· Place chicken in large kettle; cover with hot water. Simmer until tender and meat falls from bones, about 3 hours. Remove from broth; take meat off bones. Grind, using coarse blade.

• Cook liver, heart and gizzard separately; grind. Mix with chicken.
• Cook onion and garlic in oil until soft and clear. Add chicken and seasonings.
• Bring chicken broth to boil. Prepare mush, using broth, cornmeal and salt.
• Trim and brush shucks for wrapping tamales. Rinse with cold water. Place in pan, and cover with boiling water. Let stand until soft and pliable. Drain on paper toweling. Grease with oil.
• On each shuck, spread a layer of mush then a layer of chicken mixture. Roll as for jelly roll. Secure each end of shuck with string cut from corn "silk."
• Place tamales on rack in large kettle, over enough water in bottom of kettle to prevent burning. Cover kettle; steam tamales about 3 hours over low heat.
• More mush may be served with tamales. Makes 6 to 8 servings.

PRESSED CHICKEN

Grandmother teamed the chicken with hot brown-crusted biscuits

3 (3½ lb.) stewing chickens
6 to 8 c. hot water
8 tsp. salt
1 carrot, quartered
1 c. celery, chopped
12 parsley sprigs
¾ tsp. savory leaves
1 medium onion

• Cut chicken in pieces. Put in large kettle and add remaining ingredients. Bring to boil; simmer about 3 hours, until chicken is very tender.
• Remove chicken from kettle and strain broth. Return broth to heat and simmer until reduced to half its measure. Remove meat from bones; leave it in small pieces.
• Add chicken to cooked-down broth; simmer 5 minutes. Pour into 9 × 5 × 3" loaf pan, cover and weight down to press. Chill overnight. To serve cut in ½" slices. Makes 18 slices.

Chicken Pie—Superb Gift

The good New England cook who sent us this recipe for chicken pie bakes a few of them every year just after Thanksgiving Day. She stores them in her freezer. During the week-before-Christmas bustle, she delivers the pies, her Christmas gifts, to lucky friends. The pie rated exceptionally high in taste tests made in our Countryside Kitchens.

MAINE CHICKEN PIE

All chicken and gravy under crisp, flaky pastry—meaty, good

Pastry for 2-crust pie
1 (5 lb.) whole stewing chicken
1½ qts. water
2 tsp. salt
1 small onion
1 carrot
1 branch celery
3½ c. chicken broth
½ c. sifted flour
½ tsp. onion salt
½ tsp. celery salt
Few grains pepper
2 or 3 drops yellow food color

• Place chicken in large kettle and add water, 1 tsp. salt, onion, carrot and celery. Simmer, covered, until tender, 3 to 3½ hours.

· Remove chicken. Strip meat from bones, removing in large pieces. Strain broth. Refrigerate chicken and broth when cool.
· Combine flour, onion salt, celery salt, pepper and remaining 1 tsp. salt with ½ c. chicken broth. Mix until smooth.
· Put 3 c. chicken broth in skillet. Heat and add flour mixture, beating with a wire whisk to prevent lumping.
· Cook over medium heat, stirring constantly until mixture is smooth and thickened. Add food coloring if desired.
· Add chicken and blend well.
· Line 9″ deep-dish pie pan with pastry. Fill with chicken mixture. Adjust top crust, cut vents and flute edges.
· Bake in hot oven (400°) 45 minutes or until browned. Makes 6 to 8 servings.

Note: If you want to freeze this pie, cool, wrap, label and place in freezer. Cool filling before pouring in crust to freeze like unbaked pie. Cool and freeze remaining broth for gravy separately. To serve, bake frozen pie in hot oven (400°) 45 minutes to 1 hour. Chicken filling should be hot, the crust a golden brown. Make gravy from frozen broth.

CHICKEN SUPPER DISH

Keep cooked chicken and broth in freezer to fast-fix this on busy days

1 (3½ to 4 lb.) stewing chicken, cut up
3 c. hot water
1 small onion, peeled
3 celery tops
1 carrot, peeled
1 tblsp. salt
1 bay leaf
3 hard-cooked eggs, sliced
1 (6 oz.) can sliced mushrooms, drained
2 tblsp. flour
1 c. chicken broth
1 c. light cream
1 tsp. salt
⅛ tsp. pepper

· Simmer chicken in water with onion, celery tops, carrot, salt and bay leaf until fork-tender, about 2½ to 3 hours. Cut meat from bones. Strain broth. Chill meat and broth separately.
· In greased 1½-qt. casserole, arrange alternate layers of chicken, eggs and mushrooms by thirds.
· Mix flour with ¼ c. broth until smooth. Heat remaining broth with cream; stir in flour mixture and seasonings. Cook until smooth and thick; pour into casserole.
· Bake uncovered in moderate oven (350°) about 35 minutes. Makes 6 to 8 servings.

CHICKEN LOAF

Sour cream and herbs add subtle, new flavors to this favorite

1 (4 to 5 lb.) stewing chicken, cut up
1½ c. soft bread crumbs
2 eggs, beaten
⅛ tsp. rosemary leaves
Pinch of marjoram leaves
Salt
Pepper
Few grains ground nutmeg
2 branches celery, diced
1 c. dairy sour cream
2 tblsp. chicken broth (optional)

· Cook chicken in boiling, salted water until tender, about 3 hours, or

pressure cook. Remove meat from bones; cut up.
· Combine chicken with remaining ingredients; toss lightly.
· Pour into greased 8½ × 4½ × 2½" loaf pan. Set in pan of hot water and bake in moderate oven (350°) 50 minutes, until knife inserted in center comes out clean. Unmold, slice. Serves 6.

RICE AND CHICKEN JAMBALAYA

Meal-in-a-dish—extra-good tasting

½ c. chopped onion
1 c. diced celery
½ c. butter, regular margarine or chicken fat
4 c. chicken broth
1 c. uncooked rice
1½ tsp. salt
⅛ tsp. pepper
1 (4 to 5 lb.) stewing chicken, cooked and diced
1½ c. diced carrots
1 c. chopped parsley

· Cook onion and celery in butter in 2-qt. saucepan until golden brown.
· Add broth, rice and seasonings.
· Cover; cook over low heat about 20 minutes. Add chicken and carrots and cook 15 minutes more.
· Sprinkle with chopped parsley. Makes 8 servings.

CHICKEN IN CRUMB BASKETS

Crisp crumb baskets make a tasty change from traditional patty shells

Crumb Baskets:
5 c. soft bread crumbs
¼ c. minced onion
1 tsp. celery salt
⅛ tsp. pepper
½ c. melted butter or regular margarine

Chicken Filling:
⅓ c. butter or regular margarine
⅓ c. flour
½ c. light cream
1½ c. chicken broth
½ tsp. salt
⅛ tsp. pepper
1 tsp. Worcestershire sauce
1 c. cooked or canned peas
3 c. chopped cooked chicken

· To make baskets, combine crumbs with onion, seasonings and butter.
· Line 6 greased individual casseroles with crumb mixture. Press into place.
· Bake in moderate oven (375°) 15 minutes, or until crumbs are brown.
· Meanwhile, prepare filling. Melt butter, blend in flour. Add cream, chicken broth and seasonings.
· Cook until thickened, stirring constantly. Add peas and chicken. Serve in Crumb Baskets. Makes 6 servings.

CREAMED CHICKEN

Peas and pimiento make this colorful

2 c. cubed cooked chicken
1 c. cooked peas, drained
½ tsp. salt
⅛ tsp. pepper
1 tsp. grated onion
2 tblsp. chopped pimiento
1 can condensed cream of chicken or mushroom soup

· Combine all ingredients except soup. Let stand in refrigerator about 1 hour.
· Pour undiluted soup in top pan of double boiler or chafing dish.
· Add chicken mixture; blend together. Cover; heat, and serve piping hot on toast. Makes 6 servings.

CHICKEN CASSEROLE

Good use for leftover chicken

1 c. elbow macaroni
½ c. diced celery
¾ c. chicken broth
1 can condensed cream of celery soup
1 (3 or 4 oz.) can mushrooms
2 c. cut-up cooked chicken or turkey
½ c. minced parsley
½ tsp. Worcestershire sauce
Salt (optional)
¾ c. soft bread cubes
2 tblsp. butter or regular margarine

· Cook macaroni according to package directions. Drain.
· Cook celery in chicken broth (or use a chicken-flavored bouillon cube plus ¾ c. water) for 5 minutes.
· Combine cooked macaroni, celery, broth, celery soup, mushrooms, chicken, parsley and Worcestershire sauce. Add salt if needed. Pour into greased 2-qt. casserole. Sprinkle with bread cubes; dot with butter.
· Bake in moderate oven (350°) 30 to 40 minutes. Makes 8 servings.

CHICKEN CRUNCH CASSEROLE

Just the hot dish to serve with cranberry sauce and scalloped corn

2½ c. diced cooked chicken
1 can condensed cream of mushroom soup
1 c. milk
½ tsp. salt
3 c. crushed potato chips
¼ c. shredded sharp cheese
Paprika

· Combine chicken, soup, milk and salt. Heat to boiling.
· Spread 1½ c. potato chips on bottom of greased 2-qt. casserole. Pour in chicken mixture. Cover with remaining chips; sprinkle with cheese and paprika.
· Bake in moderate oven (350°) 25 to 30 minutes. Makes 6 servings.

Variation

TURKEY CRUNCH CASSEROLE: Substitute cooked turkey for chicken.

CHICKEN WITH DRESSING

Easy-to-serve baked chicken—no bones

1 (3 to 4 lb.) stewing chicken, cut up
1 branch celery
1 onion, sliced
1 tblsp. salt
3 to 4 peppercorns
1½ qts. dry bread cubes
½ tsp. rubbed sage
⅛ tsp. pepper
½ tsp. salt
¼ c. minced onion
⅓ c. butter or chicken fat
½ c. fat (from broth)
¾ c. flour
1½ tsp. salt
⅛ tsp. pepper
4 c. chicken broth
4 egg yolks, well beaten

· Place chicken, celery, onion, salt and peppercorns in water to almost cover. Simmer until chicken is tender, about 2 hours. Remove chicken from bones in good-size pieces. Arrange in 2-qt. casserole. (Cool and refrigerate if you like.)
· Combine bread cubes, sage, ⅛ tsp. pepper and ½ tsp. salt. Brown onion in butter; add to bread mixture. Spread over chicken.
· Melt fat in heavy skillet; add flour with 1½ tsp. salt and ⅛ tsp. pepper; stir until smooth. Blend in strained chicken broth; cook until thick and smooth, stirring constantly.
· Mix a little hot gravy with yolks;

pour yolks into remaining gravy. Cook over medium heat about 3 minutes, stirring constantly. Pour over casserole.

• Bake in moderate oven (375°) 35 minutes or until custard gravy is set and golden brown on top. Makes 8 servings.

MOLDED CHICKEN LOAF

Summer favorite–serve with peas and new potatoes in cream

- **2 envelopes unflavored gelatin**
- **2½ c. chicken broth**
- **4 c. diced cooked chicken**
- **Salt**
- **Pepper**
- **2 tsp. lemon juice**
- **2 tblsp. chopped parsley**
- **¾ c. finely chopped celery**
- **2 tblsp. chopped sweet pickle**
- **¼ c. chopped pimiento**
- **1 c. mayonnaise or salad dressing**

• Soften gelatin in ½ c. cold chicken broth. Heat remaining broth. Add gelatin, and stir until it dissolves.

• Add chicken, and salt and pepper to taste. Cool until mixture starts to thicken. Then fold in remaining ingredients. Pour into 9 × 5 × 3″ loaf pan. Chill several hours.

• Unmold on platter. If you like, garnish with tomato slices and green pepper rings. Makes 10 to 12 servings.

DRUMSTICKS IN BASKET

Good for a children's supper party

- **24 chicken legs (broiler-fryers)**
- **½ c. melted butter or regular margarine**
- **½ c. flour**
- **2¾ tsp. salt**
- **¼ tsp. pepper**
- **2 tsp. paprika**

• Dip chicken legs in butter to coat; then roll in mixture of remaining ingredients. Arrange 12 legs in each of 2 buttered large, shallow pans. (Make 2 pans of heavy-duty aluminum foil, each 13 × 9 × 1″; set each on a baking sheet.) Do not let chicken pieces touch. Pour any remaining butter over chicken.

• Place pans of chicken on two shelves in hot oven (425°) and bake, uncovered, 30 minutes. Turn chicken and reverse position of pans in oven (change shelves). Bake about 15 minutes longer, or until chicken is fork-tender and golden brown.

• Put paper frills on ends of chicken legs; place in basket, frilled ends out. Place on buffet surrounded by an assortment of your favorite barbecue sauces to ladle on serving plates. Makes 8 to 10 servings.

CHICKEN/TUNA PIE

Surprise–chicken and tuna baked between two flaky pastry crusts

- **1 (9½ oz.) pkg. pie crust mix**
- **¼ tsp. poultry seasoning**
- **2 tblsp. yellow cornmeal**
- **1 can condensed cream of chicken soup**
- **2 tblsp. water**
- **1 or 2 chicken bouillon cubes**
- **1 (13 oz.) jar or can boned chicken, cut in large pieces, or 2 c. cut-up cooked chicken**
- **1 (7 oz.) can tuna, flaked**

• Make pie crust by package directions for 2-crust pie; add poultry seasoning and cornmeal, before adding the liquid called for. Fit half pastry into 9″ pie pan.

• Heat soup; blend in water and bouillon cubes. Add chicken and tuna; cool and pour into pastry-lined pan. Cover with crust, make slits in center; flute edges.

• Roll out leftover pastry; cut into chicken shapes; place on top.

• Bake in hot oven (425°) 30 to 40 minutes, until filling bubbles and crust is delicately brown. Makes 6 servings.

Variation

INDIVIDUAL CHICKEN/TUNA PIES: Double recipes of pastry and filling; use 5" tart pans. Fill with chicken-tuna mixture; roll pastry and cut into 6" circles; cover filling and flute edges. Bake in hot oven (425°) about 25 minutes. (Bake pastry chickens separately.) Makes 8 pies.

OVEN CHICKEN LOAF

With mushroom sauce, this is a hostess' dream come true—also serve peas

Chicken Loaf:

3 c. chopped cooked chicken
1 c. cooked rice
2 c. soft bread crumbs
2 tsp. salt
2 c. chicken broth
4 eggs, beaten
¼ c. chopped pimiento

Mushroom Sauce:

¼ c. butter
1 c. fresh mushrooms, sliced, or 1 (4 oz.) can
¼ c. flour
½ tsp. salt
⅛ tsp. pepper
2 c. chicken broth
¼ c. light cream
½ tsp. lemon juice
⅛ tsp. paprika
Chopped parsley

• Combine chicken with rice, crumbs, salt and broth. Add eggs; stir in pimiento.

• Pour into greased 9" square baking dish. Bake in moderate oven (350°) 1 hour, or until firm.

• Meanwhile, make sauce. Melt butter; add and brown mushrooms. Stir in flour, salt and pepper. Add chicken broth and cream. Cook until thickened, stirring. Add lemon juice, paprika and parsley.

• To serve, cut warm chicken loaf in squares; serve with mushroom sauce. Makes 6 to 8 servings.

ALICE'S SCALLOPED CHICKEN

Cook the chicken days in advance, discard bones and freeze meat

1 (5 to 6 lb.) stewing chicken
1 c. chicken fat
1 c. plus 2 tblsp. flour
1 tblsp. salt
¼ tsp. white pepper
4½ c. chicken broth
2 c. milk
4 c. day-old bread, toasted and cubed
¼ c. chopped onion
1 c. chopped celery
1 tsp. salt
½ to 1 tsp. rubbed sage
⅓ c. melted butter or regular margarine

• Simmer chicken in salted water to cover until tender, 3 to 3½ hours; or pressure cook. Remove chicken from broth; take meat from bones.

• To make sauce, melt fat in heavy skillet; blend in flour, 1 tblsp. salt and white pepper. Cook over low heat until bubbly, stirring constantly.

• Slowly stir in chicken broth and milk; boil 3 minutes, stirring constantly.

• Lightly toss together bread cubes, onion, celery, 1 tsp. salt, sage and butter. Arrange in two 2-qt. baking dishes. Top with chicken; cover with sauce. Mix with fork to moisten dressing. Bake in moderate oven (350°) 1 hour. Makes 16 servings.

CHICKEN LIVERS DE LUXE

When putting chickens in freezer, save livers in amounts to make this

- **¼ c. butter**
- **1 lb. chicken livers (about 15)**
- **½ tsp. salt**
- **¼ tsp. pepper**
- **6 slices bread**
- **1½ c. dairy sour cream**
- **1 tblsp. minced onion**
- **½ tsp. salt**

• Melt butter in skillet over low heat. Brown livers in butter about 5 minutes; add ½ tsp. salt and pepper.

• Toast bread; cut each slice diagonally in 4 triangles.

• Combine sour cream, onion and ½ tsp. salt. Heat only until warm; do not boil. Place about ½ c. sour cream mixture on each plate. Arrange toast points and hot livers in cream. Makes 6 servings.

Turkey Any Day

Roast turkey for Thanksgiving dinner is as American as the Fourth of July, but nowadays it comes to the table on many other happy occasions. Even picnics: roast the bird one day, cool, refrigerate and then carry it, chilled, the next day. Carve it at the picnic spot and let everyone make his own sandwiches and help himself to potato salad.

Cooked turkey makes a splendid substitute for cooked chicken in most of the recipes in this cookbook.

PERFECT ROAST TURKEY

PREPARE THE TURKEY:

• Thaw bird if frozen. Let it thaw unwrapped in refrigerator 2 to 4 days, depending on size. Or if package is watertight, place it under running cold water until bird is pliable, 2 to 6 hours. Rinse inside and out with cold water, drain and pat dry with paper towel. Stuff if you wish. Shake bird to settle stuffing, but do not pack it. Truss turkey; brush with fat.

TO ROAST TURKEY:

In Open Pan: Place breast side up on rack in shallow pan. Do not cover pan or add water. Cover turkey loosely with foil; then press the foil tightly at ends of drumsticks and neck; do not let foil touch top or sides of bird. Cook in slow oven (325°); lift foil to baste occasionally with fat (optional). This way of cooking gives the most attractive roast turkey for carving at the table.

• When turkey is two thirds done (see Roasting Guide), cut band of skin or cord that holds drumsticks against turkey. This shortens cooking time by letting heat penetrate to inside of thighs. If you use a meat thermometer, insert it now (see directions) and continue roasting.

In Covered Pan: Some cooks like to omit the foil and cover the pan with a lid. Turkey cooked with a cover on has a steamed taste. Remove cover when turkey has an hour longer to cook so it will brown. The type of pan affects the roasting time. Turkey roasted in a shiny, light-colored pan may take as much as an hour longer than one cooked in a dark enameled or dull metal roaster.

In Foil: This is a good way to cook large turkeys, 16 to 24 lbs., for church or other community meals when carving is done in the kitchen.

The high temperature shortens cooking time.

• Place turkey breast side up in center of wide, heavy foil that's at least 12" longer than the bird. (For big bird, put two widths together with drugstore fold and press to make leakproof seal.)

• Bring one end of foil up over turkey; then bring up other end, lapping it over first end by 2 to 3". Fold tightly. Fold foil down snugly over greased breast and legs. Press remaining sides up to hold drippings. Package will not be airtight.

• Place wrapped turkey in shallow pan without rack. Roast in very hot oven (450°). Remove pan from oven 30 to 40 minutes before turkey should be done (see Roasting Guide for Cooking Turkey in Foil). Slit foil open and fold away from turkey to edge of pan. Insert meat thermometer if you use one. Return to oven until done.

ROASTING GUIDE FOR COOKING TURKEY IN FOIL

Ready-to-Cook Weight	*Approximate Cooking Time (Hours)*	*Internal Temperature*
10–13 lbs.	2¼–3	185°
14–17 lbs.	3½–4	185°
18–21 lbs.	4½–5	185°
22–24 lbs.	5½–6	185°

To Insert Thermometer: Push it into thickest part of inside thigh muscle; do not touch bone. (If you roast a stuffed turkey, you can place bulb of thermometer in the center of the stuffing. Turkey is done when temperature reaches 165°.)

TESTS FOR DONENESS:

1) Always make the pinch test: Protecting your thumb and forefinger with paper or cloth, pinch thickest part of inside thigh muscle; do not touch bone. If done, meat will feel very soft and you can move drumstick up and down easily.

2) Turkey should be done when thermometer reads 185°.

ROASTING GUIDE FOR TURKEY

Ready-to-Cook Weight	*Approximate Cooking Time (Hours)*	*Internal Temperature*
6–8 lbs.	3–3½	185°
8–12 lbs.	3½–4½	185°
12–16 lbs.	4½–5½	185°
16–20 lbs.	5½–6½	185°
20–24 lbs.	6½–7	185°

• If you do not use a thermometer, test for doneness at least 30 minutes before approximate timetable indicates turkey will be done. If you do not stuff turkey, it cooks a little more quickly. Allow cooked turkey to stand at room temperature about 20 minutes. This makes carving easier.

TURKEY GRAVY

• Remove turkey from roasting pan. Pour drippings—fat and meat juices—into pint measuring cup. Skim off fat.

• Return 3 tblsp. fat and 3 tblsp. flour to roasting pan; blend thoroughly.

• Cook slowly, stirring over low heat to brown fat and flour slightly.

• Add water, milk or giblet broth to meat juices to make 2 c. liquid. Add to fat and flour.

• Cook, stirring constantly, until smooth and thickened. Simmer about 5 minutes. Season. Makes 2 cups.

CELERY STUFFING

This recipe makes enough stuffing to fill a 12-lb. ready-to-cook turkey

1 c. chopped onion
2 c. finely chopped celery
⅔ c. melted butter or regular margarine
7 c. dry bread crumbs
2 tsp. salt
½ tsp. pepper
1½ tsp. rubbed sage
½ tsp. poultry seasoning
1⅓ c. milk
1¼ c. turkey broth (or canned chicken broth)
2 eggs, slightly beaten

• Simmer onion and celery in butter until soft, but do not brown.
• Combine with bread crumbs and seasonings.
• Add milk, broth and eggs; toss lightly.
• Stuff loosely into cavities of bird. Makes 6½ cups stuffing.

CRUMBLY BREAD STUFFING: Heat 1 c. plus 2 tblsp. butter or regular margarine in deep kettle; sauté ¾ c. minced onions until soft and tender, but do not brown. Combine with 4 qts. day-old bread crumbs, ¼ c. diced celery, 1½ tsp. poultry seasoning, ½ c. snipped parsley (optional), ¼ tsp. pepper and 2¼ tsp. salt. Heat well without browning, stirring frequently. Makes enough to stuff neck and body cavity of 10 lb. ready-to-cook turkey.

POTATO STUFFING

Potatoes keep this stuffing light—a great Pennsylvania Dutch favorite

4 lbs. baking potatoes, peeled
1 c. light cream
1 c. butter or regular margarine
16 slices dry white bread
2 c. chopped onion
1 c. chopped celery
1 tblsp. salt
1 tsp. pepper
2 tblsp. chopped parsley
Giblets, cooked and chopped
3 eggs, slightly beaten

• Boil potatoes until tender; drain. Heat cream with ⅓ c. butter and whip mixture into potatoes.
• Cut bread into small cubes; toss in ⅓ c. melted butter and toast in moderate oven (350°) 5 minutes.
• Sauté onion and celery in remaining ⅓ c. butter. Remove from heat; stir in seasonings and parsley.
• In a very large bowl, mix potatoes, giblets and onion mixture. Stir in beaten eggs, then toasted bread cubes. Fill bird (do not pack), truss and roast as usual. Or spoon into greased 13 × 9 × 2″ baking pan. Cover and bake in moderate oven (350°) 40 minutes; uncover and bake 20 minutes. Makes 12 to 13 cups.

SWEET CORN BREAD STUFFING

Especially favored in the southern homes—corn bread prevents sogginess

½ c. chopped onion
½ c. chopped green pepper
½ c. chopped celery
½ c. butter or regular margarine
2½ tsp. salt
2 tsp. rubbed sage
½ tsp. pepper
6 slices dry wheat bread, cubed
4 c. coarsely crumbled sweetened corn bread
1½ c. turkey broth or water

• Sauté vegetables in butter until tender-crisp. Stir in seasonings.
• Combine breads in a large bowl; add vegetable mixture. Stir in broth. Fill bird (do not pack), truss and roast as usual. Or spoon into greased 4-qt. casserole. Bake, covered, in moderate oven (350°) 35 minutes; uncover and bake 10 minutes more. Makes 9 cups.

TURKEY SURPRISE

For a change, spoon over waffles, fried noodles or hot biscuits

4 tblsp. shortening
½ clove garlic, finely chopped
4 tblsp. flour
2 c. turkey or chicken broth
1 tblsp. soy sauce
3 c. diced cooked turkey
Salt (optional)
Pepper (optional)
Hot cooked rice

• Melt shortening; add garlic and sauté slightly. Stir in flour and cook until bubbly, stirring constantly. Add broth, soy sauce, turkey and seasonings.
• Cook until thickened and thoroughly heated, about 20 minutes. Serve with hot cooked rice. Makes 6 servings.

Note: You can dissolve 2 chicken bouillon cubes in 2 c. boiling water and use for the broth.

TURKEY DIVAN

Your family and friends will like the way broccoli tastes in this dish

12 large slices cooked turkey
2 (10 oz.) pkgs. frozen broccoli or asparagus, cooked and drained
1 can condensed cream of chicken soup
¾ c. shredded sharp cheese

• Arrange sliced turkey on bottom of greased 11 × 7 × 1½" baking dish; cover with layer of broccoli. Pour on soup. Sprinkle top with cheese.
• Bake in moderate oven (375°) 20 to 25 minutes or until lightly browned. Makes 6 servings.

Note: You can blend 1 c. mayonnaise with 1 beaten egg white and substitute it for soup.

TURKEY SHORTCAKES

Make on busy days—takes little time

½ lb. process cheese
2 tblsp. chicken broth or milk
2 c. cubed cooked turkey or 3 (5 oz.) cans boned turkey
1½ tsp. instant minced onion
Salt
Pepper

• Place cheese and broth in double boiler. Cook over boiling water until cheese is melted, stirring occasionally to blend. Add remaining ingredients, seasoning to taste.
• Serve over toast, hot biscuits or corn bread. Makes 4 servings.

TURKEY TETRAZZINI

Just the treat to make with leftover turkey from freezer or refrigerator

1 can condensed cream of mushroom soup
1 can condensed cream of chicken soup
1 c. turkey broth or canned chicken broth
2 c. grated process cheese
6 c. cooked spaghetti (12 oz. uncooked)
4 c. diced cooked turkey
½ c. mushrooms or toasted almonds (optional)

½ c. grated Parmesan cheese
Dash paprika

• Blend soups and broth (part milk may be used). Stir in process cheese; mix with spaghetti, turkey and mushrooms. Turn into greased 11½ × 7⅜" baking dish. Sprinkle top with Parmesan cheese and paprika.
• Bake in moderate oven (350°) about 30 minutes, until bubbly and browned. Makes 8 to 10 servings.

Roast Goose

The New Mexico hostess who shares her recipe for roasting goose likes to use a stuffing containing fruits. She and her husband raise geese and select young birds for their company dinners. Weights of geese vary greatly, from about 4 to 14 lbs. ready-to-cook weight. Young goose has tender meat and cooks more quickly than a mature goose. Whatever kind you choose for your company dinner, allow from 1 to 1½ lbs. ready-to-cook weight per person.

ROAST GOOSE WITH FRUIT STUFFING

It's the fruited stuffing that's distinctive. Adds a tangy taste which is equally good in turkey or chicken —do try it

2 (6 to 8 lb.) ready-to-cook geese
Goose giblets
1 qt. water
2 (8 oz.) pkgs. herb-seasoned stuffing
2 c. fresh cranberries, washed and mashed
¼ lb. fresh mushrooms, wiped and chopped, or 2 (4 oz.) cans mushrooms, drained
1 (1 lb.) can sweetened plums, drained, pitted and quartered (reserve ½ c. juice)
1 tblsp. salt
¼ tsp. freshly ground pepper

• Simmer giblets in water until tender, about 1 hour. Time will vary with age of the goose. Reserve ½ c. cooking broth from giblets. Chop giblets finely.
• Mix together prepared poultry stuffing, mashed cranberries, mushrooms, plums and ½ c. plum juice, salt, pepper, chopped giblets and ½ c. broth from cooked giblets.
• Remove any pinfeathers from geese and singe off hairs. Fill neck and body cavities with stuffing, skewer shut and truss.
• Place breast side down on rack in a large roasting pan. Roast uncovered in slow oven (325°) 3 to 4 hours. Turn bird breast side up about two thirds of the way through the roasting time. During roasting, fat may be spooned or siphoned off as it accumulates in the pan so that it will not overbrown (use it for shortening in cooking).
• Test for doneness by moving the drumstick up and down. The joints should yield readily and the drumstick meat should feel very soft (do not undercook goose). Makes about 12 servings.

Note: If you do not wish to stuff goose, rub cavity with a split clove garlic, salt and pepper; add 1 tsp. caraway seeds. Or put quartered apples, onions or celery in cavity; discard after roasting.

STEAM-BAKED GOOSE

As fat accumulates in pan, pour it off or siphon off with poultry baster

- 1 (10 to 12 lb.) goose
- 1 tblsp. salt
- 12 c. Savory Bread Stuffing
- 2 c. hot water
- ¼ tsp. pepper
- 1 small onion, minced
- 1 clove garlic, mashed
- ½ c. coarsely ground green pepper
- 1 can condensed cream of mushroom soup

• Rub 1 tsp. salt inside body cavity of goose. Stuff cavity and neck with Savory Bread Stuffing. Skewer and lace skin openings with string. Tie legs and wings close to body. Place on rack in bottom of roaster pan, breast side up.

• Add water (add more as needed during cooking period). Add remaining salt, pepper, onion, garlic and green pepper to water. Bake, covered, in slow oven (325°) 2 hours.

• Remove from oven. Carefully skim off all goose fat from broth. Add mushroom soup; return goose to oven. Bake uncovered 2 hours longer, basting frequently with savory broth. Remove bird to serving platter and make gravy in roasting pan. Makes about 8 servings, depending on size of goose.

SAVORY BREAD STUFFING

Stuffing absorbs juices and swells. Pack loosely to avoid sogginess

- 8 c. dry bread crumbs
- 2 eggs, beaten
- 2 c. coarsely ground carrots
- 2 small onions, coarsely ground
- 1 can condensed cream of mushroom soup
- ½ lb. bulk pork sausage
- ½ lb. round steak, finely ground
- Goose heart, liver and gizzard, ground together
- 1 tsp. rubbed sage
- ½ tsp. marjoram leaves
- ⅛ tsp. ground cinnamon
- ⅛ tsp. ground nutmeg
- 2 tsp. salt

• Blend all ingredients thoroughly in large kettle or mixing bowl. Stuff goose body cavity and neck. Makes 12 cups, enough for a 10- to 12-lb. goose.

Duckling for Dinner

Some families prefer roast duckling without stuffing while others like to stuff the birds and make brown gravy. So take your choice of our recipes: Roast Ducklings in Lemon/Carrot Sauce and Roast Duckling with Orange Stuffing.

There is almost complete agreement in country kitchens that it's better to carve ducks and arrange the servings attractively on the platter before you take it to the table. Our Countryside Kitchens recommend that duck not be carved like chicken and turkey, but this way: Cut the bird in half lengthwise along the backbone with poultry or heavy kitchen shears and a sharp knife. Then cut along the breastbone on the other side. Cut each half crosswise just above thigh. You will have four pieces.

If you plan to cook a frozen duckling, put it in the refrigerator in its original wrap (unopened) 1 to 1½ days before you want to fix it. Use promptly after thawing.

ROAST DUCKLINGS IN LEMON/CARROT SAUCE

Garnish platter with slices of oranges and bananas dipped in lemon juice

2 (5 lb.) ducklings
½ lemon
Salt
Pepper
Lemon/Carrot Sauce
2 oranges, peeled and sliced
3 bananas, peeled, cut in 1″ diagonal slices and brushed with lemon juice
¼ c. chopped fresh parsley

• Rub skin of ducklings with lemon; rub cavities with salt and pepper; close cavities with skewers. Place on rack in roasting pan; roast in moderate oven (350°) about 1½ hours, or until leg joints move easily.

• Remove ducks from oven and cut into quarters with poultry shears or electric slicing knife. Replace in whole-duck shape on heat-proof serving platters. Spoon about ⅓ Lemon/Carrot Sauce over ducks; surround with orange and banana slices.

• Bake in moderate oven (350°) 10 minutes, or until heated through. Sprinkle with parsley. Serve a duck quarter with orange and banana slices to each person; pass remaining hot Lemon/Carrot Sauce. Makes 8 servings.

LEMON/CARROT SAUCE

Delightful coating for roast duck

1 medium onion, finely chopped
2 large carrots, peeled and grated
¼ c. butter (or part butter, part duck drippings)
2 tblsp. cornstarch
2 c. chicken broth
3 tblsp. lemon juice
⅓ c. sugar
Salt
Pepper
3 tblsp. chopped fresh parsley

• Sauté onion and carrots in butter until limp.

• Blend cornstarch into ¼ c. chicken broth. Stir into butter mixture. Add remaining broth, lemon juice and sugar. Season to taste with salt and pepper.

• Cook over medium heat, stirring, about 5 minutes or until sauce is clear and slightly thickened. Stir in 3 tblsp. chopped fresh parsley. Makes enough sauce for two 5-lb. ducklings.

ROAST DUCKLING WITH ORANGE STUFFING

Honey gives bird a beautiful glaze

Salt or other seasonings
1 (4 to 5 lb.) ready-to-cook duckling
Orange Stuffing
2 tblsp. honey (optional)
1 tsp. bottled browning sauce (optional)

• Lightly rub salt inside body cavity (or use seasoned salt, caraway or celery seeds or any desired seasoning).

• Stuff neck and body cavity with Orange Stuffing. Skewer and lace skin openings with string. Lift wing tips up and over back to form a natural brace. Do not truss. Place duck breast side up on rack in shallow pan. Roast uncovered in slow oven (325°) 1½ to 2 hours for medium done, 2 to 2½ hours for well done, or until thigh moves easily and drumstick meat is soft when pressed between fingers. About ½ hour before roasting time is up, brush duck with honey mixed with browning sauce. Increase heat to moderate (350°) until bird is done. Remove duck. Use brown drippings and small amount of fat in pan for gravy.

• Cut duck in quarters. Arrange stuffing in center of large platter, the duck around it. Makes about 4 servings, allowing 1¼ lbs. dressed weight per serving.

Note: You may roast duck unstuffed if you wish. For flavor put thick onion slices; cored, quartered and thickly sliced apples; sauerkraut; celery tops or some combination, such as apple, celery and onion, in body cavity. Discard after roasting.

ORANGE STUFFING

This brings out the best duck flavor

- **2 c. chopped celery**
- **1 c. boiling water**
- **¼ c. chopped green pepper (optional)**
- **⅓ c. chopped onion**
- **⅓ to ½ c. butter or shortening**
- **2 c. diced peeled oranges with juice**
- **2 tsp. grated orange peel**
- **¾ tsp. poultry seasoning**
- **1 tsp. salt**
- **¼ tsp. pepper**
- **7 to 8 c. lightly packed soft bread crumbs**

• Simmer celery in water until tender, about 10 to 15 minutes. Drain.

• Sauté green pepper and onion in butter until tender, but not brown.

• Combine oranges, peel, seasonings and crumbs; add cooked vegetables and toss together lightly. Makes enough to stuff one 5-lb. duck.

FRIED DUCKLING

Excellent served with sweet potatoes

- **1 (3 to 4 lb.) duckling**
- **1 c. flour**
- **2 tsp. salt**
- **¼ tsp. pepper**
- **2 tsp. paprika**
- **¼ c. butter or regular margarine**
- **Shortening**
- **1 c. water**

• Shake pieces of duckling, 2 or 3 at a time, in paper bag with dry ingredients to coat thoroughly.

• Heat butter and enough shortening in skillet to make ¼″ layer. Place duckling in hot fat skin side down. Brown and turn. Add water and cover tightly.

• Reduce heat and cook slowly or bake in moderate oven (350°) about 1 hour. Uncover and continue to cook about 30 minutes until duckling pieces have crisp crusts. Makes 4 to 6 servings.

chapter 3

Fish and Game Roundup

FOR MANY FARM FAMILIES fishing and hunting are the favorite sports—the best way to have a good time. Boys grow up knowing how to get their fish and game and how to dress and clean it for cooking. Their mothers and sisters know what to do with the prized quarry in their kitchens. The fondness—and respect—for these foods know no generation gap. This started in pioneer days when fish and game were essential to survival and they're still staples in thousands of country kitchens, the source of many recipes in this cookbook.

Nothing stretches the seasons for fish and game more than the home freezer. But, if you have a sportsman husband or son who loves to fish and hunt, you may wonder at times what to do with a freezer filled with "wild things." Most country families today use the bounty throughout the year, which cuts down on freezer cleanouts in the spring and extends good eating around the calendar.

A few necessary rules when using these foods: Defrost game in its original wrap. If the cut is large, put it in the refrigerator to thaw; small cuts may be defrosted at room temperature. Let fish partially or completely thaw in its original wrap. And most important of all, cook game and fish while it's still cold.

A fork is to fish what a thermometer is to candy—it will tell you when the cooking is complete. If fish flakes easily with a fork, it's done. Country people like sauces on their fried, baked and broiled fish—hence a wealth of sauce recipes in this chapter.

Cans of salmon and tuna are practically always on country cupboard shelves ready for use in making main dishes. So we have some good recipes for these and also for the ranking shellfish in rural areas—shrimp and oysters. Turkey/Oyster Casserole, which also contains ham, is an old southern treat for the after-Thanksgiving days when there's leftover turkey. For a marvelous company main dish, pin your faith on Shrimp Marengo—really special.

If wild ducks come to your kitchen, do try Texas Barbecued Duck, which rates high with most people. But there are men who prefer California Rare Duck. Our venison recipes provide some excellent eating; you'll find Venison Mincemeat elsewhere in this book (see Index). Many ranch women in the mountain states declare it makes the best mince pies.

Pointers on Freezing Fish

· *To Freeze:* Prepare as for cooking—scale, eviscerate, remove heads and fins, wash thoroughly and drain. Package in aluminum foil or plastic wrap. A good way to freeze small fish is in a block of ice. Place dressed fish in a 2-lb. coffee can or bread pan and cover with cold water. Process and freeze shellfish as near to the source of supply as possible. It is very susceptible to spoilage. Frozen unpeeled shrimp may be cooked, peeled and refrozen immediately. Shrimp cocktail, shrimp creole and cooked shrimp may be packaged in air-tight packages or containers. Crab and lobster which have been frozen and cooked may be removed from the shell and frozen immediately. Store fish in the coldest part of the freezer, near the bottom of the chest-type and on the shelves of the upright freezer.

· *To Thaw:* Always thaw fish in its original wrapper. The best way, if the wrap is water-tight, is to thaw fish under running cold water. Thaw completely or partially; cook the fish while it still is cold. The time required for thawing depends on the size of the package, from ½ hour for 1 lb. fish filets or steaks or 1 lb. package shellfish to 1¼ hours for a 4½ lb. whole fish. Thawing in the refrigerator takes much more time, about 8 hours for 1 lb. fish filets or steaks and 1 lb. package shellfish to 20 hours for a 4½ lb. fish.

· *Maximum Storage Time:* Shrimp cocktails and creole, 6 weeks; cooked peeled shrimp, 2 to 3 months; cooked unpeeled shrimp, 4 to 6 months. The storage time varies with different kinds of fish. Here are recommendations from the Institute of Agriculture, University of Minnesota, for length of storage for fish at zero temperature. Storage time is 1 to 2 months longer if the temperature of the freezer is 10° below zero.

· Lake herring, crab meat, cooked and peeled shrimp, 3 to 4 months; bullhead, catfish, sea herring, lake trout, mackerel, northern pike, pollock, rainbow trout, chum salmon, shrimp, smelt and tuna, 4 to 6 months; lake bass, bluegill, crappies, flounder, halibut, shellfish, ocean perch, rock fish, most salmon, sunfish and whitefish, 7 to 9 months; and cod, blue pike, haddock, hake, lingcod, lutefish, whiting, yellow pike (walleye) and yellow perch, 9 months or more.

FAVORITE FRIED FISH

• Pan-fried, or just "fried fish," as country people call it, is a universal favorite. It's a fast-fix main dish. You put it on to cook when the rest of the meal is just about ready. Here is the traditional way country people do it.

• Dip fish in milk, French dressing or dry white wine. Sprinkle with salt and pepper. Then roll in flour or cornmeal to coat.

• Heat ⅛″ salad oil or melted shortening in skillet, add fish and quickly cook over medium heat until fish is crisp and golden on underside. Gently turn with spatula and cook until fish browns and flakes easily with a fork. Total cooking time usually is about 8 minutes.

• Drain fish on paper towels and lift to a heated platter. Quickly add one of the garnishes described in this chapter, or make one of the fish sauces. And rush it to the table.

• Country cooks have their own imaginative touches for fried fish—see Different Fried Fish, Filets Supreme and Oven-Fried Fish.

GARNISHES FOR FRIED FISH

• Lemon, lime or orange slices sprinkled with minced pimiento, parsley or green pepper.

• Grapefruit sections dusted with paprika.

• Thick tomato slices topped with pickle relish or with thin lemon slices topped with slice of pimiento-stuffed olives.

• Canned pineapple slices, drained, topped with little haystacks of coleslaw.

• Celery sticks or fans or cheese-stuffed.

• Cucumber slices, fluted and sprinkled with tarragon vinegar.

• Pickled beet slices dotted with horse-radish sauce.

DIFFERENT FRIED FISH

A touch of ketchup and biscuit mix coating make this fish special

2 lbs. dressed fish (whole small filets or steaks from larger fish)
1 egg
2 tblsp. water
1 c. all-purpose buttermilk biscuit mix
3 tblsp. ketchup
½ c. shortening or salad oil

• Dip fish first in egg beaten with water, then in biscuit mix blended with ketchup.

• Fry slowly in heated shortening (use ⅛″ in bottom of skillet) until golden brown on both sides. Serve with lemon and parsley. Makes 6 servings.

FISH PICKLE

Another name for this treat is sour fish—a Minnesota favorite

6 to 8 (about 1 lb.) whole small fish or pieces of larger fish
2 tblsp. salad oil
½ c. water
½ c. vinegar
2 tblsp. minced onion
1 tsp. mixed pickling spice or 1 bay leaf
½ green or red pepper, seeded and diced
1 tsp. salt
⅛ tsp. pepper

• Gently simmer fish in salted water until cooked, or use leftover fried fish.

• Mix remaining ingredients together in a bowl. Add fish and gently turn in this mixture. Cover and let stand in refrigerator at least 24 hours before serving, turning fish occasionally.

• Serve cold, as a relish, or as a main dish. Makes about 2½ cups. Fish Pickle will keep in refrigerator 1 to 2 weeks.

PAN-FRIED FILETS

Take your choice of the excellent sauces to serve with browned fish

1 (1 lb.) pkg. frozen filets (ocean perch, haddock or flounder)
Melted fat or salad oil
⅓ c. fine dry cracker or bread crumbs
½ tsp. salt
1 tsp. paprika
⅛ tsp. pepper
¼ c. milk
Quick Cucumber or Egg Sauce

• Thaw filets enough to separate.
• Heat fat (⅛″ deep) in large skillet.
• Combine crumbs with seasonings.
• Dip filets in milk, then in crumbs; fry in fat over moderate heat 4 to 5 minutes, turn and brown on other side 4 to 5 minutes longer.
• Serve with Quick Cucumber or Egg Sauce. Makes 4 servings.

QUICK CUCUMBER SAUCE: Combine ½ c. mayonnaise or salad dressing, ½ c. finely chopped fresh cucumber, ¼ tsp. salt, 1 tsp. vinegar, ¼ tsp. Worcestershire sauce and 1 tsp. grated onion.

EGG SAUCE: Combine ½ c. mayonnaise or salad dressing, 1 hard-cooked egg, chopped, 2 tblsp. ketchup, 2 tsp. grated onion, ½ tsp. salt and dash of pepper (freshly ground best).

FISH IN CREAM

Really good either on platter or baked and served in a casserole

2 lbs. dressed fish
½ c. flour
1 tsp. salt
¼ tsp. pepper
¼ tsp. paprika
1 egg
1 tblsp. water
¼ c. shortening
2 medium onions, sliced
½ c. light cream
Parsley (optional)

• Dip fish in flour mixed with salt, pepper and paprika, then in egg beaten with water.
• Fry until brown on one side in heavy skillet containing heated shortening. Turn. Place onions on top of fish; cook until underside is brown. Drain fat.
• Pour cream over fish; cover and simmer until cream is absorbed. Garnish with parsley. Makes 6 servings.

Variation

FISH IN CREAM CASSEROLE: After frying, carefully remove fish and onions from skillet; place in casserole. Add cream, cover and bake in hot oven (425°) until heated, about 15 minutes.

OVEN-FRIED FISH

Oven does the frying for you—fish comes out golden, sizzling, good

½ c. butter or regular margarine
8 fish fillets or pieces
1 egg, well beaten
1 c. fine bread crumbs
Salt
Pepper

• Place butter in baking dish and place in preheated moderate oven (375°). Watch carefully while melting butter.
• Dip fish in beaten egg, then in crumbs. Coat well. Place each filet in butter, turning to coat evenly. Season to taste.
• Bake 15 to 20 minutes. Serves 6 to 8.

BAKED FISH

• Use fresh or thawed frozen fish filets or steaks. Cut in serving pieces if necessary and sprinkle on both sides with salt (or seasoned or garlic salt) and pepper.
• Combine ¼ c. melted butter and 2 tblsp. lemon juice. Add 1 tsp. minced onion if you like. Many men fish cooks like to shake in a couple drops of Tabasco sauce. Dip fish in this mixture.
• Arrange fish in greased baking pan on a bed of chopped celery, parsley or onion if you wish to add to the fish flavor. The vegetables also help to keep fish from sticking to the pan.
• Pour any leftover butter-lemon mixture over fish and bake, uncovered, in moderate oven (350°) about 30 minutes or until fish flakes easily with a fork but is still moist.
• Serve on a heated platter with one of the fish sauces in this chapter. Our recipe for Baked Trout follows.

BAKED TROUT

Snappy cheese-butter is elegant dress-up

4 to 6 fresh water trout
2 tblsp. lemon juice
¼ c. melted butter
Salt
Pepper
Blue Devil Butter

• Clean fish and rinse well in cold water. Brush with lemon juice mixed with butter. Season on both sides with salt and pepper. Place in greased pan in single layer and pour over any leftover lemon juice-butter mixture.
• Bake in moderate oven (350°) 30 minutes, or until fish flakes easily with fork. Place on warm platter and spread with Blue Devil Butter. Serves 4 to 6.

BLUE DEVIL BUTTER: Combine 6 tblsp. softened butter or regular margarine, 3 tblsp. blue cheese and 1 tblsp. anchovy paste. Dissolve ½ tsp. dry mustard in 1 tsp. white vinegar and 1 tsp. lemon juice. Blend into butter mixture. Makes about ½ cup.

BAKED NORTHERN PIKE

You may prefer to precook onion slices: Sauté them in butter

2 northern pike, cut in crosswise slices about 2″ thick
Salt
Pepper
1 large sweet onion, cut in thick slices
1 (1 lb.) can ready-seasoned stewed tomatoes
1 tsp. basil leaves

• Place slices of pike in a greased baking pan. Season with salt and pepper. Place slices of onion on fish. Spoon tomatoes over onions. Crumble basil over tomatoes.
• Bake in moderate oven (350°) about 1 hour or until fish flakes easily with fork. Number of servings depends on size of fish.

BAKED FLOUNDER WITH BACON

Spicy, colorful with tomatoes—there's a hint of bacon in the flavor

- 2 lbs. flounder filets
- 4 slices bacon
- 4 thin slices lemon
- ½ c. condensed tomato soup
- ½ c. water
- 2 bay leaves
- Salt
- Pepper
- 1 large onion, sliced
- Paprika

• Place fish on top of 2 slices bacon in greased baking dish. Cover with remaining bacon and lemon slices.
• Combine tomato soup and water. Add bay leaves, salt and pepper to taste and sliced onion. Pour over fish. Bake in moderate oven (350°) 30 minutes.
• Place on heated serving platter. Strain sauce around fish. Sprinkle with paprika. Makes 4 to 6 servings.

BAKED BASS WITH BACON

First you bake fish and then you broil it with quartered tomatoes

- 6 bass, cleaned
- ½ c. cornmeal
- 1½ tsp. salt
- 1½ tsp. paprika
- 6 bacon slices
- 3 tomatoes, peeled and cut in wedges

• Cut bass in serving pieces.
• Mix together cornmeal, salt and paprika. Dip fish in cornmeal mixture. Place in single layer in greased baking dish. Top with bacon.
• Bake in hot oven (425°) 20 minutes. Remove from oven and arrange tomatoes around fish.
• Broil 5″ from heat, about 6 minutes. Makes 6 servings.

BAKED FISH AU GRATIN

Fish cooks in oven without attention. Good with French fries

- 1 (1 lb.) pkg. frozen filets (cod, ocean perch, halibut or flounder)
- 2 tblsp. fine cracker crumbs
- 1 c. canned tomatoes
- 2 tblsp. chopped onion
- ¼ tsp. salt
- ⅛ tsp. black pepper
- 1 tblsp. butter or regular margarine
- ¼ c. shredded Cheddar cheese

• Thaw filets as directed on package.
• Grease 1-qt. shallow baking dish. Sprinkle with cracker crumbs. Lay filets on crumbs.
• Combine tomatoes, onion, salt and pepper; pour over filets. Dot with butter and cheese. Bake in moderate oven (350°) 35 minutes, until fish flakes when pierced with fork. Serves 4.

HALIBUT AU GRATIN

You can bake fish in individual casseroles if you wish—pretty

- 1 lb. fresh or frozen halibut
- 4 slices onion
- 2 bay leaves
- ¼ c. butter or regular margarine
- ¼ c. flour
- 2 c. milk
- ½ lb. Cheddar cheese, shredded
- Salt
- Pepper
- ½ c. buttered bread crumbs
- Parsley
- Paprika

• Top halibut with onion slices and broken bay leaves. Place fish in cheesecloth on perforated rack di-

rectly over boiling water. Cover tightly and steam 30 minutes.
• Meanwhile, melt butter, stir in flour, add milk and stir and cook until sauce thickens and is smooth.
• Add cheese and stir until it is melted; then season to taste with salt and pepper.
• Break halibut into serving-size pieces, discard bay leaves and place fish in buttered 1½-qt. casserole. Top with cheese sauce and sprinkle with buttered crumbs, chopped parsley and paprika.
• Bake in moderate oven (350°) 30 minutes. Makes about 4 servings.

Note: This is a recipe you can double successfully or make 2 recipes if you wish to serve the dish to more than 4.

TRADITIONAL BROILED FISH

• Preheat broiler 10 to 15 minutes.
• Lay a sheet of heavy-duty foil in a 15½ × 10½ × 1″ jelly roll pan. Brush foil with butter, margarine, shortening or salad oil.
• Sprinkle fish with salt or seasoned salt, lemon juice and, if you like, a tiny bit of herb, such as dried basil leaves.
• The distance of fish from source of heat varies with ranges and with thickness of fish filets, steaks or dressed whole fish. Here is the general timetable to use as a guide, but test fish for doneness with a fork.
• Broil filets from ¼ to 1″ thick about 2″ from heat for 8 to 10 minutes. Do not turn.
• Broil steaks from 1½ to 2″ thick about 2″ from heat, 10 to 16 minutes, turning once.
• Broil dressed whole fish 3″ from heat if fish is thin. If thick, broil 6″ from heat. Cook 5 minutes on one side, turn and cook 8 to 10 minutes longer.
• Serve on heated platter at once, garnished with lemon and chopped parsley.

BROILED LAKE TROUT

Serve with baked acorn squash, parslied potatoes, green salad tossed with olive oil and tarragon vinegar, apple pie or cobbler

4 large filets of lake trout
Salt
Pepper
¼ c. finely chopped onion
1 tsp. dried dill weed
1 c. melted butter or regular margarine
Juice of 1 lemon

• Place 4 large fish filets in 2 lightly greased 15½ × 10½ × 1″ jelly roll pans.
• Sprinkle with salt, pepper, onion and dill weed. Drizzle on ½ c. melted butter.
• Mix remaining ½ c. melted butter with juice of 1 lemon.
• Preheat broiler. Place one pan about 5″ from broiler unit. Broil about 10 minutes, or until fish flakes easily. Drizzle on lemon-butter mixture as the fish broils. Keep trout hot while you broil the other pan of fish. Makes 8 generous servings.

Note: Try this treat in October when the days begin to be chilly.

BROILED FISH

Lime juice enhances fish flavor—mayonnaise top browns temptingly

2 large fish filets
Juice of 2 limes
Mayonnaise or salad dressing
Paprika
Salt
Pepper
Parsley

• Grease a piece of heavy-duty aluminum foil well. Place on baking sheet. Turn up edges of foil so juices will not run off. Place filets on foil, skin side down. With a sharp knife, score fish in crisscross fashion. Squeeze lime juice over surface. Let stand 30 minutes before broiling.

• Preheat broiler. Spread surface of fish with mayonnaise. Place baking sheet 5″ from broiler unit. Broil 10 minutes, until fish flakes easily with a fork and mayonnaise bubbles and is brown. Sprinkle with paprika and seasonings; garnish with parsley. Makes 4 servings.

MOLDED FISH

Fish molded in gelatin and served with cold sauce refreshes in summer

6 medium fresh water trout
2 chicken bouillon cubes
2 c. hot water
1 tblsp. lemon juice
1 envelope unflavored gelatin
¼ c. cold water
Lemon slices
Olives
Sour Cream/Cucumber Sauce

• Simmer trout in chicken broth made by dissolving bouillon cubes in hot water and adding lemon juice. Remove fish to deep serving platter; let stand until cool.

• Soften gelatin in cold water. Add to hot broth in saucepan, and stir until dissolved. Chill until gelatin starts to thicken.

• Spoon half of gelatin mixture over fish; chill until firm.

• Garnish with lemon slices and olives; spoon over remaining gelatin; chill. Serve with Sour Cream/Cucumber Sauce. Makes 4 to 6 servings.

SOUR CREAM/CUCUMBER SAUCE: Combine ¾ c. dairy sour cream, ¼ tsp. prepared mustard, ½ tsp. salt, 1 tsp. grated onion, 1 tsp. chopped parsley, ½ c. chopped cucumber and juice of ½ lemon. Chill. Makes about ¾ cup.

FILETS SUPREME

Cream skillet sauce poured on cooked fish is the flavor secret

1 (1 lb.) pkg. frozen filets (haddock, flounder or ocean perch), thawed
2 tblsp. butter or regular margarine
1 medium onion, sliced
1 (3 oz.) can sliced mushrooms
1 (8 oz.) can tomato sauce
3 sprigs parsley
¼ tsp. salt
⅛ tsp. pepper
1 egg yolk
½ c. heavy cream

• Thaw frozen filets as package directs.

• Melt butter in large skillet; add onion, mushrooms, tomato sauce and parsley.

• Separate filets. Cut large filets in half; place side by side on top of tomato mixture. Sprinkle with salt and pepper. Bring to boil. Cover tightly; reduce heat and simmer 10 to 12 minutes, until tender.

• Remove filets to hot serving platter.

• Cook liquid in pan until reduced to about half. Add egg yolk to cream, and mix well. Add a little hot liquid to cream; turn into pan, stirring constantly. Bring just to boiling, but do not boil.

• Pour over filets; garnish with lemon wedges and parsley, if desired. Makes 6 servings.

TROUT AU BLEU

Sounds fancy but it's easy to fix

6 fresh trout or bass, cleaned
½ c. mild vinegar
½ c. chicken broth
1 small bay leaf
Caper Sauce

• Trim fish and split down back.
• Combine in skillet vinegar and broth (make broth by dissolving 1 chicken bouillon cube in ½ c. hot water). Add bay leaf. Simmer 10 minutes.
• Add fish to broth; simmer 15 minutes, or until tender. Remove to platter and serve with Caper Sauce. Serves 6.

CAPER SAUCE: Combine ⅓ c. melted butter or regular margarine, juice of ½ lemon and ⅓ c. capers, drained. Serve warm. Makes about ½ cup.

Superb Fish Sauces

Good cooks around the world trade recipes for their favored fish sauces. Since Europeans often are experts in handling fish in their kitchens, we sought their secrets in France, Spain and Portugal. The four sauces that follow are adaptations we made of sauces used in those countries to dress up fish and make it taste better.

You can use fresh or frozen white fish of any kind—fresh or salt water varieties from the supermarket or what the fisherman in your family brings home. Serve these sauces on broiled, baked or fried fish such as halibut, sea bass, butterfish, cod, haddock, sole, flounder, perch, mackerel, lake trout or catfish. If you use frozen fish, defrost it overnight or at least several hours in the refrigerator.

Cook the fish until it loses its translucency and breaks apart in flakes when you test it with a fork or the tip of a knife. The secret is not to cook fish too long, for that makes the flesh dry. Season it lightly with salt and pepper before adding the sauce.

Our following four recipes make enough sauce for 2 pounds of fish, about 6 servings. You may want to prepare the recipe twice if you are serving more people. It won't be a burden, for these sauces are easy and quick to make. Then we give a collection of sauce recipes that consists of favorites in the country homes of enthusiastic fishermen.

CHEESE/PIMIENTO WHIP

This festive sauce is perfect with fried, baked or broiled fish

1 (3 oz.) pkg. cream cheese, softened
1 tsp. lemon juice
⅛ tsp. salt
⅛ tsp. pepper
½ c. heavy cream, softly whipped
1 (2 oz.) jar pimientos, drained and sliced
3 tblsp. minced green onions, including part of green tops

• Beat together cream cheese, lemon juice, salt and pepper until creamy; fold into whipped cream along with pimientos and green onions.
• Drop spoonfuls of whip on servings of hot, cooked fish. Let it melt down and turn into a sauce. Makes enough whip for 2 pounds of fish, about 6 servings.

VEGETABLE/EGG SAUCE

Decorative with chopped green vegetables and yellow and white eggs

- 1 tblsp. butter
- 1 c. heavy cream
- ½ tsp. garlic salt
- ½ tsp. dry mustard
- ¼ tsp. pepper
- ⅛ tsp. salt
- 2 tblsp. finely chopped parsley
- 2 hard-cooked eggs, grated or finely chopped
- ½ c. cooked peas or frozen peas, thawed to separate
- 1 (10½ oz.) can asparagus tips, drained

• Combine butter, cream, garlic salt, dry mustard, pepper and salt in a saucepan; bring to a boil, then simmer just a few minutes to reduce slightly.

• Add remaining ingredients; heat through, stirring gently to blend.

• Spoon over hot, cooked fish; sprinkle with additional parsley. Makes enough sauce for 2 pounds of fish, about 6 servings.

FISH SAUCE PROVENÇALE

Color-bright with tomatoes and green onions—expertly seasoned

- 4 medium tomatoes, cut in sixths, seeded and peeled if you wish
- ½ tsp. sugar
- ⅓ c. finely sliced green onions (white part only)
- 2 tblsp. butter
- 1½ tblsp. lemon juice
- ½ c. butter
- ½ tsp. garlic salt
- ¼ tsp. salt
- ¼ tsp. pepper
- 4 tblsp. finely chopped parsley

• Sprinkle tomatoes with sugar.

• In large frying pan, sauté green onions in the 2 tblsp. butter, just until limp. Add tomatoes and gently cook and turn just until heated through.

• Add remaining ingredients. Gently shake and tilt pan over heat to mix ingredients and just melt butter. (Butter should be of a thick creamy consistency; do not let it melt down to a thin liquid.)

• Spoon over hot, cooked fish. Makes enough sauce for 2 pounds of fish, about 6 servings.

CUCUMBER MAYONNAISE

Great on broiled or baked fish. Use dill once, then try tarragon

- ½ c. mayonnaise
- 1 tsp. finely crumbled tarragon leaves, or ½ tsp. dill weed
- 1 tsp. lemon juice
- ½ tsp. scraped onion
- ⅛ tsp. salt
- ⅛ tsp. pepper
- 1 large cucumber, peeled and coarsely grated

• Mix together thoroughly mayonnaise, tarragon or dill, lemon juice, onion, salt and pepper. Squeeze excess moisture from cucumber; fold into mayonnaise mixture. Chill thoroughly. Makes enough sauce for 2 pounds of fish, about 6 servings.

MORNAY SAUCE

A well-seasoned cheese sauce like this complements almost all fish

- 2 tblsp. butter or regular margarine
- 2 tblsp. flour
- ½ tsp. salt
- ½ tsp. prepared mustard
- Dash of ground red pepper
- 1 c. milk

½ tsp. Worcestershire sauce
½ c. grated or shredded sharp process cheese
1 tblsp. lemon juice

• Melt butter; stir in flour, salt, mustard and red pepper.
• When well blended, add milk slowly, stirring constantly over low heat until mixture thickens and bubbles.
• Add Worcestershire sauce, cheese and lemon juice; heat to melt cheese. Makes 1½ cups.

MUSTARD/BUTTER SAUCE

Pour this zippy sauce over boiled or broiled fish just before serving

¼ c. butter
1 tsp. prepared mustard
1 tsp. lemon juice

• Heat butter until light brown; stir in mustard and lemon. Makes about ¼ cup.

JIFFY CHEESE SAUCE

A favorite with fish, but try it on vegetables and in casseroles

¼ c. butter or regular margarine
½ c. minced onion
½ c. evaporated milk
2 drops Tabasco sauce
½ lb. process sharp cheese, sliced

• Melt butter; sauté onion in butter until slightly tender. Add remaining ingredients. Heat, stirring occasionally, until blended. Makes 2 cups.

SEAFOOD SAUCE

Try this sauce the next time you make shrimp cocktail

½ c. chili sauce
⅓ c. ketchup
⅓ c. prepared horse-radish
1½ tsp. Worcestershire sauce
¼ tsp. salt
2 tblsp. lemon juice
⅛ tsp. pepper
¼ c. minced celery

• Combine all ingredients. Place in jar, cover and chill before serving. If a milder sauce is preferred, substitute ¼ c. puréed canned tomatoes for half the chili sauce. Makes 1½ cups.

TOMATO/CHEESE SAUCE

Fast fix-up for fried or baked fish. It adds bright color and flavor

1 can condensed tomato soup
1 c. grated or shredded cheese
¼ tsp. prepared mustard

• Heat all ingredients together until cheese melts. Makes about 1½ cups.

LOUIS SAUCE

Delicious on fried fish, in fish salads and with seafood cocktails

1 c. mayonnaise
¼ c. ketchup
1 tsp. prepared horse-radish
1 tsp. Worcestershire sauce
Salt
Pepper

• Mix all ingredients, adding salt and pepper to taste. Makes 1½ cups.

Fish from the Cupboard

Canned salmon and tuna on the kitchen shelf insure the makings for tasty main dishes. You will find prized recipes in this cookbook that feature these foods in delightful dishes. Here are some of them with universal appeal.

SALMON LOAF WITH SHRIMP SAUCE

Makings come from cupboard, refrigerator and freezer. Superb!

2 (1 lb.) cans salmon
¼ c. finely minced onion
¼ c. chopped parsley
¼ c. lemon juice
½ tsp. salt
½ tsp. pepper
½ to 1 tsp. ground thyme
2 c. coarse cracker crumbs
½ c. milk (about)
4 eggs, well beaten
¼ c. melted butter
Shrimp Sauce

• Drain salmon, saving liquid.
• Flake salmon into bowl; add onion, parsley, lemon juice, seasonings and cracker crumbs; mix lightly.
• Add salmon liquid plus enough milk to make 1 cup; add eggs and melted butter. Mix lightly.
• Spoon into greased 2-qt. loaf pan or casserole. Bake in moderate oven (350°) 1 hour or until loaf is set in center. Spoon Shrimp Sauce over top of loaf. Makes 8 servings.

SHRIMP SAUCE: Heat a can of condensed cream of shrimp soup according to directions on label. Add ¼ c. milk, stir until smooth.

SALMON CASSEROLE

With this have stewed or sliced tomatoes, fruit salad and cookies

½ c. cooked carrots
¼ c. cooked onions
1 (1 lb.) can salmon, flaked
1 c. cooked macaroni
1 can condensed cream of celery soup
1 tsp. salt
⅛ tsp. pepper
2 tblsp. butter or regular margarine
½ c. bread crumbs
¼ lb. process cheese, cut in strips

• Cook carrots and onions in small amount of salted water; drain.
• Place salmon in greased 2-qt. casserole; add carrots, onions and macaroni.
• Stir in soup, salt and pepper. Melt butter; toss with bread crumbs. Top casserole with crumbs and cheese.
• Bake in moderate oven (375°) about 20 minutes. Makes 4 servings.

SALMON BISCUIT ROLL

Serve with peas and tiny onions, green salad and butterscotch sundae

½ c. chopped celery
½ c. chopped green pepper
¼ c. chopped onion
2 tblsp. butter
½ c. chopped ripe olives (optional)
1 (1 lb.) can red salmon
1 can condensed cream of chicken soup
2 c. all-purpose buttermilk biscuit mix
⅔ c. milk
1 egg
1 tblsp. water
Milk
1 tblsp. lemon juice

• Sauté celery, green pepper and onion in butter until tender; add olives.
• Drain salmon; reserve liquid for sauce. Add salmon with ¼ c. of the chicken soup to vegetables; set aside.
• Combine biscuit mix and ⅔ c. milk; turn onto floured surface. Knead 12 times. Roll dough into 12 × 9″ rectangle; set aside trimmings. Cover dough with salmon mixture; roll up as for jelly roll.

Place on baking sheet, seam side down.

• Combine egg and water; glaze roll with mixture. If you wish, decorate roll with reserved dough trimmings. Brush with egg mixture. Bake in hot oven (400°) 25 minutes, until golden brown.

• Meanwhile, make sauce. Add enough milk to reserved salmon liquid to make ½ c. Combine with remaining chicken soup and lemon juice in small saucepan; heat to boiling.

• To serve, cut hot salmon roll in individual servings; spoon sauce over top of each. Makes 8 servings.

SALMON LOAF

Serve this for supper with hot biscuits, celery and carrot sticks

1 (1 lb.) can salmon
¾ c. milk
¼ c. chopped green pepper
2 eggs, well beaten
1½ c. dry bread crumbs
2 tblsp. chopped onion
¼ c. melted butter or regular margarine
2 tblsp. butter or regular margarine
2 tblsp. flour
¾ c. milk

• Drain salmon, reserving liquid for sauce. Flake; remove skin. Add ¾ c. milk, green pepper, eggs, bread crumbs, onion and ¼ c. melted butter; mix well. Spoon into greased 8½ × 4½ × 2½″ loaf pan. Pack mixture in tightly. Bake in moderate oven (350°) 50 minutes.

• Meanwhile, make sauce. Melt 2 tblsp. butter; add flour; blend well. Add ¾ c. milk and liquid from salmon; stir constantly. Cook until thick. Serve with salmon. Makes 6 servings.

TUNA FISH PIE

The pie to serve when your fisherman returns home without a catch

Pastry for 2-crust pie
½ c. chopped celery
1 small onion, minced
2 tblsp. butter or shortening
3 tblsp. flour
2 c. milk
1 chicken bouillon cube
2 (7 oz.) cans tuna, flaked
½ c. diced cooked potatoes
2 hard-cooked eggs, chopped

• Line 9″ pie pan with half of pastry; roll out top.

• Sauté celery and onion in butter until soft and clear. Blend in flour.

• Add milk, then bouillon cube; cook until thick and smooth, stirring constantly. Stir in tuna, potatoes and eggs. Turn into pastry shell. Cover with pastry; flute edges and cut steam vents.

• Bake in very hot oven (450°) 10 minutes, then reduce heat to hot (400°) and bake 20 minutes more. Makes 6 servings.

SUNDAY SUPPER CASSEROLE

Be ready for guests with this in the oven, relishes and dessert on hand

1 (12½ oz.) can tuna
1 can condensed cream of mushroom soup
1 can condensed cream of chicken soup
2 c. water
½ c. regular rice (uncooked)
½ c. chopped celery
1½ c. potato chips

• Combine all ingredients except potato chips. Pour into greased 10 × 6 × 1½″ glass baking dish.

• Crush potato chips and sprinkle over the top. Bake in moderate oven (350°) 1½ hours. Makes 6 to 8 servings.

CASHEW TUNA LUNCHEON

There are many tuna luncheon casseroles. This is one of the best

- 1 (3 oz.) can chow mein noodles
- 1 can condensed cream of mushroom soup
- ¼ c. water
- 1 (7 oz.) can chunk-style tuna
- ¼ lb. cashew nuts, salted or unsalted
- 1 c. finely diced celery
- 1 tblsp. chopped green pepper
- ¼ c. minced onion
- ⅛ tsp. salt (if cashews are unsalted)
- ⅛ tsp. pepper (optional)

• Combine all the ingredients in a 1½-qt. casserole, saving out ½ c. chow mein noodles. Sprinkle reserved noodles over the top.

• Bake, uncovered, in slow oven (325°) 40 minutes. Makes 5 servings.

Note: You can double this recipe for 10 servings. Combine ingredients in a 3-qt. casserole and bake about 50 minutes. If you want to keep the casserole warm, turn to a very slow oven (170°) until serving time. Cover if holding time is more than 1 hour.

TUNA/SPAGHETTI BAKE

Try this for covered-dish suppers

- 1 qt. block frozen Home-cooked Tomato Sauce (see Index)
- 1 c. water
- 1 bouillon cube (beef or chicken)
- 1 (8 oz.) pkg. spaghetti
- 2 (7 oz.) cans tuna
- 2 slices (3½″ square) sharp process cheese, quartered

• Heat tomato sauce and water with bouillon cube.

• Cook spaghetti by package directions; drain; return to kettle. Add tuna, coarsely broken, and tomato sauce; toss together. Place in greased 2½-qt. baking dish; top with cheese.

• Cover and bake in moderate oven (375°) 10 minutes; uncover and bake 10 minutes longer. Makes 6 servings.

Seafood Specialties

Of all shellfish from the oceans, shrimp and oysters are the most popular in country homes. With shellfish, as with other fish, the important point is to avoid overcooking. Shellfish is tender; cooking is not required for tenderizing. The Japanese like it raw. In the United States people prefer cooked fish because to them it looks more appetizing and tastes better.

SHRIMP MARENGO

Elegant main dish for special occasions

- 3 lbs. fresh or frozen shrimp
- 8 slices bacon
- 1 c. chopped onion
- 1 clove garlic, minced
- 2 (8 oz.) cans mushroom stems and pieces, undrained
- 2 (1 lb.) cans tomatoes (4 c.)
- 1 (6 oz.) can tomato paste
- 1 can chicken consommé
- 1 tsp. basil leaves
- 1¼ tsp. orégano leaves
- 1 tsp. salt
- 1 tblsp. sugar
- 3 tblsp. prepared mustard
- 3 drops Tabasco sauce

½ c. flour
½ c. water
Fluffy Rice

• Clean shrimp. Fry bacon, cut in pieces, until crisp; drain. Set bacon aside. To bacon drippings add onion and cook lightly. Add garlic, shrimp, undrained mushrooms, tomatoes, tomato paste, consommé, basil, orégano, salt, sugar, mustard and Tabasco. Cook gently 10 minutes.
• Combine flour and water to make a smooth paste. Stir into shrimp mixture and cook 1 minute, stirring all the time. Add bacon. Serve on Fluffy Rice. Makes 16 cups, or 16 servings.

FLUFFY RICE: For 16 servings, bring to a boil 7½ c. water. Add 3 c. long grain parboiled rice and 3 tsp. salt. Cover and simmer until all the water is absorbed, about 25 minutes.

SHRIMP CREOLE

Gourmet treat is beautiful with pink shrimp and green pea pods

2 tblsp. butter
½ medium green pepper, chopped
2 medium onions, chopped
½ c. chopped celery
1 (1 lb. 4 oz.) can tomatoes
1½ tsp. salt
¼ to ½ tsp. pepper
⅛ tsp. ground red pepper
1 c. water
1 tblsp. flour
1 tsp. sugar
2 c. cooked shrimp
1 pt. frozen pea pods (snow peas), partially defrosted

• Melt butter in skillet; sauté green pepper, onions and celery until tender. Add tomatoes, salt, pepper, red pepper and water. Cover, cook about 10 minutes.
• Combine flour and sugar; add enough water to make a smooth paste and stir into tomato mixture. Cook and stir until slightly thickened. Add shrimp and pea pods; cook until pea pods are tender, about 5 minutes. Serve wth Fluffy Rice. Makes 6 servings.

EASY SHRIMP CREOLE

Keep sauce on hand to make this New Orleans special extra-quick

1 lb. raw shrimp, in the shell
½ c. chopped green pepper
½ c. chopped celery
1 tblsp. salad oil
1 c. Basic Red Sauce (see Index)

• Cook shrimp; remove shells and veins.
• Cook green pepper and celery in hot oil until just soft. Add Basic Red Sauce and shrimp and heat. Serve with rice. Makes 4 servings.

OVEN-FRIED OYSTERS

Takes the work out of frying oysters. No watching while they're cooking

1½ c. flour
1¼ tsp. salt
¼ tsp. pepper
24 large oysters
2 eggs, slightly beaten
Fine bread crumbs
Salad oil
Lemon wedges

• Combine flour, salt and pepper.
• Roll oysters in flour; dip in eggs, then roll in bread crumbs. Sprinkle both sides of oysters with oil. Place in shallow pan.
• Bake in hot oven (400°) about 15 minutes, until brown. Serve with lemon wedges. Makes 5 to 6 servings.

Variation

OYSTER SANDWICHES: Use fried oysters, lettuce, thin tomato slices and crisp bacon between hot buttered toast slices.

SALMON/OYSTER PIES

Serve filling on rice instead of in pastry shells for a change

Pastry for 2-crust pie
¼ c. butter or regular margarine
¼ c. flour
1½ c. milk
1 tblsp. minced parsley
1 tblsp. lemon juice
1 pt. oysters
1 (7¾ oz.) can salmon

• Line 6 large custard cups or individual casseroles with pastry. Prick, crimp edges. Bake in hot oven (425°) 15 minutes, until browned.
• Melt butter; blend in flour, and stir in milk, ½ c. at a time. Add parsley and lemon juice.
• Cook oysters in their liquor until edges curl, about 3 minutes. Add salmon, flaked. Add both to white sauce. Heat through slowly. Pour into baked pastry shells. Makes 6 servings.

OYSTER PIE

Cranberry salad is a splendid accompaniment for this main dish

Pastry for 2-crust pie
1½ pts. oysters (3 c.)
Milk plus cream
⅓ c. butter or regular margarine
⅓ c. flour
1 tblsp. minced parsley
1 tsp. salt
Pepper to taste

• Make pastry. Divide dough in half. Roll each to ⅛″ thickness. Cut top, bottom and 4 strips for sides to fit 8″-square baking dish. Transfer pastry to baking sheet. Prick well with fork.
• Bake in very hot oven (450°) 8 to 10 minutes, until lightly browned.
• Drain oysters; reserve liquor. Add enough milk and some cream to liquor to make 3½ c. liquid.
• Melt butter in saucepan. Stir in flour. Add liquid slowly; boil 2 or 3 minutes, stirring constantly.
• Add parsley, salt, pepper and oysters. Heat again just to the boiling point.
• Fit baked crust in bottom and sides. Just before serving add hot oyster filling. Place crust on top. If you wish, garnish with gay splashes of paprika, pimiento, and green pepper. Makes 6 servings.

Note: You can bake pastry in 6 custard cups as in Salmon/Oyster Pies, and serve oyster filling in these pastry shells.

TURKEY/OYSTER CASSEROLE

Oysters, turkey and ham casserole —serve it with cranberry relish

½ c. butter or regular margarine
¼ c. flour
2 c. milk
½ tsp. salt
⅛ tsp. pepper
¼ tsp. dry mustard
2 c. diced cooked turkey
1 c. ground cooked ham
1 pt. oysters, preheated in juice
3 c. mashed potatoes
Paprika

• Melt butter; stir in flour, and blend.
• Add milk, salt, pepper and mus-

tard. Cook over low heat, stirring constantly, until smooth and thickened.

• Add turkey, ham and oysters. Pour into greased 1½-qt. casserole. Arrange mashed potatoes around edge of casserole; sprinkle with paprika.

• Bake in moderate oven (350°) 30 minutes. Makes 6 to 8 servings.

SCALLOPED OYSTERS

Perfect Sunday supper main dish

2½ c. coarse cracker crumbs
1 pt. oysters, drained
¼ c. oyster liquor
¾ c. light cream
1 tsp. Worcestershire sauce
½ tsp. salt
⅛ tsp. pepper
⅓ c. butter or regular margarine

• Arrange ⅓ of the crumbs in well-buttered, shallow 1-qt. baking dish. Cover with half the oysters; repeat layer of crumbs and remaining oysters.

• Blend liquids and seasonings; pour over oysters. Cover with remaining crumbs and dot with butter.

• Bake in moderate oven (350°) about 45 minutes. Makes 5 servings.

How to Roast Venison

The best-eating venison is stripped of all fat which isn't edible. For roasts, keep meat from drying out by larding with salt pork or bacon before cooking.

Ripen meat—hang at least 4 days to 2 weeks. If the deer is full grown, meat should be marinated.

To make marinade, chop 1 onion, 1 carrot and branch of celery. Make bouquet in cheesecloth of parsley, thyme, bay leaf and a few whole cloves. Cook 1 to 2 minutes in hot fat or salad oil, then add 1 c. vinegar. Bring to boil, and simmer about 20 minutes. Strain; then cool. Pour over venison.

Let stand 12 to 24 hours in glass, earthenware or china container—not metal. (Marinating tenderizes meat and takes away some of gaminess.)

After marinating 24 hours, lard well with salt pork and a few pieces of garlic. Roast on rack in shallow pan in moderate oven (350°) allowing 30 minutes per pound, basting frequently with drippings. Serve with red currant jelly.

VENISON STEAKS

Serve with baked potatoes, green salad and pineapple sherbet

3 tblsp. flour
1½ tsp. salt
¼ tsp. marjoram leaves
6 venison steaks, cut from the round
Fat for frying
1 small onion, peeled
4 medium carrots, peeled
½ c. diced celery and tops
1½ c. beef broth

• Mix flour, salt and marjoram; rub over meat. Brown steaks in hot fat in pressure pan.

• Add vegetables and broth; cover, and cook at 10 lbs. pressure 20 to 30 minutes, or as manufacturer directs.

• Cool normally 5 minutes, then place pan under cold water to reduce pressure quickly.

• Thicken liquid for gravy by rubbing vegetables through sieve, food mill or blender. Makes 6 servings.

VENISON PASTIES

Tastily seasoned meat-and-vegetable mixture bakes in pastry jackets

Pastry for 2-crust pie
¾ lb. venison round, thawed and cut in tiny cubes
2 potatoes, diced
2 carrots, thinly sliced
3 tblsp. minced onion
1 tsp. salt
¼ tsp. pepper
¼ to ½ tsp. thyme leaves, crushed (optional)
2 tblsp. chopped fresh parsley
4 tsp. water

• Roll out half of pie dough and place in 9″ pie pan. Mix venison and remaining ingredients. Place half of mixture on pie dough in pie pan. Fold dough over filling to make half-moon shape that fills one half of the pie pan. Seal and crimp edges of dough.

• Roll out second half of dough and place in other half of pie pan. Fill with remaining meat mixture. Fold dough over into half-moon shape; seal and crimp edges (do not cut vents in dough). You will have 2 half pies or pasties.

• Bake in moderate oven (375°) 1 hour and 10 minutes. Pierce crust and vegetables with sharp fork to be sure vegetables are tender. Makes 4 servings.

Note: Venison Pasties with chili sauce make excellent use of frozen venison in February and March. Add a salad of sliced cucumbers in oil and vinegar dressing and a hot fruit dessert, such as a compote of canned peaches and plums heated together.

VENISON/PORK PATTIES

Start your sportsman off to duck blind or woods with this for breakfast

1 lb. venison, thawed
1 lb. seasoned bulk pork sausage
1 tsp. salt
⅛ tsp. pepper
¼ tsp. thyme leaves, crushed
¼ tsp. crushed rosemary leaves (optional)

• Grind together the venison and sausage. Mix in seasonings. Flour hands and form into 8 patties.

• Pan-fry slowly about 15 minutes on each side or until patties are cooked through. Drain off fat as patties cook. Makes 4 servings.

Note: This is an excellent breakfast dish in chilly November. Also have waffles with apple slices cooked in butter.

BARBECUED VENISON

Leftover venison pot roast in barbecue sauce makes excellent sandwiches

1 (28 oz.) bottle prepared barbecue sauce
1 c. ketchup
2 tblsp. pickle relish
1 c. beef broth or pan juices from venison roast
1 small onion, chopped
2 branches celery, chopped
2 lbs. cooked rump pot roast of venison

• Mix all ingredients except venison in a large saucepan. Cook over low heat about 30 minutes or until sauce is thick.

• Slice rump roast into the bubbling sauce and simmer until meat is just heated through. Makes 5 servings of 2 hearty sandwiches per person.

Note: On an autumn day when men return home from hunting, chilled and maybe wet and hungry, these sandwiches will please. Serve "sauced" venison in buns or on halves of hard rolls crisped in oven, with coleslaw, shoestring potatoes, dark chocolate cake and coffee.

SCALLOPINE OF VENISON

Country chefs pound venison with edge of plate as for Swiss steak

2½ lbs. venison
Seasoned flour (with salt, pepper, paprika)
Fat for frying
2 medium onions, peeled and sliced
1 tsp. sugar
1 (4 oz.) can mushrooms
1¼ c. tomato purée
1¼ c. hot water

• Wipe meat with vinegar-soaked cloth–vinegar picks up hairs and clotted blood more easily.
• Cut meat into serving pieces and roll lightly in seasoned flour. Flatten slightly with edge of plate or meat pounder.
• Fry until golden brown on both sides in hot fat. Add onions after first turning.
• Place in greased casserole; add remaining ingredients. Bake in moderate oven (350°) about 2 hours, until tender. Makes 8 to 10 servings.

Tips on Freezing Game Birds

Success in freezing game birds depends to no small extent on their care after they are killed. It is important to remove the body heat as soon as possible by allowing space between them rather than by piling them in the car trunk. Deterioration is rapid when birds are stacked. Often it is best to have the birds frozen at a locker plant near the hunting grounds if the trip home is long. *Be sure birds are drawn before freezing.*

Farm people prepare game birds for freezing much the same as poultry, but they do find it desirable to pluck wild ducks and geese dry, or without scalding. They scald pheasants in hot water below the boiling point, or with a temperature of 155 to 160°.

PHEASANT WITH RICE STUFFING

Meat has lighter color than chicken or turkey because it has less fat

2 pheasants (about 2½ lbs. each)
1 tblsp. salt
1½ c. long-grain rice
3 c. water
½ c. butter or regular margarine
1 c. finely chopped celery
3 tblsp. minced onion
½ c. fresh mushrooms, sliced (or canned and drained)
⅛ tsp. rubbed sage
⅛ tsp. thyme leaves
⅛ tsp. savory leaves
Melted butter or regular margarine
6 bacon slices

• Rub 1 tsp. salt into cavity of each pheasant.
• Brown rice in dry frying pan. Transfer to saucepan; add water and 1 tsp. salt; cook until tender.
• Melt ½ c. butter in frying pan. Add celery, onion and mushrooms, and cook 10 minutes. Add to rice along with herbs. Stuff birds lightly. (Extra stuffing may be baked in covered casserole last 30 minutes of roasting time.)

• Truss the birds, brush them with melted butter. Place strips of bacon across breasts.
• Roast in covered pan in moderate oven (350°) about 2 hours, or until tender. Baste frequently.

Note: Complete the dinner menu with Curried Broccoli and Onions, lettuce tossed with Orégano Salad Dressing (see Index), hot rolls and coffee.

STUFFED PHEASANT

Cook and season mixed wild and long-grain rice to serve with this

2 (3 to 4 lb.) pheasants
Salt
Bread stuffing (your favorite recipe)
Fat for frying
1 c. water

• Clean, dress and salt inside pheasants.
• For each pound of pheasant, allow ½ c. favorite bread stuffing; stuff loosely. Sew or skewer openings together.
• Brown pheasants in hot fat in pressure pan. Add water.
• Cover and cook at 10 lbs. pressure 20 to 30 minutes (depending on age of birds), or as manufacturer directs.
• Cool 5 minutes, then place pan under cold water to reduce pressure quickly. Makes 8 servings.

Seven Good Ways to Cook Wild Ducks

Wild ducks are better eating than ever. That's what many farmers, who like to shoot ducks, and their wives, who take pride in cooking the prizes their husbands bring home, tell us. The main reason for the improvement, they say, is that the ducks themselves eat better. They get more corn, wheat and other small grains left in the fields by mechanical harvesters.

When the food editors of FARM JOURNAL wanted to find the best ways to cook wild duck, they went directly to the homes of men who like to hunt and who, with their families and friends, consider duck dinners special treats. One wild duck makes 1 or 2 servings, depending on its size. Most farmers insist that their wives cook as many ducks as people around the table.

Here are seven recipes, all different, that are the result of the quest. They come from the four major duck flyways—Atlantic, Mississippi, Central and Pacific. Home economists in our Countryside Kitchens used mallards, each weighing about 1¾ pounds, to test the recipes. You can adjust the cooking time to the size of the birds you have and to their age. When you're in doubt about age, or think the ducks lost fat during a long flight, it's a good plan to wrap the birds individually in foil when roasting them.

There are some men who like duck cooked very rare, about 22 minutes in a hot oven (400°). Our recipe for California Rare Duck is a compromise between the very-rare and the well-done versions. It was the favorite of men editors of FARM JOURNAL who shoot ducks. Several readers have written that they never liked wild duck until they tasted Texas Barbecued Duck.

TEXAS BARBECUED DUCK

Wrapping ducks in foil tenderizes and keeps them moist

2 wild ducks
2 tblsp. salad oil
Rio Grande Barbecue Sauce

• Rub ducks with oil; brown under broiler. Brush ducks with half the Rio Grande Barbecue Sauce; place 1 tblsp. sauce in each cavity. Wrap each bird closely in heavy foil; bake in shallow pan in slow oven (325°) 1 hour, or until tender. Remove foil last 15 minutes, and spoon over remainder of sauce.

To Grill Outdoors: Proceed as above, browning over hot coals and finishing over slow coals.

RIO GRANDE BARBECUE SAUCE: Sauté 2 tblsp. chopped onion in ¼ c. butter. Add ½ c. ketchup, ½ c. lemon juice, ¼ tsp. paprika, ½ tsp. salt, ¼ tsp. pepper, ¼ tsp. ground red pepper, 2 tblsp. brown sugar and 2 tblsp. Worcestershire sauce. Simmer 15 minutes.

DUCK FILETS

Layer cooked filets in electric roasters to tote and reheat for church suppers

1 wild duck
Instant meat tenderizer
2 slices bacon
2 tblsp. salad oil

• With sharp knife, remove skin from duck. Cut meat from breast in 2 filets.
• Use meat tenderizer as directed on the package. Wrap each filet loosely with bacon slice; fasten with toothpicks.
• Cook filets in hot oil over moderate heat until browned and tender, about 15 minutes per side. Serve on hot platter with ribbons of cooked bacon.

Variation

DUCK PATTIES: Omit tenderizer. Pound filets; dip in mixture of salt, pepper and flour. Round into patties; wrap bacon strip around edge; fasten with toothpick. Cook in hot oil over moderate heat until browned and tender, about 15 minutes on each side.

CALIFORNIA RARE DUCK

Pink flesh tastes like rare roast beef; skin is crisp and shiny

1 wild duck
1 tsp. salt
½ tsp. pepper
¼ tsp. garlic salt
Glaze

• Rub cavity and outside of duck with seasonings. Bake on rack in shallow pan, uncovered, in extremely hot oven (500°) 25 to 35 minutes, brushing with Glaze.

GLAZE: Ten to 15 minutes after placing duck in oven, brush several times with mixture of 2 tblsp. light or dark corn syrup and 1 tsp. bottled browning sauce.

SPICY ROAST DUCK

Serve ducks in foil packages and let everyone open his own

1 wild duck
2 tblsp. flour
½ tsp. salt
⅛ tsp. pepper
1 tblsp. whole allspice, cracked
1 bay leaf, crumbled

• Rub duck inside and out with mixture of flour, salt, pepper and allspice.
• Sprinkle bay leaf pieces over top.
• Place on rack in roaster (arranging several ducks close together helps prevent drying). Bake, covered, in slow oven (325°) 2½ to 3 hours, or until tender. It's a good idea to wrap each duck in foil the last hour of roasting.

BASTED DUCK WITH OYSTER STUFFING

Try this favorite of country people on Maryland's Eastern Shore

1 duck
1 tsp. salt
¼ tsp. pepper
1 qt. bread stuffing (your favorite)
1 c. oysters
¼ c. melted butter
¼ c. lemon juice
¼ tsp. paprika
⅛ tsp. thyme leaves

• Season duck cavity and outside of bird with salt and pepper.
• To your favorite bread stuffing, add 1 c. oysters, drained and chopped. Use oyster liquor as a part of liquid to moisten stuffing.
• Lightly stuff duck; put the remainder of the stuffing in a pan to bake with duck (baste with duck drippings).
• Place duck on a rack in a roasting pan; cover and bake in a slow oven (325°) about 2½ hours. Remove cover to brown.
• Baste often with mixture of butter, lemon juice, paprika and thyme.

WILD DUCK IN SOY MARINADE

You let the ducks stand overnight in an interesting marinade

2 wild ducks, quartered
1 (13½ oz.) can pineapple tidbits
½ c. soy sauce
1 tsp. ground ginger
¼ c. shortening or bacon drippings
1 (3 oz.) can mushrooms, drained

• Marinate ducks overnight in mixture of pineapple, soy sauce and ginger.
• Wipe meat; brown in fat. Place in shallow casserole; pour on marinade and mushrooms. Bake, covered, in moderate oven (350°) 1½ hours, or until tender (add water, if necessary).

ROAST WILD DUCK WITH PRUNE/ORANGE STUFFING

Stuffing makes it special; serve with one of your favorite barbecue sauces

2 wild ducks
2 tsp. baking soda
Salt
Pepper
2 c. day-old bread crumbs
¼ c. melted butter or regular margarine
¼ c. diced orange sections
¼ tsp. grated orange peel
¾ c. diced celery
1 c. cooked prunes, pitted and quartered
½ tsp. salt
⅛ tsp. pepper
Bacon slices or strips of salt pork

• Cover ducks with cold water to which baking soda has been added. Simmer 1 hour; remove from water; drain. Rub inside and out with salt and pepper.

• For stuffing, toast bread lightly in butter in large skillet. Add oranges and peel, celery, prunes, ½ tsp. salt and ⅛ tsp. pepper; toss together lightly. Stuff ducks lightly and truss. Place on rack, breast side up, in shallow roasting pan. Lay 4 to 6 slices bacon across each.

• Roast in moderate oven (350°), allowing 15 minutes per pound for young birds, 20 minutes for older, basting frequently with pan drippings until well done. Makes 6 to 8 servings.

Note: Other stuffing suggestions are: Add about ½ c. peanuts to your favorite bread stuffing; or sauerkraut makes an easy, delicious duck stuffing. If you do not care to stuff, place a branch of celery, a small onion and an apple inside duck to add flavor during roasting; discard before serving.

ROAST WILD GOOSE

Include cranberry, currant or other tart jelly in goose dinner menus

1 young wild goose (6 to 8 lbs. dressed)
Juice of 1 lemon
Salt
Pepper
¼ c. butter or regular margarine
¼ c. chopped onion
1 c. chopped tart apple
1 c. chopped dried apricots
3 c. soft bread crumbs (day-old bread)
½ tsp. salt
¼ tsp. pepper
4 to 6 slices bacon
Melted fat or drippings

• Rub cleaned goose inside and out with lemon juice and seasonings.

• For stuffing, melt butter in heavy skillet or saucepan. Sauté onion until soft and clear; mix in apple, apricots, crumbs, ½ tsp. salt and ¼ tsp. pepper.

• Spoon stuffing lightly into cavity. Close opening with skewers and truss bird. Cover breast with bacon slices and cheesecloth soaked in melted fat.

• Place breast side up in roasting pan. Roast in slow oven (325°), allowing 20 to 25 minutes per pound, until tender. Baste often with fat or pan drippings.

• If age of goose is uncertain, pour 1 c. water into pan and cover last hour of cooking. Makes about 6 servings.

Rabbit Recipes

We selected three of the most popular rabbit recipes from country game cooks. The dishes the recipes produced passed our own taste-testers with compliments. And a universal comment was: "This rabbit really is tender!"

ONION-STUFFED RABBIT

An old-time country favorite way of cooking rabbits and squirrels

1 rabbit (about 2 lbs.)
1½ tsp. salt
⅛ tsp. pepper
1½ c. onion slices
3 bacon slices

• Rub salt and pepper inside rabbit. Stuff with onion slices. Truss. Lay strips of bacon over rabbit.

• Wrap in aluminum foil; place in shallow baking pan. Bake in moderate oven (350°) 1½ hours. Makes 4 servings.

BRAISED RABBIT IN WINE SAUCE

With this serve buttered noodles, parsnip sticks cooked in a bit of butter and sugar, lettuce salad, cranberry pie, hot coffee

2 rabbits, cut into pieces
Flour
Salt
Pepper
Butter
¼ c. dry white wine
1 c. hot water
1 c. chopped celery
½ c. chopped parsley
1 bay leaf
¼ tsp. paprika

• Roll rabbit pieces in flour. Season with salt and pepper. In a large skillet sauté rabbit pieces in ½″ butter until well browned.

• Add remaining ingredients; cover and simmer over low heat until tender, about 1 hour. (Add more water to sauce if necessary.) Remove bay leaf before serving. Makes 8 to 10 servings.

Note: In December cook the last of the rabbits in your freezer.

RABBIT WITH VEGETABLES

The gravy almost "steals the show"

2 (3 to 4 lb.) rabbits
¼ c. flour
2 tsp. salt
2 tsp. curry powder
⅛ tsp. paprika
Fat for frying
8 potatoes, peeled
12 whole carrots, peeled
2 thick onion slices
1 c. hot water
1 bay leaf
1 c. dairy sour cream

• Skin, clean and cut up rabbits.

• Combine dry ingredients in paper bag; shake rabbit pieces in flour mixture.

• Brown meat lightly in hot fat in pressure pan.

• Add vegetables, water and bay leaf.

• Cover and cook at 10 lbs. pressure 18 to 20 minutes, or as manufacturer directs. Reduce pressure slowly.

• Arrange rabbits and whole vegetables on heated platter.

• Thicken liquid for gravy by forcing remaining vegetables through sieve, food mill or blender. Stir in cream; simmer 5 minutes. Serve hot. Makes 8 servings.

ROAST RACCOON

It's fixed this way for an Illinois community's famed coon suppers

3 to 4 raccoons, 4 to 6 lbs. each
5 tblsp. salt
2 tsp. pepper
2 c. flour
1 c. shortening
8 medium onions, peeled
12 small bay leaves

• Skin, draw and clean raccoons soon after killing. Remove, without breaking, the brown bean-shaped kernels from under forelegs and each thigh.

• Cut into pieces. Reserve meaty backs and legs for baking. Cook bony pieces in water to make broth for gravy and stuffing (recipe follows). Add small amount of seasonings. Simmer until meat is tender; strain, and use only the broth.

• Sprinkle back and leg pieces with salt and pepper. Then dredge with flour.

• Heat shortening in heavy skillet. Add meat; brown on all sides.

• Transfer pieces to roaster; add onions and bay leaves. Cover.

• Bake in moderate oven (350°) 2 hours, until tender.
• Make gravy by adding flour to drippings in pan. (Use 2 to 3 tblsp. for each cup of liquid or broth used.) Serves 24.

STUFFING: Prepare while meat roasts. Mix together 3 loaves day-old bread, crumbed; 2½ tsp. salt; 1 tsp. pepper; 2½ tsp. rubbed sage; 4 beaten eggs; 1 (1½ oz.) pkg. dehydrated onion soup mix; 4 branches chopped celery; ½ c. butter or regular margarine; and 4 c. coon broth. Bake in large shallow pan in moderate oven (350°) 30 minutes. Serves 24.

Note: Coleslaw to serve with fish and game is made this way: Sprinkle 2½ c. finely shredded cabbage with 1 tsp. salt; moisten with mayonnaise and add ½ c. each cut-up cucumber and green onions. Sprinkle with celery seeds. This makes 4 servings. Double or triple recipe for more servings.

One-dish Meal for a Crowd

You are certain to be in the South when you find this tempting and famous stew, but there's no reason why it can't be made in other areas. If squirrels are scarce or your hunters have no time to go after them, chicken makes a good substitute. The Brunswick Stew goes by different names. Squirrel Stew is one, and in some Carolina communities, it is called Squirrel Muddle.

For a large crowd the stew is cooked outdoors over coals in a big iron kettle. A southern woman says that Brunswick Stew is the perfect way to serve a lot of people without a lot of fuss.

BRUNSWICK STEW

It makes a one-dish meal for the entire neighborhood

About 70 squirrels, cut up
2 large stewing chickens, cut up
6 gals. water
2½ lbs. salt pork, chopped
2½ gals. butter beans (lima beans)
3½ gals. cubed peeled potatoes
4 gals. chopped peeled tomatoes
1 gal. cubed peeled carrots
2½ gals. freshly cut corn
1 gal. shredded cabbage (optional)
1 pod red pepper, chopped
¾ c. black pepper
1¾ c. salt
2¼ c. sugar

• Clean, dress and cut up squirrels and chickens. If your folks are not ardent squirrel hunters, increase the number of chickens. If you use all chickens, this recipe will take 24 stewing chickens.
• Bring 4 gals. water to boil in 30-gal. iron kettle. Add squirrel and chicken pieces. Cook, stirring often, until meat comes off the bone. (Take out pieces of bone before serving to small children.) Add remainder of water, as needed.
• Chop salt pork, fry out and add pork and drippings to boiling mixture. Add beans, potatoes, tomatoes, carrots and corn in order as each is prepared. Continue cooking and stirring until vegetables are tender.
• Add cabbage and seasonings, and cook, stirring, 1 hour, until stew is thick and flavors well blended. Remove kettle from the coals to serving area by hooking the handle over a heavy pole, several helpers carrying each end. Makes 15 gallons.

· The stew may be served in heavy paper bowls (the kind used for ground meat). Folks usually stand up to eat it at big community suppers or other affairs—the bowls of stew and paper cups of iced tea rest on high, temporary tables which are simply wide boards nailed to waist-high poles. You will get big mounds of spoon bread as long as it holds out.

chapter 4

Special Main Dishes

SCRAMBLED EGGS and macaroni and cheese represent main dishes firmly established in country meals. Eggs, cheese and pasta (macaroni products) have long been staples in farm kitchens. The ease with which busy women can use them to fix many superior dishes accounts in large part for their popularity. Mothers also appreciate the protein in these main dishes, which enables them to compete with the meat platter. They also know that these foods have remarkable ability to make a little meat go a long way.

Women recognized as the best cooks in their neighborhoods depend on a bountiful supply of eggs. Before poultrymen stepped up seasonal production to year-round, hens used to produce more plentifully in March, as a salute to spring. That's when egg cookery went into high gear, a country custom that continues to this day. But eggs are a staple in use every day of the year. Short-order cooks rely on a platter of eggs and bacon or ham for quick unexpected meals they are proud to serve.

Cheese is a great flavor booster as well as an important provider of protein. You will find in this chapter a galaxy of recipes in which it is an ingredient. Cheese/Bacon Pie is a splendid example. And most of our pasta dishes feature cheese. Indeed pasta and cheese complement each other. Macaroni products are mild in flavor while cheese often is aggressive or nippy in taste. This chapter tells how to cook pasta properly. Perfectly cooked macaroni products will result in success with the fascinating recipes. Try the casserole, Double Cheese Bake, a macaroni special flavorful with Cheddar and Swiss cheese, for example.

Busy Women Praise Scrambled Eggs

Few main dishes are as accommodating as scrambled eggs, often the busy woman's first choice. They are at home in all three of the daily meals—taste equally good with bacon or ham, or with such foods as cheese, tuna and corn added.

Country women frequently possess great skillet skill in scrambling eggs. They cook them—as they do all egg dishes—with low or moderate heat until done, but still moist. (Eggs keep on cooking a little even after you turn them onto a warm platter.)

SCRAMBLED EGGS

The secret of tender, scrambled eggs is to cook them over low heat and only until they are cooked throughout, but still are glossy and moist. Using water for liquid instead of milk increases tenderness, but you lose the milk's nutritional value. If you like the mottled yellow-and-white appearance, don't beat the eggs—just stir them with a fork.

Here are a few ways we vary scrambled eggs in Countryside Kitchens:

· Sprinkle grated Swiss cheese and buttered bread crumbs over the cooked eggs; broil 1 minute to brown.

· Add a little grated onion when the cooking eggs start to thicken.

· Add flaked pieces of dried beef, or crumbled, cooked bacon, a bit of finely chopped green pepper, a well-drained and chopped fresh tomato or a 2- or 4-oz. can mushroom stems and pieces.

· When in an adventurous mood use ¾ c. orange juice or dairy sour cream for the liquid.

· For a gourmet's touch, fold in a little chopped dill or chives just before serving.

PERFECT SCRAMBLED EGGS

Turn onto platter while slightly moist. They'll be just right when served

8 eggs
½ c. milk or light cream
1 tsp. salt
⅛ tsp. pepper
3 tblsp. butter, regular margarine or bacon drippings

· Break eggs into bowl and stir with fork. Mix in milk, salt and pepper.

· Melt butter in heavy skillet over medium heat, add egg mixture and reduce heat to low. (You may scramble eggs in double boiler. Takes less watching, but more time for cooking. See Index for Double-boiler Scrambled Eggs.)

· When eggs begin to set at bottom and sides, push them back with pancake turner to allow the uncooked eggs to flow to the bottom of the pan. Repeat until the eggs are just cooked through. Remove from skillet at once. Serve on warm platter. Makes 4 to 6 servings.

EGGS IN BUTTERCUPS

Pretty way to dress up scrambled eggs—toast cups look like flowers

12 slices fresh bread
Melted butter or regular margarine
8 eggs
2 tsp. salt
1 tsp. pepper
¼ c. heavy cream
Crisp-fried bacon bits (optional)

• Trim crusts from bread, save crusts for crumbs to be used later. Press slices into muffin-pan cups, brush with butter. Bake in hot oven (400°) 20 minutes.
• Beat eggs until fluffy; add salt, pepper, cream and bacon.
• Pour into greased skillet or double boiler. Cook over low heat until set, lifting occasionally with spatula to let uncooked portion run underneath.
• Spoon into toast cups. Serve immediately. Garnish with additional bacon. Makes 6 servings.

DOUBLE-BOILER SCRAMBLED EGGS

Easier to avoid overcooking than skillet method—takes less watching

3 tblsp. butter or regular margarine
12 eggs
½ c. milk
1 tsp. salt
⅛ tsp. pepper

• Melt butter in top of double boiler.
• Beat eggs slightly; add milk and seasonings. Pour into double boiler and cook over simmering, not boiling, water, scraping the cooked portions from bottom and sides of the pan until the eggs are thick and creamy flakes, but moist. Serve at once. Makes 8 servings.

CHEESE SCRAMBLED EGGS

Cheese in scrambled eggs provides a new taste, change and food value

6 eggs
6 tblsp. light cream
Salt
Pepper
3 tblsp. butter
½ c. coarsely shredded process cheese

• Combine eggs, cream and salt and pepper to taste. Stir with fork to mix.
• Melt butter in a 12″ skillet. Add eggs and cook over low heat, gently lifting egg mixture with a spoon so uncooked eggs will flow to bottom of skillet. Add cheese just before eggs are cooked; mix in lightly. Cook eggs until set, but remove from heat while they are moist. Makes 4 servings.

Note: If you like, add 2 tblsp. chopped chives or crumbled crisp bacon just before serving.

TUNA/EGG SCRAMBLE

Five-minute main dish to fix with ingredients kept in country kitchens

6 eggs
⅓ c. light cream or milk
½ tsp. salt
1 (7 oz.) can tuna
2 tblsp. butter or regular margarine

• Blend together eggs, cream and salt. Stir in tuna. Pour into hot skillet with butter. Cook over low heat, stirring occasionally, until eggs are thickened, but still moist. Makes 6 servings.

CAMP-STYLE EGGS AND CORN

Excellent cooked indoors or on outdoor grill. Start meal with tomato juice

½ lb. bulk pork sausage
1 (16 to 17 oz.) can cream style corn
6 eggs

• Brown sausage in skillet; pour off fat. Add corn.
• Beat eggs. Add to corn-sausage mixture, and cook as for scrambled eggs. Makes 6 servings.

Note: You can substitute ¼ lb. bacon, chopped, for the sausage. Or, use ¼ lb. shredded cooked ham for the meat. Sauté in 3 to 4 tblsp. fat or drippings before adding eggs. Vary the color and flavor by adding ¼ c. minced onion or scallions and 3 tblsp. finely chopped green pepper.

EGGS FOO YUNG

A speedy version of a famous Chinese dish—right for supper

4 eggs, beaten
1 (1 lb.) can bean sprouts, drained
½ c. cooked or canned chicken, chopped
1 small onion, chopped
½ tsp. salt
⅛ tsp. pepper
1 tblsp. soy sauce (optional)
2 tblsp. salad oil
Chinese Sauce

• Combine all ingredients, except oil and Chinese Sauce. Drop by spoonfuls into hot oil in skillet; spread bean sprouts gently with tip of spoon to cover egg mixture.
• Cook until little cakes set and brown on edges. Turn and brown on the other side. Add more oil to skillet if necessary as you cook additional patties. Place on hot platter and serve at once with Chinese Sauce. Makes 10 patties.

CHINESE SAUCE: Combine 1½ c. chicken broth (or 1½ c. hot water with 2 chicken bouillon cubes added) with 1 tsp. molasses and 1 tsp. soy sauce. Blend 2 tblsp. cornstarch and 2 tblsp. cold water; add to chicken broth and cook, stirring constantly, over low heat until mixture comes to a boil. Makes about 1½ cups.

Corned Beef Hash with Eggs

You'll almost always find a few cans of corned beef hash in country cupboards ready to team with eggs on a minute's notice for a satisfying main dish. Our recipe is for a skillet special you can make in 15 minutes flat while the accompanying hot rolls are baking.

If you're looking for a luncheon main dish to serve a fastidious guest, choose Eggs Benedict. With buttered asparagus or peas and a salad, you have a meal that's bound to please.

EGGS IN CORNED BEEF HASH

Delicious dish to fix for lunch when unexpected company arrives

1 tblsp. shortening or salad oil
¼ c. chopped onion
2 (1 lb.) cans corned beef hash
6 eggs
Salt
Pepper

• Heat shortening in 9 or 10″ heavy skillet. Add onion; cook 2 minutes. Add hash, breaking it up with spoon. Cook over medium heat, 6 minutes, stirring occasionally.
• Reduce heat to low; pat hash level in pan and make 6 deep hollows with back of spoon. Drop an egg into each hollow; season with salt and pepper.
• Cover skillet tightly. Cook 5 minutes or until eggs are set.
• Divide into 6 portions. With wide spatula or pancake turner, carefully lift out each portion to serving plate. Serve with ketchup or chili sauce, if desired. Makes 6 servings.

EGGS BENEDICT

Serve with a tossed green salad

6 thin small ham slices
6 eggs
3 hamburger buns or English muffins, split
Easy or Mock Hollandaise Sauce (see Index)

• Score fat edges of ham slices. Place on broiler rack, 3" from heat. Broil 3 minutes; turn.
• Poach eggs; keep warm.
• Place bun halves on broiler. Broil until light golden, but broil ham 3 minutes.
• Place ham on buns. Top with poached eggs. Pour Easy or Mock Hollandaise Sauce over all. Makes 6 servings.

EGGS IN A BASKET

The eggs are poached in milk and shredded wheat makes the basket

6 shredded wheat biscuits
2 c. milk
2 tblsp. butter or regular margarine
6 eggs
Salt
Pepper

• Halve shredded wheat biscuits lengthwise. Warm in slow oven (300°).
• Heat milk to simmering in skillet; add butter. Poach eggs in milk mixture.
• Spoon eggs and milk on top of warmed shredded wheat biscuits. Add salt and pepper to taste. Makes 6 servings.

Note: To round out the supper menu: Serve sausages, pickled beets, and peach or cherry cobbler. This easy-to-fix dish can be prepared by the junior cooks when they start to share in mealtime preparation. For variety, dissolve 1 to 2 tsp. sugar in the milk before poaching the eggs. This dish is recommended as nourishing for little shut-ins, too.

EGGS IN TOAST RINGS

Complete this supper of eggs and toast with coleslaw and ham

12 slices bread
Butter
12 eggs
Salt
Pepper

• Cut centers from bread slices with small biscuit cutter. Toast rims on one side on grill. Butter untoasted side, turn.
• Break an egg into each toast ring, season with salt and pepper. Cook until eggs are set, 12 to 15 minutes. Makes 10 to 12 servings.

Note: Instead of grilling, bake on greased baking sheet in moderate oven (350°) 15 to 20 minutes, or until eggs are set. Bread need not be toasted before baking eggs this way.

OVEN-COOKED EGGS

• Baked eggs are easy to fix and often they provide a meal change. To please the children split thick hamburger buns in halves; hollow out each half. Spread with butter or regular margarine and drop an egg in each hollow. Season with salt and bake in a slow oven (325°) about 15 minutes, or until the eggs are partly set. Top each bun half with a slice of tomato and cheese and broil until cheese starts to brown.

EGGS A LA SUISSE

Eggs and cheese are fine partners when cooked this quick and easy way

- 1 c. grated sharp cheese
- 6 eggs
- Salt
- Pepper
- ½ c. light cream

• Sprinkle half of cheese in greased 9" pie pan. Break each egg into small cup; slide on top of cheese, being careful not to break yolk. Season with salt and pepper to taste.
• Pour cream evenly over eggs and sprinkle remaining cheese on top.
• Bake in moderate oven (350°) 15 minutes. Makes 6 servings.

EGG PLATTER

Spring supper—Egg Platter, salad of leaf lettuce, rhubarb sauce, cookies

- ⅔ c. uncooked rice
- ⅓ c. melted butter or regular margarine
- 1½ c. cooked peas (fresh, frozen or canned)
- ½ c. grated process cheese
- 6 eggs

• Cook rice according to package directions. Combine with butter, peas and half the cheese.
• Spoon into greased oven platter or shallow casserole. With back of spoon, make 6 small hollows in rice mixture. Break an egg into each. Sprinkle with remaining cheese.
• Bake in moderate oven (350°) about 20 minutes, until eggs are set. Makes 6 servings.

EGGS IN SPANISH SAUCE

Serve with a green vegetable

- 2 c. canned tomatoes
- ½ small onion, sliced
- ½ bay leaf
- 3 whole cloves
- 1 tsp. sugar
- ¾ tsp. salt
- 2 tblsp. butter or regular margarine
- 2 tblsp. flour
- 3 c. cooked rice (1 c. uncooked)
- 6 eggs
- 3 tblsp. grated Parmesan or process cheese
- ½ c. buttered crumbs

• Simmer tomatoes, onion, spices, sugar and salt 10 minutes. Strain.
• Melt butter and blend in flour. Add tomato mixture; cook until thickened, stirring constantly.
• Spread rice in greased shallow 2½-qt. casserole, making six hollows in it with tablespoon. Break an egg into each nest.
• Carefully pour sauce over all. Sprinkle with cheese and crumbs.
• Bake in moderate oven (350°) 20 minutes, or until eggs are firm. Serves 6.

EGGS IN SPINACH CUPS

No need to cut up spinach when you buy the frozen chopped kind

- 2 (10 oz.) pkgs. frozen chopped spinach, cooked and drained
- 1 can condensed cream of mushroom soup
- ¼ tsp. onion salt
- 8 eggs
- Paprika

• Mix spinach with soup and onion salt. Butter 8 (6 oz.) baking cups; line with spinach; break one egg into each cup. Bake in slow oven (325°)

5. CHOW MEIN—No Chinese food delights Americans more than this vegetable-pork dish. Also have canned fried noodles, fruit for dessert. Recipe, page 39.

6. ONION PIE—This main dish ranks high in Pennsylvania Dutch country. Caraway seeds and bacon add their charms. Serve pie warm. Recipe, page 185.

7. POTATOES IN VARIETY—In Chapter 7 you'll find recipes for Puffed-up Potatoes, page 192. Cheese-topped Potatoes, page 195 (both pictured).

8. UNCOOKED TOMATO RELISH—When tomatoes ripen by basketfuls, here's a tasty way to use them. Delicious relish requires no cooking. Recipe, page 274.

15 minutes. Sprinkle with paprika. Makes 8 servings.

EGGS BAKED IN TOMATOES

• Place thin slices of peeled tomatoes in bottom of greased, large muffin-pan cups. Top each with an egg. Season with salt and pepper and sprinkle with shredded process cheese. Bake in slow oven (325°) until eggs are set, about 25 minutes. Serve on rounds of buttered toast.

Puffed-Up Omelet

Almost every woman treasures a pet recipe for a puffy omelet. The one that follows is first choice in many country kitchens. It contains a white sauce which enables the omelet to avoid an early collapse. We give you recipes for several sauces to use with it to provide flavor changes. And for good measure, we include directions for baking Omelet Pancakes, which taste superb when buttered and spread with strawberry jam.

PUFFY OMELET

Failure-proof—adding the sauce makes omelet sturdier. Try all four sauces for variety and flavor change

¼ c. butter or regular margarine
3½ tblsp. flour
1 tsp. salt
1 c. milk
4 eggs, separated
2 tblsp. shortening
Creamed Shrimp Sauce
Chopped parsley

• Melt butter in small saucepan over low heat. Blend in flour and salt; cook 1 minute, stirring constantly.

• Remove from heat; gradually stir in milk; return to heat. Cook, stirring constantly, until white sauce is thick and smooth. Cool.

• Beat egg whites until stiff enough to hold firm peaks. Then beat the yolks.

• Blend egg yolks into white sauce. Then fold in beaten egg whites.

• Heat shortening over low heat in a 10″ skillet. Pour in the omelet mixture. Cover with a close fitting lid.

• Cook over low heat 15 to 20 minutes, or until a light brown crust is formed on bottom and top is firm.

• Loosen the omelet from the sides of skillet and cut through the center down to crust in bottom. Tilt pan; fold one half over the other. Slide onto platter.

• Unfold and pour Creamed Shrimp Sauce over half of omelet. Fold other half over the sauce. Sprinkle with chopped parsley. Serve immediately with Creamed Shrimp Sauce. Serves 4.

Variation

EXTRA-SPECIAL OMELET: Just before folding omelet, spread lower half with ⅓ c. grated sharp cheese, 3 slices crisp bacon, crumbled, 1 tsp. chopped chives or parsley or ½ c. hot chopped, cooked chicken. Serve with Creamed Shrimp or Asparagus/Mushroom Sauce.

CREAMED SHRIMP SAUCE

Makes Puffy Omelet a special dish

2 tblsp. butter or regular margarine
2 tblsp. flour
½ tsp. salt
Dash of pepper
1¼ c. milk
1 tsp. grated onion
1½ c. cooked and cleaned shrimp, fresh, canned or frozen

• Blend together in a small saucepan over low heat butter, flour, salt and pepper. Cook for 1 minute. Remove from heat; add milk and onion. Cook over low heat, stirring constantly, until thick and smooth. Add shrimp. Cook long enough to heat through. Pour inside and over Puffy Omelet.

CHICKEN SAUCE WITH PEAS

Stir up this sauce while omelet cooks

¼ c. water
¼ tsp. salt
1 c. fresh or frozen peas
1 can condensed cream of chicken soup

• Heat water and salt to boiling. Add peas; cover and cook until tender, about 7 minutes.
• Heat undiluted soup, stirring until smooth. Add peas. Pour inside and over Puffy Omelet.

SHRIMP CREOLE SAUCE

Fix this before you start the omelet

2 tblsp. butter or regular margarine
¼ c. chopped onion
¼ c. chopped green pepper
1 can condensed tomato soup
¼ tsp. salt
Dash of pepper
1 tsp. sugar
1 (5 oz.) can shrimp, drained

• Melt butter in saucepan, add onion and green pepper. Cook until pepper is soft.
• Stir in undiluted soup, salt, pepper and sugar. Simmer 45 minutes, until thick.
• Just before serving, add cleaned shrimp; heat. Pour inside and over Puffy Omelet. Makes about 1½ cups.

ASPARAGUS/MUSHROOM SAUCE

Spring comes to the table the year around with this tasty trimming

12 to 15 stalks fresh or frozen asparagus
¾ c. boiling water
1 can condensed cream of mushroom soup

• Place asparagus in boiling water; cook, covered, until tender, about 15 minutes. (You can fix this sauce while the omelet puffs up and browns.) Place about 3 cooked stalks on one omelet half; fold omelet over.
• Heat undiluted soup, stir until smooth. Pour over Puffy Omelet and remaining asparagus. Makes about 1⅓ cups.

OMELET PANCAKES

Roll pancakes for a happy change

¾ c. sifted flour
1 tsp. salt
¼ tsp. pepper
¾ c. milk
6 large eggs, beaten

• Combine flour, salt and pepper in mixing bowl. Stir in milk slowly and beat to form a smooth batter.
• Stir in beaten eggs, blend well.
• Pour ½ c. batter on very hot, greased 10″ griddle; spread batter to edges.
• Cook about 20 seconds until browned. Turn, brown on other side.
• Remove to warm plate. Keep warm in oven while cooking remaining pancakes. Makes 6 pancakes.

Note: For tasty toppings, or fillings, spread pancakes with cooked bulk pork sausage, or butter and spread with cranberry sauce, jam or cinnamon-sugar mixture. Roll up if you wish.

HASTY OMELET

A delicious way to use bread crumbs

- 3 eggs, slightly beaten
- 2 c. milk
- 1 tsp. salt
- ⅛ tsp. pepper
- 3 c. coarse day-old bread crumbs

• Blend together eggs, milk, salt and pepper. Stir in bread crumbs lightly. Turn into greased heavy skillet.
• Cover tightly. Cook slowly over low heat until set and lightly browned.
• Cut in serving-size pieces, turn and brown on other side. Serve immediately, plain or, if you like, with tomato or cheese sauce. Makes 4 to 6 servings.

Deviled Eggs, Cold or Hot

What is more tempting on the summer supper or picnic table than a plate or tray of cold deviled eggs from the refrigerator? And what is more inviting for a Sunday evening supper on a cold day than a baking dish of deviled eggs hurried from the oven to table? Try the recipes that follow for hot and cold eggs, both popular in country meals.

COUNTRY-KITCHEN DEVILED EGGS

Every good cook has her pet way of making stuffed or deviled eggs, but everyone agrees that appearance has much to do with their appeal. We find in our Countryside Kitchens that putting the mashed and seasoned yolks through a pastry bag with a large star tube gives the eggs a professional look. And it's quicker to stuff the egg whites that way than with a spoon. Running the cooked yolks through a food mill assures satiny smoothness.

For a welcome surprise put a small cube of ham or cheese or tiny olive in the whites before adding the filling. Another favorite of FARM JOURNAL's food staff is to fix hard-cooked yolks by seasoning with 3 tblsp. soft butter (for 6 yolks), 2 tblsp. mayonnaise, 1 tsp. vinegar, salt and pepper.

DEVILED EGGS

Make these in the morning and chill them until suppertime

- 6 hard-cooked eggs
- 1 tsp. vinegar
- ½ tsp. salt
- ⅛ tsp. pepper
- 1 tsp. prepared mustard
- 2 tblsp. melted butter or regular margarine
- ¼ c. mayonnaise or salad dressing

• Cut eggs in halves lengthwise. Remove yolks; put through sieve, or mash with fork.
• Add remaining ingredients to yolks; whip until smooth and fluffy. Heap into white halves. Crisscross tops with tines of fork. Refrigerate. Makes 12 halves.

Note: For variety, follow egg-yolk recipe above and add 3 or 4 tblsp. of cream cheese or grated cheese, deviled or chopped ham, mashed cooked chicken livers or crisp bacon bits. Or, put bits of any of these in hollow of egg white halves before adding yolk mixture.

HOT DEVILED EGGS

Serve with peas or broccoli

¼ c. butter or regular margarine
¼ c. flour
½ tsp. salt
¼ tsp. pepper
2 c. milk
12 deviled-egg halves
½ c. dry bread crumbs
½ c. grated sharp cheese

• Melt butter over low heat; blend in flour, salt and pepper. Add milk and cook, stirring, until thick and smooth. Pour over eggs, arranged in rows in greased 8″ square baking dish. Top with crumbs, then cheese.
• Bake in moderate oven (350°) until cheese melts. Makes 6 servings.

SUNDAY-SUPPER DEVILED EGGS

You can get this ready to bake in the morning and refrigerate

½ c. chopped onion
¼ c. butter or regular margarine
2 c. precooked rice (or 4 c. cooked regular rice)
1 tsp. salt
2 c. boiling water
1 (12 oz.) can pork luncheon meat
⅛ tsp. pepper
3 tblsp. chopped parsley
⅔ c. mayonnaise
2 tblsp. light cream
3 tblsp. ketchup
12 deviled-egg halves

• Sauté onion in melted butter over low heat until golden. Add rice, salt and water. Cover; let stand 5 minutes.
• Cut meat into 3 or 4 slices; mash with fork. Add to rice mixture with pepper and parsley.
• Blend together mayonnaise, cream and ketchup. Add half this sauce to rice mixture. Spread in bottom of greased 11½ × 7⅜ × 1½″ baking dish.
• With back of spoon make depressions in rice to hold eggs. Spoon remaining sauce over indentations. Put eggs in place. Cover; bake in moderate oven (350°) 20 minutes. Makes 6 servings.

CREAMED EGGS

A country main dish to serve over many foods—we suggest six

½ c. butter or regular margarine
6 tblsp. flour
1 qt. milk
1½ tsp. salt
½ tsp. paprika
⅛ tsp. pepper
¼ tsp. Tabasco sauce
2 tsp. finely grated onion
12 hard-cooked eggs, coarsely cut

• Melt butter over low heat. Add flour, stir until bubbly (do not let brown) and add milk. Cook, stirring constantly, until mixture thickens. Add remaining ingredients. Heat thoroughly.
• Serve over split hot biscuits, toast, rice, baked potatoes, broccoli or asparagus. Makes 6 to 8 servings.

Note: Peel the hard-cooked eggs and cut in halves. Remove yolks. Chop whites and cut yolks in halves to decrease breaking during the heating.

CREAMED EGGS WITH CHEESE

Serve with tomato soup, green salad, hot rolls, Pears Cardinale (*see Index*)

12 hard-cooked eggs
⅓ c. butter or regular margarine
½ c. flour

1 c. light cream
2½ c. milk (about)
½ lb. sharp process cheese, cut up
1 tsp. salt
Dash of pepper
12 frankfurters
8 slices white bread
2 tblsp. chopped parsley

• Separately chop yolks and whites of 2 eggs; set aside for garnish.
• Quarter remaining eggs.
• Melt butter, blend in flour. Add cream slowly; cook, stirring constantly. Add milk to make a smooth, rather thin sauce. Stir in cheese, salt and pepper.
• Cover pan and simmer, without stirring, over low heat until cheese melts, 10 to 15 minutes.
• Stir to blend and add quartered eggs. Bring sauce to a boil. (If sauce gets too thick, add a little more milk.)
• Split frankfurters, and cut in halves; fry or broil until crisp and brown.
• Toast bread slices. Cut into triangles.
• Pour creamed eggs onto hot serving platter. Garnish with rows of reserved chopped eggs and parsley. Poke frankfurters part way into egg mixture around the edge of dish, alternately with toast triangles. Makes 8 servings.

CREAMED EGGS WITH PEAS

Quick-as-a-wink supper dish

1 (10 oz.) pkg. frozen peas
6 hard-cooked eggs, sliced
2 c. Medium Cream Sauce
1 (6 oz.) can fried noodles

• Cook peas as directed on package; drain. Add eggs to Medium Cream Sauce. Heat; add peas. Serve over noodles. Makes 6 servings.

MEDIUM CREAM SAUCE: Melt 4 tblsp. butter or regular margarine over low heat. Add 4 tblsp. flour, blend together and add 2 c. milk, stirring constantly. Cook until thick and smooth. Add ¾ tsp. salt. Makes 2 cups. To hasten cooking, heat 1 c. of milk and stir it in after blending in 1 cup cold milk.

Note: Instead of Medium Cream Sauce use 1 c. condensed cream of celery soup and ⅓ soup can of milk. Serve over fried noodles, hot biscuits or toast.

Dishes Enhanced with Cheese

There are four basic types of cheese—the very hard, the firm, the semisoft and the soft. The very hard cheeses are commonly used for grating—one of these which you'll find often in this cookbook is Parmesan.

In the firm cheese branch of the family the Cheddars are famous, with mild or sharp flavors, depending on their cure. Cheddar holds its flavor through heating—that's one of the reasons it's the favorite in cooking. Gouda and Swiss, the "cheese with eyes," also belong in the firm group.

Some of the best known semisoft cheeses are those with a blue mold, like the Roquefort of France and blue cheese of Denmark and the United States. Gorgonzola of Italian ancestry and Stilton, as British as John Bull, are other examples.

Soft cheeses divide into two families: the ripened dessert cheese like

Camembert; the unripened cottage, pot and cream cheeses, and the ricotta and mozzarella used in so many popular American-Italian dishes.

Then there are the process cheeses. They are natural cheeses, melted, pasteurized, and blended with an emulsifier. Heating stops the ripening, so the cheese always has a uniform flavor and texture. There's no waste and it melts smoothly and never gets stringy during cooking—one reason process cheeses are used so extensively in country kitchens.

Knowledge of the cheese families helps in buying the kind suited to the use you expect to make of it. If men are better shoppers for cheese than women, as is sometimes claimed, it's because they let their noses tell them what to buy. But taste is as important as smell and selecting the cheese best adapted to the way you wish to use it also matters greatly.

CHEESE AND NOODLE RING

Buffet supper special. To serve 12, double recipe, bake in shallow pans and serve cut in squares, creamed food on top

3 tblsp. chopped onion
3 tblsp. diced pimiento
¾ tblsp. butter or regular margarine
1 egg, slightly beaten
1 c. milk, scalded
1 c. cut-up sharp process cheese
1 tsp. salt
⅛ tsp. pepper
1½ c. cooked noodles (¾ c. uncooked)
1 c. soft bread crumbs

• Cook onion and pimiento in butter until onion is tender (do not brown).

• Combine egg, milk, cheese, salt and pepper.

• Mix noodles and bread crumbs with cheese mixture. Add onion and pimiento. Pour into greased ring mold or loaf pan. Set in pan of warm water and bake in moderate oven (350°) 1 hour.

• Unmold and serve with creamed foods, such as chicken, fish or vegetables. Makes 6 servings.

TOMATO/CHEESE RAREBIT

Good main dish for hurry-up suppers. Tomato flavor is the new addition

2 tblsp. butter or regular margarine
¼ c. chopped onion
1 can condensed tomato soup
2 c. grated Cheddar cheese (½ lb.)
1 egg, slightly beaten
Salt
Pepper
Paprika

• Melt butter; add onion and cook until tender. Add soup. When heated, add cheese; cook, stirring until cheese melts. Add egg and seasonings to taste. Cook, stirring constantly, until mixture thickens. Serve immediately on toast or crackers. Makes 4 servings.

Cheese and Egg Favorites

With cheese and eggs on hand main dish problems vanish. There are so many tasty, substantial dishes to make with them. Recipes for three classics follow: Cheese Soufflé, Cheddar Bread Bake and Cheese/Bacon Pie. Cheese and eggs also share honors in our handsome Asparagus and Egg Bake and the delightful Cheese/Bread Casserole served with Curried Dried Beef. Try all these hearty dishes and treat your guests to them.

CHEESE SOUFFLÉ

Airy soufflé wears a tall top hat. Serve pronto, as it waits for no one

1 c. milk
¼ c. butter or regular margarine
¼ c. flour
½ tsp. salt
⅛ tsp. ground red pepper
½ lb. sharp process cheese, sliced fine
4 eggs, separated

• Heat but do not scald milk.
• Melt butter in saucepan; stir in flour, milk and seasonings; cook, stirring, until smooth and thickened. Blend in cheese.
• Beat egg yolks until thick and lemon-colored; blend with a little cheese sauce; slowly stir into remaining cheese sauce. Cool slightly.
• Beat egg whites until stiff but not dry. Slowly pour cheese sauce into egg whites; gently blend. Pour into ungreased soufflé dish or 1½-qt. casserole. Make a circle through mixture 1" deep and 1" from edge of casserole. This gives soufflé a puffy top hat.
• Bake uncovered in slow oven (300°) about 1¼ hours, or until knife inserted in soufflé comes out clean. (Do not open oven door until baking time is about up.) Serve at once; break apart with two forks. Makes 4 servings.

Note: For tall soufflés, make a waxed paper collar for casserole. Measure enough paper to go around casserole plus 2" for overlap. Butter one side. With collar extending 2" above casserole, buttered side down, fasten collar with cellophane tape. Carefully remove collar before serving.

CHEDDAR BREAD BAKE

An apple-celery salad is good with this

8 slices day-old white bread
2 tblsp. butter or regular margarine
½ lb. Cheddar cheese, shredded
4 eggs, slightly beaten
2½ c. milk
½ tsp. Worcestershire sauce
½ tsp. dry mustard
1 tsp. salt

• Make four sandwiches from bread and butter. Cut into quarters or cubes.
• Place two of the cut sandwiches in the bottom of a buttered 1½-qt. casserole. Sprinkle with half the cheese. Repeat, using remaining bread and cheese.
• Combine eggs, milk and remaining ingredients; pour over layers in casserole. Refrigerate 1 hour.
• Bake in slow oven (300°) 1 hour and 15 minutes. Serve immediately. Makes 6 servings.

CHEESE/BREAD CASSEROLE

Fluffy, yellow pudding with curried sauce spooned over—tasty

5 slices bread
Butter or regular margarine
3 eggs, separated
1 c. milk
¼ tsp. salt
½ tsp. prepared mustard
½ lb. grated sharp process cheese
Curried Dried Beef

• Trim crusts from bread; spread bread generously with butter; cut into cubes. Place in greased 1½-qt. casserole.

• Beat egg yolks until foamy; add milk, salt, mustard and cheese.

• Beat egg whites until stiff; fold into yolk mixture; pour over bread.

• Bake uncovered in moderate oven (350°) 35 to 40 minutes, or until set, puffed and brown. Serve hot, topped with Curried Dried Beef or creamed vegetables. Makes 6 to 8 servings.

CURRIED DRIED BEEF: Melt ¼ c. butter in saucepan; stir in ¼ c. flour, ¼ tsp. curry powder and ⅓ c. chopped green onions. Cook 1 minute. Gradually add 2½ c. mixture of dairy half-and-half and light cream; cook until thickened, stirring constantly. Shred 1 (4 oz.) pkg. dried beef and mix into sauce. Serve hot. Makes 3 cups.

CHEESE/BACON PIE

Very rich and very delicious. Serve with tossed green salad or asparagus

Unbaked 9″ pie shell
10 slices crisp cooked bacon, crumbled
⅓ c. minced onion
1 c. shredded Swiss cheese (natural, about 4 oz.)
4 eggs
2 c. heavy or light cream
½ tsp. salt
⅛ tsp. pepper
Dash ground red pepper

• Sprinkle bacon, onion and cheese in bottom of unbaked pie shell.

• Beat eggs slightly. Beat in remaining ingredients. Pour into pie shell.

• Bake in hot oven (425°) 15 minutes. Reduce heat to slow (300°) and bake 30 minutes longer, or until knife inserted 1″ from edge comes out clean. Let stand 10 minutes before cutting into wedges. Makes 6 to 8 servings.

Note: To cut down on time, cook enough extra bacon while getting breakfast, for this main dish.

SPRING ASPARAGUS AND EGG BAKE

Asparagus contributes eye appeal and flavor; cheese and eggs add protein

18 asparagus spears
¼ c. butter or regular margarine
¼ c. flour
½ tsp. salt
1½ c. milk
1 c. shredded Cheddar cheese
⅛ tsp. ground red pepper
4 hard-cooked eggs, sliced
½ c. cracker crumbs
¼ c. melted butter or regular margarine

• Cook asparagus spears in boiling, salted water 10 to 20 minutes, or until just tender.

• In a saucepan, melt ¼ c. butter and stir in flour and salt; blend in enough milk to make a smooth paste. Stir in remainder of milk and cook over medium heat until sauce is thick, stirring constantly. While sauce is hot, stir in shredded cheese and red pepper. Stir until cheese is melted.

• In a greased 1½-qt. baking dish layer half of asparagus, sliced eggs and sauce. Repeat ingredients to make a second layer. Top with cracker crumbs mixed with ¼ c. butter.

• Bake in moderate oven (350°) 30 minutes, or until mixture bubbles. Place under broiler 2 minutes to brown top. Makes 5 servings.

Note: For 10 servings, bake 2 casseroles of this asparagus and egg treat, or double recipe and bake 45 to 50 minutes in a 3-qt. casserole.

Cottage Cheese Main Dishes

The all-star main dish featuring cottage cheese often is a salad to which it contributes valuable protein. It may be combined with canned pineapple slices or peach halves, fresh tomatoes, or several fruits or vegetables. Sometimes the choice is in a molded salad like our Cottage Cheese/Salmon Loaf. You'll also find recipes for Lasagne Casserole and Neapolitan Lasagne in this chapter; part of their goodness comes from the cottage cheese they contain.

We are including directions for making cottage cheese; they appear in the original FARM JOURNAL *Country Cookbook*. Homemade cheese does not have the same taste and texture as do commercial cheeses—it is impossible to get the same results in home kitchens as in dairies.

The homemade cheese tastes like that our grandmothers made, seasoned with salt and flavored with thick cream skimmed from crocks of milk. Duplicating this cottage cheese is a nostalgic journey. You can count on your cheese being the talk of the table.

HOW TO MAKE COTTAGE CHEESE

Pioneer families who kept cows used milk and cream in every possible way, and one of the favorite—but time-consuming—activities was cheese-making. Today's supermarket shelves offer a great variety of cheeses. Rarely do country women even dream of making this protein food for their families. But if you want to try your luck with the old-fashioned home cookery art, cottage cheese is the best kind to attempt. A farm homemaker (home economist) who still makes it shared her recipe with us. She thinks this art should not be lost—and we agree.

HOMEMADE COTTAGE CHEESE

1. Pasteurize 2 gallons of skim milk. Cool the milk to about 75° F. in can under running water. (Without a pasteurizer, heat milk to 165° F. for 30 minutes; then cool to 75°.)

2. Transfer milk to enameled pan with cover to heat curd. Add 1 c. starter. For homemade starter, sour small amount fresh (unpasteurized) skim milk by holding at room temperature 12 to 24 hours. If cheese is made regularly, save 1 c. clabbered milk before heating curd. Keep covered in cool place.

• For commercial starter, buy lactic acid culture from dairy or commercial culture laboratory. Add this to pasteurized skim milk which has been cooled to 75°. As the homemade starter has the organisms necessary for clabbering, the use of lactic acid culture is optional if you have raw milk; however it is a must with pasteurized milk and you get more uniform results.

3. After milk with starter has stood overnight at room temperature (70° to 75°), a firm clabber forms and a little whey appears on the sur-

face. If it stands too long, cheese may be rubbery and strong. In cooler weather, it may take 12 to 18 hours for milk to clabber.

4. Cut curd into ½″ squares by passing a long knife or spatula through it lengthwise and crosswise of the container. Don't change pans to cook curd—breaks it up too much!

5. Set pan of clabbered milk in a larger pan containing hot water—double boiler style. Heat slowly to separate whey and make small, firm curds. Stir gently for even heating and avoid matting. Avoid breaking curd in unnecessarily small pieces.

6. Carefully check temperature with thermometer as it nears 100° F. Test curd by gently rubbing between fingers—should feel slightly granular. (For firmer curd, heat to 110°. Family approval will tell you when to stop.) For a rather soft curd, heat to 100° F., then keep it at that temperature until curd feels grainy. Avoid overheating!

7. Pour mixture immediately into colander lined with cheesecloth. Drain 1 to 2 minutes. Shift curd on cloth by gently lifting one corner.

8. Rinse curd thoroughly with cold water to wash out all whey. (Dip cheesecloth with curd in ice water to cool faster.)

9. Remove curd from cloth; add 2 tsp. salt (1 tsp. for each pound of curd). Blend. Store, tightly covered, in cold place.

10. At serving time, fold in cream—amount depends on personal preferences. A gallon of milk makes about 1 quart cottage cheese.

COTTAGE CHEESE/SALMON LOAF

Round out supper with broccoli or spinach, buttered, and hot rolls

Cheese Layer:

1 envelope unflavored gelatin
½ c. milk
1 tsp. chopped onion
½ tsp. salt
3 c. creamed cottage cheese
1 cucumber
Pimiento

Salmon Layer:

1 envelope unflavored gelatin
¼ c. cold water
1 tblsp. lemon juice
¾ c. mayonnaise or salad dressing
1 c. finely chopped celery
2 tblsp. chopped sweet pickle or pickle relish
1 (1 lb.) can salmon

· To make cheese layer, soften gelatin in ¼ c. cold milk. Heat remaining milk until hot. Add gelatin; stir until dissolved. Add onion, salt and cottage cheese.
· Lightly oil 9 × 5 × 3″ loaf pan. Arrange pattern of unpeeled cucumber slices and pimiento pieces on bottom of pan. Cover with cottage cheese mixture. Chill until set.
· For salmon layer, soften gelatin in cold water. Heat over boiling water until gelatin dissolves. Add lemon juice. Cool slightly.
· Combine gelatin and mayonnaise. Add celery and sweet pickle.
· Drain salmon; add liquid to gelatin mixture. Remove skin and bones from salmon. Flake and add to gelatin mixture. Pour over cheese layer. Chill until firm. Unmold on platter. Serves 10.

Note: This main-dish salad is good served with dressing made by combining equal amounts of finely diced cucumber and mayonnaise. Takes about 1 c. of each.

Popular Pasta Dishes

Peaches and cream, turkey and cranberry sauce and macaroni and cheese are famous food twosomes—pairs of foods that complement each other. Not all pasta dishes contain cheese, but the favorites of the countryside combine macaroni products with cheese and often also with meat.

• For superior dishes, cook macaroni and spaghetti the correct way: Use plenty of water (for 8 ounces macaroni product, 4 servings, use 3 quarts). Too little water makes pasta sticky. Add ½ tblsp. salt to every 3 quarts water.

• Gradually add the pasta to rapidly boiling water—keep it boiling. Cook uncovered, stirring gently and occasionally with a fork, until pasta is tender but firm, 8 to 10 minutes. Cook a little less time if macaroni will be used in a casserole dish.

• Drain macaroni in strainer as soon as it is done. Rinse with cold water only if it is to be used in salad.

• You'll want to try our distinctive pasta main dishes. If you have not realized spaghetti can be glamorous, do try Timballo with Cheese Sauce.

DOUBLE CHEESE BAKE

Distinctive macaroni casserole—good with coleslaw or lettuce salad

1 c. elbow macaroni (uncooked)
¼ c. butter
1 c. soft bread crumbs
1 c. shredded Cheddar cheese
½ c. shredded Swiss cheese
½ c. slivered cooked ham
3 eggs, well beaten
1 tblsp. minced onion
1 tblsp. chopped parsley
¼ tsp. salt
⅛ tsp. pepper
1½ c. milk, scalded
Paprika

• Cook macaroni according to package directions; drain. Add butter; mix well.

• Add remaining ingredients except paprika; mix well. Turn into greased 2-qt. casserole. Sprinkle with paprika. Bake in slow oven (325°) 40 to 45 minutes. Makes 6 servings.

TIMBALLO WITH CHEESE SAUCE

Spaghetti goes glamorous in this rich-tasting, beautiful dish

1 lb. spaghetti (uncooked—break strands in halves)
⅓ c. butter
1 lb. bulk pork sausage
1 (4 oz.) can sliced mushrooms, drained
3 tblsp. finely chopped onion
⅓ c. sliced pimiento-stuffed olives
½ c. grated Parmesan cheese
2 tblsp. chopped parsley
½ tsp. salt
¼ tsp. pepper
¼ c. dry bread crumbs
2 eggs, well beaten
¼ lb. mozzarella cheese, shredded
Cheese Sauce

• Cook spaghetti 10 minutes in boiling salted water. Drain; toss with butter.

• Sauté sausage in skillet until almost done. Pour off fat; return 2 tblsp. to skillet. Add mushrooms and onion; sauté until tender.

• Toss together spaghetti, sausage

mixture, olives, Parmesan cheese, parsley, salt and pepper.

• Coat a buttered 9″ spring-form pan with bread crumbs; reserve some for top. Place half the spaghetti mixture in pan; pour eggs evenly over all. Sprinkle with mozzarella cheese; top with remaining spaghetti mixture. Sprinkle with reserved crumbs. Cover with foil; bake in moderate oven (375°) 40 minutes. Let stand 5 minutes. Serve with Cheese Sauce. Makes 6 to 8 servings.

CHEESE SAUCE: Melt ¼ c. butter or regular margarine over low heat; blend in ¼ c. flour. Add 2 c. milk and cook, stirring constantly, until thick and smooth. Stir in ¾ tsp. salt, ¼ c. Parmesan cheese and 1 tblsp. chopped parsley.

NEAPOLITAN LASAGNE

Good buffet-supper choice—add a salad

Sauce:

2 tblsp. finely chopped onion
½ tsp. minced garlic
⅓ c. salad oil
1 (2 lb. 3 oz.) can plum tomatoes, sieved
2 beef bouillon cubes
1 c. water
1 (6 oz.) can tomato paste
½ bay leaf
2 whole cloves
½ tsp. basil leaves
½ tsp. orégano leaves
½ tsp. salt
¼ tsp. pepper
¼ tsp. sugar

Filling:

1 lb. creamed cottage cheese
1 (9 oz.) pkg. frozen spinach, cooked, drained and chopped
2 eggs, slightly beaten
½ c. grated Parmesan cheese
¼ tsp. salt
¼ tsp. ground nutmeg
⅛ tsp. pepper
1 (1 lb.) pkg. lasagne noodles, cooked and drained
¼ lb. mozzarella cheese, shredded
Grated Parmesan cheese

• Sauté onion and garlic in oil. Stir in remaining sauce ingredients. Bring to boil; simmer 1 hour. Stir occasionally. Remove bay leaf and cloves.

• Blend together cottage cheese, spinach, eggs, ½ c. Parmesan cheese, salt, nutmeg and pepper. Set aside.

• Spread 1 c. sauce in 13 × 9 × 2″ baking dish. Lay a third of noodles in single layer on top. Spread with sauce; spoon on half of spinach mixture; sprinkle with a third of mozzarella cheese. Repeat layers, topping with sauce. Add remaining noodles; cover with remaining sauce. Sprinkle with mozzarella and Parmesan cheeses. Cover loosely with foil. Bake in moderate oven (350°) 40 minutes. Makes 12 servings.

HEARTY ITALIAN SPAGHETTI

Use of spaghetti sauce mix adds expert seasoning in a jiffy

1 (1½ oz.) pkg. Italian spaghetti sauce mix
1 (8 oz.) can tomato sauce
1 lb. ground beef
12 oz. spaghetti (uncooked)
½ c. shredded mozzarella cheese
1 tsp. parsley flakes (optional)

• Prepare sauce mix, adding tomato sauce as directed on package.

• Brown beef in skillet. Add spaghetti sauce and simmer.

• Cook spaghetti as directed on package; drain. Place spaghetti on platter or in large, shallow bowl. Top with sauce. Sprinkle with cheese and parsley. Makes 8 servings.

LASAGNE CASSEROLE

Mixed herbs season expertly and they're quick and easy to use

8 oz. broad noodles (uncooked)
1 tblsp. salad oil
1 (8 oz.) pkg. brown-and-serve sausages
1 (1 lb.) can tomatoes
1 (6 oz.) can tomato paste
1 tblsp. instant minced onion
1 tsp. mixed Italian herbs
1 c. drained creamed cottage cheese
¼ c. grated Parmesan cheese
1 (6 or 8 oz.) pkg. mozzarella cheese, cut in ½" strips

• Cook noodles as directed on package and drain. Return to same saucepan. Toss with salad oil to prevent sticking.

• Meanwhile, dice sausages and brown, stirring often, in medium skillet. Stir in tomatoes, tomato paste, onion and herbs. Heat to boiling and simmer, stirring occasionally, 5 minutes.

• Layer half the noodles, cottage cheese, Parmesan cheese, tomato mixture and mozzarella cheese in greased 2-qt. casserole. Repeat, trimming the top by crisscrossing mozzarella cheese strips.

• Bake in moderate oven (350°) 30 minutes, until bubbling at edges and cheese is browned. Makes 6 servings.

Note: Double recipe to serve 10 to 12.

SKILLET MACARONI AND CHEESE

Busy mothers favor this top-of-the-range way of fixing an old favorite

8 oz. elbow macaroni (uncooked)
¼ c. butter or regular margarine
1 (8 oz.) pkg. process Cheddar cheese, shredded
½ c. milk
¼ c. grated onion
1 tsp. salt
⅛ tsp. pepper

• Cook macaroni as directed on package. Drain but do not remove from saucepan. Add remaining ingredients. Cook over low heat, stirring frequently, until cheese melts, about 5 minutes. Makes 8 servings.

TUNA-MACARONI-AND-CHEESE

Just the main dish to serve when your extension club meets for lunch

2 (8 oz.) pkgs. macaroni (uncooked)
3 (7 oz.) cans tuna, drained and flaked
2 c. cooked whole kernel corn, drained (fresh, frozen or canned)
2 c. cooked peas or baby lima beans, drained (fresh, frozen or canned)
1 qt. milk
2 c. cubed Cheddar cheese
4 tsp. salt
½ tsp. pepper
½ c. dry bread crumbs
2 tblsp. butter

• Cook macaroni by package directions in boiling salted water; drain. Place in two buttered 2-qt. casseroles. Add tuna, corn and peas.

• Heat milk; add cheese and stir until it melts. Add salt and pepper. Pour over macaroni, mixing slightly.

• Top with bread crumbs; dot with butter. Bake in moderate oven (375°) 20 minutes. Makes 12 servings.

MACARONI/MEAT BALL SOUFFLÉ

Soufflé has brown top with ring of meat balls—hearty, tasty, different

1½ c. elbow macaroni (uncooked)
2 c. milk, scalded
3 tblsp. butter or regular margarine
1 c. grated or shredded sharp process cheese
1 tblsp. minced onion
½ tsp. salt
⅛ tsp. pepper
3 eggs, separated
2¾ c. lightly packed soft bread crumbs
Company Meat Balls

• Cook macaroni as directed on package, using 8 c. boiling water and 1 tblsp. salt. Cook until macaroni is tender. Drain.

• Combine milk, butter, cheese, onion, salt and pepper. Stir to melt cheese.

• Beat egg whites until stiff.

• Beat yolks thoroughly. Add a little hot milk mixture to egg yolks. Gradually add yolks to hot mixture, stirring constantly. Add bread crumbs. Mix well. Remove from heat. Fold into egg whites.

• Fill bottom of well greased 2-qt. casserole with half of macaroni. Pour in half of sauce. Add half of meat balls.

• Add remaining macaroni and sauce. Arrange remaining meat balls over top.

• Place casserole in shallow pan. Set on lower rack in oven. Add 1″ boiling water to pan. Bake in moderate oven (375°) 50 to 60 minutes, until knife comes out clean. Makes 6 to 8 servings.

COMPANY MEAT BALLS

Perfect crown for macaroni casserole

½ lb. ground beef
½ lb. ground lean pork
1 egg, slightly beaten
½ c. fine day-old bread crumbs
⅓ c. milk
1 tsp. salt
⅛ tsp. white pepper
2 tsp. minced onion
1 tsp. fat or salad oil

• Combine all ingredients except fat. Mix thoroughly. Shape into 26 balls, about 1″ in diameter.

• Heat fat in skillet over medium heat. Add meat balls and cook to brown, about 20 minutes; remove from pan. Add to macaroni casserole as directed.

MACARONI MEDLEY

New carry-along dish wins praises

1 (8 oz.) pkg. large elbow macaroni (uncooked)
1 large onion, diced
½ green pepper, diced
3 tblsp. butter
2 lbs. ground beef
1 tsp. salt
2 (8 oz.) cans tomato sauce
2 c. water
1 (1½ oz.) pkg. spaghetti sauce mix (Italian style with mushrooms)
1 (4½ oz.) can chopped ripe olives
½ lb. Cheddar cheese, grated coarsely

• Cook macaroni in salted, boiling water, as directed on package. Drain.

• Sauté onion and green pepper in

butter until soft, but do not brown. Add beef and brown. Drain off fat. Add salt, tomato sauce and water; stir in spaghetti sauce mix and simmer 10 minutes.

• Mix olives and cheese with macaroni, saving out 1 c. cheese.

• Place half the macaroni mixture in greased 13 × 9 × 2" pan; cover with half the meat mixture. Repeat.

• Bake in moderate oven (350°) 40 minutes, sprinkling with reserved 1 c. cheese the last 10 minutes of baking. Makes 8 to 10 servings.

CHILI/MAC CASSEROLE

Garlic bread is good with this. Heat it in the oven with casserole

1 c. macaroni (uncooked)
2 (16 oz.) cans chili with beans
Dill pickle slices

• Cook macaroni as directed on package. Heat chili to boiling point.

• Drain cooked macaroni and combine with chili. Place in a 1½-qt. casserole. Top with pickle slices.

• Bake in moderate oven (375°) 20 minutes. Makes 4 servings.

SPAGHETTI SOUFFLÉ

A hearty colorful supper dish—it's surprising how remarkably good it is

2 c. soft bread crumbs
½ c. melted butter
6 eggs, separated
2 c. drained, cooked spaghetti (about 5 oz. uncooked, broken in 2" lengths)
2 tblsp. chopped parsley
2 tblsp. chopped pimiento
2 tblsp. chopped green pepper
2 tblsp. chopped onion
1½ tsp. salt
2 c. milk
Mushroom Sauce

• Combine bread crumbs and butter in mixing bowl. Stir in egg yolks and all other ingredients except egg whites and Mushroom Sauce.

• Beat egg whites until stiff but not dry. Fold into spaghetti mixture.

• Pour into 2-qt. casserole or soufflé dish. Bake in moderate oven (350°) 1 hour, or until set in center. Serve with Mushroom Sauce. Serves 6 to 8.

MUSHROOM SAUCE: Sauté 1 (4 oz.) can drained mushroom stems and pieces in 3 tblsp. butter. Stir in 2 tblsp. flour, ¼ tsp. salt and ⅛ tsp. pepper. Gradually add 1 c. milk, stirring until smooth. Cook over medium heat, stirring, until of medium thickness. Makes 1¼ cups.

TUNA/TOMATO SAUCE

Designed to add fine flavor and excitement to your favorite pasta

¼ c. chopped onion
¼ c. chopped green pepper
½ tsp. finely chopped garlic
¼ c. salad oil
1 (2 lb. 3 oz.) can plum tomatoes
1 (6 oz.) can tomato paste
⅔ c. water
1 tsp. salt
½ tsp. orégano leaves
½ tsp. basil leaves
¼ tsp. ground nutmeg
¼ tsp. pepper
¼ tsp. sugar
1 (7 oz.) can solid pack tuna, drained and flaked
1 lb. pasta, cooked and drained

• Sauté onion, green pepper and garlic in oil until tender.

• Press tomatoes through sieve. Combine ingredients, except tuna and pasta. Bring to boil; simmer 35 minutes. Add tuna; simmer 10 minutes more. Serve over your favorite cooked pasta. Makes 6 to 8 servings.

chapter 5

Substantial Soups

A BIG KETTLE OF SOUP bubbling on the kitchen range—this is a familiar winter farm scene. Country soups are substantial enough to serve as the main dish in supper and luncheon menus, and sometimes for dinner.

While soups enjoy greatest prestige in cold weather, frosty versions are gaining favor for hot, humid days. Take Cucumber Cool Soup—tastes and looks cool, yet it satisfies. Frosty Spanish Vegetable Soup, which doubles for salad, is becoming popular on this side of the Atlantic.

The custom in country homes is to make soups, such as our Split Pea/Vegetable and Minestrone, in large quantity, serve part of it and then freeze the surplus. This is an application of a farm kitchen rule: Cook once for twice whenever possible.

Canned frozen condensed soups sometimes are ingredients in the soup kettle, particularly for special occasions. Cucumber Cool Soup owes some of its flavor richness to canned frozen condensed cream of potato soup and Spinach-of-the-Sea Soup to frozen condensed oyster stew and cream of shrimp soup.

Chicken and beef stock or broth frequently bolster flavors in country soups. We give you two recipes for beef stock to freeze—one for 8 quarts and the other for 2 quarts—and there's a recipe for chicken stock, too. Accompanying them are recipes for superior soups in which they star.

No balanced collection of country soup recipes omits homespun potato soups. We share with you several of our best ones, including Potato Soup with Dumplings which almost always draws ovations from men. Bean soups also are favorite farm fare.

Read through the pages of this chapter—you'll decide to make soup soon, confident that your family will be pleased!

Beef and Vegetable Soups

In many country kitchens soup-making is extended over two days. One reason is to avoid greasy soups. Cook beef and bones one day until meat is tender; then set the covered kettle in a very cold place. It's easy to lift off the congealed fat the next day, then heat for serving.

You can chill the meat and broth separately overnight in the refrigerator. To fix the soup, cut the beef in small pieces and add it and the prepared vegetables to the broth (from which the congealed fat has been skimmed), discarding the bones. Simmer gently until vegetables are tender.

Check the seasoning before ladling the steaming soup into bowls. Then inform the family and guests: soup's on!

VEGETABLE/BEEF SOUP

Recipe for this "like mother used to make" soup provides 6 quarts. Freeze some for days you're away at noon

3 lbs. shin beef with bone
3 qts. water
2 tblsp. salt
2 tsp. Worcestershire sauce
¼ tsp. pepper
1 medium onion, chopped
1 c. chopped celery
1 c. sliced carrots
1 c. sliced potatoes
1 c. shredded cabbage
1 turnip, peeled and cubed
1 (1 lb. 12 oz.) can tomatoes (3½ c.)
2 tsp. parsley flakes

• Combine beef, water, salt, Worcestershire sauce and pepper in large kettle. Cover and simmer until meat is tender, 2½ to 3 hours. Remove meat from soup; cut from bone in small pieces and return meat to soup.
• Add remaining ingredients. Simmer until vegetables are tender, about 45 minutes. Makes about 6 quarts.

Note: If desired, you may add one or two of the following loose-pack frozen vegetables: peas, corn, green beans. Add 1 c. of each vegetable that you use just long enough before serving for the vegetables to cook tender. Or you can add ⅓ c. barley, regular rice or broken-up spaghetti.

Minestrone—the Hearty Soup

There are as many versions of this substantial soup as there are women of Italian descent or chefs in Italian restaurants, both of whom make it superlatively. All versions feature many vegetables, simmered low until tender. Some of the soups contain meat and others only beef stock.

All the good cooks we consulted when we tested recipes for minestrone agreed on one point. Here's the way one woman put it: "Be sure to sprinkle a wee touch of dried basil leaves (crushed fresh ones if you have them) and grated Parmesan cheese on the soup after you ladle it into serving bowls."

We heeded the advice and were glad we did. Our own Test Kitchen variation was to add the basil to the Parmesan cheese, passing a bowl of the mixture and letting everyone help himself. This is one recipe where the bit of basil actually seems essential.

MINESTRONE

This is a big recipe for the great Italian soup—freeze the surplus

1½ lbs. shin beef with bone
1 c. dried navy beans
5 qts. water
2 tblsp. salt
½ tsp. pepper
2 c. chopped onion
1 clove garlic, minced
1½ c. diced celery
2 c. finely shredded cabbage
1½ c. diced carrots
1 medium potato, peeled and cubed
1 tblsp. parsley flakes
½ lb. ground chuck
1½ c. thinly sliced fresh or frozen zucchini or small yellow squash
1 c. frozen loose-pack green beans
1½ c. broken-up uncooked spaghetti
Grated Parmesan or Romano cheese
Basil leaves

· Place shin beef, beans, water, salt and pepper in large kettle. Cover and simmer 3 hours. (This may be done a day ahead.)

· Remove meat from mixture and cut meat from bones. Add meat to soup. Add onion, garlic, celery, cabbage, carrots, potato and parsley.

· Brown ground chuck and add to mixture. Cover and simmer until vegetables are tender, about 30 minutes. Add squash, green beans and spaghetti. Simmer until spaghetti is cooked, about 10 to 15 minutes. Taste for seasonings; you may wish to add an additional tablespoon salt. Serve in bowls and sprinkle with cheese and a pinch of dried basil leaves. Makes about 7 quarts.

OXTAIL SOUP

Vegetables thicken and season this hearty country-style beef soup

1 large oxtail (about 2½ lbs.)
Flour
Fat or salad oil
3 qts. cold water
1 tblsp. salt
⅛ tsp. pepper
1 bay leaf
2 sprigs parsley
½ c. chopped onion
½ c. diced turnips
½ c. chopped celery
½ c. diced carrots
1 tsp. Worcestershire sauce

· Have oxtail cut between joints. Singe to remove hairs; wash and dry. Dredge with flour and brown on all sides in hot fat in soup kettle. Add water, salt, pepper, bay leaf and parsley. Bring to boil and boil 10 minutes. Skim fat from broth; cover and simmer 2 or 3 hours, or until meat is tender. Remove meat from bones and add meat to broth (or serve joints in soup if time is short.

· Add vegetables and simmer until they are tender. Stir in Worcestershire sauce. Serve very hot. Makes 6 to 8 servings.

LUNCHEON MENU: Oxtail soup, toast or crackers, hard-cooked egg and shredded lettuce salad, cookies and applesauce.

CRISP CRACKERS TO SERVE WITH SOUP: Brush crackers with soft butter and sprinkle with celery seeds and paprika. Brown lightly in broiler or moderate oven (350°). Poppy seeds may be substituted for celery seeds.

BORSCH

Top bowls of hot soup at serving time with spoonfuls of dairy sour cream

2 lbs. beef or veal knuckle
4 c. diced beets
¼ c. lemon juice
3 medium onions, sliced
15 whole allspice
1 bay leaf
8 sprigs parsley
½ c. chopped green pepper
3 c. diced potatoes
4 c. chopped cabbage
2 c. canned tomatoes
Salt
Pepper

• Cover meat with water and simmer about 3 hours, or until rich broth is formed. Stir occasionally. Remove bone and skim fat from broth.

• Mix beets with lemon juice; add onions, allspice, bay leaf, parsley and green pepper. Add to broth and simmer 20 minutes. Add potatoes, cabbage and tomatoes; simmer until potatoes are tender. Season to taste. Makes 10 servings.

CAMP VEGETABLE/BEEF SOUP

Quick main-dish soup, ideal to make when you're camping or picnicking

1 lb. ground beef
1 tblsp. instant minced onion
1 c. tomato juice or 3 tblsp. ketchup plus 1 c. water
1 (10 oz.) pkg. frozen hashed brown potatoes or 2 c. shredded fresh potatoes
1 (10 oz.) pkg. frozen mixed vegetables or 1 (1 lb.) can mixed vegetables
3 c. water
2 tsp. salt
¼ tsp. pepper
1 tblsp. butter
¼ tsp. orégano leaves

• Brown meat quickly with onion. Add tomato juice; stir in remaining ingredients. Simmer until vegetables are tender. Makes 6 servings.

SPLIT PEA/VEGETABLE SOUP

You can float frankfurter or Polish sausage slices on piping hot soup

1 lb. dried split peas (2 c.)
3 qts. water
1 meaty ham bone, or 1½ lbs. ham hocks
2 tsp. salt
½ tsp. pepper
¼ tsp. marjoram leaves
1½ c. chopped onions
¾ c. chopped carrots
¾ c. chopped celery

• Combine peas and water in large kettle. Bring to a boil; simmer 2 minutes. Remove from heat, cover and let stand 1 hour.

• Add ham bone, salt, pepper, marjoram and onions. Cover and simmer 1½ hours.

• Add carrots and celery. Continue simmering until tender, 30 to 40 minutes. Add more salt if necessary. Serve piping hot. Makes about 3½ quarts.

BEAN SOUP

Stir a dash of prepared horse-radish into soup before serving to add zest

2 c. dried beans
1½ qts. water
1 ham bone or 1½ lb. ham butt
½ c. chopped onion
1 c. chopped celery and leaves
4 c. canned tomatoes
¾ c. diced peeled potatoes
1 tsp. salt
⅛ tsp. pepper

• Combine beans and water in large kettle; boil 2 minutes. Remove from heat and let stand 1 hour. Simmer beans without draining until tender, about 2 hours, adding more water if necessary.

• In the meantime simmer ham in water to cover. Skim fat from broth and add beans. Stir in remaining ingredients; simmer until potatoes are tender, about 20 minutes. Makes 10 servings.

CHICKEN GUMBO

Bring out the soup bowls and get ready for compliments

- 1 (3 to 3½ lb.) chicken, cut in pieces
- ½ lb. ham, cut in ½″ cubes
- ¼ c. salad oil
- 1 c. chopped onion (1 medium)
- ⅓ c. chopped green pepper
- 2 tblsp. chopped hot pepper
- 6 large tomatoes, peeled and chopped
- 2 c. sliced okra
- 1 qt. boiling water
- 1 bay leaf
- 2 tsp. salt
- ½ tsp. pepper
- Cooked rice (see Note)

• Cook chicken pieces and ham in salad oil in large Dutch oven until browned.

• Add remaining ingredients, except rice. Simmer until tender, about 45 minutes.

• To serve, place spoonfuls of cooked rice in soup bowls or plates. Ladle gumbo over rice. Makes 8 servings.

Note: Cook rice according to package directions. To cook regular rice, combine 1 c. uncooked rice, 1 tsp. salt and 2 c. boiling water in saucepan with tightly fitting lid. Bring to a boil; stir two or three times, lower heat, cover tightly and simmer about 14 minutes without removing lid or stirring, or until all the liquid is absorbed and rice is tender. If there is leftover rice, package and freeze it. To thaw, unwrap and let stand at room temperature 3 to 3½ hours. To reheat, cover bottom of saucepan with water, add thawed rice, cover and simmer until rice is hot and fluffy. It will be ready in 8 to 10 minutes.

IDAHO LENTIL SOUP

This 4-gallon recipe freezes well

- ½ c. bacon drippings
- ½ lb. onions, thinly sliced
- 3 large carrots, chopped
- 8 branches celery, finely chopped
- ⅓ c. flour
- 3¼ lbs. lentils, washed
- 2 meaty ham bones
- 3¼ gals. beef broth or bouillon
- 1 tblsp. sugar
- 2 tsp. pepper
- ½ tsp. garlic powder (optional)
- 2 bay leaves (optional)
- 6 frankfurters, diagonally sliced
- Salt

• Combine bacon drippings, onions, carrots and celery in 4-gal. kettle. Cook, covered, 20 minutes.

• Stir in flour, then remaining ingredients, except frankfurters and salt. Simmer, uncovered, 3 hours. After 1 hour, cut meat from bones; chop. Return meat and bones to kettle.

• Just before serving, remove the bones, add sliced frankfurters to heat; add salt to taste. Makes 50 servings.

VEGETABLE/LENTIL CHOWDER

You'll like this hearty soup. It has color and fine flavor

1½ c. lentils, washed
1 qt. water
2½ tsp. salt
¾ c. chopped onion
⅔ c. chopped green pepper
⅓ c. butter or regular margarine
½ c. chopped pimientos
1 (1 lb. 14 oz.) can tomatoes
¼ tsp. pepper

· Combine lentils, water and salt in large saucepan. Cook, covered, over medium heat 30 minutes.
· Cook onion and green pepper in butter until tender. Combine all ingredients; simmer, covered, 30 minutes. Makes 6 large servings.

BEAN PORRIDGE

Most country kitchens keep makings for this tasty, main-dish soup on hand

4 c. cooked or canned baked beans, puréed
2 c. stewed tomatoes (fresh or canned)
1 bay leaf
1 tblsp. chopped parsley
2 tblsp. chili sauce
1 c. sliced carrots
1 c. sliced celery
½ c. sliced onions
1 c. sliced peeled potatoes
2 qts. water
2 tsp. salt

· Combine bean purée, tomatoes, bay leaf, parsley and chili sauce.
· Cook remaining vegetables until just tender in 1 to 1½" water.
· Combine bean-tomato mixture, vegetables, 2 qts. water and salt. Simmer 2 hours. Serve hot. Makes 8 servings.

GREEN BEAN SOUP

Excellent hot dish for an otherwise cold meal in warm weather

1½ lb. ham bone with meat
15 whole allspice
8 to 10 sprigs parsley
4 sprigs summer savory (1 tsp. dried savory leaves)
1 small onion, minced
1½ c. diced peeled potatoes
2 c. cut green beans
½ c. light cream
1 tblsp. butter or regular margarine
2 tsp. salt

· Place ham bone in soup kettle with water to cover. Tie allspice, parsley and savory in small cheesecloth bag or put in tea ball; add to kettle. Simmer 2 hours, adding more water if needed.
· Add onion, potatoes and beans; cook until vegetables are tender, 20 to 30 minutes. Remove spice ball.
· Just before serving, blend in cream, butter and salt. Makes 8 to 10 servings.

Broth Enriches Soups

Chicken broth, as well as beef broth, is the magic seasoning in many meatless vegetable soups. Keep homemade broth in the freezer and bring some out when you're in a soup-making mood. Or buy cans from your supermarket. Once you get the habit of substituting broth for part of water or milk in vegetable soups, you'll stick to it. And you'll get out the soup kettle more frequently.
· Creamy Cauliflower Soup made with 2 c. chicken broth is an example. Enriched also with cheese and

sprinkled with chopped chives or parsley, it will tempt everyone around your dining table. Equally tasty and appealing are the other broth- or stock-flavored vegetable soups in this chapter.

CHICKEN BROTH OR STOCK

Keep this on hand in the freezer

1 large stewing chicken, or 4 lbs. chicken necks and backs
1 medium onion, peeled
2 whole cloves
1 branch celery with leaves
1 peeled carrot (optional)
2 sprigs parsley
1 tsp. salt
⅛ tsp. pepper
Boiling water

· Wash chicken and put into a kettle with vegetables and seasonings (stick cloves into onion).
· Add boiling water to cover the chicken completely. Cover and simmer gently about 2 hours, or until chicken is tender.
· Remove chicken, strip meat from bones and refrigerate for other use. Return bones to broth and simmer another 45 minutes.
· Strain broth; remove fat as directed in recipe that follows for Beef Broth. Makes about 1 quart.

BEEF BROTH OR STOCK

The foundation for superior soup

4 lbs. beef soup bones (pieces)
2½ qts. cold water
1 tsp. salt
1 bay leaf
1 medium onion, peeled
2 whole cloves
5 whole peppercorns
1 carrot, scraped
1 branch celery with leaves
2 sprigs parsley

· Remove meat from bones; cut it in small pieces. Put meat, bones, water and remaining ingredients in a kettle (stick cloves into onion). Do not cover. Simmer (do not boil) 3 hours. Strain. (Use the meat in hash or sandwiches.)

TO REMOVE FAT FROM BROTH: Skim off with spoon. Or lay a paper towel on surface of fat; when it's saturated, repeat with more towels until fat is removed. Or wrap an ice cube in a paper towel and draw across the top of the broth, changing paper as needed. Or refrigerate the broth overnight; you can then lift off the congealed fat with a spoon.

TO CLARIFY BROTH: Crush an eggshell; mix with 1 egg white and ¼ c. cold water. Stir into lukewarm defatted broth. Heat to boiling; let stand about 5 minutes and strain through two thicknesses of cheesecloth or a fine sieve. Makes 2 quarts.

Note: You can omit vegetables and seasonings in the above recipe if you are making beef broth to use in Garden Row Soup (recipe follows).

GARDEN ROW SOUP

Get out soup bowls and invite guests to share this end-of-the-garden treat

2 qts. Beef Broth (made without vegetables), clarified
2 tsp. salt
½ tsp. orégano leaves
½ tsp. marjoram leaves
½ tsp. celery seeds
⅛ tsp. ground cumin
6 peppercorns
1 clove garlic, crushed
1 large onion, chopped
¼ c. chopped parsley
4 carrots, scraped and sliced

1 large green pepper, scalded, skinned, seeded and cut in strips
1 c. green beans, cut in pieces
1 zucchini, cut in ¾″ slices
3 ears sweet corn, cut in 3″ lengths
2 large pink tomatoes, peeled and quartered

• Simmer broth with salt, spices and garlic for 30 minutes.
• Add onion, parsley, carrots, green pepper and beans; simmer 20 minutes.
• Add zucchini and corn; simmer 15 minutes. Add tomatoes; simmer 15 minutes. Makes 8 servings.

Note: Cut the corn in thin slices—they will look like rosettes in the soup.

CREAMY CAULIFLOWER SOUP

Chicken broth plays an important seasoning role in this superior soup

1 medium head cauliflower, cut in tiny flowerets
¼ c. butter
⅔ c. chopped onion
2 tblsp. flour
2 c. chicken broth
2 c. light cream
½ tsp. Worcestershire sauce
¾ tsp. salt
1 c. grated Cheddar cheese
Chopped chives or parsley

• Cook cauliflower in boiling salted water; drain, reserving liquid.
• Melt butter. Add onion and cook until soft. Blend in flour; add broth, and cook, stirring constantly, until mixture comes to a boil. Stir in 1 c. liquid drained from cauliflower (adding water if necessary to make 1 c.), cream, Worcestershire sauce and salt. Add cauliflower. Heat to boiling. Stir in cheese. Serve sprinkled with chopped chives or parsley. Makes about 2 quarts.

SALSIFY SOUP

Mock oyster stew is the Pennsylvania Dutch name for oyster-plant soups

1⅔ c. sliced peeled salsify (about ¾ lb.)
1 qt. water
1 tblsp. vinegar
2 tblsp. butter
1 tblsp. chopped onion
2 tblsp. flour
1 c. chicken broth
1 c. milk
½ tsp. salt
½ tsp. parsley flakes
⅛ tsp. pepper

• Plunge salsify slices immediately into 1 qt. water with 1 tblsp. vinegar added to prevent discoloration. Drain, and cook in 1″ boiling salted water until tender, 15 to 20 minutes.
• Meanwhile, melt butter. Add onion and cook until soft. Blend in flour, then chicken broth and milk. Cook, stirring constantly, until mixture comes to a boil. Add remaining ingredients and salsify with water in which it was cooked. Makes about 1 quart.

PURÉE OF CARROT SOUP

Absolutely delicious—surprising that carrots can taste so wonderful

2 tblsp. butter
⅔ c. chopped onions
3 c. finely chopped carrots
1 qt. chicken broth
2 tblsp. uncooked rice
½ tsp. salt
⅛ tsp. pepper
½ c. light cream
Chopped parsley (optional)

• Melt butter in large saucepan. Add onions and cook until soft. Add carrots, chicken broth, rice and seasonings. Simmer, uncovered, 30 minutes. Purée soup through a food mill.
• Return to saucepan and add cream. Heat just to boiling. Garnish with chopped parsley. Makes 5 cups.

PUMPKIN SOUP

Taste this soup and you'll know why swanky restaurants serve it

2 tblsp. butter
¼ c. chopped green pepper
2 tblsp. chopped onion
1 large sprig parsley
⅛ tsp. thyme leaves
1 bay leaf
1 (8 oz.) can tomatoes (1 c.)
1 (1 lb.) can pumpkin
2 c. chicken broth or stock
1 tblsp. flour
1 c. milk
1 tsp. salt
⅛ tsp. pepper

• Melt butter in large saucepan. Add green pepper, onion, parsley, thyme and bay leaf. Cook 5 minutes. Add tomatoes, pumpkin and chicken broth. Cover and simmer 30 minutes, stirring occasionally. Press mixture through food mill or wire strainer.
• Blend together flour and milk and stir into soup. Add salt and pepper and cook, stirring frequently, until mixture comes to a boil. Serve immediately. Serves 6.

Soups from Frozen Stock

SUPER SOUP STOCK

Wonderful to have in your freezer

10 lbs. soup bones
1 lb. soup meat chunks
2 tblsp. peppercorns
3 onions, quartered
6 cloves garlic

• Crack bones. Put into 7-qt. pressure canner, being careful not to fill above "full" mark. (If using 7- or 8-qt. pressure saucepan, use half this recipe.)
• Add soup meat, peppercorns, onions and garlic. Cover with cold water. (Stock will be highly concentrated, so it's best to add salt later, when you make soup.)
• Close pressure canner cover; bring up steam. Exhaust air, close valve when pressure reaches 15 pounds. Adjust heat to hold at 15 pounds. (Good idea to watch for about ½ hour to be sure pressure is maintained steadily.)
• Cook under pressure 4 to 8 hours. Remove from heat. Let pressure go down without opening petcock. Cool stock until it can be handled easily, and fat rises to top. Skim off fat.
• Pick out bones with kitchen tongs. Use slotted spoon to remove big bone fragments and chunks of fat and gristle; strain through cheesecloth, returning bits of lean meat to stock. Makes 8 quarts.

TO FREEZE: Dip cool stock into plastic freezer containers. (Pint size holds enough stock to make 6 or 8 servings of soup.) Cool completely; skim off any fat that forms; seal airtight. Freeze.

TO CAN: Pour cooled stock into clean pint or quart jars. Put on caps, screwing bands tightly. Process in pressure canner, 40 minutes at 10 pounds.

BEAN AND FRANKFURTER SOUP

Good with toasted cheese sandwiches, lettuce salad, ice cream

2 c. dried lima beans
4 c. water
2 c. thawed Super Soup Stock
1 onion, thinly sliced
1 tblsp. salt
½ tsp. pepper
½ tsp. dry mustard
3 tblsp. vinegar
3 tblsp. Worcestershire sauce
2 tblsp. brown sugar
1 lb. frankfurters

• Soak beans overnight in water to cover.
• Place beans in large pan. Add water, stock, onion, salt, pepper and mustard. Simmer in tightly covered saucepan about 1½ hours, or until beans are soft. Mash beans or put through food mill.
• Return bean purée to saucepan. Add vinegar, Worcestershire sauce and sugar.
• Slice frankfurters; add to soup. Bring to boil; simmer 15 minutes. Makes 6 to 8 servings.

VEGETABLE CHOWDER

Serve with piping hot corn bread and pineapple-cottage cheese salad

2 c. canned or fresh corn
2 c. chopped celery
½ green pepper, cut in thin strips
1 onion, thinly sliced
1 c. cooked tomatoes
1 tblsp. salt
⅛ tsp. pepper
2 c. thawed Super Soup Stock
¼ c. butter or regular margarine
3 tblsp. flour
2 c. milk, scalded
½ c. grated cheese
½ c. chopped pimiento
¼ tsp. paprika

• Put corn, celery, green pepper, onion, tomatoes, salt and pepper in kettle. Add thawed soup stock, bring to boil and simmer 30 minutes.
• Melt butter and stir in flour; gradually add milk and cook 5 minutes, stirring constantly until smooth and thickened; add to vegetable mixture. Add remaining ingredients, stirring until cheese is melted. Makes 6 servings.

FRENCH ONION SOUP

Dress it up with a sprinkling of cheese

¼ c. butter or regular margarine
3 onions, sliced
Salt
Pepper
4 c. water
2 c. thawed Super Soup Stock
1 tsp. Worcestershire sauce

• Melt butter in large pan; add onions. Fry until soft and yellow. Season with salt and pepper to taste.
• Add water, stock and Worcestershire sauce. Simmer slowly 45 minutes. Good served in bowls topped with circles of toast sprinkled with grated cheese. Makes 6 servings.

QUICK SOUPS

Use frozen Super Soup Stock with canned or packaged soup mixes

4 c. cold water
1 c. frozen Super Soup Stock
1 can condensed soup, or 1 pkg. soup mix

• Combine all ingredients; simmer gently until frozen stock melts and flavors blend. Makes 6 servings. If desired, two different commercial soups can be combined for new flavor treats, such as Black Bean and Onion; Tomato and Split Pea or Vegetable Noodle; Mushroom and Onion. For 2 cans, increase frozen soup stock to 2 c. and water to 8 c. Makes 12 servings.

Milk-Made Soups

• Sturdy soups made with milk have come a long way since Pennsylvania Dutch people called them "poor soups." That name suggested the availability of the main ingredient, milk, at all times in farm kitchens. It also designated the ease and speed with which a woman could make milk soups (in comparison to catching and dressing a chicken and making soup stock).
• Some of today's milk-made soups rate high, for taste as well as nourishment. Cream of Squash/Corn Soup surprises everyone with its delicate blend of fresh vegetable flavors.
• Potato soups frequently have a milk base. When you're in a nostalgic mood and hungry, do try Brown Potato Soup, a creation of Pennsylvania Dutch kitchens. The Dutch scattered chopped hard-cooked eggs or minced parsley over the bowls of hot soup just before serving.

VELVETY CHEESE SOUP

Peas and pimiento add color to this rich-in-protein hot soup

¼ c. butter
¼ c. minced onion
¼ c. flour
1 tsp. salt
4 c. milk
1 c. grated process cheese (¼ lb.)
½ c. cooked green peas
¼ c. diced pimiento

• Melt butter in saucepan. Add onion; cook until clear. Remove from heat. Blend in flour, salt and milk.
• Cook until thick, stirring constantly. Add cheese, stirring until it melts. Add peas and pimiento. Makes 6 servings.

WATER CRESS SOUP

A spring song in the soup bowl—it's yellow and green. Delicious!

2 cans condensed cream of chicken soup
2 soup cans milk
½ c. chopped water cress (about ¼ bunch)
2 hard-cooked eggs, sliced

• Empty soup into saucepan. Add milk; heat as directed on can.
• Wash water cress. Save sprigs for garnish. Chop very fine. Add to hot soup just before serving.
• Pour into soup bowls. Top each serving with egg slice and sprig of water cress. Makes 6 servings.

CORN CHOWDER

Cool chowder before serving if there's time—reheating improves its flavor

¼ lb. salt pork, diced, or 4 slices bacon
3 medium onions, chopped
3 or 4 diced peeled potatoes
½ c. water
4 c. corn, cut from cob
1 qt. milk
2 tsp. salt
⅛ tsp. pepper

• Fry pork until almost crisp; add onions and cook until golden brown —this gives a definite tang to the chowder.
• Add potatoes and water; simmer 5 minutes. Add corn and cook 5 minutes more, or until tender.
• Stir in milk, salt and pepper. Heat slowly until chowder is piping hot. Makes 6 to 8 servings.

CREAM OF SQUASH/CORN SOUP

Perfect go-with for supper sandwiches—you can easily double recipe

2 c. grated white or yellow squash
2 c. fresh corn, cut from cob
2 c. boiling water
1 c. chopped onion
½ c. chopped green pepper
6 tblsp. butter or regular margarine
6 tblsp. flour
5 c. milk
1 tblsp. salt
¼ tsp. pepper
8 slices bacon, diced, cooked and drained (optional)

• Combine squash, corn and water. Cover and simmer until tender.
• Meanwhile, cook onion and green pepper in melted butter until soft. Stir in flour. Add milk, and cook, stirring constantly, until thickened. Add to squash-corn mixture along with salt and pepper. Heat thoroughly.
• Serve in bowls. Garnish with bacon, if you like. Makes 9 cups.

Potato Soup with Dumplings

This soup ranks first with a young Iowa dairyman, whose mother taught his wife, a trained home economist, how to make it. The hearty dish with crisp crackers or rolls and a tray of relishes, such as carrot sticks, celery and pickles, frequently takes the spotlight in company suppers. And do try the four other potato soup recipes that follow; they're all substantial, unusual and good!

POTATO SOUP WITH DUMPLINGS

The dumplings are light and tasty

Soup:
1 c. diced celery
½ c. water
6 medium potatoes
2 c. water
1 medium onion, chopped
2 tsp. salt
¼ tsp. pepper
3 c. milk

Dumplings:
1 c. sifted flour
1½ tsp. baking powder
½ tsp. salt
½ tsp. sugar
1 tsp. parsley flakes
1 egg
½ c. milk

• Cook celery in ½ c. water just until tender. Do not drain.
• Peel and cube potatoes. Place in 4-qt. saucepan with 2 c. water. Add cooked celery, onion, salt and pepper. Cook until potatoes are tender. Mash slightly to eliminate definite cubes. Add milk; set aside until dumplings are mixed.
• To make dumplings, sift together flour, baking powder, salt and sugar. Stir in parsley flakes.
• Beat eggs; add milk; add to dry ingredients and mix just until moistened.
• Bring soup to a boil. Drop dump-

lings by tablespoonfuls into liquid so they don't touch. Turn heat to simmer, cover tightly; simmer gently 20 minutes. *Don't lift lid.* Makes 6 servings.

HERBED POTATO SOUP

With this hearty soup in the freezer you're always ready for supper guests

8 medium potatoes, peeled
2 onions, chopped or 2 tblsp. instant minced onion
¼ c. butter
2 tblsp. chopped parsley
½ tsp. crushed basil leaves
¼ c. flour
2 tsp. salt
½ tsp. pepper
2 c. cold milk
4 c. scalded milk
2 c. hot potato water

• Cook potatoes and onions together until potatoes are tender. Drain; save potato water. Put the potatoes through a ricer or coarse strainer.
• While potatoes cook, melt the butter in a heavy 6-qt. saucepan. Add parsley and basil. Blend in flour, salt and pepper; gradually stir in the cold milk. Add scalded milk and potato water.
• Cook over medium heat; stir constantly, until mixture thickens slightly. Stir in potatoes and onions; heat. Serve in bowls; if you like, sprinkle soup with chopped parsley, or dust with paprika. This soup freezes well. Makes 12 cups.

BROWN POTATO SOUP

The browned crumbs add oomph

2½ c. diced peeled potatoes
4 c. water
1 tblsp. salt
¼ tsp. pepper
¼ tsp. onion salt
¼ tsp. celery salt
4 c. milk
2 tblsp. butter or regular margarine
¾ c. flour

• Cook potatoes until tender in 2 c. water. While cooking, add salt, pepper, onion and celery salts.
• Drain. Add milk and remaining 2 c. water to the drained, seasoned potato water. Heat to boiling; simmer.
• While liquid simmers, cut butter into flour until mixture looks like crumbs. Brown these in small heavy skillet, stirring constantly. Stir browned crumbs into hot liquid; cook about 5 minutes, stirring.
• Add potatoes, and heat about 5 minutes more. Serve hot. Serves 6 to 8.

CREAM OF POTATO SOUP

Especially irresistible on a cold day

4 large branches celery and leaves
2 medium onions
1½ c. water
2 chicken bouillon cubes
1½ c. mashed potatoes
1 tblsp. butter
2 c. milk
Dash of paprika
Chopped chives or parsley

• Chop celery and onions; add water and simmer 30 minutes. Strain through sieve (should be about 1 cup).
• Stir bouillon cubes into strained water. While hot pour over potatoes, stirring until they dissolve. Rub through strainer to make sure no lumps remain.
• Add butter, milk and paprika and heat. Serve with chives or parsley. Makes 4 to 6 servings.

POTATO/CHEESE SOUP

Cheese, summer sausage and herbs make this soup unusual and extra-good

- 4 medium potatoes, peeled
- 1 medium onion, sliced
- 4 c. boiling water
- ⅓ c. diced summer sausage
- ½ tsp. thyme leaves
- ½ tsp. marjoram leaves
- 1½ tsp. salt
- Pepper
- 2 tblsp. butter or regular margarine
- ½ c. grated sharp cheese
- 1 tblsp. grated Parmesan cheese (optional)

• Cut potatoes in halves. Cook with onion in 2 c. boiling water, until tender. Do not drain.

• Mash potatoes. Add sausage, thyme, marjoram, salt, pepper, butter, sharp cheese and remaining boiling water. Simmer 10 minutes.

• Add grated cheese just before serving. Makes 6 servings.

Opulent Oyster Stew

Oyster stew is the classic country soup made with seafood. Early in our history, enterprising colonials transported barrels of ice-packed oysters inland and sold them during winter months. This was a replay of the custom of ancient Romans of importing oysters in snow and ice from England to feature as a delicacy in the Eternal City's feasts and banquets. Oyster suppers were popular in our prairie and coastal areas; they brought neighbors together for happy evenings.

Now oysters, once available only during the "R" months—in cold weather—are an around-the-year food. They appear in cans in supermarket freezer cases at all times. The important point is to avoid overcooking oysters. Just heat them through, or until the edges curl. This will take an average of three to five minutes only. When so handled, oysters retain their delicate flavor, plumpness and tenderness.

Here are some of our readers' favorite oyster soup recipes.

"Stretcher" Oyster Stew
Corn/Oyster Soup
Oyster Chowder
Vegetable/Oyster Stew

Oyster Stew with Potatoes

The Maryland farm woman who gave us this unusual recipe buys two or three bushels of oysters at a time. The entire family helps her shuck them—they open the shells with oyster knives, scrape out the oysters and rinse them quickly in cold water. One bushel yields 2 or 3 quarts. But even if you live far from oyster farming country and buy your oysters without shells, ready to use, you'll want to try this stew. It makes a delightful supper dish. And who can improve on the accompaniment the originator of the dish suggested—crisp coleslaw?

"STRETCHER" OYSTER STEW

Perfect to fix when oyster supply is scarce—potatoes are the "stretchers"

- 2 c. finely diced potatoes
- 1 c. water
- 2 tsp. salt
- 1 pt. oysters, drained and cut coarsely or chopped

1 pt. oyster liquor (add milk to make 1 pt.)
1/3 c. butter or regular margarine
1 c. light cream or dairy half-and-half
1/8 tsp. pepper
1/4 tsp. paprika

• Cook potatoes in water with salt added until almost soft, about 10 minutes. Add oysters and liquor and bring just to a boil. Remove from heat at once.
• Add butter, cream and seasonings. Cover and let stand about 15 minutes before serving. Makes 5 to 6 servings.

Corn/Oyster Soup

Oyster prices have soared in recent years, but the tradition of oyster stew for Christmas Eve supper lingers. We're glad to share with you the favorite recipe of a Wisconsin farmer's wife for Corn/Oyster Soup. It tastes wonderful on a holly-decorated evening or a winter day.

Corn stretches the oysters beautifully; the blend of flavors is excitingly good. So before the children hang up their Christmas stockings, why not serve them Corn/Oyster Soup, crackers, a fruit cup or salad, Christmas cookies and chocolate milk? They'll go to bed happy.

CORN/OYSTER SOUP

Call this Christmas Eve soup—it's a real special-occasion treat

1 tblsp. butter
1 tblsp. flour
1 qt. milk
1 (1 lb. 1 oz.) can whole kernel corn
1 lb. oysters (about 2 c.)
1½ tsp. salt
¼ tsp. pepper
Paprika (optional)
Chopped parsley (optional)

• Melt butter in large saucepan. Blend in flour, then milk. Cook, stirring constantly, until mixture comes to a boil. Add corn, oysters (with their liquid), salt and pepper. Simmer 10 minutes. Serve sprinkled with paprika and parsley, if desired. Makes 6 servings.

OYSTER CHOWDER

You can keep ingredients on hand to make this chowder on short notice

1 small onion, chopped
2 tblsp. butter or regular margarine
2 cans condensed oyster stew
1½ soup cans milk
1 (8 oz.) can white potatoes, drained and cubed
2 tsp. Worcestershire sauce
1 pimiento, chopped (optional)

• Cook onion in butter until tender. Add all ingredients and heat. Makes 5 cups.

VEGETABLE/OYSTER STEW

New, tasty version of oyster stew—it adds vegetables to the meal

2 medium carrots, scraped and grated
½ c. diced celery
¼ c. butter or regular margarine
1 qt. milk
1 qt. oysters
Salt
Pepper
Paprika
Minced parsley

• Sauté carrots and celery in butter until soft and tender (not brown). Add milk and bring to a boil.

• Cook oysters in own liquor until edges curl (about 5 minutes).
• Combine oyster and vegetable mixtures. Season to taste with salt, pepper and paprika. Garnish with parsley. Serve immediately, it curdles if left standing. Makes 8 servings.

Note: Tiny parboiled onions may be added with milk and vegetables.

FISH CHOWDER

This soup is to the midwest what clam chowder is to New England

4 slices of bacon, cut in pieces, or 1½" salt pork cube
2 lbs. fish filet (haddock or cod, frozen or fresh)
2 c. thinly sliced peeled potatoes
1 large onion, thinly sliced
1½ c. water
2 c. scalded milk
1½ tsp. salt
Dash of pepper
1½ tblsp. butter or regular margarine

• Place bacon in large heavy saucepan. Brown well; remove, leaving drippings.
• Cut fish filets into 1" pieces.
• Place layers of potato, onion and fish in saucepan. Add water. Cover. Bring to a boil, reduce heat; simmer 10 to 15 minutes, until potatoes and fish are just cooked.
• Add milk, seasonings, butter and bacon. Keep warm over low heat. Makes 4 generous servings.

FISH SOUP

Country fishermen say it's a fine way to cook the smallest fish

6 to 8 fish, cleaned
1 qt. water
5 parsley sprigs
2 small carrots, peeled
3 branches celery
2 medium onions, peeled
2 lemon slices
1 tblsp. salt
3 peppercorns or ¼ tsp. pepper
1 c. light cream
2 egg yolks
3 tblsp. chopped parsley, dill or chives

• Combine fish, water, parsley sprigs, carrots, celery, onions, lemon, salt and pepper in kettle. Simmer 1 to 2 hours. Strain stock.
• Beat cream and egg yolks in large bowl. Add chopped parsley.
• Pour hot stock over cream-egg mixture; blend thoroughly and serve at once. Makes 4 to 6 servings.

POTATO/SALMON CHOWDER

A hearty meal-in-a-bowl—serve with cabbage salad and crackers

6 medium potatoes, peeled and cut in ½" cubes (4 c.)
1 c. sliced carrots
1 tblsp. salt
3 c. water
1 (10 oz.) pkg. frozen peas
⅓ c. butter or regular margarine
⅓ c. chopped onion
¼ c. flour
5 c. milk
1 (1 lb.) can salmon
1 c. thinly sliced celery
½ tsp. Worcestershire sauce

• Cook the potatoes and carrots in salted water in covered pan until just tender.
• Add frozen peas. Bring to boil. Cook 1 minute.
• Remove from heat. Do not drain.
• Melt butter in a skillet. Add onion and cook until lightly browned. Add flour, stir until smooth. Cook 1

minute. Add half the milk, stirring constantly. Cook over low heat until sauce boils and thickens.

• Flake salmon; add, with the fish liquid, to the vegetables.

• Add hot white sauce, celery, Worcestershire sauce and remaining milk to the vegetables and salmon. Heat thoroughly. Serve at once. Makes 3 quarts or 12 generous servings.

CRAB BISQUE

This rich soup is an excellent supper main dish. An electric skillet helps

1 can condensed tomato soup
1 can condensed cream of celery soup
1 can condensed cream of mushroom soup
1 can condensed green pea soup
5 c. milk
1 (7½ oz.) can crabmeat
1 tsp. salt
Paprika
¼ c. chopped parsley

• Combine soups and blend. Gradually add milk. Add undrained crabmeat and salt.

• Heat slowly, stirring constantly, until just hot enough to serve. (This must be stirred while heating; it scorches easily.)

• Serve sprinkled with paprika and parsley. Makes about 11 cups.

SPINACH-OF-THE-SEA SOUP

Oyster stew and shrimp soup join frozen spinach to make this

1 (10 oz.) pkg. frozen chopped spinach
1 can condensed oyster stew
1 can condensed cream of shrimp soup
2⅔ c. milk
4 slices bacon, chopped, fried and drained (optional)

• Cook spinach in boiling salted water. Drain.

• Combine oyster stew, shrimp soup and milk. Add spinach. Simmer until thoroughly heated. Serve in soup bowls garnished with bacon. Makes 6 servings.

Frosty-Cold Soups

Serve substantial, frosty soups on hot, humid days; bubbling, hot soups on cold, stormy evenings. This makes sense: Soup helps conquer the weather. Cups of chilled soup are a good summer meal starter. Cucumber Cool Soup is refreshing and satisfying; hearty Vichyssoise, a cold potato soup, was invented in New York by a French chef. And try Frosty Spanish Vegetable Soup, a superb appetizer for summer evenings.

CUCUMBER COOL SOUP

Company special for a hot day

1 c. milk
1 medium cucumber, peeled, seeded and diced
2 cans condensed cream of potato soup
½ tsp. salt
⅛ tsp. pepper
1 c. heavy cream
Chopped chives

• Pour milk and cucumber in blender

container. Blend until cucumber is finely minced. Add 1 can soup; blend. Pour out half of mixture into bowl. Blend other can of soup with remaining mixture in blender. Combine in bowl with remaining ingredients, except chives. Chill thoroughly.
• If desired, pour into a 13 × 9 × 2″ pan and place in freezer 30 minutes before serving, chilling until mixture just begins to freeze. Stir smooth. Or chill thoroughly in refrigerator. To serve, spoon into cups; sprinkle with chopped chives. Makes 6 servings, or 5 cups.

VICHYSSOISE

Rich, cold, luscious potato soup. Make early in day and refrigerate

¼ c. unsalted butter
4 leeks, chopped
1 onion, minced
1 qt. chicken broth
1 sprig parsley
1 branch celery
Salt
Pepper
Few grains ground nutmeg
Few drops Worcestershire sauce
2 potatoes, peeled and thinly sliced
1 c. heavy cream
Chopped chives

• Melt butter over low heat. Add leeks and onion; cook slowly until tender, but not brown.
• Add chicken broth, parsley, celery, salt and pepper to taste, nutmeg, Worcestershire sauce and potatoes. Cook until potatoes are tender.
• Put through fine sieve into china or glass bowl. Stir in heavy cream; chill. Serve cold, sprinkled lightly with chives. Makes 6 to 8 servings.

TOMATO BOUILLON

Float thin lemon slices in bouillon for an attractive garnish

1 (16 to 17 oz.) can tomato juice
1 can condensed beef broth
¼ tsp. seasoned salt

• Combine all the ingredients and heat. Serve piping hot with crisp crackers. Makes 6 servings.

Note: Instead of heating Tomato Bouillon, chill and serve in juice glasses.

Frosty Vegetable Soup from Spanish Kitchens

Everyone who visits Spain when the weather is warm returns home with pleasant memories of refreshing cold *gazpacho.* And most women want to duplicate this vegetable soup in their own kitchens. We have worked out a recipe for it, knowing that many country women have the important makings in their gardens.

It takes time to chop the vegetables, but the results are worth the cost in minutes and effort. While you can use your blender for the chopping, you lose some of the desired texture. Also you can use salad oil instead of olive oil, but you get a different flavor from the truly great Spanish soup.

The ingredients are what we use in salads, but sipping your salad is different. Try this soup the next time you want something special to serve on a hot, humid day.

FROSTY SPANISH VEGETABLE SOUP

Make in morning to serve as evening meal on particularly sultry days

- 1 c. finely chopped peeled tomatoes
- ½ c. finely chopped green pepper
- ½ c. finely chopped celery
- ½ c. finely chopped peeled cucumber
- ¼ c. finely chopped onion
- 2 tsp. finely chopped or snipped fresh parsley
- 2 tsp. chopped or snipped chives
- 1 small clove garlic, minced
- 2½ tblsp. wine vinegar
- 2 tblsp. olive oil
- 1 tsp. salt
- ¼ tsp. ground pepper
- ½ tsp. Worcestershire sauce
- 2 c. tomato juice

• Combine all the ingredients in a glass bowl and stir to mix. Cover and chill thoroughly several hours. Serve in chilled cups. Makes 6 servings.

chapter 6

Sandwiches—Hearty and Dainty

NO FOOD IS MORE VERSATILE than the sandwich. It can be hearty enough to qualify for the main dish in suppers and lunches, and dainty and pretty enough for festive parties. Sandwiches are lunchbox favorites, but in country homes they also make pleasing lunches when teamed with bowls of soup, a tray of relishes, and milk or milk shakes, tea or coffee. Substantial sandwiches served with salad, a dessert like baked apples and cookies, and a beverage, make a complete meal.

Sandwiches had an unfavorable start. The Fourth Earl of Sandwich, an unpopular and corrupt eighteenth-century politician and gambler, refused to leave his card games to dine. A servant handed him greasy mutton chops inserted between bread slices. The invention prospered. The wonderful sandwiches in this book testify to their refinement.

You'll find recipes for both hot and cold sandwiches in this chapter. Notice sandwiches to fix ahead and refrigerate, and also fillings to spread in sandwiches to freeze.

Here's a secret from country kitchens: Use homemade bread for superlative sandwiches. (You'll find recipes in the bread chapter of this book and also in our *Homemade Bread* cookbook). Firm breads slice and spread better than soft ones, but if you must use the soft loaves, chill them (well wrapped) for 2 hours or longer. We culled choice sandwich recipes for this chapter. Let's start with the hot and hearty ones.

Hamburgers—Grand Champion Sandwiches

In 1904 while people across the country were singing "Meet Me in St. Louis," hamburger sandwiches were capturing the interest of people at the St. Louis world's fair. They now dominate the American sandwich scene and every family has its own favorite versions. But we give you recipes for two "loose hamburgers," or sandwich fillings that you spoon into buns. Barbecued Beef Filling, a cousin of hamburgers, is perfect for serving a crowd. (See Index for other recipes for hamburgers.)

COLORADO LOOSE HAMBURGERS

Serve with French fries, carrot sticks, milk shakes and homemade cookies

1½ lbs. ground beef
3 tblsp. shortening
1 branch celery, chopped
1 large onion, chopped
1 green pepper, chopped
½ can condensed tomato soup
1 c. ketchup
1 tblsp. celery seeds
1½ tsp. salt
¼ tsp. pepper
2 tblsp. flour
1 tblsp. brown sugar
1 tblsp. vinegar
1 tblsp. prepared mustard (optional)
Hamburger buns

• Brown meat in shortening if meat is lean; otherwise brown beef in its own fat. Add celery, onion and green pepper and simmer until tender. Add remaining ingredients, except buns.

• Cook slowly 1 hour. Serve 1 tblsp. (or more) mixture in each split hamburger bun. Makes 15 to 18 sandwiches, depending on size of buns and amount of hamburger mixture used in each.

BARBECUED BEEF FILLING

Please the crowd—take a big kettle of this to the Sunday school picnic

4½ lbs. boneless beef
3 tblsp. melted shortening or beef fat, more if needed
3 c. water
¼ c. Worcestershire sauce
1 c. tomato sauce
1 c. ketchup
4 c. chopped onions, cooked tender in melted shortening
1½ tsp. salt (or to taste)
¼ tsp. pepper

• Cut beef in 4" pieces; brown well in shortening or beef fat. Add to 3 c. water and simmer until tender, about 2 hours. Remove beef from cooking liquid and put through coarse blade of food chopper.

• Combine beef with remaining ingredients. Add enough of the cooking liquid to make filling moist but spreadable (about 2 c.)

• Heat filling and serve between hamburger buns. Makes enough filling for 50 sandwiches.

HARVEST SANDWICH SPECIAL

An extra-quick main dish for supper or lunch on a cool day

1½ c. process cheese cubes
½ c. light cream
6 slices process cheese

6 slices toast
6 (½") tomato slices
6 poached eggs
6 slices cooked bacon

• Put cheese cubes and cream in saucepan over low heat, stirring constantly to blend. Keep hot.
• Lay thin cheese slices on toast and broil to brown lightly. Top with tomato slices and then with hot eggs. Pour on cheese sauce; add bacon. Serve at once. Makes 6 servings.

BOLOGNA/CHEESE SUBMARINES

Easy way to please teen-age guests. Serve in foil so they'll stay hot

10 Coney buns (long)
Butter or regular margarine, softened
1 lb. bologna, ground
1 c. grated sharp Cheddar cheese
1 medium onion, chopped
⅓ c. sweet pickle relish, well drained
¼ c. prepared mustard
2 tblsp. mayonnaise

• Spread buns with butter. Combine remaining ingredients; spoon into buns.
• Wrap each bun in a piece of foil. (Freeze if desired. Defrost 1 hour in foil or place in oven, frozen.)
• Place foil-wrapped buns in slow oven (300°) 30 minutes. (If frozen, bake a total of 50 minutes.) Makes 10 servings.

TOASTED CHEESE TREAT

Swiss cheese also is good in this

6 tomato slices
6 slices process cheese
12 strips cooked bacon
6 hamburger buns, split and toasted

• Layer a tomato slice, a cheese slice and 2 strips bacon on each bun half. Broil until cheese melts and is golden brown. Top with remaining bun half. Makes 6 servings.

CORNED BEEF SANDWICHES

Serve these with hot vegetable soup

1 small onion, chopped
2 tblsp. butter or regular margarine
1 (12 oz.) can corned beef, shredded
1 c. ketchup
8 hamburger buns

• Cook onion in butter until soft. Stir in corned beef and ketchup. Cook over low heat, stirring frequently, 15 minutes. Serve in hot, split buns. Makes 8 sandwiches.

CHEESE BARBECUE SANDWICHES

Toasting open-face sandwiches helps to make them appealing and tasty

2 hard-cooked eggs
1 green pepper
1 small onion
6 green olives
1½ c. grated process cheese
3 tblsp. ketchup
½ tsp. Worcestershire sauce
3 hamburger buns

• Chop fine: eggs, green pepper, onion and olives. Mix with cheese, ketchup and Worcestershire sauce.
• Cut buns in halves; spread each half with cheese mixture. Toast in moderate oven (350°) to melt cheese. Serves 3.

PIZZA LOAF

Here's a new sandwich with the pizza look and taste. Serve it to company

1 long loaf French bread (1 lb.), or 4 long Italian rolls
Butter or margarine, softened
¾ lb. ground beef
½ c. grated Parmesan cheese
½ tsp. orégano leaves
1 tsp. salt
⅛ tsp. pepper
1½ tsp. minced onion
1½ (6 oz.) cans tomato paste
¼ c. sliced olives (optional)
2 ripe tomatoes, thinly sliced
8 slices process cheese

• Cut bread loaf or rolls in halves lengthwise. Spread with butter.
• Combine beef, Parmesan cheese, seasonings, onion, tomato paste and olives. Spread mixture on cut sides of bread loaf or rolls.
• (If freezing for later use, cut each half loaf into good-size servings; wrap in foil or freezer wrap. Freeze. Defrost 1½ hours in wrap.)
• Place unwrapped loaves or servings, meat side up, on baking sheet. Top with tomato slices.
• Bake in moderate oven (350°) 20 minutes. Remove from oven; top with cheese slices. Return to oven until cheese is melted, about 5 minutes. Serves 8 to 10.

TOMATO/CHEESE SAUCE

Tomato sauce and sausage get together in this hot supper sandwich special

1 (8 oz.) can tomato sauce
1 chopped onion
Parsley
1 tsp. salt
¼ tsp. pepper
1 tsp. paprika
½ lb. bulk pork sausage or hamburger
6 hamburger buns
6 slices process cheese

• Combine tomato sauce, onion, parsley, salt, pepper and paprika. Cook until thick, about 10 minutes.
• Brown sausage; break into small pieces with a fork.
• Spoon a tablespoonful of warm tomato sauce into each bun, then a spoonful of meat; top with a slice of cheese. Brown open buns in hot oven (400°) 8 to 10 minutes. Makes 6 servings.

NIPPY CHEESE LOAF

Sprinkle dried parsley flakes on cheese-topped slices before baking

1 (5 oz.) jar sharp pasteurized process cheese spread
1 tsp. Worcestershire sauce
Dash of Tabasco sauce (optional)
¼ tsp. garlic salt
1 large loaf Italian or homemade bread

• Soften cheese spread at room temperature. Stir in remaining ingredients, except bread.
• Slice bread in thick slices almost through bottom crust and spread cheese mixture generously on one side of slices.
• Wrap loaf in foil; leave foil open at top. Heat in moderate oven (375°) 15 to 20 minutes. Makes 6 to 8 servings.

CONEY ISLAND HOT DOGS

Milder than most "Coneys" with a peppy, tomato-chili flavor

1 (15 oz.) can chili con carne
1 (6 oz.) can tomato paste
1 tsp. prepared mustard
10 frankfurters
10 frankfurter buns

• Combine chili con carne, tomato paste and mustard in saucepan; heat.
• Heat frankfurters in hot water, but do not boil.
• Toast split buns. Place a frankfurter in each bun and spoon heated mixture over. Makes 10 servings.

HOT DOGS IN BREAD JACKETS: Spread fresh bread slices lightly with butter. Lay a frankfurter diagonally on each slice. Fold opposite corners of bread slice over frank and secure with toothpick. Brush top of sandwiches at fold with butter. Broil 6″ from heat to brown bread without burning and to heat frankfurter. Serve hot-dog relish at ends of sandwiches.

Note: A clever, thrifty cook invented these sandwiches to please her sons and to come out even—buns come in packages of 8, and a 1 lb. package contains 10 frankfurters. Be sure to use fresh bread so it will fold without breaking.

Country Egg Sandwiches

When you're visiting Colorado mountain country, you'll doubtless be served the Denver Sandwich. In its simplest form the filling is made of beaten egg with bits of chopped onion and crisp bacon, browned on both sides and served in buns. And if you order the sandwich in Denver restaurants, the waiter is likely to ask: "With or without green peppers?" There are now many versions of the original.

Our Deviled Denver Sandwich Filling has the green peppers, but deviled ham substitutes for the bacon. Try it, and also try Baked Egg Sandwich Loaf, developed in our Countryside Test Kitchens. You can get the loaf ready ahead to bake at mealtime.

DEVILED DENVER SANDWICH FILLING

Shake up and cook this sandwich filling at the last minute

2 eggs
1 tblsp. instant or fresh minced onion
1 tblsp. minced green pepper
1 tblsp. milk
1 (2¼ oz.) can deviled ham
1 tblsp. butter or bacon drippings

• Put ingredients, except butter, in jar. Cover and shake to blend (or use electric blender). Pour into skillet containing butter, melted, and brown on both sides. Makes filling for 2 sandwiches.

Note: Serve on split buns or between buttered bread slices.

BAKED EGG SANDWICH LOAF

Bacon and eggs in a new sandwich. Fix ahead, chill and bake at mealtime

1 tblsp. prepared mustard
1½ tsp. Worcestershire sauce
1 tsp. minced onion
1 tblsp. lemon juice
4 drops Tabasco sauce
½ tsp. salt
⅛ tsp. pepper
⅔ c. salad dressing
4 slices crisp-cooked bacon, crumbled
10 hard-cooked eggs, minced
1 (1 lb.) loaf dry white bread
3 tblsp. melted butter
2 tblsp. grated Parmesan cheese

• Combine mustard, Worcestershire sauce, onion, lemon juice, Tabasco

sauce, salt, pepper and salad dressing. Stir in bacon and eggs; mix well.
• Spread one side of each bread slice with egg salad. Stack slices back into loaf shape on a greased baking sheet. To hold, press a 3″ strip of foil around the loaf, lengthwise. Bake in very hot oven (450°) 10 minutes. Brush top with butter; sprinkle with cheese. Bake 8 minutes longer or until golden brown. Serve on a platter (remove foil strip). Makes 10 to 12 servings.

Boys' Breakfast Sandwiches

Why not have hearty, hot sandwiches for a breakfast surprise? It's a splendid way to tempt boys to eat. Mothers report that fast-fix, hot sandwiches are as well received for the first meal of the day as for lunch, supper and substantial snacks. Serve them morning, night or noon—whenever you have hungry youngsters to feed.

FRANKFURTER/EGG: Cut hot frankfurters in round slices; arrange these "pennies" on buttered toast. Top with scrambled eggs and hurry to the table.

EGG/CHEESE WITH HELP-YOURSELF TOPPINGS: Toast hamburger buns, split in halves. Top with hot scrambled eggs. Pass bowls of grated cheese and crumbled crisp bacon to sprinkle on top.

HAM/CHEESE IN FOIL: Split and butter hamburger buns. Insert a thin slice of boiled or baked ham and a slice of process American cheese in each. Wrap in foil. If you do this in the evening, store sandwich bundles in refrigerator. Put sandwiches on a baking sheet and bake in moderate oven (350°) 20 minutes, 5 minutes longer if sandwiches have been chilled. Serve in foil, opened at the top.

WAFFLED HAM: Spread bread slices on both sides with soft butter, a bit of prepared mustard folded in; put together in pairs with sliced cooked ham or luncheon meat. Toast sandwiches in waffle iron until browned, about 1 minute. Children like to brown their own.

PEANUT BUTTER/BACON: Spread peanut butter on bread slices; drizzle on a little honey. Add crumbled, crisp-cooked bacon. Heat in broiler until edges of bread are crisp. An all-boy favorite. Make it with raisin bread for a change.

BACON/EGG: Butter 2 bread slices. Cook 1 bacon slice in heavy skillet; remove and keep warm. Pour off excess fat. Break an egg into a measuring cup, season with salt and pepper and beat lightly with a fork. Pour egg into skillet; do not stir. When it is set on bottom, turn like a pancake and remove skillet from heat. Lift egg with spatula to one of the bread slices. Dot with ketchup. Add bacon, crumbled. Top with other bread slice and serve immediately. You can make 3 egg fillings at a time.

French Toast in Sandwiches

Dry bread makes the best French toast and French toast makes the best ham/cheese sandwiches. At least this is the verdict of men who have sampled our Frenched Ham

Sandwich. With French toast in the freezer, you can assemble and bake the sandwiches in half an hour. Buttered asparagus or peas and a mixed fruit salad round out the menu.

FROZEN FRENCH TOAST

Make, package and freeze French toast when you have dry bread on hand

4 eggs, beaten
2 tsp. sugar
½ tsp. salt
¼ tsp. ground nutmeg
¼ tsp. vanilla (optional)
1½ c. milk
8 slices day-old bread (very dry)
Butter or regular margarine

• Combine eggs, sugar, seasonings, vanilla and milk in large bowl; beat well. Dip each bread slice so it will absorb as much egg mixture as possible.
• Brown bread on both sides in butter in skillet over moderate heat. Cool.
• To freeze, lay slices on greased baking sheet; put in freezer. When frozen, stack slices with foil or freezer paper between; wrap, seal and freeze. Makes 8 slices.

Note: Storage time in freezer is 2 to 3 months. To serve as toast, thaw in toaster.

FRENCHED HAM SANDWICH

Hearty—a snap to fix when you have French toast in your freezer

6 slices baked ham
6 slices mild cheese
12 slices Frozen French Toast
2 tblsp. butter or regular margarine

• Place 1 slice ham and 1 slice cheese between 2 slices toast; place in shallow baking pan with melted butter. Bake in hot oven (425°) 15 to 20 minutes. Turn once. Makes 6 sandwiches.

Chicken, Turkey and Other Hot Sandwiches

SAUCY CHICKEN/CHEESE SANDWICH

Start the meal with tomato juice—also have molded fruit salad

1 can condensed cream of chicken soup
⅓ c. milk
⅓ c. shredded sharp Cheddar cheese
1 (5 to 6 oz.) can chicken, cubed, or ⅔ c. cooked cubed chicken
1 (14½ oz.) can cut asparagus, drained
6 slices toast

• Blend soup and milk in saucepan. Add cheese, chicken and asparagus. Heat until cheese is melted, stirring occasionally. Serve over toast. Makes 6 servings.

Note: Add ¼ c. sliced pimiento-stuffed olives for additional flavor and color.

FRENCH CHICKEN SANDWICH

Serve with cranberry sauce and celery

1 egg, beaten
2 tblsp. milk
4 slices bread, day old
8 slices cooked chicken
1 can condensed cream of chicken soup

• Blend together egg and milk.
• Cut bread slices diagonally. Dip in

milk-egg mixture. Brown lightly on both sides in small amount of hot fat in heavy skillet. Arrange in baking pan.

· Cover with chicken. Pour on soup. Bake in moderate oven (375°) 20 minutes. Makes 4 servings.

GRILLED TURKEY SANDWICH

Melted cheese bubbles atop turkey and spicy ham on toasted bread

8 slices bread
1 (4½ oz.) can deviled ham
8 to 12 slices cooked turkey
8 slices process cheese (8 oz. pkg.)

· Toast bread lightly on one side under broiler. Turn over and spread untoasted side with deviled ham. Cover with turkey; top with cheese slice.

· Broil until cheese is delicately browned and bubbly. Serve hot. Makes 8.

BAKED ASPARAGUS/CHEESE SANDWICH

Serve with baked ham slices, relishes and lemon meringue pie

6 thick (¾") slices firm-textured bread (like home-baked)
6 (3½" square) slices process Swiss cheese
4 eggs
2 c. milk
1 tsp. salt
⅛ tsp. pepper
¼ tsp. ground nutmeg
1 tblsp. finely chopped onion
18 cooked asparagus spears
½ c. shredded Cheddar cheese

· Trim crusts from bread slices. Arrange bread slices in bottom of 13 × 9 × 2" pan or glass dish. Top each bread slice with a slice of process Swiss cheese.

· In a bowl, beat eggs slightly; add milk, stir in seasonings and onion. Pour this mixture over sandwiches and bake in slow oven (325°) 25 minutes.

· Remove from oven. Top each bread slice with 3 cooked asparagus spears. Sprinkle on shredded Cheddar cheese. Return dish to oven and continue to bake 10 to 15 minutes, until custard sets and top is golden. Allow to stand 5 minutes before serving. Makes 6 servings.

HOT MEAT AND CHEESE DOGS

Fix ahead to bake after the gang arrives—a favorite with men and boys

8 Coney buns (long)
Butter or regular margarine, softened
1 (12 oz.) can luncheon meat, diced
½ c. process cheese spread
2 tblsp. pickle relish
3 tblsp. minced onion
1 tsp. poppy seeds
2 tsp. prepared mustard
2 tblsp. melted butter or regular margarine

· Spread buns with softened butter. Mix remaining ingredients and spoon into buttered buns. Wrap individually in foil.

· (Freeze if desired. Defrost 1 hour in foil.)

· Place foil-wrapped buns on baking sheet; heat in slow oven (300°) 20 minutes. Makes 8 servings.

More Sandwich Selections

Many sandwich-makers improvise using the ingredients on hand. And with remarkably good results, as the four recipes that follow indicate. A woman designed these sandwiches to make use of such foods as a bountiful tomato supply, leftover beef roast, canned deviled ham and mushroom soup, peanut butter and part of a loaf of raisin bread. Sandwich-making encourages experimentation. Why not add your own touches to recipes you use?

TOMATO/BACON SANDWICHES: Split buns in half, toast and butter. Lay a slice of peeled tomato on each bun half. Pour your favorite cheese sauce, heated, over tomatoes and top each sandwich with 2 slices (crisscross fashion) of crisp cooked bacon.

ROAST BEEF SANDWICHES: Cover 4 buttered toast slices with thin slices of leftover roast beef. Top with thin tomato slices and sprinkle with seasoned salt. Combine ½ c. mayonnaise with 1½ c. grated Cheddar or Parmesan cheese and brush on sandwich tops. Broil just long enough to brown.

HAM/EGG SANDWICHES: Spread toast with deviled ham. Top with hard-cooked egg slices. Heat canned condensed cream of mushroom soup, adding milk for the consistency you desire. Spoon over toast and serve at once.

BUTTER-BROWNED PEANUT SANDWICHES: Make sandwiches with peanut butter and raisin bread. Spread outside of sandwiches (both sides) with soft butter or regular margarine. Brown in heavy skillet.

Baked Bean Sandwiches

With a can of baked beans and a bottle of ketchup in the kitchen, you have the makings for quick, substantial supper sandwiches. Teamed with cabbage or apple salad and ice cream for dessert, no one goes hungry. Brown Bean Sandwiches, Boston-style, use canned bread, while Midwestern-style Baked Bean Stack-ups call for buns.

BAKED BEAN STACK-UPS

Try these quick and easy hot sandwiches—they rate with all ages

3 hot dog buns, halved
Butter or regular margarine
1 (1 lb.) can baked beans, or 2 c. leftover baked beans
3 to 4 tblsp. ketchup
⅓ lb. process cheese, shredded
6 slices bacon

• Toast cut sides of bun halves under broiler until lightly browned. Spread with butter.

• Top buns with beans, ketchup and cheese; lay a bacon slice over each. Broil about 3″ from heat until cheese is melted and bacon is crisp. Serve very hot. Makes 6 servings.

Note: You can use round hamburger buns instead of long hot dog buns. Just cut each bacon slice in half and arrange over top of each sandwich.

BROWN BEAN SANDWICHES

Don't bother to measure ketchup—just shake it on from bottle

1 (9 oz.) can brown bread
1 (about 1 lb.) can New England-style baked beans
Ketchup

· Cut bread in 10 slices; top each slice with baked beans. Shake ketchup on sandwich tops, as much as you like.
· Bake on ungreased baking sheet in moderate oven (375°) 8 to 10 minutes. Makes 5 servings.

Fish Sandwiches

Fish sandwiches are no strangers in country homes. Fried oysters tucked in buns or between bread slices are an old-time favorite in Maryland's oyster territory. Tuna sandwiches are popular everywhere. Cheese/Tuna Surprise is a splendid choice if you like to get "main dish" sandwiches ready in advance to bake at mealtime. Glazed Crab Sandwiches are special-occasion treats.

CHEESE/TUNA SURPRISE

It's fun to unwrap and eat this tasty fix-ahead family sandwich

1 c. cubed sharp cheese (¼ lb.)
1 (7 oz.) can tuna, flaked
2 tblsp. chopped onion
2 tblsp. chopped sweet pickles
3 hard-cooked eggs, chopped
2 tblsp. diced green pepper
2 tblsp. chopped pimiento-stuffed olives
½ c. mayonnaise or salad dressing
6 hot dog buns

· Combine cheese, tuna, onion, pickles, eggs, green pepper, olives and mayonnaise. Spread on buns, cut in halves lengthwise.
· Place sandwiches on baking sheet. Heat in very slow oven (250°) 30 minutes. Or wrap in foil and refrigerate a few hours if you wish to make them ahead. Heat and serve in foil. Makes 6 servings.

GLAZED CRAB SANDWICHES

Delicious for an evening company snack or a family supper or lunch

1 c. crabmeat or 1 (7½ oz.) can
2 tblsp. chopped green onion
1 tblsp. lemon juice
2 tblsp. ketchup or chili sauce
6 slices toast
½ c. mayonnaise
¼ c. grated Cheddar cheese

· Combine crab, onion, lemon juice and ketchup; mix well. Spread mixture on toast slices.
· Frost top of each sandwich with mayonnaise and cheese, mixed together. Run under broiler a few minutes or until crab mixture is heated and glazed by topping. Makes 6 sandwiches.

Note: You can put a thin slice of tomato on each slice of toast before adding crab mixture. Or top crab on each sandwich with 2 slices of avocado before adding the mayonnaise and cheese.

Frozen Sandwiches

Country women who pack lunches praise frozen sandwiches. They make them at slack times to have ready for quick use. These filling recipes make 6 sandwiches. They keep in the freezer 2 to 3 weeks in excellent condition—thaw in 3 hours. While fillings introduce pleasing variety, different breads also provide change. Package sandwiches separately in good freezer wrapping material.

BEEF AND KETCHUP FILLING

1¼ c. cooked ground beef
½ tsp. salt
1 tsp. Worcestershire sauce
⅓ c. ketchup
1 tblsp. softened butter or regular margarine

• Mix all ingredients together. Makes about 1⅓ cups, enough for 6 sandwiches.

BAKED BEAN AND SALAMI FILLING

1 (1 lb.) can baked beans (2 c.)
1 c. finely chopped salami (¼ lb.)
2 tblsp. chili sauce
2 tsp. prepared mustard

• Mix together all ingredients. Makes about 2¾ cups, enough for 6 sandwiches.

SARDINE AND PIMIENTO FILLING

2 (3¼ oz.) cans sardines
¼ c. ketchup
1 tblsp. lemon juice
2 tblsp. chopped pimiento or olives

• Combine ingredients; stir lightly. Makes about ¾ cup, enough for 6 sandwiches.

CHICKEN AND PICKLE FILLING

1¼ c. cooked, chopped chicken or tuna, flaked
¼ c. chopped pickle
1 tsp. Worcestershire sauce
⅓ c. condensed cream of chicken soup
¼ tsp. celery salt

• Combine ingredients. Makes about 1⅓ cups, enough for 6 sandwiches.

CREAM CHEESE/DRIED BEEF FILLING

1 (3 oz.) pkg. cream cheese
1 tblsp. milk (optional)
½ c. shredded dried beef
1 tblsp. prepared horse-radish
1 tblsp. light cream

• Blend cheese and milk. Stir in remaining ingredients and mix well. Makes about ¾ cup, enough for 6 sandwiches.

Note: Some country women prefer to freeze sandwich fillings in little frozen food containers to make sandwiches when needed. The best way to thaw the filling to spreading consistency is to place it in the refrigerator overnight. When salad dressing is called for, add it sparingly—just barely enough to give the filling spreading consistency.

Suggestions for Sandwich Fillings

LIVERWURST with chopped, pimiento-stuffed olives or dill pickles mixed in.

PEANUT BUTTER with orange marmalade and honey added for easy spreading.

BACON, cooked crisp and crumbled, in peanut butter.

CHEESE AND DATES, ground in equal parts, moistened for spreading consistency with orange juice. Point up flavor with a dash of grated orange peel. Add finely chopped nuts for variety.

BROWN BREAD, spread with butter and then with prepared mustard. Top with mashed baked beans, or omit mustard and add finely chopped mustard pickles to the beans.

GROUND COOKED CHICKEN and cream cheese, mixed and moistened with lemon juice.

SARDINES, canned in oil, drained, bones and skins removed, mashed with hard-cooked egg yolk. Add a dash of lemon juice.

HAM, cooked, chopped and mixed with cream cheese and finely chopped pimiento-stuffed olives or dill pickles.

ROAST BEEF, left over, chopped and mixed with chopped pickle and salad dressing.

CHICKEN, cooked, ground, with chopped pimiento added and just enough salad dressing for spreading consistency.

SALMON OR TUNA, canned, drained and mashed with pickle relish and a little salad dressing.

HAM, cooked, chopped and mixed with pickle relish and a little salad dressing.

Glamorous Sandwich Loaf

Of all cold sandwiches none surpasses Ribbon Sandwich Loaf for eye-appeal and flavor richness. To cut a loaf of bread in even lengthwise slices, trim off the crust and then make a cutting guide by inserting rows of picks in bread to mark the width of the sandwich layers.

Beat the cream cheese for the "frosting" with your electric mixer so it will be fluffy. Tint it delicately with a few drops of food color if you wish. Spread a thin layer over the loaf and then swirl on the remainder. Chill the loaf at least 30 minutes. Then cover it with a damp cloth; chill at least 2 hours.

To dramatize the loaf, slice it at the table. Use a cake server to deliver the slices to individual plates. This, of course, is a sandwich to eat with forks.

RIBBON SANDWICH LOAF

When sliced, the party sandwiches look like striped ribbon

1 loaf (14 oz. or 16 oz.) day-old bread, unsliced
Butter or regular margarine
½ lb. sharp process cheese, sliced
Egg Filling
Ham Filling
3 (3 oz.) pkgs. cream cheese
⅓ c. light cream or top milk

• Remove crust from bread. With sharp knife cut lengthwise into 6 slices. Butter one side of each slice.
• On two slices, butter side up, place sliced cheese; spread two slices with Egg Filling; then one with Ham Filling.

• Stack slices, with Ham Filling in middle. Top with remaining bread slice. Press together firmly.
• Combine cream cheese (at room temperature) with cream. Beat until smooth and fluffy. Spread mixture over top and sides of loaf. Chill loaf several hours. (For a pretty garnish, decorate top with gay pimiento flowers and green pepper leaves.) Cut in 10 (1″) slices. Makes 10 servings.

EGG FILLING: Combine 5 chopped hard-cooked eggs, 1 tblsp. chopped celery, 2 tsp. minced onion, ½ tsp. salt, ½ tsp. prepared mustard and 3 tblsp. mayonnaise.

HAM FILLING: Combine ½ lb. ground cooked ham and contents of 1 (2¼ oz.) can deviled ham with 1 or 2 tblsp. mayonnaise.

SANDWICH CAKE

Yellow cheese frosting gives the sandwich a festive Halloween look

1 (8″) round loaf rye bread
6 c. chicken salad
3 to 4 (5 oz.) jars sharp process cheese spread
2 or 3 tblsp. milk

• Remove outside crust from fresh loaf rye (or white) bread. Cut crosswise into four equal slices.
• Put slices together like layer cake, using 2 c. of your favorite chicken salad mixture between each pair bread slices, 6 c. filling in all. (Other good fillings are ham, egg, tuna, salmon and finely cut shrimp salads. Two or three kinds may be used for each "cake.")
• Frost as you would cake with cheese thinned with milk to good spreading consistency. Chill several hours. Makes 16 to 20 servings.

Bologna/Cheese Sandwiches Satisfy

Boys especially give Bologna/Cheese Sandwiches enthusiastic reception. There are two reasons for their approval. They are triple-deckers, substantial enough to appease ravenous appetites.

BOLOGNA/CHEESE SANDWICHES

Two layers of this savory filling in every sandwich make it doubly good

½ lb. bologna
½ lb. process pimiento cheese
1 small onion
⅛ green pepper (optional)
6 small sweet pickles
½ tsp. salt
6 tblsp. salad dressing or mayonnaise
1 tsp. prepared mustard
Dark or light bread
Fresh garden lettuce

• Grind bologna, cheese, onion, green pepper and pickles into a bowl. Add salt, salad dressing and mustard.
• For each sandwich, butter lightly 3 slices bread. Spread two with about ¼ c. filling. Stack together with buttered slice in middle. Insert lettuce. Makes 2½ cups filling, enough for 10 triple sandwiches.

Note: Other types of favorite ready-to-serve sausages may be substituted for bologna. Or a leftover roast will combine very well with this filling mixture.

Pretty Party Sandwiches

Occasions when distinctly party sandwiches are in order include receptions and tea parties. Make the sandwiches dainty, flavorful and with color contrasts. Our Teatime Open-Face Sandwiches arranged on a display tray meet these requirements.

If you want to fix sandwiches ahead and freeze them, read Ideas for Fancy Sandwiches, which follows the Teatime recipe. These dainties have filling spread between bread cut in fancy shapes. Spread the bread first with butter to prevent filling from soaking in and making sandwiches soggy.

TEATIME OPEN-FACE SANDWICHES

Tiny sandwiches for the tea party are so pretty that the work involved in making them is rewarding. Open-face sandwiches are especially attractive. Butter single slices of bread, crusts removed, and cut them in small, fancy shapes with a sharp knife or cookie cutters. Spread on buttered side with the filling, then garnish.

You don't need recipes for these fancies, but here are a few suggestions; they indicate how simple teatime sandwiches can be:

- Spread with currant, or other red jelly, and sprinkle with flaked coconut.
- Arrange thin slices pimiento-stuffed olives on small rounds of buttered bread. Put a little snipped parsley in the center.
- Spread bread with your favorite cheese spread; roll edges of sandwiches in finely snipped chives or parsley.
- Place small, thin cucumber slice on buttered rounds of bread; ring with thin red radish slices, cut in halves.
- Spread half of sandwich with pineapple/cheese spread, the other half with deviled ham or jelly.

CUCUMBER SANDWICHES

Refreshing American version of the English classic teatime special

- With a very sharp knife, cut off both ends of long unsliced buns (Coney buns). Then carefully slice the buns thin. Spread one side of each slice with butter and then with mayonnaise. Cut a cucumber, peeled or unpeeled, as you like, in thin slices. Let stand in ice water until crisp. Drain and dry on towels. Place a cucumber slice between two slices of bread. If you have cucumbers in your garden, try to select them with the same diameter as that of the sliced rolls. If cucumber slices are too large, trim them to fit.

Ideas for Fancy Sandwiches

Use a variety of breads and cut buttered slices in fancy shapes with cookie cutters. Make small, dainty sandwiches. Pack party sandwiches for freezing in layers with a sheet of plastic wrap between. Put only one kind of sandwich in a container to avoid mixing flavors. Pack in good freezer containers and freeze immediately.

CREAM CHEESE, softened at room temperature and whipped until very light and fluffy. Use food color to tint cheese delicate pastel colors.

LIVERWURST, spread on bread and garnished with strips or cutouts of pimientos.

PEANUT BUTTER, mixed with chopped dates with orange marmalade added for spreading consistency.

CHEESE/TUNA: 1 c. grated Cheddar cheese mixed with ½ c. tuna, drained. Add finely chopped dill pickle and a little salad dressing.

CHEESE/OLIVE: 1 (3 oz.) pkg. cream cheese mixed with 8 ripe olives, pitted and finely chopped. Point up flavors with lemon juice.

DEVILED HAM, mixed with finely chopped nuts and spread on rye bread. Use canned ham. Add a little horse-radish if desired.

BACON/CHEESE: Crumbled, crisp-cooked bacon mixed into cream cheese with a little grated orange peel added.

chapter 7

Variety in Vegetables

DID YOU EVER DIG tiny new potatoes with skins so delicate you could almost rub them off? And hurry from the garden with peas that had pods so crisp they squeaked when clutched in your hand? If so, you know how marvelous garden-fresh vegetables can taste.

Not all country families have gardens in these busy times, but usually enough people in a neighborhood grow more vegetables than they can use, to make sharing possible. The trend, though, is to greater involvement with the soil, planting, weeding and watching vegetables partly for the pleasure it provides. And for good eating!

You will find variety in the vegetables listed in this chapter's recipes. More than thirty different kinds appear, but they barely scratch the surface of our recipe collection. (Our FARM JOURNAL cookbook, *America's Best Vegetable Recipes,* features forty-one different vegetables.)

It's the country custom with fresh vegetables to use them as soon as possible after they reach the kitchen and to cook them just until they are tender–often tender-crisp. If cooking in water, the rule is to use a small amount of boiling salted water, 1 tsp. salt to 1 c. water, unless recipe directs otherwise.

Since homegrown vegetables do not remain in season year-round, country women, when they can find time, freeze and can the surplus if crops are bountiful. They also use many frozen, canned and dried vegetables from their supermarkets.

Asparagus Announces Spring's Arrival

Tender, crisp asparagus stalks bring spring to country tables. American-Chinese Asparagus is one favored way to fix the vegetable. When winter comes, frozen asparagus often finds a place, in combination with sliced hard-cooked eggs—Winter Take-Along Casserole is a delicious example.

PIE-PAN ASPARAGUS

Chicken broth and two cheeses highlight the delicate asparagus taste

¼ c. butter or regular margarine
¼ c. flour
¾ c. chicken broth
¾ c. milk
½ c. grated Cheddar cheese
¼ c. grated Parmesan cheese
½ tsp. salt
⅛ tsp. pepper
2 lbs. hot, freshly cooked medium asparagus spears (about 32 to 36)
2 tblsp. grated Parmesan cheese

• Melt butter in saucepan; blend in flour. Add chicken broth (canned or homemade) and milk and cook, stirring constantly, until mixture is thick and bubbly. Add Cheddar cheese, ¼ c. Parmesan cheese, salt and pepper; stir until cheeses melt.
• Place asparagus in 10″ pie pan. Pour sauce over. Sprinkle with 2 tblsp. Parmesan cheese. Broil until bubbly. Makes 6 servings.

AMERICAN-CHINESE ASPARAGUS

This is a superior short-cook dish

2 lbs. asparagus
⅓ c. butter or regular margarine
⅓ c. water
½ tsp. salt
⅛ tsp. pepper

• Break off each asparagus stalk as far down as it snaps easily. Cut off scales with a knife. Scrub with soft brush to remove all sand. Lay 1 or 2 stalks together on a cutting board; cut diagonally, making bias slices about 1″ long and ¼″ thick. You will have about 4 c.
• Heat butter and water to boiling in heavy skillet with tight-fitting lid. Add asparagus and seasonings. Cover and cook over high heat 5 minutes, shaking skillet occasionally. Check with fork to see if asparagus is tender-crisp. If not, cook 1 or 2 minutes longer, adding 1 tblsp. water, if necessary—it should be evaporated at end of cooking. Serves 6.

WINTER TAKE-ALONG CASSEROLE

This tasty dish is popular at potluck suppers in the country

2 (10 oz.) pkgs. frozen asparagus
1 c. chopped onion
¼ c. butter or regular margarine
6 tblsp. flour
3 c. milk
2 tsp. salt
¼ tsp. pepper
4 hard-cooked eggs, sliced
½ c. shredded Cheddar cheese
½ c. dry bread crumbs

• Cook asparagus as directed on package until barely tender; drain.

• In a large skillet, cook onion in butter until tender (not brown). Stir in flour. Add milk and cook, stirring constantly, until thickened. Mix in salt, pepper, eggs, and asparagus.
• Turn into a 2-qt. casserole. Top with cheese and crumbs. Bake in moderate oven (350°) about 30 minutes, until hot and bubbly. Makes 8 servings.

GREEN BEANS WITH ALMONDS AND MUSHROOMS

Easy-to-fix company vegetable special

6 c. cut green beans (1½ lbs.)
3 tblsp. butter or regular margarine
¼ c. coarsely chopped toasted almonds
1 (4 oz.) can mushroom slices, drained
¾ tsp. salt
⅛ to ¼ tsp. savory leaves
1 tsp. lemon juice

• Cook green beans in boiling salted water until tender; drain.
• Melt butter and add almonds and drained mushrooms. Cook until mushrooms are heated. Add to beans along with remaining ingredients. Toss. Serve immediately. Makes 8 servings.

GREEN BEANS WITH DILL

Dill gives beans a flavor lift

3 tblsp. butter or regular margarine
⅔ c. chopped onions
1 c. water
½ c. chili sauce
½ tsp. dill weed
1½ tblsp. cornstarch
2 tblsp. water
3 c. cooked or canned green beans

• Melt butter in saucepan; add onions. Sauté until soft and clear. Add water, chili sauce and dill weed.
• Blend together cornstarch and water; add smooth paste to onion mixture. Cook, stirring, until thickened.
• Combine sauce and beans. Serves 6.

GREEN BEANS WITH BACON

You can't surpass the green bean-bacon team, as this recipe proves

2 to 3 slices bacon, cut in ½″ pieces
1 (16 to 17 oz.) can French-style green beans
2 green onions, finely cut
1 tsp. lemon juice
2 tsp. cornstarch
½ tsp. sugar
Salt
Pepper

• Fry bacon until crisp; drain off fat.
• Drain beans, reserving ½ c. liquid; add beans and onions to bacon.
• Combine bean liquid and lemon juice; stir in cornstarch. Add to beans; heat until sauce is thickened; add sugar and salt and pepper to taste. Serves 4 to 6.

GREEN BEANS WITH ORANGES

Easy; combines two well-liked foods

2 (10 oz.) pkgs. frozen whole green beans
1 (11 oz.) can mandarin oranges, drained
3 tblsp. butter
Salt and pepper to taste

• Cook beans according to package directions; drain. Add orange sections and butter. Heat through; season with salt and pepper. Makes 6 servings.

GOURMET SNAP BEANS

This is an elegant, simple vegetable dish—fix it for company

2 lbs. fresh green beans
1 tblsp. salt
2 qts. boiling water
3 tblsp. butter
2 tsp. lemon juice
2 tblsp. minced fresh parsley
½ tsp. salt
⅛ tsp. pepper

• Snap or cut off ends of beans. Just before cooking, wash quickly under warm water. Add beans and 1 tblsp. salt to boiling water. Bring quickly to a boil and cook, uncovered, until tender-crisp, about 10 to 15 minutes, the exact time depending on age of beans. (Some cooks test for doneness by eating a bean.)
• Drain beans into colander. To serve them right away, melt butter in large skillet. Add drained beans and stir and heat until hot. Remove from heat, add lemon juice, parsley, ½ tsp. salt and pepper; toss to distribute. Serve at once. Makes 8 servings.

Note: You can cook the beans early in the day if you like. Drain cooked beans and put them immediately into a kettle of very cold water to cool quickly (this stops the cooking and helps them stay green and tender-crisp). Drain cooled beans, cover and refrigerate. Reheat and season just before serving.

LIMA BEAN BARBECUE

Hearty supper dish that tastes great

2 c. dried lima beans (or 4 c. cooked or canned)
2 tsp. salt
1 lb. pork sausage links
½ c. chopped onions
1 c. ketchup
¼ c. liquid from cooked beans
1 tblsp. prepared horse-radish
1 tsp. Worcestershire sauce

• Cover dried beans with 5 c. water. Boil 2 minutes and then soak 1 hour, or overnight (cooking before soaking helps soften the skin which covers beans).
• Add salt and boil gently until tender—about 45 minutes for small lima beans, about 1 hour for large. Drain.
• Fry sausage until brown.
• Mix all ingredients, except sausage.
• Place half of bean mixture in 1½-qt. casserole. Cover with half the sausages. Add remaining bean mixture. Garnish top with rest of sausages.
• Bake in hot oven (400°) 15 minutes. Makes 6 servings.

SPANISH LIMAS

Tomatoes and cheese flavor beans

1 medium onion, chopped
1 green pepper, chopped
2 tblsp. butter or regular margarine
1 c. cooked or canned tomatoes
1 tsp. Worcestershire sauce
1 tsp. salt
¼ tsp. pepper
⅛ tsp. ground red pepper
2 c. cooked frozen or canned lima beans
1½ c. grated process cheese

• Fry onion and green pepper slowly in butter until golden. Add tomatoes; simmer 10 minutes. Add seasonings and well-drained beans; combine.

• Alternate layers of bean mixture and cheese in greased 1-qt. casserole.

• Bake in moderate oven (350°) 30 minutes. Makes 6 servings.

PARTY LIMAS

Orégano does something good to limas, as do cheese, bacon and garlic

- **3 slices bacon**
- **1 to 2 cloves garlic, minced**
- **⅛ tsp. orégano leaves**
- **1 (1 lb.) can green lima beans**
- **Salt**
- **Pepper**
- **¼ c. grated Parmesan cheese**

• Cook bacon until crisp; remove and drain. Add garlic to bacon fat; cook 1 to 2 minutes. Add orégano, 2 tblsp. liquid from limas and drained limas; heat. Season with salt and pepper to taste. Just before serving, stir in crumbled bacon and cheese. Makes 4 servings.

WAX BEANS PLUS

Mild cheese heightens delicate yellow bean taste and dill enhances it

- **4 c. wax beans, cut in 1″ pieces**
- **1 (3 oz.) pkg. cream cheese, softened**
- **1 tblsp. milk**
- **¾ tsp. dill seeds**
- **½ tsp. salt**
- **⅛ tsp. pepper**
- **2 tblsp. chopped parsley**

• Cook beans in boiling salted water until just tender; drain.

• Stir together cream cheese, milk, dill seeds, salt and pepper. Add to drained hot beans and toss until cheese is hot. Sprinkle with parsley. Serves 4.

Homespun Baked Beans

It all started with the Indians who taught early colonists how to use bean pots and to depend on slow and easy cooking. Baked beans rate as a hearty farm treat that men and boys especially like. Sometimes country women open cans of baked beans from supermarkets and add their own touches. On other occasions, they make up the traditional recipes and freeze the surplus for quick heating in the future. A combination of several kinds of canned beans results in another type of dish that's especially popular along the West Coast—Western Baked Beans. These get a big hand at community suppers. The recipe comes from Washington State.

WESTERN BAKED BEANS

Four-in-one baked beans. Use 1 cup sugar for beans on the sweet side

- **8 slices bacon**
- **4 large onions, sliced and separated in rings**
- **½ to 1 c. brown sugar, firmly packed**
- **1 tsp. dry mustard**
- **½ tsp. garlic powder (optional)**
- **1 tsp. salt**
- **½ c. cider vinegar**

2 (15 oz.) cans dried lima beans, drained
1 (1 lb.) can green lima beans, drained
1 (1 lb.) can dark red kidney beans, drained
1 (1 lb. 11 oz.) jar New England-style baked beans, undrained

• Pan-fry bacon until crisp, drain on paper towels and set aside.
• Place onion rings in a large skillet and add the sugar, mustard, garlic powder, salt and vinegar. Cover and cook 20 minutes.
• Add onion mixture to the beans and stir in the bacon, crumbled. Pour into a 3-qt. casserole.
• Bake, covered, ½ hour in a moderate oven (350°). Uncover and bake ½ hour longer. Makes 12 servings.

BAKED BEANS MICHIGAN

Apples are the unusual tasty addition

2 lbs. dried navy beans
9 c. water
1 lb. salt pork, diced
3 tart apples, peeled, cored and coarsely cut
1 medium onion, chopped
½ c. brown sugar, firmly packed
½ c. molasses
3 tsp. dry mustard
3 tblsp. vinegar
¼ tsp. pepper

• Wash beans and soak overnight in water. Add salt pork; cook in kettle until beans are tender, about 1 hour.
• Pour bean mixture into a bean pot, add remaining ingredients and bake, covered, 6 hours in slow oven (300°). Add more warm water during cooking if necessary. Makes 10 servings.

BOSTON BAKED BEANS

The traditional New England dish

2 lbs. dried navy or pea beans
1 tblsp. salt
2 to 4 tblsp. brown sugar
½ c. molasses
1 tsp. dry mustard
½ to ¾ lb. salt pork

• Wash and soak beans overnight in water to cover. Drain, place in saucepan, cover with water and simmer until skins burst, 1½ to 2 hours.
• Turn beans into bean pot or heavy casserole without draining. Combine salt, brown sugar, molasses and mustard with 1 c. boiling water; pour over beans.
• Scrape pork rind and cut gashes in fat ½" apart. Press into beans leaving only rind exposed.
• Cover pot and bake in very slow oven (275°) 6 to 8 hours without stirring, but adding more water as needed to keep beans moist. Remove cover last ½ hour of baking. Makes 8 servings.

Variation

VERMONT BAKED BEANS: Omit brown sugar and molasses and add ½ c. maple syrup. Put an onion in bottom of pot before adding beans.

Indian Pinto Beans

Pinto beans are important crops in Colorado and New Mexico, where they are great favorites. You find them for sale in many states, however. The spotted beans take the spotlight in Indian Beans, an unusual and delicious dish. It's the long and easy cooking that makes them taste so good.

INDIAN BEANS

It takes time to cook pinto beans—their taste makes it time well spent

1 lb. dried pinto beans
3 qts. water
1 (1 lb.) can tomatoes
1 large onion, chopped
8 slices bacon, cut in 2″ lengths
¾ c. sliced celery
1½ tsp. salt
¾ tsp. ground cinnamon
6 tblsp. sugar
3 tblsp. vinegar

• Wash beans; place in 6-qt. kettle with 3 qts. water and bring to a simmer. Cover; cook 4 hours, or until tender.
• Mix remaining ingredients with beans and cooking water. Place in 4-qt. casserole; cover and bake in moderate oven (350°) 2 to 3 hours, or until done. Add water if necessary. Serves 10 to 12.

KIDNEY BEAN BAKE

Pickle relish adds a new flavor

2 (1 lb.) cans red kidney beans
½ tsp. salt
½ c. chili sauce
¼ c. pickle relish
1 medium onion, thinly sliced
1 tblsp. butter or regular margarine

• Drain 1 can beans and add to entire contents of second can. Add salt, chili sauce, relish and onion. Mix well. Put in 1½-qt. casserole; dot with butter. Cover and bake in moderate oven (375°) 35 minutes. Makes 4 servings.

KIDNEY BEAN RABBIT

Serve with a green or tomato salad

¼ c. chopped onion
½ c. chopped green pepper
2 tblsp. butter or regular margarine
1 (1 lb. 4 oz.) can kidney beans, drained (2½ c.)
2 tblsp. ketchup
1 tsp. Worcestershire sauce
½ tsp. salt
⅛ tsp. pepper
½ lb. process cheese, diced

• Cook onion and green pepper in butter until soft. Add beans, ketchup, Worcestershire sauce and seasonings.
• Alternate layers of bean mixture and cheese in greased 1-qt. casserole. Bake in moderate oven (350°) about 20 minutes. Makes 4 servings.

Colorful Beets

Beets add color charm to country meals the year round. It's this decorative gift of the vegetable that has much to do with the wide use of pickled beets. Country women believe that a touch of horse-radish complements most beet dishes. Fix Horse-radish Beets the next time you serve pork, and see if your family doesn't like the flavor combination.

HORSE-RADISH BEETS

You'll want to double this flavorful recipe when there's company

2 tblsp. butter or regular margarine
2 tblsp. flour
½ tsp. salt
1 c. milk

3 tblsp. prepared horse-radish
3 c. diced cooked beets

• Melt butter in saucepan. Stir in flour and salt. Gradually add milk; cook, stirring, until thick and smooth. Add horse-radish and mix well.
• Pour sauce over hot beets. Serve immediately. Makes 4 to 6 servings.

HONEYED BEETS

Honey, vinegar and onion—no wonder these beets taste extra-good

½ c. honey
2 tblsp. vinegar
2 (1 lb.) cans sliced beets
2 tblsp. butter
1 medium onion, sliced and separated into rings

• In a saucepan blend honey, vinegar and 2 tblsp. beet liquid. Add butter, beets and onion rings. Simmer until heated through, stirring occasionally. Do not overcook as onion rings should remain crisp. Makes 8 servings.

PINEAPPLE BEETS

Pleasing way to perk up beets when you serve them often

1 (13½ oz.) can pineapple chunks
½ c. water
⅓ c. cider vinegar
4 tblsp. brown sugar
1 tblsp. cornstarch
½ tsp. salt
⅛ tsp. ground ginger
2 (1 lb.) cans sliced beets, drained (4 c.)

• Drain syrup from pineapple and mix with water and vinegar. Mix brown sugar, cornstarch, salt and ginger; add vinegar mixture. Cook until thickened, stirring constantly. Add beets, then heat to boiling. Just before serving, mix pineapple into hot mixture. Serves 8.

Broccoli and Sprouts

The mother who shares this recipe with you has great respect for the orange sauce. She says it taught her children how good broccoli can be.

FRESH BROCCOLI WITH ORANGE SAUCE

1½ lbs. fresh broccoli, or 2 (10 oz.) pkgs. frozen broccoli
2 tblsp. butter or regular margarine
2 tblsp. flour
1 c. fresh orange juice
⅛ tsp. salt
Paprika

• Wash broccoli; cook in a little salted water until tender-crisp. (Cook frozen broccoli as directed on package.)
• Meanwhile, melt butter in small saucepan; blend in flour and cook a few minutes. Add orange juice and salt; cook and stir until thick and smooth.
• Drain broccoli and serve with orange sauce. Top with a sprinkle of paprika. Makes 4 to 5 servings.

BROCCOLI PLATTER

Easy sauce is a new touch, but peanuts on top are the surprise

2 tblsp. minced onion
2 tblsp. butter or regular margarine
1 c. dairy sour cream
½ tsp. poppy seeds
½ tsp. paprika
¼ tsp. salt
⅛ tsp. ground red pepper
2 lbs. cooked broccoli, salted
⅓ c. chopped salted peanuts

• Sauté onion in butter; remove from heat. Stir in sour cream, poppy seeds, paprika, salt and red pepper; heat over boiling water.
• Arrange hot broccoli on heated platter; pour warm sauce over top. Sprinkle with peanuts (or cashews for company). Makes 6 to 8 servings.

BROCCOLI AND RICE

If you use frozen chopped broccoli stir lightly just before serving

2 c. hot water
1 (1 to 1½ oz.) pkg. onion soup mix
1⅓ c. packaged precooked rice
2 tblsp. butter
1 tsp. salt
¼ tsp. pepper
1 tblsp. lemon juice
1 (10 oz.) pkg. frozen broccoli (chopped or whole stalks)

• Add hot water to onion soup mix. Stir; add rice, butter, salt, pepper and lemon juice.
• Place frozen broccoli in greased 2-qt. casserole. Pour rice mixture over. Cover with a tight-fitting lid and bake in moderate oven (375°) 45 minutes. Makes 4 servings.

BROCCOLI SOUFFLÉ

The soufflé falls slightly during baking—it's light and flavorful

1 (10 oz.) pkg. frozen chopped broccoli
3 tblsp. butter or regular margarine
3 tblsp. flour
1 c. milk
½ tsp. salt
⅛ tsp. ground nutmeg
1 tsp. lemon juice
4 egg yolks, beaten
4 egg whites, beaten until stiff

• Cook broccoli according to package directions; drain.
• Meanwhile, melt butter in saucepan; blend in flour; add milk gradually, stirring constantly. Cook and stir until thick and smooth. Add salt, nutmeg and lemon juice; mix sauce into broccoli. Add egg yolks and let stand to cool.
• About 30 minutes before serving time, turn broccoli mixture into greased 1½-qt. casserole. Carefully fold in egg whites. Bake in hot oven (400°) 25 minutes. Makes 4 to 6 servings.

CASSEROLE OF CURRIED BROCCOLI AND ONIONS

Vegetables with pronounced flavors like these are great with game

1 (10 oz.) pkg. frozen broccoli
3 tblsp. butter or regular margarine
3 tblsp. flour
½ tsp. curry powder
¼ tsp. paprika
Dash ground red pepper
1½ c. milk
½ c. grated or shredded sharp process cheese
1 (15½ oz.) can small whole onions (2 c. cooked)

• Cook broccoli as directed on package.
• Melt butter; add flour and seasonings. Blend. Add milk; cook, stirring constantly, until thickened. Add cheese; stir until melted.
• Drain onions; add to drained broccoli in greased 1½-qt. casserole.
• Pour sauce over vegetables. Bake in moderate oven (350°) 20 minutes. Makes 6 servings.

SAN MATEO BRUSSELS SPROUTS

Scatter sliced pimiento-stuffed olives over dish of sprouts for colorful trim

2 qts. Brussels sprouts (two 10 oz. tubs)
2 tblsp. butter
¼ c. lemon juice
1 c. dairy sour cream
¼ c. minced fresh parsley
½ tsp. salt
⅛ tsp. pepper
Sliced pimiento-stuffed olives (optional)

• Wash sprouts. Trim stem ends and cut an "x" in stem to hasten cooking. Remove any loose or yellow leaves. Let stand a few minutes in cool, salted water.
• Heat butter in skillet over medium heat. Drain sprouts; add to hot butter. Cover and steam about 10 minutes. Shake skillet occasionally. Check with fork to see if they are tender-crisp.
• Add lemon juice and steam 2 minutes more. Add remaining ingredients, except olives. Heat, but do not boil. Serve topped with sliced olives, if desired. Makes 6 servings.

Cook Cabbage Fast

The secret to superlative country cabbage dishes is quick cooking. The rule is to cook it, covered, in a little salted water, drain and season. It takes about 5 minutes for shredded cabbage, 10 to 15 minutes for wedges. Speedy cooking makes the vegetable taste better and it retains more vitamins.

Red cabbage is different. Cook it uncovered, in a small amount of salted water with 1 to 2 tablespoons vinegar or lemon juice added to retain (or restore) the vegetable's red color. Let it cook about 25 minutes, or until tender. For a special dish try Red Cabbage and Pineapple . . . really flavorful.

PANNED CABBAGE DE LUXE

Quick-cooked, it's at its peak

1 large onion, sliced
1 tblsp. fat
2 c. shredded cabbage
1 c. grated carrots
1 tsp. salt
⅛ tsp. pepper
1 c. boiling water

• Sauté onion in hot fat in heavy skillet until soft and clear. Add cabbage, carrots and seasonings.
• Pour water over vegetables. Cover, and simmer 12 minutes. Serve hot. Makes 6 servings.

CABBAGE WITH APPLES

A welcome variation from boiled and buttered cabbage—good with ham

1 head cabbage
1 red apple, cored and sliced
½ c. dairy sour cream
1 tblsp. butter or regular margarine
½ tsp. salt
3 tblsp. lemon juice

• Cut cabbage into 6 wedges. Cook in small amount of boiling salted water 5 minutes. Add apple; cook about 3 minutes more, until tender. Drain.
• Combine remaining ingredients. Heat through, but do not boil. Pour on cabbage. Serve hot. Makes 6 servings.

CABBAGE WITH CHEESE

Double this recipe if you like cabbage—it's excellent with pork

3 c. shredded cabbage
½ c. boiling water
1 tsp. salt
¼ c. light cream
½ c. grated process cheese

• Cook cabbage in boiling salted water until tender, about 6 to 9 minutes.
• Drain. Add cream and cheese. Place over low heat; stir until cheese melts and coats cabbage. Makes 4 servings.

CARAWAY-BUTTERED CABBAGE

Be sure to shred cabbage coarsely—use a sharp knife. A dull knife bruises cabbage and wastes vitamin C

¼ c. butter
1 tsp. caraway seeds, crushed
1 tsp. salt
2 tblsp. water
6 c. coarsely shredded cabbage

• Melt butter in saucepan. Add remaining ingredients. Steam until cabbage is tender, about 10 minutes. Stir to combine. Makes 4 servings.

FIVE-MINUTE CABBAGE

Makes its own sauce as it cooks

1¼ c. milk
8 c. finely shredded cabbage
2 tblsp. flour
¼ c. milk
2 tblsp. butter
1 tsp. salt
⅛ tsp. pepper

• Heat 1¼ c. milk in heavy skillet over medium heat. Add cabbage; cover and simmer 2 minutes.
• Meanwhile, blend together flour and ¼ c. milk. Add to cabbage along with butter, salt and pepper. Stir until mixture comes to a boil and is thickened.
• Cover and continue cooking over low heat 2 minutes. Stir. Serve in sauce dishes. Makes 6 servings.

PENNSYLVANIA DUTCH CABBAGE

Just the dish to add variety to cold-weather meals—it's sweet-sour

8 c. shredded cabbage
4 slices bacon, chopped
1 small onion, minced
2 tblsp. brown sugar
2 tblsp. flour
½ c. water
⅓ c. vinegar
½ tsp. salt
⅛ tsp. pepper

• Cook cabbage in boiling salted water until tender, 5 to 7 minutes. Drain.
• Meanwhile, cook bacon until crisp. Remove from skillet. Add onion to bacon drippings and cook until soft. Blend in brown sugar and flour. Add water and vinegar and cook, stirring constantly, until thickened. Add salt and pepper.
• Add sauce and bacon to drained cabbage; heat thoroughly. Makes 6 servings.

RED CABBAGE AND PINEAPPLE

Different, distinctive and delicious

6 c. shredded red cabbage
1 tblsp. lemon juice
½ c. boiling water
1 tblsp. butter
2 tblsp. brown sugar
1 tblsp. cornstarch

½ tsp. salt
1 (9 oz.) can pineapple tidbits
2 tblsp. vinegar

• Place cabbage, lemon juice and boiling water in skillet. Cover and cook, stirring once or twice, until cabbage is tender, 10 to 12 minutes. Stir in butter.

• Meanwhile, blend together brown sugar, cornstarch and salt. Drain juice from pineapple and blend into cornstarch mixture along with vinegar. Add cornstarch mixture and pineapple bits to cabbage. Cook, stirring, until mixture thickens and bubbles. Serve hot. Makes 6 servings.

Homemade Sauerkraut

Country cooks often make sauerkraut when there's a surplus of cabbage. They find its sharp flavor adds a pleasing change of pace in winter meals. And it's a real country convenience food–ready to serve cold in salads or appetizers and to heat in a few minutes with frankfurters for a main dish. Many families prefer it hot alongside meats. Some FARM JOURNAL readers in Pennsylvania prefer sauerkraut with turkey to the New Englander's favorite, cranberry sauce.

Use pure granulated (sack salt) salt to make sauerkraut by the following directions and do measure it accurately. The cabbage will not ferment properly if you add too much salt.

GLASS-JAR SAUERKRAUT

If you have a big crop of cabbage, it is economical to cure it in brine–to make sauerkraut. The fermented vegetable serves as a "pickle" and brings variety to winter meals when fresh vegetables are not always abundant. Good country cooks like to serve it cold with a dash of celery or caraway seeds, a few chunks of chilled, drained canned pineapple or a little pineapple juice added, for an appetizer. They know that the sharpness of its flavor, when hot, depends on how long it is cooked. For the most tang and greatest crispness, they only heat it. They cook it longer for a milder flavor.

An easy way to make sauerkraut is to ferment the cabbage in glass fruit jars. Here are directions:

1. Remove and discard outer leaves from firm, matured heads of cabbage. Wash, drain, cut in halves or quarters and remove and discard cores.

2. Shred 5 lbs. cabbage at a time with a shredder or sharp knife. It should be no thicker than a dime.

3. Sprinkle 3½ tblsp. salt over shredded cabbage (5 lbs.) and mix thoroughly by hand.

4. Pack into clean glass jars, pressing cabbage down firmly with wooden spoon. Fill to within 1½" to 2" from jar top. Be sure juice covers cabbage. A quart jar holds about 2 lbs. cabbage.

5. Wipe off jar top. Cover cabbage with pads of cheesecloth, edges tucked down against inside of jar. Hold cabbage down by crisscrossing two dry wood strips (some good kraut makers first coat the strips with melted paraffin) so they catch under the neck of the jar. Wipe off jar, put on lid, but *do not seal tightly*.

6. Set filled jars in shallow pans or on folded newspapers–the brine may overflow during fermentation.

Keep at room temperature (70° F.) for top-quality sauerkraut.

7. Skim film every few days if it forms. If directions have been followed carefully and correct temperature maintained, little or no film should form.

8. Keep cabbage covered with brine. If necessary add more weak brine made by dissolving 1½ tblsp. salt in 1 qt. water.

9. Let ferment about 10 days, or until liquid settles and bubbles no longer rise to the surface. Remove the cheesecloth and wood strips and add more weak brine if needed. (Some women fix 1 extra qt. cabbage for every 4 qts. to use in refilling jars when fermentation ends and shrinkage occurs.)

10. If sauerkraut is to be used soon, wipe mouths of jars and seal tightly; keep in a cool place. If it is to be stored longer than a few weeks, remove lids and set jars in a pan of cold water. Water should extend to shoulder of jars. Bring water slowly to a boil; then remove jars. Add boiling weak brine to sauerkraut, if needed to fill the jar to within ½″ from top. (To make brine, dissolve 1½ tblsp. salt in 1 qt. water.) Wipe off jar rims. Adjust lids. Process in boiling water bath (212° F.) 30 minutes for quart jars.

• Remove jars from canner and complete seals unless closures are self-sealing type.

Note: For 20 to 25 lbs. cabbage, use ½ lb. salt. Makes 8 to 10 quarts.

SAUERKRAUT TIPS

From good cooks famed for excellent sauerkraut, we learned of these good ways to use sauerkraut.

SAUERKRAUT SANDWICH: Make a round, open-face hot dog sandwich. Slice the frankfurters to make "pennies" and arrange them around the outer edges of buns cut in crosswise halves. Put a spoonful of sauerkraut in center of each sandwich. Serve with knife and fork. Buns may be toasted and buttered, frankfurter slices heated in a little water and well drained.

SCALLOPED SAUERKRAUT: Scallop sauerkraut with Cheddar cheese slices.

SAUERKRAUT/CARROT SALAD: Combine chilled sauerkraut and shredded carrots.

STONE-JAR SAUERKRAUT

• Prepare 40 to 50 lbs. cabbage as directed for Glass-Jar Sauerkraut. Shred and salt 5 lbs. cabbage at a time.

1. To 5 lbs. cabbage, add 3½ tblsp. salt. Mix thoroughly.

2. Pack firmly and evenly with a potato masher into a stone jar (or crock) that has been washed in soapy water, rinsed and scalded.

3. Repeat shredding and salting cabbage until jar is filled to within 5″ from top. Press firmly (do not pound) with masher to extract enough juice to cover cabbage by the time jar is filled. Keep cabbage covered with juice.

4. Cover with two or three layers of white, clean cloth, tucking edges down against inside of jar. On top, place a scalded, heavy plate that just fits inside the jar or a paraffined board. Weight it down with a fruit jar filled with water (or with a stone–not limestone–or paraffined brick), so that juice comes over plate.

5. Fermentation will begin the day following the packing. It works faster at high temperatures and the kraut is more likely to spoil at a high temperature. The best quality product is made at room temperature (70° F.).

6. Give the kraut daily care. Remove the film as it forms and wash and scald the cover cloth as often as necessary to remove mold and film.

7. When bubbling stops (in 2 or 3 weeks—or 4 weeks in cold weather), tap jar or crock gently. If no bubbles rise, fermentation has ended.

8. Pack into clean qt. jars to within 1″ of top. Cover with sauerkraut juice. If you need more juice, add a weak brine (1½ tblsp. salt to 1 qt. water). Set jars in a pan of cold water. Water should extend to shoulder of jars. Bring water slowly to a boil; remove jars. Wipe off jar rims. Adjust lids. Process in boiling water bath (212° F.) 30 minutes for quart jars.

• Remove jars from canner and complete seals unless closures are self-sealing type. Makes 15 to 18 quarts.

Note: If you eat sauerkraut often and will use your supply before winter ends, it will hold in the stone jar in a cold room (55° F. or lower).

SAUERKRAUT ANSWERS

Q. What makes sauerkraut turn pink?
A. The color is caused by certain kinds of yeast. They often grow when the salt is not evenly distributed, or when too much salt is used, and when the cabbage is too loosely packed in a crock or stone jar.

Q. What causes soft sauerkraut?
A. The salt content may be too low. High temperatures during curing also have a softening effect. Use of containers not cleaned thoroughly sometimes causes this trouble, as does improper packing of cabbage which traps air.

Q. Why is sauerkraut sometimes slimy?
A. Certain bacteria are responsible and usually they flourish when not enough salt is used and the temperatures are too high.

Q. What makes sauerkraut darken at times?
A. Failure to clean the cabbage properly, uneven salting and a high curing temperature may be at fault.

Q. Is use of too much salt harmful?
A. Yes, it prevents fermentation.

Q. Can you prevent the formation of a white film?
A. The trick is to cover the sauerkraut and adjust the weights so very little kraut juice or kraut is exposed to the air. This treatment discourages the growth of this yeast.

BUTTERED CARROT STICKS

Bake this along with your oven dinner

6 medium carrots
¼ c. water
½ tsp. salt
2 tblsp. butter or regular margarine

• Peel carrots and quarter lengthwise. Place in 1-qt. casserole. Add water and salt. Bake in moderate oven (350°) 50 minutes.

• Serve buttered. Makes 6 servings.

CREAMY CARROTS

Mayonnaise is the surprise seasoning

8 medium carrots
½ c. boiling water
½ tsp. salt
1 tsp. sugar
3 tblsp. mayonnaise or salad dressing
2 tblsp. light cream

• Wash and scrape carrots. Cut into quarters, lengthwise.
• Put carrots, boiling water, salt and sugar in saucepan. Cover. Cook until tender but still a little firm, 15 to 20 minutes. Drain.
• Blend mayonnaise and cream; pour over carrots, and mix lightly. Serve immediately. Makes 5 to 6 servings.

WALNUT CARROTS

Walnuts add crunchy note and flavor to bright carrots, expertly seasoned

5 c. (3″) carrot sticks (32 young carrots)
1½ c. water
½ tsp. salt
½ c. melted butter or regular margarine
2 tsp. honey
½ tsp. salt
¼ tsp. coarse pepper
2 tblsp. lemon juice
¼ tsp. grated lemon peel
½ c. coarsely broken walnuts

• Cook carrots in water with ½ tsp. salt added, just until tender. Drain well.
• Meanwhile, heat remaining ingredients except the walnuts. Pour this topping over hot carrots. Toss in walnuts. Makes 8 servings.

POLKA DOT CARROTS

Olive-green rings with bright red centers decorate and flavor carrots

6 medium carrots
¼ c. butter
1 tblsp. minced onion
½ tsp. salt
½ tsp. sugar
⅛ tsp. pepper
½ c. sliced pimiento-stuffed olives

• Peel carrots and cut in ¼″ slices. Cook in boiling salted water until tender; drain.
• Meanwhile, melt butter. Add onion and cook until onion is soft. Add to carrots along with remaining ingredients. Heat thoroughly. Makes 6 servings.

CARROT PATTIES

For company, serve these with ham and eggs or with syrup or honey

1½ c. grated raw carrots
3 tblsp. grated onions
3 c. bread crumbs
¾ tsp. baking powder
2 eggs, beaten
¼ c. milk
½ tsp. salt
⅛ tsp. pepper
3 tblsp. butter or bacon fat

• Combine all ingredients, except butter. Mix well and form into patties similar to potato cakes, about 3″ in diameter (there should be 12).
• Heat butter in a skillet; brown patties lightly on both sides. Makes 6 servings.

GOLDEN CARROTS SUPREME

Try this simple French recipe

¼ c. butter or regular margarine
¾ c. chicken broth

9. TOSSED GREEN SALAD—The variety of greens and salad dressings is endless; recipes in this cookbook will serve as starters for your own ingenuity. Recipes, page 211.

10. GARDEN SALAD LOAF—Capture the refreshing flavors and brightness of fresh vegetables in this make-ahead, wiltproof salad. Recipe, page 221.

11. JELLIED BEEF MOLD – Beef in jellied loaf waiting in the refrigerator brings peace of mind to hostess when company is coming. Recipe, page 225.

12. SUMMER SALAD DRESSINGS—Glorify your salads with Italian Tomato, Sweet-sour Bacon, Creamy Thousand Island and Orange/Honey Dressings. Recipes, pages 227-228.

2 tsp. salt
⅛ tsp. pepper
2 tsp. sugar
5 c. diagonally sliced (¼″) carrots
2 tsp. lemon juice
¼ c. chopped parsley

• Add butter to boiling chicken broth. Stir in salt, pepper, sugar and carrots. Simmer, covered, until carrots are tender-crisp, about 10 minutes.
• Stir in lemon juice and parsley. Makes 6 servings.

CAULIFLOWER WITH SHRIMP SAUCE

Shrimp sauce and toasted almonds enhance this hostess special

1 head cauliflower
1 can condensed cream of shrimp soup
½ c. dairy sour cream
½ tsp. salt
⅛ tsp. pepper
¼ c. slivered, toasted almonds

• Separate cauliflower into flowerets. Cook in boiling salted water until tender; drain.
• Meanwhile, blend together soup, sour cream, salt and pepper in saucepan. Heat, but do not boil.
• Place cauliflower in serving bowl. Top with shrimp sauce, then toasted almonds. Makes 4 to 6 servings.

PARMESAN CAULIFLOWER

Browned butter and cheese season delightfully; keep hot in covered dish

1 large head cauliflower
¼ c. butter or regular margarine
3 tblsp. dry bread crumbs, toasted
2 tblsp. grated Parmesan cheese
Paprika

• Separate cauliflower into flowerets. Cook in small amount of boiling salted water until tender, about 10 minutes. Drain.
• In heavy skillet, over medium heat, brown butter until delicate brown (watch that it does not burn). Coat cooked cauliflower with butter; toss with bread crumbs. Sprinkle cheese over top. Garnish with paprika. Makes 4 to 6 servings.

CORN ON THE COB

A native of the Americas, corn is high in popularity. Farm women call it the king of vegetables. While available to some extent throughout the year, the peak season is from May to September.

Select ears with fresh green husks. The cobs should be filled with kernels. The kernels of fresh corn spurt a thin milky juice when punctured with a thumbnail. If the milk is thick or the skin of the kernel is tough or rubbery, the corn is too old.

Allow 2 ears corn for each serving. Two ears yield about 1 c. fresh kernels.

Farm families like to gather corn as near mealtime as possible. If the ears must be held, put them, unhusked, in refrigerator. Use quickly.

When ready to cook, husk the corn and remove silk.

Cover ears with boiling unsalted water, cover and cook 3 to 5 minutes. Or cover ears with cold water and cook, covered, just until the water reaches a boil. Lift out of water with tongs, drain and serve at once. Pass butter or margarine, salt and pepper.

OVEN-ROASTED CORN

Let it rain—corn roasted in oven tastes like corn cooked over coals

12 ears sweet corn, including husks
Savory Butter

• Pull back husks on freshly picked sweet corn, leaving husks fastened to the stem end. Remove silk.
• Spread kernels generously with Savory Butter. Pull husks around corn and tie a string snugly around ear, close to open end.
• Lay corn ears in a large roasting pan. Bake in moderate oven (350°) 40 minutes. Remove strings; remove husks, if you wish, and serve. Makes 12 ears.

SAVORY BUTTER

Spread on corn for exciting flavor

• Combine ¾ c. soft butter or regular margarine with 2½ tsp. salt. Season with one of the following:

ORÉGANO: Add 1½ tsp. orégano leaves and ½ tsp. garlic salt.

CHIVES: Add 2 tsp. dried chopped chives.

ONION: Add 2 tsp. minced green onion.

BARBECUE: Add 1½ tsp. barbecue spice.

BROILED CORN IN HUSKS

Choose corn in the milk stage for top flavor and tenderness

• Pick 12 ears of corn about 2 hours before mealtime.
• Remove thick outer husks.
• Turn back inner husks and remove silk, being careful not to detach husks from ear. Pull husks back around ears.
• Soak in ice water 1 hour.
• Preheat broiler. Shake excess water from corn. Arrange on rack, about 4″ from heat.
• Broil 7 minutes on one side; turn with tongs or fork and continue broiling on all sides until corn is done, about 30 minutes. Or roast in moderate oven (350°) 40 minutes.
• Serve right in husks so that corn keeps steaming hot with butter and salt, and pepper, if desired.

CORN CURRY

A favorite in our Test Kitchens; mild curry flavor makes it special

¼ c. butter or regular margarine
3 c. frozen or canned corn
2 tblsp. chopped green pepper
2 tblsp. chopped red pepper or pimiento
3 tblsp. chopped onion
½ tsp. curry powder
¾ c. dairy sour cream
½ tsp. salt
⅛ tsp. pepper

• Melt butter in skillet. Add vegetables and curry powder; cook over low heat until vegetables are just tender, 8 to 10 minutes.
• Stir in sour cream, salt and pepper. Heat through, stirring constantly. Makes 6 servings.

CORN "OYSTERS"

Corn puffs up like oysters in cooking

6 ears select corn (fresh-picked or frozen-thawed)
3 egg yolks, well beaten

¼ c. flour
½ tsp. baking powder
¾ tsp. salt
¼ tsp. pepper
3 egg whites, stiffly beaten

• Slash down each row of kernels with a sharp knife, then cut from cob. (Easier than grating and just as effective for getting every bit of milky kernel.) Add egg yolks; blend.
• Sift together flour, baking powder, salt and pepper. Stir into corn-egg mixture; blend. Gently fold in egg whites.
• Drop by spoonfuls onto hot, well-greased griddle. Fry until nicely browned. Makes 4 servings.

CORN CUSTARD PUDDING

They'll want second helpings—you'd better bake two casseroles of this

2 c. frozen loose-pack whole kernel corn
2 c. milk or dairy half-and-half
2 tblsp. melted butter or regular margarine
1 tblsp. sugar
1 tsp. salt
⅛ tsp. white pepper
3 eggs, beaten

• Add corn, milk, butter, sugar, salt and pepper to eggs; stir to combine well. Turn into a well-greased 1½-qt. casserole. Place in pan of hot water; bake in moderate oven (350°) 45 minutes, or until pudding is set. Makes 4 servings.

Note: You can substitute 1 (1 lb.) can cream style corn for frozen whole kernel corn, but use 1 c. milk or dairy half-and-half instead of 2 c.

Variations

To the ingredients for Corn Custard Pudding make the following additions:

CHEESE/PEPPER CORN PUDDING: Add ½ c. grated sharp process cheese and ¼ c. finely chopped green pepper.

HAM/CORN CUSTARD PUDDING: Add ½ c. finely chopped cooked ham.

MUSHROOM/CORN CUSTARD PUDDING: Add ½ c. chopped mushrooms.

SOUTHWESTERN CORN BAKE

A vegetable dish that's highly prized by Southwestern hostesses—do try it

2 (16 to 17 oz.) cans cream style corn
2 eggs, beaten
¾ c. yellow cornmeal
1 tsp. garlic salt
6 tblsp. salad oil
1 (4 oz.) can green chili peppers, finely cut
2 c. grated Cheddar cheese

• Mix together all ingredients except chili peppers and cheese.
• Divide mixture in half. Place one half in a greased 8″ square baking dish.
• Mix together chili peppers and cheese; lay on top of corn mixture in dish. Cover with the remaining corn mixture.
• Bake in moderate oven (350°) 35 minutes. Makes 8 servings.

CORN/OYSTER SCALLOP

Serve this tasty dressed-up corn with fried chicken or pork chops

2 (10 oz.) cans condensed oyster stew
1 (1 lb.) can cream style corn
1 (1 lb.) can whole kernel corn, drained
1¼ c. cracker crumbs, crushed medium fine
1 egg, slightly beaten
½ tsp. salt
⅛ tsp. pepper
2 tblsp. pimiento strips
2 tblsp. melted butter
½ c. cracker crumbs

• Combine oyster stew, corn, 1¼ c. cracker crumbs, egg, salt, pepper and pimiento. Pour into greased 2-qt. casserole. Combine butter and ½ c. cracker crumbs. Sprinkle around edge of corn mixture.
• Bake in moderate oven (350°) 1 hour, or until knife inserted halfway between center and edge comes out clean. Makes 8 servings.

CORN WITH CREAM CHEESE

This creamy corn is the company special of a busy Iowa farm woman

¼ c. milk
1 (3 oz.) pkg. cream cheese
1 tblsp. butter
½ tsp. salt
⅛ tsp. pepper
2 (12 oz.) cans whole kernel corn, drained (3 c.)

• Combine milk, cream cheese, butter, salt and pepper in saucepan. Cook over low heat, stirring constantly, until cheese melts and is blended. Add corn and heat. Makes 6 servings.

HOMEY SCALLOPED CORN

Watch the traffic when they spy scalloped corn at the church supper

4 slices bacon, chopped
1¼ c. crushed saltine crackers
1 medium onion, chopped
2 eggs, beaten
1 (1 lb.) can cream style corn
1 (4 oz.) can pimientos, drained and chopped
1 c. milk
1 c. grated Cheddar cheese
¼ tsp. salt
¼ tsp. pepper

• Cook bacon until crisp; remove from skillet. Combine 2 tblsp. bacon fat with ¼ c. cracker crumbs; set aside.
• Cook onion in remaining bacon drippings until tender. Add remaining crumbs; mix and brown slightly.
• Combine onion-crumb mixture with eggs, corn, pimientos, milk, cheese, bacon, salt and pepper. Pour into greased shallow 1½-qt. casserole. Top with reserved crumbs. Bake in moderate oven (350°) about 45 minutes. Serves 6.

TWENTIETH-CENTURY HOMINY

Grandmother used wood ashes to make hominy—a trick learned from the Indians. We've modernized the recipe, and think you will like it

1 qt. shelled corn (husked field corn)
2 tblsp. baking soda
1 tsp. salt

• Wash corn, add 2 qts. cold water and soda; cover and soak overnight.
• In morning bring to boil (in enamel kettle) in water in which corn soaked. Cook 3 hours or until hulls loosen. Add more water if necessary.

• Drain off water; wash corn in cold water, rubbing vigorously until hulls are removed. Bring corn to a boil with 2 qts. cold water, drain. Repeat. Add salt. Makes 1 quart. Butter and serve hot or pass gravy to ladle over hominy. Some good cooks like to fry hominy in a skillet with bacon drippings added.

HOMINY/ALMOND CASSEROLE

Hominy goes fancy for the ham or pork chop company dinner

1 can condensed cream of mushroom soup
½ c. light cream or evaporated milk
1 tsp. celery seeds
1 tblsp. Worcestershire sauce
4 drops Tabasco sauce (about)
1 (14½ oz.) can hominy, yellow or white whole kernel
½ c. slivered almonds
2 tblsp. corn flake crumbs
1 tblsp. melted butter or regular margarine

• In a saucepan, combine soup, cream, celery seeds, Worcestershire sauce and Tabasco. Simmer gently a few minutes to blend flavors.
• Meanwhile, drain hominy; add to hot sauce together with almonds. Turn into greased 1-qt. casserole.
• Combine crumbs and melted butter; sprinkle over casserole. Bake in moderate oven (350°) 25 to 30 minutes. Makes 4 servings.

Deep Purple Eggplant

Eggplant is one of the best-liked vegetables in many parts of the world–the Middle East, Greece and Italy, for instance. In some American families it is not appreciated. If you need to overcome this unfortunate attitude, try Eggplant Parmigiana, a real treat. If your family likes pizza, let Italian Eggplant win friends for the vegetable. A California grower's wife invented the recipe to please her husband who immigrated from Italy when a young man. She scored success with this creative dish and so will you.

EGGPLANT PARMIGIANA

Our taste-testers voted this the blue ribbon eggplant dish

2 medium eggplants (2 lbs.)
½ c. flour
½ tsp. salt
⅛ tsp. pepper
¼ to ½ c. olive oil
2 (8 oz.) cans tomato sauce (2 c.)
1 (8 oz.) pkg. mozzarella cheese, thinly sliced
½ c. grated Parmesan cheese

• Peel eggplants and cut in ½" slices. Sprinkle with salt. Spread out in layer on board or paper toweling; let stand 20 minutes. Pat dry with paper toweling.
• Dip each slice in mixture of flour, ½ tsp. salt and pepper.
• Heat ¼ c. olive oil. Brown eggplant quickly. Cooking quickly over medium high heat will keep eggplant from absorbing a lot of oil. Drain on paper toweling. Continue cooking eggplant slices, adding more oil if necessary.
• Pour ¼" tomato sauce in bottom of greased 2-qt. casserole. Top with one third of eggplant slices, one third of remaining tomato sauce and one third of cheeses. Continue layers. Cover and bake in hot oven (400°) 20 minutes. Remove cover and continue baking 10 minutes. Makes 6 servings.

ITALIAN EGGPLANT

Pizza-like with yellow and red top

- 1 medium eggplant
- Salt
- 1 egg, slightly beaten
- 1 c. corn flake or bread crumbs
- ⅔ c. salad oil
- ¼ tsp. pepper
- 2 tblsp. chopped parsley
- ¼ c. grated Parmesan cheese
- 6 slices mozzarella cheese (6 oz.)
- 1 (8 oz.) can tomato sauce

• Peel eggplant if desired; cut in ½″ slices. Sprinkle with salt. Dip in egg and then in crumbs. Dry on rack a few minutes.

• Pour oil into skillet to the depth of ⅛″ and heat. Brown eggplant slices on both sides in hot oil. Place slices in a shallow baking pan, overlapping if necessary. Sprinkle with pepper, parsley and Parmesan cheese; top with mozzarella cheese slices. Pour tomato sauce over all.

• Bake in moderate oven (350°) 20 to 25 minutes. Makes 6 servings.

EGGPLANT CLAMBAKE

A bargain in good flavors

- 2 large eggplants
- 2 (7½ oz.) cans minced clams, drained
- 2 c. cracker crumbs
- 2 tblsp. melted butter or regular margarine
- 2 eggs, beaten
- Salt
- Pepper
- 2 tblsp. milk (optional)
- Butter or regular margarine

• Peel eggplants; cut in 1″ thick slices. Let stand in water 20 minutes.

• Cook slices in boiling salted water until soft, about 15 minutes; drain and mash. (Makes about 2 c.)

• Add clams, 1½ c. cracker crumbs, melted butter, eggs, salt and pepper to taste and milk, if mixture seems dry.

• Place in 2-qt. baking pan. Cover with remaining crumbs. Dot with butter and bake in slow oven (325°) about 40 minutes, or until brown on top. Makes 6 servings.

CREAMED KALE AND ONIONS

Good with pork chops

- 1½ lbs. kale, cleaned
- 2 lbs. small white onions, peeled (about 12)
- ¼ c. shortening
- 3 tblsp. flour
- 1½ c. milk
- Seasonings

• Cook kale in boiling salted water (enough to come halfway up on vegetable) until tender, about 15 minutes.

• Cook onions in boiling salted water until tender, about 15 minutes.

• Drain; combine vegetables.

• Make white sauce of shortening, flour, milk and seasonings you prefer (salt, pepper, etc.). Pour over kale and onions. Serve hot. Makes 6 servings.

Note: You can use liquid drained from cooked vegetables for all or part of milk in making the sauce.

SWISS CHARD WITH CHEESE

Once you team chard with cheese they'll go steady in your kitchen

- 2 lbs. Swiss chard
- 2 tblsp. butter or regular margarine
- 2 tblsp. flour
- 1 tsp. salt
- ½ c. milk

½ lb. diced process cheese
½ c. bread crumbs
2 tblsp. melted butter

• Cut stalks from washed chard leaves in 1″ pieces. Place in bottom of large kettle; cover with boiling salted water (½ tsp. salt to 2 c. water). Cover; cook 5 minutes. Add torn leaves and continue cooking until tender, about 5 minutes. Drain thoroughly in colander, pressing out liquid. You should have 5 c. chard.
• Meanwhile, melt butter. Blend in flour and salt. Add milk and cook, stirring constantly, until mixture comes to a boil. Add cheese, stirring until cheese is melted and blended. Place chard in greased 2-qt. casserole. Stir in sauce.
• Toss crumbs with melted butter; sprinkle over casserole. Bake in moderate oven (350°) until bubbly, about 25 minutes. Makes 6 servings.

KOHLRABI IN CREAM SAUCE

Select small to medium bulbs with fresh green leaves to make this

1 qt. cubed peeled kohlrabi bulbs (4 to 6)
Kohlrabi leaves
2 tblsp. butter or regular margarine
3 tblsp. flour
½ c. milk
Salt
Pepper

• Cook kohlrabi cubes in boiling salted water until tender, 15 to 20 minutes.
• Cook the leaves in boiling salted water in another pan, discarding any that appear old and tough, for 20 minutes.
• Drain kohlrabi cubes, reserving ½ c. liquid. Drain greens and chop coarsely (use blender, if available).
• In another saucepan, melt butter, add flour and cook, stirring in reserved vegetable liquid and milk gradually. When thickened, add kohlrabi cubes and greens. Check for seasonings, adding more salt, if needed, and pepper to taste. Makes 4 to 6 servings.

Note: Use 2 tblsp. flour for sauce when leaves are not used (they tend to thin the sauce).

ONION PIE
(Zwiebel Kuchen)

A main-dish pie of German origin

1½ c. sifted flour
¾ tsp. salt
1½ tsp. caraway seeds
½ c. shortening
2 to 3 tblsp. water
3 c. peeled onions, thinly sliced
3 tblsp. melted butter, regular margarine or fat
½ c. milk
1½ c. dairy sour cream
1 tsp. salt
2 eggs, well beaten
3 tblsp. flour
Bacon slices, cooked crisp

• To make pastry, combine 1½ c. flour, ¾ tsp. salt and caraway seeds. Add shortening; cut into flour until mixture resembles coarse cornmeal. Stir water in lightly with fork; stir until mixture adheres and follows fork around bowl. Turn onto floured board; roll to ⅛″ thickness. Fit into 10″ pie pan; flute edges.
• Bake in hot oven (425°) 10 minutes, or until lightly browned.
• Meanwhile, make filling. Sauté onions in butter until lightly browned. Spoon into pastry shell.
• Add milk, 1¼ c. sour cream and salt to eggs.

• Blend 3 tblsp. flour with remaining ¼ c. sour cream. Combine with egg mixture; pour over onion.
• Bake in slow oven (325°) 30 minutes, or until firm in center. Garnish with crisp bacon. Makes 8 servings.

GLAZED ONIONS

Excellent choice for a turkey dinner

18 small white onions, peeled
¼ c. butter
1 to 2 tsp. sugar

• Peel onions; cut slice from stem and root ends. Cook, covered, in salted water (½ tsp. salt to 1 c. water) until just tender, about 25 minutes. Drain.
• Melt butter in heavy skillet; add onions. Cook over medium heat, shaking pan so onions roll around and start to brown on all sides.
• Sprinkle with sugar and continue rolling skillet around so sugar will give onions a shiny glaze. Makes 6 to 8 servings.

FRENCH ONIONS AND RICE

Absolutely delicious with poultry

¼ c. long-grain rice
2 qts. boiling water
1 tsp. salt
¼ c. butter or regular margarine
4 c. thinly sliced large white or yellow onions (about 3)
½ tsp. salt
⅛ tsp. paprika
2 tblsp. grated Parmesan cheese

• Drop rice into rapidly boiling water with 1 tsp. salt added; boil uncovered 5 minutes; drain at once.
• Melt butter in 2-qt. casserole in oven; stir in onions. Add ½ tsp. salt and stir onions in butter until nicely yellowed and coated. Then add rice and stir to distribute evenly. Cover and bake in slow oven (325°) 1 hour. Sprinkle with paprika and cheese. Makes 8 servings.

Cold Weather Parsnips

Home gardeners in New England do not dig parsnips until after the ground thaws in the spring. The peak season for the vegetable in supermarkets stretches from January through March. There's a reason for the timing. The flavor of parsnips sweetens after exposure to the cold weather. Many interesting ways to prepare this root vegetable developed in country kitchens. Two typical rural combinations are Glazed Parsnips to serve with pork and Parsnips Country-style, good with roast beef. You'll find both recipes easy to fix—tasty, too.

GLAZED PARSNIPS

Honey-orange glazed parsnips tempt appetites with a gourmet flavor

3 c. diagonally sliced (½″) parsnips
¾ c. boiling water
½ tsp. salt
2 tblsp. butter
1 tblsp. honey
¼ c. orange juice
1 tsp. grated orange peel

• Cook parsnips in water and salt until tender, about 10 minutes. Drain and remove from saucepan.
• Heat remaining ingredients together in saucepan. Combine with parsnips. Serve hot. Makes 6 servings.

PARSNIPS COUNTRY-STYLE

If you're fond of parsnips, you'll like these golden brown patties

8 to 10 medium parsnips (2 lbs.)
½ tsp. onion salt
½ tsp. salt
⅛ tsp. pepper
1 egg, beaten
⅓ c. fine bread crumbs
2 tblsp. butter or regular margarine

• Peel parsnips. Cut in halves crosswise. Then halve or quarter lengthwise to make strips about the same size. Cook in boiling salted water until tender. Remove cores if woody.
• Mash parsnips. Beat in seasonings and egg. Chill well.
• Make 6 patties. Coat with bread crumbs. Cook patties on both sides in melted butter until golden brown. Makes 6 servings.

PARSNIP CASSEROLE

Ham and mushrooms glamorize these

3 c. mashed cooked parsnips
Seasonings
1 c. cubed cooked ham
1 c. canned mushrooms, drained
1 c. shredded sharp process cheese
½ c. crushed ready-to-eat cereal

• Season hot parsnips with salt, pepper, seasoned salt, etc.
• Mix ham, mushrooms and cheese.
• Alternate layers of parsnips and ham mixture in greased 2-qt. casserole. Sprinkle top with cereal crumbs.
• Bake in moderate oven (350°) 25 minutes. Makes 6 servings.

Variation

PARSNIP/CHEESE CASSEROLE: Omit ham and mushrooms; use 3 c. sliced cooked parsnips and ⅔ c. diced process cheese. Alternate layers of parsnips and cheese. Bake in moderate oven (350°) 30 minutes. Top with slices of crisp-cooked bacon. Makes 6 servings.

Green Garden Peas

June is the time of roses and garden peas in the Midwest and it's difficult to determine which are more anticipated and enjoyed, the flowers or vegetables.

NEW PEAS IN CREAM

Garden peas at their country-best

4 c. shelled peas
2 tsp. sugar
2 tsp. salt
Pea pods
1 small green onion with top, chopped
Water
2 tblsp. butter
½ tsp. pepper
1 c. light cream

• Cook peas with sugar, salt, 5 or 6 pea pods, onion and enough water to cover for 10 to 15 minutes, or until just tender (water should almost evaporate). Add butter and hold over heat to melt. Add pepper and cream. Heat but do not cook. Makes 6 to 8 servings.

NEW PEAS, 12 WAYS

WITH MINT: Cook 2 or 3 fresh mint leaves with the peas.

WITH MINT JELLY: Omit sugar and add 3 to 4 tblsp. mint jelly to peas with butter. Hold over heat to melt. Add pepper and cream and heat to warm.

WITH PIMIENTO: Add ¼ c. chopped pimiento to peas just before adding cream.

WITH SOUR CREAM AND CHIVES: Add 3 tblsp. chopped chives to peas before buttering. Then add 1 c. dairy sour cream instead of light cream and heat to warm; do not cook.

WITH POTATOES: Cook 12 small new peeled whole potatoes until just tender. Mix with peas before adding cream.

WITH MUSHROOMS: Sauté 1 c. drained canned sliced mushrooms in 1 tblsp. butter. Mix with peas before adding cream.

WITH ONIONS: Cook 1 c. sliced small green onions (use tops, too) in boiling salted water, until just tender, 8 to 10 minutes. Add to peas before buttering.

WITH CARROTS: Cook 1½ c. thinly sliced carrots until just tender. Add to peas before buttering.

WITH CELERY: Cook ¼ c. chopped celery in small amount of water until tender. Add to peas before buttering.

WITH BACON: Sprinkle ½ c. finely crumbled crisp-cooked bacon over top of peas just before serving.

WITH HAM: Cut ham slices (boiled or baked) in thin strips 1″ in length. Mix with peas just before serving.

WITH LETTUCE LEAVES: Line saucepan with several leaves of leaf lettuce, wet from washing. In center place peas, salt, pepper, sugar, tops of small green onions and 3 or 4 tblsp. water. Cover and cook until tender. Discard lettuce; season peas with cream.

GOURMET PEAS

Very good and very simple to fix

1 (10 oz.) pkg. frozen peas
¼ c. chicken broth (canned or homemade)
2 to 4 tblsp. dairy sour cream
Salt

· Cook frozen peas in broth until barely tender. Drain off reserve for later use, if desired. Stir sour cream into peas; heat only until cream is hot and peas are coated. Add a little salt, if necessary. Makes 4 servings.

PEAS AND CABBAGE

People are surprised to find this simple combination so tasty

1½ c. fresh peas, or 1 (10 oz.) pkg. frozen peas
1 small head cabbage, chopped
Salt
Pepper
2 tblsp. butter

· Cook peas in boiling salted water in saucepan until tender; drain. Cook cabbage in another saucepan in a small amount of water until tender-crisp; drain.
· Combine vegetables; add salt and pepper to taste and butter. Serves 6.

TEXAS BLACK-EYED PEAS AND RICE

Barbecue sauce adds the right zip

- 2 (10 oz.) pkgs. frozen black-eyed peas
- 1 c. chopped onion
- 1 qt. water
- 1 tblsp. salt
- ⅔ c. rice
- 10 slices bacon, diced
- ⅔ c. barbecue sauce
- ¼ tsp. pepper
- 2 tblsp. bacon drippings

• Place peas, onion, water and salt in large saucepan. Cover; bring to a boil. Reduce heat and simmer 30 minutes. Add rice and continue simmering until rice is tender, 20 to 25 minutes. Stir occasionally.

• Cook bacon; remove from skillet.

• Combine pea mixture, barbecue sauce, half of bacon, pepper and bacon drippings. Place in greased 2-qt. casserole. Top with remaining bacon.

• Bake in moderate oven (350°) 30 minutes. Makes 8 servings.

Heat-and-eat Potato Treats from Your Freezer

Many FARM JOURNAL readers have asked our food editors how to freeze potatoes when they're at their peak quality so they will store successfully in their freezers. This was the incentive that initiated work in our Test Kitchens to determine the best way to do it. We discovered how to handle potatoes so you can freeze them successfully for up to two months.

The trick is to cook the potatoes and freeze them in ready-to-use shapes so they go directly from freezer to range or oven. It's important not to let the potatoes thaw before heating; thawing softens them and makes them mushy.

Many homemakers now use our recipes to stock their freezers with several meals of hashed browns and fluffy mashed potatoes. Frequently they cook double amounts, use one and freeze the other. Here are the directions:

FROZEN HASHED BROWN POTATOES

Cook two skilletfuls of these golden, crisp-crusted potatoes for 8 or 9

To Freeze:

• Boil baking-type potatoes in their jackets until just tender but still firm, 10 to 15 minutes (1 medium potato makes about 1 c. grated). Drain, cool and peel. Grate potatoes on a coarse grater.

• Line a 10" skillet with aluminum foil, bringing foil up to cover sides. Mix 1½ tsp. salt with 4 c. grated potatoes. Pack in foil-lined skillet, pressing down firmly. Remove from skillet with foil. Seal, label and freeze. Repeat to stock your freezer.

To Cook:

• Heat ½ c. shortening over medium heat (350° in electric skillet) in same skillet in which potatoes were shaped for freezing. Remove foil and add the disk of frozen potatoes (shortening will spatter, so quickly cover the skillet). Cook 5 minutes over medium heat. Uncover and continue cooking 10 to 12 minutes, or until potatoes are browned on the bottom. Cut into 4 wedges; turn each piece separately with spatula or pancake turner. Continue cooking 5 minutes, or until attractively browned. Makes 4 generous servings.

BASIC MASHED POTATOES

Freeze these plain or make into one of our five interesting variations

4 lbs. boiling potatoes
1 c. milk (amount varies with moisture in potatoes)
¼ c. butter
1½ tsp. salt

· Peel potatoes. Boil until soft; drain. Press potatoes through a ricer or mash.
· Heat milk, butter and salt together. Gradually whip in until the potatoes are smooth and fluffy.
· Form into shapes that are ready to use with no thawing. Freeze by directions in variations that follow.

Variations

POTATO PUFFS: Add ½ c. grated Cheddar cheese or 2 egg yolks to Basic Mashed Potatoes. Chill. Form into balls; roll in mixture of ¾ c. corn flake crumbs and 3 tblsp. Toasted Sesame Seeds (see Index). Freeze on tray until firm. Package, label and return to freezer. Makes 48 small or 24 medium balls.

To Serve: Place frozen puffs on baking sheet. Brush lightly with melted butter. Bake in hot oven (400°) 20 minutes for small puffs and 30 minutes for medium puffs. To serve without freezing, omit brushing with butter and bake puffs only until they brown, 5 to 10 minutes.

SNOWCAPS: Add 2 egg yolks to Basic Mashed Potatoes. Spoon hot potatoes in mounds on baking sheet. Cool; freeze until firm. Remove from baking sheet; place in plastic bags. Seal, label and return to freezer. Use to top meat and vegetable casseroles. Makes 24.

PIMIENTO NESTS: Add ½ c. chopped, drained pimiento to Basic Mashed Potatoes. Line a 1½-qt. casserole with aluminum foil. Spoon half the potato mixture into casserole. Shape into a nest, building up the sides to top of casserole. Remove from casserole with foil to hold shape of the nest. Reline casserole with foil and shape remaining potato mixture. Cool; freeze nests until firm. Remove from freezer; package, seal and label. Return to freezer. Serve with chicken filling (see recipe for Chicken in Potato Nest). Makes 2.

CHEESE NESTS: Add ½ c. grated Cheddar cheese to hot Basic Mashed Potatoes; omit the pimiento and proceed as for Pimiento Nests. Serve with onion filling (see recipe for Cheese/Onion Pie).

POTATO NESTS: Omit the pimiento and shape like Pimiento Nests.

CHICKEN IN POTATO NEST

For company use two Pimiento Nests and double other ingredients

1 frozen Pimiento Nest
4 tblsp. melted butter or regular margarine
2 tblsp. flour
1 c. chicken broth
Salt
Pepper
1 (4 oz.) can sliced mushrooms, drained
½ c. diced celery
1 c. diced cooked chicken

· Remove wrapper from frozen Pimiento Nest. Place in casserole in which it was shaped originally. Drizzle with 2 tblsp. melted butter. Cover and bake in hot oven (400°) 30 minutes. Uncover and bake 30 minutes.

• In the meantime, combine remaining 2 tblsp. butter and flour in heavy saucepan. Slowly add broth; stir constantly until sauce is smooth and thick. Season with salt and pepper. Add remaining ingredients; heat. Spoon hot mixture into baked Pimiento Nest. Makes 6 servings.

CHEESE/ONION PIE

Potatoes make the crust for this pie —serve with fish, ham or chicken

1 frozen Cheese Nest
2 tblsp. melted butter
1 beef bouillon cube
½ c. boiling water
2 c. chopped onions
¼ c. butter or regular margarine
3 tblsp. flour
1 c. milk
Salt
Pepper

• Remove wrapper from frozen Cheese Nest. Place in casserole in which it was shaped originally. Drizzle with 2 tblsp. melted butter. Cover and bake in hot oven (400°) 30 minutes. Uncover and bake 30 minutes.

• In the meantime, dissolve bouillon cube in boiling water. Add onions, cover and simmer until tender; drain.

• Melt ¼ c. butter in heavy saucepan. Add flour to make a smooth paste. Add milk slowly; stir constantly until white sauce is smooth and thick.

• Season with salt and pepper. Add drained onions. Spoon onion mixture into baked Cheese Nest for serving. Makes 6 servings.

REFRIGERATOR MASHED POTATOES

Taste good, like baked potatoes served with sour cream and chives

5 lbs. potatoes (9 large)
2 (3 oz.) pkgs. cream cheese
1 c. dairy sour cream
2 tsp. onion salt
1 tsp. salt
¼ tsp. pepper
2 tblsp. butter or regular margarine

• Cook peeled potatoes in boiling salted water until tender. Drain.

• Mash until smooth (no lumps). Add remaining ingredients and beat until light and fluffy. Cool.

• Cover and place in refrigerator. May be used any time within two weeks.

• To use, place desired amount in greased casserole, dot with butter and bake in moderate oven (350°) until heated through, about 30 minutes. Makes 8 cups, or 12 servings.

Note: If you use the full amount, heat in a 2-qt. casserole and dot with 2 tblsp. butter.

POTATO ROSES

A new shape for mashed potatoes. Make the day before and refrigerate

4 lbs. baking potatoes
¼ c. butter
1 tblsp. minced onion
1½ tsp. salt
⅛ tsp. pepper
1 tblsp. minced parsley
2 tblsp. grated Parmesan or Romano cheese
1 egg
Paprika
½ c. melted butter

• Peel potatoes; cut in halves and cook in boiling lightly salted water until tender. Mash slightly.
• Place potatoes in large mixer bowl; beat until light and fluffy. Add 1/4 c. butter, onion, salt, pepper, parsley, cheese and egg. Whip until well mixed. Cool.
• Moisten hands; shape potato mixture into balls, about 3/4 c. each. Place on greased baking sheet; flatten slightly on bottom.
• To form roses, dip forefinger in water; make an indentation in center of each potato ball. Swirl finger clockwise to make a spiral. If you wish, cover and chill overnight.
• Before baking, sprinkle lightly with paprika and drizzle 1/2 c. melted butter over roses. Bake in very hot oven (450°) 8 minutes. Let set a few minutes. Makes 10 servings.

Perennial Favorite—Fried Potatoes

In the Great Plains kitchens fried potatoes are the dish good cooks serve with steaks and hamburgers. The first recipe comes from France —the four that follow are from cattle ranches on the prairies.

PUFFED-UP POTATOES

Two-step fried potatoes—one of many wonderful French importations

8 large potatoes
Shortening or salad oil
Salt

• Peel potatoes; cut in even 1/8" slices. Soak 4 minutes in ice water; pat dry on paper toweling.
• Heat shortening in deep kettle to 300°. Cook a few slices at a time at this temperature until light brown and half-done, about 10 minutes. Remove from kettle; drain on paper toweling.
• After frying all potatoes at 300°, heat shortening to 400°. Add more shortening, if needed.
• Finish frying potatoes, a few at a time, turning constantly. (They will puff quickly.) Drain on paper toweling. Keep hot in oven while frying the rest. Sprinkle with salt; serve at once. Makes 6 to 8 servings.

FRENCH FRIED POTATOES

Double recipe—use one batch and freeze the other for quick browning

6 medium potatoes, peeled
Cold water
Fat for frying
Salt
Pepper

• Cut potatoes lengthwise, then crosswise into 3/8" strips. Rinse in cold water; dry thoroughly between towels.
• Fry small amounts in deep, hot fat (360°) about 5 minutes, until tender but not brown. Drain on paper toweling; repeat with remaining batches.
• To prepare for freezing, cool to room temperature. Package, seal, label, date and freeze. Recommended storage time is 1 month.
• To serve, arrange potatoes on baking sheet; put in hot oven (425°) 10 minutes, or until brown, turning once.
• Quickly season with salt and pepper to taste. Serve at once. Makes 6 servings.

HASHED BROWN POTATOES

Brown and crisp on outside—tasty

3 c. cubed cooked potatoes (about 4)
¼ c. minced onion
¼ c. minced parsley or spinach
3 tblsp. flour
1½ tsp. salt
½ tsp. pepper
¼ c. light cream
3 tblsp. bacon drippings

• Combine potatoes with onion, parsley, flour, salt and pepper; toss lightly to mix well. Stir in cream.
• Heat 2 tblsp. drippings in heavy 8″ skillet. Spread potato mixture in skillet, packing down with spatula. Brown over medium heat until bottom is crusty, 10 to 15 minutes. (Shake pan constantly from side to side to prevent sticking.) Lift to hot platter, browned side up. Scrape and wipe pan free of crumbs with paper towel.
• Heat 1 tblsp. drippings in skillet. Slide potato "pancake" back into skillet, browned side up. Brown 5 to 10 minutes, shaking constantly, and firming edges with spatula. Turn onto hot platter; cut in wedges to serve. Makes 6 servings.

POTATO SUNFLOWERS

Shaggy shreds make the potato petals of this country favorite

4 medium potatoes
¼ c. melted shortening or salad oil
Salt
Pepper
Garlic salt

• Coarsely shred peeled potatoes.
• Heat shortening in heavy skillet. Drop rounded tablespoons of potatoes in fat. Spread a little, keeping the cakes thin. Fry until golden brown on both sides, about 5 minutes.
• Drain on paper toweling; sprinkle with salt, pepper and garlic salt. Serve at once. Makes 6 servings.

OVEN-FRIED POTATOES

No fuss to fix the crisp, brown potato slices that are mealy inside

4 medium potatoes, peeled
3 tblsp. melted fat
1 tsp. salt
⅜ tsp. pepper
⅜ tsp. paprika

• Cut potatoes crosswise in ⅜″ slices. Brush with melted fat.
• Bake in hot oven (425°), basting frequently with fat until tender and golden brown on both sides.
• Sprinkle with salt, pepper and paprika, and serve hot. Makes 5 servings.

OVEN FRENCH FRIES

A wise selection for a fast-fix meal

Potatoes, cut in ⅜″ strips or slices
Melted butter
Salt
Corn flake crumbs

• Dip potatoes (allow 1 medium potato for each serving) in melted butter, sprinkle with salt and roll in crumbs. Spread in baking pan, one layer deep. Bake in moderate oven (375°) 45 minutes, or until done.

COUNTRY-FRIED POTATOES

A favorite since pioneer days

⅓ c. lard
6 c. sliced peeled potatoes, ¼″ thick
1 c. sliced onions
2 tsp. salt
¼ tsp. pepper
Chopped parsley (optional)

· Heat lard in heavy skillet (bacon drippings or other fat or oil may be used). Arrange in skillet a layer of potatoes, then one of onions; repeat.
· Sprinkle with salt and pepper. Sauté, covered, over low heat, about 15 minutes. Uncover; increase heat slightly and sauté 10 minutes longer, or until potatoes are crisp and brown on underside. Do not stir.
· Sprinkle with parsley. Fold in half like an omelet and serve on a hot platter. Makes 4 to 6 servings.

Note: You can omit onions and use shredded instead of sliced potatoes.

BROWN POTATOES

Perfect companion for roast beef

12 medium potatoes
2 c. chopped beef suet
Salt
Pepper

· Peel potatoes and cut in lengthwise halves. Boil 8 minutes in salted water; drain.
· Place beef suet in shallow pan; melt in oven.
· One hour before dinner, add potatoes and bake in slow oven (325°) about 1 hour, or until tender. Turn occasionally to brown potatoes evenly. Season with salt and pepper. Makes 8 servings.

Note: If you're roasting beef and do not have room in oven for a pan of potatoes, you can boil peeled whole medium-size potatoes 15 minutes, drain and put in pan around roast to cook 45 minutes. Turn to brown evenly.

POTATO/CHEESE SCALLOP

You won't go wrong on this

1 medium onion, thinly sliced
2 tblsp. melted butter or regular margarine
6 medium potatoes (about 2 lbs.)
1 c. grated sharp process cheese
2 tblsp. flour
2 tsp. salt
⅛ tsp. pepper
2½ c. milk
¼ c. finely crushed cracker crumbs or potato chips

· Cook onion slices in butter until lightly browned.
· Peel and slice potatoes. Place one fourth of potatoes in bottom of greased 2-qt. baking dish. Add one fourth each: onion slices, cheese, flour, salt and pepper. Repeat layers. Pour milk over top. Sprinkle with crumbs.
· Cover and bake in moderate oven (350°) 1 hour. Remove cover the last 15 minutes. Makes 6 servings.

POTATOES IN BUTTERMILK

These are a perfect ham or bacon go-with for breakfast—or any meal

2 tblsp. butter or regular margarine
2 c. chopped peeled raw potatoes
½ tsp. salt
⅛ tsp. coarse grind pepper
1 c. thick buttermilk
Paprika

· Heat butter in a skillet (electric one is excellent); add potatoes and toss and cook until potatoes begin to brown. Add salt, pepper and buttermilk; simmer slowly until potatoes are tender and liquid thickened. Sprinkle a little paprika on each serving. Makes 4 servings.

SKILLET-SCALLOPED POTATOES

They're luscious with cream and cheese

6 medium potatoes
¼ c. shortening or bacon drippings
1 medium onion, chopped
1 tsp. salt
¼ tsp. pepper
¼ c. light cream
⅓ c. process sharp cheese spread

• Peel potatoes; slice thinly.
• Heat shortening in large skillet. Add potatoes, onion and seasonings. Fry potatoes slowly over low heat until golden brown, turning frequently.
• Pour on cream; add cheese, stirring gently to mix. Cover; cook slowly 10 minutes, or until potatoes are tender. Makes 6 servings.

FARM POTATOES WITH EGGS

Give thanks to Pennsylvania Dutch women who invented this simple treat

4 c. sliced boiled potatoes
¼ c. butter, regular margarine or bacon drippings
Salt
Freshly ground pepper
2 tblsp. minced parsley, or 1 tsp. parsley flakes
2 eggs, slightly beaten

• Fry potatoes in butter until nicely browned; add salt and pepper to taste.
• Combine parsley and eggs; stir into potatoes at the moment they are being dished up (do not let pan remain on heat after eggs are in). Serve as a breakfast dish with broiled ham or bacon. Makes 4 servings.

CHEESE-TOPPED POTATOES

Perfect to serve with hamburgers

6 baking potatoes
Salt
½ c. melted butter or regular margarine
Process cheese slices
Parsley

• Scrub potatoes well. Cut diagonally, with skins on, in 1½" slices. Spread in greased 13 × 9 × 2" baking pan. Sprinkle with salt; brush with butter.
• Bake uncovered in hot oven (400°) 30 minutes, or until tender. Remove from oven and top with cheese slices (about 6). Return to oven about 5 minutes, or until cheese is melted. Garnish with sprigs of parsley. Makes 6 servings.

SCALLOPED SWEET POTATOES AND APPLES

A marvelous flavor combination

8 medium sweet potatoes, cooked
4 medium apples, cored and cut in rings
½ c. brown sugar, firmly packed
½ c. pecans, halves or pieces
1 tsp. salt
½ tsp. ground mace
2 tblsp. butter or regular margarine

• Peel sweet potatoes and cut in lengthwise slices about ½" thick. Arrange layers of potato slices, apples, brown sugar, pecans and seasonings in greased 2-qt. casserole.
• Cover and bake in moderate oven (350°) 50 minutes. Makes 6 servings.

STUFFED BAKED SWEET POTATOES

You can stuff and refrigerate these a few hours before baking them

6 medium sweet potatoes
3 tblsp. butter
½ c. orange juice
1 tsp. salt
1 (8½ oz.) can crushed pineapple
½ c. chopped pecans

• Bake scrubbed sweet potatoes in moderate oven (375°) until tender, 45 minutes to 1 hour. Cut strip off top of each potato. Spoon potato out of shell. Combine with butter, orange juice and salt, and whip.

• Stir in pineapple. Spoon back into sweet potato shells. Sprinkle with nuts. Bake in moderate oven (375°) until thoroughly hot, about 12 minutes. Makes 6 servings.

BAKED SWEET POTATOES WITH ORANGE MARMALADE

Bake these sweets alongside your pork roast—they're good oven partners

8 medium sweet potatoes, cooked and peeled
¼ c. brown sugar, firmly packed
½ tsp. salt
1 c. light cream or evaporated milk
½ c. orange marmalade
16 marshmallows

• Cut potatoes in 1″ slices. Place in greased 13 × 9 × 2″ pan. Sprinkle with brown sugar and salt. Pour cream over. Bake in moderate oven (350°) 45 minutes. Remove from oven.

• Spread marmalade over potatoes; top with marshmallows. Return to oven and bake until marshmallows are lightly browned, 15 to 20 minutes. Serves 8.

OVEN-CANDIED SWEET POTATOES

Fine escort for ham or pork chops

¼ c. butter
½ c. dark corn syrup
2 tblsp. water
¼ c. brown sugar, firmly packed
½ tsp. salt
6 medium sweet potatoes, cooked and peeled

• Melt butter. Stir in corn syrup, water, brown sugar and salt.

• Cut potatoes in halves lengthwise. Dip in corn syrup mixture, coating all sides. Place in 13 × 9 × 2″ pan. Pour remaining syrup over top.

• Bake in slow oven (325°) until tender and glazed, about 1 hour and 15 minutes. Baste occasionally. Serves 6.

SUNSHINE POTATO BALLS

A Christmas special as pretty on the table as glitter balls on the tree

¼ c. melted butter
¼ c. milk
2 tblsp. sugar
½ tsp. salt
¼ tsp. pepper
4 c. mashed cooked sweet potatoes
18 to 20 miniature marshmallows
3 c. coarsely crushed corn flakes

• Beat butter, milk, sugar, salt and pepper into potatoes; form 2″ balls with marshmallow centers; roll in corn flakes.

• Place in greased 13 × 9 × 2″ baking pan. Bake in moderate oven (375°) 25 to 35 minutes. Or freeze; then bake without defrosting 45 minutes. Makes 18 to 20 potato balls.

MAPLE SWEET POTATOES

The maple flavor complements sweet potatoes, gives them a nice glaze

½ c. maple syrup
¼ c. butter or regular margarine
1 (17 oz.) can vacuum pack sweet potatoes, drained

• Combine syrup and butter in saucepan; bring to a boil and cook until thickened.
• Add sweet potatoes; simmer until hot, basting occasionally with glaze. Makes 4 servings.

GLAZED SWEET POTATOES

Easy to fix, extra-good, attractive—pink glaze glistens over sweets

½ c. apple jelly
1 tsp. red cinnamon candies (red hots)
2 tblsp. butter
½ tsp. salt
2 (17 oz.) cans vacuum pack sweet potatoes, drained

• Melt apple jelly, candies and butter in skillet. Add salt and stir to blend.
• Add sweet potatoes. Turn to coat thoroughly with mixture. Cover and cook over low heat 5 minutes. Uncover. Turn potatoes again and continue cooking until thoroughly heated, 2 or 3 minutes. Makes 6 to 8 servings.

PLUMP SWEET POTATO CROQUETTES

Cranberry sauce gives color—the tart taste is nice with the sweets

1 (17 oz.) can vacuum pack sweet potatoes, drained and mashed
1 egg, slightly beaten
1 tsp. grated orange peel
1 tblsp. brown sugar
½ tsp. salt
¾ c. finely chopped pecans
1 tblsp. melted butter or regular margarine
Canned whole cranberry sauce

• Combine sweet potatoes, egg, orange peel, brown sugar and salt. Form into 12 balls by rolling heaping tablespoonfuls of the mixture in the nuts. Place on greased baking sheet. Make a large thumbprint in each ball to form a nest. Dribble with butter.
• Bake in hot oven (425°) 20 minutes, or until brown. Place a spoonful of cranberry sauce in center of each. Makes 12 croquettes.

Hungry for Salsify

Memories of how good salsify, or oyster plant, tastes influenced a woman with her husband and children, to move from a California city back to the Iowa farm where she grew up. That's what a FARM JOURNAL food editor discovered when she asked her hostess why the family had changed from an urban to a rural home. She gave many reasons, including pure air and her belief that the country is a good place to bring up children. Then she confessed her homesickness for vegetables that tasted like those back on the farm. "Vegetables in California markets did not always taste like vegetables in our farm garden," the homemaker said. "Often I couldn't find my favorites. I actually longed in autumn for salsify. Now we grow it." Her recipe for Salsify Cakes follows.

SALSIFY CAKES

Serve these with ham and eggs, or with maple syrup or honey

1½ lbs. salsify (about 6 roots)
1 tsp. vinegar
½ tsp. salt
⅛ tsp. pepper
3 to 4 tblsp. butter or margarine
⅛ tsp. garlic powder
Flour

• Cut off tops and wash salsify; peel thinly with vegetable peeler; cut in 1″ lengths. Drop immediately in cold water to cover with vinegar and salt added. Bring to a boil and cook, covered, until tender enough to mash, 15 to 20 minutes. Drain thoroughly.

• Mash salsify, adding pepper, 1 tblsp. butter and garlic powder. Form in flat cakes about 3″ in diameter; dredge lightly with flour. Cook in remaining butter. Makes 12 cakes, or 6 servings.

SALSIFY/OYSTER CASSEROLE

Oyster stew bolsters salsify's faint oyster taste in this delightful dish

1½ lbs. salsify (about 6 roots)
1 tsp. vinegar
½ tsp. salt
2 eggs
1 (6 oz.) can evaporated milk, undiluted
1 can condensed oyster stew
1 c. coarse cracker crumbs
Salt
Pepper
1 tblsp. butter or regular margarine
⅛ tsp. paprika

• Cut off tops of salsify; wash and peel thinly with vegetable peeler. Cut in ½″ slices (you'll have 3½ to 4 c.), and plunge into cold water containing vinegar to prevent discoloration. Drain. Barely cover with boiling water; add ½ tsp. salt and cook until tender, about 15 minutes. Drain, and cool.

• Beat eggs; add evaporated milk and oyster stew (there should be 12 to 15 small oysters, actually tiny ones).

• Place salsify in greased 1½-qt. casserole. Pour oyster stew mixture over, distributing the oysters about. Add crumbs and fold in slightly. Add more salt, if necessary, and a little pepper. Dot with butter and sprinkle with paprika. Bake in moderate oven (350°) 40 to 45 minutes, or until set. Makes 6 to 8 servings.

CHEESE-CREAMED SPINACH

The kind of vegetable dish you'll be proud to offer guests—it's distinctive

3 (10 oz.) pkgs. frozen chopped spinach
1 (1 to 1½ oz.) envelope onion soup mix
2 c. dairy sour cream
½ c. grated Cheddar cheese

• Cook spinach as directed on package; drain. Combine with onion-soup mix and dairy sour cream. Spoon into greased 2-qt. casserole. Top with cheese.

• Bake in moderate oven (350°) until heated throughout, about 25 minutes. Makes 8 to 10 servings.

GREEN RICE

An old friend—as popular as ever and a perfect companion to chicken

3 c. cooked rice (1 c. uncooked)
1 c. chopped spinach
2 eggs, well beaten
1 c. milk
1 tsp. Worcestershire sauce
1¼ tsp. salt

2 tsp. grated onion
¼ c. butter or regular margarine
½ c. grated sharp cheese

• Toss rice and spinach together with fork. Add eggs, milk, Worcestershire sauce, salt and onion. Toss gently to mix, using care not to mash rice.
• Pour into greased 2-qt. baking dish; dot with butter and sprinkle on cheese.
• Bake in slow oven (325°) 30 to 40 minutes. Makes 8 servings.

Note: Add a few chopped blanched almonds, if you like. You can use ½ c. chopped parsley for half the spinach.

SQUASH MEDLEY

A much praised vegetable casserole

4 fresh medium unpeeled summer squash, or 4 c. frozen summer squash
½ green pepper, chopped
2 ripe tomatoes, peeled and chopped
6 slices bacon, fried and crumbled
1½ c. shredded process cheese
⅓ c. chopped onion
½ tsp. salt
½ c. fine bread crumbs
2 tblsp. butter

• Parboil squash (zucchini for 3 minutes; yellow crooknecks or small white pattypans, 5 minutes; and white scallops, 15 to 20 minutes). If you use frozen squash, do not parboil.
• To make filling, combine remaining ingredients, except crumbs and butter. Mix well.
• Slice parboiled squash thinly. Place in baking dish, alternating squash and filling. Top with bread crumbs and dabs of butter.
• Bake in moderate oven (375°) 35 minutes. Makes 6 to 8 servings.

PUFFED-UP ZUCCHINI

Light and tender—almost like a soufflé. Serve with roast meats

4 c. chopped zucchini
1 c. chopped onion
¼ c. water
2 tblsp. butter or regular margarine
½ tsp. salt
⅛ tsp. pepper
1 tblsp. grated horse-radish
1 egg, slightly beaten
1 c. coarse cracker crumbs
3 tblsp. butter or regular margarine

• Combine zucchini and onion in saucepan. Add water, cover and cook until tender, about 15 minutes. Drain well. Mash zucchini; add 2 tblsp. butter, salt, pepper and horse-radish. Cool.
• Add egg and mix thoroughly. Pour into greased 1-qt. baking dish. Top with crumbs that have been browned in the 3 tblsp. butter.
• Bake in moderate oven (350°) 30 minutes. Makes 6 servings.

SHORT-CUT ZUCCHINI

Don't bother to peel the zucchini

1 lb. small zucchini
¼ c. butter or regular margarine
¼ tsp. garlic salt
⅛ tsp. pepper
2 tblsp. water
2 tblsp. grated Parmesan cheese

• Slice zucchini (do not peel). Melt butter in skillet; add zucchini, seasonings and water.
• Cover tightly and simmer over low heat about 10 minutes. Sprinkle with cheese. Simmer an additional 5 minutes. Makes 3 servings.

SUMMER SQUASH WITH SOUR CREAM

Young squash is a natural convenience food—no peeling, no seeds big enough to need removing

- 2 lbs. squash, cut in 1" strips
- 1 tsp. salt
- ⅓ c. chopped onion
- 2 tblsp. butter or regular margarine
- 1 c. dairy sour cream
- 4 tsp. flour
- Paprika

• Sprinkle squash with salt; let stand 1 hour to improve flavor; drain.

• Cook squash and onion in butter over low heat. When squash is tender, add sour cream mixed with flour. Bring to a boil; remove from heat. Sprinkle with paprika. Makes 6 servings.

MAPLE BUTTERED SQUASH

Country cooking at its best—squash flavored with butter and maple syrup

- 1 (3 to 3½ lb.) Hubbard squash
- 2 tblsp. maple syrup
- 2 tblsp. butter or regular margarine
- 1 tsp. salt
- Dash pepper
- Chopped chives or green onion

• Cut squash in large pieces; place in large baking pan. Cover with foil and bake in moderate oven (350°) about 1¼ hours, or until squash is tender.

• Scoop out pulp and put through a sieve. Stir in syrup, butter, salt and pepper. If mixture is thin, simmer gently to reduce moisture. Otherwise, heat just to boiling; turn into serving dish and garnish with chopped chives. Makes 4 to 6 servings.

BAKED BUTTERNUT SQUASH

Squash bakes to delicious perfection with practically no oven-watching

- 1 (3 to 3½ lb.) butternut squash
- Salt
- Pepper
- 1 tblsp. butter or regular margarine
- 3 to 4 tblsp. water
- ⅓ c. toasted pecan halves

• Wash squash; remove seeds at full, round end; cut in ½" slices. Overlap slices in 13 × 9 × 2" baking pan. Sprinkle with salt and pepper to taste; dot with butter. Add water; cover tightly with foil.

• Bake in hot oven (400°) 35 to 40 minutes, or until squash is tender. Serve topped with pecans. Makes 4 servings.

SQUASH CASSEROLE SPECIAL

Serve orange-yellow squash and green peas with chicken—a real feast

- 3 c. hot mashed butternut squash
- ¼ c. butter
- 1 tsp. salt
- ⅛ tsp. pepper
- 1 tsp. minced onion
- ¼ c. milk
- 3 eggs, well beaten
- ¼ c. buttered bread crumbs

• To hot squash add butter; beat until butter melts. Stir in salt, pepper and onion.

• Blend milk into eggs; add to squash.

• Pour into greased 1½-qt. casserole; top with bread crumbs. Set in pan of warm water and bake in moderate oven (350°) about 45 minutes, until knife inserted in center comes out clean. Serves 6.

ACORN SQUASH WITH CREAMED ONIONS

Creamed onions de luxe fill baked squash cups for an extra-good dish

- **3 acorn squash**
- **Salt**
- **2 lbs. small onions, peeled (about 4 c.)**
- **½ c. light raisins**
- **2 tblsp. butter or regular margarine**
- **2 tblsp. flour**
- **¼ tsp. salt**
- **1½ c. milk**
- **¼ tsp. ground nutmeg**

• Wash squash; cut in halves lengthwise, and remove seeds. Place squash, cut side down, in shallow baking pan; add a few tablespoons water to pan. Bake in hot oven (400°) 30 minutes. Turn cut side up; sprinkle with salt and continue baking 25 to 30 minutes, until tender.

• Cook onions in boiling salted water, covered, about 30 minutes, or until tender. Drain.

• Simmer raisins in water to cover 10 minutes; drain.

• Melt butter; blend in flour and ¼ tsp. salt. Add milk all at once. Cook and stir until sauce is thickened. Blend in ¼ tsp. nutmeg. Gently stir in onions and raisins. Spoon into cooked squash halves; sprinkle with additional nutmeg. Makes 6 servings.

CORN-STUFFED TOMATOES

Choose firm ripe tomatoes and tender corn; serve with chicken

- **10 medium tomatoes**
- **4 c. cooked corn, or 2 (1 lb.) cans whole kernel corn, drained**
- **1 tsp. salt**
- **¼ tsp. pepper**
- **¼ c. melted butter or regular margarine**

• Wash tomatoes, slice off tops, scoop out pulp. Combine pulp in bowl with remaining ingredients.

• Stuff tomatoes with mixture. Place in greased muffin-pan cups. Bake in moderate oven (375°) about 20 minutes. Makes 10 servings.

TOMATOES WITH BREAD STUFFING

Red tomatoes hold expertly seasoned stuffing–pretty and delectable

- **8 tomatoes**
- **1 c. chopped onion**
- **½ c. chopped celery with leaves**
- **¼ c. butter**
- **1 tblsp. parsley flakes**
- **½ tsp. basil leaves**
- **¼ tsp. instant minced garlic**
- **1 tsp. salt**
- **⅛ tsp. pepper**
- **5 c. bread cubes**

• Cut slice off top of each tomato. Scoop out center and save. Turn tomatoes upside down to drain.

• Cook onion and celery in butter until soft. Chop tomato centers and add to onion mixture along with parsley, basil, garlic, salt and pepper. Cook until mixture thickens, about 15 minutes. Stir occasionally.

• Add bread cubes. Place tomato shells in muffin-pan cups. Fill with bread stuffing. Bake in moderate oven (350°) 30 minutes. Makes 8 servings.

BAKED TOMATO HALVES

Just bake these seasoned tomatoes in the oven—no last-minute fuss

6 tomatoes
2 tblsp. chopped onion
2 tblsp. butter
½ c. bread crumbs
2 tblsp. chopped parsley
½ tsp. salt
⅛ tsp. pepper

• Cut stem end out of tomatoes. Cut tomatoes in halves and place in 13 × 9 × 2" baking pan.
• Cook onion in butter until soft. Add remaining ingredients and toss. Spread mixture on top of tomato halves.
• Bake in hot oven (400°) until lightly browned, about 25 minutes. Makes 6 servings as a vegetable, 12 as a garnish.

SAVORY TOMATO SKILLET

Ripe tomatoes cook to perfection in buttery sauce for this country treat

¼ c. butter or regular margarine
½ c. finely chopped onion
2 tblsp. chopped parsley
½ tsp. salt
¼ tsp. thyme leaves
⅛ tsp. pepper
6 whole tomatoes, peeled and cored

• Melt butter in skillet. Add onion, parsley, salt, thyme and pepper. Add tomatoes, cored side down.
• Cover and cook 5 minutes. Turn tomatoes carefully, basting with butter mixture. Cover and continue cooking 5 minutes. Serve in sauce dishes with sauce spooned over. Makes 6 servings.

TOMATOES COUNTRY-STYLE

Seasoning tomatoes with celery seeds is a favored farm kitchen custom

2 slices bacon
1 small onion
1 (1 lb.) can tomatoes
¼ tsp. celery seeds
Salt
Pepper

• Cook bacon until crisp; remove from skillet and drain.
• Slice onion and separate into rings; cook in bacon fat until tender, but not brown. Add tomatoes and celery seeds; heat. Season with salt and pepper to taste. Serve topped with crumbled bacon. Makes 4 servings.

TOMATOES AU JUS

Old-time favorite always in style

2 tblsp. butter or regular margarine
1 small onion, finely chopped
2 tblsp. minced parsley
1 (28 oz.) can tomatoes
⅛ tsp. pepper
1 tsp. Worcestershire sauce
Salt to taste

• Combine butter, onion, parsley and juice drained from tomatoes; cook down to about half.
• Add tomatoes, pepper, Worcestershire sauce and salt; heat. Serve in sauce dishes. Makes 5 servings.

STEWED TOMATOES SUPREME

The parsley decorates, the crackers add crispness and a taste of cheese

1 (1 lb.) can stewed tomatoes
¼ c. crushed appetizer cheese crackers
1 tblsp. chopped parsley

• Heat tomatoes in saucepan. Serve in individual sauce dishes, topping each serving with a spoonful of crackers and a sprinkling of parsley. Makes 4 servings.

When the Tomatoes Are Ripe

Big tomato crops challenge country people to find ways to extend the enjoyment of the vegetable throughout the year. "If you have bushel baskets and tubs filled with red-ripe, fat, juicy tomatoes on your back porch," says an upstate New York gardener, "you get busy and figure out a way to salvage some of them to use during the winter."

She developed a two-in-one canning idea that works like a charm. After each picking, she cooks the tomatoes and converts them into two products that please her family and friends. They also cut down on grocery bills and give meals a homegrown flavor. One is Tangy Tomato Cocktail, the other, Spicy Spaghetti Sauce. Once you have these two tomato specialties in your cupboard, you'll find many occasions and ways to use them.

BASIC TOMATO MIXTURE

Both cocktail and sauce start with this

20 lbs. firm ripe tomatoes, about 60 medium-size tomatoes
2 tblsp. salt
1 tsp. celery salt
3 tblsp. Worcestershire sauce
2 tsp. onion powder
¼ tsp. Tabasco sauce

• Wash tomatoes, cut in halves and remove stem ends (no peeling necessary). Remove any spoiled or green spots (they can ruin the mixture).

• Place tomato halves in a large canning kettle over high heat. Add salt, celery salt, Worcestershire sauce, onion powder and Tabasco sauce. Bring to a full boil, stirring frequently to prevent sticking. Cook 5 minutes. Remove from heat and ladle mixture into a food mill, colander or large sieve. Strain off any liquid that pours through easily. Stir just enough to let the juice pour through. Use it to make the cocktail.

TANGY TOMATO COCKTAIL: Taste the juice to make sure it is well seasoned. If you wish, add another 1 tsp. celery salt. If juice is too tart, add 1 to 2 tblsp. sugar. Heat mixture just until boiling, pour into quart canning jars, adjust lids and process in a boiling water bath 10 minutes. Makes about 4 quarts.

SPICY SPAGHETTI SAUCE: Transfer the juicy tomato pulp into another container without passing through a food mill, colander or sieve. Add 1 tblsp, dried orégano leaves, 2 cloves garlic, peeled and quartered, and 2 tblsp. Worcestershire sauce. Place in the electric blender, about 2 c. at a time; blend until smooth. Make sure tomato skins are blended. (If you want to remove all the small bits of tomato skin and seeds, run this mixture through a colander, food mill or sieve after blending.) Heat mixture until boiling. Pour into pint canning jars, adjust lids and process 10 minutes in a boiling water bath. Makes about 7 pints.

BROILED TOMATOES

Tempting accompaniment to broiled steak, lamb chops or hamburgers

- 3 tblsp. melted butter or regular margarine
- ½ c. coarse cracker crumbs
- 2 tblsp. minced parsley
- ¼ tsp. thyme leaves
- ½ tsp. salt
- ⅛ tsp. pepper
- 4 medium ripe tomatoes

· Combine butter, crumbs, parsley, thyme, salt and pepper; mix well.

· Cut stem end from tomatoes; cut in halves crosswise. Spread crumb mixture on cut sides.

· Place on rack in preheated broiler, about 4″ from heat. Broil until tomatoes are heated through and topping is lightly browned, 3 to 5 minutes. Serve immediately. Makes 4 servings.

COUNTRY-FRIED GREEN TOMATOES

If you don't count calories, you'll like these tomatoes with hot, rich cream gravy poured over the top

- 6 medium green tomatoes, sliced
- 1 tblsp. sugar
- ½ c. flour
- ½ tsp. salt
- ¼ tsp. pepper
- ¼ c. butter

· Sprinkle tomatoes with sugar; let stand about 15 minutes. Combine flour, salt and pepper and coat tomato slices.

· Melt 2 tblsp. butter in skillet. Brown tomatoes slowly on both sides. Remove each batch to ovenproof platter and keep hot in oven until all tomatoes are cooked. Add more butter if needed. For crisp slices, serve as is. Or add ½ c. light cream or dairy half-and-half to skillet. Heat, stirring into drippings, and pour over tomatoes. Makes 6 servings.

WHIPPED TURNIPS

Taste-testers named this the best turnip dish they ever tasted—mild

- 4 c. mashed cooked turnips
- 2 c. soft bread crumbs
- ½ c. melted butter
- 2 tblsp. sugar
- 2 tsp. salt
- ¼ tsp. pepper
- 4 eggs, slightly beaten

· Combine turnips with bread crumbs. (To prepare soft bread crumbs, remove crusts from fresh bread; cut or tear in tiny cubes.)

· Blend in remaining ingredients. Place in greased 2-qt. casserole. Bake in moderate oven (350°) 1 hour and 15 minutes, or until set. Makes 8 servings.

TURNIPS IN CHEESE SAUCE

If your family doesn't fancy turnips, try this and win them over

- 3 c. sliced peeled turnips
- ¼ c. butter or regular margarine
- ¼ c. flour
- 1½ c. light cream
- 1 c. shredded process cheese
- 1 tblsp. minced chives

· Cook sliced turnips in boiling salted water 8 to 10 minutes. Drain; cover to keep hot.

· Melt butter in saucepan; stir in flour. Add cream; cook, stirring, until thickened. Add cheese, and stir until melted.

· Add turnips to sauce. Sprinkle with chives. Makes 6 servings.

Note: New Englanders refer to yellow and white turnips, but in some areas the yellow ones are called rutabagas. White turnips are more delicate in flavor, but they may be used interchangeably.

BAKED TURNIPS WITH PEANUTS

Unusual turnip dish of Dutch origin

3 c. sliced cooked turnips
1 medium onion, sliced
1 c. chopped peanuts
2 tblsp. butter
2 tsp. salt
½ tsp. paprika
Chopped parsley

• Arrange turnips, onion and peanuts in well greased 1½-qt. baking dish. Dot with butter, add salt and paprika. Bake uncovered in moderate oven (350°) 15 minutes. Sprinkle with parsley. Makes 6 servings.

Variation

BAKED RUTABAGAS WITH PEANUTS: Substitute cooked rutabaga for turnips.

GOLDEN RUTABAGA RING

Limas in cheese sauce fill the ring

4 to 6 c. mashed rutabagas
3 tblsp. butter
½ to ¾ tsp. salt
⅛ tsp. pepper
2 (10 oz.) pkgs. frozen lima beans
¼ lb. pasteurized process cheese spread
½ tsp. salt
⅛ tsp. pepper

• Whip mashed rutabagas with butter, ½ to ¾ tsp. salt and ⅛ tsp. pepper. Arrange on round serving platter around a form. (An empty 1 lb. 13 oz. can from which both ends have been removed, and stood upright, makes a good form.)
• Meanwhile, cook limas in boiling salted water; drain. Add cheese, stirring until cheese is melted. Add ½ tsp. salt and ⅛ tsp. pepper.
• Place limas in center of can on platter. Carefully lift can; serve immediately. Makes 8 servings.

SWEDISH RUTABAGAS

An heirloom recipe shared by the granddaughter of a good Swedish cook

2 medium rutabagas, peeled, quartered and sliced ¼" thick
2 tblsp. brown sugar
½ tsp. ground ginger
½ tsp. salt
⅛ tsp. pepper
2 tblsp. butter

• Cook rutabagas in boiling salted water; drain.
• Meanwhile, combine brown sugar, ginger, salt and pepper; mix thoroughly. Add with butter to rutabagas. Stir gently over low heat until sugar melts, 2 to 3 minutes. Makes 6 servings.

RUTABAGA/POTATO CASSEROLE

Complete the main course with pork sausage and buttered green beans

2 medium potatoes
2 medium rutabagas
½ c. flour
1 tsp. baking powder
1 tsp. salt
⅛ tsp. pepper
4 eggs, well beaten
¼ c. milk
¼ c. melted butter or drippings

• Peel potatoes and rutabagas; cover with cold water and let stand.

• Sift together flour, baking powder and seasonings.
• Blend half of dry ingredients with eggs. Stir in milk and butter; mix.
• Drain vegetables; grate fine or use blender.
• With wooden spoon, quickly mix remaining dry ingredients with vegetables. Work quickly to avoid dark potatoes. Blend in egg mixture.
• Place in greased 1-qt. casserole. Set in pan of hot water with level at least ⅔ up side of casserole.
• Bake in slow oven (325°) 1 hour. Makes 6 servings.

VEGETABLES IN FOIL

Tuck the silvery packages in the oven—forget about them for an hour

6 medium carrots
6 small whole onions
3 branches celery
1 medium green pepper
Salt
6 tblsp. Basic Red Sauce (see Index)

• Peel carrots and onions; clean celery. Remove seeds from green pepper. Cut carrots in quarters lengthwise, celery in diagonal strips and green pepper in lengthwise strips. Leave onions whole.
• Place vegetables on 6 pieces of aluminum foil, dividing them evenly. Sprinkle salt over them and add 1 tblsp. Basic Red Sauce to each of the 6 groups. Close foil around vegetables, using drugstore wrap and folding ends. Do not wrap tightly.
• Bake in hot oven (400°) 50 to 60 minutes or until vegetables are tender. Serve steaming hot in foil, opening tops of packages and folding edges back. Makes 6 servings.

chapter 8

Superior Salads and Dressings

CHILLED LEAFY VEGETABLES so crisp that they crackle, tossed with your favorite dressing, make a health-brimming green salad neither your husband nor men guests will shun. You know all the talk about men not liking salads is a myth.

Many of the favorite salad recipes sent to us come from country kitchens. Since women plan meals to please their husbands and families, the increasing flow of salad recipes to our food editors indicates progress in good nutrition and taste-changing.

The recipes in this chapter divide into four groups: fruit, vegetable, molded (gelatin) and substantial salads. With them we give you excitingly different salad dressings. Good salad-makers depend on a variety of dressings to provide distinction and superior flavors to their salads.

Molded salads are great travelers. They're easy to carry and women appreciate being able to make them the day before or early in the morning to serve in the evening. If you do not have the size mold specified in the recipe, fill the possible substitutes with water and measure them in cupfuls. Then you will know how much they hold and which one is the best selection. Be sure to chill the gelatin mixture until it's thick as an unbeaten egg white before you add vegetables, fruits or nuts. Drain the foods before you add them or the liquid may thin the gelatin. To hasten thickening, set the pan containing the gelatin mixture in the freezing compartment of the refrigerator or in a pan of ice water. Remove when the thickening begins. If "overset," soften over hot water before you add fruit or other ingredients.

Many women like to remove gelatin from molds this way: Top mold with a plate and invert. Dip a kitchen towel in hot water, wring it out and wrap it around the mold; press into the depressions made by the design. If the salad does not slip out easily, repeat until it does.

Choose the salad from this chapter that complements the remainder of the meal. Those with pronounced flavor like our Farmhouse Green Salad with Cheese/Garlic Dressing hold their own with steaks, roast beef and lamb. Juicy, cooling fruit salads taste wonderful with Mexican-type dishes; apple salads are great with ham and pork. Some fruit salads double for dessert. Our Frozen Fruit Salad/Dessert is an excellent example. Make a big batch of it before the holiday season. If you want the perfect gift from your kitchen, a quart of this salad will fill the bill.

Apple Salad Specials

When we looked in our bulging recipe files of choice fruit salads, the number of tempting apple salads impressed us. We share some of these —Frozen Apple Salad comes as a favorite from a hospitable home economist, wife of an Iowa dairyman, who loves to entertain friends. Fruit Salad Plate provides perfect refreshment for a women's luncheon. While the salad proper does not contain apples, it owes much of its superior taste to Apple/Honey Dressing.

SEPTEMBER APPLE SALAD

Surprise—apples and cucumbers pair off in this delightful salad

2 c. diced unpeeled apples
2 c. diced peeled cucumbers
½ tsp. salt
¼ c. lemon juice
½ c. salad dressing
¼ c. chopped nuts (optional)
Lettuce

• Toss apples and cucumbers with salt; sprinkle with lemon juice. Mix in salad dressing and nuts. Serve chilled on lettuce. Makes 6 servings.

POINSETTIA SALAD

Red, cinnamon apples make the petals

6 medium apples
1½ c. water
1 c. sugar
6 very thin lemon slices
¼ c. red cinnamon candies
8 pineapple slices
1 hard-cooked egg yolk

• Peel and core apples; cut each into 8 lengthwise slices.

• Put water, sugar, lemon and cinnamon candies in saucepan; bring to boil. Add apples; simmer slowly in syrup until tender but firm, about 10 minutes. Chill in syrup until serving time.

• Place pineapple slices on individual salad plates. Arrange 6 drained apple slices on pineapple to form flower petals.

• Rub egg yolk through sieve; sprinkle a bit in center of apples. Add a few sprigs of greens for stem. Makes 8 servings.

WALDORF VARIATION SALAD

Lemonade makes this salad refreshing

4 peeled oranges cut in sections
4 red apples, cut into wedges

1 c. sliced celery
1 (13½ oz.) can pineapple chunks
1 (6 oz.) can frozen lemonade concentrate, slightly thawed

• Toss all ingredients together. Chill well. Makes about 8 servings.

CRUNCHY APPLE SALAD

This bright fruit salad is refreshing

1 c. diced unpeeled apples
1 c. diced bananas
1 tblsp. lemon juice
½ c. drained pineapple tidbits
½ c. raisins
½ c. coarsely chopped pecans
⅓ c. mayonnaise

• Place apples, bananas and lemon juice in a bowl and toss. Add pineapple, raisins and pecans.
• Toss slightly. Add mayonnaise. Toss just until mayonnaise is mixed thoroughly. Spoon into individual lettuce cups or into a salad dish. Serves 6.

FROZEN APPLE SALAD

Reduce sugar to ¼ c. if you prefer a less sweet frozen salad

1 (8½ oz.) can crushed pineapple
2 eggs, beaten
½ c. sugar
⅛ tsp. salt
3 tblsp. lemon juice
2 c. chopped unpeeled apples
½ c. chopped celery
1 c. heavy cream, whipped

• Drain pineapple; save juice. Add enough water to juice to make ½ c. liquid; stir into eggs. Add sugar, salt and lemon juice. Cook over medium heat, stirring, until mixture thickens, about 5 minutes. Cool.
• Fold drained pineapple, apples, celery and whipped cream into cooled dressing. Spoon into 8" square dish or pan; cover and freeze.
• To serve, place frozen salad in refrigerator about 30 minutes. Cut in squares and serve on lettuce. Makes 9 servings.

FRUIT SALAD PLATE

A fruit plate for your luncheon party —serve with hot rolls and coffee

1 head lettuce
1 bunch escarole
3 oranges, peeled
3 grapefruit, peeled
2 doz. cooked prunes
1 (1 lb. 2 oz.) can Queen Ann cherries or dark sweet cherries
1 (1 lb. 14 oz.) can peach halves
2 red apples
Orange or grapefruit juice
2 (8 oz.) cartons creamed cottage cheese
2 c. fresh or frozen whole strawberries
Lime or pineapple sherbet
Apple Honey Dressing

• Wash and crisp greens. Section oranges and grapefruit (remove membrane). Pit prunes. Drain canned fruit. Slice and core apples; cover with orange or grapefruit juice to avoid darkening.
• Place greens on salad plates with mound of cottage cheese in center of each. Top with peach half, cut side up. Arrange other fruits around cottage cheese.
• Just before serving, fill peach half with sherbet, and serve with Apple/ Honey Dressing. Makes 6 salads.

APPLE/HONEY DRESSING

Let guests ladle this over their salads

⅓ c. sugar
¼ tsp. dry mustard
½ tsp. paprika
¼ tsp. salt
½ c. smooth applesauce
¼ c. strained honey
3 tblsp. lemon juice
1 tblsp. vinegar
¼ tsp. grated lemon peel
1 tsp. celery seeds
½ c. salad oil

• Combine all ingredients, except oil, in bowl. Mix well. Add oil slowly, beating thoroughly. Chill. Shake or beat well before serving. Makes 1½ cups.

CANTALOUPE SALAD

Cool-looking and cool-tasting—really refreshing on a sizzling day

2 medium cantaloupes, chilled
4 c. green seedless grapes
1 c. mayonnaise or salad dressing
⅓ c. frozen orange juice concentrate

• Cut cantaloupes lengthwise into 6 sections; remove seeds and peel.
• Place each section on a crisp lettuce leaf and heap stemmed grapes around melon.
• Combine mayonnaise with frozen orange juice concentrate; mix well and pass to ladle over salads. Serves 12.

Bowl Fruit Salads

Country people like to help themselves to mixed fruit salads. Bowls of it frequently make the rounds at the table. One favored make-ahead is the old-fashioned Overnight Salad, luscious with whipped cream. Another example is Glazed Fruit Salad, which contains no fat. Canned apricot pie filling provides the glaze. The flavors of fruits in these salads blend and mellow during the night while the hostess rests so she will be in good form next day while preparing the remainder of the party food.

OVERNIGHT SALAD

Grandmother's 24-hour salad-dessert

2 eggs
¼ c. white vinegar
¼ c. sugar
2 tblsp. butter
1 c. heavy cream, whipped
1 (1 lb. 4 oz.) can pineapple tidbits, drained
2 c. seedless grapes, halved
2 oranges, peeled and diced
2 c. quartered or miniature marshmallows

• Beat eggs in top of double boiler. Add vinegar, sugar and butter. Cook over boiling water, stirring until thick. Cool.
• Fold in whipped cream, fruits and marshmallows. Chill 24 hours. Serve in lettuce cups. Makes 8 to 10 servings.

Note: You can substitute 1 (1 lb. 1 oz.) can light cherries, drained, pitted and halved for the grapes.

GLAZED FRUIT SALAD

It's apricot pie filling that makes salad glisten—also adds fine flavor

1 (1 lb. 4 oz.) can pineapple chunks
1 (1 lb. 13 oz.) can fruit cocktail
2 (11 oz.) cans mandarin oranges
7 or 8 sliced peeled bananas

2 tblsp. lemon juice
1 (1 lb. 6 oz.) can apricot pie filling

• Drain the canned fruits thoroughly. Mix all the ingredients together and chill several hours, or overnight. Makes 12 servings.

Big-batch Hospitality Salad

A smart hostess works out ways to serve superior food to friends on short notice. One excellent plan is to fix a large fruit salad and freeze it. Then when guests come, all you have to do is make coffee or tea and slice the salad.

We share with you the salad-dessert recipe of an Iowa extension home economist who makes nine quarts of the luscious fruit mixture every year right after Thanksgiving. Then she's ready to welcome guests throughout the holiday season. She calls it Hospitality Salad-Dessert. Her friends call it good!

FROZEN FRUIT SALAD-DESSERT

Serve attractive slices of this luscious frozen treat to holiday drop-in guests

4 (1 lb. 4 oz.) cans crushed pineapple
2 (1 lb.) cans sliced peaches
2 c. fresh white seedless grapes, halved, or 2 (1 lb. 4 oz.) cans
1½ c. maraschino cherries, cut in eighths
½ lb. marshmallows, quartered (30)
2 tsp. crystallized ginger, finely chopped
1 envelope unflavored gelatin
¼ c. cold water
1 c. orange juice
¼ c. lemon juice
2½ c. sugar
½ tsp. salt
2 c. coarsely chopped pecans
2 qts. heavy cream, whipped, or 10 envelopes dessert topping mix, whipped, or 1 qt. heavy cream and 5 envelopes dessert topping mix, whipped
3 c. mayonnaise

• Drain fruit; save 1½ c. pineapple syrup. Cut peaches in ½" cubes. Combine fruit, marshmallows and ginger.
• Soften gelatin in cold water.
• Heat pineapple syrup to boiling. Add gelatin; stir to dissolve. Add orange and lemon juices, sugar and salt; stir to dissolve. Chill.
• When mixture starts to thicken, add fruit mixture and nuts. Fold in whipped cream and mayonnaise.
• Spoon into 1-qt. cylinder cartons (paper, plastic or metal). Cover and freeze. Makes 9 quarts.
• To serve, remove from freezer and thaw enough to slip out of carton. Cut in 1" slices. Serve salad on lettuce; garnish with cherries. For dessert, top with whipped cream. Each quart makes 6 to 8 servings.

Note: You can substitute 1½ c. ground raw cranberries or 3 (1 lb.) pkgs. frozen whole strawberries for the cherries. Thaw, drain strawberries. Substitute juice for some of the orange and pineapple juices.

Tossed Green Salads

Some country hostesses confess they rarely use a recipe to make tossed salads. They rub the bowl with a cut garlic clove, add bite-size pieces of lettuce or other greens (tender, baby spinach leaves, beet greens and dandelion greens are favorites) and toss them with bottled salad dressing from their supermarkets. The one point these saladmakers emphasize is that they combine vegetables and dressing at the last minute before serving to avoid wilting. Sometimes, for the sake of variety, they add non-leafy vegetables, such as cauliflower, onions, celery, green peppers, tomatoes and pickled beets.

We give you four recipes for exceptionally good and different green salads developed by home economists in our Countryside Test Kitchens. They have won more than their share of compliments from hostesses and their guests—you will like them.

FARMHOUSE GREEN SALAD WITH CHEESE/GARLIC DRESSING

The dressing adds a distinctive note to all kinds of green salads

¼ lb. bacon
1 head lettuce, broken into bite-size pieces
1 c. chopped celery
2 hard-cooked eggs, chopped
Cheese Garlic Dressing

• Fry bacon until crisp; drain and crumble into bits.
• Combine bacon, lettuce, celery and eggs in bowl; toss with Cheese/Garlic Dressing. Makes 6 servings.

CHEESE/GARLIC DRESSING: Stir together 1 tblsp. cheese garlic salad dressing mix, 1 c. dairy sour cream and 2 tblsp. lemon juice.

GARDEN SALAD BOWLS

Spicy red beets and crisp greens make picture-pretty individual salads

2 qts. mixed greens (leaf lettuce, romaine, escarole or tender beet greens)
½ c. onion slices
½ c. canned chick-peas, drained (optional)
1 c. pickled beet slices, well drained
Cottage Blue Cheese Dressing

• Wash and drain greens well; break into bite-size pieces before measuring.
• Toss together greens, onion slices and chick-peas; divide into 8 or 10 individual salad bowls. Top each bowl with about 4 beet slices and 2 tblsp. Cottage/Blue Cheese Dressing.

COTTAGE/BLUE CHEESE DRESSING

It's creamy with a mild cheese taste

2 tblsp. vinegar
⅛ tsp. salt
3 drops Tabasco sauce
⅔ c. mayonnaise
½ c. crumbled blue cheese
⅓ c. creamed cottage cheese

• In a small bowl, blend vinegar, salt and Tabasco sauce; blend in mayonnaise and beat until smooth.
• Stir in blue cheese and cottage cheese. Makes 1⅓ cups.

CATALINA TOSSED SALAD

Perfect salad for the barbecue crowd —equally at home in indoor meals

2 qts. mixed greens (leaf or romaine lettuce, spinach leaves or tender beet greens)
3 tomatoes, cut in wedges

- 1 c. raw cauliflowerets
- ½ c. crumbled blue cheese
- ½ c. crumbled cooked bacon
- ½ tsp. salt
- ¼ tsp. pepper
- ½ c. Honey French Dressing

• Wash and drain greens well; shake dry in a dish towel. Break into bite-size pieces before measuring.
• Add tomato wedges, cauliflowerets, blue cheese and bacon. Refrigerate until serving time.
• When ready to serve, add seasonings and Honey French Dressing; toss to coat all the greens. Makes 8 to 10 servings.

HONEY FRENCH DRESSING

Honey is the magic in this dressing

- 1 tsp. salt
- ¼ tsp. pepper
- 1 tsp. dry mustard
- ⅓ c. cider vinegar
- 2 tblsp. honey
- 1 c. salad oil

• In a small bowl, mix salt, pepper and dry mustard; stir in vinegar and honey. Slowly add the salad oil while beating with a rotary beater or electric mixer. Makes about 1⅓ cups.

BERMUDA TOSSED SALAD

Sesame seeds and garlic croutons are the exciting flavor and texture accents

- 1 qt. lettuce (leaf or romaine)
- 1 qt. young spinach leaves
- 3 tomatoes, cut in wedges
- ½ c. sweet onion rings
- 3 tblsp. Toasted Sesame Seeds
- ½ to 1 tsp. salt
- ¼ tsp. pepper
- ½ c. Honey French Dressing
- 1 to 3 c. Garlic Croutons

• Wash and drain leaves well; break into bite-size pieces before measuring.
• Add tomato wedges, onion rings and Toasted Sesame Seeds. Refrigerate until serving time.
• When ready to serve, add seasonings and Honey French Dressing; top with Garlic Croutons. Makes 8 to 10 servings.

TOASTED SESAME SEEDS: Spread sesame seeds in shallow pan and place in moderate oven (350°). Remove pan when seeds are a pale brown. It will take about 20 minutes, but watch them to prevent overbrowning, which destroys the seeds' finest flavors.

GARLIC CROUTONS: Trim crusts from 5 slices of day-old bread; cut into ½" cubes. In a heavy skillet, heat ⅓ c. salad oil and 1 crushed clove garlic. Add bread cubes; sauté until golden brown and crisp. Makes 3 cups.

FLOATING VEGETABLE SALAD

An old-fashioned country salad

- 3 large tomatoes, peeled and sliced rather thick
- 1 medium onion, thinly sliced
- 1 green pepper, seeded and sliced in rings
- 1 cucumber, thinly sliced
- 1½ tsp. salt
- ¼ tsp. pepper
- 3 tblsp. vinegar
- 3 tblsp. salad oil
- 1 tsp. paprika
- ½ tsp. dry mustard
- ½ tsp. celery seeds

• Arrange layers of vegetables in bowl. Sprinkle each with salt and pepper.
• Combine remaining ingredients and pour over vegetables; cover and chill

several hours, gently lifting vegetables occasionally to distribute dressing. Makes 6 servings.

CUCUMBER/SOUR CREAM SALAD

An inviting choice for a meal that features fried chicken or fish

1 tblsp. sugar
1½ tsp. salt
1 c. dairy sour cream
3 tblsp. grated onion
2 tblsp. white vinegar or lemon juice
4½ c. thinly sliced peeled cucumbers (6 medium)

· Blend together sugar, salt, sour cream, onion and vinegar. Stir in cucumbers. Chill at least 2 hours.
· Serve in lettuce cups for salad or on the tray with other relishes. Makes about 6 cups, the exact amount depending on size of cucumbers.

Variation

CUCUMBER SALAD WITH DILL: Stir 1 tsp. dill seeds into Cucumber/Sour Cream Salad. Omit sugar if you like a tart salad.

MARINATED TOMATOES

Garnish with chopped parsley

5 large ripe tomatoes
¼ c. salad oil
1½ tblsp. lemon juice
½ clove garlic, minced
½ tsp. salt
½ tsp. orégano leaves
⅛ tsp. pepper

· Peel tomatoes; cut in thick slices.
· Combine remaining ingredients. Pour over tomatoes. Chill thoroughly, stirring once or twice. Makes 6 servings.

Refrigerator Cabbage Salads

Generations of country saladmakers have depended on cabbage to brighten meals, add crunchy texture and contribute pleasing flavor contrast. Today's women follow suit by fixing delightful cold salads, like tossed Red and Green Cabbage Salad with Sour Cream Dressing and warm ones, such as Hot Slaw with Apples, made in a skillet.

The newer type cabbage salads are those you can keep on hand to serve quickly. Cabbage/Onion Salad is the specialty of a Kansas ranch wife who keeps a bowl of it in her refrigerator much of the time. She can spoon it up quickly to serve with hamburgers or steak when cattle buyers visit the ranch. Stay-crisp Cabbage Salad is another good ready-to-go salad. The recipe for our Sauerkraut Salad comes from Missouri, where men like its sharp flavor and often tote it on fishing trips. It's a good "keeper."

RED AND GREEN CABBAGE SALAD

Simple to fix, colorful salad that perks up meals featuring pork or ham

4 c. shredded green cabbage
4 c. shredded red cabbage
½ medium onion, minced
Sour Cream Dressing

· Toss cabbages and onion together with Sour Cream Dressing. Makes 8 to 10 servings.

SOUR CREAM DRESSING: Mix together 2 c. dairy sour cream, 6 tblsp. vinegar, ¼ c. sugar, 1 tblsp. salt, ¾ tsp. dry mustard and pepper to taste. Makes about 2¼ cups dressing.

HOT SLAW WITH APPLES

From skillet-to-table farm salad

6 c. cabbage, finely shredded
3 tblsp. water
3 tblsp. lemon juice
2 tblsp. sugar
3 tblsp. butter or salad oil
1½ tsp. salt
½ tsp. caraway seeds, or 2 tsp. Toasted Sesame Seeds (see Index)
1 large unpeeled apple, thinly sliced

• Place all ingredients except the apple slices in a skillet; cook, uncovered, over medium-high heat, stirring, until the cabbage is tender-crisp, about 3 minutes.
• Reduce heat to low; add apple, cover and cook 1 minute longer. Serve at once. Makes 8 servings.

CABBAGE/ONION SALAD

Use green cabbage and white onions or white cabbage and red onions. It wilts slightly but has crisp texture

1½ qts. shredded cabbage (1 large head)
2 large onions, thinly sliced and separated in rings
1 c. sugar
1 c. vinegar
1 tsp. salt
1 tsp. celery seeds
1 tsp. dry mustard
¼ tsp. pepper
1 c. salad oil

• Alternate cabbage and onions in bowl, with onions for top layer.
• Combine sugar, vinegar, salt, celery seeds, mustard and pepper in saucepan. Bring to a boil. Remove from heat; add salad oil.
• Drip the hot mixture over cabbage and onions; do not stir. Cover and refrigerate 24 hours or longer before serving. Makes about 12 cups.

STAY-CRISP CABBAGE SALAD

This refrigerator salad does not wilt because gelatin coats the vegetables

8 c. shredded cabbage
2 carrots, shredded
1 green pepper, cut in thin strips
½ c. chopped onion
¾ c. cold water
1 envelope unflavored gelatin
⅔ c. sugar
⅔ c. vinegar
2 tsp. celery seeds
1½ tsp. salt
¼ tsp. pepper
⅔ c. salad oil

• Shred cabbage fine with sharp knife. Mix with carrots, green pepper and onion. Sprinkle with ½ c. cold water; chill.
• Soften gelatin in ¼ c. cold water.
• Mix sugar, vinegar, celery seeds, salt and pepper in saucepan. Bring to a boil. Stir in softened gelatin. Cool until slightly thickened; beat well. Gradually beat in salad oil.
• Drain vegetables; pour dressing over top. Mix lightly until all vegetables are coated with the dressing. Serve immediately, or cover and store in refrigerator; stir just before serving to separate pieces. Makes 8 servings.

SAUERKRAUT SALAD

Ideal salad to tote to picnics—sauerkraut pickles the other vegetables and insures good keeping for hours

2 c. sauerkraut (1 lb. can)
½ c. sugar
½ c. thinly sliced celery
½ c. thin strips green pepper
½ c. shredded carrot
¼ c. chopped onion

• Cut sauerkraut strands in shorter pieces with scissors. Stir in sugar and let stand 30 minutes.

• Add remaining ingredients. Cover bowl tightly and chill in refrigerator at least 12 hours. Serve on lettuce if you wish. Makes 8 servings (about ½ c. each).

CARROT/CHIVE SALAD

Brilliant colors—marvelous flavors

⅓ c. salad oil
¼ c. vinegar
½ tsp. salt
1 tblsp. chopped fresh chives, or ½ tsp. dried chives
2 tblsp. syrup drained from canned pineapple
3 c. coarsely shredded carrots
1 (13½ oz.) can pineapple tidbits
Chopped chives (for garnish)

• Mix oil, vinegar, salt, chives and syrup drained from pineapple.

• Mix carrots and drained pineapple tidbits; pour over the oil-vinegar mixture. Toss lightly. Chill at least 4 hours. Serve in shallow bowl; garnish salad with chopped chives. Makes 6 to 8 servings.

Glamorous Gelatin Salads

Just as the home gardener proudly gathers her loveliest blossoms to carry to a friend, we select recipes for some of our most tempting and tasty molded salads to present to you in this chapter. Gelatin salads often are table show-offs. Their sparkling jewel colors and fancy shapes attract the eye.

What could be more handsome and appetizing on a hot summer day than Mint Julepeach Salad, with balls of ripe peaches and melons in lemon flavor gelatin? Or color-bright fresh vegetables in trim Garden Salad Loaf for supper on a sultry day? And on a snowy winter evening, what better way to put sunshine on the table than via Sun Gold Fruit Salad? When it's Halloween time with the countryside in brilliant dress and the new apple crop harvested, Cider Mold Salad speaks the country language eloquently!

CIDER MOLD SALAD

Delightfully different apple salad

3 (3 oz.) pkgs. orange gelatin
2 c. boiling apple cider or juice
3¾ c. cold apple cider or juice
½ c. seedless white raisins
½ c. apple cider or juice
2 large apples, cut in cubes (peeled or unpeeled)
½ c. chopped walnuts

• Dissolve gelatin in boiling cider. Add cold cider. Chill until slightly jelled.

• In the meantime, soak white raisins in ½ c. cider about 30 minutes. Drain raisins, discarding cider. Add raisins, apples and walnuts to gelatin. Pour into 2½-qt. mold and chill until firm.

• To serve, run a knife around edge of salad. Dip mold into warm water for a few seconds. Unmold on platter. Garnish with frosted grapes or greens. Makes 9 to 12 servings.

APPLE/CHEESE SALAD

The fruit in this salad is applesauce flavored with little cinnamon candies

¼ c. red cinnamon candies
1 (3 oz.) pkg. cherry flavor gelatin
1 c. hot water
1½ c. sweetened applesauce (canned or homemade)
1 (8 oz.) pkg. cream cheese
½ c. chopped nuts
½ c. finely cut celery
½ c. mayonnaise or salad dressing

• Mix cinnamon candies and gelatin, pour on hot water; stir to dissolve. Stir in applesauce. Pour half of mixture into 8″ square pan. Chill.

• Blend together cream cheese (room temperature), nuts and celery; add mayonnaise. Spread in layer over firm apple mixture. Pour on remaining apple mixture. Chill until firm, unmold; garnish with small bunches of sugared grapes, if you like. Makes 6 servings.

AVOCADO/STRAWBERRY RING

Beautiful salad for a buffet table

2 (3 oz.) pkgs. lemon or lime flavor gelatin
1 tsp. salt
2 c. boiling water
1¼ c. cold water
3 tblsp. lemon juice
2 ripe avocados, mashed
¼ c. mayonnaise
3 c. fresh strawberries
Honey Dressing

• Dissolve gelatin and salt in boiling water. Add cold water and lemon juice. Chill until slightly thickened.

• Combine avocados and mayonnaise; blend well. Stir into gelatin thoroughly.

• Pour into 4-cup ring mold or 8 individual ring molds. Chill until firm. Unmold and fill center with strawberries. Serve with Honey Dressing. Makes 8 servings.

HONEY DRESSING: Combine ½ c. dairy sour cream, 3 tblsp. honey and ⅛ tsp. ground mace.

FROSTED CRANBERRY SALAD

If it's easier, you can make this salad a few days ahead and freeze it

1 (8½ oz.) can crushed pineapple
1 (1 lb.) can whole cranberry sauce
2 (3 oz.) pkgs. raspberry flavor gelatin
1 (8 oz.) pkg. cream cheese
2 tblsp. salad dressing
1 c. heavy cream, or 1 envelope dessert topping mix, whipped
½ c. coarsely chopped walnuts
1 chopped peeled tart apple

• Drain pineapple and cranberry sauce, reserving liquid; add enough water to make 2 c. liquid. Bring to a boil. Dissolve gelatin in hot liquid. Chill until partially set.

• Beat softened cream cheese (room temperature) and salad dressing together until fluffy. Gradually beat in gelatin; fold this mixture into the whipped cream or topping mix. Set aside 1½ c. of this mixture for topping. Add drained fruits, nuts and apple to the remaining cheese mixture. Pour into a 11½ × 7⅜ × 1½″ glass dish; refrigerate until surface sets, about 20 minutes.

• Frost with reserved cheese mixture. Chill several hours, or freeze. If frozen, remove salad to refrigerator 1 hour before serving. Makes 12 servings.

CRANBERRY SALAD

Black walnuts are the country trick

4 c. cranberries
½ c. water
3 c. sugar
2 (3 oz.) pkgs. lemon flavor gelatin
1 c. boiling water
2 c. diced celery
1 c. chopped black walnuts
Crisp lettuce or salad greens

· Combine cranberries and water in saucepan; simmer until skins burst. Add sugar. Cook 3 minutes more.
· Combine gelatin and boiling water; stir to dissolve gelatin. Chill until syrupy.
· Fold in cranberries, celery and nuts. Pour into 2-qt. mold or 8 individual molds. Chill until firm.
· Unmold on lettuce or other greens. Makes 8 servings.

ELISABETH'S FRUIT SALAD

You make this ranch salad with dried prunes and apricots—delicious

1 (3 oz.) pkg. lemon flavor gelatin
1 c. hot water
1 c. cold water
1 tblsp. lemon juice
1 c. cooked dried prunes
½ c. cooked dried apricots
1 (3 oz.) pkg. cream cheese
¼ c. chopped walnuts

· Dissolve gelatin in hot water. Add cold water and lemon juice. Chill until syrupy.
· Pit cooked prunes. Cut prunes and apricots in small pieces.
· Whip cream cheese (at room temperature) until smooth.
· Whip thickened gelatin until frothy. Mix in cream cheese until smooth.
· Fold in prunes, apricots and nuts.
· Pour into 8″ square pan or 6 individual molds. Chill; serve on crisp lettuce leaves. Makes 6 servings.

GREEN GAGE PLUM SALAD

It makes any meat taste better

1 (1 lb. 4 oz.) can green gage plums
1 (3 oz.) pkg. lemon flavor gelatin
Juice of 1 lemon
½ tsp. salt
¾ c. slivered toasted almonds
Crisp lettuce cups
Salad dressing

· Drain juice from plums; add water to make 2 c. liquid. Heat to boiling, and pour over gelatin. Add lemon juice and salt; stir to dissolve. Cool until thickened.
· Pour 2 tblsp. gelatin into each of 6 individual molds or baking cups. Chill until firm. Chill remaining gelatin until syrupy.
· Pit and chop plums. Fold with almonds into gelatin. Spoon over clear gelatin in molds. Chill until firm.
· Serve in lettuce cups with salad dressing. Makes 6 servings.

SUN GOLD FRUIT SALAD

Make salad one day, frost it the next

2 (3 oz.) pkgs. orange flavor gelatin
2 c. boiling water
1½ c. cold water
1 (11 oz.) can mandarin oranges
1 (8¾ oz.) can apricot halves
1 c. seedless white grapes, fresh or canned
2 large bananas, sliced
Fluffy Topping
¼ c. grated American cheese

• Dissolve gelatin in boiling water; add cold water. Refrigerate until syrupy.

• Drain fruit, reserving 1 c. liquid. Fold fruit into gelatin mixture; pour into a 9 × 5 × 3″ loaf pan or an 11½ × 7⅜ × 1½″ glass dish. Refrigerate overnight.

• Unmold salad and frost with Fluffy Topping. Sprinkle top with cheese. Refrigerate until topping sets, about 1 hour. Makes 12 servings.

FLUFFY TOPPING: Combine 6 tblsp. sugar and 2 tblsp. cornstarch in a heavy saucepan. Blend in 1 egg, slightly beaten, and the 1 c. reserved fruit liquid. Cook, stirring constantly, over low heat until thickened. Remove from heat; stir in 2 tblsp. butter and 1 tblsp. lemon juice. Cool. Whip 1 c. heavy cream, or 1 envelope dessert topping mix; fold into the cooled mixture.

MINT JULEPEACH SALAD

Ginger and mint enhance peach-melon flavors in this refreshing salad

2 (3 oz.) pkgs. lemon flavor gelatin
1½ c. hot water
½ c. frozen lemonade concentrate, undiluted
1 (7 oz.) bottle ginger ale, chilled
⅛ tsp. peppermint extract
2 c. fresh peach balls
1 c. honey dew melon balls
1 c. seedless green grapes, cut in halves

• Dissolve gelatin in hot water. Add lemonade concentrate, ginger ale and peppermint extract. Stir to dissolve. Chill until partially set.

• Fold in remaining ingredients. Turn into a 1½-qt. mold or 8 individual molds. Chill. Makes 8 servings.

GOLDEN GLOW SALAD

As this picture-pretty salad chills, it separates into two distinct layers

24 marshmallows
½ c. pineapple juice (drained from crushed pineapple plus water)
1 (3 oz.) pkg. lemon flavor gelatin
1½ c. boiling water
¾ c. crushed pineapple, drained
¾ c. grated raw carrots
1 (5 oz.) jar cream cheese with pineapple (⅔ c.)

• Melt marshmallows in pineapple juice over low heat, folding over and over until smooth.

• Dissolve gelatin in boiling water.

• Blend pineapple, carrots and cheese.

• When the gelatin is cool, blend together all the ingredients; pour into a 1-qt. ring mold. Serve garnished with watercress or lettuce and with salad dressing. Makes 6 servings.

MOLDED GRAPEFRUIT SALAD

Especially good with pork and chicken

1 (3 oz.) pkg. lime flavor gelatin
1 c. boiling water
¼ tsp. ground ginger
1 c. grapefruit juice
1 c. grapefruit pieces
½ c. diced celery
1 c. creamed cottage cheese

• Dissolve lime flavor gelatin in boiling water. Add ginger and grapefruit juice. Chill until mixture starts to congeal.

• Add grapefruit pieces, celery and cottage cheese. Mix well.

• Pour into a 5- to 6-cup mold. Chill until firm. Unmold on crisp greens. Serve with mayonnaise or salad dressing. Makes 6 servings.

TART CHERRY SALAD MOLD

Excellent salad to serve with ham

- 2 (1 lb.) cans tart red cherries
- 2 (8½ oz.) cans crushed pineapple
- 1 c. sugar
- 4 (3 oz.) pkgs. cherry flavor gelatin
- 3 c. ginger ale
- 1 c. chopped nuts (optional)
- ¾ c. shredded coconut

· Drain fruits, reserving juices. Add water to juices to make 3¼ c.; add sugar. Bring to a boil; stir in gelatin until dissolved.

· Add fruit and ginger ale. Chill until very thick, but not set.

· Stir in nuts and coconut. Pour into a 2-qt. ring mold. Chill until set. Makes 12 to 14 servings.

Note: You may substitute 2 (1 lb.) cans frozen tart red cherries. Use juice as directed; reduce sugar to ⅓ c.

BEET PERFECTION SALAD

Zippy in flavor and colorful—just right with pork or chicken

- 2 envelopes unflavored gelatin
- ½ c. cold water
- 1½ c. hot beet juice or boiling water
- 1 c. cider vinegar
- Juice of 1 lemon
- 1 tblsp. prepared horse-radish
- ½ c. sugar
- 1 tsp. salt
- 2 c. finely shredded cabbage
- 2 c. coarsely shredded or diced cooked beets

· Soften gelatin in cold water; add hot liquid to dissolve. Stir in vinegar, lemon juice, horse-radish, sugar and salt. Chill until thick and syrupy.

· Fold in cabbage and beets. Pour into 1½-qt. mold or 8 individual molds. Makes 8 servings.

KRIS KRINGLE WREATH SALAD

Fix this one day to serve the next

Layers 1 and 2:

- 1 envelope unflavored gelatin
- ½ c. cold water
- ¾ c. hot water
- ½ tsp. salt
- 1 tblsp. lemon juice
- Green pepper
- Pimiento
- 1 (8 oz.) carton creamed cottage cheese

Layer 3:

- 4 c. tomato juice
- 1 bay leaf
- 1 tblsp. chopped onion
- ½ tsp. celery salt
- Dash ground red pepper
- 2 envelopes unflavored gelatin
- ½ c. cold water
- 1 tsp. Worcestershire sauce
- 1 tsp. lemon juice
- Crisp salad greens

· Soften gelatin in cold water; add hot water and salt. Stir to dissolve gelatin. Add lemon juice. Pour 3 tblsp. gelatin mixture into 8″ ring mold; chill until firm. Arrange holly leaf pattern cut from green pepper with small pimiento rounds for berries over gelatin. Add 3 or 4 tblsp. liquid gelatin. Chill.

· Mix remaining gelatin with cottage cheese. Pour over first layer.

· For 3rd layer, combine tomato juice, bay leaf, onion and seasonings; simmer 15 minutes. Remove bay leaf.

· Soften gelatin in cold water.

· Add Worcestershire, lemon juice and gelatin to hot tomato mixture. Cool.

• Pour over cottage cheese layer; chill. Unmold; garnish with greens. Makes 8 to 10 servings.

Summer Supper

Garden Salad Loaf
Assorted Cheese   Deviled Eggs
Buttered Green Beans
Hot Rolls
Cookies
Milk   Iced Tea

The salad, cheese and deviled eggs are make-ahead foods from the refrigerator; the cookies are from freezer or package. Last-minute chores consist of cooking the green beans and heating the rolls. Use regular or instant tea, whichever you prefer.

GARDEN SALAD LOAF

Cool and beautiful—shimmering gelatin holds fresh garden vegetables

2 green peppers, cut in small strips
4 chopped green onions (include tops)
20 radishes, thinly sliced
2 medium carrots, thinly sliced
4 small tomatoes, cut in thin wedges
¾ c. French dressing
2 envelopes unflavored gelatin
¼ c. sugar
1 tsp. salt
2⅔ c. very hot water
½ c. vinegar
2 tblsp. lemon juice
2 c. shredded chicory or lettuce
1 c. coarsely torn spinach or shredded cabbage
¼ c. minced parsley

• Combine peppers, onions, radishes, carrots and tomatoes; marinate in French dressing 15 minutes or more.

• Combine gelatin, sugar and salt; add hot water and stir to dissolve ingredients. Add vinegar and lemon juice. Chill until gelatin thickens.

• Drain vegetables well. Fold marinated vegetables, chicory, spinach and parsley into gelatin mixture. (Chicory, spinach and parsley do not wilt easily, but you may use lettuce or shredded cabbage, too.) Pour into oiled 8½ × 4½ × 2½" loaf pan; chill until firm.

• Unmold on platter. Serves 10 to 12.

Note: You can omit unflavored gelatin and sugar; substitute 2 (3 oz.) pkgs. lemon flavor gelatin and 3½ c. very hot water. Follow same procedure.

FANCY TOUCHES: For a design of vegetables on top of mold when you turn it out, pour about ½ c. dissolved gelatin mixture into loaf pan and let set. On this arrange an interesting pattern with radish slices, green pepper and tomato strips. Spoon a little of gelatin mixture over vegetables to "anchor" them; let set before adding vegetable-gelatin mixture. A border of tomato wedges may be arranged around outer edge of mold for color.

Substantial Salads

Country people lead active lives and much of their food is hearty. Salads are no exception to the rule. Occasionally they take the main role in suppers and luncheons. Jellied Egg Salad, teamed with toasted sandwiches and a cold or hot drink, makes a satisfying summer supper. Regal Chicken Salad and hot rolls please women at bridge luncheons, and Hot Chicken Salad, accompanied by a green vegetable, such as asparagus, broccoli or beans, guarantee the hostess an enthusiastic reception for Sunday evening company supper. When peas reach their flavor peak in the home garden, invite friends to come to supper and serve delicately flavored pink and green Pea/Shrimp Salad.

Potato Salads of many kinds hold their own on country picnic and home tables. Baked German Salad and Salad Niçoise, an import from the area around Nice, France, share honors with the typical American varieties of which our Sweepstakes Potato Salad is a splendid example. Try these and other substantial salads in this chapter. We predict you'll make them again and again.

JELLIED EGG SALAD

Serve as main course for supper with toasted cheese sandwiches, peas

2 (3 oz.) pkgs. lemon flavor gelatin
1¼ c. boiling water
2 c. cold water
3 tblsp. lemon juice
1 c. mayonnaise
4 tblsp. pickle relish, drained
1 tsp. salt
¼ c. chopped onion
2 tblsp. chopped pimiento
6 hard-cooked eggs, chopped (reserve 1 egg yolk for garnish)

• Dissolve gelatin in boiling water. Add cold water and chill in refrigerator until syrupy. Stir in lemon juice, mayonnaise, pickle relish, salt, onion and pimiento. Fold in eggs.

• Spoon into a 2-qt. mold. Chill until firm. Serve on lettuce or watercress; garnish salad with sieved hard-cooked egg yolk. Makes 8 large servings.

REGAL CHICKEN SALAD

Best-ever chicken salad! The proof is in its taste, so make it soon

4 c. diced cooked chicken
1 (1 lb. 4½ oz.) can pineapple chunks, drained
2 c. seedless green grapes
1 c. chopped celery
⅔ c. coarsely chopped dry salted peanuts
Salt
¼ tsp. tarragon leaves
1 c. mayonnaise
2 tblsp. lemon juice
2 tblsp. juice drained from pineapple

• Combine chicken, drained pineapple (reserve juice), grapes, celery and peanuts. Taste for salt (salted nuts may furnish enough). Stir in tarragon.

• Combine mayonnaise, lemon juice and 2 tblsp. pineapple juice. Gently fold into chicken mixture. Serve on lettuce with parsley or small celery leaves for garnish. Makes 8 servings.

HOT CHICKEN SALAD

Clever way to dress up leftover turkey or chicken to serve on cold days

¼ c. minced onion
⅔ c. chopped green pepper
3 c. chopped celery
¼ c. butter
4 c. cooked chicken or turkey, cut into chunks
2 tblsp. lemon juice
2 tsp. salt
1 c. mayonnaise
½ to 1 c. toasted almonds, slivered

• Sauté onion, green pepper and celery in butter until tender, but do not brown.

• Stir in chicken, lemon juice and salt. Cover skillet and place over low heat until ingredients are hot. Just before serving, remove skillet from heat and lightly stir in the mayonnaise and almonds. Makes 8 to 10 servings.

Variation

CRISP-TOPPED SALAD: Sprinkle the Hot Chicken Salad with 1½ c. crushed potato chips and ½ c. grated Swiss cheese. Heat under broiler until top of salad is golden brown.

SWEEPSTAKES POTATO SALAD

It's glamorous with radish-pineapples, egg water lilies and crisp greens

4 c. cold boiled potatoes, diced
¾ c. sliced green onions
⅓ c. radish slices
3 hard-cooked eggs, cubed
½ c. mayonnaise or salad dressing
¾ c. dairy sour cream
2½ tblsp. herb vinegar
1½ tsp. salt
¾ tsp. celery seeds

· Combine potatoes, onions, radishes and hard-cooked eggs.
· Blend remaining ingredients; mix lightly with potato mixture. Chill.
· Serve in salad bowl lined with endive or leaf lettuce, and garnish with hard-cooked eggs (we cut them with an egg slicer) and radish-pineapples (tuck 1″ lengths of sliced green onion tops in holes cut in radishes). Makes 6 servings.

Variations

CARROT: Add 1 c. shredded carrots to vegetables before mixing with dressing.

CUCUMBER: Add 1 c. diced cucumber to vegetables before adding dressing.

CELERY: Omit celery seeds; add 1 c. chopped celery to vegetables.

GREEN PEPPER/ONION: Substitute ¼ c. chopped onion and ⅓ c. chopped green pepper for green onions.

HAM: Add 1 c. chopped ham or luncheon meat before adding dressing.

BACON: Add 8 strips crisp-cooked bacon, crumbled, before adding dressing.

SHRIMP: Add 1 c. (5 oz. can) cooked shrimp to vegetables.

SHARP CHEESE: Add 1 c. sharp cheese, cubed, to salad before final mixing.

BAKED GERMAN POTATO SALAD

This ranch house special is in the oven when guests arrive—it's tasty

¾ c. diced bacon
1 c. chopped celery
1 c. chopped onion
3 tblsp. flour
1⅓ c. water
⅔ c. cider vinegar
⅔ c. sugar
3 tsp. salt
½ tsp. pepper
8 c. cubed cooked potatoes (about 8 medium)
1 c. sliced radishes
½ c. chopped dill pickle (optional)

· Cook bacon in large skillet; drain off fat. Measure fat and return ¼ c. to skillet. Add celery and onion; cook 1 minute. Blend in flour. Stir in wa-

ter and vinegar; cook, stirring constantly, until mixture is thick and bubbly. Stir in sugar, salt and pepper.
• Pour mixture over potatoes and bacon in a greased 3-qt. casserole; mix lightly. Cover; bake in moderate oven (350°) 30 minutes.
• Remove from oven. Stir in radishes and dill pickle. Serve at once. Makes 10 to 12 servings.

SALAD NIÇOISE

Add this special potato salad to your recipe collection for company meals

- 9 medium potatoes, cooked and cut
- 1 c. Oil/Vinegar Dressing
- ½ c. chopped sweet onion
- 3 c. hot, cooked green beans
- Salad greens
- 4 tomatoes
- 4 hard-cooked eggs
- Pitted large ripe olives
- Anchovy filets
- Chopped fresh parsley, basil or savory
- 1 or 2 (7 oz.) cans tuna, chilled

• Cook potatoes in their jackets. Just as soon as they can be handled, peel and cut in thin slices (⅛"). Put into a bowl and drizzle over ¼ c. Oil/Vinegar Dressing. Add the onion, toss gently and cover. Let stand at room temperature until cool; then refrigerate.
• Pour 3 tblsp. of the Oil/Vinegar Dressing over the hot, drained green beans; cover. Let stand at room temperature until cool; then refrigerate.
• To serve, toss green beans and potato slices together gently, adding more Oil/Vinegar Dressing to coat vegetables if needed. Mound in the center of a large chilled chop plate. Arrange crisp salad greens around the edges.
• Arrange tomatoes, peeled and quartered, and quartered eggs alternately around the potato salad. Tuck olives between tomatoes and eggs. Garnish top of salad with anchovy strips. Sprinkle salad with parsley. If not ready to serve, cover with foil and refrigerate.
• At serving time, turn chilled tuna onto a chilled plate and garnish with lemon quarters and greens. Or if you prefer, make clusters of tuna chunks with the tomatoes and eggs around the salad.
• Take a cruet of the Oil/Vinegar Dressing or a bowl of mayonnaise to the table. Pass so guests can add more dressing to the salad. Makes 8 to 12 servings.

OIL/VINEGAR DRESSING: Shake together in a covered jar or bottle ¾ c. salad oil (the French use olive oil), ¼ c. red wine vinegar, ¼ tsp. salt, ¼ tsp. dry mustard and ⅛ tsp. black pepper (freshly ground in pepper mill is traditional kind). Makes 1 cup.

SHRIMP SALAD

Louisiana salad with peppy seasonings

- 1 lb. shrimp, cooked, or 2 (5 oz.) cans, cleaned
- 1 c. coarsely chopped celery
- 2 hard-cooked eggs, coarsely chopped
- 3 tblsp. diced dill pickle
- ½ c. mayonnaise or salad dressing
- 1 tblsp. lemon juice
- 1 tblsp. ketchup
- ½ tsp. Worcestershire sauce
- ¾ tsp. salt
- ¼ tsp. pepper
- Lettuce

• Chill shrimp and if large, cut in halves or quarters.

• Toss together shrimp, celery, eggs and pickle with mayonnaise which has been combined with lemon juice, ketchup, Worcestershire sauce and seasonings. Serve on crisp lettuce or salad greens. Garnish top with shrimp and egg. Makes 4 servings.

Note: You may want to double this recipe for 8 servings.

PEA/SHRIMP SALAD

Picture-pretty green and pink salad

1 lb. cooked shrimp, shelled and deveined
4 c. shelled peas
1 c. dairy sour cream
½ c. mayonnaise
1 tblsp. lemon juice
½ tsp. salt
½ tsp. dill weed
4 hard-cooked eggs, chopped
¼ c. chopped sweet pickle or pickle relish
2 tblsp. chopped green onion
1 c. sliced celery
Lettuce

• Chill shrimp.
• Cook peas until barely tender. Pour into colander; cool under cold running water. Chill.
• Combine sour cream, mayonnaise, lemon juice, salt and dill weed. Chill.
• Just before serving, combine all ingredients except lettuce. Serve in lettuce cups. Makes 6 servings.

RICE/BEAN SALAD

The excellence of this take-along salad was a nice treat in our Test Kitchens

1 c. cooked rice
1 (1 lb.) can kidney beans, drained
2 hard-cooked eggs, chopped
½ c. sweet pickles, chopped
¼ c. chopped onion
¼ c. chopped celery
¼ c. chopped green pepper
½ tsp. salt
¼ tsp. pepper
⅓ c. mayonnaise or salad dressing
Crisp lettuce or other greens

• Combine all ingredients, except lettuce, in mixing bowl. Chill in refrigerator. Serve on crisp lettuce or greens. Makes 6 to 8 servings.

Note: For the best flavor combine ingredients while rice is hot.

JELLIED BEEF MOLD

A Kansas rancher's favorite summer supper dish. It's refreshing

1½ lbs. boneless chuck beef
1 c. hot water
1 envelope unflavored gelatin
⅓ c. chopped celery
¼ c. chopped onion
¼ c. cubed dill pickles
1 can condensed beef consommé
½ tsp. salt
⅛ tsp. pepper
12 pimiento-stuffed olives, sliced
Strips of pimiento
Parsley
Pimiento-stuffed olives

• Simmer beef in water until tender. Remove meat; put through food chopper using coarse blade. There should be 2 c. ground beef.
• Cool broth; soften gelatin in 2 tblsp. broth.
• Cook celery and onion in remainder of broth until tender, but still slightly firm, about 10 minutes. Drain, save broth. Mix celery, onion and pickles with meat.
• Add enough broth to consommé to make 2 c.; heat. Add softened gelatin; stir to dissolve. Pour thin layer of gelatin into 9 × 5 × 3″ loaf pan; chill. To remainder of gelatin mix-

ture add salt, pepper and beef mixture.

• Arrange olive slices and pimiento strips in design over gelatin in pan. Spoon in beef mixture; chill.

• To serve, unmold on platter. Garnish with parsley and olives. Serves 8.

MOLDED SALMON SALAD

Splendid accompaniments are: peas, hot rolls and chocolate sundaes

2 envelopes unflavored gelatin
¼ c. cold water
3 tblsp. lemon juice
1 c. hot water
1 (1 lb.) can salmon, cleaned and flaked
¾ c. mayonnaise or salad dressing
1 c. diced celery
¼ c. chopped green pepper
1 tsp. minced onion
½ tsp. salt
⅛ tsp. pepper
Crisp lettuce leaves

• Soften gelatin in cold water and lemon juice.

• Dissolve in hot water; chill until thickened and syrupy.

• Fold in remaining ingredients except lettuce. Pour into oiled 2-qt. mold. Chill until firm.

• Unmold on lettuce. Makes 6 servings.

TUNA/ONION SALAD

Serve with hot rolls, biscuits or muffins

1 c. mayonnaise or salad dressing
2 tblsp. lemon juice
2 (7 oz.) cans tuna
12 green onions
4 c. diced cooked potatoes
½ c. chopped celery
12 midget gherkins, sliced
Fresh garden lettuce
1 large carrot

• Combine mayonnaise and lemon juice in mixing bowl. Drain oil from tuna into bowl; blend. Flake and add tuna.

• Cut 4 green onions into thin slices.

• Add cut onions, potatoes, celery and gherkins to tuna. Toss just enough to mix. Chill before serving.

• Serve on crisp lettuce leaves. For color, garnish with carrot rings strung on green onions. Makes 8 servings.

GOLDEN MACARONI SALAD

Mustard gives zip, beans add protein and cabbage provides texture

1 (8 oz.) pkg. shell macaroni, cooked and drained
6 c. chopped cabbage
½ c. chopped celery
½ c. green pepper strips
¼ c. minced onion
2 (1 lb.) cans red kidney beans, drained
3 eggs, slightly beaten
½ c. sugar
1 (9 oz.) jar prepared mustard
3 tblsp. butter
½ tsp. salt
¼ tsp. pepper

• Toss together macaroni, cabbage, celery, green pepper, onion and kidney beans.

• Blend together remaining ingredients in top part of double boiler. Cook over simmering water about 5 minutes or until mixture thickens slightly. Cool. Pour over vegetables; toss together lightly. Makes 10 to 12 servings.

Make-ahead Salad Dressings

Busy farm women know that an easy way to add variety and superior flavor to salads is to have several kinds of dressings stored in the refrigerator. Each of the following four recipes yields a pint of dressing that will stay fresh for a month if tightly capped. Let the dressings chill at least a day before you use them. They are excellent on tossed greens and many other salads. Experiment with them and your adventures in salad-making will please you, your family and friends.

CREAMY THOUSAND ISLAND DRESSING

Good with lettuce or cabbage

½ c. salad dressing
½ c. chili sauce
1 tsp. Worcestershire sauce
Dash of Tabasco sauce
½ tsp. salt
¼ tsp. paprika
2 tblsp. chopped celery
2 tblsp. pickle relish
2 tblsp. chopped pimiento-stuffed olives
1 tsp. minced onion
1 hard-cooked egg, chopped
½ c. dairy sour cream

• Combine salad dressing, chili sauce, Worcestershire, Tabasco, salt and paprika in 1-qt. bowl. Stir in celery, relish, olives, onion and egg; mix well. Fold in sour cream. Chill. Makes 1 pint.

SWEET/SOUR BACON DRESSING

Right for potato and macaroni salads

4 slices bacon
2 tblsp. chopped onion
3 tblsp. sugar
3 tblsp. white vinegar
½ c. water
1⅓ c. salad dressing

• Fry bacon until crisp and brown. Drain bacon and crumble into small pieces. Set aside.

• Sauté onion in bacon drippings until tender. Add sugar, vinegar and water; bring to boiling point. Cool. Combine mixture with salad dressing; beat until smooth. Mix in bacon. Chill. Makes 1 pint.

ITALIAN TOMATO DRESSING

Perfect on tomatoes and cucumbers

½ c. salad oil
⅓ c. cider vinegar
1 (8 oz.) can tomato sauce
½ tsp. salt
2 tblsp. sugar
1 tsp. dry mustard
1 tsp. paprika
½ tsp. orégano leaves
2 tsp. Worcestershire sauce
½ clove garlic, finely chopped
2 tsp. finely chopped onion
1 tblsp. finely chopped celery
2 tblsp. salad dressing

• Combine all ingredients in 1-qt. mixing bowl. Beat at medium speed 2 minutes. (Or blend in blender for 15 seconds on high speed.) Chill. Makes 1 pint.

ORANGE/HONEY DRESSING

Tasty glaze for gelatin fruit salads

- ¼ tsp. paprika
- ½ tsp. dry mustard
- 1 tsp. salt
- ½ tsp. celery salt
- ½ c. honey
- 3 tblsp. lemon juice
- 2 tblsp. cider vinegar
- 3 tblsp. frozen orange juice concentrate, thawed
- 1 c. salad oil

• Combine dry ingredients in 1-qt. mixer bowl. Add honey, lemon juice, vinegar and orange juice concentrate; blend well. Beating constantly, slowly add oil; beat 5 minutes longer at medium speed. (Or blend all ingredients in blender for 20 seconds at high speed.) Chill. Shake before serving. Makes 1 pint.

Two Great Dressings for Country Fruit Salads

POPPY SEED SALAD DRESSING

Grapefruit sections on lettuce with this dressing—simply wonderful

- 1 c. sugar
- ½ tsp. salt
- 1 tsp. dry mustard
- 1½ tsp. paprika
- ½ c. vinegar
- 1½ c. salad oil
- 1 tsp. grated onion
- 2 tblsp. poppy seeds

• Mix sugar, salt, dry mustard, paprika and vinegar together thoroughly.

• Add oil gradually, beating constantly.

• Add onion and poppy seeds; shake to mix thoroughly. Makes 2½ cups.

SHERBET SALAD DRESSING

A wonderful frosty-cold dressing. Spoon it on your fruit salads

- 2 tblsp. flour
- ¼ c. sugar
- ¼ tsp. salt
- 1⅓ c. fresh orange juice
- 2 tblsp. fresh lemon juice
- 2 egg yolks, slightly beaten
- 1 tblsp. grated orange peel
- 3 tblsp. salad oil
- ½ c. raspberry sherbet

• In top of double boiler combine flour, sugar and salt. Add orange and lemon juices. Cook, stirring constantly, until mixture thickens.

• Stir 2 tblsp. hot mixture into egg yolks; gradually add yolks to hot sauce. Stir and cook 1 minute. Remove from heat and stir in orange peel and salad oil. Cool and chill.

• Just before serving, fold in sherbet. Serve over fruit salad. Makes 2 cups.

Note: Use orange, pineapple, lemon, lime or any other flavor of sherbet.

ORÉGANO SALAD DRESSING

Toss lettuce with this dressing for the pheasant or fish dinner

- ¾ c. vinegar
- 1 tblsp. salt
- 1 tblsp. sugar
- 1 tsp. orégano leaves
- 2 tsp. pepper
- 1½ tblsp. sweet basil
- 2 cloves garlic, split
- ¾ c. salad oil

• Combine all ingredients, except oil. Let marinate 24 hours.

• Strain vinegar; add oil. Shake vigorously. Makes 1½ cups.

SHORT-CUT SALAD DRESSING

Resembles Thousand Island dressing —try it on lettuce wedges

½ c. mayonnaise
2 tblsp. Basic Red Sauce (see Index)
1 hard-cooked egg, finely chopped
Salt to taste

• Combine all ingredients. Chill until ready to use. Makes about ¾ cup.

chapter 9

Homemade Breads and Country Butter

WHEN A CHILD WALKS INTO a country kitchen after school and confronts the tantalizing fragrance of homemade bread cooling on the counter top he knows he is lucky. And when he spreads butter on a faintly warm slice of bread and tastes, he knows the true meaning of good eating. More children today are enjoying this experience in the revival of baking yeast breads. Young women who are rather new in this culinary art crave the satisfaction of creating something special with their hands. And they are finding, as did their grandmothers, that kneading dough relieves frustrations–and is good therapy as well!

Three kinds of breads are basic–white, whole wheat and rye. You'll find our best recipes for these and other highly prized loaves in this chapter. There are also recipes for light-as-a-feather rolls and superior coffee breads that the country hostess serves with pride.

Be sure to use *all-purpose flour* unless another kind is specified. It contains more gluten than other flours. You knead yeast breads to develop this protein which, stretched by yeast, makes the loaf's framework.

You'll observe that many recipes advise letting dough rise until doubled. Use your finger, not your eyes, to determine this stage. Insert it ½″ into the dough; if the indentation remains, the dough is doubled.

This chapter divides into two parts, yeast and quick breads. Biscuits, corn breads, coffee breads, pancakes, waffles and fruit-nut breads are examples of quick breads–those leavened by baking powder and/or baking soda. The trick in making these treats is to avoid beating or manipulating the batter or dough more than necessary. It's important *not* to develop the gluten, for these are tender breads.

For a special bonus, this chapter has a postscript. Because butter contributes so much to the enjoyment of homemade breads, we give you easy, straight-from-the-farm directions for making country butter with heavy cream in your electric mixer.

Pointers on Freezing Yeast Breads

To Freeze Yeast Breads and Rolls:

• Bake before freezing, cool to room temperature and, if you like, slice loaves of bread. Wrap in foil or plastic wrap, or place in polyethylene bags.

• To thaw, heat in covered container or in aluminum foil wrapper in moderate oven (350°) 20 to 25 minutes, or let stand in its wrapper at room temperature from 2 to 3 hours. If sliced, thaw in toaster.

To Freeze Coffee Breads and Sweet Rolls:

• Bake before freezing. Remove from baking sheet, cool at room temperature and wrap in foil or plastic wrap. Coffee breads and sweet rolls are best frosted or glazed just before serving.

• To thaw, follow directions for yeast breads and rolls. Frosted and glazed breads must be thawed in their wrappers at room temperature 2 to 3 hours.

• *Maximum Storage Time:* Yeast breads and rolls, 9 to 12 months; coffee breads and sweet rolls, 9 months.

BEST-EVER WHITE BREAD

This is a 2-loaf recipe—dough is easy to handle, loaves are plump

2 c. milk
2 tblsp. sugar
2 tsp. salt
1 tblsp. lard or shortening
1 pkg. active dry yeast
¼ c. warm water (110 to 115°)
6 to 6½ c. sifted flour

• Scald milk. Stir in sugar, salt and lard. Cool to lukewarm.

• Sprinkle yeast on warm water; stir to dissolve. Add yeast and 3 c. flour to milk mixture. Beat with spoon until batter is smooth and sheets off spoon. Or beat with electric mixer at medium speed until smooth, about 2 minutes, scraping bowl occasionally.

• Add enough remaining flour, a little at a time, first by spoon and then with hands, to make a dough that leaves the sides of the bowl. Turn onto lightly floured board; cover and let rest 10 minutes.

• Knead until smooth and elastic, 8 to 10 minutes. Round up into a ball and put into lightly greased bowl; turn dough over to grease top. Cover and let rise in warm place until doubled, about 1½ hours. Punch down, cover and let rise again until almost doubled, about 45 minutes.

• Turn onto board and shape into ball. Divide in half. Shape into loaves and place in 2 greased 9 × 5 × 3″ loaf pans. Cover and let rise until doubled, about 1 hour.

• Bake in hot oven (400°) 35 minutes, or until deep golden brown. Place on wire racks and let cool away from drafts. Makes 2 loaves.

Note: Just double the recipe for Best-ever White Bread if you want to bake 4 loaves.

HONEY WHOLE WHEAT BREAD

Voted tops by Nebraska wheat growers

- 2 pkgs. active dry yeast
- 5 c. warm water (110 to 115°)
- 6 tblsp. lard or other shortening
- ¼ c. honey
- 4 c. whole wheat flour
- ½ c. instant potatoes (not reconstituted)
- ½ c. nonfat dry milk
- 1 tblsp. salt
- 6½ to 8 c. sifted flour

· Sprinkle yeast on ½ c. warm water; stir to dissolve.

· Melt lard in 6-qt. saucepan; remove from heat, add honey and remaining 4½ c. warm water.

· Mix whole wheat flour (stirred before measuring), instant potatoes, dry milk and salt. Add to saucepan; beat until smooth.

· Add yeast and beat to blend. Then with wooden spoon mix in enough flour, a little at a time, to make a dough that leaves the sides of the pan. Turn onto lightly floured board and knead until smooth and satiny and small bubbles appear, 8 to 10 minutes.

· Place in lightly greased bowl; turn dough over to grease top. Cover and let rise in warm place until doubled, 1 to 1½ hours. Punch down dough, turn onto board and divide in thirds. Cover and let rest 5 minutes. Shape into 3 loaves and place in greased 9 × 5 × 3″ loaf pans. Cover and let rise until doubled, about 1 hour.

· Bake in hot oven (400°) about 50 minutes, or until bread tests done. Remove from pans and cool on wire racks. Makes 3 loaves.

Note: You may use 1 c. unseasoned mashed potatoes in place of instant potatoes. Combine with the honey-water mixture.

Extra-good Rye Bread

Swedish women make many kinds of rye breads, all of them good. Usually they flavor their loaves with grated orange peel, caraway seeds or anise seeds. Our Swedish Rye Bread Supreme recipe comes from a farmer's wife in McPherson County, Kansas, who lived in Sweden until she was of high school age. You have a choice of flavorings. Try all three and see which one gets the most compliments.

SWEDISH RYE BREAD SUPREME

Take your pick of caraway or anise seeds or orange peel for flavoring

- ¼ c. brown sugar, firmly packed
- ¼ c. light molasses
- 1 tblsp. salt
- 2 tblsp. shortening
- 1½ c. boiling water
- 1 pkg. active dry yeast
- ¼ c. warm water (110 to 115°)
- 2½ c. rye flour
- 2 to 3 tblsp. caraway seeds
- 3½ to 4 c. sifted flour

· Combine brown sugar, molasses, salt and shortening in large bowl; pour on boiling water and stir until sugar is dissolved. Cool to lukewarm.

· Sprinkle yeast on warm water; stir to dissolve.

· Stir rye flour (stir before measuring) into brown sugar-molasses mixture, beating well. Stir in yeast and caraway seeds; beat until smooth.

· Mix in enough flour, a little at a time, first with spoon and then with hands, to make a smooth soft dough. Turn onto lightly floured board; knead until satiny and elastic, about 10 minutes. Place dough in lightly greased bowl; turn dough over to grease top. Cover and let rise in warm place until dough is doubled, 1½ to 2 hours.

· Punch down; turn dough onto lightly floured board and divide in half. Round up dough to make 2 balls. Cover and let rest 10 minutes. Shape into loaves and place in 2 greased 8½ × 4½ × 2½" loaf pans. Cover and let rise in a warm place until almost doubled, 1½ to 2 hours.

· Bake in moderate oven (375°) 25 to 30 minutes, covering with sheet of aluminum foil the last 15 minutes if loaves are browning too fast. Turn onto wire racks to cool. Brush loaves with melted butter while warm if you like a soft crust. Makes 2 loaves.

Variations

ORANGE-FLAVORED RYE BREAD: Omit caraway seeds and use instead 2 tblsp. grated orange peel.

ANISE-FLAVORED RYE BREAD: Omit caraway seeds and use 1 tsp. anise seeds.

ROUND LOAF RYE BREAD: Shape the 2 balls of dough by flattening them slightly instead of shaping into oblongs. Place loaves on opposite corners of greased baking sheet instead of in loaf pans. Let rise and bake as directed for Swedish Rye Bread Supreme.

ITALIAN BREAD

Long kneading is the key to correct texture for Italian and French breads

2 pkgs. active dry yeast
2½ c. warm water (110 to 115°)
7¼ to 7¾ c. sifted flour
1 tblsp. salt
Yellow cornmeal
1 egg white, slightly beaten
1 tblsp. cold water

· Sprinkle yeast on warm water; stir to dissolve.

· Add 2 c. flour and beat thoroughly; stir in salt. Stir in 4½ c. flour (about) a cupful at a time; the dough will be stiff.

· Turn onto a lightly floured board, cover with a clean towel and let rest 10 to 15 minutes. Knead 15 to 25 minutes, until dough is smooth and very elastic, working in ¾ to 1¼ c. more flour. Do not underknead.

· Place in lightly greased bowl; turn dough over to grease top. Cover and let rise in a warm place free from drafts until doubled, about 1½ hours. Punch down, let rise again until doubled, about 1 hour.

· Turn onto lightly floured board, divide in half, cover and let rest 10 minutes.

· Roll each half in a 15 × 12" rectangle; the dough will be about ¼" thick. Starting with the long side, roll up tightly, sealing each turn well with the hands. Roll the ends between hands to taper them and place diagonally, seam side down, on greased baking sheet sprinkled with cornmeal. Cut slits ⅛" deep and 2" apart on tops of loaf. Combine egg white and cold water. Brush on tops and sides of loaves. Cover with towel wrung from water, but do not let it touch the bread; prop it with iced tea glasses turned upside down. Let rise in warm place until doubled, 1 to 1½ hours.

• Place a large, shallow pan on the floor or low rack of a moderate oven (375°); fill with boiling water. Bake loaves about 20 minutes, or until light brown. Brush tops and sides again with egg white-water mixture. Bake 20 minutes longer until golden brown. Cool. Makes 2 loaves.

Variations

ITALIAN BREAD—ROUND LOAVES: Shape each half of dough into a ball instead of into a long loaf. Place on baking sheet sprinkled with cornmeal and with sharp knife make 3 or 4 cuts ⅛" deep on tops of loaves. Brush with egg white-water mixture and let rise and bake like Italian Bread.

FRENCH BREAD: Much French Bread is made exactly like Italian Bread, but sometimes either 1 tblsp. sugar or 1 tblsp. melted shortening is added.

ORANGE/NUT-GLAZED RAISIN BREAD

Rich golden loaves, so delicious . . . The orange glaze contains walnuts

1 c. milk
1½ tsp. salt
½ c. sugar
½ c. soft butter or shortening
2 pkgs. active dry yeast
¼ c. warm water (110 to 115°)
5¼ to 5¾ c. sifted flour
2 eggs
1 tsp. grated orange peel
1 tsp. ground ginger
1½ c. raisins
Orange/Nut Glaze

• Scald milk. Pour over salt, sugar and butter in large bowl. Blend and cool to lukewarm.

• Sprinkle yeast on warm water; stir to dissolve. Add to milk mixture with 2½ c. flour. Beat 2 minutes with electric mixer at medium speed, scraping bowl occasionally. Or beat with spoon until smooth, about 100 strokes.

• Beat in eggs, orange peel, ginger, raisins and ½ c. flour. Then mix in enough remaining flour, a little at a time, first with spoon and then with hands, to make soft dough that leaves sides of bowl.

• Turn onto lightly floured board. Knead just until smooth, about 50 strokes. Round up in ball. Place in a lightly greased bowl; turn dough over to grease top. Cover and let rise in warm place until doubled, 1 to 1½ hours.

• Punch down and let rest for 15 minutes. Divide in half. Shape into loaves and place in 2 greased 8½ × 4½ × 2½" or 9 × 5 × 3" loaf pans. Make 3 diagonal slashes ¼" deep across top of each.

• Cover and let rise in warm place only until doubled, about 1 hour.

• Bake in moderate oven (375°) 40 to 50 minutes. Cover with sheet of foil after first 20 minutes of baking if loaves are browning too fast. Remove loaves from pans; place on wire racks. Spread Orange/Nut Glaze on tops, then cool. Makes 2 loaves.

ORANGE/NUT GLAZE: Blend 1 c. sifted confectioners sugar, 2 tsp. soft butter and ½ c. finely chopped walnuts; add 2 to 4 tblsp. orange juice to make glaze of spreading consistency.

CINNAMON TWIST BREAD

Lovely to look at—wonderful to eat

1 c. milk
¼ c. shortening
½ c. sugar
2 tsp. salt
2 pkgs. active dry yeast
½ c. warm water (110 to 115°)
6 c. sifted flour
2 eggs, slightly beaten
½ c. sugar
1 tblsp. ground cinnamon
1 tblsp. soft butter

• Scald milk; stir in shortening, ½ c. sugar and salt. Cool to lukewarm.

• Sprinkle yeast on warm water in large bowl; stir to dissolve. Stir in 3 c. flour, eggs and milk mixture. Beat with electric mixer 2 minutes at medium speed, scraping bowl occasionally. Or beat by hand until batter sheets off spoon. Mix in enough remaining flour with hands, a little at a time, to make a soft dough that leaves the sides of bowl. Turn out onto lightly floured board; knead until smooth, about 10 minutes. Place in lightly greased bowl; turn dough over to grease top. Cover and let rise in warm place until doubled, about 1½ hours.

• Punch down; cover and let rise again until almost doubled, about 30 minutes. Turn onto board; divide in half. Round up each half to make a ball. Cover and let rest 10 minutes.

• Roll each half into a 12 × 7″ rectangle. Combine ½ c. sugar and cinnamon; save out 1 tblsp. for topping. Sprinkle dough rectangles evenly with sugar-cinnamon mixture. Sprinkle 1 tsp. cold water over each rectangle. Spread smooth with spatula. Roll as for jelly roll, starting at narrow end. Seal long edge; tuck under ends. Place, sealed edge down, in 2 greased 9 × 5 × 3″ loaf pans. Cover and let rise until almost doubled, 45 to 60 minutes.

• Brush tops of loaves with soft butter and sprinkle with reserved sugar-cinnamon mixture.

• Bake in moderate oven (375°) 35 to 40 minutes. Cover tops of loaves with aluminum foil the last 15 minutes of baking, if necessary, to prevent excessive browning. Remove from pans and cool on wire racks. Makes 2 loaves.

OLD-FASHIONED OATMEAL BREAD

Loaves with tempting homemade look and taste go fast at bake sales

2 c. milk
2 c. quick-cooking rolled oats
¼ c. brown sugar, firmly packed
1 tblsp. salt
2 tblsp. shortening
1 pkg. active dry yeast
½ c. warm water (110 to 115°)
5 c. sifted flour (about)
1 egg white
1 tblsp. water
Rolled oats

• Scald milk; stir in 2 c. rolled oats, brown sugar, salt and shortening. Remove from heat and cool to lukewarm.

• Sprinkle yeast on warm water; stir to dissolve.

• Add milk mixture and 2 c. flour to yeast. Beat with electric mixer on medium speed, scraping the bowl occasionally, 2 minutes. Or beat with spoon until batter is smooth.

• Add enough remaining flour, a little at a time, first with spoon and then with hands, to make a soft dough that leaves the sides of the bowl. Turn onto floured board;

knead until dough is smooth and elastic, 8 to 10 minutes. Place in lightly greased bowl; turn dough over to grease top. Cover and let rise in warm place until doubled, 1 to 1½ hours. Punch down and let rise again until nearly doubled, about 30 minutes.

• Turn onto board and divide in half. Round up to make 2 balls. Cover and let rest 10 minutes. Shape into loaves and place in greased 9 × 5 × 3″ loaf pans. Let rise until almost doubled, about 1 hour and 15 minutes. Brush tops of loaves with egg white beaten with water and sprinkle with rolled oats.

• Bake in moderate oven (375°) about 40 minutes. (If bread starts to brown too much, cover loosely with sheet of aluminum foil after baking 15 minutes.) Makes 2 loaves.

Piping Hot Rolls

Beautifully browned rolls hot from the oven lift many a meal above the commonplace. Our delicious Rich Hot Rolls recipe truly is versatile. From it you also can fashion luscious Cinnamon and Butterscotch Rolls. Dough for Refrigerator Rolls is handy to have on hand ready to bake. And country women, who like to bake ahead, say Twice-baked Rolls (or brown and serve) really have a fresh taste when you heat and brown them 7 to 10 minutes just before serving.

If you want your hamburgers to be the best ever for special occasions, bake the buns for them. We tell you how to make them of uniform shape and size.

RICH HOT ROLLS

Light, tender, rich, delicious

¾ c. milk
½ c. shortening
½ c. sugar
1 tsp. salt
2 pkgs. active dry yeast
½ c. warm water (110 to 115°)
4¼ to 4¾ c. sifted flour
2 eggs

• Scald milk; add shortening, sugar and salt. Cool to lukewarm.

• Sprinkle yeast on warm water; stir to dissolve.

• Add 1½ c. flour to milk mixture; beat well by hand or with electric mixer at low speed 1 minute. Beat in eggs and yeast.

• Gradually stir in enough remaining flour, a little at a time, to make a soft dough that leaves the sides of bowl. Turn onto lightly floured board; knead until smooth, satiny and no longer sticky, 5 to 8 minutes.

• Place in lightly greased bowl; invert to grease top. Cover and let rise in warm place until doubled, 1 to 1½ hours. Punch down and turn onto board. Divide in half and shape as desired (see How to Shape Rolls in Index).

• Brush tops lightly with melted butter; let rise until doubled, 30 to 45 minutes.

• Bake in hot oven (400°) 12 to 15 minutes, or until golden brown. Makes about 30 rolls, exact number depending on shape and size.

Variations

PLAIN ROLLS (less rich): Reduce sugar to ¼ c. and shortening to ⅓ c. in recipe for Rich Hot Rolls.

CINNAMON ROLLS: Divide risen dough for Rich Hot Rolls in half.

Roll each half into a 16 × 8″ rectangle. Combine 1 c. sugar, ½ c. melted butter and 1 tblsp. ground cinnamon. Spread half of mixture on each rectangle. If you like, scatter ⅓ c. raisins over each rectangle. Roll lengthwise as for jelly roll; seal edges. Cut in 1″ slices. Place, cut side down, in 2 well-greased 9″ square pans. Cover and let rise until doubled, 30 to 40 minutes. Bake in moderate oven (375°) 20 to 25 minutes. Remove to wire racks. Makes 32 rolls.

Note: Frost rolls with Confectioners Sugar Frosting (see Index), if you like.

BUTTERSCOTCH ROLLS: Use one half of risen dough for Rich Hot Rolls. Roll dough into a 16 × 8″ rectangle. Brush with ¼ c. melted butter. Sprinkle with ⅓ c. brown sugar, firmly packed, combined with 1 tsp. ground cinnamon. Roll lengthwise as for jelly roll; seal edges. Cut in 1″ slices.

• Pour ¼ c. melted butter into a 9″ square pan; grease sides of pan. Stir ½ c. brown sugar, firmly packed, and 1 tblsp. light corn syrup into butter in pan; mix well. Heat slowly, stirring constantly, until mixture is syrupy and spreads evenly over bottom. Remove from heat. Sprinkle with ⅓ c. finely chopped pecans.

• Place rolls, cut side down, over syrup mixture. Cover and let rise until doubled, 30 to 45 minutes. Bake in moderate oven (375°) about 20 minutes. Cool 3 minutes in pan; then invert on rack (place waxed paper under rack to catch any drippings). Makes 16 rolls.

REFRIGERATOR ROLLS

Make rolls any time up to 3 to 5 days after the dough has chilled 2 hours

2 pkgs. active dry yeast
1¾ c. warm water (110 to 115°)
½ c. sugar
1 tblsp. salt
5½ to 6 c. flour
1 egg
¼ c. soft shortening, butter or regular margarine

• Sprinkle yeast over warm water in large bowl; stir to dissolve. Add sugar, salt and about half the flour. Beat with electric mixer on medium speed 2 minutes, or by hand until mixture is smooth.

• Add egg and shortening. Beat to mix. Mix in remaining flour with hands or a spoon until dough is easy to handle. Shape into a ball and place in lightly greased bowl; turn greased side of dough up. Cover tightly with aluminum foil, or place bowl in a plastic bag.

• Put dough in refrigerator and let rise at least 2 hours, or until doubled before using. Punch down dough every day until you use it. Two hours before you want to serve hot rolls, punch down dough and shape (see Index for How to Shape Rolls). Brush tops with melted butter; cover and let rise in warm place until nearly doubled, about 1½ hours.

• Bake in hot oven (400°) 12 to 15 minutes. Makes about 3 dozen average size rolls.

Note: Dough may be kept up to 5 days in refrigerator with 45° or lower temperature.

TWICE-BAKED ROLLS

Keep on hand ready to brown quickly—rolls have fresh, home-baked taste

1 pkg. active dry yeast
¼ c. warm water (110 to 115°)
¼ c. scalded milk, cooled to lukewarm
¼ c. sugar
2¼ tsp. salt
¼ c. melted shortening
4½ c. sifted flour (about)

· Sprinkle yeast on warm water; stir to dissolve. Stir in lukewarm milk, sugar, salt, shortening and 2½ c. flour. Beat until smooth. Stir in remaining flour to make a soft dough that leaves the sides of bowl.

· Turn dough onto lightly floured surface; knead until smooth and satiny, about 5 minutes. Put in lightly greased bowl, turn greased side of dough up; cover and let rise in warm place until doubled, about 1½ hours.

· Punch down, and turn dough onto lightly floured surface; divide into 24 pieces of equal size. Shape each piece into a ball. Place about 3″ apart on greased baking sheet (or in greased muffin-pan cups), cover and let rise until doubled, about 45 minutes.

· Bake in very slow oven (275°) 20 to 30 minutes. *Do not let rolls brown.* Remove from baking sheet and cool at room temperature.

· Wrap rolls in plastic wrap or aluminum foil and store in refrigerator for several days or in freezer up to 2 to 3 months. To serve, brown rolls in hot oven (400°) 7 to 10 minutes. Makes 2 dozen rolls.

Note: You can form dough in other shapes.

HOW TO SHAPE ROLLS

CLOVERLEAFS: Shape dough in long rolls 1″ in diameter. Cut off 1″ pieces and form each into a small ball. Place 3 balls in each greased muffin-pan cup. Balls should touch bottom of cups and fill them half full. Brush with melted butter or regular margarine.

FOUR-LEAF CLOVERS: Place 2″ ball of dough in each greased muffin-pan cup. With scissors cut surface of each ball in half and then across again to make fourths.

BUTTERHORNS: Roll dough ¼″ thick, brush with melted butter or regular margarine and cut in 12″ circle. Cut circle in 16 pie-shaped pieces. Starting at wide or curved end, roll up. Place, point end down, on greased baking sheet, 2″ apart.

CRESCENTS: Make like Butterhorns, but curve ends of each roll on baking sheet to make crescent shapes.

FAN-TANS: Roll dough ⅛″ thick into an oblong. Brush with melted butter or regular margarine. Cut in strips 1½″ wide. Stack 6 strips; cut in 1½″ pieces. Place cut side down, in greased muffin-pan cups.

PAN ROLLS: Shape dough in 2″ balls. Dip in melted butter or regular margarine. Place in greased round layer cake pans, letting balls just touch one another.

DINNER ROLLS: Shape dough in 2″ balls. Roll each ball with floured hands until 4″ long. Roll ends between hands to taper. Place on greased baking sheet, 2″ apart.

PARKERHOUSE ROLLS: Roll dough ¼″ thick on lightly floured board; cut in rounds with 2½″ floured biscuit or cookie cutter. Brush with melted butter. Make a crease in each round just off center with back of table knife. Fold larger side of each round over other side, overlapping slightly. Seal end edges. Brush with melted butter; place rolls about 1″ apart on greased baking sheet.

BUTTERFLY ROLLS: Roll dough into rectangle about ¼″ thick, 6″ wide. Brush with melted butter or regular margarine and roll like a jelly roll. Cut in 2″ widths. Make a depression down center of each with a small wooden handle. Place on greased baking sheet.

EASTER BUNNIES: Shape dough into long ropes ¾ to 1″ in diameter; cut in 10 to 12″ lengths. Tie in loose knots, bringing ends straight up to make ears. Press in raisins for eyes. Brush with 1 egg yolk beaten with 1 tblsp. water. Let rise on greased baking sheet. After baking and while still warm, frost lightly with Confectioners Sugar Frosting (see Index), tinting some of frosting a pale pink for bunnies' ears.

Roll dough into an oblong about 12″ long and a scant ½″ thick. Cut in strips ½″ wide, 6″ long, and shape rolls as follows:

SNAILS: Hold one end of strip on greased baking sheet and twist. Wind strip round and round to make coil. Tuck end under.

FIGURE 8S: Hold one end of strip in one hand; twist other end, stretching strip slightly until the two ends, when placed together on greased baking sheet, make a Figure 8.

TWISTS: Make like Figure 8s, but give each circle of Figure 8 an additional twist before placing on greased baking sheet.

KNOTS: Form loop of strip and ease one end through loop to make a knot. Press ends down on greased baking sheet.

ROSEBUDS: Form twisted strip into a loop; pull one end up through center of loop (making a knot) and bring other end over the side and under.

BRAIDS: Form several ropes of dough ½″ in diameter. Braid 3 ropes into a long braid. Repeat with other ropes. Cut braids into 3½″ lengths. Pinch together at both ends; then gently pull to lengthen braids. Lay on greased baking sheets; brush lightly with melted butter.

PERFECT BUNS

Buns are uniform in size and shape if you bake them in 4″ foil tart pans

½ c. milk
2 tblsp. sugar
1½ tsp. salt
¼ c. shortening
1 pkg. active dry yeast
½ c. warm water (110 to 115°)
3 c. sifted flour
1 egg, beaten
1 egg (for glaze)
2 tblsp. water
½ tsp. sesame or poppy seeds (optional)

• Scald milk; pour into bowl over sugar, salt and shortening. Stir; cool to lukewarm.
• Sprinkle yeast on warm water; stir to dissolve.
• Add yeast, 1½ c. flour and beaten egg to milk mixture. Beat with electric mixer at medium speed until bat-

ter is smooth, about 2 minutes; or beat by hand. Mix in remaining flour, a little at a time, with spoon or hands. Cover and let rest 15 minutes.

• Toss dough onto floured board until it no longer is sticky. Divide into 12 equal portions. Shape each portion into a smooth ball. (Dough may be somewhat sticky and difficult to shape into a ball. If so, toss each ball into a little flour on the board.)

• Place each ball in a greased 4″ foil tart pan (the disposable kind). Flatten tops of buns by pressing dough down gently with fingertips. Set pans on two baking sheets; cover, let rise in warm place until doubled. (If you do not have tart pans, you can bake the buns on greased baking sheets, but their shape may not be uniform.) If oven is not in use, place buns in oven with pan of boiling water on oven floor.

• Brush with mixture of 1 egg, beaten with 2 tblsp. water. If desired, sprinkle each bun with sesame or poppy seeds.

• Bake in hot oven (400°) 12 minutes, changing position of baking sheets during baking. Cool 5 minutes; turn out on wire racks. Buns may be frozen. Serve warm or cool. Makes 12 buns.

Yeast Coffee Breads

Styles come and go as do the seasons, but the coffee hour remains part of the pattern of farm life. It's the best excuse to pause briefly between breakfast and noon for people whose working day starts early.

In winter when the men work nearby in the barnyard and feedlot, the warmth of a cheerful kitchen and thoughts of full-bodied coffee and yeast breads draw them to the house both morning and midafternoon. And in summer they frequently have coffee or iced tea in the field from a vacuum jug, plus sandwiches made from homemade breads.

Recipes for coffee breads that follow are at home in country breakfasts as well as supper. And sometimes are served with canned or frozen fruit for dessert. They're good any time!

FINNISH COFFEE BREAD

You can divide dough and make 1 coffee bread and 1 plain round loaf

2 pkgs. active dry yeast
2 c. warm water (110 to 115°)
1 egg (room temperature)
6 to 7 c. sifted flour
½ tsp. ground cardamom
⅓ c. sugar
2 tsp. salt
¼ c. soft butter or shortening
Thin Confectioners Sugar Icing

• Sprinkle yeast on warm water; stir to dissolve.

• Blend in egg, 3 c. flour, cardamom, sugar and salt. Beat with electric mixer at medium speed about 2 minutes (or about 100 strokes by hand), until batter is smooth. Add butter and enough remaining flour, a little at a time, first with spoon and then with hand, to make a fairly soft dough that leaves the sides of bowl.

• Turn onto lightly floured board. Knead until smooth and elastic, about 8 minutes. Place in greased bowl and turn dough over to grease top. Cover and let rise in warm place until doubled, about 1 hour.

Punch down dough, turn over, cover and let rest 10 minutes.
• Turn out onto board; divide in half. Cut each half into 3 equal parts.
• Roll each part under hand to make a strip 11 to 12″ long. Braid 3 strips, starting from the center and braiding to each end, pinching ends to seal. Place in greased 9 × 5 × 3″ loaf pan. Repeat with remaining 3 strips.
• Cover and let rise in warm place until doubled, about 45 minutes.
• Bake in hot oven (400°) 40 to 50 minutes, covering with sheet of foil during last 15 minutes to prevent browning too much. Remove from pans and place on wire cooling racks. After loaves are slightly cooled, brush with Thin Confectioners Sugar Icing. Makes 2 loaves.

THIN CONFECTIONERS SUGAR ICING: Add 1 tblsp. plus 2 tsp. light cream to 1 c. sifted confectioners sugar, and stir until icing is smooth.

Variations

FINNISH BREAD—ROUND LOAVES: Turn risen dough onto board; divide into 2 parts. Shape into 2 round loaves and place in 2 greased 9″ round layer cake plans. Make 3 or 4 slashes on tops of loaves with very sharp knife. Cover, let rise until doubled; bake and cool like Finnish Coffee Bread. Omit icing. Makes 2 round loaves.

FINNISH BRAIDS: Turn risen dough onto board; divide in half. Cut one half into 4 parts. Shape 3 parts into strands 12″ long. Place on greased baking sheet and braid, starting at center and braiding to each end. Seal ends. Cut remaining part into 3 parts; shape into strands 9″ long; braid and place on top of large braid, tucking ends into large braid. Repeat with other half of dough. Cover, let rise until doubled; bake (20 to 25 minutes), cool and frost like Finnish Coffee Bread. Makes 2 braids.

CARAMEL TWISTS

Make dough one day, bake rolls the next—serve with coffee

Dough:
4½ c. sifted flour
¼ c. sugar
1 tsp. salt
¾ c. butter or regular margarine
1 pkg. active dry yeast
¼ c. warm water (110 to 115°)
3 egg yolks, beaten
1 c. milk, scalded and cooled to lukewarm

Caramel Coating:
⅔ c. butter or regular margarine
¼ c. light corn syrup
1½ c. light brown sugar, firmly packed
1 c. chopped walnuts

Filling:
½ c. brown sugar, firmly packed
1 tsp. ground cinnamon
Soft butter

• Combine flour, sugar and salt in mixing bowl. Cut in butter until size of small peas.
• Sprinkle yeast on warm water; stir to dissolve. Add to flour mixture along with beaten egg yolks and milk. Beat until thoroughly mixed and smooth. Cover bowl and chill in refrigerator overnight.
• When ready to bake, prepare caramel coating by melting butter in a small saucepan. Stir in the syrup. Spread this mixture in bottoms of two 15½ × 10½ × 1″ jelly roll

pans. Sprinkle ¾ c. brown sugar and ½ c. chopped nuts evenly in each pan.

• To make filling, mix the brown sugar and cinnamon. Divide into thirds.

• Cut dough in three equal parts for easy handling. Roll each third into a 15 × 10″ rectangle. Brush center lengthwise third of each rectangle with soft butter, then sprinkle with filling mixture.

• Fold a third of each rectangle over the third and sprinkle with filling mixture (you'll use ⅓ of filling mixture for each rectangle of dough). Fold remaining third over two layers. Cut crosswise into strips 1″ wide.

• Grasp ends of strips firmly and twist in opposite direction; seal ends firmly in fan shape. Place dough strips in pans about 1″ apart. Allow to rise about 30 minutes in a warm place.

• Bake in moderate oven (350°) about 25 minutes. Invert pans immediately on large sheets of foil. Allow pans to remain inverted about 1 minute before removing. Makes about 30 twists.

EASTER EGG BREAD

Gay Easter eggs in breakfast bread

12 eggs in shell, uncooked
Easter egg coloring
½ c. milk
½ c. sugar
1 tsp. salt
½ c. shortening
Grated peel of 2 lemons
2 pkgs. active dry yeast
½ c. warm water (110 to 115°)
2 eggs (at room temperature)
4½ c. sifted flour (about)
1 egg, beaten
Tiny colored candies

• Wash 12 uncooked eggs. Tint shells with egg coloring; set aside.

• Scald milk; add sugar, salt, shortening and lemon peel. Cool to lukewarm.

• Sprinkle yeast on warm water; stir to dissolve. Add to milk mixture with the 2 eggs, slightly beaten, and 2½ c. flour. Beat until smooth.

• Stir in enough remaining flour, a little at a time, to form a dough that is easy to handle. Turn onto lightly floured board and knead until smooth and elastic, 5 to 8 minutes. Place in lightly greased bowl; turn dough over to grease top. Cover and let rise in warm place until doubled, about 1 hour.

• Punch down; cover and let rise again until almost doubled, about 30 minutes.

• Make 2 large braided rings or 12 individual rings as follows:

LARGE RINGS: Divide dough into 4 parts. Form each part into a 36″ rope. On a greased baking sheet, shape 2 of the ropes into a very loosely braided ring, leaving space for 6 eggs. Repeat with other 2 ropes of dough for second ring. Insert 6 tinted eggs in spaces in each ring.

INDIVIDUAL RINGS: Divide dough into 12 parts. Form each part into a ring around a tinted egg.

• Cover; let rise until doubled.

• Brush evenly with beaten egg. Sprinkle with tiny decorating candies.

• Bake in moderate oven (375°) 15 minutes for individual rings, 20 minutes for large rings, or until lightly browned. Serve warm. Makes 2 large or 12 individual rings.

Note: Easter Egg Bread can be baked the day before. Refrigerate.

13. BAKED BEANS and APPLE PIE—Almost every family enjoys these great American originals. See favorite recipes for them, pages 168, 406.

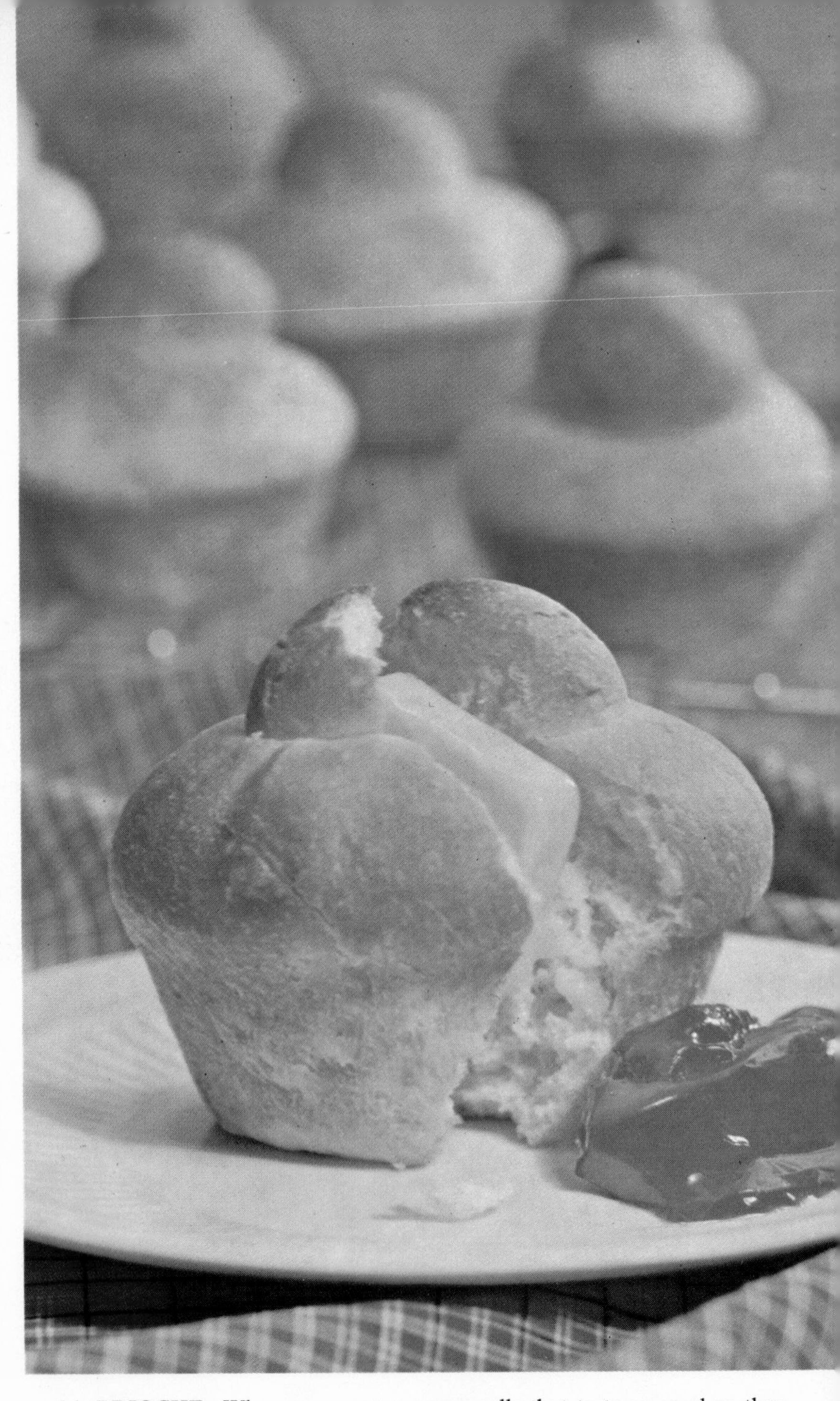

14. BRIOCHE—When you want to serve rolls that taste as good as they look, bake feather-light brioche. Wonderful with coffee. Recipe, page 247.

15. HELP-YOURSELF DESSERT—Assemble several kinds of cheese and apple and/or pear slices on tray. Tell guests dessert is ready—they'll come and get it.

16. APPLE DUMPLINGS—When trees in orchards bend low with fruit, it's time to bake whole apples wrapped in pastry jackets. Recipe, page 335.

At serving time, reheat in moderate oven (350°) 8 minutes.

CLASSIC SWEET DOUGH

Starting point for wonderful breads —the dough will make 3 loaves

2 c. milk
½ c. butter or regular margarine
½ c. sugar
2 tsp. salt
2 pkgs. active dry yeast
½ c. warm water (110 to 115°)
2 eggs, beaten
9½ to 10 c. sifted flour

• Scald milk; stir in butter, sugar and salt. Cool to lukewarm.
• Sprinkle yeast on warm water; stir to dissolve.
• Add milk mixture, eggs and 4½ c. flour to yeast; beat until smooth. Stir in enough remaining flour, a little at a time to make a slightly stiff dough. (If you want to make Grecian Feast Loaf, remove one third of dough at this point.)
• Turn dough onto lightly floured board, cover and let rest 5 minutes. Knead until smooth and elastic, about 5 minutes. Put in greased bowl; turn dough over to grease top. Cover and let rise until doubled, about 1 hour.
• Punch down, turn onto board, divide into thirds and use to make the following:

APRICOT CRESCENTS

Twin loaves with hearts of gold

⅓ of Classic Sweet Dough
2 c. Apricot Filling
2 tblsp. melted butter
2 tblsp. sugar

• Divide dough in half. Roll each half into a 12 × 8″ rectangle. Spread each with 1 c. Apricot Filling. Starting at long edge, roll as for jelly roll. Seal edge.
• Place on greased baking sheet and shape in crescents. Make slashes on tops with scissors 1½″ apart. Brush with butter; sprinkle with sugar.
• Cover; let rise in warm place until doubled, about 30 minutes.
• Bake in moderate oven (350°) 25 to 30 minutes. Remove to wire racks to cool. Makes 2 loaves.

APRICOT FILLING: Combine in a heavy saucepan 2 c. dried apricots (11 oz. pkg.) and 1 c. water. Cover and simmer until apricots are tender. Add ¼ c. butter or regular margarine, stir and mash until butter is melted. Add 1½ c. sugar and stir to dissolve; beat well. Cool and add 1 c. chopped walnuts. Makes 3 cups.

DATE BRAID

Filling peeks through slits in loaf

⅓ of Classic Sweet Dough
2 c. Date Filling

• Roll dough into a 14 × 8″ rectangle. Place on greased baking sheet.
• Reserve ¼ c. Date Filling. Spread remaining filling in 3″ strip lengthwise on center of rectangle. At each side of filling cut from edge of dough to filling at 2″ intervals. You will have 7 strips on each side.
• Bring strips from opposite sides to center, crossing them and then tucking in on sides. Spoon reserved filling into the open spaces. Cover, let rise in warm place until doubled, 30 to 45 minutes.
• Bake in moderate oven (350°) 25 to 30 minutes. Place on wire rack to cool. Frost with Confectioners Sugar Frosting (see Index) while still warm.

DATE FILLING: Combine in heavy saucepan 1 (8 oz.) pkg. dates, chopped or finely cut with scissors, 1 c. chopped pecans, ¼ c. brown sugar, firmly packed, ⅔ c. water and 1 tblsp. lemon juice. Cook, stirring constantly, until of spreading consistency, 3 to 5 minutes. Cool before using. Makes 2 cups.

SWEDISH TEA RING

For Yuletide centerpiece put candle in center of pretty bread wreath

- **¼ c. soft butter or regular margarine**
- **¼ c. sugar**
- **1 tsp. grated lemon peel**
- **½ c. ground almonds**
- **⅓ of Classic Sweet Dough**
- **1 c. mixed candied fruits, chopped**

• Cream butter and sugar; stir in lemon peel and almonds. Mix well.

• Roll dough into a 14 × 10″ rectangle. Sprinkle sugar mixture evenly over dough. Arrange candied fruits evenly over the top. Roll up from the long side as for jelly roll; seal edge. Place, sealed edge down, in ring on lightly greased baking sheet. Seal ends together firmly. Snip dough with scissors from edge of circle three fourths of the way to center every 1½″. Turn cut pieces on their sides. (If you're making this bread for Christmas, place greased custard cup in center to keep hole round for non-drip candle.)

• Cover and let rise until doubled, 45 minutes to 1 hour.

• Bake in moderate oven (350°) 25 to 30 minutes. Cool on wire rack.

Note: You can frost Swedish Tea Ring with Confectioners Sugar Frosting (see Index).

GRECIAN FEAST LOAF

The 3-leaf-clover loaf is an Easter and Christmas tradition in Greece

- **⅓ of Classic Sweet Dough (before kneading)**
- **½ c. currants**
- **1 tsp. grated lemon peel**
- **¼ tsp. ground mace**
- **1 egg, beaten (for glaze)**

• Remove one third of Classic Sweet Dough when mixed, before kneading. Work in the currants, lemon peel and mace; knead until dough is smooth and elastic, 3 to 5 minutes. Place in lightly greased bowl; turn dough over to grease top. Cover, let rise in warm place until doubled, about 1 hour.

• Punch down, turn onto floured board and divide into 3 equal parts. Shape each part into a smooth ball and arrange on greased baking sheet to form a 3-leaf clover. Leave ¾″ between the 3 balls.

• Cover and let rise in warm place until doubled, about 1 hour. Brush each ball of dough with beaten egg.

• Bake in moderate oven (350°) about 25 minutes. Cool on wire rack.

CINNAMON LEAF RING

Let everyone pull off his serving

- **2 pkgs. active dry yeast**
- **2 c. milk, scalded and cooled to warm (110 to 115°)**
- **¾ c. shortening**
- **¼ c. butter or regular margarine**
- **½ c. sugar**
- **2 tsp. salt**
- **4 egg yolks or 2 eggs, beaten**
- **6 c. sifted flour (about)**

1 c. melted butter or regular margarine (about)
2 tblsp. ground cinnamon
2 c. sugar

• Sprinkle yeast over warm milk; stir to dissolve.
• Cream shortening and ¼ c. butter; add ½ c. sugar and salt. Cream until light and fluffy. Add egg yolks, yeast and enough flour to make a soft dough that leaves the sides of bowl.
• Turn out on lightly floured board; knead until smooth and elastic. Place in greased bowl; turn greased side of dough up. Cover and let rise until doubled, about 1 hour.
• Turn dough out onto board; roll about ¼″ thick. Cut into rounds with 2″ biscuit cutter. Dip each in melted butter, then in mixture of cinnamon and 2 c. sugar. Stand up in 2 well buttered 8½ × 2¼″ ring molds until rings are filled. (Make rolls from any leftover dough.) Cover and let rise until light, about 30 minutes.
• Bake in moderate oven (350°) about 25 minutes. Cool slightly on racks before turning out. Makes 2 rings, or 20 to 25 servings.

Variations

KOLACHES: Make ½ recipe Cinnamon Leaf basic dough. Shape into small balls (about 1½″) and place on greased baking sheets; let rise. Brush with melted butter or regular margarine. Make deep hole in center of each with thumb; then press out with forefinger to make the hole larger. Fill them with a fruit filling (recipe follows). Bake in moderate oven (375°) about 15 minutes. Makes 4 dozen buns. To give a special occasion touch to the Kolaches, sprinkle a fine dusting of confectioners sugar over tops before serving.

FRUIT FILLINGS: Cook together slowly, stirring until thickened: 2 c. dried apricots, finely cut, ¾ c. sugar, ¾ c. water and 1 tblsp. lemon juice. Cool. Or use 2 c. mashed cooked prunes for the apricots.

ORANGE TWISTS: Make ½ recipe basic dough, adding 1½ tsp. grated orange peel to dough. Roll into rectangles 18 × 10″. Spread with well blended mixture of grated peel of 1 orange, ¾ c. sugar and ⅓ c. soft butter or regular margarine. Roll up lengthwise; cut into 1½″ slices; with back of shears, indent center of each slice. Place on greased baking sheet and let rise. Bake in hot oven (400°) 15 to 20 minutes. Makes about 4 dozen rolls. While still warm, brush with following glaze: Bring to boil ½ c. sugar, ¼ c. light corn syrup and ¼ c. hot water; simmer 1 minute, stirring once or twice. Set aside to cool until rolls are removed from oven.

CINNAMON/RAISIN AND CURRANT BUNS: Make ½ recipe basic dough. Roll into rectangles 18 × 9″. Spread with mixture of 2 tsp. ground cinnamon and ½ c. sifted brown sugar, firmly packed; sprinkle with ½ c. seedless raisins or dried currants and drizzle with 2 tblsp. dark corn syrup. Roll up and cut into 1″ slices. Place in very well greased muffin-pan cups, each containing 1 tblsp. corn syrup; let rise. Bake in moderate oven (350°) 20 to 25 minutes. Makes about 4 dozen rolls.

HONEY-FILLED COFFEE CAKE

Breakfast bread has sparkling top, rich filling; slices a swirl pattern

2 pkgs. active dry yeast
¼ c. warm water (110 to 115°)
½ c. shortening
2 tsp. salt
¼ c. sugar
1 c. scalded milk
2 eggs, beaten
4½ c. sifted flour
Melted butter
Honey Filling

• Sprinkle yeast over warm water; stir to dissolve.
• Combine shortening, salt and sugar in large bowl; add scalded milk. Stir until shortening is melted, then cool to lukewarm.
• Add eggs and yeast; mix well.
• Gradually add flour, beating thoroughly after each addition. Turn onto lightly floured board; knead until smooth and elastic.
• Place in greased bowl and turn dough over to grease top. Cover; let rise in warm place until doubled, about 1½ hours.
• Punch down dough; turn over, cover and let rest 10 minutes. Turn out onto floured board. Divide dough in half, keeping one half covered with cloth.
• Roll out other half into a 16 × 12″ rectangle. Brush with melted butter and spread with half the Honey Filling. Roll like jelly roll; seal edges.
• Cut into 1″ slices. Make bottom layer in greased 10″ tube pan, placing slices cut side down so they barely touch. Arrange remaining slices in layers, covering up the spaces, with no slice directly on top of another.
• Prepare remaining half of dough in same manner, placing slices on top in layers as before. Cover and let rise in warm place until doubled, about 30 minutes.
• Bake in moderate oven (350°) 45 to 60 minutes, or until sides and top are well browned. (If bread browns too soon, cover with foil the last half of baking.) Loosen bread from pan; turn out on rack to cool.

HONEY FILLING: Combine ½ c. honey, ¼ c. sugar, grated peel of 1 orange or lemon, 1 tblsp. orange or lemon juice, 1 tsp. ground cinnamon, ⅓ c. finely cut raisins, ⅓ c. finely chopped nuts and 1 tblsp. melted butter or regular margarine.

Note: If desired, you can pour a glaze over cake, made by combining ½ c. honey, ½ c. sugar, 1 tblsp. butter or regular margarine and 1 tblsp. coarsely grated orange peel. Simmer until thick, about 5 minutes. Pour glaze over cake.

Election Coffee Cake

It's called a cake, but it's a yeast-leavened coffee bread. More than a century ago this fruit- and nut-studded loaf, according to legend, was the payoff of Connecticut politicians to men who voted the straight party ticket. Today its only connection with politics is that many hostesses, especially in New England, serve it at informal parties on election day. It's a good choice if you're looking for something tasty to serve with coffee to guests in front of your television set, while listening to vote counts.

You can bake the bread days ahead and freeze it (but then omit the frosting). To use, thaw the loaf in its wrapper at room temperature for several hours; frost shortly before serving. Or if you prefer, wrap the frozen bread in aluminum foil and heat it in a hot oven (400°) 30 minutes to 1 hour. Cool slightly before you spread the frosting on top, letting it dribble temptingly down the sides of the loaf.

ELECTION DAY CAKE

Good to serve at election day parties

- **2 pkgs. active dry yeast**
- **1½ c. warm water (110 to 115°)**
- **2 tsp. sugar**
- **4½ c. sifted flour**
- **¾ c. butter or regular margarine**
- **1 c. sugar**
- **1 tsp. salt**
- **1½ tsp. ground cinnamon**
- **¼ tsp. ground cloves**
- **¼ tsp. ground mace**
- **½ tsp. ground nutmeg**
- **2 eggs**
- **1½ c. raisins**
- **½ c. chopped citron**
- **¾ c. chopped nuts**
- **Confectioners Sugar Frosting**

• Sprinkle yeast on warm water; stir to dissolve. Add 2 tsp. sugar and 1½ c. flour and beat well by hand, or 2 minutes with electric mixer at medium speed. Cover and let rise in warm place until bubbly, about 30 minutes.

• Meanwhile, cream butter and 1 c. sugar until light and fluffy.

• Sift remaining 3 c. flour with salt, cinnamon, cloves, mace and nutmeg.

• When yeast mixture is bubbly, add eggs to creamed butter and sugar and beat well. Combine with yeast mixture. Add remaining dry ingredients (flour, salt and spices), a little at a time, beating with spoon after each addition. Beat until smooth.

• Stir in raisins, citron and nuts. Pour into well greased and floured 10″ tube pan. Cover and let rise in warm place until doubled, about 1½ hours.

• Bake in moderate oven (375°) 1 hour. Cool in pan 5 minutes; turn out on rack to finish cooling. While faintly warm, spread with Confectioners Sugar Frosting. Makes 12 to 16 servings.

CONFECTIONERS SUGAR FROSTING: To 1 c. sifted confectioners sugar add enough milk or light cream to make mixture of spreading consistency. Add ½ tsp. vanilla and a dash of salt (or flavor with ½ tsp. lemon juice and ¼ tsp. grated lemon peel). Stir until smooth. Spread on coffee breads or rolls.

BRIOCHE

Light, delicately yeasty, golden

- **1 c. milk**
- **½ c. butter or regular margarine**
- **1 tsp. salt**
- **½ c. sugar**
- **2 pkgs. active dry yeast**
- **¼ c. warm water (110 to 115°)**
- **4 eggs, beaten**
- **1 tsp. grated lemon peel**
- **5 c. sifted flour (about)**
- **Melted butter**

• Scald milk; stir in ½ c. butter, salt and sugar. Cool to lukewarm.

• Sprinkle yeast on warm water; stir to dissolve.

• Combine eggs and lemon peel and add with yeast to milk mixture. Beat in flour, a little at a time, to make a soft dough you can handle.

• Turn onto floured board; knead lightly until dough is smooth and satiny. Place in greased bowl; turn dough over to grease top. Cover and let rise in warm place free from drafts until doubled, about 2 hours. Punch down and turn out on floured board. Knead lightly.

• Shape two thirds of the dough into smooth balls about 2″ in diameter. Shape remaining dough in 1″ balls. Place large balls in greased muffin-pan cups. Flatten balls slightly; make a deep indentation in each with finger or the handle of a wooden spoon. Shape small balls like teardrops and set one firmly in the indentation in each ball in muffin-pan cups. Brush with melted butter. Cover and let rise until doubled, about 1 hour.

• Bake in hot oven (425°) about 10 minutes. Remove from pans at once. Place on wire racks. Serve warm; or wrap cold rolls in aluminum foil and heat a few minutes in oven before serving. Makes 3 dozen rolls.

Hot Cross Buns

Shiny, brown rolls, topped with white frosting crosses, are as English as roast beef and Yorkshire pudding. The recipes came with the early settlers and caught on from the start. Now the buns come to thousands of breakfast and luncheon tables, mostly during the Easter season.

You can bake the rolls ahead and freeze them, providing you omit the frosting. It takes only a few minutes to add it the day of serving. Put the frozen rolls on a baking sheet and run them in a hot oven (400°) for 10 minutes. Cool 5 minutes, add the frosting and serve pronto.

When you bake Hot Cross Buns, you are making bread that has stood the test of time. English people first made them to honor the Goddess of Spring. When the Christian faith came to the country, bakers bowed to changing times and added the cross.

HOT CROSS BUNS

Easter buns with frosting crosses—traditionally served on Good Friday

¼ c. milk
⅓ c. sugar
¾ tsp. salt
½ c. shortening
2 pkgs. active dry yeast
½ c. warm water (110 to 115°)
3 eggs
4 c. sifted flour (about)
¾ c. currants
1 egg white
1 tsp. cold water
White Frosting

• Scald milk, add sugar, salt and shortening; cool to lukewarm.

• Sprinkle yeast on warm water; stir to dissolve.

• Add eggs, yeast and 1 c. flour to milk mixture; beat with electric mixer at medium speed about 2 minutes, occasionally scraping the bowl. Stir in currants and enough remaining flour, a little at a time, to make a soft dough that is easy to handle. Beat well. Place in lightly greased bowl; turn dough over to grease top. Cover and let rise until doubled, about 1½ hours. Punch down. Turn onto lightly floured board.

• Roll or pat to ½″ thickness. Cut in rounds with 2½″ biscuit cutter;

shape cutouts in buns. Place about 1½" apart on greased baking sheets. Cover and let rise until doubled, about 1 hour.

- With a very sharp knife, cut a shallow cross on top of each bun. Brush tops with unbeaten egg white mixed with cold water.
- Bake in moderate oven (375°) 15 minutes, or until golden brown. Cool on wire racks about 5 minutes. Then, with tip of knife or teaspoon, fill in crosses on buns with White Frosting. Best served warm. Makes about 18 buns.

WHITE FROSTING: Combine 1 c. sifted confectioners sugar, ½ tsp. vanilla and 2 tblsp. hot water. Mix until smooth.

Variation

FRUITED HOT CROSS BUNS: With currants stir in 3 tblsp. finely chopped candied orange peel and 3 tblsp. finely chopped citron.

OLD VIRGINIA SALLY LUNN

Rich, light, tender, almost cake-like yeast bread, yet not sweet—delicious

2 c. milk
1 c. shortening
2 pkgs. active dry yeast
½ c. warm water (110 to 115°)
3 eggs, beaten
¼ c. sugar
2 tsp. salt
6 c. sifted flour

- Scald milk, add shortening to melt. Cool to lukewarm.
- Sprinkle yeast on warm water; stir to dissolve. Add to lukewarm milk mixture.
- Stir in eggs, sugar and salt. Mix well. Stir in flour and beat thoroughly. Cover and let rise in warm place until doubled, about 1 hour.
- Punch down. Spoon into greased 9" ring mold or tube pan; let double again.
- Bake in moderate oven (350°) 50 minutes to 1 hour. Makes 16 servings.

CINNAMON/PECAN ROLLS

Nut-dotted cinnamon rolls—gooey and truly luscious eating

1 pkg. active dry yeast
1 c. milk, scalded and cooled to warm (110 to 115°)
6 tblsp. shortening
6 tblsp. butter or regular margarine
¾ c. sugar
1 tsp. salt
2 egg yolks or 1 egg, beaten
3 c. sifted flour (about)
Melted butter or regular margarine
½ c. brown sugar, firmly packed
2 tsp. ground cinnamon
1 c. corn syrup
1 c. brown sugar, firmly packed
¼ c. butter
1½ c. pecans

- Sprinkle yeast on warm milk; stir to dissolve.
- Cream shortening and 2 tblsp. butter; add ¼ c. sugar and salt; cream together until light and fluffy. Add yolks, yeast and enough flour to make soft dough that leaves the sides of bowl. Turn out on lightly floured cloth or board; knead until smooth and elastic. Place in greased bowl; turn greased side of dough up. Cover; let rise until doubled.
- Divide in half; roll into 2 rectangles, 18 × 9", about ¼" thick. Brush with melted butter.
- Mix together remaining ½ c. sugar, ½ c. brown sugar and cinnamon; sprinkle each piece of dough with half of mixture. Roll like jelly roll, cut into 1" slices.

• Mix together corn syrup, 1 c. brown sugar and ¼ c. butter; heat slowly or in top of double boiler. Place 1 tblsp. syrup and 4 to 5 pecans, rounded side down, in greased muffin-pan cups (about 36). Drop dough slices, cut side down, in syrup; cover and let rise until doubled.

• Bake in hot oven (400°) 12 to 15 minutes. Remove from oven, flip over pans at once. Remove rolls, pecan side up, onto large tray. Let pans stand over rolls a minute, so syrup drains onto them. Makes 3 dozen.

POTATO DOUGHNUTS

Keep some of these potato doughnuts in the freezer to serve with coffee

1¾ c. milk
½ c. shortening
½ c. sugar
½ c. mashed potatoes
1 pkg. active dry yeast
½ c. warm water (110 to 115°)
2 eggs, beaten
½ tsp. vanilla
6½ to 7 c. sifted flour
1 tsp. baking powder
2 tsp. salt

• Scald milk; stir in shortening, sugar and mashed potatoes. Cool to lukewarm. Blend well.

• Sprinkle yeast over warm water and stir until yeast is dissolved. Add to milk mixture. Stir in beaten eggs and vanilla.

• Sift 6½ c. flour with baking powder and salt; add gradually to yeast mixture, mixing well after each addition. Add another ½ c. flour if needed to make a soft dough you can handle (use no more than necessary). Turn into greased bowl; turn dough over to grease top. Cover and let rise in warm place until doubled, about 1½ hours.

• Roll to ½″ thickness on floured board. Cut with floured doughnut cutter, reserving centers to make Pecan Rolls (recipe follows).

• Place cut-out doughnuts on waxed paper; cover with cloth and let rise in warm place until doubled, about 30 minutes.

• Fry a few doughnuts at a time in hot salad oil (375°). Drain on absorbent paper. Spread warm doughnuts with a thin glaze made of confectioners sugar and milk, or shake them in a bag containing sugar to coat them. Makes about 4 dozen doughnuts.

PECAN ROLLS FROM POTATO DOUGHNUT CENTERS: Lightly grease 12 medium-size (2½″) muffin-pan cups. In the bottom of each cup, place 1 tsp. brown sugar, 1 tsp. light corn syrup, ½ tsp. water, 3 pecan halves and 3 or 4 raisins. Arrange 4 doughnut centers on top, cover with cloth and let rise in warm place until doubled, about 30 minutes. Bake in moderate oven (350°) 25 to 30 minutes. Makes 12 rolls.

Yeast-leavened Country Specialties

Waffles, buckwheat cakes and sour dough biscuits and hot cakes bring cheer to the table especially on chilly days. Like homemade pizza, they are hostess specialties. You can roll and freeze our pizza dough ready to fill and bake on short notice. Serve it hot from the oven to the teen-age youngsters after the game, skiing or swimming.

YEAST WAFFLES

Change of pace and taste in waffles

2 c. milk
1 pkg. active dry yeast
½ c. warm water (110 to 115°)
⅓ c. melted butter
1 tsp. salt
1 tsp. sugar
3 c. sifted flour
2 eggs, slightly beaten
½ tsp. baking soda

• Scald milk; cool to lukewarm.
• Sprinkle yeast on warm water in large bowl; stir to dissolve.
• Add milk, butter, salt, sugar and flour to yeast; mix thoroughly with rotary or electric mixer until batter is smooth. Cover and let stand at room temperature overnight.
• When ready to bake, add eggs and baking soda. Beat well. Bake on preheated waffle iron. Makes 6 to 8 waffles.

BUCKWHEAT CAKES

To please the men, keep the starter ready and the griddle handy to use

1 c. sifted flour
3½ c. buckwheat flour
1 tsp. salt
1 pkg. active dry yeast
4 c. warm water (110 to 115°)
2 tsp. sugar
2 tblsp. dark brown sugar
¾ tsp. baking soda
1 tblsp. salad oil

• Combine flours. Stir in salt.
• Sprinkle yeast on ¼ c. warm water; stir to dissolve.
• Dissolve 2 tsp. sugar in remaining 3¾ c. warm water; cool to lukewarm. Add lukewarm water mixture and yeast to flours. Stir to mix thoroughly. Cover and let stand overnight or several hours at room temperature. Batter should no more than half fill bowl.
• When ready to bake pancakes, stir down batter and add brown sugar, baking soda and oil. Stir to mix.
• Dip batter with ¼-cup measure; bake on lightly greased, preheated griddle (hot enough that a few drops of water dropped on it dance about). Brown on both sides, turning once. Serve hot with butter or margarine and table syrup. Makes 5 cups batter.

STARTER FOR MORE BUCKWHEAT CAKES

• The leftover batter becomes the starter. Pour it into a glass or plastic container with tight fitting lid. Fill container no more than half full of batter. Cover and place in refrigerator. It will keep several days.

HOW TO USE BUCKWHEAT CAKE STARTER

• Remove starter from refrigerator the night (or several hours) before you wish to bake cakes. Pour it into a mixing bowl and add 1 c. lukewarm water for every cup buckwheat flour you add to starter. Stir to blend, cover and let stand at room temperature.
• When ready to bake cakes, stir down batter. Add 1 tsp. salt, 2 tblsp. brown sugar, ¾ tsp. baking soda and 1 tblsp. salad oil. Stir to blend.
• Bake like Buckwheat Cakes, saving out batter to store in refrigerator to make starter for the next batch of pancakes.

SOUR DOUGH STARTER

Good beginning for country specials

½ pkg. active dry yeast (1¼ tsp.)
2 c. sifted flour
2 tblsp. sugar
2½ c. water

• Combine the ingredients in a stone crock or glass or pottery bowl. Beat well. Cover with cheesecloth and let stand 2 days in a warm place.

SOUR DOUGH BISCUITS

These biscuits are light and fluffy—they have that marvelous tangy taste

1½ c. sifted flour
2 tsp. baking powder
¼ tsp. baking soda (½ tsp. if Starter is quite sour)
½ tsp. salt
¼ c. butter or regular margarine
1 c. Sour Dough Starter
Melted butter

• Sift dry ingredients together. Cut in ¼ c. butter with pastry blender. Add Starter, and mix.
• Turn dough out on a lightly floured board. Knead lightly until satiny.
• Roll dough ½" thick. Cut with floured 2½" cutter. Place biscuits in well greased 9" square baking pan. Brush with melted butter. Let rise about 1 hour in a warm place.
• Bake in hot oven (425°) 20 minutes. Makes 10 biscuits.

Note: To replenish Starter, stir in 2 c. warm (not hot) water and 2 c. flour.

SILVER DOLLAR HOTCAKES

Serve with butter and lots of "lick," the cowboy's term for sweet syrup

1 c. Sour Dough Starter
2 c. flour
2 c. milk
1 tsp. salt
2 tsp. baking soda
2 eggs
3 tblsp. melted shortening
2 tblsp. sugar

• About 12 hours before mealtime, mix Starter, flour, milk and salt; let stand in a bowl covered with cheesecloth. Set in a warm place.
• Just before baking cakes, remove 1 c. batter to replenish Starter in crock. To the remaining batter in the bowl, add baking soda, eggs, shortening and sugar. Mix well.
• Bake cakes the size of silver dollars on a lightly greased, hot griddle. For thinner hotcakes, add more milk to the batter. Makes about 30 cakes.

POPULAR PIZZA

A treat for teens! Keep dough in freezer ready to fill and bake

1 pkg. active dry yeast
1¼ c. warm water (110 to 115°)
3½ to 4 c. sifted flour
½ tsp. salt
Pizza Filling

• Sprinkle yeast on warm water; stir to dissolve. Add 2 c. flour and salt. Beat thoroughly. Stir in remaining flour. Turn onto lightly floured board and knead until smooth and elastic, about 10 minutes.
• Place in lightly greased bowl; turn dough over to grease top. Cover and let rise in warm place until doubled, about 30 minutes.

• Turn onto board and knead just long enough to force out large bubbles. Divide in half. Roll each half to make an 11″ circle. Stretch each circle to fit an oiled 12″ pizza pan. Add filling (recipes follow).

• Bake in very hot oven (450°) 20 to 25 minutes. Exchange position of pans on oven racks once during baking to brown pizzas the same. Makes 2 pizzas.

Note: If you do not have pizza pans, use baking sheets. Roll each half of dough into a 12 × 10″ rectangle, or one that almost fills your baking sheet. Place on oiled baking sheets and build up edges slightly. Fill and bake like pizzas in round pizza pans.

PIZZA FILLINGS

HAMBURGER FILLING: Spread 1 (8 oz.) can pizza sauce over dough in each pizza pan (you'll use two 8-oz. cans). Brown 1 lb. ground beef in skillet and drain; divide in half and sprinkle evenly over sauce in pizza dough. Then sprinkle evenly over each pizza 1½ c. shredded mozzarella cheese (about 12 oz. cheese for both pizzas). Bake as directed.

HAM AND SALAMI FILLING: Spread 1 (8 oz.) can pizza sauce over dough in each pizza pan. Alternate strips of boiled ham and salami on sauce (about 4 slices ham and 6 slices salami, cut in strips, for both pizzas). Sprinkle each pizza with 1½ c. shredded mozzarella cheese. Bake.

SAUSAGE FILLING: Spread 1 (8 oz.) can pizza sauce over dough in each pizza pan. Brown 1 lb. bulk pork sausage in skillet, drain and divide in half. Spread evenly over sauce in pizza dough. Then sprinkle 1½ c. shredded mozzarella cheese over each pizza. Bake as directed.

CHOICE OF PIZZA FILLINGS: Fill dough in each pizza pan with 1 (8 oz.) can pizza sauce and sprinkle on each 1½ c. shredded mozzarella cheese. Cook 1 lb. pizza sausage in skillet, drain and divide in half. Sprinkle evenly over pizza dough in pans filled with sauce and cheese. Or instead of pizza sausage, top with anchovies, mushrooms, sliced ripe olives, sardines or miniature frankfurters. Bake as directed.

To Freeze Pizza Dough: When you divide the risen dough in half, roll each into an 11″ circle. Place in oiled pizza pan with double thickness of waxed paper between circles. (Or roll each half of dough into a 12 × 10″ rectangle, place on oiled baking sheet with waxed paper between rectangles.) Wrap and freeze. Keeps up to 1 week.

To Use Frozen Pizza Dough: Remove from freezer and let stand at room temperature 20 minutes. With fingers pull and stretch circles to cover pizza pans. (Or stretch rectangles of dough almost to edges of baking sheet and make small rim around edge.) Fill and bake as directed.

Quick Hot Breads

Hot quick breads appeared on the American scene soon after the first colonists stepped ashore. From the Indians they learned the wonders of maize and how to grind it and make corn breads. Sailing vessels, plying the West Indian trade, delivered barrels of molasses to

New England. Homemakers used it to sweeten a steamed bread which became the traditional Boston Brown Bread served Saturday evening with baked beans—a team just as popular today.

Biscuits helped win the West. They were so favored by cowboys in cow camps, who gave their cooks a universal nickname, the "biscuit shooter." Here are some excellent recipes for country quick hot breads popular with thousands of today's American families.

POINTERS ON FREEZING QUICK BREADS

To Freeze Biscuits, Coffee Breads, Muffins, Nut Breads, Waffles:

· Bake, cool at room temperature and wrap in aluminum foil or plastic wrap. Stack waffles before wrapping, separating layers with wrap. You can freeze unbaked baking powder biscuit cutouts. Place them in frozen food containers, separating layers with wrap.

· To thaw, let stand at room temperature in original wrap or heat in a slow to moderate oven (325 to 350°) until as warm as you like them. Thaw waffles in electric toaster. Partially thaw unbaked baking powder biscuit cutouts before baking them.

Maximum Storage Time: Two to three months. Unbaked baking powder biscuit cutouts may be stored only for a brief time, less than 1 month.

SWEET POTATO BISCUITS

Serve piping hot with plenty of butter and jelly, or jam, or honey

2 c. sifted flour
4 tsp. baking powder
1 tsp. salt
⅔ c. shortening
1 c. cooked, mashed sweet potatoes
3 tblsp. milk

· Sift together dry ingredients. Cut in shortening. Blend in sweet potatoes. Add enough milk to make a soft dough (this will depend on moisture in potatoes).

· Knead lightly. Roll ¾" thick on lightly floured board. Cut with floured 2" biscuit cutter.

· Place on ungreased baking sheet and bake in hot oven (400°) 20 minutes, or until brown. Makes about 15 biscuits.

PUMPKIN BISCUITS

Bring a change to bread basket with these tasty, colorful biscuits

2 c. sifted flour
3 tblsp. sugar
4 tsp. baking powder
½ tsp. salt
½ tsp. ground cinnamon
½ c. butter or regular margarine
⅓ c. chopped pecans
½ c. light cream or dairy half-and-half
⅔ c. canned pumpkin

· Sift together flour, sugar, baking powder, salt and cinnamon.

· Cut in butter with pastry blender until mixture looks like coarse meal or crumbs. Stir in pecans.

· Combine cream and pumpkin; stir into flour mixture just enough to moisten dry ingredients. You will have a stiff dough. Turn dough onto a lightly floured board and knead gently a few times.

· Roll out to ½" thickness. Cut with 2" cutter. Place 1" apart on greased baking sheet.

· Bake in hot oven (425°) until golden brown, about 20 minutes.

Serve at once. Makes about 20 biscuits.

BISCUIT FAN-TANS

Fancy biscuits that go together fast —perfect with fruit salad and coffee

2 c. sifted flour
3 tblsp. sugar
4 tsp. baking powder
½ tsp. cream of tartar
½ tsp. salt
½ c. shortening
⅔ c. milk
2 tblsp. melted butter
¼ c. sugar
1 tblsp. ground cinnamon

· Sift together flour, 3 tblsp. sugar, baking powder, cream of tartar and salt into mixing bowl.

· Cut in shortening until mixture resembles coarse meal or crumbs. Add milk and stir with fork to moisten all ingredients. Turn onto lightly floured surface and knead gently 20 times.

· Roll dough into a 12 × 10″ rectangle. Brush with melted butter.

· Combine ¼ c. sugar and cinnamon; sprinkle evenly over dough.

· Cut lengthwise into 5 strips, 2″ wide. Stack strips, one on top of the other. Cut in 12 (1″) pieces. Place cut side down in well greased muffin-pan cups.

· Bake in hot oven (425°) about 15 minutes. Remove carefully from pan with spatula so fan-tans will hold their shape. Serve while warm. Makes 12.

CRUSTY HOT BISCUITS

Brown-crusted, tender biscuits

2¼ c. sifted flour
4 tsp. baking powder
½ tsp. cream of tartar
½ tsp. salt
2 tblsp. sugar
⅓ c. lard
⅔ c. milk
1 egg

· Sift together dry ingredients. Cut lard into mixture to make coarse crumbs. Add milk, then the egg. Mix with fork until dough follows fork around bowl.

· Knead on floured board five or six times. Roll or pat to ½″ thickness; cut with 2″ cutter.

· Place on ungreased baking sheet about ¾″ apart and bake in very hot oven (450°) 10 to 12 minutes. Makes 16 medium biscuits.

DROP BISCUITS

Serve these cream biscuits with honey

2 c. sifted flour
1 tblsp. baking powder
1 tsp. salt
2 eggs, beaten
¾ c. heavy cream

· Sift together dry ingredients. Add eggs and cream. Stir to mix (dough should be lumpy and soft). Drop from tablespoon onto ungreased baking sheet.

· Bake in hot oven (400°) 15 minutes. Makes 12 large biscuits.

HUSH PUPPIES

This corn bread for fish fries is equally good in home fish meals

1 c. sifted flour
1 c. cornmeal
4 tsp. baking powder
1 tsp. salt
¼ tsp. garlic powder (optional)
1 egg, slightly beaten
⅔ c. buttermilk or milk
¼ c. finely chopped onion

• Stir together to mix thoroughly flour, cornmeal, baking powder, salt and garlic powder.
• Add egg, buttermilk and onion. Mix well.
• Drop batter by rounded teaspoonfuls into deep hot fat (375°). Cook, turning frequently, about 3 to 5 minutes, until golden brown. Makes about 2 dozen.

FARMER'S SPOON BREAD

Spoon fluffy hot bread onto plate, serve with butter and eat with fork

1 c. white or yellow cornmeal
1½ c. boiling water
1 tblsp. softened butter or regular margarine
3 eggs, separated
1 c. buttermilk
1 tsp. salt
1 tsp. sugar
1 tsp. baking powder
¼ tsp. baking soda

• Put cornmeal in large bowl; stir in boiling water. Continue to stir until cool to prevent lumping.
• Blend in butter and egg yolks. Stir in buttermilk, salt, sugar, baking powder and soda.
• Beat egg whites until soft peaks form; fold into cornmeal mixture. Pour into greased 2-qt. casserole.
• Bake in moderate oven (375°) 45 to 50 minutes. Serve at once with butter. Makes 8 servings.

VIRGINIA SPOON BREAD FOR A CROWD

Serve hot with a spoon—an excellent escort for Brunswick Stew (see Index)

6 c. white cornmeal
4 qts. milk
2 doz. eggs
½ c. butter or regular margarine
3 tblsp. salt

• Put cornmeal into large kettle; add milk. Mix thoroughly and cook over medium heat until mixture thickens, stirring constantly. Remove from heat.
• Separate eggs. Beat whites until stiff; then yolks until thick and lemon-colored.
• Add yolks to cornmeal mixture; add butter and salt. Blend well; then fold in egg whites.
• Pour into 4 ungreased 13 × 9 × 2″ pans. Bake in moderate oven (350°) 45 to 55 minutes. Makes 50 servings.

SOUTHERN CORN BREAD

It upholds fame of Southern cooking

2 eggs
2 c. buttermilk
1 tsp. baking soda
2 c. white cornmeal
1 tsp. salt

• Start oven heating to 450°. Generously grease a 9″ square pan; heat in oven while mixing batter.
• Beat eggs; add buttermilk.
• In bowl, stir together baking soda, cornmeal and salt. Add egg mixture all at once; beat with rotary beater or electric mixer until smooth. Pour into heated pan.
• Bake in very hot oven (450°) 20 to 25 minutes, or just until set. Serve hot, cut in squares, with butter. Makes 9 servings.

Note: Some Southern women add 1 tsp. sugar to the other dry ingredients.

GOLDEN CORN BREAD

This is Yankee-style corn bread

1 c. sifted flour
¼ c. sugar
4 tsp. baking powder
¾ tsp. salt
1 c. yellow cornmeal
2 eggs
1 c. milk
¼ c. soft shortening

• Sift together into bowl flour, sugar, baking powder and salt. Stir in cornmeal.
• In a small bowl beat eggs with fork; add milk and shortening. Add all at one time to cornmeal mixture. Stir with fork until flour is just moistened. Even if batter is lumpy, do not stir any more.
• Pour into well-greased 9″ square pan. Bake in hot oven (425°) 20 to 25 minutes, or until done. Cut in squares and serve hot with butter. Makes 9 servings.

Variation

BACON CORN BREAD: Add ⅓ c. crumbled, crisp cooked bacon to batter for Golden Corn Bread just before pouring into greased baking pan.

BOSTON BROWN BREAD

Traditional escort for baked beans

1 c. rye flour
1 c. yellow cornmeal
1 c. flour
2 tsp. baking soda
1 tsp. salt
¾ c. molasses
2 c. buttermilk

• Mix dry ingredients; stir in molasses and buttermilk, mixing well, but do not beat. Fill 1½-qt. mold two thirds full.
• Cover with tight-fitting lid or aluminum foil. Place on rack in tightly covered kettle, containing a small amount of boiling water; steam 3 to 3½ hours, or until wooden pick inserted in center comes out clean. Keep water boiling over low heat throughout cooking, adding more if necessary. (To add, lift lid and quickly add boiling water.) Immediately remove from mold. Serve hot with butter. Makes enough for one 7″ tube mold or four 1-lb cans. Makes 8 to 10 servings.

REFRIGERATOR BRAN MUFFINS

For crusty tops sprinkle a bit of cinnamon and sugar on batter in pans

1 c. boiling water
3 c. whole bran cereal
2 c. buttermilk
1½ c. sugar
⅔ c. shortening
4 eggs
4 c. sifted flour
2½ tsp. baking soda
1 tsp. salt

• Pour boiling water over whole bran cereal. Mix well, cool; stir in buttermilk.
• Cream sugar and shortening until fluffy. Add eggs and beat well.
• Sift together flour, soda and salt.
• Stir cooled bran mixture into creamed mixture. Stir in dry ingredients just to barely moisten (batter will not be smooth). Don't overmix.
• Store in tightly covered container in refrigerator overnight, or until needed. Can be stored up to 3 days.
• Spoon batter into greased muffin-pan cups. Bake in hot oven (425°)

about 20 minutes. Makes 3 dozen muffins.

Note: You can bake half of the batter (or any amount you want) at one time, the remaining batter later. Or, for 18 muffins, you can cut this recipe in two—just use half of all the ingredients.

Quick Coffee Breads

When you want to stir up and bake a coffee bread in a hurry, try our sour cream Sugar-top Coffee Cake. Or if blueberries are in season, bake Blueberry Kuchen (best when served faintly warm). Hot cakes, or doughnuts, still disappear fast in country homes. Serve them with coffee to friends who stop by for a friendly visit. You can depend on an enthusiastic reception for our doughnuts and Cocoa Balls.

SUGAR-TOP COFFEE CAKE

Better make a couple of these coffee cakes if you're serving more than six

1 egg
¾ c. sugar
1 tblsp. melted butter or regular margarine
1 c. dairy sour cream
1 tsp. vanilla
1½ c. sifted flour
2 tsp. baking powder
¼ tsp. baking soda
¾ tsp. salt
Brown Sugar Topping

• Beat egg until frothy; beat in sugar and butter. Cream until light and fluffy. Add sour cream and vanilla; blend well.

• Sift dry ingredients together; add to the sour cream mixture. Blend well. Pour into a greased 8″ square pan. Sprinkle with Brown Sugar Topping.

• Bake in moderate oven (375°) 25 to 30 minutes, or until cake tests done. Serve warm. Makes 6 servings.

BROWN SUGAR TOPPING: Mix ½ c. brown sugar, firmly packed, 2 tblsp. flour, ½ tsp. ground cinnamon and 2 tblsp. softened butter until crumbly.

GERMAN BLUEBERRY KUCHEN

Delicate, fine-grained coffee cake for breakfast or dinner dessert

1½ c. sifted flour
2 tsp. baking powder
½ tsp. salt
¾ c. sugar
¼ c. soft shortening
⅔ c. milk
1 tsp. vanilla
½ tsp. grated lemon peel (½ lemon)
1 egg
1 c. fresh blueberries
3 tblsp. sugar
1 tsp. grated lemon peel

• Sift together flour, baking powder, salt and ¾ c. sugar. Add shortening, milk, vanilla and ½ tsp. grated lemon peel. Beat with electric mixer on medium speed 3 minutes, or 300 strokes by hand.

• Add egg and beat with mixer 2 minutes longer (200 strokes by hand).

• Turn into greased 8″ square pan.

• Lightly stir together blueberries, 3 tblsp. sugar and 1 tsp. grated lemon peel. Sprinkle over batter in pan.

• Bake in moderate oven (350°) 40 to 45 minutes, or until lightly browned. Cool slightly in pan. Cut in squares and serve warm. Makes 6 to 9 servings.

CINNAMON COFFEE SQUARES

Try these at your next coffee party, or tote to the men in the field

- **3 c. sifted flour**
- **2 tsp. baking powder**
- **2 tsp. ground cinnamon**
- **½ tsp. baking soda**
- **½ tsp. salt**
- **1 c. butter**
- **2 c. brown sugar, firmly packed**
- **2 eggs**
- **1 c. hot black coffee**
- **2 c. sifted confectioners sugar**
- **⅓ c. butter**
- **1½ tsp. vanilla**
- **Dash salt**
- **2 tblsp. milk**

• Sift together flour, baking powder, cinnamon, soda and ½ tsp. salt.

• Cream together 1 c. butter, brown sugar and eggs until fluffy. Alternately add dry ingredients and coffee, beating after each addition.

• Pour into greased 13 × 9 × 2″ baking pan. Bake in moderate oven (350°) 35 minutes, or until cake tests done. Cool.

• Combine remaining ingredients. Mix until smooth. Frost cooled cake and cut in squares. Makes about 12 servings.

MARMALADE COFFEE CAKE

You'll want to share this coconut-crowned quick bread with friends

- **¼ c. shortening**
- **½ c. sugar**
- **1 egg, beaten**
- **1 tblsp. grated orange peel**
- **1¾ c. sifted flour**
- **2 tsp. baking powder**
- **½ tsp. salt**
- **½ c. milk**
- **3 tblsp. melted butter or regular margarine**
- **1 c. flaked or shredded coconut**
- **¾ c. orange marmalade**
- **1 tblsp. sugar**

• Cream shortening; add ½ c. sugar and mix well. Add egg and orange peel.

• Sift together dry ingredients; add alternately with milk to creamed mixture. Beat after each addition.

• Spread dough in greased 9″ square pan. Brush top with 1 tblsp. butter.

• Blend coconut with marmalade; add remaining butter. Drop by spoonfuls on dough; spread evenly over top; sprinkle with 1 tblsp. sugar.

• Bake in moderate oven (375°) 25 to 30 minutes. Serve warm. Makes 9 to 12 servings.

Doughnuts to Dunk

The family used to hang around the kitchen on doughnut frying days. Children settled for fried cakes with glasses of cold milk, but most adults poured coffee to go with this perfect food for dunking. While fewer doughnuts are homemade today, there are red letter occasions, such as Halloween and Shrove Tuesday, when they come from kettles for quick tossing in paper bags of sugar. And the old description of well-received foods holds—they disappear like fried hot cakes!

BAKED DOUGHNUT PUFFS

You bake these in muffin pans—less work than frying doughnuts

2 tblsp. shortening
½ c. sugar
1 egg
2 c. sifted flour
½ tsp. salt
1 tblsp. baking powder
½ tsp. ground nutmeg
½ c. milk
½ c. chopped walnuts
¼ c. confectioners sugar
½ tsp. ground cinnamon
¼ c. melted butter

· Cream shortening, sugar and egg until light and fluffy.
· Sift together flour, salt, baking powder and nutmeg. Add alternately with milk to creamed mixture. Mix well (this will be a stiff dough). Stir in nuts.
· Drop from tablespoon into well greased small size muffin-pan cups. Bake in hot oven (400°) 20 minutes.
· Combine confectioners sugar and cinnamon in paper bag. Dip top of doughnuts in melted butter; shake 2 or 3 at a time in sugar. Serve hot. Makes 1 dozen.

CHOCOLATE CAKE DOUGHNUTS

Mashed potatoes and chocolate make these extra good with coffee

1½ c. sugar
¼ c. melted butter or regular margarine
1 c. cold mashed potatoes
2 eggs, beaten
3 c. sifted flour
2 tblsp. baking powder
1 tsp. salt
1 tsp. ground nutmeg
½ c. cocoa
½ c. milk

· Stir sugar, butter and mashed potatoes into eggs; whip until creamy.
· Sift flour, baking powder (2 tblsp. is right), salt, nutmeg and cocoa together; add alternately with milk to egg mixture. Mix well. Chill 2 hours.
· Roll ½" thick on lightly floured board. Cut with doughnut cutter; fry in hot fat (365°) 3 minutes. Drain on paper toweling. Makes 2 dozen.

NEW JERSEY DOUGHNUTS

Lemon-nutmeg flavor is a good cook's secret that wins compliments

½ c. butter
1 c. sugar
2 eggs
1 tsp. grated lemon peel
4½ c. sifted flour
2 tsp. baking powder
2 tsp. salt
2 tsp. ground nutmeg
1 c. milk

· Cream butter and sugar; add eggs and lemon peel; beat until light and fluffy.
· Sift flour with baking powder, salt and nutmeg; add alternately with milk to creamed mixture. Mix well. Roll out on lightly floured board, and cut with doughnut cutter.
· Fry in hot fat (365°) 3 minutes. Drain on paper toweling. Makes 2 dozen.

COCOA DOUGHNUT BALLS

You skip rolling and cutting dough by quickly shaping with spoon

2 eggs, well beaten
⅔ c. sugar
2 tblsp. melted butter or regular margarine

1 c. milk
1 tsp. almond extract
3¼ c. sifted flour
2 tblsp. cocoa
1 tblsp. baking powder
¼ tsp. salt
Fat for deep frying
Confectioners sugar

• Combine eggs, sugar, butter, milk and almond extract; mix to blend.
• Sift together dry ingredients; slowly add to first mixture. Beat until smooth.
• Heat fat to 370° (browns 1″ bread cube in 1 minute). Dip balls of dough with spoon; slide into hot fat. Turn frequently to brown on all sides. Drain on paper toweling. Roll in confectioners sugar. Makes 3 to 4 dozen.

SWEET MILK DOUGHNUTS

Assorted homemade doughnuts on tray at coffee parties create excitement

4¼ c. sifted flour
3½ tsp. baking powder
1 tsp. salt
½ tsp. ground nutmeg
¼ tsp. ground cinnamon
3 eggs
1 tsp. vanilla
¾ c. sugar
3 tblsp. soft butter or regular margarine
¾ c. milk
Fat for frying

• Sift together flour, baking powder, salt and spices.
• Beat eggs; add vanilla and sugar. Beat well. Mix in butter.
• Add milk and sifted dry ingredients alternately. Mix into a soft dough.
• Turn dough onto lightly floured board. Knead lightly for 30 seconds, then roll out ⅓″ thick. Cut with floured doughnut cutter. Remove trimmings.
• Lift each doughnut on a wide spatula and carefully ease into deep hot fat (375°). Put as many into fat at a time as can be turned easily.
• Fry about 3 minutes, until completely brown on both sides. Lift from fat with a long fork. Do not pierce. Drain on paper toweling.
• Form trimmings into a ball. Make into doughnut balls or re-roll and cut with doughnut cutter. Fry as above. Serve plain, sugared or frosted (see variations). Makes about 2 dozen.

Variations

DROPPED DOUGHNUTS: Drop dough by spoonfuls into deep hot fat (375°). Use 2 teaspoons which have been dipped into the fat first, so dough won't stick to them. Take a rounded portion of dough on one spoon, push off into fat with other spoon. Or, roll dough in balls with floured hands and drop into fat. Turn as soon as they rise to top. Fry until golden brown on both sides.

SUGARED DOUGHNUTS: While doughnuts are still warm, dip into bowl of granulated sugar or mixture of sugar and ground cinnamon (½ c. sugar to ½ tsp. cinnamon). Or, when doughnuts have cooled, shake in paper bag containing confectioners sugar.

FROSTED DOUGHNUTS: Doughnuts frost best while still warm. Dip into Plain Frosting or any other flavors given below. For a special touch, dip top of frosted doughnut into dish of chopped walnuts, pecans, almonds or peanuts. Or dip into a dish of finely cut shredded coconut.

PLAIN FROSTING: Mix together 1¾ c. sifted confectioners sugar, 3 tblsp. hot water, 2 tsp. melted butter or regular margarine and ½ tsp. vanilla.

Variations in Frostings

CHOCOLATE: Add to Plain Frosting, 1 square unsweetened chocolate, melted, and an additional 2 tsp. hot water. Mix.

ORANGE: Omit vanilla. Add to Plain Frosting in place of water, 3 tblsp. orange juice and 1 tsp. grated peel.

MAPLE: Omit vanilla. Add to Plain Frosting ¼ tsp. maple flavoring.

PEPPERMINT: Omit vanilla. Add to Plain Frosting ¼ tsp. peppermint extract and 2 drops red food color.

Fruit and Nut Breads

Spread thin slices of tasty fruit and nut breads with butter and you have perfect companions to tea, coffee and hot fruit drinks. The moist loaves, carefully wrapped, will keep several days in the refrigerator, months in the freezer. They also make thoughtful gifts to friends and they enjoy brisk sales at food bazaars.

FRESH APPLE BREAD

This fruity quick bread makes compliment-winning cheese sandwiches

2 c. sifted flour
1 tsp. baking powder
½ tsp. baking soda
½ tsp. salt
⅓ c. shortening
1 c. sugar
1 egg
⅓ c. orange juice
¾ c. raisins
¼ c. chopped nuts
1 c. finely chopped apples
1 tblsp. grated orange peel

• Sift together flour, baking powder, soda and salt.
• Cream shortening; add sugar gradually. Add egg; beat thoroughly.
• Add dry ingredients and orange juice alternately to creamed mixture; blend well after each addition. Add remaining ingredients; mix well.
• Pour into 3 well greased 1-lb. cans. Bake in moderate oven (350°) 45 minutes. Makes 3 loaves.

APPLE/NUT BREAD

A sandwich special from the heart of apple land—Washington State

½ c. butter or regular margarine
1 c. sugar
2 eggs, unbeaten
1 tsp. vanilla
1½ tblsp. dairy sour cream
2 c. sifted flour
1 tsp. baking powder
1 tsp. baking soda
½ tsp. salt
1 c. chopped nuts
1 c. chopped unpeeled apples

• Cut butter into sugar; add eggs, one at a time, mixing well after each addition. Blend in vanilla and sour cream.
• Sift together dry ingredients; add nuts. Combine with first mixture. Stir in apples. Pour into greased 9 × 5 × 3″ loaf pan or 2 small loaf pans.
• Bake in slow oven (325°) about 1 hour. Makes 1 large or 2 small loaves.

CARROT SANDWICH BREAD

This makes marvelous sandwiches

1 c. finely grated raw carrots
1 c. brown sugar, firmly packed
1 tsp. baking soda
1 tblsp. melted shortening
1 c. boiling water
2 eggs
2½ tsp. baking powder
1 tsp. salt
1½ c. sifted flour
1 c. whole wheat flour
1 c. chopped walnuts

• Combine carrots, brown sugar, baking soda and shortening in a large bowl. Pour on boiling water and stir just to mix. Set aside until cool.

• Beat eggs with a fork and add to cooled carrot mixture. Sift in baking powder, salt and all-purpose flour. Stir in whole wheat flour. Fold in walnuts. Pour into greased 8½ × 4½ × 2½" loaf pan. Let stand 5 minutes.

• Bake in moderate oven (350°) 1 hour. Remove from pan and cool on wire rack. Bread slices better if allowed to stand, wrapped in aluminum foil or plastic wrap, in a cold place overnight. Makes 1 loaf.

GLAZED LEMON BREAD

Ideal for tea party sandwiches when sliced thin and spread with butter

⅓ c. melted butter
1¼ c. sugar
2 eggs
¼ tsp. almond extract
1½ c. sifted flour
1 tsp. baking powder
1 tsp. salt
½ c. milk
1 tblsp. grated lemon peel
½ c. chopped nuts
3 tblsp. fresh lemon juice

• Blend well the butter and 1 c. sugar; beat in eggs, one at a time. Add almond extract.

• Sift together dry ingredients; add to egg mixture alternately with milk. Blend just to mix. Fold in peel and nuts.

• Turn into a greased 8½ × 4½ × 2¾" ovenproof glass loaf pan. Bake in slow oven (325°) about 70 minutes, or until loaf tests done in center.

• Mix lemon juice and remaining ¼ c. sugar; immediately spoon over hot loaf. Cool 10 minutes. Remove from pan; cool on rack. Do not cut for 24 hours (it will slice easily). Makes 1 loaf.

Note: If you bake this bread in a metal 8½ × 4½ × 2½" loaf pan, use a moderate oven (350°).

PEACHY OATMEAL BREAD

You'll enjoy this as a dessert or a coffee cake. Eat it with a fork

1¾ c. sifted flour
¾ c. sugar
4½ tsp. baking powder
¾ tsp. salt
1½ tsp. ground cinnamon
¾ tsp. ground nutmeg
¼ tsp. ground cloves
1½ c. quick-cooking rolled oats
½ c. chopped nuts
⅔ c. milk
1 egg, slightly beaten
½ c. melted butter or regular margarine
1 (1 lb. 14 oz.) can cling peaches, well drained
⅓ c. brown sugar, firmly packed
3 tblsp. melted butter or regular margarine

· Sift together flour, sugar, baking powder, salt and spices. Stir in oats and chopped nuts.
· Combine milk, egg and ½ c. melted butter. Stir into dry ingredients until moistened. Do not beat.
· Pour batter into 8″ square baking pan. Bake in moderate oven (375°) 40 to 45 minutes. Cool in pan.
· Chop or slice peaches. Arrange on cooled bread. Sprinkle with brown sugar and dribble 3 tblsp. melted butter on top. Broil 4″ from broiler unit until topping bubbles and tops of peaches begin to brown. Makes about 9 servings.

Note: You can freeze this bread if you wish. Defrost and add topping just before serving.

PINEAPPLE/DATE LOAF

Tastes like a mellow fruitcake—improves after standing overnight

¼ c. soft butter or regular margarine
½ c. sugar
1 egg
¼ tsp. lemon extract
1 (8½ oz.) can crushed pineapple
¼ c. chopped nuts
2½ c. sifted flour
2½ tsp. baking powder
¼ tsp. baking soda
1 tsp. salt
½ c. finely chopped, pitted dates
¼ c. water
¼ c. chopped maraschino cherries, well drained

· Cream butter and sugar; add egg and lemon extract. Drain pineapple, reserving liquid. Add crushed pineapple and nuts to creamed mixture.
· Sift dry ingredients together. Add dates and mix well, separating date pieces with your fingers. Stir dry ingredients into creamed mixture alternately with reserved pineapple juice plus ¼ c. water. Fold in the chopped maraschino cherries.
· Pour into a greased 9 × 5 × 3″ loaf pan. Bake in moderate oven (375°) about 55 minutes. Cool in pan 10 minutes. Remove from pan; cool completely. Makes 1 loaf.

SWEET POTATO/NUT BREAD

Sweet and moist, extra light. This big recipe makes loaves and muffins

½ c. soft butter or regular margarine
½ c. shortening
2⅔ c. sugar
4 eggs
2 c. cold, mashed sweet potatoes
3½ c. sifted flour
1 tsp. salt
1 tsp. ground cinnamon
1½ tsp. ground nutmeg
2 tsp. baking soda
1 c. chopped walnuts
⅔ c. cold, strong black coffee

· Cream butter, shortening and sugar. Add eggs, one at a time, mixing well after each addition. Blend in sweet potatoes.
· Sift together dry ingredients; add nuts. Stir into creamed mixture alternately with cold coffee.
· Pour batter into 2 greased 9 × 5 × 3″ loaf pans and 8 greased muffin-pan cups. Bake in moderate oven (375°) 1 hour for loaves and 25 minutes for muffins, or until they test done in center.
· Cool 10 minutes; remove from pans and cool completely. Makes 2 loaves plus 8 muffins.

Pancakes and Waffles

Among the quick hot breads farm families esteem highly are pancakes and waffles, in a wide assortment. Served with plenty of butter and sweet syrup, they can't be surpassed. While packaged mixes are often used, every household treasures at least a few "from scratch" recipes for special occasions—Sunday evening guest suppers or Sunday morning breakfasts. We give you some of the most praised recipes from our collection.

SOUR CREAM/BLUEBERRY PANCAKES

Light, fluffy pancakes with that interesting flavor sour cream adds

1 c. sifted flour
3 tsp. baking powder
¼ tsp. salt
1 tblsp. sugar
1 egg
1 c. milk
¼ c. dairy sour cream
2 tblsp. melted butter
½ c. blueberries

• Sift together flour, baking powder, salt and sugar.
• Beat together egg, milk and sour cream.
• Pour milk mixture over dry ingredients and blend with rotary beater until batter is just smooth. Stir in butter. Fold in blueberries.
• Pour 2 tblsp. batter onto hot griddle for each cake. (Pour 1 tblsp. batter onto hot griddle for each cake if you want silver-dollar-size pancakes. If you have the time this is a festive way to serve them.) Brown on one side until golden. Turn and brown on the other side. If cakes brown too fast, lower heat. Serve hot with butter and maple syrup or Maine Blueberry Syrup (recipe follows). Makes 12 pancakes using 2 tblsp. batter, or 24 silver-dollar-size pancakes.

Variation

SOUR CREAM PANCAKES: Prepare batter for Sour Cream/Blueberry Pancakes, but omit the blueberries. If you have leftover batter, cover and store in the refrigerator. It will keep 2 or 3 days, but it will thicken. When you are ready to use it, add 1 to 2 tblsp. milk in which you dissolve ½ tsp. baking powder for each cup of batter. Bake as directed.

MAINE BLUEBERRY SYRUP: Simmer together 2 c. blueberries, ½ c. sugar, ½ c. water and a thin slice of lemon to make a syrup. This takes about 10 minutes. Makes about 2½ cups.

CAMPERS' CORN PANCAKES

For breakfast with syrup and butter or for supper with creamed chicken

1 egg, slightly beaten
½ c. milk
2 tblsp. salad oil
1½ c. pancake mix
1 (1 lb.) can cream style corn

• Combine egg, milk and oil. Stir into mix along with corn. Blend ingredients.
• Bake on griddle over high heat. Makes 12 to 14 (4") pancakes.

APPLE GRIDDLECAKES

Quick with the butter and syrup

2 c. sifted flour
5 tsp. baking powder
2 tsp. salt
3 tblsp. sugar
1 tsp. ground cinnamon
2 c. milk
6 tblsp. melted shortening or salad oil
2 eggs, beaten
1 c. finely chopped unpeeled apples

• Sift together flour, baking powder, salt, sugar, and cinnamon.
• Add milk, shortening and flour mixture to eggs; beat until smooth. Fold in apples.
• Heat griddle or heavy frying pan slowly until moderately hot. Test temperature by sprinkling a few drops of water on it—if they "dance," temperature is right. Or use electric griddle, following manufacturer's directions.
• Grease griddle very lightly before baking. Pour on about ¼ c. batter for each cake. Bake until top is bubbly and edges dry; turn and brown on other side. Makes 2½ dozen cakes 4 to 5″ in diameter or one dozen 6 to 7″ in diameter.

Variation

SOUR MILK GRIDDLECAKES: Substitute 2¼ c. buttermilk for sweet milk. For leavening use 1 tsp. baking soda and 1 tblsp. baking powder.

CORN GRIDDLECAKES

You can bake tiny cakes and serve with maple syrup like corn fritters

1 c. sifted flour
2 tsp. baking powder
1 tsp. sugar
½ tsp. salt
2 eggs, well beaten
¾ c. milk
2 tblsp. melted butter or regular margarine
1 c. whole kernel corn

• Sift together flour, baking powder, sugar and salt. Beat in eggs, milk and butter until batter is smooth. Stir in corn.
• Drop from ⅓-cup measure on preheated griddle and bake until golden brown on both sides. Serve hot with butter and syrup for breakfast. Makes 9 to 10 griddlecakes.

Note: You can double this recipe, Then you'll need 1 (1 lb.) can corn.

AM/NOR PANCAKES

Americanized Norwegian favorite —bake either on griddle or waffle iron

1½ c. buttermilk
3 egg yolks
¼ c. melted shortening
1½ c. sifted flour
1 tblsp. baking powder
½ tsp. baking soda
¼ tsp. salt
3 egg whites, beaten stiff

• Combine buttermilk, yolks and shortening in bowl.
• Sift together dry ingredients and add buttermilk mixture, stirring only until smooth. Fold in egg whites.
• Bake on lightly greased hot griddle, using 2 tblsp. batter for each cake and browning on both sides. Makes 18.

SUNDAY SUPPER WAFFLES

Country women vote the waffles made with four eggs a top favorite

2 c. sifted flour
4 tsp. baking powder

1 tsp. salt
2 c. milk
4 eggs, separated
1 c. melted butter, regular margarine or salad oil

• Start heating waffle iron.
• Sift together flour, baking powder and salt.
• Combine milk and egg yolks. Beat egg whites until stiff.
• Add milk-egg yolk mixture to dry ingredients; beat with electric mixer at high speed, or with rotary beater, just enough to moisten dry ingredients.
• Stir in slightly cooled butter. Fold in egg whites, leaving little fluffs of them showing in batter.
• Pour batter from pitcher onto center of lower grid until it spreads to about 1″ from edges. Gently close lid at once; do not open during baking.
• Bake until steaming stops or signal light shows waffle is done.
• Loosen waffle with fork and lift it from grid. Place on warm plate. Reheat waffle iron before pouring on more batter. Makes about 8 waffles.

Variations

BUTTERMILK WAFFLES: Follow recipe for Sunday Supper Waffles, but use 3 tsp. baking powder and 1 tsp. baking soda, and substitute 2 c. buttermilk for the milk. Do not separate eggs; beat them until foamy, and mix with buttermilk.

RANCH BREAKFAST WAFFLES: Reduce butter in Sunday Supper Waffles to 6 tblsp. to ½ c., or use 6 tblsp. to ½ c. bacon fat (drippings) instead of the butter. Use 2 instead of 4 eggs; do not separate eggs, beat them and mix with the milk.

HAM WAFFLES: Sprinkle 2 tblsp. finely chopped cooked ham over batter as soon as you pour it on waffle grid.

CORN WAFFLES: Add 1 c. drained, whole kernel corn (canned) to batter. This is an excellent base for creamed ham or chicken.

CHEESE WAFFLES: Add ½ c. grated process cheese to batter.

NUT WAFFLES: Sprinkle 2 tblsp. coarsely chopped pecans or walnuts over batter as soon as you pour it on the grids. You can break the nuts with fingers instead of chopping them.

BACON WAFFLES: Cook 6 slices bacon until crisp; drain and crumble into the batter for Sunday Supper Waffles.

WHOLE WHEAT WAFFLES

When short of time to bake whole wheat bread, make these waffles

2 c. whole wheat flour
2 tsp. baking powder
¾ tsp. salt
3 eggs, separated
1½ c. milk
¼ c. melted shortening

• Combine flour, baking powder and salt; stir to mix. (Stir whole wheat flour before measuring.)
• Beat egg whites; set aside.
• Beat egg yolks, add milk and shortening. Add all at once to flour mixture and beat until flour is moistened.
• Fold in egg whites, leaving little fluffs of them showing in batter. Pour onto preheated waffle iron; bake until steaming stops or signal light indicates waffle is baked. Serve

hot with butter or margarine and syrup, honey or apple butter. Makes 6 (7″) waffles.

RICE BUTTERMILK WAFFLES

Tender delicate waffles with luscious peachy spread . . . serve with bacon

3 eggs, separated
2 c. buttermilk
6 tblsp. melted shortening
2 c. sifted flour
½ tsp. salt
1 tblsp. baking powder
1 tsp. sugar
½ tsp. baking soda
1 c. cooked rice (cooked in salted water)
Peach Butter

· Beat egg yolks until thick and lemon-colored. Add buttermilk and shortening.
· Sift together flour, salt, baking powder, sugar and baking soda. Add to egg yolk-buttermilk mixture. Stir until smooth. Stir in rice.
· Fold in egg whites, beaten stiff.
· Bake on hot waffle iron. Serve with Peach Butter. Makes 8 (7″) waffles.

PEACH BUTTER: Beat ½ c. butter until fluffy. Beat in ½ c. peach preserves and a dash of ground nutmeg. Beat again; pass to spread on hot waffles. Vary the spread by substituting apricot or apricot/pineapple preserves for peach preserves. Makes 1 cup.

For Special Occasions: Homemade Mixer-butter

Remember how Grandmother used to churn butter? And how wonderful hot, brown-topped biscuits, corn breads and delicate light rolls tasted with little golden pools of it melting on them? Few country cooks now have the time to make butter. But there are the once-in-a-blue-moon occasions when the homemade kind adds charm that makes everyone sit up and take notice. Table conversation revolves around it and if handled carefully, the butter tastes good enough to deserve the spotlight.

When cream is available, and important guests are coming, butter making frequently returns briefly to the good cook's kitchen. The children no longer count strokes and take turns lifting the churn's dasher up through the cream and pushing it down again. The electric mixer handles the job. The work is in the precise preparation of the cream which so greatly affects the quality of the end product.

The directions for making country-fresh butter that follow came to FARM JOURNAL from an Iowa farm woman. We have used them successfully in our Countryside Test Kitchens and think you will have good luck with them when you wish to try your hand with an old country culinary art.

HOW TO MAKE BUTTER

Collect 1 to 1½ qts. heavy cream from separator (or buy it at the store, in which case omit pasteurizing step). Pasteurize it in an electric pasteurizer or by the flash method (heat it until it begins to rise in the pan, remove from the heat, let the cream settle, and repeat two more times). Cool the cream by setting the pan in cold water. Pour into a glass jar, cover and store several days in the refrigerator. Cream must be at least twenty-four hours old to churn well. Use cream with at least thirty per cent butter fat. (You can buy heavy cream at most markets.)

Ripen the cream by letting it stand at room temperature from 4 to 6 hours. It will thicken and become mildly sour. This procedure helps give the butter a mild, good taste.

Cool cream again in refrigerator.

Pour cream into larger bowl of the electric mixer. Use no more than 1½ qts. cream to prevent spattering. Add a few drops of butter color if desired. Beat at high speed until flecks of butter begin to form. Then turn to low speed until butter separates from milk. Watch to keep the spattering to a minimum. Push down the sides of the bowl with spatula as cream whips.

Pour off the buttermilk.

Add cold water, about as much as there was buttermilk. Let beater run at lowest speed. Pour off water; repeat.

Add a scant tablespoon of salt. Let beater mix it into butter. Remove beaters, scrape off butter with spatula and work out water with a spatula by pressing butter against side of bowl. Be sure to work out all the water.

Mold butter in a butter press or empty it into a container with tightly fitting lid. Store in refrigerator, or in freezer for longer periods of time.

One quart cream makes about 1 pound butter, although it depends on how heavy the cream is.

chapter 10

Relish Sampler

RELISHES DO FOR MEAT and poultry, what strawberries do for shortcake, fudge frostings for cake. No wonder generations of farm women have depended on them to add color, flavor, texture and temperature contrast to their meals. Back of the shiny jars of pickles on pantry shelves are proud women who created such relishes as Best-ever Piccalilli, Fermented Dill Pickles and Rummage Pickle. These well-established relishes and newer specialties, like Sliced Zucchini Pickles, deserve much credit for the splendid reputation country meals enjoy.

There are two big families of relishes—those you fix in fairly small amounts to use right away and those you freeze or can for the future. Serve-soon relish recipes appear first in this chapter. Lovely Blushing Peaches (currant jelly imparts the rosy flush) taste best if warm when they accompany beef, pork, lamb or chicken to the table. You make refrigerator relishes ahead and chill them for quick service. Country women watch for signals to fix and chill certain relishes. One farmer's wife says when her husband starts talking about the duck season opening, she makes Spiced Orange Slices and puts them in the refrigerator. This relish is a true delight with duck, wild or domestic.

Relishes with an eye to the future are those you freeze and can—spiced fruits and vegetables, pickles in great variety, and jellies, jams, marmalades, preserves and fruit honeys. This chapter is a sampler of favorites from our large recipe collection. They are typical of those in the *Farm Journal Freezing & Canning Cookbook*.

When you look at recipes for frozen jellies, jams and spreads that require no cooking, you'll be hungry for the biscuits, waffles and ice cream these tasty treats glorify. Notice the short-cook jellies and jams and then turn to the longer-cook type—recipes like those your grandmother used:

Ground Cherry Marmalade, Rosy Watermelon Rind Preserves or Tomato Preserves concocted from the small, pear-shaped yellow tomatoes or the big red ones.

If you're trying to think of a Christmas gift to make for your friends, how about a spiced fruit or vegetable? Red and green Pineapple Pickles, for instance—as delicious on the mainland as on Hawaii's palm-fringed shores, where the recipe originated. Remember, too, what great money-makers relishes are at food sales.

SPICED APPLES GLACÉ

Ideal meat accompaniment—pretty served in crystal compotes on buffets

6 large apples
2 c. sugar
3 c. water
6 thin lemon slices
3 whole cloves
1 tblsp. grated orange peel
1 (1") stick cinnamon
6 maraschino cherries
2 tsp. cornstarch
¼ c. cold water
Red food color

• Peel and halve apples; remove stem ends. Core. (You can remove cores easily with a melon ball scoop.)

• Combine sugar and water in a large skillet. Bring to boil. Add lemon slices, cloves, orange peel and cinnamon, then apples. Simmer, uncovered, over moderate heat until apples are tender but still firm, about 15 minutes. Turn apples once during cooking.

• Remove apple halves and lemon slices to serving dish. Garnish with cherries.

• Bring syrup to a rolling boil and boil until it forms a very thin syrup, about 5 minutes.

• Dissolve cornstarch in ¼ c. cold water; stir into syrup. Cook about 2 minutes more until slightly thickened. Add a few drops red food color. Cool slightly and pour over apples. Makes 6 dessert servings; more as meat accompaniment.

SPICY APPLE RELISH

Chili sauce adds spice—cook relish in a skillet about 10 minutes

4 medium apples
2 tblsp. butter or regular margarine
1 tblsp. honey
1 c. chili sauce

• Cut unpeeled apples in wedges, removing cores.

• Melt butter in skillet, add honey and chili sauce, mix thoroughly and heat. Add apples, coating them with the chili-sauce mixture, and cook until slightly soft, about 10 to 12 minutes, turning occasionally to baste fruit. Serve hot or cold as meat relish and garnish. Makes 6 servings.

GLAZED APRICOTS

Serve on platter of chicken or meat —bright garnish and super-fine eating

1 (1 lb.) can apricot halves
1 tblsp. butter or regular margarine
1 tblsp. brown sugar
1 stick cinnamon

· Drain syrup from apricots. Add butter, sugar and cinnamon to syrup and boil 3 minutes. Gently add apricots. Reduce heat and simmer 5 minutes. Serve hot with poultry or meat. Serves 6.

APPLE/CRANBERRY RELISH

This soft jellied sauce tastes marvelous with poultry or meats

1 (1 lb.) pkg. fresh cranberries
¾ c. sugar
1½ c. boiling water
1 (3 oz.) pkg. lemon flavor gelatin
1 c. sweetened applesauce

· Combine cranberries, sugar and water; bring to a boil. Boil rapidly 5 minutes, or until cranberries pop.
· Pour hot cranberry mixture over gelatin in 2-qt. casserole; stir to dissolve gelatin. Blend in applesauce. Cover and refrigerate overnight. Makes 8 servings.

APPLE/PINEAPPLE SCALLOP

Serve hot as a tangy companion to meats or warm for dessert

1 (1 lb. 4½ oz.) can pineapple chunks
¼ c. sugar
1 tblsp. cornstarch
¼ tsp. salt
¼ c. lemon juice
3 c. sliced, tart cooking apples
4 slices dry bread, broken into coarse crumbs
¼ lb. process cheese, shredded

· Drain pineapple; reserve ¾ c. liquid. Combine dry ingredients in heavy saucepan; add pineapple liquid. Cook, stirring constantly, until thickened. Remove from heat; stir in lemon juice and set aside.
· Layer fruit, crumbs and cheese in buttered 2-qt. casserole. (Pour on sauce before adding last layer of crumbs and cheese.) Cover; bake in moderate oven (350°) about 1 hour or until apple slices are tender. Makes 8 servings.

PICKLED CARROTS

Fix several days before serving and chill—wonderful with shrimp

1 lb. carrots, peeled
3 cloves garlic, minced
2 tblsp. coarsely chopped onion
3 tblsp. salad oil
¼ c. vinegar
1½ tsp. salt
½ tsp. dry mustard
⅛ tsp. pepper
1 tblsp. whole pickling spices
1 medium onion, peeled and thinly sliced

· Cut carrots lengthwise in ¼″ slices; then cut in strips about ¾″ wide and 3″ long.
· Cook garlic and chopped onion in salad oil until almost tender, about 5 minutes (do not let brown).
· Stir in vinegar, salt, dry mustard, pepper, pickling spices, tied in a cheesecloth bag, and carrots. Cover and simmer about 5 minutes (carrots should be crunchy and crisp). Remove pickling spices.
· Arrange the carrot mixture in a shallow dish; top with a layer of sliced onions. Cover and refrigerate until time to serve, spooning some of liquid over carrots from time to time.
· Serve cold on plate, surrounded with short lengths of celery and cherry tomatoes. Makes 10 to 12 servings.

SPICY PEACH PICKLES

They bring fancy prices in gourmet shops but are easy to fix at home

1 (1 lb.) can peach halves
1 (3″) stick cinnamon
1 tsp. whole cloves
1 tsp. whole allspice
¼ c. white vinegar

• Drain syrup from peaches into saucepan. Add spices and vinegar. Simmer 5 minutes.
• Pour over peaches, cover and refrigerate overnight, at least 8 hours. Serve as relish with chicken or meats. Makes 6 to 8 servings.

Note: Save the syrup after peaches are served. Heat and pour over more drained canned peaches, apricots, pears or pineapple. Chill.

4-VEGETABLE RELISH

Excellent with fried chicken. A summer substitute for salad

3 large tomatoes, peeled and cut in wedges
½ c. chopped green pepper
½ c. grated peeled cucumber
1 tblsp. grated onion
½ tsp. seasoned salt
½ tsp. salt
⅛ tsp. pepper

• Combine all ingredients. Chill ½ hour or longer to blend flavors. Serves 6.

CRANBERRY RELISH

You can omit apples for a more pronounced orange flavor

4 medium oranges, seeded
2 lbs. cranberries
4 medium unpeeled apples, cored
4 c. sugar

• Take the yellow peel from oranges; trim off and discard white part. Put orange pulp and yellow peel, cranberries and apples through food chopper. Add sugar and mix well.
• Cover and refrigerate. Or pour into glass jars, leaving ½″ head space. Seal and freeze. Makes 4 pints.

OREGON CRANBERRY SAUCE

Little trouble to make—no sieving. Many berries stay whole

1 lb. cranberries (4 c.)
2 c. sugar
2 tblsp. water
Dash of salt

• Wash cranberries and lift from water into large saucepan. Add sugar, water and salt. Stir to mix sugar and berries.
• Cover saucepan and set on heat. Cook only until berries start to pop. Remove lid and lightly stir, using care not to crush berries. Cook 2 minutes. Let the mixture boil up; then boil 1 minute longer. Makes about 3½ cups.

SPICED ORANGE SLICES

Sweet-tart relish brings out good flavor in duck, pork or chicken

8 whole medium oranges, unpeeled
5 c. sugar
3 c. water
1¼ c. vinegar
24 whole cloves
2 sticks cinnamon

• Select oranges with unblemished skins. Simmer whole oranges in enough water to cover, until tender, about 20 minutes. Drain, cool and slice fairly thin.
• Combine sugar, water, vinegar

and spices. Bring to a boil. Add sliced oranges and simmer 20 minutes. Remove cinnamon sticks.

· Spoon orange slices into 6 hot pint jars. Pour on cooking liquid to cover. Place 2 or 3 cloves from liquid in each jar. Seal, and refrigerate. Makes 6 pints.

BLUSHING PEACHES

Serve these color-bright beauties hot

1 c. water
½ c. sugar
3 tblsp. currant jelly
2 tblsp. lemon juice
1½ tsp. grated lemon peel
4 large peaches

· Combine water, sugar, jelly, lemon juice and peel in fry pan. Cover, and simmer 5 minutes until jelly is dissolved.

· Peel and cut peaches in halves. Place cut side down in syrup in fry pan. Cover and simmer 10 minutes. Turn cut side up; cover, and cook 5 minutes more.

· Remove peaches from syrup into a dish. Cook syrup, stirring constantly, until it begins to jell (2 drops run together in a sheet when mixture is dropped from edge of spoon). Pour mixture over peaches. Serve hot. Makes 8 servings.

REFRIGERATOR SPICED PRUNES

Perfect with meats—they'll keep in refrigerator several weeks

1 lb. prunes (about 42)
4 c. water
⅓ c. vinegar
⅓ c. dark brown sugar, firmly packed
3 sticks cinnamon
1 tblsp. whole cloves

· Combine all ingredients in a saucepan (tie cloves in a piece of cheesecloth). Bring to a boil and simmer 7 minutes. Remove cloves.

· Cool, cover and chill in the refrigerator 24 hours or longer. Serve as a relish or garnish with meats or poultry. Allow 2 prunes to a serving.

UNCOOKED TOMATO RELISH

Use as baked-on topping for meat loaf or with roast pork or lamb

18 medium tomatoes
2 branches celery
2 green peppers
2 sweet red peppers
4 medium onions
½ c. finely ground horse-radish
⅓ c. salt
2½ c. sugar
½ tsp. pepper
½ tsp. ground cloves
2 tsp. ground cinnamon
3 tblsp. whole mustard seeds
3 c. cider vinegar

· Scald tomatoes; remove skins and as many seeds as possible. Chop into small pieces; should make about 3 quarts chopped tomatoes.

· Put celery, peppers and onions through food chopper, using coarse grind. Use the finest grind for horse-radish.

· Combine vegetables and salt; let stand overnight in refrigerator. Drain thoroughly in a strainer. Add sugar, spices, mustard seeds and vinegar. Mix well.

· Pack in hot jars; seal and store in the refrigerator. Should keep for several months. (Do not store at room temperature.) Makes about 4 quarts.

Uncooked Jelly for Freezing

You can use frozen fruit juice concentrates, canned and bottled juices as well as juices extracted from fresh fruits—which, of course, have the freshest flavor. You can store these jellies successfully in the refrigerator for 3 to 4 weeks. They will keep their flavor 6 months or longer in the freezer at 0° F. or a lower temperature. Once you open them, continue using.

TART CHERRY JELLY

Sparkling, cherry-red—serve with hot rolls when ham is on platter

4¾ c. sugar
3 c. fresh cherry juice
1 pkg. powdered fruit pectin
½ c. water

· Add sugar to 1¼ c. cherry juice; stir thoroughly.
· Slowly add pectin to water. Heat almost to boiling point, stirring constantly. Pour hot pectin into remaining 1¾ c. cherry juice. Stir until pectin is completely dissolved. Let pectin mixture stand 15 minutes, but stir it occasionally.
· Add the juice-sugar mixture; stirring until all the sugar is dissolved. Pour into containers; cover with tight lids.
· Let stand at room temperature until set, overnight or at least 6 hours. Freeze or refrigerate. Makes 5 to 6 half pints.

Note: Frozen cherries may be used. Grind whole frozen cherries and thaw. Pour into jelly bag and allow juice to drain. Squeeze bag to obtain the maximum quantity of juice. If juice is from commercially frozen cherries, reduce sugar to 4¼ c.

Variation

BERRY JELLIES: Follow recipe for Tart Cherry Jelly using juice from fresh berries instead of the cherry juice. Reduce the sugar from 4¾ c. to 4½ c. Use blackberries, black raspberries, boysenberries, loganberries or red raspberries.

CONCORD GRAPE JELLY

Spoon on lettuce leaves to garnish dinner plates—good with veal, chicken and especially sliced cold roast pork

1 pkg. powdered fruit pectin
2 c. lukewarm water
1 (6 oz.) can frozen grape juice concentrate
3¼ c. sugar

· Dissolve pectin in water in a 2-qt. bowl. Add pectin slowly, stirring constantly until completely dissolved. Let stand 45 minutes, stirring occasionally (stir, do not beat).
· Thaw grape juice concentrate by setting can in cold water. Pour it into a 1-qt. bowl. Add 1½ c. sugar to the juice. Mix thoroughly (all sugar will not dissolve).
· Add remaining 1¾ c. sugar to the dissolved pectin. Stir until sugar dissolves.
· Add the juice mixture to the pectin mixture. Stir until all the sugar dissolves.
· Pour into containers. Cover with tight lids. Let stand at room temperature about 24 hours or until set. Freeze or refrigerate. Makes 5 to 6 half pints.

Variation

BOYSENBERRY JELLY: Make like Grape Jelly substituting 1 (6 oz.) can frozen boysenberry juice concentrate for the grape juice concentrate.

ORANGE/LEMON JELLY

Right flavor accent for eggs and egg dishes—and simply great with duck

- **1 pkg. powdered fruit pectin**
- **2 c. lukewarm water**
- **1 (6 oz.) can frozen orange juice concentrate**
- **¼ c. strained fresh lemon juice**
- **4½ c. sugar**

· Dissolve pectin in water in a 2-qt. bowl. Add the pectin slowly, stirring constantly until completely dissolved. Let stand 45 minutes, stirring occasionally (not beating).

· Thaw orange juice by placing can in cold water. Then pour juice into a 1-qt. bowl. Add the lemon juice and 2½ c. sugar. Mix thoroughly (all sugar will not dissolve).

· Add the remaining 2 c. sugar slowly to the dissolved pectin. Stir until sugar dissolves.

· Add juice mixture to pectin mixture. Stir constantly until all the sugar dissolves.

· Pour into containers. Cover with tight lids. Let stand at room temperature overnight or until set. Freeze or refrigerate. Makes 5 to 6 half pints.

Uncooked or Frozen Jams

If the jams seem a little stiff when you open them for serving, stir gently to soften. Or if they "weep" when cut, stir to blend them. They will mold or ferment if kept at room temperature more than a few days, so always store in refrigerator.

Jams from Frozen Fruit

STRAWBERRY JAM

As delicious spooned over vanilla ice cream as it is on hot breads

- **2 (10 oz.) pkgs. frozen, sweetened strawberries**
- **3 c. sugar**
- **1 pkg. powdered fruit pectin**
- **1 c. water**

· Thaw frozen berries and grind or blend in blender to make a purée.

· Add sugar, mix thoroughly and let stand 20 minutes, stirring occasionally.

· Combine powdered pectin and water and boil rapidly for 1 minute, stirring constantly.

· Remove from heat. Add the fruit to the pectin; stir for 2 minutes.

· Pour into clean containers; cover with tight-fitting lids. Let stand at room temperature 24 hours. If jam does not set, refrigerate until it does.

· Freeze at 0° F. or lower, or refrigerate. Makes 4 to 5 half pints.

Variations

Omit powdered pectin and water and use ½ c. liquid fruit pectin. No heating is necessary.

CHERRY JAM: Put frozen tart cherries through food chopper. Add 2 tsp. lemon juice. Use cherries instead of strawberries.

PEACH JAM: Mash frozen peaches when thawed. Stir in 1 tsp. powdered ascorbic acid or 3 tblsp. lemon juice. Substitute for strawberries.

RED RASPBERRY JAM: Use 3 (10 oz.) pkgs. of frozen raspberries and 4 c. sugar. Follow recipe for Strawberry Jam.

Jams from Fresh Fruits

FRESH STRAWBERRY JAM

Keeps that luscious fresh berry taste and is so easy to make

2 c. finely mashed or sieved strawberries
4 c. sugar
1 pkg. powdered fruit pectin
1 c. water

• Combine fruit and sugar. Let stand 20 minutes, stirring occasionally.
• Boil powdered pectin and water rapidly for 1 minute, stirring constantly. Remove from heat. Add berries and stir about 2 minutes.
• Pour into containers and cover. Let stand at room temperature 1 hour. Refrigerate until set.
• Store in freezer. Once opened, keep in refrigerator. Makes 5 to 6 half pints.

Variations

Omit powdered pectin and water. Use ½ c. liquid fruit pectin. No heating is necessary.

APRICOT JAM: Add 1 tsp. powdered ascorbic acid or 3 tblsp. lemon juice to finely mashed and measured fresh apricots. Substitute apricots for strawberries.

BLACK RASPBERRY JAM: Substitute black raspberries for strawberries.

CHERRY JAM: Pit tart cherries and put through food chopper. Measure and substitute for strawberries.

PEACH JAM: Add 1 tsp. powdered ascorbic acid or 3 tblsp. lemon juice to mashed peaches to keep them from darkening. Measure peaches and substitute for strawberries.

Uncooked Spreads

Spreads are less sweet than jams and they hold more of the delicate fresh fruit taste and aroma. You add more pectin but since it controls the consistency, you can use a little less of it if you prefer thinner spreads, more if you like thicker spreads. Make up a test batch to determine if you wish to use more or less pectin. Add light corn syrup to reduce the formation of sugar crystals during storage.

The best way to make the fruit purée is to use a food mill, an electric mixer with a 1-qt. bowl, or a blender. Or you can mash the fruit very fine.

To make a luscious topping for ice cream, thin the spread when you open it with light corn syrup to the consistency you like.

You can store these spreads in the refrigerator several weeks—in the freezer at 0° or lower they will keep a year.

BLUEBERRY SPREAD

Use either wild or "tame" berries—perfect on pancakes or waffles

¼ c. powdered fruit pectin
2 tblsp. sugar
1 c. sieved blueberries
¾ c. sugar
2 tblsp. light corn syrup
2 tblsp. lemon juice

• Combine pectin and the 2 tblsp. sugar; mix thoroughly. Add the finely sieved berries and mix at low speed for 7 minutes.
• Add remaining sugar, corn syrup and lemon juice. Mix 3 minutes longer.
• Pour into freezer containers and secure lids. Let stand at room temperature overnight or until jellied. Freeze. Makes 2 half pints.

CONCORD GRAPE SPREAD

Marvelous teamed with roast pork, fried chicken, ham, hot toast

¾ c. powdered fruit pectin
3 c. sugar
4 c. unsweetened grape juice
½ c. light corn syrup

• Mix pectin and ½ c. sugar. Add grape juice and mix at low speed for 7 minutes. Add the remaining sugar and corn syrup. Mix 3 minutes longer.
• Pour into containers, secure lids. Let stand at room temperature for 24 hours. Store in freezer or refrigerator. Makes 6 half pints.

Note: Any fruit you can purée or chop very finely may be used to make these spreads. Peach, nectarine and pear spreads are delicious when fresh, but they are not good keepers.

STRAWBERRY SPREAD

It's strawberry season whenever you have this on the table

1 c. powdered fruit pectin
3½ c. sugar
4 c. puréed or finely mashed strawberries, fresh or frozen without sugar
½ c. light corn syrup
2 to 3 tblsp. lemon juice

• Mix the pectin and ½ c. sugar. Add the puréed berries and mix at low speed for 7 minutes.
• Add remaining ingredients and mix 3 minutes longer.
• Pour into containers, fasten lids. Let stand at room temperature 24 hours. Store in freezer or refrigerator. Makes 6 half pints.

Variations

APRICOT SPREAD: Add 4 tsp. ascorbic acid to 4 c. puréed apricots and follow recipe for Strawberry Spread.

BERRY SPREADS: Substitute raspberries, loganberries, boysenberries or blackberries for the strawberries.

Quick-cook Jellies and Jams

ORANGE JELLY

For gifts, scatter sequins on top of paraffin topping before it sets

2 c. water
1 pkg. powdered fruit pectin
3½ c. sugar
1 (6 oz.) can frozen orange juice concentrate, thawed

• Mix water and pectin in saucepan; bring quickly to full rolling boil; boil hard 1 minute; add sugar and concentrate; stir until dissolved (don't boil).
• Remove from heat; pour into hot sterilized glasses; add paraffin; cool. Makes about 5 half pints.

Note: If you use standard jelly jars, there's no need to use paraffin. Just fill to within ⅛" of top; seal at once with regular home canning cap.

Variations

TANGERINE JELLY: Substitute frozen tangerine juice for orange.

PINEAPPLE JELLY: Substitute pineapple juice for orange.

MARJORAM JELLY

Really good with all meats, but superfine with lamb and chicken

2 tblsp. marjoram leaves
1 c. boiling water
⅓ c. lemon juice
3 c. sugar
½ c. liquid fruit pectin

• Combine marjoram and water. Let stand 15 minutes. Strain through fine mesh cheesecloth. Measure liquid and add water to make 1 c.
• Strain lemon juice through cheesecloth. Combine lemon juice, sugar and herb liquid in a saucepan. Place over high heat. Bring to a boil; stir in pectin. Stirring constantly, bring to a full boil. Boil ½ minute. Remove from heat. Skim. Pour into hot sterilized jars; seal. Makes 3 half pints.

APRICOT JAM

The rich, tangy-sweet taste does something good to buttered toast

3 c. diced apricots
¼ c. lemon juice
7 c. sugar
½ bottle liquid fruit pectin

• Mix apricots, lemon juice and sugar. Boil until apricots are soft. Remove from heat; stir in pectin. Stir and skim for 5 minutes.
• Pour into hot sterilized jars; seal. Makes 3½ pints.

BLUEBERRY/RASPBERRY JAM

Flavors of red berries and blueberries complement one another

1 pt. blueberries
1 qt. red raspberries
7 c. sugar
1 bottle liquid fruit pectin

• Crush berries; measure 4 c. (if necessary, add water to make full amount).
• Add sugar, mix well. Heat to full rolling boil; boil hard 1 minute, stirring constantly. Remove from heat; stir in pectin; skim.
• Ladle into hot sterilized jars; seal. Makes 10 half pints.

BLUEBARB JAM

Use fresh rhubarb and unsweetened frozen berries to make this

3 c. finely cut rhubarb
3 c. crushed blueberries
7 c. sugar
1 bottle liquid fruit pectin

• Combine rhubarb and blueberries in large saucepan, add sugar; mix.
• Place over high heat; bring to full, rolling boil and boil hard 1 minute, stirring constantly. Remove from heat, add pectin. Stir and skim for 5 minutes. Ladle into hot sterilized jars. Cover at once with thin layer paraffin. Makes about 9 half pints.

PEACHY PEAR JAM

Good choice for a meal featuring a chicken-rice casserole

3½ c. mashed peaches and pears
6½ c. sugar
Juice of 2 lemons
½ tsp. ground cinnamon
½ tsp. ground nutmeg
½ bottle liquid fruit pectin

· Mix all ingredients, except pectin.
· Place over high heat and bring to a full rolling boil. Boil hard for 1 minute, stirring constantly.
· Remove from heat; stir in pectin. Skim. Stir and skim for 5 minutes.
· Pour into hot sterilized jars; seal. Makes 4 pints.

Longer-cook Jellies and Jams

Some women call this the old-fashioned method because it's the one their grandmothers followed. No one denies that the jellies and jams are delicious, but making them takes more time and skill than the other types containing liquid or powdered pectin.

It is important to know when the jelly or jam has cooked enough. The safest way is to use a jelly, candy or deep-fat thermometer. The correct point for your altitude is determined this way: Note the temperature at which the mixture boils, then add 8°. That is the point when the jelly or jam is ready to remove from the heat. Or put a little jelly or jam on a small plate and set in refrigerator, removing the kettle from the heat. If the fruity mixture in refrigerator jells in a few minutes, it is cooked enough.

APPLE/GERANIUM JELLY

This old-fashioned delicacy sells fast in city gourmet shops

6 c. apple juice (about 5 lbs. apples)
4 c. sugar
12 rose geranium leaves

· Prepare juice by removing stem and blossom ends of tart, red apples. Slice and put in kettle with water, barely to cover. Cook until very tender. Turn into a jelly bag and let juice drip into bowl.
· Measure 6 c. juice into large kettle; bring quickly to a boil. Add sugar, stirring until dissolved. Boil rapidly until jellying point is reached.
· Quickly place 2 small (or 1 large) rose geranium leaves in each hot sterilized jar. Skim jelly and pour into jars; seal. Makes 6 half pints.

Note: If apples are not tart, test juice for pectin before making jelly.

Variation

MINT JELLY: Omit geranium leaves. Delicately tint jelly just before pouring into jars with green food color; add ½ tsp. peppermint extract.

CRAB APPLE JELLY

Spread between folds of a puffed-up omelet or use to glaze baked ham

5 lbs. crab apples
8 c. water
Sugar
1 tsp. vanilla (optional)

· Remove stem and blossom ends from washed crab apples, cut in halves and place in large kettle. (Red fruit makes the most colorful jelly.) Add water and cook until fruit is very soft, about 10 minutes.
· Strain mixture through jelly bag, but do not force juice through bag.
· Measure juice. You should have about 7 c. Stir in ¾ c. sugar for every cup of juice. Bring to a boil quickly and cook rapidly until jellying point is reached.
· Skim off foam, stir in vanilla and pour into hot sterilized jars. Makes about 4 half pints.

Note: The amount of jelly depends

on the juiciness of the fruit, so the yield may vary.

TWO-STEP GRAPE JELLY

Make it this way and you'll not find crystals in the amethyst

3½ lbs. Concord grapes
½ c. water

· Select ¼ underripe and ¾ ripe grapes. Wash and remove stems. Place in kettle, crush, add water, cover and bring quickly to a boil over high heat.
· Lower heat and simmer 10 minutes. Let juice drip through jelly bag.
· Cover juice and let stand in a *cool place overnight.* Strain through two thicknesses of damp cheesecloth to remove crystals.

Second Step

4 c. grape juice
3 c. sugar

· Pour juice into large kettle; stir in sugar. Boil over high heat until jellying point is reached.
· Remove from heat; skim off foam quickly. Pour at once into hot sterilized jars or glasses; seal. Makes about 4 half pints or 5 (6 oz.) glasses.

GOOSEBERRY JAM

Excellent with meats. Use ripe berries for the attractive color

2 qts. gooseberries (or 1 qt. ground gooseberries)
4 c. sugar
Juice of 1 lemon

· Remove both ends from the gooseberries. Wash. Grind with medium-coarse blade of food chopper.
· Combine all ingredients in a wide kettle. Cook until mixture clings to the wooden spoon, showing it has begun to thicken. Stir constantly while cooking. Ladle into hot sterilized jars; seal. Makes 4 half pints.

Note: Half-ripe or ripe berries may be used. With half-ripe or green berries, omit lemon juice.

FAVORITE STRAWBERRY JAM

Add 1 tblsp. lemon juice to 1 c. berries if they're very ripe and sweet

8 c. strawberries
6 c. sugar
Lemon juice (optional)

· Wash, drain, hull and crush berries. Add sugar and cook slowly, stirring constantly until sugar dissolves. Bring quickly to a boil and boil rapidly until the jellying point is reached.
· Pour or ladle hot jam into hot sterilized jars; seal. Makes 6 half pints.

APPLE/RASPBERRY JAM

Apples stretch the red raspberry flavor without hiding it—good with chicken

9 c. sugar
2 c. water
6 c. finely chopped tart apples (about 2 lbs.)
3 c. red raspberries, washed and drained

· Combine sugar and water; boil until mixture spins a thread.
· Stir in apples and boil 2 minutes. Add raspberries and boil 20 minutes longer, stirring often. Pour into hot sterilized jars; seal. Makes 5 pints.

RED PLUM JAM

A deep red jam with a slightly tart taste. Excellent with meats

5 lbs. red plums (about 11¼ c.) pitted and chopped
½ c. water
Sugar

· Cook plums in water until soft. Put through food mill. Add sugar, 1½ c. to each cup plum purée.
· Boil rapidly to jelly stage, approximately 10 minutes. Ladle into hot sterilized jars; seal. Makes 6 pints.

PLUM/RASPBERRY JAM

If raspberries are scarce, capture their flavor with this recipe

3 lbs. prune plums, ground (5 c.)
5 c. sugar
1 (10 oz.) pkg. frozen raspberries

· Put ripe, firm plums through food chopper using medium blade.
· Combine plums and sugar in a 5- or 6-qt. pan. Add raspberries. Mix together.
· Bring to boil; reduce heat and simmer until thick, about 40 minutes. Stir occasionally. Pour into hot sterilized jars. Seal at once. Makes 8 half pints.

STRAWBERRY/RHUBARB JAM

Spread jam on sponge cake slices and dust with confectioners sugar

3 c. strawberries
3 c. diced rhubarb
6 c. sugar

· Mash strawberries. Cut rhubarb into ½" pieces. Combine and mix. Add 4 c. sugar; bring to a rolling boil and boil 4 minutes.
· Add 2 c. sugar and boil again for 4 minutes. Pour into hot sterilized jars; seal. Makes 2½ pints.

Apple Butter with the Old-Fashioned Taste

Grandmother made apple butter for two important reasons that are just as valid today: it tastes exceptionally good and it makes use of the sound parts of culls or windfalls. Once apple butter cooked for long hours in big black kettles over fires built in the yard. Someone had to stir it constantly so neighbors came over to take their turns at the stirring and to visit. Our Oven Apple Butter needs little stirring (about once every half hour—three times in all). And its taste matches that of the most delicious apple butters of yesteryear.

OVEN APPLE BUTTER

Delicious on hot biscuits or rolls

2 qts. water
2 tblsp. salt
6 lbs. apples, cored, peeled and sliced
2 qts. sweet cider
3½ to 4 c. sugar
1 tsp. ground cinnamon
½ tsp. ground cloves
½ tsp. ground allspice

· Combine water and salt. Add apples. Drain well but do not rinse slices.
· Put through food chopper, using finest blade. Measure pulp and juice (there should be 2 qts.).
· Combine with cider. Place in large enamel pan. Center pan in moderate oven (350°). Let mixture

simmer about 3 to 3½ hours until cooked down about half and is thick and mushy. Stir thoroughly every half hour.

• Put mixture through sieve or food mill; it should yield 2¼ to 2½ quarts.

• Combine sugar and spices; add to sauce and return to oven. Continue simmering about 1½ hours or until thick, stirring every half hour. To test, pour small amount onto cold plate. If no liquid oozes around edge, apple butter is cooked.

• Pour into hot jars; adjust lids and process in boiling water bath (212°) 10 minutes. Remove jars and complete seals unless closures are self-sealing kind. Makes 2 quarts.

Preserves, Marmalades and Fruit Honeys

Open the storage cupboard doors in country homes and you'll see jars of tempting preserves, marmalades and fruit honeys on the shelves. These are some of the treats farm women like to can when fruits are in season and plentiful. The jars carry fond remembrances of summer tastes to winter meals.

QUINCE GINGER

This is the kind of relish country women make to give meals a lift

6 lbs. ripe quince
4 lbs. sugar
2 c. water
1 tblsp. grated fresh ginger root
4 lemons, sliced thin

• Peel and core quince; cut into small pieces.

• Combine sugar and water; stir to dissolve. Boil 5 minutes. Add chopped quince, ginger root and lemon slices.

• Simmer 2 hours, until fruit is transparent and deep red in color. Pour into hot jars and seal; adjust lids. Process in boiling water bath (212°) 5 minutes. Remove jars and complete seals, unless closures are self-sealing type. Makes 5 pints.

Note: If fresh ginger root is unavailable, use a small piece of the dried root, but discard before sealing glasses.

TOMATO PRESERVES

These old-fashioned preserves in a glass dish enhance country meals

5 lbs. firm, red or yellow tomatoes
5 lbs. sugar
1 lemon, sliced thin
Small piece ginger root, or 1 tsp. ground ginger

• Skin and cut up tomatoes. Add remaining ingredients.

• Simmer slowly until thick, stirring frequently, about 45 minutes. Remove ginger root, if used.

• Pour into hot sterilized glasses. Seal at once. Makes about 4 (6 oz.) glasses.

TART CHERRY PRESERVES

No preserves provide a more welcome taste when served with ham

1 lb. ripe, firm tart cherries
1 lb. sugar

• Pit cherries; add sugar. Boil to 240° on candy thermometer, or until thick.

• Seal in hot sterilized pint jars. Makes about 2 pints.

STRAWBERRY PRESERVES

An heirloom recipe for a great national favorite—colorful and luscious

4 c. hulled strawberries
3 c. sugar

· Add sugar to berries and let stand 10 minutes or until juices start to flow. (Some cooks like to cover them and leave in the refrigerator overnight.)

· Put berry-sugar mixture in a 4-qt. kettle and bring to a boil, stirring constantly until sugar dissolves. Cook until berries are tender, about 3 minutes. Let stand overnight.

· Next morning bring preserves to a boil and boil 1 minute. Cover the preserves, remove from heat and let stand 2 minutes. Stir gently about 5 minutes, skimming if necessary.

· Pour or ladle into hot sterilized jars and seal, or if you live in a warm climate, adjust lids and process at the simmering point in boiling water bath (212°) 15 to 20 minutes.

· Remove jars from canner and complete seals unless closures are self-sealing type. Makes 3 half pints.

ROSY STRAWBERRY PRESERVES

Cook a batch daily while getting lunch during the strawberry season

1 qt. halved strawberries
4 c. sugar
1 tblsp. vinegar (or lemon juice)

· Combine strawberries and sugar. Stir lightly and let stand 1 hour in flat-bottomed shallow pan.

· Bring to a boil and cook 10 minutes, stirring constantly. Add vinegar; boil 3 minutes longer. Remove from heat, cover and let stand 24 hours.

· Bring to a boil and ladle into hot sterilized jars; seal. Makes 2 pints.

RED RASPBERRY PRESERVES

A state fair champion. Spoon on vanilla ice cream for a treat

4 c. whole raspberries
4 c. sugar
Juice of 1 lemon

· Place raspberries in kettle with sugar and lemon. Bring slowly to a boil over low heat, *shaking* all the while. *Do not stir*. Continue shaking and boil for 5 minutes.

· Remove from heat. Cover; let stand several hours or overnight. Heat and seal in hot sterilized jars. Makes 7 half pints.

PEACH PRESERVES

Heat and blend ¼ c. butter and ½ c. preserves to dress up waffles

1½ qts. peaches, diced
1 orange, diced, and grated peel
Juice of 2 lemons
1 c. chopped maraschino cherries
6 c. sugar

· Mix all ingredients and cook until of desired consistency.

· Pour into hot sterilized jars; seal. Makes 3½ pints.

CANTALOUPE PRESERVES

A country woman captured blue ribbons at a state fair with this recipe

2 lbs. firm, ripe cantaloupe
1¾ lbs. sugar (4 c.)
Juice of 1 lemon

· Peel cantaloupe and cut into thin

slices 1″ long. Mix sugar and cantaloupe; let stand overnight.

· Add lemon juice; cook until clear. Pour into hot sterilized jars; seal. Makes about 2 pints.

ROSY WATERMELON RIND PRESERVES

Perfect to serve with venison

1 very large, firm watermelon
1 c. salt
4 c. cider vinegar
2 c. strained red cherry juice (from fresh, cooked or canned cherries)
12 c. sugar
4 sticks cinnamon
2 tblsp. whole cloves

· Remove rind from watermelon. Peel off outside skin, then cut rind into 3″ strips (there should be 12 cups of cut-up rind). Place strips in a large jar. Cover with water to which 1 c. salt has been added. Let stand overnight.

· The next morning, drain off all water. Place rind and 2 qts. fresh water in a large saucepan. Boil for 10 minutes. Drain.

· In a 6-qt. kettle bring vinegar, cherry juice and sugar to a boil. Add spices, tied loosely in a cheesecloth bag, and simmer 10 minutes. Remove spices. Drop cooked melon strips into hot syrup. Cook until syrup thickens and is transparent.

· Put a cinnamon stick and 3 whole cloves into each hot jar, then fill with boiling hot preserves. Adjust lids. Process in boiling water bath (212°) 15 minutes. Remove jars and let cool. Complete seals unless closures are self-sealing type. Makes 8 to 10 pints.

ORANGE MARMALADE

Spread a thin layer on pumpkin pie and top with whipped cream

4 oranges
2 lemons
Water
Sugar

· Wash fruit and slice very thin without peeling it. Remove seeds and cores.

· Measure the sliced fruit and for each cup add 3 c. cold water; let stand 24 hours.

· Heat mixture to boiling; boil 15 minutes and again let stand 24 hours.

· On the third day, measure 3 cups of the mixture into a large saucepan; add 3 c. sugar and boil rapidly, stirring frequently, about 20 minutes or until the jellying point is reached. Stir and skim for a few minutes to prevent floating. Pour into hot sterilized jars; seal.

· Repeat in 3-cup batches until all has been used. Cooking in small amounts gives a more delicate marmalade. Makes about 5 pints.

PINEAPPLE/CARROT MARMALADE

Make this spun-gold spread in spring when fresh fruit is scarce

4 lbs. raw carrots, peeled
3 lemons
1 (1 lb. 4½ oz.) can crushed pineapple (2 c.)
4 c. sugar
1 c. orange juice

· Put carrots and unpeeled lemons through food chopper. Add pineapple, sugar and orange juice; cook until clear, stirring occasionally.

• Pour into hot sterilized jars; seal at once. Makes 4½ pints.

GROUND CHERRY MARMALADE

Lovely yellow color, crystal clear and delicate, yet rich in flavor

3 c. ground cherries (husk tomatoes)
2 c. cooked pears, drained and diced finely
¾ c. water
½ c. drained, crushed pineapple
¼ c. lemon juice (2 lemons)
7 c. sugar
½ bottle liquid fruit pectin

• Husk and wash the ground cherries. Combine with pears and water; simmer 25 minutes.
• Add pineapple, lemon juice and sugar and bring quickly to a full rolling boil. Add pectin; boil rapidly for 3 minutes.
• Remove from heat and alternately skim and stir marmalade for 3 minutes. Pour into hot sterilized jars; seal. Makes 7 half pints.

PEACH HONEY

On grapefruit or toast it makes winter meals taste like spring

1 large orange
12 large peaches, peeled
Sugar

• Put orange, including peel, and peaches through the food chopper. Measure the mixture and add an equal amount of sugar.
• Cook until of desired consistency, approximately 20 minutes. Pour into hot sterilized jars; seal. Makes 5 pints.

LEMON/CARROT MARMALADE

Adds a cheerful spot of color and a sprightly flavor to any meal

12 large carrots, grated (9 c.)
9 c. sugar
Juice of 3 lemons
Juice of 1 orange
⅛ tsp. salt

• Scrape carrots and grate coarsely; add sugar (use equal amounts carrots and sugar). Let stand overnight.
• Add fruit juice and salt. Bring to boiling, and simmer 2 hours. Stir often, and skim when necessary. Seal in hot sterilized glasses. Makes about 11 (6 oz.) glasses.

Note: Orange and lemon peel sliced very thin without any of the white membrane makes a nice addition.

AMBER GRAPE MARMALADE

Depend on this company special to please your guests—it's delicious

1⅓ c. Concord grapes
2⅔ c. seedless green grapes
½ c. water
2 c. unsweetened applesauce
3½ c. sugar
2 tsp. grated lemon peel

• Slip skins off Concords and discard; add pulp to seedless grapes; add water.
• Cook until soft, put through sieve or food mill. Sieve applesauce, add to mixture. Bring to boil, stirring frequently.
• Add sugar and lemon peel. Simmer until thick and jelly-like. (Two drops of mixture should run together and sheet from metal spoon.)
• Pour into hot sterilized glasses or jars. Seal immediately. Makes 2½ pints.

REBA'S PEAR HONEY

Honey-colored if cooked no longer than necessary for right consistency

4 c. peeled, crushed pears
3 c. sugar
¼ tsp. salt
1 lemon, ground

• Combine all ingredients and cook in a heavy pan, stirring occasionally, about 15 minutes or until of spreading consistency. Pour into hot sterilized jars; seal. Makes 2½ pints.

Variation

ORANGE/PEAR HONEY: Use 1 orange, ground, instead of lemon.

PEAR HONEY

You are sure to like honey with lemons added, but try all three

5 lbs. Kieffer pears
10 c. sugar
2 (8½ oz.) cans crushed pineapple (2 c.)

• Peel pears, remove hard core and discard. Put pears through food chopper, using coarse blade.
• Combine pears, sugar and pineapple; cook until mixture is thick and pears are clear. Pour into hot sterilized jars and seal or cover with paraffin. Makes 7 pints.

Variations

LEMON/PEAR HONEY: At the beginning of the cooking period, add 1 c. lemon juice or 2 lemons very thinly sliced.

AMBROSIA PEAR HONEY: At end of cooking period, add ½ c. shredded coconut.

PEACH/PLUM JAM

Blending of two fruits is flavor secret; plums add rich color

4 c. peaches (about 3 lbs.)
5 c. red plums
8 c. sugar
1 lemon, thinly sliced

• Peel and pit peaches. Pit plums. Cut fruits in small pieces or chop. Measure into large kettle. Add sugar and lemon (very thinly sliced) and stir to mix well.
• Boil rapidly, stirring constantly, until jellying point is reached, or until thick. Remove from heat; skim and stir alternately for 5 minutes. Ladle into hot sterilized jars; seal. Makes 12 half pints.

Success with Homemade Pickles and Relishes

Heed these rules:
• Start with fresh, firm fruits and vegetables free from blemishes. Wash thoroughly.
• Use a clear vinegar of 4 to 6% acid content. (Look on bottle label for acid content.) White distilled vinegar gives pickles and relishes the best color; it should always be used with light fruits. Cider vinegar may darken pickles, but many country women prefer it for its flavor and aroma.
• Use fresh spices for best flavor.
• Use either cane or beet sugar. Some recipes call for brown sugar for added flavor when darker color is not objectionable.

· Water containing iron may darken pickles. In regions where hard water is chemically treated, boil it, let cool and remove film.

· Prepare jars by washing thoroughly in hot, soapy water and rinsing well; or wash them in an electric dishwasher. Jars need not be sterilized when pickles will be processed. Keep them warm in a pan of water set over low heat so they will not break when filled with hot food. If pickles or relishes will not be processed, sterilize jars and keep them warm until filled. Fill to within ⅛″ of top, wipe off spill and seal at once.

· To process pickles and relishes, fill hot jars to within ½″ from top (be sure liquid covers vegetables or fruits); wipe off any spill and adjust lids following manufacturer's directions. Process in boiling water bath by placing jars on rack in a deep container holding enough boiling water to cover tops of jars by 2″. Quickly bring water back to a boil and start counting time when it begins to boil; boil gently and steadily for recommended time. Remove jars at once; do not disturb self-seal lids. Cool jars, well separated, on a rack or folded towel away from drafts.

· Store pickles properly. Check all the seals. (Jars that are not sealed should be refrigerated and used.) Label and store in a cool, dark, dry place. Make certain that the liquid in the jars covers the fruits and vegetables during storage and when opened. Keep opened jars in refrigerator.

· Discard, without tasting, any pickles that have a bad odor or that appear moldy, mushy or gassy when opened.

Quick Process Pickles

Short-cut pickling methods today rank first in popularity. They eliminate the brining process which often is tedious. This section starts with recipes for quick-cure pickles and relishes, but further on you will find several recipes for longer-cure pickles.

Tangy Fruit Pickles

A lively debate question: Which fragrance is the more pleasing—yeast bread baking in the oven or peach pickles simmering in spicy syrup on a bright summer morning? Everyone agrees that peach, pear, crab apple, quince and pineapple pickles contribute lovely color and delightful flavors to meals. Here are recipes for fruit pickles.

SPICED APPLE STICKS

This relish is spiced to make meats taste better—especially pork

12 medium apples, peeled and cored
3 qts. water
3 tblsp. vinegar
1 c. sugar
½ c. light corn syrup
1 c. vinegar
⅔ c. water
2 tsp. whole cloves
1½ sticks cinnamon

· Cut apples into eighths and cover with water and vinegar.

• Combine all other ingredients in kettle. Bring slowly to a boil.
• Add well-drained apples; cover and boil 3 minutes, stirring occasionally.
• Pack apple sticks in hot jars and cover with liquid; adjust lids. Process in boiling water bath (212°) 15 minutes.
• Remove jars from canner and complete seals unless closures are self-sealing type. Makes 4 pints.

CALIFORNIA APRICOT PICKLE

Hostess helper that's spicy, colorful and excellent with lamb

4 qts. apricots
Whole cloves
4 c. sugar
4 c. brown sugar, firmly packed
1 qt. vinegar
6 (3″) sticks cinnamon

• Stick each apricot with 2 or 4 cloves.
• Bring sugars, vinegar and cinnamon sticks (may be tied in cheesecloth) to a boil. Add 2 qts. apricots and simmer gently until soft. Remove fruit and repeat with remaining apricots.
• Remove cinnamon. Fill hot jars with fruit to within ½″ from top; pour on syrup, making certain it covers fruit. Adjust lids. Process in boiling water bath (212°) 20 minutes. Remove jars and complete seals unless closures are self-sealing type. Makes 6 pints.

Note: You can substitute peeled peaches or pears for apricots. Use 8 c. white sugar instead of equal parts of white and brown.

CINNAMON APPLE RINGS

Candy does the spicing and tinting —glamorous relish to serve with pork

18 tart apples
6 c. sugar
3 c. water
1 (9 oz.) pkg. red cinnamon candies
3 drops red food color

• Cut cored, peeled apples in rings.
• Combine sugar, water, cinnamon candies and food color. Bring to a boil; boil 3 minutes.
• Add apples to syrup; cook until transparent.
• Pack in hot jars. Cover with syrup; adjust lids. Process in boiling water bath (212°) 25 minutes. Remove jars from canner and complete seals unless closures are self-sealing type. Makes 4 pints.

Note: Drop rings in lightly salted water before cooking to keep them from discoloring. We tested this recipe with Jonathan apples, but other tart varieties may be used.

SPICED BLUEBERRIES

Blueberry fans praise this as an accompaniment to ham and bacon

3 qts. blueberries
1 c. vinegar
1 c. sugar
2 tblsp. whole cloves

• Combine all ingredients in large kettle and bring to a boil. Simmer, stirring often until liquid begins to jell, about 20 to 25 minutes.
• Pour into hot jars; adjust lids. Process in boiling water bath (212°) 5 minutes. Remove jars and complete seals unless closures are self-sealing type. Makes 2 pints.

CANTALOUPE PICKLE

Delicious way to salvage slightly underripe melons. Try it

1 medium underripe cantaloupe
1 qt. vinegar
2 c. water
1 tsp. ground mace
2 (3″) sticks cinnamon
2 tblsp. ground cloves
4 c. sugar

· Peel cantaloupe and cut in 1″ sections. Cut sections crosswise.
· Combine vinegar and water in kettle; bring to a boil; add spices, tied loosely in cheesecloth. (Or if you prefer to leave spices in pickles, do not tie them in cheesecloth.)
· Place cantaloupe in a nonmetal container. Bring the vinegar water to a boil and pour over cantaloupe. Let stand overnight.
· In morning, drain cantaloupe; bring vinegar-water mixture to a boil. Add sugar and cantaloupe and cook until melon pieces are transparent, about 1 hour. Remove spice bag.
· Fill hot pint jars with cantaloupe. Keep syrup boiling. Add syrup to jars to within ½″ from top. Make certain it covers the melon. Adjust lids. Process in boiling water bath (212°) 5 minutes. Remove jars and complete seals unless closures are self-sealing type. Makes 2 pints.

Note: A medium syrup is desirable. If it is too thin, boil it longer. Keep the jars of cantaloupe pickles warm by setting them in a kettle of hot water until syrup is ready. You can use 2 c. white and 2 c. brown sugar instead of all white sugar, if you like.

Pickled Cherries

If you like really tart relishes, pickled cherries are for you. Some cooks trim the stems slightly and leave these "handles" on the fruit. Wrap the jars of pickles in heavy brown paper when storing them in the fruit closet. The covering will protect their color.

PICKLED CHERRIES

Use the largest sweet cherries you can find to make this relish

2 qts. cherries, stemmed
¼ c. sugar
2 doz. whole cloves
1 (3″) stick cinnamon
2½ c. vinegar

· Select large cherries; wash and stem but do not pit.
· Mix sugar, spices, tied in bag, and vinegar. Cook for 5 minutes.
· Add cherries, cook slowly until tender. Remove from heat; let stand overnight.
· In morning, remove spices. Drain syrup from cherries; pack them in hot jars. Boil syrup rapidly until slightly thick.
· Pour boiling hot over cherries; adjust lids. Process in boiling water bath (212°) 5 minutes. Remove jars and complete seals unless closures are self-sealing type. Makes 2½ pints.

CRAB APPLE PICKLE

Be sure to leave stems on apples to add to their appetite appeal

4 lbs. crab apples
2½ c. vinegar

2 c. water
4 c. sugar
1 tblsp. whole cloves
3 (3″) sticks cinnamon
1 tsp. whole ginger

• Wash and remove blossom ends of crab apples; do not remove stems. Prick each apple in several places.
• Bring vinegar, water and sugar to a boil. Add spices tied in bag.
• Cook half of the crab apples in the syrup for 2 minutes; remove. Repeat until all the crab apples are cooked. Pour syrup with spice bag over apples; let stand overnight.
• Remove spice bag. Pack apples in hot pint jars. Bring syrup to a boil. Pour over fruit.
• Adjust lids. Process in boiling water bath (212°) 30 minutes.
• Remove jars from canner and complete seals unless closures are self-sealing type. Makes 4 to 5 pints.

FROZEN SPICED CRAB APPLES

Color is gorgeous, flavor is orchard-fresh—a treat in any meal

16 small ripe crab apples
½ c. sugar
½ c. cold water
6 whole cloves
⅛ tsp. salt
3 strips lemon peel

• Use firm crab apples; wash and remove the blossom ends but leave the stems on.
• Combine remaining ingredients in saucepan; mix thoroughly. Prick apples in several places and put upright in the saucepan and cover loosely. Place over low heat and cook 10 minutes. Do not stir. (Low heat prevents apples from overcooking.)
• Remove from heat and set in a cool place until cold. Do not disturb apples.
• Pick up apples by stems and pack them in freezer containers (airtight). Stagger them so that the second layer fits between stems of first layer. Strain juice in pan over the apples. Seal and freeze. Let thaw for 1 to 2 hours before serving. Makes about 1 pint.

QUINCE PICKLE

The taste is pleasing, the color is a tempting apricot-peach

8 quince, peeled, cored and quartered
Whole cloves
2 oranges, sliced, seeds removed
6 c. sugar
2 c. vinegar
1 (3″) stick cinnamon
1 firm apple, peeled, cored, diced

• Cook quince in a little water until tender; drain, reserving the liquid.
• Stick 2 cloves in each quince piece.
• Combine sliced oranges, sugar, vinegar, 1½ c. liquid from quince (add water if measure is short), cinnamon and apple. Simmer over low heat 10 minutes. Add quince and simmer gently 30 minutes.
• Fill hot jars with fruit and pour on syrup to within ½″ from top. Make certain syrup covers fruit. Adjust lids. Process in boiling water bath (212°) 20 minutes. Remove jars and complete seals unless closures are self-sealing type. Makes 6 pints.

SWEET QUINCE PICKLE

In many country homes this is the favorite relish with cold cuts

7 lbs. ripe, yellow quince
8 c. sugar
2 c. vinegar
1 (3″) stick cinnamon
2 tblsp. mixed pickling spices
2 c. boiling water

• Cut fruit, cored, but not peeled, in ⅓″ slices. Weigh. Simmer in a little water until tender. Drain and place in a crock, glass jars, pottery or enamel-lined pan with tight lid.
• Combine sugar, vinegar, spices and boiling water. Bring to a boil and boil 2 minutes. Immediately pour over the fruit. Make certain syrup covers fruit. Cover tightly and store in cool, dark place (or refrigerate if weather is warm) for 14 days. Use as needed. Makes 7 to 8 pints.

Note: Instead of placing cooked fruit in crock, you may heat and pack it into hot jars. Pour on boiling syrup to cover fruit and adjust lids. Process in boiling water bath (212°) 20 minutes (unless refrigerated). Remove jars and complete seals unless closures are self-sealing type.

PEACH PICKLE

Enjoy the golden pickle; add juice to mayonnaise for fruit salads

4 lbs. peaches (about 16 medium)
1 tblsp. whole cloves
2 qts. water
2 tblsp. vinegar
4 c. sugar
1½ c. vinegar
¾ c. water
1 tsp. whole ginger
2 (3″) sticks cinnamon

• Pour boiling water over peaches; let stand until skins slip off easily when dipped into cold water. Peel.
• Stick a clove in each peach. Pour on 2 qts. water with the 2 tblsp. vinegar added.
• Combine sugar, 1½ c. vinegar and ¾ c. water. Add ginger, remaining cloves and cinnamon, tied in cheesecloth bag. Bring to a boil; add drained peaches; cover, boil until tender, about 10 minutes. Let stand overnight.
• Drain, saving liquid; remove spice bag. Pack peaches into hot pint jars. Bring syrup to a boil and pour over peaches, leaving ½″ head space. Make certain peaches are covered with syrup.
• Adjust lids. Process in boiling water bath (212°) 30 minutes.
• Remove jars from canner and complete seals unless closures are self-sealing type. Makes 4 to 5 pints.

PEAR PICKLES

Improves most menus; keep a few jars on hand to spice up guest meals

3½ lbs. ripe pears (about 14 to 16 medium)
1 qt. water
1 tblsp. vinegar
2½ c. sugar
1¼ c. vinegar
1 c. water
2 tsp. whole ginger
2 tblsp. whole cloves
7 (3″) sticks cinnamon

• Wash, peel and core pears. Place at once in 1 qt. water with 1 tblsp. vinegar added.
• Combine sugar, 1¼ c. vinegar and 1 c. water; bring to a boil. Add spices

tied in cheesecloth. Cover; boil 5 minutes. Remove spices. Put pears in hot pint jars. Add syrup to within ½″ from top of jar. Make certain pears are covered with syrup. Adjust lids. Process in boiling water bath (212°) 15 minutes.

• Remove jars from canner and complete seals unless closures are self-sealing type. Makes 3 to 4 pints.

GOURMET GINGER PEARS

Serve as a relish with meats; as a luscious spread on toast

- 4 lbs. fresh pears
- ⅓ c. finely chopped ginger root (2 oz.)
- ¼ c. fresh lemon juice
- 5 c. sugar
- 2 tsp. grated lemon peel
- ¼ c. vinegar

• Wash, peel, quarter and core pears. (If extra large, cut them into eighths.)

• Soak ginger in lemon juice while soaking pears.

• Add sugar to pears and mix well to coat each piece. Cover and let stand overnight or 6 to 8 hours.

• Stir lemon-soaked ginger into pears.

• Cook, uncovered, over medium-low heat until pears are tender and clear, about 1 hour, stirring frequently. (Cooking time depends upon ripeness of pears.) Add lemon peel and vinegar 5 minutes before cooking time is up.

• Pack in hot jars, filling to within ½″ from top. Adjust lids. Process in boiling water bath (212°) 20 minutes. Remove jars and complete seals unless closures are self-sealing type. Makes 7 half pints.

PINEAPPLE PICKLES

To make red and green pickles, tint hot syrup with food colors. Recipe comes from Hawaii where the pickles are a universal favorite

- 2 medium pineapples
- 1½ c. sugar
- ¾ c. water
- ⅓ c. vinegar
- 10 whole cloves
- 1 (3″) stick cinnamon

• Cut pineapple in ¼″ crosswise slices; peel and remove eyes. Cut slices into quarters; remove cores.

• Combine remaining ingredients and bring to a boil. Add pineapple; simmer 30 minutes. Continue simmering while packing fruit in one hot jar at a time, filling each jar with syrup to within ½″ from top. Make certain liquid covers fruit. Adjust lids. Process in boiling water bath (212°) 20 minutes. Remove jars and complete seals unless closures are self-sealing type. Makes 2 pints.

Farm-kitchen Vegetable Pickles

Some farm people believe food for picnics, church suppers and community feasts is not complete without plenty of cool, crunchy pickles. And some farmers hold that there's nothing they'd rather sit down to on a blowy, autumn day, when they come cold and hungry to dinner, than a deep brown pot roast or stew with a big bowl of dill pickles nearby.

Pickle-making is not the extensive project in rural homes it once was, but in almost every household a few favorites are "put up" every year. Take your pick of those you think will appeal especially to your family and friends. So much praise for Fermented Dill Pickles has come to our Countryside Test Kitchens that we include this recipe, even though it takes time to make these pickles. The fermentation has much to do with the fine flavor, as it does with the tried-and-true 14-Day Sweet Pickles.

BEST-EVER PICCALILLI

Tastes good like what grandmother made—just right with chicken

22 medium green tomatoes, quartered
1 pt. small onions
6 green peppers, quartered lengthwise
6 sweet red peppers, quartered
1½ qts. vinegar
3½ c. sugar
¼ c. salt
1½ tsp. ground allspice
1½ tsp. ground cinnamon
4 tsp. celery seeds
½ c. mustard seeds

• Wash vegetables; put through food chopper, using medium blade. Drain.
• Place vegetables in a large kettle; add 1 qt. vinegar. Boil 30 minutes, stirring frequently. Drain and discard liquid. Return vegetables to kettle and add remaining vinegar, sugar, salt and spices. Simmer 3 minutes. Keep mixture simmering while packing jars.
• Pack into one hot jar at a time. Fill to within ½" of jar top. Adjust lids. Process in boiling water bath (212°) 5 minutes. Remove jars and complete seals unless closures are self-sealing type. Makes 6 to 7 pints.

RUMMAGE PICKLE

Another old-time relish that makes good use of late autumn vegetables

2 qts. green tomatoes
1 small head cabbage
3 sweet green peppers
3 sweet red peppers
1 large ripe cucumber
3 large onions
1 qt. red tomatoes
6 c. celery
½ c. salt
1½ c. vinegar
1½ c. water
4 c. sugar
1 tsp. dry mustard

• Chop all vegetables first, discarding pepper seeds and peeling onions.
• Add salt and let stand overnight. In the morning, drain and discard liquid.
• Add vinegar, water, sugar and mustard to vegetables. Bring to a boil and simmer about 1 hour or until clear.
• Pack into hot jars; adjust lids. Process in boiling water bath (212°) 5 minutes. Remove jars and complete seals unless closures are self-sealing type. Makes 14 pints.

SLICED ZUCCHINI PICKLES

They make hamburgers taste better. Also try the dilled version

1 qt. vinegar
2 c. sugar
½ c. salt
2 tsp. celery seeds
2 tsp. ground turmeric
1 tsp. dry mustard
4 qts. sliced, unpeeled zucchini
1 qt. onions, sliced

• Bring vinegar, sugar, salt and spices to a boil; pour over zucchini and onions and let stand 1 hour.

• Bring to a boil; cook 3 minutes.
• Pack in hot jars; adjust lids. Process in boiling water bath (212°) 5 minutes. Remove jars and complete seals unless closures are self-sealing type. Makes 6 to 7 pints.

Variation

DILLED ZUCCHINI PICKLES: Substitute 2 tsp. dill seeds for turmeric.

RED PEPPER RELISH

Lemon gives this relish of ripe, sweet peppers a fruity taste

12 medium red peppers
2 c. chopped onions
2 c. white vinegar
3 c. sugar
4 tsp. salt
1 lemon, sliced
4 tsp. whole allspice
½ tsp. ground ginger

• Remove stems and seeds from peppers. Cover peppers with boiling water; let stand 5 minutes; drain. Repeat; drain well. Then put through coarse blade of food chopper. Should measure about 4 c.
• Combine all ingredients (tie spices in cloth bag). Boil 30 minutes. Let stand overnight.
• Bring to boil; simmer 10 minutes. Pour at once into hot pint jars; adjust lids. Process in boiling water bath (212°) 10 minutes. Remove jars and complete seals unless closures are self-sealing type. Makes about 3 pints.

PICKLED BEETS

Slice beets with corrugated cutter to give them a fancy look

24 small beets
1 c. cooking liquid
1 pt. vinegar
1¼ c. sugar
2 tblsp. salt
6 whole cloves
1 (3″) stick cinnamon
3 medium onions, sliced

• Remove beet tops, leaving roots and 1″ stems. Cover with boiling water; cook until tender. Drain, reserving 1 c. cooking liquid. Remove skins; slice.
• Combine cooking liquid, vinegar, sugar and salt. Add spices tied in a cheesecloth bag. Heat to boiling point.
• Add beets and onions. Simmer 5 minutes. Remove spice bag. Continue simmering while quickly packing beets and onions into one hot pint jar at a time. Fill to within ½″ of jar top. Adjust lids. Process in boiling water bath (212°) 10 minutes.
• Remove jars from canner and complete seals unless closures are self-sealing type. Makes 4 pints.

Note: Sliced beets may be cut in fancy shapes. "Save the scraps," a Minnesota country cook suggests. "Chop or grind them and combine with shredded cabbage for salad. Add a little horse-radish to the salad dressing."

Blender-made Ketchup

One Wisconsin country woman lets her blender chop the vegetables when she makes ketchup. She practically eliminates pot watching and stirring by cooking the tomato mixture in the oven. If you have an electric saucepan, oven roaster or a controlled surface unit or burner on your range, it also will cut out the necessity of constant watching and stirring.

BLENDER KETCHUP

Use dead-ripe tomatoes, white vinegar, and spices tied in cloth bag

48 medium tomatoes (about 8 lbs.)
2 ripe sweet red peppers
2 sweet green peppers
4 onions
3 c. vinegar
3 c. sugar
3 tblsp. salt
3 tsp. dry mustard
½ tsp. ground red pepper
½ tsp. whole allspice
1½ tsp. whole cloves
1½ tsp. broken stick cinnamon

· Quarter tomatoes; remove stem ends. Add peppers, seeded and cut in strips, and onions, peeled and quartered. Mix.
· Put vegetables in blender container, filling jar ¾ full. Blend at high speed 4 seconds; pour into large kettle. Repeat until all vegetables are blended.
· Add vinegar, sugar, salt, dry mustard, red pepper and remaining spices, tied loosely in thin muslin bag. Simmer, uncovered, in slow oven (325°) or in electric saucepan until volume is reduced one half. Remove spices.
· Pour into hot jars. Adjust lids. Process in boiling water bath (212°) 10 minutes. Remove jars and complete seals unless closures are self-sealing type. Makes 5 pints.

Variation

BLENDER APPLE/TOMATO KETCHUP: Add 2 c. thick applesauce to the cooked ketchup and mix thoroughly.

KETCHUP WITHOUT BLENDER

· Use same ingredients as in recipe above.
· Quarter tomatoes, peel onions and discard stems and seeds from peppers. Chop. Cook until tender, about 15 minutes. Put through sieve or food mill.
· Add remaining ingredients and simmer until you have half the amount you started with, or the consistency you like. The yield is less than if you use the blender. Recipe makes 3 pints.

Variation

APPLE/TOMATO KETCHUP: Add about 1 c. thick applesauce.

BEST-EVER BREAD-AND-BUTTERS

The ice cubes help keep the thin cucumber slices from breaking

4 qts. sliced cucumbers (40 to 50)
½ c. salt
Ice cubes
2 qts. sliced onions
1 qt. vinegar
4 c. sugar
1 tblsp. celery seeds
2 tblsp. mustard seeds
1 tblsp. ground ginger
1 tsp. ground turmeric (optional)
½ tsp. white pepper (optional)

· Gently stir salt into thinly sliced cucumbers. Cover with ice cubes; let stand 2 or 3 hours or until cucumbers are crisp and cold. Add more ice if it melts. Drain; add onions.
· Combine remaining ingredients; bring quickly to a boil and boil 10 minutes.
· Add cucumber and onion slices and bring to boiling point. Pack at

once in hot jars. Adjust lids. Process in boiling water bath (212°) 30 minutes.

• Remove jars from canner and complete seals unless closures are self-sealing type. Makes 8 pints.

FISH FRY CHOW-CHOW

Perfect to serve with any fish

5 lbs. cucumbers (6 large)
6 medium onions
¼ c. salt
2½ c. white vinegar
1 c. dark brown sugar, firmly packed
1 c. light brown sugar, firmly packed
2 tblsp. prepared mustard
4 tsp. ground turmeric
4 tsp. cornstarch
1 (4 oz.) jar pimiento, drained and chopped
1 medium green pepper, chopped

• Peel and cut cucumbers in ¼" slices. Slice onions thinly. Place in bowl and sprinkle with salt. Cover; refrigerate overnight.

• Drain off any liquid. Chop cucumbers and onions.

• Combine vinegar and sugars. Blend together mustard, turmeric and cornstarch. Add enough vinegar mixture to make a thin paste. Stir paste into vinegar mixture. Bring to a boil, stirring frequently. Add cucumbers and onions; bring to a full rolling boil. Add pimiento and green pepper.

• Ladle into hot jars; adjust lids. Process in boiling water bath (212°) 5 minutes. Remove jars and complete seals unless closures are self-sealing type. Makes 5 pints.

SHORT-CUT CHILI SAUCE

Swirl some of this into baked beans

3 qts. chopped peeled tomatoes
3 c. chopped celery
2 c. chopped onions
1 c. chopped green pepper
¼ c. salt
2 c. sugar
¼ c. brown sugar, firmly packed
1½ tsp. pepper
1½ tsp. mixed pickling spices
1 c. white vinegar

• Combine tomatoes, celery, onions, green pepper and salt. Let stand overnight. Drain in colander, but do not press vegetables.

• Place vegetable mixture in large kettle and add sugars, pepper, pickling spices tied in a cheesecloth bag and vinegar. Bring to a boil; reduce heat and simmer, uncovered, 15 minutes. Remove spices.

• Ladle into hot jars; adjust lids. Process in boiling water bath (212°) 10 minutes. Remove jars and complete seals unless closures are self-sealing type. Makes 5½ pints.

SWEET CORN RELISH

Go-along with almost any meat

10 c. fresh, frozen or canned whole kernel corn
7 c. shredded cabbage
2 c. chopped onions
¾ c. chopped green pepper
¾ c. chopped sweet red pepper
2 tblsp. dry mustard
1½ tsp. flour
½ tsp. ground turmeric
4 c. cider vinegar
2 c. sugar
2 tblsp. salt

• Combine corn, cabbage, onions, green and red pepper in a large kettle.

• Mix together mustard, flour and turmeric. Add ¼ c. vinegar to mustard mixture; stir to blend well. Add mustard mixture, remaining vinegar, sugar and salt to vegetables, mixing well.

· Bring vegetables to a boil; reduce heat and simmer, uncovered, 15 minutes. Ladle into hot jars; adjust lids. Process in boiling water bath (212°) 15 minutes. Remove jars and complete seals unless closures are self-sealing type. Makes 8 pints.

MINTED ONION RINGS

Delicious with lamb or veal—they make you want to grow more mint

1 qt. vinegar
¼ c. sugar
2 c. fresh mint leaves, or ¼ c. dried mint flakes
Few drops green food color
4 c. peeled, sliced onions
4 pimientos, thinly sliced

· Combine vinegar, sugar and mint, tied in cheesecloth, in saucepan. Heat gently 10 minutes; remove from heat.

· Stir in food color. Add onions and pimientos; heat to boiling. Remove mint. Pour into hot jars; adjust lids. Process in boiling water bath (212°) 5 minutes. Remove jars and complete seals unless closures are self-sealing type. Makes 4 half pints.

Variation

PEPPER ONION RINGS: Substitute 4 sweet red peppers, thinly sliced, for the pimientos.

PICKLED ONIONS

Quick and easy version of the old-fashioned onion pickles. Good!

4 qts. small onions
1 c. salt
¼ c. pickling spices
2 qts. vinegar
2 c. sugar

· Peel onions. Add salt and let stand overnight.

· In the morning, put in colander and rinse thoroughly with cold water to remove all salt. Drain.

· Tie spices loosely in a bag; boil 10 minutes with vinegar and sugar. Discard spices.

· Pack onions into hot jars. Pour boiling hot vinegar mixture over. Adjust lids. Process in boiling water bath (212°) 5 minutes. Remove jars and complete seals unless closures are self-sealing type. Makes 8 pints.

GREEN TOMATO PICKLES

Sliced pickles are spicy and sharp with a sweet tang—tasty

2 qts. sliced green tomatoes
3 tblsp. salt
2 c. vinegar
⅔ c. dark brown sugar, firmly packed
1 c. sugar
3 tblsp. mustard seeds
½ tsp. celery seeds
1 tsp. ground turmeric
3 c. sliced onions
2 large, sweet red peppers, chopped
1 hot green or red pepper, chopped

· Mix tomatoes and salt. Let stand about 12 hours. Drain.

· Heat vinegar, sugars and spices to a boil; add sliced onions and boil gently 5 minutes. Add the drained tomatoes and peppers; bring slowly to a boil. Simmer 5 minutes, stirring occasionally with a wooden spoon.

· Pack into hot jars. Be sure syrup covers vegetables. Adjust lids. Process in boiling water bath (212°) 5 minutes. Remove jars and complete seals unless closures are self-sealing type. Makes 9 half pints.

INDIAN PICKLE

Splendid way to salvage green tomatoes—sells well at bazaars

4 lbs. green tomatoes
4 lbs. ripe tomatoes, peeled
3 medium onions, peeled
3 sweet red peppers, seeded
3 green peppers, seeded
1 large cucumber
7 c. chopped celery
⅔ c. salt
3 pts. vinegar
3 lbs. brown sugar
1 tsp. dry mustard
1 tsp. white pepper

• Chop coarsely all the vegetables. Sprinkle with salt and let stand 12 hours or overnight.
• In the morning, drain well, discard liquid and add remaining ingredients.
• Bring to a boil and simmer slowly about 30 minutes, stirring occasionally. Pour into hot jars; adjust lids. Process in boiling water bath (212°) 5 minutes. Remove jars and complete seals unless closures are self-sealing type. Makes about 6 pints.

EASY SWEET DILLS

If you're tired of your dill pickles, make these treats from them

2 qts. dill pickles, sliced (8 to 10 pickles)
4 cloves garlic, crushed (optional)
2⅓ c. vinegar
2 tblsp. whole allspice
1 tblsp. peppercorns
4 c. sugar
1 c. brown sugar, firmly packed

• Drain dill pickles.
• Make a pickling syrup of garlic, vinegar, spices and sugars. Simmer 5 minutes. Add pickle slices; heat to a boil.
• Pack in hot jars; adjust lids. Process in boiling water bath (212°) 5 minutes. Remove jars and complete seals unless closures are self-sealing type. Makes 2 quarts.

EXTRA-GOOD SWEET DILL PICKLES

Use dill-size cucumbers. Short on cooking time; long on flavor

6 cucumbers
Ice water
Onion slices or clove garlic
Dill, fresh or dried
1 c. sugar
1 c. water
1 pt. vinegar
⅓ c. salt

• Soak whole cucumbers in ice water 3 to 4 hours. Drain. Slice or cut in strips. Place in hot jars along with onions and a generous amount of dill.
• Combine sugar, water, vinegar and salt; bring to boil. Pour over pickles to within ½" from jar top. Adjust lids. Process in boiling water bath (212°) 20 minutes (start to count the processing time as soon as hot jars are placed into the actively boiling water). Remove jars from canner and complete seals unless closures are self-sealing. Makes 3 pints.

FRESH-PACK DILLS

Speedy way to make crisp dills

17 to 18 lbs. (3 to 5") cucumbers
1½ c. salt
2 gals. water
6 c. vinegar
¾ c. salt
¼ c. sugar
9 c. water
2 tblsp. whole pickling spices
Dill heads, fresh or dried
Whole mustard seeds

• Wash cucumbers; cover with brine made by adding 1½ c. salt to 2 gallons water. Let stand overnight. Drain.

• Combine vinegar, ¾ c. salt, sugar, 9 c. water and pickling spices, tied loosely in cloth bag. Heat to boiling.

• Pack cucumbers into hot quart jars. Add 3 dill heads and 2 tsp. mustard seeds to each jar. Pour boiling vinegar mixture, spice bag removed, over cucumbers to within ½″ of jar tops. Adjust lids. Process in boiling water bath (212°) 20 minutes.

• Remove jars from canner and complete seals unless closures are self-sealing type. Makes 7 quarts.

FERMENTED DILL PICKLES

Best-liked FARM JOURNAL *dill pickles*

20 lbs. (3½ to 5½″) cucumbers (about ½ bushel)
½ c. whole mixed pickling spices
2 to 3 bunches fresh dill
2 c. vinegar
1½ c. salt
2 gals. water
10 to 20 cloves garlic, peeled (optional)

• Cover cucumbers with cold water. Wash thoroughly, using a vegetable brush, handling gently to avoid bruising. Take care to remove any blossoms. Drain on rack or wipe dry.

• Place half the pickle spices and a layer of dill in a 5-gallon crock or stone jar. Fill with cucumbers to 3 to 4″ from top of crock. Mix vinegar, salt and water and pour over the cucumbers. Place a layer of dill and remaining spices over the top of cucumbers. Add garlic, if you wish.

• Cover with a heavy china or glass plate or lid that fits inside the crock and use a weight, such as a glass jar filled with water on top of the cover to keep cucumbers under the brine. Cover loosely with clean cloth. Keep pickles at room temperature and remove film daily when formed. Film may start forming in 3 to 5 days. Do not stir pickles around in jar but be sure they are completely covered with brine, using original proportions.

• In about 3 weeks the cucumbers become olive-green and any white spots inside the fermented cucumbers will be eliminated by processing.

• Pack the pickles, along with some of the dill, into clean, hot jars; add garlic, if desired. Cover with boiling brine to ½″ of top of jar. Adjust lids. Put jars into canner containing boiling water; be sure the water comes an inch or two over the jar tops. Cover the canner tightly and start to count the processing time. Continue heating and process for 15 minutes.

• Remove jars from canner immediately. Set jars on a wire rack several inches apart to cool. Complete seals unless closures are self-sealing type. Makes 9 to 10 quarts.

Note: Use of garlic gives dills the flavor of pickles sold in delicatessens. The original brine is usually cloudy as a result of yeast development during the fermentation period. If this cloudiness is objectionable, fresh brine may be used to cover the pickles when packing them. Make it with the same proportions of vinegar, salt and water as in the original brine. The fermentation brine is generally preferred for added flavor; it should be strained and heated to boiling.

14-DAY SWEET PICKLES

Adaptation of an heirloom recipe long prized in country kitchens

3½ qts. (2") pickling cucumbers (4 lbs.)
1 c. coarse pickling salt
2 qts. boiling water
½ tsp. powdered alum
5 c. vinegar
3 c. sugar
1½ tsp. celery seeds
4 (2") sticks cinnamon
1½ c. sugar

• Wash cucumbers carefully; cut in lengthwise halves and place in stone crock, glass, pottery or enamel-lined (unchipped) pan.

• Prepare brine by dissolving salt in boiling water; pour over cucumbers. Weight cucumbers down with a plate almost as large as the crock and lay a stone or paraffined brick (not marble or limestone) on plate to keep cucumbers under the brine. Let stand 1 week.

• On the 8th day, drain; pour 2 qts. fresh boiling water over cucumbers. Let stand 24 hours.

• On the 9th day, drain; pour 2 qts. fresh boiling water mixed with alum over cucumbers. Let stand 24 hours.

• On the 10th day, drain; pour 2 qts. fresh boiling water over cucumbers. Let stand 24 hours.

• The next day, drain. Combine vinegar, 3 c. sugar, celery seeds and cinnamon; heat to boiling point and pour over cucumbers.

• For the next 3 days, drain, retaining liquid. Reheat this liquid each morning, adding ½ c. sugar each time. After the last heating, on the 14th day, pack pickles into hot jars. Remove cinnamon sticks; pour boiling hot liquid over pickles; adjust lids. Process in boiling water bath (212°) 5 minutes. Remove jars and complete seals unless closures are self-sealing type. Makes 5 to 6 pints.

ICICLE PICKLES

The color of these sweet pickles is exceptionally good—so is the taste

4 qts. (3") cucumbers
2 c. salt
1 gal. boiling water
1½ tblsp. powdered alum
2½ qts. vinegar
5 lbs. sugar
2 tblsp. whole allspice

• Cut cucumbers in quarters, lengthwise. Dissolve salt in boiling water; pour over cucumbers in crock; weight down with plate; let stand 1 week.

• Drain; add 1 gal. fresh boiling water; let stand 24 hours; drain. Add alum to 1 gal. fresh boiling water; pour over pickles; let stand 24 hours; drain.

• To make syrup, combine vinegar, sugar and allspice; heat to boiling and boil 20 minutes. Pour over cucumbers in crock. Let stand 3 days.

• Pack pickles in hot, sterilized jars; reheat syrup to boiling; boil 10 minutes; pour over pickles. Seal at once. Process in boiling water bath (212° F.) 5 minutes. Makes 5 pints.

CRISP PICKLES

Easy to make—but they take 10 days

10 medium cucumbers
Water
8 c. sugar
1 qt. vinegar
5 tblsp. salt
2 tblsp. mixed whole pickling spices
2 tsp. celery seeds

• Cover cucumbers with boiling water. Let stand overnight. Drain. Repeat process for 4 successive days (add fresh boiling water, let stand overnight and drain).

· On the 6th morning, slice cucumbers into ¼ to ½″ slices.

· To make syrup, combine sugar, vinegar, salt and spices, loosely tied in cheesecloth bag, and heat to boiling. Pour over slices. Let stand overnight.

· The next morning, drain the vinegar syrup, reheat to boiling and again pour over the cucumber slices. Repeat this process 3 more days.

· On the tenth day, pack slices in one hot, sterilized jar at a time. Bring syrup to a boil; remove spices. Pour hot syrup over slices in jars one at a time, filling to the top. Seal each at once. Process in boiling water bath (212° F.) 5 minutes. Makes 5 pints.

chapter 11

Desserts for All Seasons

COUNTRY WOMEN tune their desserts to the seasons. Lemon Mist with cheerful Sunshine Sauce is a saga of spring. So are Molded Rhubarb Swirl and Strawberry Shortcake Royale with velvety ice cream sauce.

Summer features such delights as Fresh Blueberry and Fresh Peach Cobblers—country favorites as tasty as pie but easier to make, fresh fruit compotes, and homemade ice creams and sherbets so cool and smooth.

In harmony with autumn are treats like plump apple dumplings, Chunky Cider Applesauce and Snowy Apple Squares (a kind of big pie baked in a jelly roll pan), and apple-cranberry specials.

Winter fills country kitchens with the come-hither aroma of gingerbread (see our special recipes for it), Pumpkin Pudding Cake and Sweet Potato Pudding. Flaming Plum Pudding is a traditional Christmas dessert, sometimes challenged by such lusciousness as Cherries on Snow.

This chapter also contains new-type, year-round desserts, many of them made from frozen fruits and ice cream kept on hand in home freezers. It also presents updated versions of old-fashioned classics, such as Custard Bread Pudding, Apple Tapioca and a variety of rice puddings.

Let this collection of recipes lead you through a whole year of wonderful country desserts. Your family and friends will compliment you, and guests will beg for your recipes. Start your campaign with our chilled fruit desserts which follow.

Gorgeous Fresh Fruit Compotes

Country women excel with fruit desserts. When berries, peaches, pears and other fruits are in season, country cooks usually have a supply grown on their own land or from neighbors who share their surplus. Fruit compotes are gaining prestige not only because they look beautiful and have refreshing flavors, but also because they are so easily made without heating the kitchen and are lower in calories than many desserts.

You can mix the fruits or layer them in a large glass bowl. A generous-sized brandy snifter makes a fascinating container for compotes on the buffet table and to tote to potluck suppers. This also answers handsomely for a centerpiece.

By marinating the fruits in flavored syrups you come up with some marvelous tastes. These syrups also are good on ice cream. Here are recipes for a basic Fresh Fruit Compote with Maraschino Cherry Sauce along with compotes featuring fresh strawberries, peaches and pears. Some country women use frozen berries and peaches or drained canned fruits when fresh are not available.

FRESH FRUIT COMPOTE

Substitute any fresh fruits in season —green grapes, for instance

2 (3 oz.) pkgs. cream cheese
½ c. pecans, finely chopped
2 c. pitted Bing cherry halves
2 c. pitted plums, cut in quarters
1 c. Maraschino Cherry Sauce
2 bananas
2 c. red raspberries, washed and drained

• Soften cream cheese; roll into very small balls; coat with nuts. Cover and refrigerate.

• Fold together cherries, plums and Maraschino Cherry Sauce. Cover and refrigerate until serving time.

• Slice bananas (if you take this to a potluck, dip slices in lemon juice). Fold bananas and raspberries into fruit mixture. Spoon into large glass bowl. Top with cream cheese balls or place a few cream cheese balls on individual servings of fruit. Makes 10 to 12 servings.

MARASCHINO CHERRY SAUCE: In a saucepan, combine ¾ c. sugar and 1 tblsp. cornstarch. Stir in ¼ c. light corn syrup, ¼ c. maraschino cherry juice, ¼ c. strained orange juice and ½ c. water.

• Bring to boil and cook about 3 minutes until sauce is clear and slightly syrupy. Remove from heat. Chop 6 maraschino cherries, then crush with fork (skins will pop off; remove them). Add crushed cherries and 3 drops red food color to sauce. Refrigerate in covered container. Makes 1¼ cups.

PEARS IN MINT SAUCE

Light, cooling dessert refreshes on lazy, warm summer days

4 fresh ripe pears
½ c. Mint Sauce
1 c. fresh blackberries (optional)

• Peel pears and slice thinly. Coat slices with Mint Sauce. Refrigerate in covered container about 2 hours.

• Spoon pear slices into dessert dishes; garnish with fresh blackberries. Makes 4 servings.

MINT SAUCE: In small saucepan, mix ¾ c. sugar and 1 tblsp. cornstarch. Stir in ¼ c. light corn syrup and 1 c. water. Bring to boil and simmer about 3 minutes until sauce is clear and slightly syrupy. Remove from heat; stir in 1 tblsp. lemon juice, 8 drops oil of peppermint (or ½ tsp. peppermint extract) and 6 drops green food color. Store in covered container in refrigerator. Makes 1¼ cups.

STRAWBERRIES WITH ORANGE MOLD

Charming party dessert—lovely colors, wonderful flavor blend

1 qt. orange ice or sherbet
1 qt. fresh whole strawberries
½ c. Maraschino Cherry Sauce (see Index)

• Soften orange ice or sherbet; stir until smooth. Spoon into 8 individual molds that have been rinsed with ice water. Freeze. (Or freeze scoops of sherbet on metal tray until very firm.)

• Wash and hull strawberries. Refrigerate until serving time.

• To serve, place individual serving dishes in freezer until very cold. Unmold orange ice into cold serving dishes by wrapping a cloth dipped in warm water around each mold. Spoon ½ c. whole strawberries and 1 tblsp. Maraschino Cherry Sauce over each serving. (If you are a wine cook, try 2 tblsp. port wine instead of the cherry sauce.) Serve quickly. Makes 8 servings.

PEACHES IN MARASCHINO CHERRY SAUCE

Dreamy, light dessert—ideal for ending a warm-weather meal

4 large fresh peaches
½ c. Maraschino Cherry Sauce (see Index)
½ c. green grapes, cut in halves (optional)

• Peel and slice fresh peaches. Combine with Maraschino Cherry Sauce. Store in covered container in refrigerator until serving time. Fold in grapes. Makes 4 servings.

PEARS CARDINALE

Fruit is tinted an attractive red in this pretty, light dessert

1 (10 oz.) pkg. frozen red raspberries in syrup
1 (1 lb. 13 oz.) can large pear halves, chilled
2 tblsp. cornstarch
¼ c. sugar
2 tblsp. toasted slivered almonds

• Defrost raspberries. Drain well, reserving liquid. Drain pear halves, reserving liquid.

• Pour liquid from drained raspberries into a 1-cup measure. Add enough pear liquid to make 1 c.

• Mix cornstarch and sugar in a small saucepan. Gradually stir in the 1 c. fruit liquid. Cook over moderate heat, stirring constantly, until clear and thickened. Simmer gently for 3 minutes. Cool to room temperature.

• Fill cavities of pear halves with well drained raspberries and invert in individual glass serving dishes. Allow 1 pear half per serving.

• Spoon raspberry glaze over pear halves. Sprinkle toasted almonds over glazed pears. Refrigerate until serving time (up to 2 hours). Makes about 7 servings, depending on number of pear halves in can.

CHUNKY CIDER APPLESAUCE

You can add some heavy cream and a shake of cinnamon—yummy

- **9 c. sliced peeled apples**
- **½ c. apple cider**
- **1 tblsp. lemon juice**
- **½ c. sugar**
- **⅛ tsp. salt**
- **½ tsp. ground nutmeg**

• Combine apples, cider and lemon juice in 3-qt. saucepan. Bring to boil over medium heat and simmer until apples are tender, about 20 minutes.

• Add sugar, salt and nutmeg; cook 1 minute longer. Break up apples into chunks. Cool and refrigerate until serving time. Makes about 1 quart.

Popular Make-ahead Desserts

Refrigerator and freezer desserts enjoy great prestige on country tables today. Delicious taste and good looks have something to do with their popularity, but busy women especially rejoice that you can make them ahead and avoid some of the last-minute rush in getting meals. Swiss Strawberry Rice is simple and a farm family favorite that's at its best thoroughly chilled. If you have ripe strawberries, sugar them a little and use instead of frozen berries.

SWISS STRAWBERRY RICE

Use fresh berries when in season

- **1 c. uncooked rice**
- **3 c. milk**
- **½ c. sugar**
- **½ tsp. salt**
- **2 eggs, beaten**
- **½ c. heavy cream**
- **1 tsp. almond extract**
- **1 (10 oz.) pkg. frozen sliced strawberries**

• Cook rice in milk in top of double boiler until tender, stirring occasionally, about 1 hour. Add sugar and salt.

• Add a little hot mixture gradually to beaten eggs. Stir eggs into remaining hot mixture. Blend well; cook 1 minute and cool.

• Whip cream; add almond extract and fold into rice. Chill. Serve with partly thawed strawberries. Makes 6 servings.

RASPBERRY/RICE SURPRISE

New kind of honeyed rice pudding

- **1 c. uncooked rice**
- **3 c. boiling water**
- **¾ tsp. salt**
- **½ c. sugar**
- **2 tblsp. honey**
- **¼ tsp. almond extract**
- **1 c. heavy cream, whipped**
- **1 tblsp. cornstarch**
- **½ c. sugar**
- **¼ c. cold water**
- **2 c. red raspberries**
- **1 tblsp. lemon juice**

• Cook rice in boiling water with salt added until tender and fluffy (liquid should be absorbed by rice). Blend in ½ c. sugar, honey and almond extract. Chill. Fold in whipped cream.

17. MOLDED RHUBARB SWIRL—Celebrate spring with this dazzling pink, red and white mold made with rhubarb and strawberry gelatin flavor. Recipe, page 313.

18. HOMEMADE ICE CREAM—Pictured from top to bottom: Grape, Cinnamon, Coffee/Walnut and basic Vanilla Ice Cream. All come from one recipe, page 316.

19. GLORIFIED RICE PUDDING—This airy lemon-rice soufflé is a new version of rice pudding. Serve it pronto to prevent a collapse. Recipe, page 332.

20. FUDGE/LEMON CAKE and TWO-TONE POUND CAKE—The chocolate-lemon flavor is superb; cocoa gives pound cake a new look and taste. Recipes, pages 355, 387.

• To make sauce, mix cornstarch and ½ c. sugar. Add cold water and stir until smooth. Add raspberries and lemon juice. Bring to a boil; reduce heat and simmer 5 minutes. Chill. Top each serving of rice with raspberry sauce. Makes 6 servings.

ORANGE TAPIOCA PUDDING

A gay-as-sunshine company dessert

2 eggs, separated
6 tblsp. sugar
2 c. milk
3 tblsp. quick-cooking tapioca
¼ tsp. salt
1 tblsp. grated orange peel
1 tblsp. lemon juice
Mandarin oranges
Flaked coconut
Orange sherbet

• Beat egg whites until foamy. Gradually add 3 tblsp. sugar. Beat until soft peaks form.
• Beat yolks slightly. Add milk, 3 tblsp. sugar, tapioca, salt and orange peel. Bring to boil over low heat, stirring.
• Remove from heat. Add lemon juice. Slowly add a little hot mixture to egg whites; mix well. Quickly stir in remaining mixture. Pour into dessert dishes. Chill. Garnish with mandarin or fresh orange sections, coconut and sherbet. Makes 6 to 8 servings.

FROSTY APPLE DESSERT

Frozen rose-tinted applesauce treat

3 c. applesauce
¾ c. sugar
2 tblsp. lemon juice
¼ tsp. salt
Red food color
3 c. heavy cream
Cranberry Topping

• Combine applesauce, sugar, lemon juice and salt. Stir in a few drops of red food color.
• Whip cream; fold into apple mixture. Pour into 2-qt. baking dish. Cover and freeze until firm.
• Remove from freezer and whip until fluffy. Refreeze. Spoon Cranberry Topping over each serving. Serves 10 to 12.

CRANBERRY TOPPING: Combine 1 tblsp. cornstarch, ¼ c. sugar and ½ c. water. Bring to a boil. Add 1 c. canned whole cranberry sauce; cook until thick and clear. Cool. Makes about 1½ cups.

RASPBERRY DESSERT

Excellent to fix ahead for a crowd

2 (10 oz.) pkgs. frozen red raspberries in syrup
1 c. water
½ c. sugar
2 tsp. lemon juice
4 tblsp. cornstarch
¼ c. cold water
50 regular marshmallows
1 c. milk
2 c. heavy cream, or 2 envelopes dessert topping mix
1¼ c. graham cracker crumbs
¼ c. chopped nuts
¼ c. melted butter

• Heat raspberries with 1 c. water, sugar and lemon juice.
• Dissolve cornstarch in ¼ c. cold water; stir into raspberries and cook until thickened and clear. Cool.
• Melt marshmallows in milk over boiling water; cool thoroughly.
• Whip heavy cream or dessert topping mix and fold into marshmallow mixture.
• Mix graham cracker crumbs, nuts

and butter in a 13 × 9 × 2″ pan. Press firmly into bottom of pan.

• Spread marshmallow-cream mixture over crumbs. Spread raspberry mixture over top. Refrigerate until firm. Makes 15 to 18 servings.

REFRIGERATOR CAKE

End dinner the chocolate-cream way

- **2 (4 oz.) bars sweet cooking chocolate**
- **5 eggs, separated**
- **1 tsp. vanilla**
- **12 lady fingers**
- **1 c. heavy cream**

• Melt chocolate in top of double boiler over boiling water.

• Beat egg yolks well; add vanilla and yolks to chocolate; beat well.

• Beat egg whites until stiff; fold into chocolate mixture.

• Line a 1-qt. bowl or mold with waxed paper. Pour a little chocolate mixture into bottom of mold.

• Line sides of bowl with lady finger halves, pushing ends into filling to keep upright. Add layer of lady fingers, then remaining filling. Top with lady fingers. Refrigerate 12 to 24 hours.

• Unmold on dish. Remove paper.

• Whip cream. Add frills with cake decorator or spread cream over dessert. (For buffet serving, cut cake into pieces before adding whipped cream. Dip knife into hot water before cutting each slice.) Makes 8 servings.

Frozen Summer Desserts

With a frozen dessert in the freezer, you're always ready to treat company or your family regardless of how busy you are. You can keep Velvety Lime Squares, Vanilla Almond Crunch and Raspberry Swirl, frozen and then snugly wrapped in foil, in your freezer for weeks. They will be easier to cut if you allow them to stand at room temperature 20 minutes before cutting and serving.

VELVETY LIME SQUARES

You can thaw this several hours in refrigerator before serving

- **1 (3 oz.) can flaked coconut**
- **½ c. vanilla wafer crumbs**
- **2 tblsp. melted butter**
- **2 tblsp. sugar**
- **2 (3 oz.) pkgs. lime flavor gelatin**
- **2 c. boiling water**
- **1 (6 oz.) can frozen limeade concentrate**
- **Few drops green food color**
- **1 qt. plus 1 pt. vanilla ice cream, softened**
- **⅛ tsp. salt**
- **Pecans (optional)**

• Carefully toast ½ c. coconut in moderate oven (375°) about 5 minutes, until lightly browned. Set aside.

• Combine remaining coconut, crumbs, butter and sugar. Lightly press into 11 × 7 × 1½″ pan and bake in moderate oven (375°) 6 to 7 minutes. Cool.

• Dissolve gelatin in boiling water. Add limeade concentrate, food color, ice cream and salt; stir until dissolved. Pour into crust. Top with reserved toasted coconut and garnish with pecans, if you wish. Freeze until firm. Cover tightly. Return to freezer. Serves 6 to 8.

VANILLA ALMOND CRUNCH

Try serving with chocolate sauce

1 (4 oz.) pkg. slivered almonds
¼ c. melted butter
1 c. crushed rice cereal squares
½ c. light brown sugar, firmly packed
½ c. flaked coconut
⅛ tsp. salt
½ gal. vanilla ice cream, softened

• Toast almonds in the melted butter. Remove half of almonds from butter and set aside.

• Combine crushed cereal, brown sugar, coconut and salt with remaining almonds and butter. Pat mixture gently into 13 × 9 × 2″ pan. Bake in moderate (375°) oven 5 minutes. Cool.

• Spread ice cream over cooled crust. Decorate top with reserved almonds. Freeze until firm. Cover tightly, and return to freezer. Makes 10 servings.

RASPBERRY SWIRL

Undertones of creamy cheesecake make this an all-season favorite dessert

¾ c. graham cracker crumbs
3 tblsp. melted butter
2 tblsp. sugar
3 eggs, separated
1 (8 oz.) pkg. cream cheese
1 c. sugar
⅛ tsp. salt
1 c. heavy cream
1 (10 oz.) pkg. frozen raspberries, partially thawed

• Thoroughly combine crumbs, melted butter and 2 tblsp. sugar. Lightly press mixture into well greased 11 × 7 × 1½″ pan. Bake in moderate oven (375°) about 8 minutes. Cool completely.

• Beat egg yolks until thick. Add cream cheese, sugar and salt; beat until smooth and light.

• Beat egg whites until stiff peaks form.

• Whip cream until stiff and fold with egg whites into cheese mixture.

• In a mixer or blender, crush raspberries to a pulp. Gently swirl half of fruit pulp through cheese filling; spread mixture into crust. Spoon remaining purée over top; swirl with a knife. Freeze, then cover and return to freezer. Makes 6 to 8 servings.

CRISPY SUNDAE CRUNCH

Delicious make-ahead dessert with ice cream between crisp crusts

2 tblsp. butter
¼ c. light brown sugar, firmly packed
1 c. oven-toasted rice cereal, crushed
⅓ c. walnuts
⅓ c. flaked coconut
1 qt. vanilla ice cream

• Melt butter in skillet; add brown sugar and heat slowly, stirring until blended. Add crushed rice cereal. Toss well to coat with butter-sugar mixture. Remove from heat; add nuts and coconut.

• Reserve ⅔ c. cereal mixture for topping. Spread remaining cereal mixture into an 8″ square pan. Spread ice cream on top. Sprinkle the ⅔ c. cereal mixture over the ice cream. Freeze. Cut in squares to serve. Makes 9 servings.

Variation

CRISPY SUNDAE CRUNCH FOR A CROWD: Double the recipe; use a

13 × 9 × 2″ pan. Reserve 1⅓ c. cereal mixture to spread over top of ice cream. Makes 18 servings.

FROZEN STRAWBERRY FLUFF

Easy to make with an electric mixer

1¼ c. crisp cookie crumbs
⅓ c. butter
2 egg whites
1 tblsp. lemon juice
1⅓ c. sugar
2 c. fresh strawberries
1 c. heavy cream, whipped

• Mix crumbs and butter; press into bottom of buttered 9″ square pan or 7″ round spring-form pan. Bake in moderate oven (350°) 8 minutes. Cool.

• Beat egg whites and lemon juice slightly in large bowl of electric mixer; gradually beat in sugar and berries. Beat at high speed 12 to 15 minutes, until mixture is fluffy and has large volume.

• Fold in whipped cream. Spread over crumb crust. Freeze overnight. Cut in squares or wedges to serve. Garnish with fresh berries. Makes 9 servings.

Variations

PEACH FLUFF: Use 2 c. sliced ripe peaches instead of strawberries. Garnish with peach slices.

RASPBERRY FLUFF: Use fresh raspberries instead of strawberries.

BLUEBERRY FLUFF: Use fresh blueberries instead of strawberries.

CALORIE-CUTTING FRUIT FLUFF: Substitute whipped nonfat dry milk for whipped cream. Sprinkle ½ c. nonfat dry milk over ½ c. ice water. Add 1 tblsp. lemon juice and beat until stiff.

DOUBLE-FROZEN FLUFF: Instead of fresh berries or peaches, use 1 (10 oz.) pkg. sweetened frozen berries or peaches; use 1 c. sugar instead of 1⅓ cups.

SHORT-CUT STRAWBERRY FLUFF: Omit the buttered crumbs. Prepare the Strawberry Fluff as directed and spread in a 9″ square pan. Freeze. Cut in squares or wedges and serve with angel food cake.

MINCEMEAT/LEMON STACK CAKE

Keep this dessert on hand and you'll be ready for last-minute company

1 (18½ oz.) pkg. lemon cake mix
Confectioners sugar
1 c. mincemeat
1 qt. vanilla ice cream, softened

• Prepare cake as directed on package. Bake in paper-lined 15½ × 10½ × 1″ jelly roll pan. Chill or let stand several hours so tender cake may be easily handled. Invert onto a piece of heavy-duty aluminum foil, dusted with confectioners sugar; carefully remove paper from cake. Cut cake crosswise in half.

• Blend mincemeat into softened ice cream. Quickly spread on one cake half. Invert other cake half onto ice cream; use foil to assist in turning one half over the other.

• Quickly cut cake into 12 pieces. Freeze; wrap well. Move dessert from freezer to refrigerator a half hour before serving. Serve with a tart lemon sauce, warmed. Makes 12 servings.

BANANA SPLITS

Ideal dessert to serve a crowd

- 30 ripe bananas
- 2 gals. strawberry ice cream (or other flavor)
- Marshmallow Sauce
- 1 lb. chopped nuts

· Peel bananas and slice into 50 sauce dishes. Top each with scoop (No. 9 dipper) of ice cream.
· Spoon on Marshmallow Sauce; sprinkle with nuts. Makes 50 servings.

MARSHMALLOW SAUCE

Perfect topper for banana splits and chocolate ice cream

- 1 lb. regular marshmallows
- 2 lbs. sugar
- 2 c. water
- 1 c. egg whites, unbeaten (about 10)
- 1 tblsp. vanilla

· Cut marshmallows into quarters.
· Combine sugar and water; stir to dissolve. Boil to make thin syrup, 228° on candy thermometer.
· Add marshmallows; cook until melted and smooth, stirring constantly.
· Beat egg whites until stiff; slowly add syrup to whites, beating constantly until mixture is fluffy and well blended.
· Blend in vanilla. Makes enough sauce for 50 banana splits or sundaes.

Beautiful Molded Gelatin Desserts

Molded gelatin desserts are among the most gorgeous and luscious refrigerator desserts. Hostesses like to make them a day before their parties. Cherries on Snow looks like Christmas, but it's pretty and tasty at any time. You'll find molded dessert recipes for all seasons and occasions in our collection.

CHERRIES ON SNOW

As appropriate for the Fourth of July as for Merry Christmas

- 1½ c. graham cracker crumbs
- 1 tblsp. sugar
- ¼ c. melted butter
- 1 envelope unflavored gelatin
- ¼ c. cold water
- ¼ c. milk
- 1 (8 oz.) pkg. cream cheese
- ½ c. sifted confectioners sugar
- 2 tsp. grated lemon peel
- 2 envelopes dessert topping mix
- 1 (1 lb. 5 oz.) can cherry pie filling

· Mix cracker crumbs, sugar and melted butter. Press into bottom of 8" spring-form pan. Line sides with waxed paper.
· Soften gelatin in cold water.
· Heat milk, stir in gelatin and heat until gelatin melts. Set aside.
· Beat cream cheese with confectioners sugar until smooth. Add gelatin and lemon peel and beat until well blended.
· Prepare topping mix according to package directions. Fold into the cream cheese mixture.
· Pour filling into spring-form pan. Refrigerate until firm. Gently spread cherry pie filling on top and refrigerate until serving time, overnight if possible. Cut in wedges to serve. Serves 9.

LEMON MIST

Beautiful light dessert that's a superb choice for springtime meals

- 2 tblsp. unflavored gelatin
- ½ c. cold water
- 1 c. boiling water
- ½ c. sugar
- ¼ tsp. salt
- ½ c. lemon juice
- 1 tsp. grated lemon peel
- 2 egg whites
- Sunshine Sauce

· Sprinkle gelatin over cold water to soften. Add boiling water, sugar and salt, stirring until dissolved. Stir in lemon juice and peel. Chill until syrupy.

· Beat gelatin mixture until frothy. Add unbeaten egg whites (always select eggs that have no cracks when they are to be used raw). Continue beating until mixture is light, fluffy and begins to mound, about 10 minutes. Pour into serving dish. Chill until set. Serve with Sunshine Sauce. Makes 8 servings.

SUNSHINE SAUCE: Combine ⅓ c. sugar, ⅛ tsp. salt, ½ c. water and 2 tblsp. lemon juice in the top of a double boiler; add 2 egg yolks and 1 egg. Beat just enough to blend. Place over gently simmering water and beat constantly with a rotary beater until mixture thickens, 8 to 10 minutes. Cool.

· Beat cooled lemon mixture until smooth. Stir in ½ c. light cream. Makes 2 cups sauce.

LEMON/CHOCOLATE DESSERT

Lower in calories than many desserts —weight-watchers praise it

- 1 (14½ oz.) can evaporated milk
- 1 (3 oz.) pkg. lemon flavor gelatin
- ¾ c. sugar
- 1½ c. boiling water
- 3 tblsp. lemon juice
- 1 tblsp. grated lemon peel
- 25 chocolate wafers (thin, icebox type, 2⅜" in diameter), finely crushed
- ¼ c. melted butter

· Chill can of evaporated milk overnight in refrigerator.

· Mix gelatin and sugar; dissolve in boiling water. Chill until almost completely set; stir in lemon juice and peel.

· In a large mixing bowl whip milk until it resembles soft whipped cream. Add gelatin mixture and continue whipping about 2 minutes.

· In a 13 × 9 × 2" pan, place chocolate wafer crumbs, reserving about 1 tblsp. crumbs. Add melted butter and mix; press firmly into bottom of pan. Pour in whipped mixture; sprinkle on reserved chocolate crumbs. Refrigerate until serving time. Makes 15 to 18 servings.

LEMON/BLUEBERRY GELATIN MOLD

Try this cool make-ahead dessert for supper on a warm summer day

First layer:

- 1 (3 oz.) pkg. Concord grape or lemon flavor gelatin
- ¼ tsp. salt
- 1¼ c. boiling water
- ½ c. grape juice
- 1 c. fresh or frozen unsweetened blueberries

Second layer:

- 1 (3 oz.) pkg. lemon flavor gelatin
- 1 c. boiling water
- ½ c. cold water
- 2 tblsp. lemon juice

- 2 (3 oz.) pkgs. cream cheese or ¾ c. whipped-type creamed cottage cheese

• To prepare first layer, dissolve gelatin and salt in boiling water. Stir in grape juice. Chill until partially set. Fold in blueberries. Pour into 6-c. mold and chill until firm.

• To prepare second layer, dissolve gelatin in boiling water. Add cold water and lemon juice. Chill just until cooled and syrupy.

• If you use cream cheese, beat until softened. Add cooled gelatin to cream cheese or cottage cheese and beat until mixture is light. Pour over blueberry layer. Chill until firm. Unmold. Makes 6 servings.

LEMON DAFFODIL DESSERT

This light dessert is an ideal ending for a heavy meal

- 6 eggs, separated
- 1 c. sugar
- ⅓ to ½ c. lemon juice
- 1 tsp. grated lemon peel
- 1 envelope unflavored gelatin
- ½ c. cold water
- 1 (11 oz.) loaf angel food cake
- 1 c. heavy cream

• In top of a double boiler, combine slightly beaten egg yolks, ½ c. sugar, lemon juice and peel. Cook over simmering water, stirring constantly, until mixture thickens. Remove from heat; stir in gelatin, which has been softened in cold water. Cool until partially set.

• Meanwhile, rub cake gently with clean dish towel to remove loose outside crumbs. Tear cake into bite-size pieces. Set aside.

• Beat egg whites until foamy; gradually beat in remaining ½ c. sugar to make soft meringue that holds a peak. Whip ½ c. cream and fold into meringue; carefully fold this mixture into gelatin mixture. Fold in cake pieces.

• Spoon into shallow oblong 3-qt. glass dish. Refrigerate overnight to set. Cut into squares; top with remaining ½ c. cream, whipped. Serves 10 to 12.

MOLDED RHUBARB SWIRL

Use pink-red rhubarb so tender the stalks won't string when cut

- 1 c. graham cracker crumbs
- 4 tsp. sugar
- 3 tblsp. melted butter or regular margarine
- 3 c. finely diced fresh rhubarb
- ½ c. sugar
- 1 (3 oz.) pkg. strawberry flavor gelatin
- 1 c. boiling water
- ½ c. sugar
- ¼ c. flour
- 1 c. milk
- 1 tsp. vanilla
- 2 tsp. unflavored gelatin, softened in 2 tblsp. cold water
- 2 c. heavy cream, whipped

• Combine crumbs, 4 tsp. sugar and butter; press into bottom of 2-qt. oblong casserole or 8" spring-form pan, greased on bottom only. Bake in moderate oven (350°) 7 minutes. Cool. Line sides of spring-form pan with waxed paper.

• Meanwhile, cover fruit with ½ c. sugar; let stand 1 hour. Then simmer in a heavy saucepan only until rhubarb loses crispness. Drain, reserving liquid. Add enough cold water to rhubarb liquid to make ¾ c.

• Dissolve strawberry gelatin in boiling water. Stir in the ¾ c. water-fruit liquid. Chill until syrupy.

• Combine ½ c. sugar, flour and milk in a heavy saucepan. Bring to a boil; then reduce heat and cook, stirring constantly, 2 minutes, or until thickened. Remove from heat. Stir in vanilla and unflavored gelatin; let stand 5 minutes. Then fold in whipped cream.

• Whip strawberry gelatin mixture until fluffy. Fold in rhubarb; then fold in half of whipped cream mixture. Alternately spoon the strawberry gelatin mixture and the remaining whipped cream mixture into crumb-lined pan; swirl with a knife. Chill overnight. Makes 9 servings.

MINCEMEAT REFRIGERATOR DESSERT

A luscious filling in gingersnap crust

2 c. gingersnap crumbs
⅓ c. melted butter
1½ tblsp. unflavored gelatin
5 tblsp. cold water
2 c. prepared mincemeat
4 eggs, separated
¼ c. butter
½ c. lemon juice
½ c. sugar
1 c. heavy cream, whipped, or 1 (2 oz.) pkg. dessert topping mix, whipped

• To make crust, combine crumbs and ⅓ c. melted butter; mix thoroughly. Reserve ½ c. for topping; pat remaining crumbs in bottom of 13 × 9 × 2" pan and refrigerate while you make filling.

• To make filling, soften gelatin in 5 tblsp. cold water. Combine mincemeat, slightly beaten egg yolks, ¼ c. butter and lemon juice in heavy saucepan. Cook over low heat, until slightly thickened, about 15 minutes. Stir constantly. Remove from heat; add gelatin, stir until dissolved. Refrigerate.

• When mincemeat mixture chills and begins to thicken, prepare a soft meringue of the egg whites and sugar. Fold meringue and whipped cream or topping mix into mincemeat mixture. Gently pour into crumb-lined pan. Sprinkle with reserved crumb mixture. Chill several hours. Makes about 12 servings.

PUMPKIN PARFAIT

Delicious light dessert to make ahead for your Thanksgiving dinner

1 envelope unflavored gelatin
¼ c. cold water
3 eggs, separated
½ c. sugar
1¼ c. cooked or canned pumpkin
½ c. milk
¼ tsp. salt
½ tsp. ground cinnamon
½ tsp. ground nutmeg
¼ tsp. salt
½ c. sugar
1 c. heavy cream, or 1 (2 oz.) pkg. dessert topping mix
1 tsp. sugar
½ tsp. rum flavoring
Chopped nuts

• Soak gelatin in cold water.

• Beat egg yolks (save the whites for later). Add ½ c. sugar, pumpkin, milk, ¼ tsp. salt, cinnamon and nutmeg. (For added flavor, grind your own cinnamon and nutmeg.) Cook in a heavy saucepan over low heat, stirring constantly, until thickened. Mix in gelatin until completely dissolved. Chill about 2 hours in refrigerator.

• Beat egg whites and ¼ tsp. salt until stiff.

· Remove pumpkin mixture from refrigerator and beat until fluffy. Add ½ c. sugar while beating.
· Fold in beaten egg whites and return to refrigerator for 1 hour.
· Whip the cream or dessert topping mix. Add 1 tsp. sugar and rum flavoring. Fold whipped cream into pumpkin mixture, reserving a bit of the cream for topping.
· Place the mixture in sherbet or parfait glasses and return to the refrigerator until ready to serve. Top each with a spoon of whipped cream; sprinkle with nuts. Makes about 6 servings.

Note: Recipe can be doubled for a big guest list.

RICE SUPREME

This classic rice pudding has gelatin base with bright cherry crown

½ c. rice
1½ qts. boiling water
1 qt. milk
¾ c. sugar
1 tsp. salt
1 tblsp. butter
3 envelopes unflavored gelatin
½ c. cold water
2 c. heavy cream
2 tblsp. vanilla
Cherry Sauce

· Pour rice into boiling water. Boil briskly 2 minutes. Drain, then rinse with cold water.
· Return to pan. Add 2 c. milk, 1 tblsp. sugar and salt. Bring to boil; add butter. Cover and simmer 20 minutes (do not stir).
· Pour rice mixture into bowl. Add remaining milk and sugar. Cool.
· Soften gelatin in cold water 5 minutes. Heat slowly until gelatin dissolves. Add to rice. Chill until thick enough that kernels don't sink.
· Whip cream, adding vanilla gradually, as you whip. Fold into rice.
· Pour into oiled, 2-qt. mold. Cover with foil. Chill overnight. Serve with Cherry Sauce. Makes 8 to 10 servings.

CHERRY SAUCE: Bring 3 c. pitted tart cherries, 1 c. water, 1 tblsp. lemon juice and ⅔ c. sugar to a boil. Blend together 2 tblsp. cornstarch and ¼ c. water. Stir into sauce. Cook, stirring until thick and clear, 2 to 3 minutes. Remove from heat and add 2 tblsp. butter. (Sauce should be tart, but a little more sugar may be added if desired.) Chill before serving. Makes about 5 cups.

STRAWBERRY CREAM DESSERT

Coconut crust has strawberry and cream filling with gelatin base

1 c. graham cracker crumbs
1 (3½ oz.) can flaked coconut
¼ c. melted butter or regular margarine
2 eggs, separated
1 (3 oz.) pkg. lemon flavor gelatin
1 c. boiling water
2 tblsp. lemon juice
¼ c. sugar
1 c. heavy cream
2 c. strawberries, sliced

· Combine crumbs, ½ c. coconut and butter. Blend in 2 egg yolks. Pat mixture into bottom of 2-qt. rectangular baking dish. Bake in moderate oven (350°) 15 minutes. Cool.
· Brown remaining coconut in oven.

· Dissolve gelatin in boiling water. Add lemon juice. Chill until consistency of thick syrup.
· Beat egg whites until frothy. Add sugar gradually, beating until stiff peaks form. Set aside.
· Whip cream until soft peaks form. Add thickened gelatin. Beat until mixture is thick and creamy. Fold in egg whites, then strawberries.
· Spread mixture on crust. Top with browned coconut. Refrigerate until firm. Makes 10 servings.

STRAWBERRY WHIP DESSERT

Use your electric blender to speed making this colorful dessert

½ c. boiling water
1 (3 oz.) pkg. strawberry flavor gelatin
15 marshmallows, cut in halves
½ c. cold water
1 (10 oz.) pkg. frozen strawberries in syrup, partially defrosted
1 tsp. lemon juice
1 c. heavy cream

· Place boiling water and gelatin in blender. Cover; blend on "low" until gelatin is dissolved. Add marshmallows, cold water, strawberries and lemon juice. Cover and blend on "low" until smooth (rest hand on container lid). Remove contents from the container; chill until partially set.
· Fold in blender-whipped heavy cream and refrigerate in 6 to 8 individual serving dishes or an 8″ square pan. Chill until firm. Serve with crisp cookies. Makes 6 to 8 servings.

STRAWBERRY BAVARIAN CREAM

Excellent dish to take to club luncheon. You can double the recipe

1 (3 oz.) pkg. strawberry flavor gelatin
2 c. hot water
1 c. heavy cream, whipped
2 c. strawberries, sliced

· Combine gelatin and hot water according to package directions. Chill until syrupy.
· Fold in whipped cream and strawberries. Turn into sherbet or parfait glasses, or chill in 1-qt. mold until set. Makes 6 servings.

Note: Raspberries or other fruit may be substituted for strawberries.

Homemade Ice Creams and Sherbets

You're in luck if you have an ice cream freezer, whether hand or electrically operated. Our ice cream and sherbet recipes are among the best you'll ever taste.

We give you two recipes for vanilla ice cream. One is the traditional country-style dessert made with milk, cream, sugar and eggs, with vanilla for flavoring. A newer recipe contains these same ingredients plus packaged vanilla pudding and gelatin. Try both kinds and see which takes first place with your family, and also try the variations. And a superlative in good eating is apple pie topped with our homemade Cinnamon Ice Cream! If you're a weight-watcher, Frozen Vanilla Custard merits your attention. So do the excellent variations of this basic recipe.

HOW TO FREEZE AND RIPEN ICE CREAM

1. Pour the cool ice cream mixture into the freezer can. Fill can two thirds to three fourths full to leave room for expansion. Fit can into freezer; follow manufacturer's directions if using an electric freezer.

2. Adjust the dasher and cover. Pack crushed ice and rock salt around the can, using 6 to 8 parts ice to 1 part salt. Turn the dasher slowly until the ice melts enough to form a brine. Add more ice and salt, mixed in the proper proportions, to maintain the ice level. Turn the handle fast and steadily until it turns hard. Then remove the ice until its level is below the lid of the can; take the lid off. Remove the dasher.

3. To ripen the ice cream, plug the opening in the lid. Cover the can with several thicknesses of waxed paper or foil to make a tight fit for the lid. Put the lid on the can.

4. Pack more of the ice and salt mixture (using 4 parts ice to 1 part rock salt) around the can, filling the freezer. Cover the freezer with a blanket, canvas or other heavy cloth, or with newspapers. Let ice cream ripen at least 4 hours, sherbet 1 hour. Or put the can in the home freezer to ripen.

Note: If you buy ice by the pound, you can use 20 lbs. ice to about 1 lb. rock salt for a 1-gal. freezer. Freezing is faster if the salt is increased (4 parts ice to 1 part salt), but the product will not be as smooth.

STORING ICE CREAM IN FREEZER

Ice cream, if left in its original container, retains its top quality about three weeks. To extend its storage life, place a sheet of plastic wrap directly on the unused portion in the container and overwrap the container with aluminum foil, plastic wrap or freezer paper.

COUNTRY-STYLE VANILLA ICE CREAM

Be sure to try the delicious variations

1 qt. milk
2 c. sugar
¼ c. flour
½ tsp. salt
4 eggs, slightly beaten
1 tblsp. vanilla
1½ qts. light cream, or dairy half-and-half

• Scald milk. Mix sugar, flour and salt. Add enough hot milk to sugar-flour mixture to make a thin paste. Stir paste into hot milk. Cook over low heat, stirring constantly, until mixture thickens slightly, about 15 minutes.

• Add hot mixture gradually to beaten eggs and cook over low heat, stirring constantly, until mixture thickens slightly, about 2 minutes (do not cook longer or eggs may curdle).

• Cool quickly in refrigerator. Do not allow mixture to cool at room temperature.

• Add vanilla and light cream to cooled mixture. Pour into freezer can; fill only two thirds full to allow for expansion. Freeze and ripen by basic directions (see "How to Freeze and Ripen Ice Cream" above). Makes 1 gallon.

Variations

CHOCOLATE ICE CREAM: Add 4 squares unsweetened chocolate to milk before scalding. After scalding, beat with rotary beater until chocolate flecks disappear. Increase sugar by ½ c. and prepare according to directions for freezing Country-Style Vanilla Ice Cream.

PEANUT BUTTER ICE CREAM: Omit 1 c. light cream. Stir a small amount of the custard mixture gradually into ½ c. peanut butter to blend well. Add to rest of the mixture in the freezer can.

STRAWBERRY ICE CREAM: Omit 3 c. light cream. Add 1 qt. washed and hulled strawberries which have been mashed and sweetened with ½ c. additional sugar. Add a few drops of red food color if you wish.

PEACH ICE CREAM: Omit 3 c. light cream. Add 1 qt. crushed fresh peaches mixed with ¾ c. additional sugar.

HOMEMADE VANILLA ICE CREAM

Ice cream is light and refreshing

- 2 tblsp. unflavored gelatin
- 3 c. milk
- 2 c. sugar
- ¼ tsp. salt
- 6 eggs
- 1½ qts. light cream
- 1 (3¾ oz.) pkg. vanilla instant pudding
- 5 tsp. vanilla

· Soften gelatin in ½ c. cold milk.

· Scald 1½ c. milk and stir into gelatin mixture until it dissolves. Add sugar and salt, stirring until dissolved. Add remaining 1 c. milk.

· Beat eggs at high speed of electric mixer for 5 minutes. Add light cream, pudding mix, vanilla and milk mixture.

· Pour into 1-gallon ice cream freezer container. Freeze and ripen by basic directions (see "How to Freeze and Ripen Ice Cream" in Index). Makes 3½ quarts.

GRAPE ICE CREAM: Substitute 3 c. grape juice for milk. Proceed as above, reducing light cream to 5 c. and sugar to 1¼ c.; omit vanilla. Add the juice of 1 lemon.

CINNAMON ICE CREAM: Slowly melt ⅔ c. cinnamon candies (red hots) with the 1½ c. milk. Proceed as above, reducing sugar to 1¼ c. and vanilla to 1 tblsp.

COFFEE/WALNUT ICE CREAM: Add ¼ c. instant coffee powder with pudding mix. Reduce vanilla to 1 tblsp. After ice cream is frozen, stir in 1 c. coarsely chopped, toasted walnuts. Repack.

PEPPERMINT STICK ICE CREAM: Melt ½ c. crushed peppermint stick candy with the 1½ c. milk. Proceed as above, reducing sugar to 1¼ c. and vanilla to 1 tblsp. After cream is frozen, stir in ½ c. crushed peppermint stick candy; repack.

FROZEN VANILLA CUSTARD

Lower in calories than most ice creams

- 3 qts. skim milk
- 2 c. sugar
- 6 tblsp. flour
- 2 tsp. salt
- 8 eggs, slightly beaten
- 2 envelopes unflavored gelatin, softened in ¼ c. cold water
- 3 tblsp. vanilla

· Scald milk in top of double boiler. Mix sugar, flour and salt and add a little of the hot milk. Blend well and add to milk in double boiler. Cook over boiling water until bubbles form at the edge of the pan.
· Remove from heat. Add the hot mixture gradually to the eggs. Return to double boiler and cook over simmering, not boiling, water, stirring constantly, until mixture coats a wooden spoon.
· Remove from the heat; gradually stir the hot mixture into the gelatin, stirring until the gelatin completely dissolves. Refrigerate until custard thickens, about 2 hours, or until it reaches 70°. (You can cook the custard a day ahead and refrigerate it.) Add vanilla to cooled custard.
· Pour into freezer can. Freeze and ripen by basic directions (see "How to Freeze and Ripen Ice Cream" in Index). Makes 1 gallon. 105 calories per ½ cup serving.

Variations

FROZEN COFFEE CUSTARD: Omit vanilla. Reserve 1 c. custard and add to it ¼ c. instant coffee powder. When custard is partly frozen, add coffee-custard mixture and continue freezing until firm. 105 calories per ½ cup serving.

FROZEN BANANA CUSTARD: Add 5 large, very ripe bananas, mashed (about 2 c.), and ¼ tsp. yellow food color. Freeze. 117 calories per ½ cup serving.

FROZEN PEPPERMINT STICK CUSTARD: Add ¼ tsp. green food color to chilled custard. Partially freeze. Add 1 c. crushed green and white peppermint stick candy, or omit food color and add red and white peppermint stick candy; freeze. 125 calories per ½ cup serving.

FROZEN STRAWBERRY CUSTARD: Omit 1 tsp. salt and 1 c. milk when making custard. Partially freeze. Add 2 c. sliced, fresh strawberries sweetened with 2 tblsp. sugar. Freeze until firm. 109 calories per ½ cup serving.

COCONUT/HONEY ICE CREAM

The honey-coconut-pineapple flavor is superb—make this for company

1½ c. honey
4 eggs, slightly beaten
3 c. heavy cream
2 tsp. vanilla
½ tsp. lemon extract
½ tsp. salt
3 c. milk
1 (3½ oz.) can flaked coconut
2 (8½ oz.) cans crushed pineapple

· Add honey to eggs; mix well. Add cream, flavorings, salt and milk; stir until well blended. Chill.
· Pour into freezer can; fill two thirds full. Partly freeze by basic directions (see "How to Freeze and Ripen Ice Cream" in Index).
· When partly frozen, add coconut and pineapple; continue freezing until crank turns hard. Remove dasher and let ripen. Or spoon into freezer containers; seal and store in freezer. Makes 1 gallon.

Note: To intensify coconut flavor, add 2 tsp. coconut extract with lemon extract and vanilla.

FRUITED VELVET ICE CREAM

Mixed fruit flavors make this special

1½ qts. light cream
1 c. eggs, beaten
1½ c. sugar
1 tsp. vanilla
½ c. chopped nuts
½ c. diced banana
½ c. drained diced pineapple (canned)
½ c. chopped maraschino cherries
½ c. chopped fresh strawberries
¼ c. sugar
2 tsp. fresh lemon juice
½ tsp. salt

· Combine cream, eggs and 1½ c. sugar. Cook over very low heat, stirring constantly, until mixture coats the back of a metal spoon. Cool quickly in refrigerator. Add vanilla. Pour into freezer can; fill two thirds full.

· Combine nuts, fruits, ¼ c. sugar, lemon juice and salt. Let stand 5 minutes. Add to mixture in freezer can. Freeze and ripen by basic directions (see "How to Freeze and Ripen Ice Cream" in Index). Makes 1 gallon.

GOLDEN GLOW ICE CREAM

Excellent use for leftover egg yolks

¼ c. grated orange peel
2 c. milk
1 c. sugar
1 c. light corn syrup
½ tsp. salt
8 egg yolks, beaten
2 c. light cream
4 c. fresh orange juice

· Place orange peel in small cheesecloth bag. Scald with milk in top of double boiler.

· Add sugar, corn syrup and salt to egg yolks, which have been mixed with some of the hot milk. Add the sugar-egg mixture to remaining hot milk.

· Cook, stirring constantly, until mixture coats spoon; cool.

· Stir in cream and orange juice. Pour into freezer can; fill only two thirds full to allow for expansion. Freeze and ripen by basic directions (see "How to Freeze and Ripen Ice Cream" in Index). Makes 1 gallon.

ORANGE PEKOE TEA ICE CREAM

Try this distinctive company dessert

2½ c. milk, scalded
6 whole cloves
1 tblsp. grated orange peel
2 tblsp. orange pekoe tea
1 envelope unflavored gelatin
⅓ c. cold water
¼ tsp. salt
¾ c. sugar
4 egg yolks, slightly beaten
¾ c. honey
4 egg whites, stiffly beaten
3 c. light cream

· Scald milk with cloves and orange peel. Add tea; let stand 5 to 8 minutes over hot water.

· Soften gelatin in water.

· Strain milk; return to double boiler top. Add salt, sugar and egg yolks, which have been mixed with some hot milk. Cook, stirring constantly, until thickened.

· Remove from heat, add softened gelatin; blend thoroughly. Add honey. Cool.

· When cold, fold in egg whites and cream. Pour into freezer can; fill only two thirds full to allow for expansion. Freeze and ripen by basic directions (see "How to Freeze and

Ripen Ice Cream" in Index). Makes 1 gallon.

HOSTESS TRICKS WITH ICE CREAM

Mold ice cream for special occasions

ICE CREAM IN ORANGE SHELLS: Pack ice cream or sherbet into scooped-out orange shells, then freeze. Do this a day or two ahead. Green leaf garnish gives a fresh-from-the-grove look.

BUFFET PARTY DESSERT: The day before your party, scoop ice cream balls onto a cold metal tray; return to freezer to firm up. Chill your prettiest *metal* bowl; fill it with ice cream balls; put bowl in freezer. At serving time, add nuts and fruits. Guests make their own sundaes. No last-minute scooping.

ICE CREAM BIRTHDAY CAKE: Pack ice cream into a 9" spring-form cake pan, return to freezer. Next day decorate like a cake, with candles. For a fancier cake, line the pan with vanilla ice cream and freeze it hard. Then freeze scoops of different flavors, and use them—along with more vanilla—to fill in center of lined pan. Sprinkle colored sugar over a paper cut-out design on top, and add candy to decorate base of cake.

ICE CREAM PETITS FOURS

Serve these tiny decorative ice cream pieces on party plates—they'll go fast

To Use Brick Ice Cream:

1. On chilled metal tray, set over pan of ice, cut half-gallon bricks of ice cream into 24 squares, or 18 diamonds, or 16 rectangles. Place on individual pieces of waxed paper. Freeze firm at least 24 hours.
2. Whip 2 c. heavy cream; divide in fourths. Tint one a delicate pink, one green, one yellow; leave one white.
3. Work on chilled tray over ice. Remove ice cream from freezer one piece at a time; frost with whipped cream; decorate with tiny candies or pastel-colored decorating sugars, nuts or whipped cream designs. (You can leave some petits fours unfrosted and roll sides in tinted coconut or finely chopped nuts.) Return to freezer immediately so they will hold shape.
4. When petits fours are frozen firm, transfer to cupcake papers; package in flat box. Wrap and freeze.

To Use Bulk or Homemade Ice Cream:

1. Place 6" strip of heavy aluminum foil in bottom of 8" square pan with ends of foil extending over edges of pan. Pack ½ gallon soft ice cream evenly in pan; freeze until very firm. Turn ice cream out of pan onto chilled tray set over pan of ice. Proceed as directed for brick ice cream.
2. To make round shapes, pack ice cream in 6 oz. juice cans; freeze firm. Cut other end out of can; push out ice cream; cut in half. Decorate by directions for brick ice cream.

Six Popular Ice Cream Pies

Hundreds of women have won countless compliments for their ice cream pies since the recipes for them were printed in FARM JOURNAL. They are different from the usual because the pie "shells" are ice cream, not pastry. In appearance and taste they rival many elaborate, intricate desserts that are more work to make.

You can wrap the pies after freezing and keep them in the freezer ready to serve on short notice when you need a special dessert. These pies prove that the simplest country dishes frequently are best in taste and tops in good looks.

ICE CREAM PIE SHELL

· Line 8″ pie pan with 1 pt. vanilla or favorite ice cream flavor. For a more generous "crust," use 1½ pts. Cut ice cream in ½″ slices; lay on bottom of pan to cover. Cut remaining slices in half; arrange around pan to make rim. Fill spots with ice cream where needed. With tip of spoon, smooth "crust." Freeze until firm before adding the filling.

CRANBERRY/NUT PIE

This all-around favorite is a perfect ending for chicken dinners

Ice Cream Pie Shell
2 c. fresh or frozen raw cranberries
1 c. sugar
1 c. heavy cream
½ c. chopped nuts

· Put cranberries through food chopper, using fine blade. (Grind your cranberries frozen—less juicy.) Add sugar; let stand overnight.
· Whip cream. Mix cranberries and nuts. Fold in whipped cream. Pour into Ice Cream Pie Shell. Freeze. To serve, cut in wedges.

CHOCOLATE/PEPPERMINT PIE

Use pink-and-white peppermint ice cream shells to hold chocolate filling

2 Pink Peppermint Ice Cream Pie Shells
1 tblsp. cocoa
½ c. sugar
1 (4 oz.) pkg. chocolate pudding and pie filling
1 tsp. vanilla
2 c. heavy cream

· Combine cocoa and sugar. Add to pudding mix and prepare as directed on package. Cool; add vanilla.
· Whip cream and fold into chocolate mixture. Pour into peppermint Ice Cream Pie Shells. Freeze. To serve, cut in wedges.

BUTTERSCOTCH/PECAN PIE

Nice to serve with coffee for afternoon or evening refreshments

2 Ice Cream Pie Shells
¼ c. brown sugar, firmly packed
1 (4 oz.) pkg. butterscotch pudding and pie filling
1 tsp. vanilla
2 c. heavy cream
½ c. chopped pecans

· Add sugar to pudding mix. Prepare as directed on package. Cool; then add vanilla.
· Whip cream. Add nuts to butterscotch mixture. Fold in whipped cream. Pour into Ice Cream Pie Shells. Freeze. To serve, cut in wedges.

Note: You can omit nuts and use butter pecan ice cream shells.

SPICY PUMPKIN PIE

Use butter almond or butter pecan ice cream to make pie shell

Ice Cream Pie Shell
1 c. cooked or canned pumpkin
1 c. sugar
¼ tsp. salt
¼ tsp. ground ginger
1 tsp. ground cinnamon
¼ tsp. ground nutmeg
1 c. heavy cream

• Mix together pumpkin, sugar, salt and spices. Cook over low heat 3 minutes. Cool.

• Whip cream; fold into pumpkin mixture. Pour into Ice Cream Pie Shell. Freeze. To serve, cut in wedges.

FROZEN STRAWBERRY/ VANILLA PIE

Good as juicy, ripe strawberries and vanilla ice cream—everyone's favorite

2 Ice Cream Pie Shells
1 (10 oz.) pkg. frozen strawberries, sliced (use fresh ones in season)
2 c. heavy cream
¼ c. confectioners sugar
½ tsp. vanilla
Red food color

• Partially thaw berries.

• Whip cream; add sugar, vanilla and food color. Fold in strawberries. Pour into Ice Cream Pie Shells. Freeze. To serve, cut in wedges.

SWEET 'N' TART LEMON PIE

Excellent make-ahead dessert choice to top off that fish dinner

Ice Cream Pie Shell
3 eggs
½ c. sugar
¼ tsp. salt
¼ c. lemon juice
1 c. heavy cream

• Beat together 1 whole egg and 2 yolks. Add sugar, salt and lemon juice. Cook over low heat, stirring constantly until thick. Cool.

• Beat egg whites until stiff; then whip cream (no need to wash beaters). Fold cream into lemon mixture. Next, fold in whites. Pour into Ice Cream Pie Shell. Freeze. To serve, cut in wedges.

STRAWBERRY PARFAIT RING

Fancy party strawberry dessert to fix ahead and freeze—it's glamorous

1 c. sugar
⅓ c. boiling water
Red food color (optional)
4 egg whites
1 tsp. vanilla
⅛ tsp. salt
2 c. heavy cream, whipped
Strawberries (about 1½ qts.)
Flaked or shredded coconut
Whipped Cream Puffs

• Cook sugar with water until syrup spins a thread (235°). Add a few drops of red food color if you wish a pink mold.

• Beat egg whites until stiff; gradually add hot syrup; continue beating until cool and light. Add vanilla and salt.

• Fold in the whipped cream; pour into a 2-qt. ring mold and freeze.

• At serving time unmold and fill center with berries. Sprinkle a fluff of coconut on top. If ring is not tinted, use coconut tinted pink. Border the ring with Whipped Cream Puffs, one for each serving. Makes 12 to 16 servings.

WHIPPED CREAM PUFFS: Whip 1 c. heavy cream until fairly stiff. Drop from spoon onto baking sheet or flat pan to make little mounds, and freeze. Garnish each puff with a whole strawberry just before serving.

Variation

INDIVIDUAL STRAWBERRY PARFAIT RINGS: Freeze parfait mixture in individual angel food pans or ring molds. To serve, turn out on dessert plates and fill centers with fresh or frozen strawberries. (Other berries or sliced peaches may be used.)

Calorie-conscious cooks may wish to omit the whipped cream garnish.

Marvelous Country Sherbets

AVOCADO SHERBET

Smooth sherbet with a buttery taste

1 envelope unflavored gelatin
2 tblsp. cold water
½ c. sugar
½ c. milk
⅔ c. mashed avocado
⅛ tsp. salt
¼ c. chopped pecans
½ c. orange juice
¼ c. lemon juice
1 egg white, stiffly beaten

· Soften gelatin in water; dissolve over boiling water. Dissolve sugar in milk. Add avocado, salt, pecans and juices. Stir in the gelatin.
· Fold in beaten egg white. Freeze in refrigerator tray, stirring occasionally. Makes 4 to 6 servings.

COUNTRY GRAPE SHERBET

Garnish with fresh strawberries for a picture-pretty trim

1 c. dairy sour cream
1 c. milk
1½ c. sugar
1 egg, well beaten
1 c. grape juice (Concord)
¼ c. lemon juice

· Combine ingredients and beat until sugar dissolves.
· Pour into two refrigerator trays or loaf pans and freeze until nearly firm.
· Turn mixture into chilled bowl and beat until fluffy and smooth. Work fast and do not let mixture melt.
· Return to trays and freeze until firm. Makes 6 servings.

Note: It's a good idea to buy a couple of ice cube trays to use for freezing desserts. When trays are used interchangeably for foods and ice cubes, washing them may destroy their finish, making ice cube removal difficult.

LEMON/PINEAPPLE SHERBET

Serve with chocolate cake for a treat

2 c. sugar
1¼ c. lemon juice
1 (8½ oz.) can crushed pineapple, undrained
1½ qts. milk
1 c. heavy cream, whipped
2 egg whites, stiffly beaten

· Dissolve sugar in lemon juice by heating slightly and stirring; add pineapple and cool.
· Pour this mixture and milk into a 1-gallon ice cream freezer container. Freeze by basic directions until mixture reaches slush stage, about 10 minutes (see "How to Freeze and Ripen Ice Cream" in Index).
· Meanwhile, fold whipped cream into beaten egg whites; open freezer container and fold into partially frozen sherbet mixture. Freeze. Remove dasher. Let sherbet ripen 1 hour before serving. Makes about 3½ quarts.

STRAWBERRY/BUTTERMILK SHERBET

Angel food cake is an ideal companion

2 c. fresh strawberries, sliced
¼ c. sugar
1 envelope unflavored gelatin
⅓ c. strawberry juice

1½ c. buttermilk
½ c. sugar
2 tblsp. lemon juice

• Combine strawberries and ¼ c. sugar and mash well. Let stand 10 minutes then strain off ⅓ c. juice. Set aside remaining crushed berries.
• Soften gelatin in the ⅓ c. strawberry juice. Dissolve over hot water. Add to buttermilk along with the remaining crushed berries, ½ c. sugar and lemon juice, stirring well to dissolve sugar.
• Pour into two refrigerator trays or loaf pans. Freeze until mushy. Beat in mixing bowl until smooth. Return to refrigerator trays or pans. Freeze until firm. Garnish with whole berries. Makes 6 to 8 servings.

FRESH STRAWBERRY SHERBET

Its coral-red color brightens meals

4 qts. fresh strawberries, sliced
4 c. sugar
2⅔ c. milk
⅔ c. orange juice
⅛ tsp. ground cinnamon

• Mix strawberries and sugar; let stand until juicy (about 1½ hours). Mash, or purée in blender. Strain out seeds (optional, but we prefer seedless sherbet).
• Add milk, orange juice and cinnamon. Mix well. Pour into freezer can. Freeze by basic directions (see "How to Freeze and Ripen Ice Cream" in Index). (Or pour mixture into refrigerator trays or loaf pans; freeze about 3 hours; stir 2 or 3 times.) Makes about 1 gallon.

Variations

PINK AND WHITE PARFAIT RING: Spoon strawberry sherbet and soft vanilla ice cream in alternating layers in chilled ring mold. Freeze. When frozen, unmold on serving plate; return to freezer. To serve, fill center with fresh berries for color-bright garnish.

STRAWBERRY/LEMON PARFAIT: Spoon strawberry and lemon sherbets alternately into parfait glasses or tumblers. Return to freezer until time to serve. Garnish with fresh berries.

CHOCOLATE/STRAWBERRY RING: Spoon sherbet into ring mold. Freeze. When frozen, unmold on plate; return to freezer. To serve, fill centers with scoops of chocolate ice cream.

WATER SHERBET: Use water instead of milk. Sherbet is smoother and tastes better when made with milk, however.

TUTTI-FRUTTI ICE

For individual servings freeze ice in paper cups set in a shallow pan

1 qt. cranberries
2 c. water
1 c. sugar
1 (10 oz.) pkg. frozen raspberries
¼ c. lemon juice
1 tsp. grated orange peel
½ c. orange juice

• Combine cranberries, water and sugar; bring to a rapid boil over high heat. Cook 10 minutes or until cranberry skins pop. Remove from heat; add raspberries. Stir until raspberries are thawed.
• Run mixture through a food mill to make a smooth pulp. Stir in remaining ingredients; pour into large mixing bowl. Put in freezer. When mixture is partially frozen, beat at high speed in mixer. Return to freezer.

· Before ice is firm, beat once more, at high speed (beat until ice becomes lighter in color; don't expect fine crystals). Put into freezer containers, cover and freeze. Makes 2 quarts.

FROZEN AMBROSIA

Perfect light dessert to follow the Thanksgiving turkey and trimmings

4 c. orange juice
½ c. lemon juice
3 c. sifted confectioners sugar
2 c. heavy cream
2 tblsp. sugar
2 tsp. vanilla
Slivered salted almonds or peanuts

· Mix together orange juice, lemon juice and confectioners sugar.
· Whip cream; blend in sugar and vanilla.
· Pour fruit juice into 2 refrigerator trays. Spoon whipped cream over top, but do not mix together (juice and cream will be separate layers). Freeze until firm.
· Spoon into sherbet dishes or a compote; top with almonds or peanuts. Makes 8 to 10 servings.

Baked Fruit Desserts and Puddings

When snow blows in cold drifts across fields, warm baked fruit desserts and puddings come into their own. These hearty farm desserts pleasingly satisfy hunger and provide excellent nutrition. Several of them are year-round favorites. Most of them bake with little or no attention.

Look carefully at the recipes for apple desserts and select one to try. They're genuine favorites with country families.

BIG APPLE BARS

Both Apple and Apple/Apricot Bars are tasty with ice cream on top

1 c. sifted flour
½ tsp. salt
½ tsp. baking soda
½ c. light brown sugar, firmly packed
1 c. quick-cooking rolled oats
½ c. shortening
2 tblsp. butter or regular margarine
2½ c. tart apple slices
¼ c. sugar
Butter pecan or vanilla ice cream

· Sift flour with salt and baking soda. Stir in brown sugar; mix in rolled oats. Cut in shortening until mixture is crumbly. Press half of this mixture firmly into bottom of greased 8" square pan or baking dish. Dot with butter. Add apple slices and sprinkle with ¼ c. sugar. Cover with rest of crumbs.
· Bake in moderate oven (350°) 45 minutes, until top is golden.
· Cut in 6 large bars. Serve cold or faintly warm with ice cream or your favorite sauce. Makes 6 servings.

Variation

APPLE/APRICOT BARS: Substitute 1 c. canned drained and chopped apricots for 1 c. of the apple slices.

APPLE MACAROON

A crisp, golden cookie crust spreads over the apple filling

4 medium-size peeled apples
¼ to ½ c. sugar (depending on tartness of apples)
½ tsp. ground cinnamon
½ c. pecan pieces
½ c. coconut
¼ c. shortening
¼ c. butter, softened

½ c. sugar
1 egg, well beaten
¾ c. sifted flour
½ tsp. vanilla

• Thinly slice apples into 10" pie pan. Sprinkle with ¼ to ½ c. sugar and cinnamon. Top with pecans and coconut.
• Make a batter of remaining ingredients by creaming together shortening and butter until fluffy. Add ½ c. sugar gradually. Stir in well-beaten egg, blending well. Add flour and stir in gently but thoroughly. Stir in vanilla. Spread batter over top of apples.
• Bake in moderate oven (375°) until top is crisp and golden, about 35 minutes. Top with whipped cream, if desired. Makes 8 servings.

APPLE PINWHEELS IN SYRUP

Apples in pastry bake in a rich spicy sauce—serve with whipped cream

Pastry for 2-crust pie
4 c. grated apples
1 tsp. ground cinnamon
¾ c. sugar
½ c. dark brown sugar, firmly packed
¼ tsp. salt
¼ c. butter
½ tsp. vanilla
2 c. hot water

• Roll pastry into 14 × 12" rectangle.
• Combine apples and cinnamon, spread over pastry evenly; then roll up as for jelly roll. Slice in 1½" pieces, sealing edges with toothpicks, and place in 11 × 7 × 1½" pan, sealed side down. Bake in hot oven (400°) 15 minutes.
• Combine remaining ingredients in 2-qt. saucepan and bring to a full boil. Pour over apple pinwheels. Return to oven and bake 15 to 20 minutes more, basting twice, until apples are tender. Makes 8 servings.

APPLE/CRANBERRY CRISP

Dessert is slightly tart—add ice cream topping for a sweet touch

2 c. cranberries
3 c. unpeeled red apple slices
¾ c. sugar
½ c. butter
1 c. quick-cooking rolled oats
½ c. flour
½ c. brown sugar, firmly packed
½ c. chopped nuts

• Combine cranberries, apple slices and ¾ c. sugar in bottom of 2-qt. casserole.
• Melt butter; stir in remaining ingredients. Spread over berries and apples.
• Bake in moderate oven (350°) 1 hour. Makes 6 servings.

Note: Make 2 casseroles of this dessert for more or larger servings.

CRANBERRY TRENTON DESSERT

Happy, tart-sweet ending for dinners featuring pork or chicken

3 c. chopped cranberries
3 c. chopped tart apples
1 tblsp. cornstarch
⅓ c. light brown sugar, firmly packed
¾ c. sugar
1 tsp. salt
1 tsp. vanilla
1 c. instant oatmeal
½ c. light brown sugar
⅓ c. sifted flour
2 tblsp. crushed corn flakes
¼ c. butter
½ c. chopped nuts

· Combine cranberries, apples, cornstarch, ⅓ c. brown sugar, ¾ c. sugar, ½ tsp. of the salt and vanilla. Pour into a buttered 11 × 7 × 1½″ baking dish.

· Mix together oatmeal, ½ c. brown sugar, flour, corn flakes and remaining ½ tsp. salt. Cut in butter until mixture is crumbly; stir in nuts. Sprinkle evenly over top of cranberry mixture.

· Bake in moderate oven (350°) 35 to 40 minutes. Serve warm or cold. Top with whipped cream if you wish. Makes 10 servings.

SNOWY GLAZED APPLE SQUARES

Apples bake between two crusts in jelly roll pan. Top is glazed

2½ c. sifted flour
½ tsp. salt
1 c. shortening
2 eggs, separated
Milk
1½ c. crushed corn flakes
5 c. sliced peeled tart apples (about 8 medium)
1 c. sugar
1½ tsp. ground cinnamon
1¼ c. sifted confectioners sugar
3 tblsp. water
½ tsp. vanilla

· Combine flour and salt in bowl. Cut in shortening.

· In a measuring cup, beat egg yolks with enough milk to make ⅔ c. Add to flour mixture; toss lightly.

· Divide dough almost in half. Roll larger portion to fit a 15½ × 10½ × 1″ jelly roll pan. Sprinkle with corn flakes. Spread apples over flakes.

· Combine white sugar and cinnamon; sprinkle over apples.

· Roll out remaining dough. Place on top; seal edges.

· Beat egg whites until foamy; spread on crust. Bake in moderate oven (350°) 1 hour.

· Meanwhile, make glaze by combining confectioners sugar, water and vanilla.

· When dessert is done, remove from oven and cool slightly, then spread with glaze. To serve, cut in squares. Makes 6 to 8 servings.

BAKED APPLE TAPIOCA

The perfect selection for an oven meal—good cinnamon-apple flavor

5 c. sliced, peeled, firm cooking apples
2½ c. water
¼ tsp. ground cloves
½ c. quick-cooking tapioca
½ c. red cinnamon candies (red hots)
½ c. sugar
½ tsp. salt
¼ c. butter
¼ c. lemon juice

· Arrange apples in a greased 3-qt. casserole.

· Combine water, cloves, tapioca, candies, sugar and salt and bring to a boil over medium heat, stirring constantly. Continue cooking at hard boil for 1 minute.

· Remove from heat; add butter and lemon juice; stir until butter melts.

· Pour over apples. Cover and bake in moderate oven (375°) about 45 minutes, or until apples are tender. Serve warm with whipped cream or vanilla ice cream sprinkled lightly with cinnamon. Makes 8 servings.

HONEY-BAKED QUINCE

A country dessert always in style

6 quince, peeled and cored
2 tblsp. honey
⅛ tsp. grated lemon peel
1 tblsp. sugar
Water
Cream

· Place quince in shallow baking dish. Fill each with honey with lemon peel added. Sprinkle with sugar. Add water to cover bottom of pan.

· Bake in moderate oven (350°) 1½ hours or until soft, basting occasionally. Serve with cream, plain or whipped. Makes 6 servings.

BLUEBERRY UPSIDE-DOWN CAKE

Cake mix makes this a quickie dessert

¼ c. butter or regular margarine
½ c. sugar
2 c. fresh or frozen unsweetened blueberries, thawed
1 tsp. grated lemon peel
1 (8½ oz.) pkg. yellow cake mix
1 tsp. grated lemon peel
½ c. heavy cream, whipped (optional)

· Melt butter in 8″ square baking pan. Sprinkle sugar evenly over butter.

· Mix blueberries and 1 tsp. lemon peel; sprinkle over sugar.

· Prepare yellow cake mix according to package directions, stirring in 1 tsp. lemon peel at end of mixing. Spread batter over berries.

· Bake in moderate oven (375°) for 30 minutes or until cake tests done. Let stand 10 minutes. Turn out on platter. Serve warm. Top with whipped cream at the table if you wish. Serves 9.

CHOCOLATE UPSIDE-DOWN CAKE

Syrup sinks to bottom and cocoa cake rises to top during baking

1 c. sifted flour
¾ c. sugar
1½ tblsp. cocoa
2 tsp. baking powder
½ tsp. salt
2 tblsp. melted butter
¾ c. milk
1 tsp. vanilla
¾ c. chopped nuts
½ c. chocolate syrup
1 c. hot water

· Sift together flour, sugar, cocoa, baking powder and salt. Add butter, milk, vanilla and nuts. Stir until well mixed. Pour into greased 8″ square baking pan.

· Mix chocolate syrup and hot water. Pour over batter in pan.

· Bake in moderate oven (350°) 35 minutes. Makes 9 servings.

Superior Baked Puddings

Baked puddings give chilly evening suppers an unforgettable finish. These cherished desserts have other virtues than superior flavors. Mothers of growing children prize them for the good food value they contain, such as milk and eggs. Some are low in fat content.

We give you recipes for a trio of such baked puddings—Fruit Pudding Cake and Zuider Zee and Sweet Chocolate Puddings—plus several other favorites.

SWEET CHOCOLATE PUDDING

Crunchy coconut-nut topping on baked pudding tastes wonderful

1 (4 oz.) bar sweet cooking chocolate
1 tblsp. butter or regular margarine
1 (14½ oz.) can evaporated milk
1 c. sugar
2 tblsp. cornstarch
½ tsp. salt
2 eggs
1 tsp. vanilla
1 (3½ oz.) can flaked coconut
½ c. chopped nuts

· Melt chocolate with butter in a saucepan over low heat. Stir until blended. Remove from heat and gradually stir in evaporated milk.
· Mix together sugar, cornstarch, salt. Beat in eggs and vanilla. Gradually stir in chocolate mixture. Pour into greased 8″ square baking pan.
· Combine coconut and nuts. Sprinkle over top of pudding.
· Bake in moderate oven (375°) 40 minutes or until top puffs and cracks slightly.
· Cool before serving. Serve plain or with whipped topping or a scoop of ice milk. Makes 9 servings.

FRUIT PUDDING CAKE

It's the tender cake topping on fruit filling that names this dessert

1 (1 lb. 5 oz.) can prepared pie filling—blueberry or cherry
3 tblsp. soft butter or margarine
½ c. sugar
1 c. sifted flour
½ tsp. salt
1 tsp. baking powder
½ c. milk
2 tsp. grated orange or lemon peel
1 tblsp. sugar

· Pour pie filling into a 10 × 6 × 1½″ baking dish.
· Cream together butter and ½ c. sugar.
· Sift together flour, salt and baking powder. Add to creamed mixture alternately with milk. Stir in orange or lemon peel. Spread batter over pie filling. Sprinkle on 1 tblsp. sugar.
· Bake in moderate oven (350°) 40 minutes or until batter is lightly browned and tests done. Makes 6 to 8 servings.

ZUIDER ZEE PUDDING

The crisp zwieback crust holds satiny smooth cornstarch pudding

1 c. zwieback crumbs (12 slices)
½ tsp. ground cinnamon
3 tblsp. sugar
¼ c. soft butter or regular margarine
½ c. sugar
3 tblsp. cornstarch
¼ tsp. salt
2 c. milk
3 eggs, separated
1 tsp. vanilla
¼ tsp. cream of tartar
6 tblsp. sugar

· Mix zwieback crumbs with cinnamon, 3 tblsp. sugar and butter. Set aside ¼ c. for topping. Line bottom and sides of 10 × 6 × 1½″ baking dish with remaining crumbs. Bake in moderate oven (350°) 10 minutes.
· Mix ½ c. sugar, cornstarch and salt in a saucepan; stir in milk. Cook over medium heat, stirring constantly until pudding boils and thickens. Stir a little hot pudding into 3 slightly beaten egg yolks and return to saucepan. Bring just to boiling point, stirring constantly. Add vanilla; pour into crust. Cool 25 minutes.

• Make a meringue by beating 3 egg whites with cream of tartar and 6 tblsp. sugar.

• Carefully cover pudding with meringue, spreading to edges to seal. Sprinkle on reserved crumbs.

• Bake in hot oven (425°) about 5 minutes, or until meringue is nicely browned. Serve warm or cold. Makes 6 servings.

Variation

QUICK ZUIDER ZEE PUDDING: Make zwieback crust. Substitute 1 (3¼ oz.) pkg. of cooked vanilla pudding or pie filling for pudding mixture. Cover with meringue and bake as above.

CUSTARD BREAD PUDDING

An old-fashioned custard bread pudding that men always praise

2⅔ c. milk
¼ c. butter
3 eggs
½ c. sugar
1 tsp. vanilla
¼ tsp. salt
3 c. (1″) day-old bread cubes, top crusts removed
⅛ tsp. ground nutmeg
¼ tsp. vanilla
¼ tsp. cream of tartar
¼ c. sugar

• Scald milk; add butter and cool.

• Add 3 egg yolks and 1 egg white to ½ c. sugar; beat to mix well. Add cooled milk, 1 tsp. vanilla, and salt.

• Place bread cubes in buttered 1½-qt. casserole. Pour egg-milk mixture over bread. Sprinkle nutmeg on top.

• Set casserole in a pan containing at least 2″ warm water. Bake in moderate oven (350°) 45 to 60 minutes, until knife inserted halfway between center and edge comes out clean. Remove from oven.

• Make meringue by beating remaining 2 egg whites with ¼ tsp. vanilla and cream of tartar until soft peaks form; gradually add ¼ c. sugar, beating constantly. Beat until stiff peaks form and all the sugar is dissolved. Swirl on warm pudding, making sure meringue covers pudding edges. Bake in moderate oven (350°) about 15 minutes, until meringue is golden brown. Serve warm or cool. (Cool out of drafts.) Makes 6 servings.

Note: You can omit vanilla from pudding and add 1 tblsp. lemon juice and ½ tsp. grated lemon peel.

FOUR-SEASONS RICE PUDDING

Fruit topping is the gala note. Vary it with the season

3 c. cooked rice
1 qt. milk
3 eggs, slightly beaten
¾ c. sugar
1 tsp. salt
3 tblsp. melted butter or regular margarine
2 tblsp. ground cinnamon
Whole cooked cranberries
2 c. whole cranberry sauce

• Heat cooked rice and milk in top of double boiler.

• Combine eggs, sugar, salt and butter.

• Pour rice and milk into greased 2½-qt. baking dish. Slowly pour egg mixture over top and mix well.

• Bake in moderate oven (350°) 40 minutes. Spoon rice into serving dish.

• Decorate top with crisscross lines of cinnamon, placing a whole cooked cranberry in each square.

• To serve, ladle a generous spoonful of cranberry sauce over each serving. Makes 8 to 10 servings.

Note: For a spring version, substitute chilled rhubarb sauce for cranberries. Cut rhubarb in 1″ pieces, add 1 c. sugar to 4 c. rhubarb and pour ½″ water into saucepan. Cover and simmer until tender. Or use 3 parts rhubarb to 1 c. strawberries, cooking as for rhubarb sauce. In winter, pour grape juice over the pudding. Whipped cream may be used as garnish.

GLORIFIED RICE PUDDING

This really is a glamorous soufflé—serve quickly, it will not hold too long

- **1 (3½ oz.) pkg. lemon pudding and pie filling**
- **⅓ c. sugar**
- **1¼ c. milk**
- **¼ c. butter**
- **1 c. cooked rice**
- **½ c. flaked coconut**
- **1 tsp. vanilla**
- **2 egg yolks**
- **5 egg whites**

· Combine pudding mix and sugar in a small, heavy saucepan; gradually add milk. Bring to boil over medium heat, stirring constantly. Remove from heat; add butter, rice, coconut, vanilla, then egg yolks. Cool to lukewarm.

· Beat egg whites until stiff peaks form. Fold into cooled pudding. Pour into 1½-qt. soufflé dish or straight-sided casserole. Bake in moderate oven (350°) 50 minutes. Makes 6 to 8 servings.

MINCEMEAT BROWN BETTY

A change from mincemeat pie—easier to make and really good-tasting

- **2 c. coarse dry bread crumbs**
- **4 apples, sliced in eighths**
- **1 c. prepared mincemeat**
- **½ c. sugar**
- **¼ tsp. ground cinnamon**
- **¼ tsp. salt**
- **3 tblsp. lemon juice (1 lemon)**
- **¼ c. water**
- **2 tblsp. butter or regular margarine**

· Put ⅓ of crumbs into bottom of buttered 1½- to 2-qt. casserole; cover with half of apples and half of mincemeat.

· Mix together sugar, cinnamon and salt; sprinkle half over mincemeat.

· Add layer of crumbs; then one of apples and mincemeat; sprinkle with remaining sugar mixture.

· Top with remaining crumbs; pour lemon juice and water over all; dot with butter.

· Cover; bake in moderate oven (350°) 20 minutes; uncover; bake 15 minutes longer. Serve hot or cold with plain or whipped cream. Makes 4 to 5 servings.

FLAMING PLUM PUDDING

Top pudding with sugar cubes soaked in lemon extract. Light the cubes at serving time, carry flaming to table

- **½ c. butter**
- **1½ c. brown sugar, firmly packed**
- **2 eggs**
- **1 tsp. vanilla**
- **1 c. grated peeled carrots**
- **1 c. grated peeled apples**
- **½ c. raisins**
- **1 c. pecans, coarsely chopped**
- **1 c. sifted flour**
- **1 tsp. baking soda**
- **½ tsp. salt**
- **1 c. fine dry, white bread crumbs**
- **Caramel Sauce**

· Cream butter and sugar. Beat in eggs and vanilla; stir in carrots, apples, raisins and nuts.

· Sift together flour, soda and salt;

stir into creamed mixture. Add crumbs and mix well.

· Spoon into well-oiled 1½-qt. mold. Cover securely with mold lid or several thicknesses of waxed paper tied in place with string.

· Place mold on a rack in covered kettle of boiling water. (Water should come halfway up on the mold.) Steam for 3 hours. Unmold pudding onto serving plate; flame if you wish (directions follow). Serve hot with warm Caramel Sauce. Makes 8 to 10 servings.

CARAMEL SAUCE: Combine ½ c. brown sugar, firmly packed, 1 tblsp. cornstarch and ⅛ tsp. salt in small saucepan. Add 1 c. boiling water; cook until thickened and clear, stirring constantly. Remove from heat and stir in 2 tblsp. butter and 1 tsp. vanilla.

TO FLAME PUDDING: Soak sugar cubes in lemon extract tinted with red food color. Just before serving, place 2 or 3 cubes on top of pudding or several around sides, not touching pudding (use a metal or flame-proof dish). Light the cubes.

PERSIMMON/DATE PUDDING

It's a custom in persimmon country to freeze the fruit pulp to make this

1¼ c. sifted flour
1½ tsp. baking soda
1½ tsp. baking powder
½ tsp. salt
1 c. sugar
½ c. soft bread crumbs
1 c. native persimmon pulp (skinned)
1 c. chopped dates
1 c. chopped walnuts
1 tsp. vanilla
1½ tblsp. melted butter
½ c. milk

· Sift together flour, soda, baking powder, salt and sugar. Add remaining ingredients. Mix well.

· Line an 8½ × 4½ × 2½″ loaf pan with brown paper and grease. Spoon in pudding mixture.

· Bake in moderate oven (350°) 1½ hours. Serve hot or cold with hard sauce, ice cream or whipped cream. Makes 10 to 12 servings.

Note: Pudding keeps 2 to 3 weeks in refrigerator, or wrap and freeze.

PRUNE PUDDING

Guests never dream this is so simple —it tastes rich and elegant

1 c. sifted flour
1 tsp. baking soda
¼ tsp. salt
¼ tsp. ground cinnamon
1 c. seedless raisins
1 c. chopped walnuts
1 c. sugar
1 c. cooked, mashed prunes
1 tblsp. melted butter
1 tsp. vanilla
¾ c. milk
Whipped cream or Sherry Sauce

· Sift together flour, baking soda, salt and cinnamon; combine with raisins and nuts.

· Add sugar to soft, mashed prunes; add melted butter and vanilla and mix well.

· Combine dry ingredients with prune mixture and milk, blending thoroughly.

· Pour into greased 8″ square pan; bake in slow oven (325°) 1 hour. Serve warm with whipped cream, lemon sauce or Sherry Sauce. Makes 8 servings.

Variations

APRICOT PUDDING: Substitute dried apricots for the prunes.

APRICOT/PRUNE PUDDING: Use ½ c. each prunes and dried apricots.

SHERRY SAUCE

If you cook sauce over direct heat, let it come just to a boil

- 2 eggs
- 2 c. sugar
- 1 c. sherry wine
- ½ c. butter or margarine

· Beat eggs well in top of double boiler. Add sugar and mix. Stir in sherry and butter. Cook over simmering (not boiling) water, stirring constantly until smooth and thickened. Serve hot. Makes 3 cups, or 12 servings.

SWEET POTATO PUDDING

Garnish servings of pudding generously with ice cream

- 4 c. cooked, mashed sweet potatoes
- ½ c. heavy cream
- 1 tsp. grated lemon peel
- Juice of ½ lemon
- ½ tsp. ground cinnamon
- ½ tsp. ground ginger
- ¼ tsp. ground cloves
- 3 eggs, separated
- 1 (3½ oz.) can flaked coconut
- ⅓ c. brown sugar, firmly packed
- ⅓ c. slivered almonds

· Beat potatoes, cream, lemon peel, juice, spices and egg yolks until smooth. Reserve ⅓ c. coconut; fold remaining coconut into sweet potato mixture.

· Beat egg whites until soft peaks form; gradually beat in brown sugar to make a stiff meringue. Fold into sweet potato mixture. Spoon into buttered 2-qt. casserole; top with reserved ⅓ c. coconut and almonds.

· Bake in moderate oven (375°) 55 minutes, or until inserted knife blade comes out clean. Serve warm. Makes 8 servings.

APPLE PUDDING CAKE

Best when faintly warm with ice cream or whipped cream on top

- ½ c. butter or regular margarine
- 1 c. sugar
- 1½ c. grated peeled apples
- 2 c. flour
- 1 tsp. baking soda
- 1 tsp. ground cinnamon
- 1 tsp. ground allspice
- 1 tsp. salt
- 1 c. walnuts, chopped
- 1 c. raisins
- 1 tblsp. butter
- ½ c. sugar
- Grated peel and juice of 1 orange

· Cream ½ c. butter and 1 c. sugar until light and fluffy. Blend in grated apples.

· Sift together dry ingredients and stir into apple mixture.

· Stir in nuts and raisins. Spread batter in a lightly greased and floured 13 × 9 × 2" pan. Bake in moderate oven (350°) 40 minutes.

· Combine 1 tblsp. butter, ½ c. sugar, orange peel and juice; bring to a boil over moderate heat. Reduce heat and simmer until sugar is dissolved. Pour hot topping over cake when it comes from the oven. Cut in individual servings. Makes 12 servings.

PUMPKIN PUDDING CAKE

Cool, wrap in foil and freeze if you like—heat in foil to serve

- 1⅔ c. sifted flour
- 1⅓ c. sugar
- ¼ tsp. baking powder

1 tsp. baking soda
1 tsp. salt
1 tsp. ground cinnamon
¼ tsp. ground ginger
⅓ c. soft shortening
1 c. cooked, mashed or canned pumpkin
⅓ c. water
1 egg
⅔ c. raisins
⅓ c. walnuts or pecans

• Sift together dry ingredients into mixing bowl; add shortening, pumpkin and water. Beat 2 minutes on medium speed of electric mixer or until ingredients are all well mixed. Add egg, beat 2 minutes longer. Stir in raisins and nuts.
• Pour into a 1½-qt. ring or Turk's head mold that has been well greased and lightly dusted with fine, dry bread crumbs. Bake in moderate oven (350°) about 45 minutes, or until cake tests done. Serve warm with whipped cream or lemon sauce. Makes 8 servings.

RHUBARB PUDDING CAKE

Serve in dessert bowls. Pass a pitcher of cream to pour over

4 c. diced fresh rhubarb
1 c. sugar
¾ c. water
¼ c. shortening
½ c. sugar
1 egg
½ tsp. vanilla
1 c. sifted flour
2 tsp. baking powder
¼ tsp. salt
½ c. milk

• Cook rhubarb, 1 c. sugar and water until rhubarb is tender; keep hot.
• Cream shortening and ½ c. sugar; beat in egg and vanilla.
• Sift together flour, baking powder and salt; add alternately with milk to creamed mixture.
• Pour batter into greased 9″ square pan. Spoon hot rhubarb sauce over batter. Bake in moderate oven (350°) 40 minutes. Makes 9 servings.

APPLE DUMPLINGS

The fruity basting syrup provides a different delicious flavor

Pastry for 2-crust pie
3 tblsp. butter or regular margarine
¾ tsp. ground cinnamon
¾ tsp. ground allspice
¾ tsp. ground nutmeg
⅓ c. sifted brown sugar, firmly packed
8 medium apples, peeled and cored
3 tblsp. orange marmalade
1½ c. boiling water
1½ c. sugar
3 tblsp. fruit juice (orange, lemon, pineapple, apricot, etc.)
Red food color (optional)
Cream or Strawberry Hard Sauce

• Make paste of butter, spices and brown sugar.
• Roll out pastry ⅛″ thick; cut into eight (6″) squares. Place apple in center of each; put marmalade (or jelly) in cavity, and spread spicy paste over each apple.
• Moisten edges of pastry; bring points together over apple; seal sides firmly. Roll leftover pastry; cut into "streamers" to lay across tops of dumplings.
• Place in greased 15½ × 10½ × 1″ jelly roll pan or large baking dish; bake in moderate oven (375°) 30 minutes.
• While apples are baking, make syrup of water, 1½ c. sugar and

fruit juice; simmer to dissolve sugar. Pour over apples; bake 10 to 20 minutes more, basting frequently, to give attractive glaze. A little food color may be added to syrup. Serve warm with cream. Makes 8 servings.

OLD-TIME APPLE DUMPLINGS

Apples wear jackets of baking powder biscuit dough instead of pastry

2 c. sifted flour
2 tsp. baking powder
½ tsp. salt
½ c. shortening
⅔ c. milk
6 baking apples
⅓ c. sugar
¼ tsp. ground cinnamon
1 tblsp. butter or regular margarine
Milk (for tops)
Sweet-Sour Sauce

· Sift together flour, baking powder and salt; cut in shortening. Stir in milk; mix until soft dough is formed.
· Turn out on board and knead lightly. Roll ⅛″ thick. Cut dough into 6 squares.
· Peel and core apples. Place an apple on each square of dough. Combine sugar and cinnamon; sprinkle into center of each apple. Add ½ tsp. butter to each.
· Moisten edges of dough and press corners up over apples; brush with milk. Place in greased baking pan.
· Bake in moderate oven (350°) 30 minutes. Serve with Sweet-Sour Sauce. Makes 6 servings.

SWEET-SOUR DESSERT SAUCE: Heat together 2 c. water, ⅓ c. vinegar and ⅓ c. butter or regular margarine. Combine ⅓ c. flour, 1 c. sugar, 1 tsp. ground cinnamon and ⅛ tsp. ground nutmeg; mix thoroughly. Stir into hot mixture; cook over low heat, stirring until thickened. Pour warm over apple dumplings. Makes about 2½ cups.

COUNTRY PEACH DUMPLINGS

Rich biscuit dough surrounds these sweetened and "honeyed" big peaches

3 c. sifted flour
4 tsp. baking powder
1 tsp. salt
⅔ c. shortening
1 c. milk
6 large ripe peaches, peeled
12 tblsp. sugar
¼ tsp. ground nutmeg
6 tsp. honey
6 tsp. butter
2 tblsp. sugar

· Sift together flour, baking powder and salt. Cut in shortening until mixture is crumbly. Stir in milk.
· Knead dough slightly on lightly floured surface. Divide into sixths. Roll each piece of dough ⅛″ thick. Cut into a 7″ square. Place a peach in center of each square. Top each with 2 tblsp. sugar, a dash of nutmeg and 1 tsp. honey.
· Moisten edges of dough with water; fold up around each peach, firmly pressing edges to seal. Cut 6 leaf shapes, about 2″ long, from remaining rolled dough. Use a knife to mark veins in leaves. Moisten end with water and attach to dumpling. Repeat with remaining dough.
· Place dumplings in 13 × 9 × 2″ baking pan. Dot each with 1 tsp. butter; sprinkle evenly with the 2 tblsp. sugar. Bake in hot oven (400°) about 35 to 40 minutes, until golden brown. Remove from pan and serve warm. Makes 6 servings.

Pioneer Desserts–Cobblers and Shortcakes

Among the early American desserts that farm families prize highly today are the fruit and biscuit combinations in the form of cobblers and shortcakes. Made with fresh berries or other fruits, and soft rich biscuit dough, they are real family favorites. The ease and speed with which you can fix them also popularizes them with the cook!

FRESH BLUEBERRY COBBLER

Lemon accents delicate berry taste

1½ c. sugar
½ c. flour
1 tsp. salt
2 qts. fresh blueberries
3 tblsp. lemon juice
3 tblsp. butter
2 c. sifted flour
4 tsp. baking powder
2 tblsp. sugar
1 tsp. salt
½ c. shortening
⅔ c. milk
1 egg, slightly beaten

• Mix 1½ c. sugar, ½ c. flour and 1 tsp. salt; combine with blueberries and lemon juice. Pour into a greased 13 × 9 × 2″ (3-qt.) baking pan; dot with butter.

• Place in a preheated hot oven (400°) about 15 minutes; be sure that mixture is hot and bubbling.

• In the meantime, mix the topping. Sift together 2 c. flour, baking powder, 2 tblsp. sugar and 1 tsp. salt. Cut in shortening until mixture resembles coarse meal. Add milk and slightly beaten egg to dry ingredients. Stir with fork to blend well.

• Remove hot blueberry mixture from oven. Drop topping mixture onto hot blueberries, making 12 biscuits. Return to hot oven (400°); bake about 20 minutes, or until biscuits are browned. Makes 12 servings.

CHERRY COBBLER

Tastes like cherry pie and that's good

1 (1 lb. 4 oz.) can pitted tart cherries, undrained (2 c.)
½ c. sugar
1 tblsp. quick-cooking tapioca
2 tblsp. butter
⅛ tsp. salt
4 drops almond extract
Cobbler Topping

• Combine cherries, sugar and tapioca. Cook, stirring constantly, until mixture is thick and clear, about 15 minutes. Stir in butter, salt and almond extract.

• Pour hot mixture into 1½-qt. casserole or baking pan. Add Cobbler Topping at once.

• Bake in hot oven (400°) about 20 minutes, or until crust is browned. Serve warm with cream or vanilla ice cream. Makes 6 servings.

COBBLER TOPPING: Sift together 1 c. flour, 1 tblsp. sugar, 1½ tsp. baking powder and ¼ tsp. salt. Cut in ¼ c. butter or regular margarine until mixture resembles coarse crumbs. Mix ¼ c. milk and 1 slightly beaten egg. Add all at once to dry ingredients. Stir just to moisten. Drop by spoonfuls over hot cherry mixture and bake as directed.

Note: If you like more cherry filling, double the recipe, but use the same quantity of Cobbler Topping.

Variation

RHUBARB COBBLER: To 4 c. rhubarb, cut in 1″ pieces, add 1 c. sugar and 2 tblsp. cornstarch, mixed together. Add 1 tblsp. water and bring to a boil. Cook and stir about a minute. Add 2 tblsp. water. Pour into 8″ round baking dish. Dot with 1½ tblsp. butter. Add Cobbler Topping to hot rhubarb filling as directed for Cherry Cobbler, only add 2 tsp. grated orange peel to flour in making topping. Bake in hot oven (400°) 20 minutes, or until crust is browned. Serve with cream or vanilla ice cream. Makes 6 servings.

WINTER CHERRY COBBLER

Keep canned cherries in the cupboard to make this quickie dessert

1½ c. sugar
3 tblsp. cornstarch
3 (1 lb.) cans pitted tart cherries
¼ c. butter or regular margarine
3 c. sifted flour
¼ c. sugar
4½ tsp. baking powder
1½ tsp. salt
½ c. plus 1 tblsp. butter
1½ c. milk
Sugar (for topping)
Cinnamon (for topping)

· Stir together 1½ c. sugar and cornstarch in a saucepan. Drain fruit, reserving juice; arrange cherries in 13 × 9 × 2″ baking pan. Stir juice into dry ingredients in saucepan. Bring to a boil; boil 1 minute. Stir constantly. Pour 1½ c. hot sauce over fruit. Save rest of sauce. Dot fruit with ¼ c. butter.

· Sift together flour, ¼ c. sugar, baking powder and salt. Cut in ½ c. plus 1 tblsp. butter as for pastry. Lightly stir in milk; spoon batter over hot fruit. Sprinkle lightly with sugar and cinnamon.

· Bake in hot oven (400°) 30 minutes, or until topping is golden brown. Serve warm with reserved sauce. Pass a pitcher of dairy half-and-half or heavy cream. Makes 12 servings.

Variation

WINTER PEACH COBBLER: Prepare as directed for Winter Cherry Cobbler, except substitute 4 (1 lb.) cans sliced peaches for the cherries and decrease the sugar from 1½ c. to ½ c.

CONCORD GRAPE COBBLER

Freeze filling to extend grape season

10 c. stemmed and washed grapes
2 c. sugar
2½ tblsp. quick-cooking tapioca
¼ tsp. salt
⅛ tsp. ground cinnamon
2 tblsp. lemon juice
1 tblsp. butter
Biscuit Lattice

· Slip skins from grapes; set aside. Heat pulp to boiling; rub through coarse sieve or food mill to remove seeds. Discard seeds.

· Combine sugar, tapioca, salt and cinnamon. Add lemon juice and grape pulp. Cook until thickened, stirring.

· Remove from heat; add skins; mix.

· Pour into 8″ square baking pan. Dot with butter. Add Biscuit Lattice.

· Bake in hot oven (400°) about 20 minutes, or until lattice crust is golden. Makes 9 servings. This filling will make 2 (8″ or 9″) pies.

BISCUIT LATTICE: Sift together 1½ c. sifted flour, 2¼ tsp. baking powder, 1 tblsp. sugar and ¼ tsp. salt. Cut in ¼ c. butter or regular margarine. Make well in center; add ¼ c. milk and 1 egg, slightly beaten, all at once; stir with fork into soft dough. Turn out on lightly floured pastry cloth and knead dough 10 times. Roll dough into 7 × 9″ rectangle; cut in seven 9″ strips. Place 4 strips on hot filling one way, lattice other 3 strips opposite way. Start with center strip. Bake.

TO FREEZE COBBLER FILLING: Pour hot filling into 8″ square foil-lined baking pan; cool and freeze.

• Remove block of filling from pan; overwrap and return to freezer. It will keep 3 to 4 months.

TO SERVE: Return unthawed filling to pan. Dot with butter. Bake in hot oven (400°) about 35 to 40 minutes until bubbling hot, stirring occasionally.

• Remove from oven, cover with Biscuit Lattice; return to oven and bake about 20 minutes. Serve warm.

FRESH PEACH COBBLER

Batter Topping and Spiced Honeyed Cream make this a real treat

1½ tblsp. cornstarch
¼ to ⅓ c. brown sugar, firmly packed
½ c. water
4 c. sweetened sliced peeled peaches
1 tblsp. butter
1 tblsp. lemon juice
Batter Topping
1 tblsp. sugar
Spiced Honeyed Cream

• Mix cornstarch, brown sugar and water. Add peaches and cook until mixture is thickened, about 15 minutes. Add butter and lemon juice. Pour into an 8″ round baking dish.

• Drop spoonfuls of Batter Topping over hot peach mixture. Sprinkle with white sugar. Bake in hot oven (400°) 40 to 50 minutes. Serve warm, in bowls, with Spiced Honeyed Cream. Makes 6 servings.

BATTER TOPPING: Combine ½ c. sifted flour, ½ c. sugar, ½ tsp. baking powder, ¼ tsp. salt, 2 tblsp. soft butter and 1 egg, slightly beaten. Beat with spoon until batter is smooth.

• Drop by spoonfuls over hot peach mixture, spreading evenly. It spreads over peaches during baking. Bake as directed.

SPICED HONEYED CREAM: Beat 1 c. heavy cream until thick. Add 2 tblsp. honey and ½ tsp. ground cinnamon. Beat to mix. Makes 1⅔ cups.

PEACH COBBLER RING

Plain, it's coffee bread; with cream and sliced peaches, a wonderful dessert

2 c. flour
4 tsp. baking powder
1 tblsp. sugar
½ tsp. salt
½ c. shortening
⅔ c. milk
2 tblsp. soft butter
¼ c. brown sugar, firmly packed
1 tblsp. flour
1 tsp. ground cinnamon
1 c. diced fresh peaches
Melted butter (for top)

• For dough, sift together 2 c. flour, baking powder, white sugar and salt; cut in shortening until mixture resembles coarse crumbs. Add milk all at once; stir to form soft dough. Turn out on lightly floured board and knead 6 to 8 times. Roll into 18 × 9″ rectangle.

· To fill, spread dough with 2 tblsp. butter. Sprinkle with mixture of brown sugar, 1 tblsp. flour and cinnamon; cover with peaches.

· Roll up like jelly roll. Place on ungreased baking sheet and form into circle. Make slits from outside edge of circle almost into center every 2″. Turn each cut on its side. Brush with butter. Bake in hot oven (400°) 25 to 30 minutes. Serve warm with cream, and spoon additional sliced peaches over top. Makes 6 servings.

PEACH/APRICOT COBBLER

Two fruits unite in the filling of this blue-ribbon treat. Try it

1 (1 lb. 13 oz.) can sliced peaches
1 (8¾ oz.) can apricot halves
½ c. sugar
1 tblsp. cornstarch
1 tblsp. butter or regular margarine
¼ tsp. ground cinnamon
1 c. sifted flour
1 tblsp. sugar
1½ tsp. baking powder
½ tsp. salt
3 tblsp. shortening
½ c. milk

· To make filling, drain peaches and apricots, reserving juices. Add enough peach juice to apricot juice to make 1 c.

· Combine ½ c. sugar and cornstarch in saucepan. Blend in juice and cook over medium heat, stirring constantly, until mixture comes to a boil. Cook 1 minute longer.

· Remove from heat and stir in butter and cinnamon. Add fruits to thickened juice and pour into 1½-qt. casserole. Place in hot oven (400°) while you prepare topping.

· To make topping, sift together flour, 1 tblsp. sugar, baking powder and salt. Cut in shortening until mixture resembles coarse crumbs. Stir in milk to make a soft dough.

· Drop by spoonfuls over hot fruit. Bake in hot oven (400°) about 30 minutes, until top is lightly browned. Serve warm with cream. Makes 6 servings.

STRAWBERRY SHORTCAKE ROYALE

Ice cream sauce surprises and delights

⅓ c. shortening
2½ c. all-purpose buttermilk biscuit mix
3 tblsp. sugar
1 tsp. vanilla
¾ c. milk
1 qt. strawberries, cut in halves
⅓ c. sugar
Triple Cream Sauce

· Cut shortening into biscuit mix until crumbly.

· Combine 3 tblsp. sugar, vanilla and milk; stir into biscuit mixture and beat 15 strokes. Pat into two well-greased 8″ round layer cake pans. Bake in hot oven (425°) 12 to 15 minutes or until golden brown. Cool.

· Meanwhile, sprinkle berries with ⅓ c. sugar. Let stand 30 minutes. Spread half of the sweetened berries on a shortcake layer. Top with second cake layer. Add remaining berries. Spoon Triple Cream Sauce over shortcake. Makes 6 to 8 servings.

TRIPLE CREAM SAUCE: Combine 1 c. softened ice cream, ½ c. dairy sour cream, ¼ c. sugar and 1 tsp. vanilla. Whip 1 c. heavy cream until quite stiff. Thoroughly fold whipped cream into ice cream mixture. Chill. Makes 3 cups.

WHIPPED CREAM SHORTCAKE

Whipped cream-egg biscuits make wonderful berry or peach shortcakes

- **3 c. sifted flour**
- **2 tblsp. baking powder**
- **1 tsp. salt**
- **¼ c. finely chopped nuts (optional)**
- **1 egg**
- **1 c. heavy cream**
- **2 tblsp. sugar**
- **1 tsp. vanilla**
- **1 qt. strawberries, cut in halves, or sliced fresh peaches**
- **⅓ c. sugar**

• Sift together flour, baking powder and salt. Stir in nuts.

• Combine egg, cream, sugar and vanilla. Whip until mixture stands in soft peaks.

• Fold cream mixture into dry ingredients until all flour is moistened. Gather dough into ball. Knead on floured board 8 to 10 times. Roll out ½″ thick.

• Cut three 4″ biscuits, three 2¾″ biscuits and six 1¼″ biscuits.

• Place on ungreased baking sheet. Brush with cream. Bake in hot oven (450°) 12 to 15 minutes.

• Split large and medium-size biscuits. Make tiers of biscuit halves, sugared berries or peaches and whipped cream. Top with tiny biscuits. Serve with strawberries or sliced fresh peaches and more whipped cream. Makes 6 servings.

Gingerbread Comes in Variety

Our gingerbread recipes are unusual and special. Apple Gingerbread, developed in our Countryside Kitchens, makes its own luscious topping. Chocolate/Orange Torte Gingerbread is guest-worthy—an exciting flavor combination and so easy to fix. Coffee and Cream Ginger Roll requires more work, but it's glamorous and delicious. Regardless of which kind of gingerbread you bake, do follow the established country custom of having plenty of hot coffee on hand to accompany the spicy dessert.

Top warm gingerbread with fluffs of whipped cream, whipped topping mix, or with ice cream dollops. Serve it warm or cool with your favorite lemon sauce. A country dessert that always pleases.

APPLE GINGERBREAD

For a crowd stack two of these gingerbreads—a dramatic dessert

- **½ c. whole bran cereal**
- **½ c. light molasses**
- **¼ c. softened shortening**
- **¼ c. boiling water**
- **1 egg**
- **1 c. sifted flour**
- **½ tsp. baking soda**
- **½ tsp. baking powder**
- **½ tsp. ground ginger**
- **¼ tsp. ground cloves**
- **¼ tsp. salt**
- **6 c. thin slices peeled apple**
- **¼ c. melted butter**
- **¼ c. light corn syrup**
- **Milk**

• Mix bran, molasses, shortening and water. Add egg, and beat with rotary beater; let stand 5 minutes.

• Sift together flour, soda, baking powder, spices and salt; add to bran mixture and stir only until blended. Pour into greased 8″ square pan.

Bake in moderate oven (350°) 20 minutes.

• Arrange apple slices in layers over top. Brush with mixture of butter and syrup. Bake 10 minutes longer, or until apples are tender.

• Remove from oven, brush apples with milk and broil just a few minutes to brown edges of apple slices (for a change, sprinkle chopped walnuts over apple slices). Serve warm. Makes 12 servings.

GINGER/LEMON PUDDING CAKE

Molasses enriches the taste

- 3 eggs, separated
- 2 tblsp. light molasses
- 6 tblsp. sugar
- 2 tblsp. flour
- 1 tblsp. melted butter or regular margarine
- 1 tsp. ground ginger
- 1/16 tsp. salt
- 1 c. milk
- 2 tsp. grated lemon peel
- ¼ c. lemon juice

• Beat egg yolks in a mixing bowl. Beat in molasses and sugar, then flour, butter, ginger, salt, milk, lemon peel and lemon juice to make a smooth mixture.

• Beat egg whites until stiff but not dry. Fold into batter.

• Pour mixture into greased 1½-qt. baking dish. Set in pan of hot water about 1″ deep. Bake in slow oven (325°) 55 minutes or until top is browned and knife inserted halfway deep into center comes out clean.

• Spoon into serving dishes. Serve warm, topped with whipped cream. Makes 5 to 6 servings.

SPICY GINGERBREAD SQUARES

A long-keeper. Serve warm or cold with a hot lemon sauce

- 2 c. sifted flour
- ½ c. sugar
- ½ tsp. salt
- 1 tsp. baking soda
- 2 tsp. ground ginger
- 1½ tsp. ground cardamom
- 1 tsp. ground allspice
- 1 tblsp. grated orange peel
- 3 eggs
- ½ c. light molasses
- 1 c. buttermilk
- ½ c. melted butter

• Sift together dry ingredients into a large mixing bowl. Stir in orange peel.

• In a separate bowl, beat eggs until thick, light and foamy. Add molasses in a stream, beating constantly. Gradually beat in buttermilk.

• Add half of buttermilk-molasses mixture to dry ingredients. Beat with a spoon until well blended. Add remaining buttermilk-molasses mixture in two parts, beating well after each addition.

• Gradually add butter and beat with spoon until batter is blended and smooth. Pour into greased 8″ square baking pan.

• Bake in moderate oven (350°) 45 to 50 minutes or until toothpick inserted in center comes out clean. Serves 9.

PECAN GINGER LOAF

Serve with a brick of cream cheese (soft, for spreading) and fruit

- ½ c. soft butter or regular margarine
- 1½ c. sugar
- 2 eggs

1⅔ c. unsifted flour
¾ tsp. salt
1 tsp. baking soda
¼ tsp. baking powder
2 tsp. ground ginger
½ tsp. ground cinnamon
½ tsp. ground nutmeg
¼ tsp. ground cloves
⅓ c. water
1 c. cooked, mashed pumpkin
½ c. finely chopped pecans

• Cream together butter and sugar with electric mixer. Add eggs, one at a time, and beat until mixture is light and fluffy.

• Sift together dry ingredients, add to creamed mixture alternately with water. Beat well after each addition. Add pumpkin and beat until well blended. Stir in chopped pecans. Turn into greased 9 × 5 × 3″ loaf pan and spread smooth.

• Bake in moderate oven (350°) 60 to 70 minutes, or until toothpick inserted in center comes out clean. Cool in pan 10 minutes, then turn out on rack to cool thoroughly. Makes 1 loaf.

WHOLE WHEAT GINGERBREAD

It's spicy, not too sweet and contains nuts, raisins and candied lemon peel

½ c. butter or regular margarine
2 tblsp. sugar
¾ c. light molasses
1 c. sifted flour
1 c. stirred whole wheat flour
½ tsp. salt
¾ tsp. baking soda
1 tsp. ground ginger
½ tsp. ground cinnamon
½ tsp. ground mace or nutmeg
½ c. chopped walnuts
½ c. raisins
3 tblsp. minced candied lemon peel
2 eggs
½ c. milk

• Melt butter in a saucepan. Add sugar and molasses; stir to blend.

• Sift together the dry ingredients into a large mixing bowl (include chaff from whole wheat flour). Stir in nuts, raisins and lemon peel.

• Beat eggs and milk together and add to dry ingredients along with molasses mixture. Stir to moisten. Then beat mixture with a wooden spoon for about 70 strokes. Turn into a greased 8″ square baking pan.

• Bake in moderate oven (350°) 40 minutes or until cake tests done. Serve warm or cool. Makes 10 servings.

COFFEE AND CREAM GINGER ROLL

Egg whites leaven this guest special

5 eggs, separated
½ tsp. cream of tartar
1 c. sifted confectioners sugar
3 tblsp. sifted flour
¼ tsp. salt
1/16 tsp. pepper
1½ tblsp. instant coffee powder
1½ tsp. ground ginger
1 tsp. ground allspice
1 tsp. ground cinnamon
1 tsp. ground nutmeg
1 tsp. ground cardamom (optional)
½ tsp. ground cloves
Sifted confectioners sugar
1½ c. heavy cream
½ c. sifted confectioners sugar
1½ tsp. vanilla
Amber Candy Shatters or fruit to garnish

• Beat egg whites (at room temperature) with cream of tartar until soft peaks form. Gradually add ½ c. of sifted confectioners sugar, beating until stiff peaks form.

· In a separate bowl, beat egg yolks until thick and light colored.

· Sift together 3 times the remaining ½ c. confectioners sugar, flour, salt, pepper, coffee and spices. Fold into egg yolks until just blended. Gently fold yolk mixture into egg whites. Spread gently and evenly in a 15½ × 10½ × 1″ jelly roll pan which has been greased, lined with waxed paper and the waxed paper greased.

· Bake in moderate oven (350°) 15 minutes or until cake springs back when touched lightly. Turn out on a towel sprinkled with sifted confectioners sugar. Quickly and gently peel off paper. Starting at narrow end, roll cake and towel together; cool thoroughly on rack.

· Whip heavy cream, gradually adding the ½ c. confectioners sugar and vanilla. Unroll cake and spread with cream. Roll up again and roll onto serving platter. Chill thoroughly, at least 3 hours.

· Sprinkle lightly with confectioners sugar. Slice to serve and top with Amber Candy Shatters or accompany each slice with fruit. Makes 10 servings.

AMBER CANDY SHATTERS: In a heavy fry-pan, cook ½ c. sugar over medium heat, stirring, until sugar melts and turns a golden brown (be careful not to scorch). Pour into buttered shallow pan to cool and harden. Break into pieces, then crush with rolling pin.

CHOCOLATE/ORANGE TORTE GINGERBREAD

This is unusual; a conversation piece! Icing complements ginger flavor

1 (14 oz.) pkg. gingerbread mix
1 tsp. ground ginger
1 tsp. ground cinnamon
2 tblsp. melted butter
Orange-Sliver Chocolate Icing

· Stir together gingerbread mix, ginger and cinnamon. Then prepare the gingerbread according to package directions *except* add the 2 tblsp. melted butter along with the water called for in the package directions.

· Pour into greased 9″ round layer cake pan. Bake according to package directions.

· Cool in pan 10 minutes, then remove from pan and cool on rack. When cake is cool, place on serving platter; spoon Orange-Sliver Chocolate Icing over top, allowing it to drizzle down cake sides. Makes 8 servings.

ORANGE-SLIVER CHOCOLATE ICING: Combine ½ c. orange marmalade, 3 oz. (½ c.) semisweet chocolate pieces and a few grains of salt in top of double boiler. Heat over hot water, stirring occasionally until chocolate melts and mixture is shiny.

Favorite Desserts for Company

Country people believe that mixing good food with conversation best expresses hospitality. When friends drive over to spend the evening, refreshments are in order.

Hostesses like to serve a superb dessert with coffee. Frequently it's a wonderful torte cheesecake, or some other cakelike dessert, such as Elegant Chocolate Log. For the festive valentine social season, this chapter offers two specialties. Cream Puff Valentine is the favorite of a gracious, young Oregon farm woman who entertains delightfully in her charming hill-top home. Or do you want first to try the heart-shaped Banana/Berry Torte developed in our own Countryside Test Kitchens?

ELEGANT CHOCOLATE LOG

Place log on tray or platter and serve at table to dramatize dessert

5 egg yolks
1 c. sifted confectioners sugar
¼ c. sifted flour
½ tsp. salt
3 tblsp. cocoa
1 tsp. vanilla
5 stiffly beaten egg whites
1 c. heavy cream, whipped
2 tblsp. sugar (about)
8 to 12 marshmallows, cut up
½ square unsweetened chocolate
1 c. confectioners sugar
Light cream
¼ c. finely chopped pecans

• Beat egg yolks until thick and lemon-colored. Sift 1 c. confectioners sugar, flour, salt and cocoa together 3 times; beat into egg yolks until well blended. Add vanilla; fold in egg whites.

• Bake in greased and paper-lined 15½ × 10½ × 1″ jelly roll pan in moderate oven (375°) 15 to 20 minutes. Lightly dust clean dish towel with confectioners sugar; loosen cake around edges with spatula. Invert on towel. Lift off pan and carefully peel off paper. With a sharp knife, cut off cake's crisp edges. Roll up cake gently, from narrow end, by folding edge of cake over and then tucking it in; continue rolling cake, lifting towel higher with one hand as you guide the rolling with the other hand, rolling the towel in the cake (to prevent cake sticking). Let cool on rack (wrap tightly in towel to hold it in shape).

• Unroll cake on towel; spread with whipped cream, sweetened to taste with about 2 tblsp. sugar and with marshmallows added. Roll like jelly roll.

• For frosting, melt chocolate; add 1 c. confectioners sugar and enough light cream to make frosting of spreading consistency. Spread over cake and immediately sprinkle with chopped nuts. Makes 8 to 10 servings.

Banana/Berry Torte for Valentine Dessert

For a dazzling valentine dessert Banana/Berry Torte is an excellent choice. You can bake the heart-shaped meringue crust, fill and freeze for a few hours or up to a couple of weeks. When you want to serve it, take the torte from the freezer and decorate it with a border of glistening glazed banana slices. Refrigerate it until time to serve. Directions for making this gorgeous treat follow.

BANANA/BERRY TORTE

Make and freeze meringue to simplify completing dessert on party day

Meringue shell:
5 egg whites (room temperature)
¼ tsp. salt
¼ tsp. cream of tartar
1 tsp. vanilla
1¼ c. sugar (sifted)

Cream filling:
2 (3 oz.) pkgs. cream cheese
1 tblsp. lemon juice
½ c. sifted confectioners sugar
½ c. mashed ripe bananas
Few drops red food color
1 (10 oz.) pkg. frozen strawberries, thawed
1 c. heavy cream, whipped

Glazed banana slices:
2 tblsp. cornstarch
¼ c. sugar
6 tblsp. water
1 tsp. lemon juice
Reserved strawberry juice
¼ tsp. red food color (about)
2 bananas

· To make meringue shell, beat egg whites, salt, cream of tartar and vanilla until frothy. Gradually add sugar, beating until stiff peaks form (about 10 minutes).

· Cover a baking sheet with heavy brown paper. Draw a heart shape, 12" high on the paper. Spread meringue to edges of heart shape; build up sides 2" to make a shell.

· Bake in very slow oven (250°) 1½ hours. Turn off heat; leave meringue in closed oven 3 hours. Remove from paper with spatula.

· To make filling, soften cream cheese; beat in lemon juice, confectioners sugar, mashed bananas and food color.

· Drain strawberries, reserving juice (refreeze juice, if you wish). Fold berries and whipped cream into cheese mixture. Spoon filling into meringue shell. Wrap carefully and freeze.

· On the day you plan to serve the torte, combine cornstarch, white sugar, water, lemon juice, reserved strawberry juice and food color in small saucepan. Cook over medium heat until glaze is thick and clear; cool slightly.

· Remove filled meringue from freezer; unwrap.

· Peel bananas; score with a fork; slice. Arrange slices on filling; spoon glaze over bananas. Refrigerate 1 to 3 hours. Makes 12 servings.

CREAM PUFF VALENTINE

Beautiful year-around company dessert

1 c. water
½ c. butter
1 c. sifted flour
4 eggs
Cream Filling
2 (10 oz.) pkgs. frozen strawberries, thawed and drained
Confectioners sugar

· Fold a 9 × 8½" piece of paper in half lengthwise. Sketch half of a heart on it; cut out. Open paper to full heart; trace with pencil on baking sheet. Grease sheet lightly.

· Heat water and butter to boiling; reduce heat. Add flour. Stir vigorously over low heat until mixture forms a ball (about 1 minute). Remove from heat.

· Beat in eggs, one at a time, beating until smooth after each addition. Drop mixture by spoonfuls, with sides touching, onto heart outline on baking sheet.

• Bake in hot oven (400°) 45 minutes. Cool on rack. Cut off top. Fill shell with Cream Filling; top with strawberries. Replace top. Dust with confectioners sugar. Serve at once. Makes 8 servings.

CREAM FILLING: Mix 1 (3¼ oz.) pkg. vanilla pudding and pie filling with 1½ c. milk. Follow package directions for cooking. Cool. Then fold in 1 c. heavy cream, whipped, and 1 tsp. vanilla.

ORANGE ANGEL TORTE

You can fix the base for this lovely torte one day, the filling the next

1 c. thinly sliced candied red and green cherries
1½ c. chopped nuts
2 c. flaked coconut
¾ c. fine soft white bread crumbs
6 egg whites (⅞ c.)
1 tsp. cream of tartar
½ tsp. salt
2 c. sugar
1 tsp. vinegar
1 tsp. vanilla
Orange Filling
2 c. heavy cream, whipped, or 2 envelopes dessert topping mix, whipped
Cherry Flowers

• Line a 15½ × 10½ × 1″ jelly roll pan with brown paper; grease and lightly flour paper.
• Combine fruit, nuts, coconut and crumbs in a large bowl; mix to coat fruit, nuts and coconut with crumbs.
• Bring egg whites to room temperature. Add cream of tartar and salt. Beat at high speed of electric mixer or portable beater to soft peak stage. Slowly beat in sugar, vinegar and vanilla. Beat 10 minutes to the stiff peak stage. Fold into the fruit-nut mixture.
• Turn mixture into the prepared pan. Spread evenly over paper, building the edges higher. Bake in moderate oven (375°) 25 minutes, or until lightly browned. Cool. Transfer torte to a tray; cut paper from edges, but not from bottom.
• Spread chilled Orange Filling over the top of the raised edges. Cover with whipped cream or dessert topping mix, prepared by package directions. Decorate with Cherry Flowers. Refrigerate overnight before serving, or freeze unwrapped, then wrap for storage. Thaw 30 minutes before serving frozen torte. Makes 24 servings.

ORANGE FILLING: Mix ½ c. flour, 1½ c. sugar and ½ tsp. salt in saucepan. Gradually add 2½ c. orange juice, then 6 slightly beaten egg yolks (½ c.) and 2 tblsp. butter or regular margarine. Cook over medium heat until thick. Cover and cool, then refrigerate.

CHERRY FLOWERS: Cut 12 red candied cherries in quarters, 3 green candied cherries in eighths. Group 2 red slices and 1 green slice together on top of Orange Angel Torte to make 24 flowers, one for each serving.

ORANGE/BUTTERSCOTCH TORTE

Make this luscious dessert that makes at least 18 servings a day ahead

6 eggs
1¼ c. sugar
¾ tsp. almond extract
¼ c. sifted flour
1 tsp. baking powder
¼ tsp. salt
2 c. graham cracker crumbs
1 c. chopped walnuts
Orange/Butterscotch Sauce
2 c. heavy cream

· Beat eggs on high speed of electric mixer for 5 minutes. Gradually add sugar, beating until soft peaks form (about 5 minutes). Add almond extract.

· Sift together flour, baking powder and salt; add graham cracker crumbs. Fold crumb mixture, about ½ c. at a time, into beaten eggs. Fold in nuts. Pour into greased 13 × 9 × 2″ pan.

· Bake in slow oven (325°) 30 to 35 minutes. Cool; turn out on plate.

· Make Orange/Butterscotch Sauce. Spread two thirds of sauce over cake.

· Whip heavy cream until stiff peaks form. Spread whipped cream over top and sides of cake. Dribble remaining sauce in lines over whipped cream; cut through whipped cream with knife several times for a marbleized effect.

· Refrigerate at least 8 hours. Cut in 18 to 21 pieces.

ORANGE/BUTTERSCOTCH SAUCE: Combine in saucepan 1 c. brown sugar, firmly packed, ¼ c. butter, ½ c. frozen orange juice concentrate, 2 tblsp. flour, 1 beaten egg and ¼ tsp. salt. Bring to boil over medium heat; cook until thick (about 4 minutes), stirring constantly. Cool slightly.

FRUIT/NUT TORTE

Nut curls for garnish: Shave nuts thin with vegetable parer or knife

1 c. Brazil nuts, halved, or ¾ c. whole blanched almonds
2 c. walnut or pecan halves
1 c. whole candied red and green cherries, mixed
1 c. raisins or sliced dates
1½ c. sifted flour
1 tsp. salt
4 eggs
2 egg yolks
1¼ c. sugar
1 tblsp. vanilla
2 egg whites
¼ c. sugar
¼ c. sifted confectioners sugar
1 tblsp. sugar (for top)
¼ c. Brazil nut curls (for top)

· Fit two lengths of brown paper into a 9″ square pan; allow 1½″ extension beyond pan edges. Grease lightly to settle papers into the pan.

· Combine nuts and fruit in a large bowl. Toss with ½ c. flour.

· Sift remaining 1 c. flour with the salt.

· Beat eggs and egg yolks until thick and lemon-colored. Gradually beat in 1¼ c. sugar and vanilla, beating until cream-colored. Fold in dry ingredients. Pour over the fruit-nut mixture; fold until completely mixed. Turn into prepared pan.

· Bake in moderate oven (375°) 50 to 60 minutes, or until cake tester comes out clean when inserted in center of the torte. (When the torte is a medium brown, cover it with paper or foil for remainder of baking time.)

· Meanwhile, prepare topping. Beat egg whites until peaks form. Gradually beat in ¼ c. sugar and the confectioners sugar; continue beating until stiff and glossy.

· Take torte from the oven, remove paper cover and spread the topping evenly over crust. Be sure to cover edges. Sprinkle with remaining 1 tblsp. sugar and Brazil nut curls. Return to oven for 15 minutes, or until lightly browned.

· Cool in pan 30 minutes. Lift from pan by paper liner onto wire rack. Loosen paper from meringue edges. When cold, cut paper off sides, but leave it on the bottom of the torte. Serve cut in slices or small squares, plain or topped with whipped cream. Makes 24 servings.

FROZEN PINEAPPLE TORTE

You can make and freeze this dessert a few days before you entertain guests

- 3 egg yolks
- ⅛ tsp. salt
- ½ c. sugar
- 1 (8½ oz.) can crushed pineapple (save juice)
- 2 tblsp. lemon juice
- 3 egg whites
- 2 tblsp. sugar
- 1 tsp. grated lemon peel
- 1 c. heavy cream, whipped
- 1 c. vanilla wafer crumbs

• Beat egg yolks slightly; add salt and ½ c. sugar and beat a little more. Add pineapple juice (drained from crushed pineapple) and lemon juice. Cook over hot, not boiling, water until custard coats the spoon; stir constantly while cooking. Add the pineapple and cool.

• Make a meringue with egg whites and 2 tblsp. sugar. Fold in the pineapple custard, lemon peel and whipped cream.

• Coat the sides of a greased 13 × 9 × 2″ baking pan with ½ c. vanilla wafer crumbs. Pour custard into pan and sprinkle remaining vanilla wafer crumbs over the top. Cover and freeze.

• Place dessert in refrigerator about 30 minutes before serving. It then will cut easily. Makes 8 to 10 servings.

RASPBERRY TORTE

Marshmallow sauce enhances berries

- 1¼ c. flour
- ¼ c. sugar
- ¼ tsp. salt
- 1 c. butter or regular margarine
- 3 tblsp. cornstarch
- 1 c. sugar
- 2 (10 oz.) pkgs. frozen red raspberries, thawed
- 45 regular marshmallows
- 1 c. milk
- 1 c. heavy cream, whipped

• To make crust, combine flour, ¼ c. sugar and salt in bowl. Cut in chilled butter until mixture resembles coarse crumbs. Pat in bottom of ungreased 13 × 9 × 2″ pan. Bake in moderate oven (350°) 15 to 18 minutes, until lightly browned. Cool.

• For filling, combine cornstarch and 1 c. sugar in saucepan. Add raspberries and cook, stirring constantly, until mixture comes to a boil and is clear. Cool slightly. Pour over crust. Chill.

• To make topping, place marshmallows and milk in a saucepan; cook over low heat, stirring frequently, until marshmallows are melted. Cool. Fold whipped cream into marshmallow mixture; spread over chilled raspberry filling. Chill. Makes 12 servings.

POINSETTIA CHEESECAKE

Perfect to serve with coffee at parties

- 1¼ c. graham cracker crumbs (about 18 crackers)
- ¼ c. sugar
- ½ c. butter or regular margarine
- 1 c. creamed cottage cheese, sieved
- 2 (3 oz.) pkgs. cream cheese
- 2 eggs
- ½ c. sugar
- 1 tsp. vanilla
- ¼ tsp. salt
- ½ c. dairy sour cream
- 2 tblsp. sugar
- ½ tsp. vanilla
- 3 maraschino cherries, quartered
- 3 citron strips

· Combine crumbs and ¼ c. sugar.
· Melt butter; cool. Mix thoroughly with crumbs. Press mixture onto bottom and sides of a well greased 9″ spring-form pan (or other round pan with deep sides). Bake in moderate oven (350°) 8 minutes. Cool.
· Blend until smooth cottage cheese, cream cheese, eggs, the ½ c. sugar, 1 tsp. vanilla and salt. Pour into crust. Bake in moderate oven (350°) about 18 minutes, or until set.
· Blend together sour cream, 2 tblsp. sugar and ½ tsp. vanilla. Spread over top of cheesecake.
· Arrange cherries and citron, poinsettia fashion, over cream topping. Chill overnight. Makes 8 servings.

SIMPLE COUNTRY CHEESECAKE

Nutritious cottage cheese provides delicate flavor and smooth texture

3 c. cottage cheese, drained
5 eggs, slightly beaten
¼ tsp. salt
1 tsp. vanilla
¼ tsp. almond extract
1 c. sugar
¾ c. sifted flour
1½ c. milk
Tangy Jam Sauce

· Press cottage cheese through sieve (or blend with 1 c. of the milk in blender until smooth). Add eggs, salt, vanilla and almond extract to cheese; blend thoroughly.
· Combine sugar and flour; slowly blend into cheese mixture. Add milk. Pour into buttered 9″ square pan. Set dish in pan of water. Bake in moderate oven (350°) 1 hour or until knife inserted halfway between side and center comes out clean. (Surface may be pale.) Cool. Cut in squares and serve with Tangy Jam Sauce and whipped cream. Makes 9 servings.

TANGY JAM SAUCE: Combine ½ c. strawberry jam, ½ tsp. lemon juice and ¼ tsp. vanilla; blend thoroughly.

BOSTON CREAM PIE

This historic dessert is a one-egg cake with velvety custard filling; top it with chocolate icing and it's called Chocolate Cream Pie

2 c. sifted cake flour
1¼ c. sugar
2½ tsp. baking powder
1 tsp. salt
⅓ c. shortening
1 c. milk
1 tsp. vanilla
¼ tsp. almond extract (optional)
1 egg, unbeaten
Custard Cream Filling

· Sift dry ingredients into mixing bowl. Add shortening, milk, vanilla and almond extract. Beat 2 minutes, using medium speed on electric mixer or 300 strokes by hand.
· Add egg; beat 2 minutes more. Pour into two greased 8″ or 9″ round layer cake pans.
· Bake in moderate oven (350°) 25 to 30 minutes. Cool on racks. Use one layer to make Boston Cream Pie; freeze the other for use later.
· Split cooled cake layer in crosswise halves. Spread Custard Cream Filling over lower half. Cover with top half. Dust with confectioners sugar. Or spread with Chocolate Icing.

CUSTARD CREAM FILLING

One of the great delicacies of country kitchens—be sure to try the variations

1 c. milk, scalded
½ c. sugar

3 tblsp. cornstarch
⅛ tsp. salt
2 eggs, slightly beaten
1 tblsp. butter or regular margarine
1 tsp. vanilla

· Gradually add milk to mixture of sugar, cornstarch and salt. Cook slowly, stirring constantly, until mixture thickens, about 10 to 15 minutes.

· Add about ½ c. hot mixture to eggs and blend; carefully combine both mixtures and cook about 3 minutes, stirring constantly.

· Remove from heat; blend in butter and vanilla. Cool. Makes 1¼ cups.

Variations

BANANA CUSTARD CREAM FILLING: Spread custard filling between halves of split cake layer. Cover custard with banana slices (1 medium to large banana, sliced and sprinkled with lemon juice) and top with remaining cake.

PINEAPPLE CUSTARD CREAM FILLING: Combine 1 c. cooled filling with ½ c. drained crushed pineapple just before spreading between split cake. Pineapple may also be added to all the following variations.

ORANGE/PINEAPPLE CUSTARD CREAM FILLING: Add 1 tsp. grated orange peel to pineapple filling.

COCONUT CUSTARD CREAM FILLING: Add ⅔ c. flaked or cut shredded coconut to custard filling.

CHOCOLATE ICING: Blend together 2 tblsp. butter or shortening, 2 squares unsweetened chocolate, melted, ¼ tsp. salt and ½ tsp. vanilla. Add 2¼ c. sifted confectioners sugar alternately with ¼ to ⅓ c. milk; beat until smooth. If thinner glaze is desired, add a little more milk.

chapter 12

Country Cakes and Frostings

IF YOU WERE FORTUNATE enough to grow up in the country, you will remember . . . how your fork cut through wedges of moist, fresh-baked and frosted chocolate cake . . . the aroma of spicy applesauce cake baking in the oven . . . thin slices of homemade fruitcake at Christmas on a holly-decorated plate . . . the smell of fresh air and the soothing feel of sunshine when you carried warm cake to the field for your father's coffee break . . . gorgeous cakes on the table waiting to escort hand-cranked ice cream and ripe strawberries at the social . . . your mother's special hickory nut cake in your lunchbox.

If you grew up in the country, these nostalgic memories will make you hungry. They'll take you "back home." You'll realize what this cherished collection of country cake recipes contributes to good home cooking.

You do not have to live on a ranch or farm to bake these wonderful cakes. You can use the recipes in your town or city kitchen. The cakes will bring you a fresh taste of the quiet, open spaces during the different seasons. Many of these updated simplified recipes will tempt you.

During a year there are many baking days and happy occasions you will want to celebrate by serving a luscious home-baked cake.

In this chapter, the shortening-type layer and loaf cakes come first, followed by foam-type specials in which eggs take a leavening role.

Pointers on Freezing Cakes

To Freeze Unfrosted Cakes: Cool cake thoroughly, place on cardboard and cover with aluminum foil or plastic wrap. Or if you wish, package cake in family-sized portions. Some cakes, especially angel and sponge types are not solid when frozen. It is a good idea to protect such cakes from crushing by placing the wrapped, frozen cake in a sturdy box. Unfrosted cakes freeze better than frosted cakes.

· To thaw, let cakes stand unwrapped at room temperature for 1 to 3 hours, the time depending on the size of the cake. Or for quicker thawing, place in a very slow oven (250 to 300°) for a short time, but watch carefully so cake will not dry out.

To Freeze Frosted Cakes: Avoid frostings that change texture in freezing. Confectioners sugar and fudge frostings freeze best. Whipped cream and boiled frostings freeze well, but will stick to the wrap, so it is difficult to wrap the frosted cakes. Therefore it is best to freeze the frosted cake before wrapping. It also helps to insert wooden picks around the top edge of the cake and the sides to hold the wrapping away from the frosting. Avoid freezing cakes with custard and fruit fillings; they make cakes soggy.

· To thaw, place loosely-wrapped cake in refrigerator for 3 to 4 hours.

Maximum Storage Time: Unfrosted cakes, 4 to 6 months; frosted cakes, 2 to 3 months; fruitcakes, much longer.

Fudge Cake Holds Its Popularity

Once again, our special-occasion Favorite Fudge Cake takes the spotlight. The recipe for this delicate, butter-flavored, chocolate three-layer cake was number one in the original *Country Cookbook.* It captured so many praises through the years that it now appears first in the cake chapter of this revised cookbook. With women busier than ever and packaged cake mixes so convenient, we also give you a two-layer variation made with a mix. The date filling is the same; the chocolate frosting is easier and quicker to make.

Read, too, the other chocolate cake recipes on the following pages. All make excellent cakes. To single out one, there's an oblong Cinnamon/Chocolate Cake that is especially versatile. It's ideal for the men's coffee break in the field, coffee parties in the home and to share at church and community suppers.

FAVORITE FUDGE CAKE

Luscious cake, but fragile. Handle gently when filling and frosting

¾ c. butter or regular margarine
2¼ c. sugar
1½ tsp. vanilla
3 eggs
3 squares unsweetened chocolate, melted
3 c. sifted cake flour
1½ tsp. baking soda
¾ tsp. salt
1½ c. ice water
Date Cream Filling
Fudge Frosting

· Cream together butter, sugar and vanilla. Add eggs, and beat until light and fluffy. Add melted chocolate and blend well.

· Sift together dry ingredients; add alternately with water to chocolate mixture. Pour batter into three 8" round layer cake pans which have been greased and lined with waxed paper.

· Bake in moderate oven (350°) 30 to 35 minutes. Cool on racks. Put layers together with Date Cream Filling. Frost with Fudge Frosting, spreading on sides of cake first and a little over the top edge. Frost top last.

DATE CREAM FILLING: Combine 1 c. milk and ½ c. chopped dates in top of a double boiler.
• Combine 1 tblsp. flour and ¼ c. sugar; add 1 beaten egg, blending until smooth. Add to hot milk mixture. Cook, stirring, until thick. Cool.
• Stir in ½ c. chopped nuts and 1 tsp. vanilla. Spread between layers.

Variation

CHOCOLATE/DATE CAKE: Use 1 (18½ oz.) pkg. devil's food cake mix and bake two 8″ layers by package directions. Cool. Put together with Date Cream Filling (made with half a recipe): Use ½ c. milk, ¼ c. chopped dates, 1½ tsp. flour, 2 tblsp. sugar, 1 egg yolk, beaten, ¼ c. chopped nuts and ½ tsp. vanilla. Frost top and sides of cake with Confectioners Sugar Fudge Frosting.

FUDGE FROSTING

Twice as good as fudge candy when teamed with the chocolate butter cake

2 c. sugar
¼ tsp. salt
1 c. light cream
2 tblsp. light corn syrup
2 squares unsweetened chocolate

• Combine sugar, salt, cream, corn syrup and chocolate. Cook over low heat, stirring until sugar dissolves. Cover saucepan for 2 or 3 minutes. Remove lid and cook to the soft ball stage (234°). Beat to spreading consistency. Add a little hot water if frosting becomes too stiff to spread evenly, sifted confectioners sugar if too thin. Frosts sides and top of three 8″ layers.

CONFECTIONERS SUGAR FUDGE FROSTING

Superior quick, easy frosting—no worry about cooking to right stage

2 tblsp. butter or margarine
3 squares unsweetened chocolate
2¼ c. sifted confectioners sugar
6 tblsp. light cream
Dash of salt
1 tsp. vanilla

• Melt butter and chocolate over boiling water, stirring to blend. All at once add 1½ c. confectioners sugar, light cream and salt. Beat with spoon until smooth.
• Cook over low heat, stirring constantly, until bubbles appear around edge of saucepan. Add vanilla and remaining ¾ c. confectioners sugar, ¼ c. at a time, beating after each addition until smooth.
• Set in bowl of ice water, stirring occasionally, until thick enough to spread evenly. Makes enough to generously frost top and sides of an 8″ three-layer cake, or to spread between layers and on sides and top of an 8 or 9″ two-layer cake.

Note: You can use 6 tblsp. evaporated milk, undiluted, instead of light cream.

FUDGE RIBBON CAKE

There's a surprise cheese layer in this rich chocolate cake

2 tblsp. butter
¼ c. sugar
1 tblsp. cornstarch
1 (8 oz.) pkg. cream cheese
1 egg

2 tblsp. milk
½ tsp. vanilla
2 c sifted flour
2 c. sugar
1 tsp. salt
1 tsp. baking powder
½ tsp. baking soda
½ c. shortening
1½ c. milk
2 eggs
4 squares unsweetened chocolate, melted
1 tsp. vanilla
Easy Chocolate Frosting

• Cream together butter, ¼ c. sugar and cornstarch. Add cheese and beat until fluffy. Add 1 egg, 2 tblsp. milk and ½ tsp. vanilla; beat until creamy. Set aside.

• Grease and flour bottom of 13 × 9 × 2" pan.

• To make cake batter, combine flour, 2 c. sugar, salt, baking powder and soda. Add shortening and 1 c. milk; blend at lowest speed of mixer. Beat 1½ minutes at low speed or 225 strokes by hand. Add 2 eggs, chocolate, 1 tsp. vanilla and ½ c. milk; continue beating 1½ minutes at low speed.

• Spread half of batter in pan. Spoon on cheese mixture, spreading carefully to cover batter. Top with remaining batter; spread to cover. Bake in moderate oven (350°) 50 to 55 minutes, until cake springs back when touched lightly in center. Cool on rack, then frost with Easy Chocolate Frosting.

EASY CHOCOLATE FROSTING: Bring ⅓ c. milk and ¼ c. butter to a boil; remove from heat. Blend in 1 (6 oz.) pkg. semisweet chocolate pieces. Stir in 1 tsp. vanilla and 2¼ c. sifted confectioners sugar until of spreading consistency.

FUDGE/LEMON CAKE

Company special; three rich, firm-textured fudge cake layers put together and covered with Chocolate/Lemon Frosting to make a torte

½ c. butter
2 c. sugar
4 eggs
4 squares unsweetened chocolate, melted
2 c. sifted flour
1 tsp. salt
2 tsp. baking powder
1¼ c. milk
2 tsp. vanilla
Chocolate/Lemon Frosting

• Cream butter and sugar until light and fluffy. Beat in eggs, one at a time. Add melted chocolate and blend.

• Sift dry ingredients together; add alternately with milk and vanilla to the creamed mixture.

• Grease the sides of three 9" round layer cake pans; dust with cocoa. Line bottoms of pans with ungreased paper. Divide batter evenly between the pans.

• Bake in moderate oven (350°) about 30 minutes, or until the cake is done.

• Cool on racks about 5 minutes; remove from pans and cool completely on racks. Spread Chocolate/Lemon Frosting between cake layers and on top of cake. Decorate with shaved chocolate pieces, if you wish.

CHOCOLATE/LEMON FROSTING: Cream ½ c. butter with 1 c. sifted confectioners sugar, 3 squares sweet cooking chocolate, melted, and 1 egg. Add 3 c. sifted confectioners sugar, 1 tsp. vanilla (optional), ¼ tsp. salt and grated peel of 1 lemon (about 1 tblsp.). Beat until smooth. If frosting is too thick to spread, add milk. Stir in 1 c. chopped nuts.

CINNAMON/CHOCOLATE CAKE

A good, big cake to tote. Subtle taste of spice makes it different

¼ c. cocoa
1 c. water
¾ c. shortening
2½ c. sifted flour
1 tsp. baking soda
1 tsp. salt
1 tsp. ground cinnamon
2 c. sugar
2 eggs
½ c. buttermilk
1 tsp. vanilla
Simple Chocolate Icing

• Mix cocoa and water in a saucepan; add shortening. Bring mixture to a boil. Cool slightly.
• Sift together flour, baking soda, salt and cinnamon.
• Blend together (do not beat) sugar and eggs in a large mixing bowl. Blend in cocoa mixture.
• Add sifted dry ingredients alternately with buttermilk, stirring after each addition until well blended. Stir in vanilla.
• Pour into greased 15½ × 10½ × 1″ jelly roll pan. Bake in hot oven (400°) 20 minutes. Cool on rack, then frost with Simple Chocolate Icing.

SIMPLE CHOCOLATE ICING: Melt ½ c. butter or margarine in ¼ c. milk in small saucepan. Mix ¼ c. cocoa with 3 c. sifted confectioners sugar and stir into milk mixture. Add 1 tsp. vanilla. Spread on cake. Top with ½ c. chopped nuts.

CHOCOLATE/CHERRY CAKE

This special-occasion beauty will serve 12. Keep in refrigerator

1 tblsp. flour
½ tblsp. cocoa
2 c. sifted cake flour
¾ tsp. salt
2 tsp. baking powder
1 (4 oz.) bottle maraschino cherries
½ c. butter
1½ c. sugar
2 eggs
4 squares unsweetened chocolate, melted
1⅓ c. evaporated milk
2 tsp. red food color
Devil's Creme
Chocolate candy kisses

• Combine 1 tblsp. flour and cocoa. Lightly grease two 9″ round layer cake pans; dust with flour/cocoa mixture.
• Sift together 2 c. cake flour, salt and baking powder. Set aside.
• Drain cherries, reserving juice. Chop cherries, and set aside.
• Cream butter; gradually add sugar and blend until light and fluffy. Add eggs, chocolate, evaporated milk, reserved cherry juice and food color. Beat until smooth. Blend in dry ingredients. Fold in cherries.
• Bake in prepared pans in moderate oven (350°) 25 to 30 minutes. Remove from pans and cool on racks. Carefully split cake layers.
• Put layers together and top with Devil's Creme; reserve ½ c. Creme to decorate top. (We used a cake decorator—#30 tip—to pipe frosting on.) Decorate with chocolate candy kisses. Refrigerate to set Creme. Makes 12 servings.

DEVIL'S CREME: Stir together ¼ c. powdered chocolate drink mix, ¼

c. sifted confectioners sugar, 1 tsp. vanilla and 2 c. heavy cream. Chill; whip until stiff.

POTATO CHOCOLATE CAKE

Cake is rather moist and it stays fresh several days when covered

½ c. milk
3 squares unsweetened chocolate
1 c. shortening
1¾ c. sugar
1 c. hot unseasoned mashed potatoes
4 eggs, separated
2 c. sifted cake flour
1 tblsp. baking powder
⅛ tsp. salt
1 tsp. vanilla
¼ c. sugar

· Heat milk slowly in saucepan. Add chocolate, and stir to melt. Cool.
· Cream shortening and 1¾ c. sugar until light and fluffy.
· Combine chocolate mixture with potatoes. Add to creamed mixture. Beat in egg yolks.
· Sift together flour, baking powder and salt; stir into batter. Add vanilla.
· Beat egg whites until stiff, adding the ¼ c. sugar gradually. Fold into batter. Pour into 3 greased waxed paper-lined 8″ round layer cake pans.
· Bake in moderate oven (350°) 30 minutes. Cool on racks and frost as desired.

CHOCOLATE NUT LOAF

Rich with chocolate, tender and moist—you'll enjoy every crumb

1 c. butter or regular margarine
2 c. sugar
5 eggs, well beaten
2 squares unsweetened chocolate, melted
1 tsp. vanilla
2½ c. sifted cake flour
1 tsp. baking soda
¼ tsp. salt
1 c. buttermilk
1 c. chopped walnuts
Confectioners sugar (for top)

· Cream butter well, add sugar gradually. Beat until light and fluffy.
· Add eggs and melted chocolate. Blend well. Add vanilla.
· Sift together flour, baking soda and salt; add alternately with buttermilk to first mixture. Fold in nuts.
· Pour batter in 2 greased 8 × 4½ × 2½″ loaf pans. Bake in slow oven (325°) 1 hour. Cool on racks.
· Sprinkle tops with confectioners sugar or spread with your favorite white or chocolate frosting. In our Countryside Test Kitchens we filled ridges on top with confectioners sugar.

POLKA DOT PICNIC CAKE

There's no frosting to melt before time to serve at summer picnics

1¼ c. chopped dates
1 c. hot water
¾ c. butter or regular margarine
1 c. sugar
2 eggs
2 c. sifted flour
1 tsp. baking soda
½ tsp. salt
1 tsp. vanilla
1 (6 oz.) pkg. semisweet chocolate pieces
½ c. chopped nuts

· Mix chopped dates and hot water; set aside to cool.
· Cream together butter and sugar. Add eggs and beat until fluffy.
· Sift together flour, soda and salt. Add to creamed mixture alternately with date mixture. Mix well after

each addition. Stir in vanilla and ½ c. chocolate pieces. Spread batter in greased 13 × 9 × 2″ baking pan.

• Top with remaining chocolate pieces and the nuts. Bake in moderate oven (350°) about 35 minutes.

Country Cake Walks

Raise money and are fun

Cake walks are popular in many country communities. They provide entertainment for a crowd and raise money for worthy causes. Here is the way to set the stage for a jolly evening.

Draw the face of a clock, as large as possible, on the floor. Write numbers representing the day's 12 hours near the outer rim of the circle. Draw a line on both sides of a number to the center, making triangles. Repeat until there are 12 triangles of equal size.

The master of ceremonies brings out a home-baked cake to tempt everyone with the prize someone will win. Twelve people walk at a time. They pay for the chance to try for the cake.

Each person stands at the outer edge of a triangle. Walking starts with the music and ends simultaneously with it. Then the master of ceremonies asks a child to draw one of the 12 numbers in a hat or basket. The person standing in the triangle with the number corresponding to the one drawn gets the cake.

The cakes of the evening are trophies worth capturing. The best cooks in the neighborhood vie with each other in decorating them. The idea is to produce a cake that is showy and glamorous—and delicious.

CHERRY CROWN CHOCOLATE CAKE

Cherry crown adds glamour—cake is fancy enough for cake walks

2 (9″) baked chocolate-cake layers
2 tblsp. butter or regular margarine
¼ c. brown sugar, firmly packed
2 tblsp. heavy cream, or dairy sour cream
16 maraschino cherries, drained and halved
1 recipe Glossy Fudge Frosting (see Index)

• Place one chocolate-cake layer on baking sheet.

• Melt butter, stir in brown sugar and cream and add cherries. Spread mixture on cake layer, spreading out to edges all around.

• Place cake in broiler 6″ to 8″ from heat and broil until bubbly all over and golden brown, 2 to 3 minutes. Use this for the top layer of cake.

• Put layers together and frost sides of cake with Glossy Fudge Frosting. Leave top unfrosted with the cherries showing.

Applesauce and Other Fruit-Flavored Cakes

No fruit successfully competes with apples for the frequency of appearance on country tables. They're so versatile. Apple and applesauce cakes are special favorites. Our Applesauce Fruitcake retains its popularity from one holiday season to the next. It sells well at bazaars and makes for a welcome Christmas gift. Another much complimented cake in this chapter is Marshmallow/

Applesauce Cake, which makes its own inviting topping while it bakes. Chopped raw apples take the fruit role in Nobby Apple Cake instead of applesauce. Serve it with ice cream and everyone will end the meal in a happy mood.

You will find these apple recipes in this chapter and also some for cakes made with other fruits, such as dates, prunes, raisins, bananas and orange and lemon juices. (They also are listed in the Index.)

APPLESAUCE FRUITCAKE

Many people enjoy this more than traditional Christmas fruitcake

3 c. thick applesauce
1 c. shortening
2 c. sugar
1 lb. dates, pitted and chopped
1 lb. light or dark raisins
1 lb. nuts, coarsely chopped
¼ lb. candied cherries, quartered
¼ lb. candied pineapple, chopped
¼ lb. citron, finely chopped
4½ c. sifted flour
4 tsp. baking soda
1 tsp. ground nutmeg
2½ tsp. ground cinnamon
½ tsp. ground cloves
1 tsp. salt

• Boil applesauce, shortening and sugar together 5 minutes, stirring occasionally. Let stand until cool.
• Line four 1-lb. coffee cans with waxed paper. (Or use any desired pans which together will hold 11 cups when filled three fourths full. Molds which can't be lined with waxed paper should be well greased and floured.)
• Mix fruit and nuts together in a 3-qt. mixing bowl. Sift together flour, soda, nutmeg, cinnamon, cloves and salt over fruit and nuts, mixing until each piece of fruit is coated.
• Stir in cooled applesauce mixture. Turn into prepared cans. Bake in very slow oven (250°) about 2 hours, or until wooden pick inserted in center of cake comes out clean. When cakes are as brown as desired, cover with brown paper. Remove baked cakes from cans; cool on racks. Store in moisture-proof wrapping in a cold place, or freeze. (Cakes frozen in cans with tight lids need not be wrapped.)
• Let mellow at least 2 weeks before cutting. Before serving, bring to a boil ½ c. light corn syrup and ¼ c. water. Cool to lukewarm; pour over cold cakes for a shiny glaze. Decorate immediately with candied fruit and whole nuts. Makes 4 cakes.

FIRST PRIZE APPLESAUCE CAKE

It's the hint of cocoa that makes this cake's flavor distinctive

4 c. sifted flour
4 tsp. baking soda
1¼ tsp. salt
2 tsp. ground cinnamon
½ tsp. ground nutmeg
½ tsp. ground cloves
2 tblsp. cocoa
1 c. salad oil
2 c. sugar
3 c. unsweetened applesauce, heated
½ c. raisins
½ c. chopped walnuts
Caramel Frosting

• Sift together flour, soda, salt, spices and cocoa.
• In a large mixing bowl combine oil and sugar. Beat until well blended. Stir in hot applesauce, blending thoroughly. Add dry in-

gredients, blending well. Stir in raisins and walnuts.

· Turn batter into two well greased and floured 9″ square pans. Bake in hot oven (400°) 15 minutes; then reduce oven temperature to moderate (375°) and bake about 15 minutes longer. Remove to racks. Let stand in pans 5 minutes. Remove from pans and complete cooling on racks. Fill and frost with Caramel Frosting.

CARAMEL FROSTING: Melt ½ c. butter in saucepan over low heat. Stir in 1 c. dark brown sugar, firmly packed, and ¼ tsp. salt. Bring to a boil over medium heat; boil hard 2 minutes, stirring constantly. Remove from heat. Stir in ¼ c. milk. Return pan to heat and bring to a full boil. Remove from heat, cool to lukewarm. Stir in 2 c. confectioners sugar and beat until smooth. If frosting is too thick, beat in a little milk.

MARSHMALLOW/ APPLESAUCE CAKE

You push marshmallows into cake batter in pan just before baking; they rise to the top during baking and make topping. Easier than frosting

2¾ c. flour
2 c. sugar
1½ tsp. baking soda
1½ tsp. salt
¼ tsp. baking powder
1 tsp. ground cinnamon
½ tsp. ground cloves
½ tsp. ground allspice
½ c. shortening
2 eggs
2 c. unsweetened applesauce
1 c. walnut halves
20 large marshmallows (¼ lb.)

· Sift together flour, sugar, soda, salt, baking powder and spices.

· Add shortening, eggs and applesauce. Beat until smooth and blended.

· Stir in walnuts. Pour into greased and floured 13 × 9 × 2″ pan. Press whole marshmallows into batter to bottom of pan—in 4 rows, 5 in each row.

· Bake in moderate oven (350°) about 50 minutes. Cool on rack.

OREGON APPLE DAPPLE

Top servings of this unfrosted cake with ice cream—excellent "combo"

¼ c. butter or regular margarine
1 c. sugar
1 egg
1 c. sifted flour
1 tsp. baking soda
¼ tsp. salt
1 tsp. ground cinnamon
¼ tsp. ground nutmeg
1 tsp. vanilla
2 c. grated tart apples
½ c. chopped walnuts

· Cream together butter and sugar. Beat in egg to mix well.

· Stir together flour, soda, salt and spices. Stir into creamed mixture. Stir in vanilla, apples and nuts.

· Bake in a greased 8″ square pan in moderate oven (350°) about 45 minutes. Serve warm with sauce or ice cream. Excellent served with Elin's Sauce, which will keep in the refrigerator 2 to 3 months.

ELIN'S SAUCE: Heat ½ c. butter or margarine, ½ c. light cream and 1 c. sugar to boiling point and simmer, stirring occasionally, 20 minutes.

NOBBY APPLE CAKE

The wife of a New England apple grower invented this fine cake recipe

- **3 tblsp. butter or regular margarine**
- **1 c. sugar**
- **1 egg, beaten**
- **½ tsp. ground cinnamon**
- **½ tsp. ground nutmeg**
- **½ tsp. salt**
- **1 tsp. baking soda**
- **1 c. sifted flour**
- **3 c. diced peeled apples**
- **¼ c. chopped nuts**
- **1 tsp. vanilla**

· Cream butter and sugar; add eggs and mix well.

· Sift together dry ingredients. Add to creamed mixture. Stir in apples, nuts and vanilla.

· Pour into greased 8″ square pan. Bake in moderate oven (350°) 40 to 45 minutes. Serve hot or cold, plain or with whipped cream or ice cream topping.

BANANA LAYER CAKE

Excellent use for very ripe bananas

- **2 c. mashed bananas** (4 or 5)
- **¼ c. milk**
- **1 c. shortening**
- **2 tsp. vanilla**
- **2 c. sugar**
- **4 eggs, unbeaten**
- **4½ c. sifted cake flour**
- **4 tsp. baking powder**
- **1 tsp. salt**

· Combine bananas and milk.

· Cream together shortening and vanilla; gradually add sugar, beating until light and fluffy. Add eggs, one at a time, beating well; mix until light and fluffy.

· Sift together flour, baking powder and salt. Add alternately with bananas and milk to creamed mixture, beating smooth after each addition.

· Pour into 3 greased 9″ round layer cake pans. Bake in moderate oven (350°) 30 to 35 minutes. Cool layers, wrap and freeze. When ready to use, thaw and frost as desired. Chocolate frosting is a good choice.

ORANGE BUTTER CAKE

Keep this cake in the refrigerator until you're ready to serve it

- **1 c. butter**
- **2 c. sugar**
- **4 eggs**
- **3 c. sifted flour**
- **3 tsp. baking powder**
- **¼ tsp. baking soda**
- **½ tsp. salt**
- **1 c. milk**
- **¼ c. orange juice**
- **1 tsp. vanilla**
- **1 tblsp. grated orange peel**
- **Pineapple Filling**
- **1 c. heavy cream, whipped**

· Cream butter and sugar; beat in eggs one at a time.

· Sift dry ingredients together; add alternately with the remaining ingredients, except filling and whipped cream, to creamed mixture. (Do not pour orange juice and milk into the same cup.)

· Pour batter into 3 paper-lined 9″ round layer cake pans. Bake in moderate oven (350°) about 35 minutes.

· Cool on racks about 5 minutes before removing from pans; complete cooling on wire racks. Put cooled layers together with Pineapple Filling. Spread filling on top of cake. Frost the sides with whipped cream.

PINEAPPLE FILLING: Combine ¼ c. cornstarch, 1 c. sugar and 3 tblsp. orange juice in saucepan. Stir in 1 tsp. grated orange peel, ½ c. butter and 1 (1 lb. 4 oz.) can crushed pineapple, undrained. Cook over low heat until thick and glossy, stirring constantly. Cool before spreading on cake.

PRUNE CAKE DE LUXE

Chocolate complements the fruity flavor. For dessert, reheat foil-wrapped unfrosted cake; serve with ice cream or lemon sauce. For tea, cut in 1" squares and roll in confectioners sugar

2 c. sifted flour
1 tsp. baking soda
¼ tsp. salt
2 tsp. ground cinnamon
1 tsp. ground nutmeg
¼ c. cocoa
½ c. shortening
1½ c. sugar
1 egg
2 c. pitted, cooked prunes, chopped, and juice
2 c. seedless raisins
1 c. coarsely chopped walnuts

· Sift together flour, baking soda, salt, spices and cocoa.
· Cream shortening; gradually add sugar, creaming until mixture is light and fluffy. Add unbeaten egg and beat into mixture until well blended.
· Alternately add prunes and juice (there should be at least ½ c. juice) with sifted dry ingredients to creamed mixture. Start and end with dry ingredients. Add raisins and nuts.
· Bake in well greased 13 × 9 × 2" pan in moderate oven (350°) about 1¼ hours, or until done (test with a toothpick). Let stand in pan on rack to cool, or cool 10 minutes and then remove to rack to complete cooling. Frost with confectioners sugar frosting, if desired.

BOILED RAISIN CAKE

Tastes mighty good like country raisin cakes Grandma baked

1½ c. sugar
¼ c. cocoa
2½ c. water
⅔ c. butter
2 c. raisins
2 tsp. ground cinnamon
½ tsp. ground cloves
½ tsp. ground nutmeg
½ tsp. ground allspice
½ tsp. salt
3½ c. sifted flour
2 tsp. baking powder
1 tsp. baking soda
1 c. chopped walnuts

· Mix sugar and cocoa. Add water, butter, raisins, spices and salt. Boil 4 minutes. Cool to room temperature.
· Sift together flour, baking powder and soda. Add to raisin mixture and mix until well blended. Stir in walnuts. Pour into greased 13 × 9 × 2" pan. Bake in moderate oven (350°) 35 minutes or until done. Remove from oven and cool on rack.

DATE/OATMEAL CAKE

Ideal hearty cake to pack in lunchboxes and to tote to potlucks

1 c. quick-cooking rolled oats
1½ c. dates, cut in pieces
1¾ c. boiling water
1 c. brown sugar, firmly packed
1 c. sugar
¾ c. shortening
3 eggs
2 c. sifted flour

2 tsp. baking powder
1½ tsp. salt
1 tsp. baking soda
1 tsp. ground cinnamon
Lemon/Butter Cream Frosting

· Place oats and dates in bowl; pour on water. Stir; let stand 20 minutes.
· Gradually add sugars to shortening, creaming well. Add eggs, one at a time, beating after each addition. Stir in oatmeal mixture.
· Sift together flour, baking powder, salt, soda and cinnamon. Add to above mixture and mix well.
· Pour into 13 × 9 × 2″ paper-lined pan. Bake in moderate oven (350°) 45 to 50 minutes. Cool on rack. Frost with Lemon/Butter Cream Frosting.

LEMON/BUTTER CREAM FROSTING: Cream together ¼ c. soft butter and ¼ tsp. grated lemon peel. Add 2 c. sifted confectioners sugar alternately with 2 tblsp. lemon juice, creaming well after each addition, until frosting is of spreading consistency.

RIBBON CAKE

Fruited cake bakes in layers—you put them together and frost in white

1 c. butter
2½ c. sugar
4 eggs
4 c. sifted cake flour
1 tblsp. baking powder
1 c. milk
½ c. raisins
1 c. dried currants
1 c. finely cut citron
1 tblsp. molasses
1 tsp. ground cinnamon
1 tsp. ground cloves
1 tsp. ground nutmeg
Butter Frosting

· Cream butter and sugar. Beat in eggs.
· Sift flour with baking powder; add alternately with milk to creamed mixture, beating until well blended.
· Pour 2⅔ c. batter into a greased and floured 9″ round layer cake pan. Add remaining ingredients, except frosting, to rest of batter. Pour into 2 greased and floured 9″ round layer cake pans.
· Bake in moderate oven (350°) about 35 minutes. Cool; put layers together and frost cake's sides and top with Butter Frosting.

BUTTER FROSTING: Blend together ¾ c. butter and 5 c. sifted confectioners sugar. Stir in ¼ c. light cream and ½ tsp. lemon extract until frosting is of spreading consistency.

Surprisingly Different Fruitcakes

Many women treasure their mothers' and grandmothers' fruitcake recipes and fondly dream, when the first thoughts of the Christmas holidays arrive, of baking these old-fashioned loaves. One look at the recipes, yellow with age, reminds them of the giant-size yields and the time required to bake these cakes. The search for tasty substitutes starts. This annual post-Thanksgiving kitchen drama inspired us to offer you smaller and simpler recipes that yield big dividends in taste.

Both Large Dark and White Fruitcakes bake in tube pans; Frozen Fruitcake eliminates the baking, and Fruitcake Delicious, although less sweet than some cakes, is perhaps the over-all first choice. Certainly it's easy to get ready for the oven, for neither nuts nor dates require chopping.

If you line your pans with brown or waxed paper, you may find it more convenient to substitute aluminum foil. This is the way we often do it in our Countryside Test Kitchens: Line pans with foil; grease foil. (If you let foil extend a little over the top edge of the pans, you'll have help in removing cake from pans.) If you plan to wrap the cooled cake to freeze or store in a cold place, let the foil extend over the sides of the pan, folding it back. When you are ready to wrap the cake, bring the foil up over the top and double-fold securely.

LARGE DARK FRUITCAKE

Molasses helps give dark color and wonderful old-fashioned flavor

5 eggs, separated
½ c. molasses
¼ c. grape juice
1 c. butter or regular margarine
1 c. sugar
1⅓ c. raisins
½ lb. cut-up candied pineapple
½ lb. whole candied cherries
1¼ c. chopped dates
¼ lb. chopped citron
¼ lb. chopped orange peel
¼ lb. chopped lemon peel
1¾ c. cut pecans
2 c. sifted flour
½ tsp. ground nutmeg
½ tsp. ground cloves
½ tsp. ground mace
1 tsp. ground cinnamon
1 tsp. baking soda

· Beat egg yolks; combine with molasses and grape juice.

· Cream butter and sugar. Add egg yolk mixture. Blend well.

· Combine fruit and nuts; mix with 1 c. flour to coat.

· Warm in slow oven (325°) 5 minutes.

· Sift remaining 1 c. flour with spices and soda.

· Beat egg whites until peaks form and fold into creamed mixture. Stir in fruits and nuts and dry ingredients.

· Pour into 9″ tube pan, bottom greased, then lined with brown paper, also well greased. Bake in slow oven (300°) 2 hours.

· Put on rack to cool. Wrap in foil and store in cold place (it freezes well).

WHITE FRUITCAKE

Worth the time it takes to make this favorite Southern fruitcake

2 lbs. white raisins, chopped
2 c. orange juice
4½ c. sifted cake flour
¼ tsp. baking powder
½ tsp. salt
1 lb. diced candied cherries
1 lb. diced candied pineapple
½ lb. diced preserved citron
¼ lb. diced candied lemon peel
¼ lb. diced candied orange peel
1 lb. almonds, blanched and slivered
2 c. butter or regular margarine
2¼ c. sugar
8 to 10 medium eggs
1 fresh coconut, grated or shredded

· Wash raisins; chop. Combine with 1 c. orange juice; let stand overnight.

· Save 1½ c. flour to mix with candied fruit and nuts. Sift remaining 3 c. flour with baking powder and salt.

· Mix candied fruit and nuts with reserved 1½ c. flour.

· Cream butter, add sugar and beat

well. Add eggs, one at a time, beating well after each addition.

• Gradually add dry ingredients, beating after each addition. Add coconut, floured fruit and nuts, raisins and remaining orange juice. Beat well.

• Divide batter evenly in 2 well greased 9 or 10″ tube pans. Bake in very slow oven (250°) about 2½ hours, or until done. Or, bake in 4 greased, paper-lined 9 × 5 × 3″ loaf pans at the same temperature and for same length of time.

• Cool 30 minutes on racks. Remove from pans; cool completely. Wrap in waxed paper or foil; store in airtight container in a very cold place or freeze.

HOW TO PREPARE FRESH COCONUT: Pierce eyes of shell with ice pick; drain out milk. Heat in moderate oven (350°) 30 minutes. Cool, break shell—meat falls free. Peel off all the crisp brown skin. Grate or shred.

MARDI GRAS CAKE

You can bake this glamorous cake a day before your yuletide party

1 c. butter
1 (8 oz.) pkg. cream cheese, softened
1½ c. sugar
1½ tsp. vanilla
4 large eggs
2¼ c. sifted cake flour
2 tsp. baking powder
¼ c. sifted cake flour
2 c. mixed candied fruit (1 lb.)
½ c. coarsely chopped pecans
½ c. finely chopped pecans

• Thoroughly blend butter, softened cream cheese, sugar and vanilla. Add eggs, one at a time, beating well after each addition.

• Sift together 2¼ c. cake flour and baking powder. Add to batter and blend well.

• Combine ¼ c. cake flour with candied fruit and ½ c. coarsely chopped pecans. Fold into batter. Spoon batter into 10″ bundt or tube pan that has been greased and sprinkled with finely chopped nuts.

• Bake in slow oven (325°) 70 to 80 minutes, or until cake tests done. Cool in pan 5 minutes. Remove from pan; cool on rack.

• Sprinkle with sifted confectioners sugar. Garnish with candied cherries and candied pineapple if you wish.

FROZEN FRUITCAKE

Busy women delight in this no-bake cake. So do their friends

2 c. milk
½ c. sugar
¼ c. flour
¼ tsp. salt
2 eggs, beaten
1 tsp. vanilla
1 c. light raisins
2 c. vanilla wafer or macaroon crumbs
½ c. candied red cherries, halved
¼ c. candied mixed fruits
1 c. broken pecans
1 c. heavy cream, whipped

• Scald milk in top of double boiler.

• Mix together sugar, flour and salt, and add to milk all at once. Cook over hot water about 3 minutes until smooth and medium thick, stirring constantly.

• Pour hot milk over beaten eggs and return to double boiler. Cook until thick, about 3 minutes, stirring constantly. Add vanilla. Cool.

• Stir raisins, crumbs, cherries, mixed fruits and nuts into cooked mixture. Fold in cream. Pour into greased and waxed paper-lined

8½ × 4½ × 2½″ loaf pan. Cool completely; wrap and freeze. Makes 8 servings.

Note: To decorate top of fruitcake, arrange a few whole nut meats and candied red and green cherries on waxed paper in bottom of mold before pouring in batter.

FRUITCAKE DELICIOUS

Nuts and dates are not chopped—you cut them when you slice cake

1½ c. sifted flour
1½ c. sugar
1 tsp. baking powder
1 tsp. salt
2 lbs. pitted dates (do not chop)
2 lbs. shelled walnuts
1 lb. shelled Brazil nuts
1 (8 oz.) jar maraschino cherries, drained
5 large eggs, beaten
1 tsp. vanilla

· In large bowl, sift together flour, sugar, baking powder and salt.

· Add dates, nuts and cherries; stir to coat well.

· Combine eggs and vanilla. Mix into flour-nut mixture. (Easy way is to use your hands.)

· Spoon into 3 greased 8½ × 4½ × 2½″ loaf pans.

· Bake in slow oven (325°) 1 hour. Cool before slicing or freezing.

LAST-MINUTE FRUITCAKES

You can bake these little cakes in soup cans at the last minute for they need no mellowing. Since you candy the pineapple and cherries they cost less. If you bake cakes ahead, freeze them in the cans

4 c. sifted flour
2 tsp. baking powder
1½ tsp. ground nutmeg
2 tsp. ground cinnamon
½ tsp. salt
2 c. butter
2 c. brown sugar, firmly packed
12 eggs
3 c. coarsely chopped pecans
Candied Pineapple, cut up
Candied Cherries, halved
1 tblsp. grated lemon peel

· Sift together flour, baking powder, nutmeg, cinnamon and salt. Reserve ⅓ c. of this mixture.

· Cream butter and brown sugar. Add eggs, one at a time, beating well. Gradually add flour mixture, mixing well. Add lemon peel.

· Toss ⅓ c. flour with fruit-nut mixture. Stir into batter.

· Spoon into 12 greased and floured 10½ oz. cans, filling 1″ from top. Bake in very slow oven (275°) 1 hour 15 minutes or until cakes test done. Cool on racks.

Note: Before serving, you can frost fruitcakes with an icing made by combining 2 c. sifted confectioners sugar, 1 tblsp. soft butter, 1 tblsp. milk and ½ tsp. vanilla. Blend well. Drizzle over cakes. Decorate with candied fruit.

CANDIED PINEAPPLE AND CHERRIES: Drain 2 (1 lb. 14 oz.) cans sliced pineapple; reserve syrup. Combine 2 c. sugar, ½ c. light corn syrup and 1⅔ c. pineapple syrup in a heavy 10″ skillet. Cook over medium heat, stirring constantly, until mixture boils. Cook until temperature reaches 234° on candy thermometer.

· Add a third of the pineapple slices; bring to a boil. Reduce heat; simmer 25 minutes or until pineapple is transparent around edges. Remove from skillet; drain on wire rack. Repeat with remaining pineapple, cooking a third at a time. Then add 3 (8 oz.) jars maraschino cherries, drained. Simmer for 25 minutes. Let dry 24 hours at room temperature.

HOLIDAY FRUITCAKE

Some hostesses prefer to bake fruitcake in tiny cupcake pans and glaze them. We give directions. Fruitcake Bonbons are finger food

1 lb. mixed candied fruit (2 c.)
1 (4 oz.) can chopped citron
1 lb. dates, pitted
½ lb. whole candied cherries (1 c.)
1 c. raisins
1 c. pecan halves
1 c. walnut halves
4 c. sifted flour
1 tsp. salt
1 tsp. ground cinnamon
1 tsp. ground cloves
½ tsp. ground nutmeg
1 c. butter
2 c. sugar
4 eggs
1 tsp. baking soda
1½ c. buttermilk
Orange juice

• Prepare baking pans—you can use one 10″ tube pan or three 8 × 4¼ × 2¼″ foil pans: Cut parchment or brown paper liners for bottoms of pans; grease each paper with unsalted fat. Top with one layer waxed paper. Grease all paper and inside of pan generously.

• Prepare and measure fruit; cut it in pieces the size of dates. (Leave nuts, cherries and dates whole.)

• Sift together flour, salt and spices. Use enough of this flour mixture to coat all fruit pieces.

• Cream butter and sugar until light and fluffy; beat in eggs, one at a time. Add soda to remaining flour mixture; add alternately with buttermilk to creamed mixture. Mix batter with fruits and nuts. Spoon into prepared pan or pans.

• To decorate, lay nuts and large fruit pieces on top to form a design.

• Bake cake in a slow oven (300°). This amount in a 10″ tube pan bakes in 2½ hours; 1-pound amounts bake in about 1¼ hours.

• Cool cake out of pan on rack. When completely cool, apply orange juice or cider to entire cake with pastry brush. Wrap in waxed paper, then in foil. Store in covered container in cool place. After two weeks, unwrap and brush again with orange juice or cider.

Variation

FRUITCAKE BONBONS: Line 1¼″ muffin-pan cups with paper bonbon cups. Fill cups three fourths full with batter. Bake in slow oven (300°) 40 to 50 minutes (place pan of water in oven so cakes will stay moist). Remove from pans. Cool on rack.

• Remove paper cups from cakes. Set cakes on racks over foil or waxed paper. Spoon Tinted Bonbon Glaze over tops and down sides of cakes. Let stand until glaze is firm. If first coat of glaze is too thin, repeat. The glaze that drips off may be scraped up, melted over hot water and reused. Makes 11 dozen.

TINTED BONBON GLAZE: Mix ¼ c. water, 1 tblsp. light corn syrup, 3 c. sifted confectioners sugar and ⅛ tsp. salt in top of double boiler. Heat just until lukewarm, stirring occasionally. Remove from hot water and add 1 tsp. vanilla. Divide and tint different colors with food color. Cool slightly.

Celebrate the Harvest Season with Pumpkin Cake

Orange pumpkins and deep yellow winter squash heaped at roadside stands signal country women when it's time to bake a pumpkin cake. FARM JOURNAL's Pumpkin Cake, which you also can make with winter squash, enjoys wide acceptance across country. This maple-flavored, pumpkin-nut layer cake is put together with fluffy, brown sugar-sweetened Harvest Moon Frosting. Bake this cheerful cake for a cozy supper on a chilly Sunday evening or tote it to a potluck. You'll get a lot of compliments on it.

PUMPKIN CAKE

Country women consider this a "must" for autumn and Thanksgiving

½ c. shortening
1 c. sugar
1 c. brown sugar, firmly packed
2 eggs, beaten
1 c. cooked, mashed pumpkin or winter squash
3 c. sifted cake flour
4 tsp. baking powder
¼ tsp. baking soda
½ c. milk
1 c. chopped walnuts
1 tsp. maple flavoring
Harvest Moon Frosting

• Cream shortening and slowly add sugars, eggs and pumpkin.
• Sift together flour, baking powder and soda; add alternately with milk to creamed mixture. Fold in walnuts and maple flavoring.
• Pour into 3 greased 8″ round layer cake pans. Bake in moderate oven (350°) 30 minutes. Cool on racks. Put cake layers together with Harvest Moon Frosting. Frost sides, bringing frosting slightly over top edge. Frost top.

HARVEST MOON FROSTING: Combine in double boiler 3 egg whites, 1½ c. brown sugar, firmly packed, dash of salt and 6 tblsp. water. Beat well; place over rapidly boiling water. Cook 7 minutes, beating constantly, or until frosting will stand in peaks. Remove from boiling water; add 1 tsp. vanilla. Beat until thick enough to spread. Makes enough frosting for a 3-layer cake.

TO COOK PUMPKIN: Select bright-colored, firm, unblemished pumpkins. Three pounds raw pumpkin make 3 c. cooked, mashed pumpkin. Cut pumpkin in half; remove seeds and stringy portion. Cut in small pieces and peel. Cook, covered, in 1″ boiling salted water 25 to 30 minutes, or until tender. Drain and mash. Season as recipe directs. Cook winter squash the same way, except for butternut squash; it cooks in 12 to 15 minutes.

Poppy Seed Cake with Velvety Filling

The trick in baking beautiful poppy seed cakes is to keep the tiny seeds evenly distributed throughout the layers. In our recipe, shared by a Nebraska woman of Bohemian ancestry, you soak the seeds in milk before stirring it into the batter; encourages the seeds to stay put during baking. The traditional Custard Filling, pale gold and luscious, gets lively competition from the quick-and-easy Bride's Custard Filling, a real compliment winner. Some of our taste-testers actually prefer it. Try both.

POPPY SEED LAYER CAKE

The crisp, blue-black seeds are evenly distributed throughout cake

¼ c. poppy seeds
1 c. milk
⅔ c. shortening
1½ c. sugar
1 tblsp. baking powder
3 c. sifted cake flour
1 tsp. salt
4 egg whites, stiffly beaten
Custard Filling

· Add poppy seeds to milk. Refrigerate 1 to 2 hours.
· Cream shortening with sugar until light and fluffy.
· Sift together baking powder, flour and salt. Add dry ingredients and poppy seed milk alternately to creamed mixture.
· Fold in egg whites, half at a time. Pour into two waxed paper-lined 8" round layer cake pans.
· Bake in moderate oven (375°) 30 minutes. Remove from pans to racks. Cool, then put together with Custard Filling. Sprinkle top of cake with confectioners sugar. Refrigerate until time to serve.

CUSTARD FILLING

Use either this traditional recipe or the quick, new variation

⅓ c. sugar
2 tblsp. flour
⅛ tsp. salt
1 egg, slightly beaten
¾ c. scalded milk
½ tsp. vanilla
¼ tsp. almond extract (optional)
½ c. chopped walnuts (optional)
½ c. heavy cream, whipped

· Combine sugar, flour and salt in top of double boiler. Stir in egg; add milk and blend thoroughly. Cook over boiling water 5 minutes, stirring constantly. Cook 5 more minutes, stirring occasionally. Refrigerate until cold.
· Add vanilla and almond extract. Add nuts; fold in whipped cream. Spread between two 8 or 9" cake layers.

Variation

BRIDE'S CUSTARD FILLING: Prepare 1 (3¼ oz.) pkg. vanilla pudding and pie filling by package directions, but use 1½ c. milk instead of 2 cups. Cover surface of pudding with plastic wrap or waxed paper and refrigerate until cold. Remove from refrigerator and fold in ½ c. heavy cream, whipped. Spread half of mixture between layers of Poppy Seed Layer Cake. Spread remaining filling on top of cake. Sprinkle with 2 tblsp. chopped nuts. Chill until ready to serve.

HICKORY NUT CAKE

For best flavor, cover this cake and let stand a day before serving

½ c. butter or shortening
1½ c. sugar
1 tsp. vanilla
2 c. sifted cake flour
2 tsp. baking powder
¼ tsp. salt
¾ c. milk
1 c. finely chopped hickory nuts
4 egg whites, stiffly beaten

· Cream together butter, sugar and vanilla until fluffy.

· Sift together flour, baking powder and salt; add alternately with milk to creamed mixture. Beat until smooth. Fold in nuts and egg whites. Pour into 2 greased 8″ square pans.

· Bake in moderate oven (350°) 35 minutes. Cool on racks. Just before serving you may put layers together and frost with sweetened whipped cream. Sprinkle chopped hickory nuts over top.

SWEET CREAM CAKE

Speedy to mix—no creaming. Cake is light, feathery and flavorful

2½ c. sifted flour
1¾ c. sugar
3 tsp. baking powder
½ tsp. salt
1⅓ c. heavy cream
⅓ c. milk
1 tsp. vanilla
3 eggs
Coffee Butter Frosting

· Sift dry ingredients into mixing bowl. Add cream, milk and vanilla. Mix to dampen dry ingredients. Beat 1 minute at medium speed of electric mixer, or 150 vigorous strokes by hand.

· Add eggs and mix 1 minute longer.

· Pour into 2 paper-lined 8″ round layer cake pans. Tap sharply on table top to remove air bubbles. Bake in moderate oven (350°) about 40 minutes.

· Cool cake in pans on rack about 10 to 15 minutes. Remove from pans; take off paper, and turn cake right side up on rack to finish cooling. Frost with Coffee Butter Frosting or your favorite chocolate frosting.

COFFEE BUTTER FROSTING

⅓ c. butter
3 c. confectioners sugar
1½ tsp. instant coffee powder
3 tblsp. light cream

· Cream butter. Sift sugar and coffee powder together. Add gradually to butter, creaming until light and fluffy.

· Add cream as frosting becomes thick. Makes enough to frost top and sides of two 8″ cake layers.

Variations

CITRUS FROSTING: Omit coffee and cream; substitute orange or lemon juice and 2 tsp. grated orange or ½ tsp. lemon peel.

PINEAPPLE OR STRAWBERRY FROSTING: Omit coffee and cream. Add ⅓ c. drained crushed pineapple or ¼ c. crushed fresh or frozen strawberries.

CHOCOLATE FROSTING: Stir 3 squares unsweetened chocolate, melted, into the creamed butter and sugar. Use 1½ tsp. vanilla instead of coffee if you wish.

BROWN BUTTER FROSTING: Lightly brown the butter in heavy skillet over medium heat; blend with the sugar.

VANILLA FROSTING: Omit instant coffee powder and add 1½ tsp. vanilla.

Superior Frostings with Syrup

Sometimes it's a simple, quick trick that works magic in the

21. LAST-MINUTE FRUITCAKES—Golden cakes baked in soup cans make charming Christmas gifts. You candy pineapple and cherries to add to batter. Recipe, page 366.

22. FORMAL WEDDING CAKE—Take your choice of this stately bride's cake or a smaller, round Informal Wedding Cake. Recipes, pages 375, 377.

23. HONEY-FILLED COFFEE CAKE—Everyone at the coffee party enjoys breaking his serving from this loaf with luscious filling. Recipe, page 246.

24. APPLE PIZZA PIE–The dramatic, giant pie has a spicy filling and thin crust. Makes 12 servings. It's best eaten warm. Recipe, page 407.

kitchen. That's exactly what Basic Sugar Syrup does with frostings. Try our Glossy Fudge Frosting and Peanut Butter Frosting and see if you don't agree.

Keep a jar of the syrup handy in the refrigerator. Also use it to sweeten beverages. And when you have an elegant cake that deserves an out-of-the-world frosting, or a plain one that needs a glamorous coverlet, put the syrup to work for you.

BASIC SUGAR SYRUP

2 c. sugar
1 c. water

• Boil sugar and water together 1 minute. Pour into jar. Cool, cover and store in the refrigerator. Makes approximately 2 cups.

Note: Frostings made with Basic Sugar Syrup in higher altitudes (above 3500 feet) take longer and more beating than in lower altitudes to become thick enough to stay on the cake.

GLOSSY FUDGE FROSTING

Frosting has a fudge-like grain—Basic Sugar Syrup is the secret

1 (6 oz.) pkg. semisweet chocolate
2 tblsp. butter or regular margarine pieces
⅓ c. Basic Sugar Syrup

• Melt butter over hot (not boiling) water. Remove from heat before the water boils.
• Add chocolate pieces to butter over hot water and stir until melted, blended and thick.
• Add Basic Sugar Syrup gradually, stirring after each addition until blended. Mixture will become glossy and smooth.
• Remove from hot water and cool until of spreading consistency. Spread thinly over cake. Apply quickly by pouring a small amount at a time on top of cake; as it runs down on sides, spread with spatula. Frost top of cake last. Makes frosting for two 8″ layers, or a 13 × 9 × 2″ cake.

CHOCOLATE/BUTTERSCOTCH FROSTING

An easy-does-it rich frosting

1 (6 oz.) pkg. butterscotch-flavored morsels
1 square unsweetened chocolate
½ c. Basic Sugar Syrup

• Melt butterscotch morsels and chocolate over hot, not boiling, water. (Remove from heat just before boiling point is reached.)
• Add Basic Sugar Syrup gradually to butterscotch-chocolate mixture, stirring until blended after each addition. (Mixture becomes glossy and smooth.)
• Remove from hot water and cool until of spreading consistency. In warm weather, it may be necessary to set pan in ice water to cool quickly. Enough frosting for two 8″ cake layers or a 13 × 9 × 2″ cake.

PEANUT BUTTER FROSTING

Fluffy frosting is perfect on spice, chocolate and yellow cakes—try it

¾ c. crunchy peanut butter
¾ c. cold Basic Sugar Syrup

• Whip peanut butter with mixer (or wooden spoon). Add syrup gradually, beating all the time.

Makes enough frosting for tops and sides of two 8 or 9″ cake layers or a 13 × 9 × 2″ cake.

Buttermilk Cake Is Flavor-rich

Tender, light buttermilk cakes remain popular in today's country kitchens. No wonder–they taste so marvelous. They used to come fragrant from ovens on churning day when women enjoyed plentiful supplies of buttermilk, the by-product. But gradually most homemakers turned butter-making over to dairies with an enthusiasm that matched that of their husbands and sons who gave up milking the cows by hand. Buttermilk for use in cake-making began to come in bottles and now in cartons.

Our collection of country cakes contains several updated recipes for buttermilk specials. Blue Ribbon Banana Cake, a rather fancy layer cake, took top honors at a county fair. Cocoa flavored Brown Mountain Cake bakes in an oblong pan. In our Countryside Test Kitchens we decided it reached the peak of taste perfection when topped with chocolate frosting. A perfect companion for ice cream.

BLUE RIBBON BANANA CAKE

Coconut flakes baked on batter give cake an interesting surface

¾ c. shortening
1½ c. sugar
2 eggs
1 c. mashed bananas
½ tsp. salt
2 c. sifted cake flour
1 tsp. baking soda
1 tsp. baking powder
½ c. buttermilk
1 tsp. vanilla
½ c. chopped pecans
1 c. flaked coconut
Creamy Nut Filling
White Snow Frosting

· Cream together shortening and sugar until fluffy. Add eggs; beat 2 minutes at medium speed. Add mashed bananas. Beat 2 minutes.
· Sift together dry ingredients. Add to creamed mixture along with buttermilk and vanilla. Beat 2 minutes. Stir in nuts.
· Turn into 2 greased and floured 9″ round layer cake pans. Sprinkle ½ c. coconut on each layer. Bake in moderate (375°) oven 25 to 30 minutes. Remove from pan. Cool layers, coconut side up, on racks.
· Place first layer coconut side down and spread on Creamy Nut Filling. Top with second layer, coconut side up. Swirl White Snow Frosting around sides and about 1″ around top edge, leaving center unfrosted.

CREAMY NUT FILLING: Combine ½ c. sugar, 2 tblsp. flour, ½ c. cream and 2 tblsp. butter in heavy saucepan. Cook until thickened. Add ½ c. chopped pecans, ¼ tsp. salt and 1 tsp. vanilla. Cool.

WHITE SNOW FROSTING: Cream together 1 egg white, ¼ c. shortening, ¼ c. butter, ½ tsp. coconut extract and ½ tsp. vanilla until well blended. Gradually add 2 c. sifted confectioners sugar, beating until light and fluffy.

BROWN MOUNTAIN CAKE

Cake slices neatly. It's an ideal escort for homemade ice cream

1 c. butter
2 c. sugar
3 eggs
3 c. sifted flour
1 tsp. baking soda
½ tsp. salt
3 tblsp. cocoa
1 c. buttermilk
1 tsp. vanilla
½ c. warm water

• Cream butter and sugar until light and fluffy. Beat in eggs, one at a time. Sift together flour, baking soda, salt and cocoa; add alternately with buttermilk to creamed mixture. Stir in vanilla and warm water.

• Pour batter into lightly greased and floured 13 × 9 × 2″ pan. Bake in moderate oven (350°) about 45 minutes, or until the cake tests done.

• Cool cake on rack. Frost with your favorite chocolate frosting.

LUSCIOUS BUTTERMILK CAKE

Instead of frosting, cut cake and serve with Lemon-Butter-Egg Sauce

1 c. shortening
2¼ c. sugar
2 tsp. vanilla
1 tblsp. lemon juice
1 tsp. grated lemon peel
6 large eggs, separated
3 c. sifted flour
1 tsp. baking powder
½ tsp. baking soda
1 tsp. salt
¾ c. buttermilk
Lemon-Butter-Egg Sauce

• Beat together shortening and 1½ c. sugar. Blend in vanilla, lemon juice and peel. Add egg yolks, one at a time, blending just until smooth after each addition.

• Sift together flour, baking powder, soda and salt. Add alternately with buttermilk to first mixture, blending until smooth.

• Beat egg whites until frothy, then gradually beat in remaining ¾ c. sugar until egg whites stand in stiff peaks. Fold into batter.

• Spoon batter into 10″ tube pan that has been greased and dusted with fine bread crumbs. Bake in moderate oven (350°) about 1 hour and 15 minutes, or until cake tests done. Cool on rack.

LEMON-BUTTER-EGG SAUCE: In a small saucepan, combine ½ c. butter or margarine, 1 c. sugar, ¼ c. water, 1 well-beaten egg and 3 tblsp. lemon juice. Cook over medium heat, stirring constantly, just until mixture comes to a boil. Makes about 1½ cups.

ORANGE CANDY CAKE

Moist, sweet cake—has fruitcake flavor but is less expensive

1 c. butter
2 c. sugar
5 eggs
1 tblsp. vanilla
1 (8 oz.) pkg. dates, cut up
1 (1 lb.) pkg. candy orange slices, cut up
2 c. pecans, chopped
1 (4 oz.) can shredded coconut
4 c. sifted flour
½ tsp. baking soda
1 tsp. salt
¾ c. buttermilk
Lemon Syrup

• Cream butter and sugar until light

and fluffy. Beat in eggs, one at a time. Add vanilla.

· Mix dates, candy, nuts and coconut with ¼ c. flour.

· Sift remaining flour with baking soda and salt. Alternately fold into creamed mixture with buttermilk.

· Fold in the date mixture. Spoon into well greased and floured 10″ tube pan.

· Bake in slow oven (300°) 2½ hours.

· Remove cake from oven and at once pour on the Lemon Syrup. Set pan on rack and let cool. When the cake is cooled thoroughly, remove it from pan. Wrap snugly in aluminum foil and refrigerate 1 day or longer before serving. The flavors blend during the refrigeration and the cake slices more easily.

LEMON SYRUP: Mix together 1 tsp. grated lemon peel, 1 tsp. grated orange peel, ¼ c. lemon juice, ¼ c. orange juice and ½ c. confectioners sugar, sifted.

SPICY PRUNE CAKE

Work fast—pour hot glaze on cake as soon as it comes from oven

1 c. salad oil
1½ c. sugar
3 eggs
2 c. sifted flour
½ tsp. salt
1 tsp. baking powder
1 tsp. baking soda
1 tsp. ground cinnamon
1 tsp. ground nutmeg
1 tsp. ground allspice
1 c. cooked and mashed prunes
1 c. buttermilk
1 c. chopped pecans
Caramel Glaze

· Cream together oil and sugar. Add eggs one at a time, beating well after each addition.

· Sift together dry ingredients. Add alternately to creamed mixture with prunes and buttermilk. Stir in pecans.

· Pour into greased and floured 13 × 9 × 2″ pan. Bake in moderate oven (350°) 35 minutes. Put pan on rack. Pour hot Caramel Glaze over cake.

CARAMEL GLAZE: Combine 1 c. sugar, ½ c. buttermilk, ½ tsp. baking soda, 1 tblsp. corn syrup, ½ c. butter, and ½ tsp. vanilla in medium-size saucepan. Bring to a boil over low heat and boil 10 minutes; stir occasionally.

BLACKBERRY JAM CAKE

When friends stop by, serve this cake from freezer with coffee

1 c. raisins
1 (8½ oz.) can crushed pineapple
1 c. butter
1 c. sugar
5 eggs
1 c. blackberry jam
2½ c. sifted flour
1 tsp. baking soda
1 tsp. ground cinnamon
1 tsp. ground nutmeg
½ tsp. ground cloves
⅔ c. buttermilk
1 c. chopped pecans

· Soak raisins for several hours or overnight in pineapple and juice.

· Cream butter and sugar until light and fluffy. Add eggs, one at a time, beating after each one. Stir in jam.

· Sift together dry ingredients. Add alternately to creamed mixture with buttermilk.

· Stir in fruit mixture and pecans.

• Pour batter into paper-lined 13 × 9 × 2″ pan. Bake in moderate oven (350°) 50 to 55 minutes. Cool on rack.
• Dust with sifted confectioners sugar to serve.

When Wedding Bells Ring

Letters from brides-to-be and their mothers start pouring in to FARM JOURNAL's Food Department about the time the first crocus pokes up its head. The steady flow continues until June, when it tapers off. In just about every letter we find this question: "Won't you please rush me a recipe for a beautiful wedding cake that's not too difficult to make?"

In answer to these requests we developed two prize bridal cake recipes—one a big glamorous one with yellow roses for the church wedding, and the other a smaller dainty cake with pastel-pink trim for the simple home wedding.

• If you are not an experienced hand with a cake decorator, make your frosting designs on waxed paper before you attempt to put them on the cake. It's surprising how practice brings improvement. Or perhaps you can call on the champion cake-baker in your community to help you. Almost every neighborhood has at least one woman clever at cake decorating.

FORMAL WEDDING CAKE

Bake three oblong cakes and three 9″ square cakes for this beauty

3 c. sifted cake flour (see Note)
4 tsp. baking powder
1½ tsp. salt
5 egg whites
6 tblsp. sugar
⅔ c. shortening
1⅔ c. sugar
1⅓ c. milk
1½ tsp. vanilla
¼ tsp. almond extract

• Sift together flour, baking powder and salt twice.
• Beat egg whites until foamy. Add 6 tblsp. of sugar, 1 tblsp. at a time, beating until mixture stands in soft peaks.
• Cream shortening; add 1⅔ c. sugar gradually. Cream until light and fluffy.
• Add flour, alternately with milk, a small amount at a time, beating after each addition until smooth. Add egg whites and flavorings; beat thoroughly (about 1 minute).
• Grease or line pans with waxed paper. Batter fills two 9″ square pans or one 13 × 9 × 2″ pan.
• Bake in moderate oven (350°). Cakes in square pans take 30 to 40 minutes, in oblong pans, 35 to 50 minutes.
• Cool cakes on racks 10 minutes. Loosen from sides of pan, turn out and remove paper. Turn right side up to cool. To keep from drying, cover or wrap as soon as cooled. Make recipe 5 times; assemble cake. Makes about 100 servings.
• You will have one and one-half 9″ square cakes left over to sample. To make cake to serve 40 you will have one-half 9″ cake left over for a sampler. You can make the Formal Cake and the small edition with packaged white cake mix. Layers will not be so thick unless you add more batter—enough to fill the pans ½ to ⅔ full.

Note: Use 3 c. plus 2 tblsp. flour in batter when baking cake in one large pan.

FROSTING THE CAKE: When cake is assembled, frost top and sides of whole cake. Start at top and work toward bottom layers. As each tier is finished, smooth it with spatula or glaze (see Frosting Facts which follow). When cake is frosted, work down–decorating top tier first, bottom tier last. Spread a layer of frosting over surface of cardboard or other board. (We used an 18″ square of white Masonite, with a piece of waxed paper 13 × 12″ in the center when we made this cake.) Put trim around cake and edge of board.

CUTTING THE CAKE: The small top tier is removed for the bride. (She may wish to wrap and freeze it to serve on her first anniversary.) Cut each layer of the middle tier into 16 square pieces (a total of 32). Cut each of the larger layers of the bottom tier into 36 pieces (a total of 72).

ORNAMENTAL FROSTING

Make this recipe twice to frost the glamorous Formal Cake

½ c. butter or regular margarine
½ tsp. salt
12 c. confectioners sugar, sifted
5 egg whites, unbeaten
½ c. light cream
2 tsp. vanilla

· Cream butter; add salt. Gradually add about 1 c. sugar, blending after each addition.

· Add remaining sugar alternately —with eggs first, then with cream, until of right consistency to spread. Beat smooth after each addition. Add vanilla; blend. (While frosting cake, keep bowl of frosting covered with damp cloth to prevent crust that makes roughness, clogs decorating tube.) Makes 6 cups.

TO ASSEMBLE FORMAL CAKE: Use one and a half large oblong cakes for each of two bottom layers. Place one cake, top side down, on waxed paper. Cut another oblong cake in half, lengthwise; frost cut side. Push it, top side down, against long side of whole cake to complete bottom layer. Center it on cardboard or other board to give it a firm foundation. Frost top; add second layer in same manner.

· Spread frosting on the bottom of a 9″ square cake. Place frosted side down, on the two bottom layers, centering it. Frost top of square cake; add another 9″ square.

· Cut third 9″ layer in four equal squares. Put two of them together with frosting for the top tier.

TIPS FOR THE CAKE BAKER: Before you start making the cake, check pan sizes and supplies needed. Use pliable spatulas to spread frosting; a short (4″) blade is best for sides of cake. You can make your own decorating bag from heavy waxed or parchment paper, but for inexperienced cake-makers, it's easier with a cake decorating set.

· Make certain you have freezer space or other proper storage if you bake cake a day ahead. You can give it a thin glaze the day before you frost and decorate it to save time.

FROSTING FACTS: Sift confectioners sugar before using it. Tiny lumps clog tube and keep it from making clear-cut designs.

· Apply thin glaze to cake before frosting, to anchor crumbs. Make glaze by adding hot water to some of the frosting, about 1 tblsp. to 1 c. frosting.

· To tint frosting, mix about ¼ tsp. of food color with 1 tblsp. frosting. Add small amounts of this color base to your frosting. Tint enough frosting for whole cake, as it's difficult to match colors with another batch.

· Frosting used in tube should be a little thicker or heavier than that for spreading with spatula. Just add a little sifted confectioners sugar.

· It's a good idea to practice putting designs on a piece of waxed paper, baking sheets or backs of pans.

Pretty Easier-to-make Wedding Cake

If you are not talented with a pastry tube, bake our Informal Wedding Cake. This will give you a smaller cake. You will need to use the pastry tube only to put frosting, tinted a pastel pink, around the rim of the serving plate. Arrange flowers on the Formal or Informal Wedding Cake just before serving. Use pink roses if you trim the rim of the serving plate with frosting tinted pink. If baking the Formal or Informal Wedding Cake for a golden wedding reception use yellow roses and make the rim on the plate for the Informal Wedding Cake with frosting tinted a delicate yellow.

INFORMAL WEDDING CAKE

Dainty pink frosting around cake on rim of plate adds charm

2¾ c. sifted cake flour
4 tsp. baking powder
1 tsp. salt
1¾ c. sugar
⅔ c. shortening
1¼ c. milk
4 egg whites, unbeaten
2 tsp. vanilla
½ tsp. almond extract

· Grease or line bottoms of cake pans with waxed paper. (We used a 4-tier round cake pan set. Pans measure about 9″, 7″, 5″ and 3″ in diameter.

· Sift together flour, baking powder, salt and sugar.

· Add shortening and 1 c. of the milk. Mix at low speed until flour is dampened. Beat 2 minutes at low speed of mixer or 300 strokes by hand.

· Add egg whites, remaining milk and flavorings; beat 1 minute or 150 strokes by hand. Pour into pans, filling ½ to ⅔ full. It takes about half the batter to fill the 9″ and the 3″ pans, remaining batter to fill the 7″ and the 5″ pans.

· Bake in moderate oven (350°) about 20 minutes for 2 small cakes, 30 minutes for larger cakes. Cool cakes on racks 5 minutes. Loosen from sides of pan, turn out on rack, remove paper. Turn right side up to cool. Makes 20 servings.

Note: You may use 2 (17 to 20 oz.) packages white cake mix. The first package will fill the two large pans. Half the batter from second package will fill two small pans. (Make single layer or cupcakes from remaining batter for pre-wedding sampling.)

BASE FOR INFORMAL CAKE: Place 12″ silver paper doily in center of your serving plate. Put a few dabs of frosting under center of doily and at various spots to hold it on plate.

FROSTING THE CAKE: Use 1 recipe of Ornamental Frosting. These are generous amounts. Coat all layers with a thin glaze (see Frosting Facts).

· It will take about 3 c. frosting to cover all the layers. Tint remaining frosting.

· Place 4 strips of waxed paper under edges of bottom cake layer. Then frost sides and top of layer. Paper will keep doily free of any drips. Remove waxed paper when frosting is completed.

· Add second tier and frost; repeat with remaining two tiers. Dip small spatula in hot water to smooth sides and top ready for decorations. Tint 2 c. frosting a delicate pink using red food color.

· As a finishing touch, outline a fluffy design of the pastel pink frosting around rim of the serving plate.

CUTTING THE CAKE: Cut top tier in half. Cut remaining layers in pie-shaped pieces. Makes about 20 servings.

Salad Oil Shortening with Lovely Cakes

Collections of prized country cake recipes always include layers and loaves in which salad oil rather than butter, margarine or homogenized shortening provides the necessary fat. When we culled our extensive files, we pulled out a few of these specialties—14-Carat Cake, for instance. Among its qualifications for recognition are its remarkable keeping qualities when stored in the refrigerator ready to slice on short notice. This explains why many hostesses champion the big cake. Carrot/Pecan Spice Cake, although quite different, is another carrot-salad oil cake that excels in taste. And Ambrosia Chiffon and Rocky Mountain Cake are lovely and luscious. These productions will please your family and friends. You'll want to make them often.

ROCKY MOUNTAIN CAKE

Black walnuts are the rocks in this recipe shared by a ranch woman

2 c. sifted flour
1½ c. sugar
1 tblsp. baking powder
1 tsp. salt
1 tsp. ground cinnamon
½ tsp. ground nutmeg
½ tsp. ground allspice
½ tsp. ground cloves
7 eggs, separated
2 tblsp. caraway seeds
½ c. salad oil
¾ c. ice water
½ tsp. cream of tartar
Rocky Mountain Frosting

· Sift flour, sugar, baking powder, salt and spices together several times.

· Combine egg yolks, caraway seeds, oil and water in large bowl. Add dry ingredients. Beat about 30 seconds at low speed on mixer or 75 strokes by hand. (Add a few drops of lemon extract for different flavor.)

· Add cream of tartar to egg whites. Beat until stiff peaks form.

• Gradually pour egg yolk mixture over beaten whites; gently fold in.
• Pour into ungreased 10″ tube pan. Bake in slow oven (325°) 55 minutes, then increase heat to moderate (350°) and bake 10 to 15 minutes more.
• Invert pan on rack to cool cake. When completely cool, spread Rocky Mountain Frosting over top and sides of cake.

ROCKY MOUNTAIN FROSTING: In saucepan, blend ½ c. butter with 2½ tblsp. flour and ¼ tsp. salt. Cook 1 minute; do not brown. Add ½ c. milk; cook until thick. While hot, add ½ c. brown sugar, firmly packed; beat well. Add 2 c. confectioners sugar, sifted; beat until thick and creamy. Add 1 tsp. vanilla and 1 c. chopped black walnuts, or other nuts. Spread over top and sides of cake.

Note: You can make a double batch of frosting and freeze for that extra cake.

AMBROSIA CHIFFON CAKE

Light as an angel cake, rich and luscious as your best butter cakes. Be sure eggs are at room temperature

2¼ c. sifted cake flour
1½ c. sugar
1 tblsp. baking powder
1 tsp. salt
5 egg yolks
½ c. salad oil
¼ c. water
½ c. orange juice
1 tblsp. grated orange peel
½ tsp. cream of tartar
1 c. egg whites (8 or 9 eggs)
1 c. flaked coconut
Orange Satin Frosting

• Sift flour with 1 c. sugar, baking powder and salt.
• Measure into mixing bowl egg yolks, oil, water, orange juice and peel. Add sifted dry ingredients. Beat until smooth, about ½ minute at low speed of mixer, or 75 strokes by hand.
• Add cream of tartar to egg whites. Beat until soft peaks form. Gradually add remaining ½ c. sugar, beating until mixture stands in very stiff peaks. Do not underbeat.
• Chop or cut coconut into shorter lengths. Fold into egg whites with a large spoon or rubber scraper. Then gently fold egg yolk mixture into whites.
• Pour into ungreased 10″ tube pan. Bake in slow oven (325°) 1 hour or until surface springs back when touched lightly.
• Invert pan on rack to cool. A good way is to place tube of pan over inverted funnel. When cool, loosen sides with a spatula and turn out. Frost with Orange Satin Frosting. For a festive touch, add a border of coconut shreds around rim of cake.

ORANGE SATIN FROSTING: Combine in top of double boiler 2 egg whites, 1½ c. sugar, 1½ tsp. light corn syrup, ⅓ c. orange juice and dash of salt. Beat 1 minute with electric or rotary hand beater.
• Cook mixture over boiling water, beating constantly until mixture forms peaks (about 7 minutes).
• Remove from heat. Add 1 tsp. grated orange peel, 8 marshmallows, cut in pieces, and enough yellow food color to tint delicately. Beat 1 or 2 minutes, until partially cooled.

CARROT/PECAN SPICE CAKE

A spiced nut cake that keeps well if you hide it—a real treat

1¼ c. salad oil
2 c. sugar
2 c. sifted flour
2 tsp. baking powder
1 tsp. baking soda
1 tsp. salt
2 tsp. ground cinnamon
4 eggs
3 c. grated raw carrots
1 c. finely chopped pecans
Orange Glaze

• Combine oil and sugar; mix well.
• Sift together remaining dry ingredients. Sift half of dry ingredients into sugar mixture; blend. Sift in remaining dry ingredients alternately with eggs, one at a time, mixing well after each addition.
• Add carrots and mix well; then mix in pecans. Pour into lightly oiled 10″ tube pan. Bake in slow oven (325°) about 1 hour and 10 minutes. Cool in pan upright on rack. Remove from pan.
• Split cake in 3 horizontal layers. Spread Orange Glaze between layers and on top and sides.

ORANGE GLAZE: Combine 1 c. sugar and ¼ c. cornstarch in saucepan. Slowly add 1 c. orange juice and 1 tsp. lemon juice and stir until smooth. Add 2 tblsp. butter, 2 tblsp. grated orange peel and ½ tsp. salt. Cook over low heat until thick and glossy. Cool before spreading on cake.

Note: You can bake this cake, cool, wrap and freeze for 2 to 3 months. To serve, thaw cake in wrapper 2 hours at room temperature. Split in 3 horizontal layers and put together with Orange Glaze. Spread glaze on top and sides of cake.

14-CARAT CAKE

This flavorful cake keeps 2 to 3 weeks in refrigerator if covered

2 c. sifted flour
2 tsp. baking powder
1½ tsp. baking soda
1½ tsp. salt
2 tsp. ground cinnamon
2 c. sugar
1½ c. salad oil
4 eggs
2 c. finely grated raw carrots
1 (8½ oz.) can crushed pineapple, drained
½ c. chopped nuts
1 (3½ oz.) can flaked coconut (optional)
Cream Cheese Frosting

• Sift together flour, baking powder, baking soda, salt and cinnamon. Add sugar, salad oil and eggs; mix well. Add carrots, pineapple, nuts and coconut; blend thoroughly.
• Pour into three 9″ round layer cake pans that have been greased and floured.
• Bake in moderate oven (350°) 35 to 40 minutes. Remove from oven, cool a few minutes in pans. Turn out on racks and cool thoroughly. Fill layers and frost top and sides of cake with Cream Cheese Frosting.

CREAM CHEESE FROSTING: Combine ½ c. butter or margarine, 1 (8 oz.) pkg. cream cheese and 1 tsp. vanilla; cream well. Gradually add 1 lb. confectioners sugar (sifted if lumpy), beating well. If mixture is too thick to spread, add a small amount of milk.

DATE/NUT CAKE

This Florida cake has rung up a fine sales record at food bazaars

4 eggs
1 c. sugar
½ c. salad oil
1 tsp. salt
1 c. sifted flour
1 lb. pitted dates
4 c. pecan halves

• Combine eggs, sugar and oil. Beat well.

• Add remaining ingredients, mixing well.

• Place in greased, and floured 9 × 5 × 3″ loaf pan. Start cake in cold oven. Bake in slow oven (300°) 2 hours.

Exquisite Southern Belles

Southern kitchens were the origin of many elegant cakes. Most of the recipes are too much work for popular use today, but Lane Cake still appears on red-letter occasions. It's a white layer cake with the left-over egg yolks salvaged in the rich filling to which pecans and raisins impart their flavor.

When the recipe for Lemon Cheese Cake first made its bow in the original *Country Cookbook*, women wrote to Countryside Test Kitchens asking if we forgot to list cheese among the ingredients. These letters did not come from the South. It was there that the cake got its name—the filling (also spread on top of cake) has a slight curd *resembling* cheese.

LANE CAKE

This superior cake is a favorite in Alabama and Georgia kitchens

1 c. butter or regular margarine
2 c. sugar
3¼ c. sifted cake flour
2 tsp. baking powder
1 c. milk
1 tsp. vanilla
8 egg whites, stiffly beaten
Raisin/Nut Filling
Southern Frosting

• Cream together butter and sugar. Sift together flour and baking powder and add to creamed mixture alternately with milk and vanilla. Fold in egg whites. Pour into three 9″ round layer cake pans. Bake in moderate oven (350°) 30 to 35 minutes, until golden brown. Cool on racks. Spread Raisin/Nut Filling between cooled layers. Frost sides and top of cake with Southern Frosting.

RAISIN/NUT FILLING: Cream together ½ c. butter or margarine and 1 c. sugar. Add 8 egg yolks, beaten, and cook in double boiler until thick. Add 1 c. seeded raisins, chopped, 1 c. chopped pecans and 1 tsp. vanilla.

SOUTHERN FROSTING: Dissolve 2½ c. sugar, ⅛ tsp. salt and ⅓ c. dark corn syrup in ⅔ c. water. Cook until mixture reaches boiling point. Meanwhile, beat 2 egg whites until foamy. Pour 3 tblsp. sugar mixture into egg whites; continue beating eggs until stiff but not dry. Add 1 tsp. vanilla. Boil syrup mixture to 240° on candy thermometer, or until it spins a thread at least 10″ long when dropped from edge of spoon. Then pour syrup slowly over egg whites, beating until frosting is thick, cool and of good spreading consistency. Spread over cake. If the frosting becomes hard, add a drop or two of hot water to the mixture. This frosting does not form a crust that cracks when cake is cut. Makes enough frosting for a 3-layer 9″ cake.

LEMON CHEESE CAKE

Cake contains no cheese but buttery filling has hint of cheese-like curd

1 c. butter
2 c. sugar
1 tblsp. baking powder
3 c. sifted cake flour
¾ c. milk
6 egg whites, stiffly beaten
Lemon Cheese Cake Filling

· Cream together butter and sugar with mixer, beating until light and fluffy.

· Sift together baking powder and flour; add alternately with milk to creamed mixture. Fold in egg whites. Pour into 3 greased 8″ round layer cake pans.

· Bake in moderate oven (350°) 25 to 30 minutes, or until top springs back when lightly touched. Cool on racks.

· Put layers together with Lemon Cheese Cake Filling, and spread filling over top. Sprinkle with coconut, if desired. White icing may be used to frost sides of cake.

LEMON CHEESE CAKE FILLING: Combine ½ c. butter, 1 c. sugar, 6 egg yolks, grated peel and juice of 2 lemons in top of double boiler. Cook over hot water, stirring constantly until thick. Cool.

FRESH COCONUT CAKE

Fresh or frozen coconut is perishable—use cake pronto after frosting

2¾ c. sifted cake flour
4 tsp. baking powder
¾ tsp. salt
¾ c. butter or shortening
1½ c. sugar
4 egg whites
1 tsp. vanilla
1 tsp. almond extract
1 c. milk or coconut milk
Tropical Frosting
½ lb. fresh coconut

· Sift together flour, baking powder and salt three times.

· Cream butter well, then add 1 c. sugar and blend well.

· Beat egg whites until fluffy. Gradually add ½ c. sugar, beating until stiff peaks form.

· Add flavorings to milk and add milk alternately with dry ingredients to creamed mixture. Beat well.

· Fold egg white mixture into batter. Pour into 3 greased 8″ round layer cake pans.

· Bake in moderate oven (350°) 25 to 30 minutes. Cool on racks.

· Spread Tropical Frosting between layers, topping with freshly grated coconut. Cover top and sides of cake and pile with freshly grated (or frozen) coconut. Keep in refrigerator until serving time, or freeze.

TROPICAL FROSTING: Combine 2 c. sugar, 1 c. water, ⅛ tsp. salt and 1 tsp. white vinegar in a heavy saucepan. Cook over medium heat, stirring constantly until clear. Without stirring, cook until mixture forms a thin thread when dropped from spoon (242° on candy thermometer). Beat 3 egg whites until stiff. Add hot syrup, beating constantly. Continue beating until frosting holds shape. Add ½ tsp. vanilla, and blend well.

ITALIAN CREAM CAKE

Italians serve chocolate and lemon ice creams together. The luscious flavor combination inspired us to develop this fascinating cake

1 (1 lb. 3 oz.) pkg. lemon chiffon cake mix
Chocolate/Spice Filling
Lemon/Fruit Filling
1½ c. heavy cream
¼ c. sifted confectioners sugar

· Prepare cake mix according to package directions. Bake in 10″ tube pan.

· When cake has cooled, remove from pan and slice in 5 layers. Fill layers alternately with Chocolate/Spice and Lemon/Fruit Filling.

· Whip heavy cream with confectioners sugar; frost top and sides of cake. Chill several hours.

CHOCOLATE/SPICE FILLING: Prepare 1 (4 oz.) pkg. chocolate pudding and pie filling as directed on package, using 1½ c. milk and adding ½ tsp. ground cinnamon. Cover and cool to room temperature. Whip ½ c. heavy cream; fold into pudding. Add 2 tblsp. slivered toasted almonds. Chill 15 minutes.

LEMON/FRUIT FILLING: Prepare 1 (3¼ oz.) pkg. vanilla pudding and pie filling as directed on package, using 1½ c. milk. Cover and cool to room temperature. Add 2 tsp. lemon juice and 1 tblsp. grated lemon peel. Whip ½ c. heavy cream; fold into pudding. Add ⅓ c. drained pineapple tidbits and ¼ c. drained, quartered maraschino cherries. Chill 15 minutes.

DOUBLE DELIGHT CAKE

Chocolate ice cream is the filling, chocolate frosting covers cake

1 (17 to 18½ oz.) pkg. yellow cake mix
3 pts. chocolate ice cream
Chocolate Frosting

· Prepare cake mix as directed on package. Bake in 13 × 9 × 2″ pan. Cool.

· Cut cake in thirds to make 3 loaves. Split each loaf in halves to make 2 layers. Place in freezer until frozen.

· Spread bottom slice of one loaf with 1 pt. ice cream, softened by stirring or beating with electric mixer. Top with other half of loaf. Return to freezer. Repeat with other two loaves.

· When the 3 loaves are frozen, frost tops and sides with Chocolate Frosting. Frost one loaf at a time, leaving others in freezer. Freeze, then wrap.

· To serve, let wrapped loaf stand at room temperature about 30 minutes. Slice and serve. Each loaf serves 8.

CHOCOLATE FROSTING: Blend together ½ c. butter or margarine, 5 c. confectioners sugar, 6 tblsp. cream, 3 tsp. vanilla and 5 squares unsweetened chocolate, melted. Beat until smooth.

JELLY JEWEL CAKE

Bits of bright red jelly sparkle in the sour cream filling

- 1 (18½ oz.) pkg. white cake mix
- 8 drops green food color (about)
- 12 drops yellow food color (about)
- 1 c. tart red jelly (currant, strawberry or raspberry)
- 1 pt. dairy sour cream, or 1 pt. heavy cream, whipped
- 3 medium bananas, thinly sliced
- ½ c. shredded coconut, fluffed

• Prepare cake batter as directed on package; before last beating period divide batter in half.
• Add green color to half the batter; yellow to other half. Finish beating.
• Pour into four 8″ round layer cake pans. Bake as directed on package 10 minutes. Cool on rack.
• Place ½ c. jelly in bowl; break in small pieces with fork; add sour cream, folding only 3 or 4 times.
• Spread green layer with jelly mixture; top with sliced bananas. Repeat with yellow and other green layer. Top with yellow layer; spread with remaining jelly, broken with fork; sprinkle coconut around edge.

HOLIDAY CRANBERRY CAKE

If you are using frozen berries, put them through food chopper unthawed

- 1 (18½ oz.) pkg. lemon cake mix
- 1 (3 oz.) pkg. cream cheese, softened
- ¾ c. milk
- 4 eggs
- 1¼ c. ground cranberries
- ½ c. ground walnuts
- ¼ c. sugar
- 1 tsp. ground mace (optional)

• Blend cake mix, cream cheese and milk; beat with mixer 2 minutes at medium speed. Add eggs; blend and beat for 2 additional minutes.
• Thoroughly combine cranberries, walnuts, sugar and mace; fold into cake batter. Pour into well-greased and floured 10″ tube or bundt pan.
• Bake in moderate oven (350°) 1 hour or until done. Cool 5 minutes. Remove from pan. Cool on rack. Dust with confectioners sugar if you wish.

Lard Cakes Made by Meringue Method

If you live in the country or visit there, you probably know how wonderful lard cakes can be. At least you do if you ever tasted cakes made by the meringue method, which home economists in our Countryside Test Kitchens developed. The first step in combining the ingredients for these cakes is to beat the egg whites with the sugar instead of creaming together the lard and sugar. This technique produces superior, light and fluffy layers and loaves. The quartet of lard cake recipes that follows are among our favorites. You'll like them as much as we do.

CHOCOLATE LARD CAKE

Velvety, moist cake with tempting light-chocolate color—it goes fast

- 2 eggs, separated
- ½ c. sugar
- ⅓ c. lard
- 1¾ c. sifted cake flour
- 1 c. sugar
- ¾ tsp. baking soda
- 1 tsp. salt
- 1 c. plus 2 tblsp. buttermilk
- 2 squares unsweetened chocolate, melted
- Glossy Fudge Frosting (see Index)

• Beat egg whites until frothy. Gradually beat in ½ c. sugar. Continue beating until very stiff and glossy.
• In another bowl, stir lard to soften. Add sifted dry ingredients and ¾ c. buttermilk. Stir to moisten dry ingredients; then beat 1 minute, medium speed, on mixer. Scrape sides and bottom of bowl constantly.
• Add remaining buttermilk, egg yolks and melted chocolate. Beat 1 minute, scraping bowl constantly.
• Fold in egg whites. Pour into 2 greased and floured 8″ round layer cake pans or 13 × 9 × 2″ pan. Bake in moderate oven (350°) 30 to 35 minutes. Cool on rack 10 minutes. Remove from pans.
• Brush crumbs from cake while warm to facilitate frosting. Frost with Glossy Fudge Frosting.

FEATHER SPICE LARD CAKE

Meltingly rich, tender cake—you'll make it again and again

2 eggs, separated
½ c. sugar
⅓ c. lard
2¼ c. sifted cake flour
1 tsp. baking powder
1 tsp. salt
¾ tsp. baking soda
¾ tsp. ground cinnamon
¾ tsp. ground cloves
1 c. sugar (brown or white)
1 c. plus 2 tblsp. buttermilk
Peanut Butter Frosting (see Index)

• Beat egg whites until frothy. Gradually beat in ½ c. sugar. Continue beating until very stiff and glossy.
• In another bowl, stir lard to soften. Add sifted dry ingredients and ¾ c. buttermilk. Beat 1 minute, medium speed on mixer. Scrape bottom and sides of bowl constantly.
• Add remaining buttermilk and egg yolks. Beat 1 minute, scraping bowl constantly.
• Fold in egg white mixture.
• Pour into 2 greased and floured 8″ round layer cake pans, or a 13 × 9 × 2″ pan. Bake in moderate oven (350°) 30 to 35 minutes. Cool on rack 10 minutes, then remove from pans. Frost with Peanut Butter Frosting or Broiled Caramel Glaze.

Variation

MOCHA SPICE LARD CAKE: Omit the cloves. Increase cinnamon to 1½ tsp. and add 2 tsp. instant coffee powder. Bake as directed for Feather Spice Lard Cake.

BROILED CARAMEL GLAZE

A quick way to put a two-layer cake together when you're in a hurry

¼ c. butter
½ c. brown sugar, firmly packed
2 tblsp. heavy cream

• Melt butter; stir in sugar and cream.
• Place cake layers on baking sheet, one at a time. Spread each layer evenly with butter mixture, spreading out to edges.
• Place cake in broiler 6 to 8″ from heat, and broil until bubbly and golden brown, 2 to 3 minutes. Broil each layer separately.
• When second layer is removed from broiler, place on cake plate immediately and place first layer on it. Layers will hold together, and glaze will have run down the side to give cake a finished, appetizing look. Makes enough glaze for 2 (8 or 9″) layers.

Variations

CARAMEL/NUT GLAZE: Remove

glazed top layer from broiler; sprinkle immediately with chopped nuts.

PINEAPPLE GLAZE: Spread top layer with glaze, dip well-drained pineapple tidbits in some of the glaze mixture and arrange in sunburst effect on top of cake at least 1″ from edge all around. Broil like plain Caramel Glaze.

SOUR CREAM/CARAMEL GLAZE: Use dairy sour cream for heavy cream.

ORANGE LARD CAKE

Dress up cake by sprinkling coconut on freshly spread frosting

2 eggs, separated
½ c. sugar
⅓ c. lard
2¼ c. sifted cake flour
1 c. sugar
2½ tsp. baking powder
1 tsp. salt
¼ tsp. baking soda
¾ c. milk
⅓ c. orange juice, fresh or reconstituted frozen
¼ tsp. almond extract
Orange Butter Cream Frosting

· Beat egg whites until frothy. Gradually beat in ½ c. sugar. Continue beating until very stiff and glossy.
· In another bowl stir lard to soften. Add sifted dry ingredients and milk. Beat 1 minute, medium speed on mixer. Scrape bottom and sides of bowl constantly.
· Add orange juice, egg yolks and almond extract. Beat 1 minute longer, scraping bowl constantly.
· Fold in egg white mixture.
· Pour into 2 greased and floured 9″ round layer cake pans. Bake in moderate oven (350°) 25 to 30 minutes.
· Cool layers in pan on rack 10 minutes; then remove from pans. Frost with Orange Butter Cream Frosting.

ORANGE BUTTER CREAM FROSTING: Cream ½ c. butter. Gradually add 3 c. sifted confectioners sugar alternately with ⅓ c. frozen orange juice concentrate, thawed, creaming well after each addition until mixture is light and fluffy.

YELLOW LARD CAKE

A light, fluffy cake with an old-time country taste—it's good

2 eggs, separated
½ c. sugar
⅓ c. lard
2¼ c. sifted cake flour
1 c. sugar
3 tsp. baking powder
1 tsp. salt
1 c. plus 2 tblsp. milk
1½ tsp. vanilla
Peanut Butter Frosting (see Index)

· Beat egg whites until frothy. Gradually beat in ½ c. sugar. Continue beating until very stiff and glossy.
· In another bowl stir lard to soften. Add sifted dry ingredients, ¾ c. milk and vanilla. Beat 1 minute, medium speed on mixer. Scrape sides and bottom of bowl constantly.
· Add remaining milk and egg yolks. Beat 1 minute, scraping bowl constantly.
· Fold in egg whites.
· Pour into 2 greased and floured 9″ round layer cake pans. Bake in moderate oven (350°) 25 to 30 minutes. Cool layers on rack 10 minutes; then remove from pans.
· Brush crumbs from cake while warm for ease in frosting. Frost with Peanut Butter Frosting.

FUDGE PUDDING CAKE

Made with lard, it's chocolate all the way—moist fudgy cake

⅓ c. lard
3 squares unsweetened chocolate
¾ c. sugar
2 tblsp. cornstarch
1 c. milk
2 c. sifted flour
1 c. sugar
1¼ tsp. baking soda
½ tsp. salt
¾ c. milk
2 eggs
Glossy Fudge Frosting (see Index)

· Melt lard in 2- to 3-qt. saucepan over low heat. Add chocolate and stir until melted. Remove from heat.
· Mix ¾ c. sugar and cornstarch thoroughly. Stir into chocolate mixture. Add 1 c. milk; stir and cook over low heat until smooth and thick. Remove from heat and cool to room temperature. (Set pan in cold water to speed cooling.)
· Sift remaining dry ingredients together 3 times. Add ½ to chocolate mixture, blend and beat ½ minute (75 strokes). Add ¾ c. milk and blend. Add remaining dry ingredients, blend, beat 1 minute (150 strokes).
· Add eggs, blend and beat ½ minute (75 strokes).
· Bake in paper-lined 13 × 9 × 2" pan in moderate oven (350°) about 35 minutes. Cool on rack.
· When cool, spread Glossy Fudge Frosting thinly over cake. Apply quickly by pouring a small amount at a time on top of cake; as it runs down on sides, spread with spatula. Frost top last.

New Flavors in Pound Cakes

Pound cakes are easier to make, more attractive and taste better than ever. Our great-grandmothers made them with one pound of each ingredient—hence the name. But batter was stiff and extremely difficult to beat. We adapted the recipes to fit modern ingredients and introduced some interesting flavors. Brown Sugar Pound Cake with a Walnut Glaze is a beauty and Two-tone Pound Cake is handsome enough for a party. Both are simply delicious.

TWO-TONE POUND CAKE

Chocolate batter swirls in center of cake, making it picture-pretty

1¼ c. butter
2½ c. sugar
5 eggs
2½ c. sifted flour
1¼ tsp. baking powder
½ tsp. salt
1 c. less 2 tblsp. milk
2 tsp. vanilla
¼ c. cocoa, sifted
Confectioners sugar (for top)

· Cream butter; gradually add sugar and beat until light and fluffy. Beat in eggs, one at a time, creaming well after each addition.
· Sift together flour, baking powder and salt. Add them alternately with the milk and vanilla to the creamed mixture.
· Take out 2 c. cake batter and blend the cocoa into it.
· Alternately spoon the light and chocolate batters into a greased and

floured 10″ tube pan or a 10″ cast aluminum bundt pan.

· Bake in slow oven (325°) 70 minutes for a 10″ tube pan, or 90 minutes for bundt pan, or until cake tests done.

· Cool in pan about 10 minutes. Invert cake on wire rack and remove the pan. Cool cake thoroughly. Sift on confectioners sugar.

POUND CAKE

Moist cake with silky grain retains old friends, always wins new ones

1 c. butter
2 c. sugar
4 eggs, unbeaten
1 tsp. vanilla
1 tsp. lemon extract
3 c. sifted flour
½ tsp. baking soda
½ tsp. baking powder
¾ tsp. salt
1 c. buttermilk

· Cream together butter and sugar thoroughly. Add eggs, one at a time. Beat at medium speed with electric mixer 2½ minutes. Add flavorings.

· Sift together dry ingredients and add to creamed mixture alternately with buttermilk. Beat 3½ minutes at medium speed. Do not overbeat or cake will fall.

· Place in 10 × 5 × 3″ large loaf pan (may overflow smaller pan). Bake in slow oven (325°) 1 hour and 10 minutes, or until done.

JEWELED POUND CAKE

Bright candied fruit bits give traditional cake a new festive look

¼ c. candied cherries
¼ c. candied orange peel
¼ c. citron
¼ c. candied pineapple
6 tblsp. light corn syrup
2 c. butter (1 lb.)
1¼ c. sugar
2 tsp. vanilla
½ tsp. salt
10 eggs, separated
4 c. sifted cake flour
1¼ c. sugar

· Chop fruits.

· Grease three 9 × 5 × 3″ loaf pans. Pour 2 tblsp. syrup into bottom of each pan and sprinkle an equal quantity of fruits into each pan.

· Cream butter until fluffy. Add 1¼ c. sugar, vanilla and salt gradually, while beating. Continue beating with electric mixer until mixture is light and fluffy and no sugar particles remain, about 5 to 7 minutes. If beating by hand, cream until very light and fluffy.

· Beat egg yolks until light and lemon-colored; combine with creamed mixture. Blend in flour.

· Beat egg whites until soft peaks form. Gradually add remaining 1¼ c. sugar, beating constantly. Continue beating until whites stand in stiff peaks.

· Fold meringue into cake batter; blend well, but do not beat. Pour into prepared loaf pans over fruit.

· Bake in slow oven (325°) 80 minutes for metal pans, 10 minutes less for glass pans. Turn out of pans; cool upside down on racks. Makes 3 loaves.

Note: Keep this cake in the freezer to slice and serve to drop-in guests. To dress up cake, cut in squares and top with whipped cream and fruit—berries, sliced peaches and bananas, or strawberries, fresh or frozen. Or serve it with ice cream and a sundae sauce. For a change, pour pudding sauce, orange or lemon, over the cake just before serving.

BROWN SUGAR POUND CAKE

You pour confectioners sugar frosting with walnuts over hot cake

1 c. butter
½ c. shortening
1 lb. light brown sugar
1 c. sugar
5 eggs
3 c. sifted flour
½ tsp. salt
1 tsp. baking powder
1 c. milk
1 tsp. vanilla
1 c. chopped walnuts
Walnut Glaze

· Beat together butter and shortening; gradually add sugars, creaming until mixture is light and fluffy. Beat in eggs one at a time.

· Sift together dry ingredients; add alternately with milk and vanilla to the creamed mixture. Stir in nuts.

· Pour batter into greased and floured 10" tube pan. Bake in moderate oven (350°) 1 hour and 15 minutes, or until done when tested with a straw. Cool on rack 10 minutes, then remove from pan and place on rack over a piece of waxed paper. Pour Walnut Glaze over hot cake. If icing falls onto the waxed paper, scoop it up and put it back on the cake.

WALNUT GLAZE: Cream 1 c. sifted confectioners sugar and 2 tblsp. butter. Add 6 tblsp. cream, ½ tsp. vanilla and ½ c. chopped walnuts. Blend well.

Beautiful Angel Food and Sponge Cakes

Tulip and daffodil season seems to bring on angel food and sponge cakes. We give you updated recipes for these gorgeous, delicately sweet cakes. And they also use packaged angel food cake mixes with great success.

Be sure to try our toppings that glamorize angel food cakes even when you make yours from a mix. Orange Cream Sauce, Fast-fix Fruit and Pink Party Toppings and Spicy Cherry Glaze (recipes in this chapter) glorify angel food. And do bake Grand Champion Sponge Cake with Creamy Pineapple Frosting—it's a pure delight.

CHAMPION ANGEL FOOD CAKE

You bake the batter in ring molds for zephyr-light Twin Wedding Ring cakes

1¼ c. sifted cake flour
1¾ c. sifted sugar
1½ c. egg whites (10 to 11)
1½ tsp. cream of tartar
¼ tsp. salt
1 tsp. vanilla

· Sift together flour and ¾ c. sugar twice.

· In large mixer bowl beat egg whites, cream of tartar, salt and vanilla until foamy. Beat in remaining 1 c. sugar, 2 tblsp. at a time, using mixer on high speed. Beat until meringue holds stiff peaks that still are glossy and moist.

· Divide flour-sugar mixture in 4 parts. With rubber spatula, gently fold each portion into meringue until flour-sugar mixture disappears. Push batter into ungreased 10″ tube pan. Gently cut through batter once with spatula to remove air bubbles. Do not lift it out of batter.

· Bake in moderate oven (375°) 35 to 40 minutes, or until cake springs back when lightly touched with finger. Invert pan and let cake cool before removing.

TWIN WEDDING RING CAKES

Rings frosted white, filled with colorful ice cream are festive

· Push batter for Champion Angel Food cake into 2 aluminum ring molds, about 10½″ in diameter, 2½″ deep. Bake in moderate oven (375°) about 25 minutes, or until cake tests done when touched with finger. Frost with 7-Minute Frosting and place on cake tray.

· At serving time, fill cake centers with strawberry ice cream. Round, half-gallon cartons of ice cream are about the same size as center of cake. Cut through cartons crosswise to obtain an ice cream circle for each cake. Cut cardboard away, and slip ice cream into center of cake. Cut in wedges to serve. Two cakes make 25 servings.

7-MINUTE FROSTING: Combine 2 egg whites, 1½ c. sugar, ⅛ tsp. salt, ⅓ c. water, 1 tblsp. light corn syrup and 1 tsp. vanilla in top of double boiler; beat with rotary beater 1 minute.

· Place over boiling water and beat about 7 minutes, stopping a few times to clean beater and sides of pan with scraper.

· Remove from boiling water when frosting stands in glossy peaks (has more body than a meringue). Continue beating until frosting is cool and thick enough to hold firm swirls. Makes enough frosting for two 8 or 9″ layers or one 9 or 10″ tube cake.

The Cake That Is an Angel

Give a farm woman a big angel food cake and watch what happens. Without a fairy's wand, she transforms it into a spectacular dessert. And what a variety of flavors she can add—peach, lemon, mocha and pineapple are classics.

The hostess prides herself on tricks to use when she wants to dress up an angel cake especially for company. Here are recipes for some special sauces culled from files in FARM JOURNAL Test Kitchens and from farm hostesses.

ORANGE CREAM SAUCE

Keep this tangy, smooth sauce in your refrigerator, an angel cake in freezer—your refreshments are ready

6 egg yolks
⅔ c. sugar
⅔ c. orange juice
2 tsp. grated orange peel
1 tsp. grated lemon peel
⅛ tsp. salt
2 tblsp. lemon juice
1 c. dairy sour cream

· Lightly beat egg yolks in top of double boiler. Blend in the remaining ingredients except the sour cream. Cook, stirring constantly, over simmering (not boiling) water until thick, about 15 minutes. Chill.

· Stir until smooth; blend in sour cream. Spoon on sliced cake. Garnish with orange slices. Makes about 3 cups.

Note: If you want to serve a thicker sauce, refrigerate it several hours after you add the sour cream.

FAST-FIX FRUIT TOPPING

Topping keeps well in refrigerator—handy to dress up cake slices

1 (1 lb. 4½ oz.) can pineapple chunks
1 (11 oz.) can mandarin oranges
1 c. orange marmalade

• Drain fruits; stir in marmalade. Heat and serve warm or cold on angel cake slices. Makes 3 cups.

PINK PARTY TOPPING

Pretty pink fluffy sauce on white cake makes a festive party dessert. It's so good and so easy to fix

1 c. miniature marshmallows
1 (10 oz.) pkg. frozen red raspberries or strawberries
1 c. heavy cream, whipped

• Pour marshmallows and frozen berries into a bowl. Cover; refrigerate overnight. Before serving, fold in whipped cream. Makes 3 cups.

SPICY CHERRY GLAZE

For a showy dessert spoon glaze on a whole cake—also pretty on slices

1½ c. drained, pitted tart canned cherries, 1 (16 to 17 oz.) can
Juice drained from cherries
8 whole cloves
3 sticks cinnamon
2 tblsp. cornstarch
¼ c. sugar
¼ tsp. salt
⅓ c. light corn syrup
1 tblsp. butter
Red food color

• Combine cherries, ½ c. cherry juice and spices in a saucepan. Bring to a boil. Reduce heat; simmer 5 minutes.

• Stir together cornstarch, sugar and salt. Stir in 2 tblsp. cold cherry juice and corn syrup. Gradually stir in the hot liquid drained from the heated cherries. Remove whole spices from cherries; pour cornstarch mixture over cherries in saucepan. Cook, stirring frequently, over low heat until mixture thickens. Reduce heat and simmer 5 minutes. Remove from heat and stir in butter and enough food color to make sauce a regal red.

• Cool slightly. Spoon over a 10″ angel food cake. Let glaze set about 2 hours before cutting. Makes 2 cups sauce.

Note: If you use sweetened frozen cherries, use 2 tblsp. sugar in making sauce instead of ¼ cup.

LEMON JELLY CAKE

Yellow and white ribbon cake with fresh lemon taste—good make-ahead

1 (9 or 10″) angel food cake
1 envelope unflavored gelatin
1½ c. sugar
4 tblsp. cornstarch
⅛ tsp. salt
⅓ c. water
2 egg yolks, beaten
2 tblsp. butter or regular margarine
¼ tsp. grated lemon peel
⅓ c. fresh lemon juice
½ c. dairy sour cream
½ c. chopped nuts
Lemon Fluff Frosting

• Cut cool cake in 3 equal layers.

• Combine gelatin with ¼ c. sugar and set aside.

• Combine remaining 1¼ c. sugar, cornstarch and salt. Add water; cook over low heat, stirring constantly, until mixture thickens and boils. Stir ½ c. hot mixture into egg yolks; stir this back into hot mixture. Return to heat and cook 1 minute, stirring constantly.

• Remove from heat and add gelatin-sugar mixture. Stir until gelatin dissolves; stir in butter. Continue to stir until mixture starts to set but is still "soupy." Add lemon juice and peel; fold in sour cream and nuts. Cool. Spread between layers of cake. Frost top and sides of cake with Lemon Fluff Frosting, tinted yellow.

LEMON FLUFF FROSTING: In double boiler, combine 1 egg white (2 tblsp.), ¾ c. sugar, ⅛ tsp. cream of tartar or 1½ tsp. light corn syrup and 3 tblsp. water. Place over boiling water and beat with rotary beater or electric mixer until mixture stands in stiff peaks. Scrape bottom and sides of pan occasionally. Fold in 2 tsp. grated lemon peel and tint a delicate yellow with food color.

MOCHA-FROSTED CAKE

For hostesses who like to stay out of the kitchen to visit with their guests

1 (3¾ oz.) pkg. chocolate pudding and pie filling
1½ tblsp. instant coffee powder
1⅓ c. milk
1 c. heavy cream, whipped
1 (10″) angel food cake, split into three equal layers
2 (¾ oz.) chocolate-coated toffee bars, crushed

• Prepare pudding as directed on package, adding coffee and milk. Chill. Beat smooth; fold in half of the whipped cream. Spread half of the chocolate-cream mixture between the cake layers.

• Fold second half of whipped cream into remaining chocolate-cream mixture. Spread on top and sides of cake. Sprinkle with crushed candy. Chill several hours before serving. Makes 12 servings.

Note: This cake freezes well. First, freeze it uncovered. When firm, wrap and return to freezer. To serve, place cake, uncovered, in refrigerator 3 hours to reach serving temperature.

CHOCOLATE ANGEL FOOD CAKE

Orange/Cheese Frosting adds a touch of delightful richness to the cake

¾ c. sifted cake flour
¼ c. cocoa
¼ tsp. salt
1¼ c. egg whites (10 to 12 eggs)
1 tsp. cream of tartar
1¼ c. sifted sugar
1 tsp. vanilla
Orange/Cheese Frosting

• Sift flour and cocoa together 4 times.

• Add salt to egg whites. Beat until frothy. Add cream of tartar. Beat until stiff peaks form.

• Fold sugar into whites, ¼ c. at a time. Add vanilla. Fold in flour mixture, 2 tblsp. at a time.

• Pour batter into ungreased 10″ tube pan. Bake in moderate oven (375°) 1 hour.

• Invert pan and let cake cool in pan on rack about 1 hour before taking it out to be frosted. Remove any loose cake crumbs, so frosting will go on smoothly. Frost with Orange/Cheese Frosting.

ORANGE/CHEESE FROSTING: Blend together 1 (3 oz.) pkg. cream cheese and 1 tblsp. orange juice. Gradually add 2½ c. sifted confectioners sugar, blending well. Add ½ tsp. grated orange peel; blend again. Makes enough to frost a 10″ tube cake.

YELLOW ANGEL CAKE

For a fancy company cake, frost with confectioners sugar frosting and trim with colored gumdrops, cut and shaped like flowers with fingers

6 eggs (about), separated (you need ½ c. yolks, ¾ c. whites)
½ c. cold water
1⅓ c. sugar
½ tsp. vanilla
½ tsp. orange extract
½ tsp. almond extract
1½ c. sifted cake flour
¼ tsp. salt
¾ tsp. cream of tartar

· Beat egg yolks until very thick and lemon colored. Add water. Beat until thick. Add sugar gradually, beating constantly, about 10 minutes with electric mixer at highest speed. Fold in flavorings.

· Sift flour and salt together at least 3 times. Carefully fold into egg yolk mixture.

· Beat egg whites until foamy. Add cream of tartar. Beat until stiff, just enough to form glossy peaks (not as stiff as for regular angel food). Fold into batter. Pour into ungreased 10″ tube pan.

· Bake in moderate oven (350°) about 1 hour. Invert and let cool in the pan on rack about 1 hour. Frost with 7-Minute Frosting (see Index) or your favorite chocolate frosting, if desired.

ICE CREAM CAKE

A dazzling make-ahead party cake—colorful as confetti and delicious, too

1 (10″) angel food cake
1 qt. strawberry ice cream
1 qt. chocolate ice cream
1 qt. pistachio ice cream
2 c. heavy cream

· Cut cool cake, made from packaged mix or bakery bought, crosswise in 4 equal layers.

· Spread tops of 3 bottom layers with ice cream, using a different flavor for each. (You can choose your favorites.) Do one at a time, starting with strawberry, and place immediately in freezer. Proceed with chocolate ice cream; stack on top of strawberry in freezer. Then follow with layer spread with pistachio ice cream. Add top layer of cake. Work fast so ice cream does not melt.

· Whip cream and use to frost cake. Store in freezer until serving time. Makes 20 servings.

SWEETHEART PARTY CAKE

Hostesses rate this pink-iced cake perfect for serving at parties

1 (10 oz.) pkg. frozen strawberries
1 envelope unflavored gelatin
2 c. heavy cream
2 tblsp. sugar
1 (9 or 10″) angel food cake

· Thaw strawberries and drain well. Over juice in dish, sprinkle gelatin; let stand until it softens. Set dish in pan of hot water and stir until gelatin dissolves. Combine with berries. Barely cool—do not let mixture congeal.

· Whip cream; add sugar. Fold in strawberry mixture. (Strawberry

mixture may appear too thin, but it will mix well into whipped cream.)
· Cut angel food cake in two layers. Spread strawberry-cream mixture generously over the bottom layer. Adjust top layer and spread remaining strawberry-cream over top and sides of the cake. Refrigerate at least 2 hours before serving. Makes 10 to 12 servings.

EASTER LAYER CAKE

This cake is between a sponge and angel food; it's a cheerful yellow. You cut unfrosted layers in wedges and pass an elegant sauce

5 egg whites
⅛ tsp. cream of tartar
¼ tsp. salt
1 tsp. vanilla
1 c. sugar
3 egg yolks
2 tblsp. orange juice or water
1 tsp. lemon juice
1 c. sifted cake flour
Fluffy Orange Sauce

· Place egg whites, cream of tartar, salt and vanilla in mixing bowl. Beat with electric mixer or hand beater until mixture is just stiff enough to hold glossy peaks (less beating than for angel foods).
· Add ½ c. sugar, a little at a time, folding in well after each addition.
· In separate bowl, beat egg yolks with orange and lemon juice. Beat in remaining ½ c. sugar until mixture is thick and lemon colored.
· Fold yolks into egg white mixture. Sift in flour gradually; fold lightly to mix well. Pour batter into 2 ungreased 8″ round layer cake pans.
· Bake in slow oven (325°) 25 minutes. Invert pans on rack to cool, about 45 minutes. Remove cakes with spatula. To serve, cut in wedges and pass a pitcher of Fluffy Orange Sauce.

FLUFFY ORANGE SAUCE: Combine juice and grated peel of 1 orange, 2 egg yolks, beaten, and ½ c. light corn syrup or sugar in top of double boiler. Cook 5 minutes, stirring constantly, until slightly thickened. Cool.
· Just before serving, fold in 1 c. heavy cream, whipped. Makes 2½ cups.

Variation

EASTER ICE CREAM CAKE: Place 8″ layer of cake on a serving plate. Pack ice cream firmly into chilled 8″ round layer cake pan. (You can freeze ice cream in advance.) Turn ice cream out quickly onto cake and top with second cake layer. Freeze or serve at once.

County Fair Cake Winners

Haven't you pitied the judges of cakes at county fairs? With so many beautiful loaves and layers on the tables before them, it's far from easy to pick the winner. They have to be extra good. In this chapter we include three cakes that won ribbons; Grand Champion Sponge Cake follows–see Index for Blue Ribbon Banana Cake and First Prize Applesauce Cake.

GRAND CHAMPION SPONGE CAKE

The pineapple frosting gives this winner a festive party look

1¼ c. sifted flour
1 c. sugar
½ tsp. baking powder
½ tsp. salt

6 egg whites
1 tsp. cream of tartar
½ c. sugar
6 egg yolks
¼ c. water
1 tsp. vanilla
Creamy Pineapple Frosting

• Sift together flour, 1 c. sugar, baking powder and salt.

• In a large mixing bowl, beat egg whites until frothy. Add cream of tartar. Gradually beat in ½ c. sugar, a little at a time; beat until whites form stiff, not dry peaks.

• In a small bowl, combine egg yolks, water, vanilla and sifted dry ingredients. Beat at a medium high speed for 4 minutes or until mixture is light and fluffy. Fold yolk mixture gently, but thoroughly into beaten egg whites. Turn into an ungreased 10″ tube pan. Bake in moderate oven (350°) about 45 minutes. Invert pan on rack to cool. Frost with Creamy Pineapple Frosting.

CREAMY PINEAPPLE FROSTING: Cream together ¼ c. butter and ¼ c. shortening. Gradually add 3 c. sifted confectioners sugar; beat until light and fluffy. Blend in 1 (8½ oz.) can crushed pineapple, drained, ⅛ tsp. salt, ¼ tsp. vanilla and ½ tsp. grated lemon peel.

BUTTER SPONGE CAKE

An excellent use for egg yolks left over after baking angel food

11 egg yolks
2 c. sifted sugar
1 c. milk, scalded
1 tsp. vanilla
2¼ c. sifted cake flour
2 tsp. baking powder
½ c. melted butter
Fluffy Frosting (optional)

• Beat together egg yolks and sugar until light-colored and fluffy. Add milk and vanilla.

• Sift together flour and baking powder. Add to egg yolk mixture. Fold in butter.

• Bake in 2 greased 8″ square pans in moderate oven (350°) 30 to 40 minutes. Cool on racks. If you wish, put layers together and cover with Fluffy Frosting.

FLUFFY FROSTING: Mix 1 c. sugar, 4 egg whites, 1 tblsp. corn syrup and ⅛ tsp. cream of tartar in top of double boiler. Set over hot water and stir constantly until mixture becomes very hot. Pour into mixing bowl and beat by hand or with electric mixer until it stands in peaks.

Note: For an appealing chocolate trim, use a potato peeler and remove thin shavings from back of semisweet chocolate bar, barely heated. The shavings will curl. Scatter them on top of white-frosted cake.

SPONGE CAKE CHOCOLATE ROLL

To make a country jelly roll, cool rolled cake 10 minutes, unroll; spread with jelly, reroll and sprinkle with confectioners sugar

¾ c. sifted cake flour
1 tsp. baking powder
¼ c. sugar
4 large eggs
¼ tsp. salt
½ tsp. cream of tartar
1 tsp. vanilla
½ c. sugar
Chocolate Filling

• Sift together 3 times, cake flour, baking powder and ¼ c. sugar.

• Combine eggs, salt, cream of tartar and vanilla in large mixer bowl. Beat at high speed on electric mixer, until mixture stands in peaks. Add ½ c. sugar, 2 tblsp. at a time. Continue beating at high speed until mixture again stands in peaks.

· Carefully fold dry ingredients into egg mixture.

· Grease a 15½ × 10½ × 1″ jelly roll pan and line with waxed paper so that paper extends above sides. Pour in batter. Bake in moderate oven (375°) 13 minutes. Cool on rack 1 minute.

· Loosen sides and turn out onto towel sprinkled with confectioners sugar. Trim edges with sharp knife. Peel off waxed paper. Fold towel over long side of cake and roll cake in towel to "set" roll while cake is warm.

· Cool, unroll and spread with Chocolate Filling to within 1″ of edges. Roll up cake and chill 2 to 3 hours. Slice into 10 servings.

CHOCOLATE FILLING: Scald ¾ c. milk in top of double boiler. Add ¼ c. sugar, 2 tblsp. flour and ⅛ tsp. salt, and blend. Add 1 egg, slightly beaten. Cook over boiling water 5 minutes, stirring constantly. Blend in 2 squares unsweetened chocolate, melted. Cover and cook 5 minutes longer, stirring occasionally. Chill. Whip ½ c. heavy cream and add 1 tsp. vanilla. Fold into chilled mixture.

Variation

LEMON SPONGE CAKES: Bake sponge roll; cut into 12 equal portions. Spread 6 pieces with half of Lemon Filling. Place remaining 6 pieces on top. Put a generous spoonful of Lemon Filling on each; sprinkle with ½ c. slivered toasted almonds. Makes 6 servings.

LEMON FILLING: Blend together ¾ c. sugar, ¼ c. cornstarch and ¼ tsp. salt. Slowly stir in 1¼ c. boiling water. Bring mixture to a boil. Reduce heat and boil 1 minute, stirring to keep smooth. Remove from heat. Slowly add ⅓ of hot mixture to 2 slightly beaten egg yolks, then add yolks to hot mixture in pan. Cook over low heat 2 minutes, stirring constantly. Remove from heat. Add ¼ c. lemon juice, 2 tsp. grated lemon peel, 1 tblsp. butter or regular margarine and a dash of salt. Stir until butter is melted and mixture is well blended. Cool.

chapter 13

Popular Pies from Country Kitchens

CUT A PIECE OF JUICY CHERRY PIE, fresh peach or apple pie spiced just right. Our Apple Pizza Pie is a good choice. Or Tawny Pumpkin Pie—set it on the kitchen table where the youngsters will see it when they return from the football game. They'll really anticipate dinner.

Country women make their homemade pies count for more than good eating, important as that is. They never underestimate pie power. Their skill in baking marvelous pies lifts spirits, promotes contentment, and brightens rainy days. No gift gets a warmer welcome from the new neighbor down the road or a bereaved family, than a tempting fresh pie just taken from the oven.

Pie customs change along the countryside. Those jolly pie suppers in one-room schoolhouses belong to grandmothers' memories, but women today rake in cash at food sales with their pies. They're big moneymakers for churches and other worthy causes. People like pie—it's been a genuine favorite since colonial days.

This chapter contains some of our best pie recipes. We could fill the cookbook with our collection; in fact, we did compile a whole book of them (FARM JOURNAL'S *Complete Pie Cookbook*). But pies are so popular that new recipes and improvements in old ones continue to come from farm homes and our Countryside Test Kitchens. The recipes in this chapter start with pie crusts, for no pie is better than its pastry.

Pointers on Freezing Pastry and Pies

To Freeze Pastry: Wrap both baked and unbaked pie shells in their pans with aluminum foil or plastic wrap. Unbaked rounds of pastry should be frozen separately, then wrapped and overwrapped as for pastry shells. (Graham cracker and cookie crusts freeze well.)

· To thaw, let pastry rounds stand at room temperature until pliable. Bake unbaked shells without thawing. Unwrap baked shells and let stand at room temperature or place in moderate oven (350°) about 6 minutes.

Maximum Storage Time: Baked shells, 4 to 6 months; unbaked pastry and shells, maximum about 2 months.

To Freeze Pies: Pies may be baked before or after freezing, but it is best to freeze baked pies. Unbaked pies often have a soggy undercrust. Cool baked pies rapidly; place in freezer (they freeze faster when unwrapped). Keep level while freezing. When frozen, wrap in aluminum foil or plastic wrap.

· To thaw, unwrap baked pies and let stand at room temperature 2 to 4 hours. Or unwrap and let stand at room temperature a short time; then put in moderate oven (350°) on the lower shelf before pie starts to thaw. Heat until just warm, about 30 minutes. If using lightweight aluminum pie pans, set pies on baking sheet before placing in oven.

· Thaw the unbaked pie by placing it on the lower shelf of a very hot oven (450°) 10 to 15 minutes; reduce heat to 350° and complete baking. Always thaw chiffon pies at room temperature.

Maximum Storage Time: Baked pies, 4 to 6 months; unbaked pies, 2 to 3 months; chiffon pies, 1 month.

To Freeze Pie Fillings: Freeze fruit fillings in foil-lined pie pans. Remove the frozen fillings from pans, overwrap and return to freezer. Package the filling for pumpkin, squash and sweet potato pies in freezer containers. Omit cloves, which increase in strength when frozen; cinnamon and nutmeg do not change.

· To thaw, place unwrapped, frozen fruit pie filling in pastry-lined pan, add top crust and bake in hot oven (425°) 10 to 20 minutes longer than for pies with unfrozen filling. Or thaw filling at room temperature until you can almost stir it; add to pastry-lined pan. Partially thaw pumpkin, squash and sweet potato pie fillings in original container, pour into pastry-lined pan and bake 10 to 15 minutes longer than for pies without a cold filling.

Maximum Storage Time: Fruit fillings, 2 to 3 months; pumpkin, squash and sweet potato pie fillings, 5 weeks.

Perfect Pastry

If there's one baking skill that country women admire above all others, it's the ability to make excellent pie crust. Some of them prefer traditional Flaky Pastry, while others hold Pastry Made with Oil in especially high esteem (tender, but somewhat more mealy than pie crusts made with shortening or lard). We give recipes for both kinds—take your pick.

Flaky Pastry

This is the traditional or standard pie crust. Make it with solid fats, except butter and margarine. Measure shortening or lard in nested measuring cups. Press it into the cup to avoid air pockets and level it off with a knife or spatula.

FLAKY PASTRY FOR 2-CRUST PIE

When baked this pastry has a "bloom" or soft luster, not a dull surface

2 c. sifted flour
1 tsp. salt
¾ c. shortening or ⅔ c. lard
4 to 5 tblsp. cold water

• Combine flour and salt in mixing bowl. Cut in shortening with pastry blender or with two knives until mixture is the consistency of coarse cornmeal or tiny peas.
• Sprinkle on cold water, 1 tblsp. at a time, tossing mixture lightly and stirring with fork. Add water each time to the driest part of mixture. The dough should be just moist enough to hold together when pressed gently with a fork. It should not be sticky.
• Shape dough in smooth ball with hands, and roll. Or if you are not ready to make the pie, wrap it in waxed paper and refrigerate 30 minutes or until ready to fill and bake pie.
• Makes crust for one 8 or 9″ two-crust pie, two 8 or 9″ pie shells, eight or nine 4″ tart shells, one 9 or 10″ pie with latticed top or topping for two 8 or 9″ deep-dish pies.

TO MAKE 2-CRUST PIE

• Divide dough in half and shape in 2 flat balls, smoothing edges so there are no breaks.

Bottom Crust: Press 1 dough ball in flat circle with hands on lightly floured surface. Roll it lightly with short strokes from center in all directions to ⅛″ thickness, making a 10 to 11″ circle. Fold rolled dough in half and ease it loosely into pie pan with fold in center. Unfold and fit into pan, using care not to stretch dough. Gently press out air pockets with finger tips. Make certain there are no openings for juices to escape.
• Trim edge even with pie pan. Then roll top crust.

Top Crust: Roll second ball of dough like the first one (for bottom crust). Put filling in pastry-lined pan. Fold pastry circle in half; lift it to the top of the pie with fold in center. Gently unfold over top of pie. Trim with scissors to ½″ beyond edge of pie. Fold top edge under bottom crust and press gently with fingers to seal and to make an upright edge. Crimp edge as desired.
• Cut vents in top crust or prick with fork to allow steam to escape. (Or cut vents before placing pastry on top of pie.) Bake as pie recipe directs.

FLAKY PASTRY FOR 1-CRUST PIE

This makes a fork-tender, delicately crisp crust that does not crumble

1 c. sifted flour
½ tsp. salt
⅓ c. plus 1 tblsp. shortening or ⅓ c. lard
2 to 2½ tblsp. cold water

· Combine ingredients as directed for Pastry for 2-Crust Pie, traditional method. Shape 1 smooth ball of dough. Makes enough for one 8 or 9″ pie shell or top crust for 1½-qt. casserole.

TO MAKE PIE SHELL

Unbaked: On lightly floured surface roll Pastry for 1-Crust Pie. Roll it lightly from the center out in all directions to ⅛″ thickness, making a 10 to 11″ circle. Fold rolled dough in half and ease it loosely into pie pan, with fold in center. Gently press out air pockets with finger tips and make certain there are no openings for juices to escape.
· Fold under edge of crust and press into an upright rim. Crimp edge as desired. Refrigerate until ready to fill.

Baked: Make pie shell as directed for Unbaked Pie Shell, pricking entire surface evenly and closely (¼ to ½″ apart) with a 4-tined fork. Refrigerate ½ hour. Meanwhile, preheat oven. Bake pie shell in very hot oven (450°) from 10 to 15 minutes, or until browned the way you like it. Cool before filling.

FLAKY PASTRY FOR (10″) 2-CRUST PIE

3 c. sifted flour
1½ tsp. salt
1 c. plus 2 tblsp. shortening or 1 c. lard
6 tblsp. water

· Combine as directed in recipe for Flaky Pastry for 2-Crust Pie.

FLAKY PASTRY FOR (10″) 1-CRUST PIE

1⅓ c. sifted flour
½ tsp. salt
½ c. shortenng or ¼ c. plus 3 tblsp. lard
3 to 4 tblsp. cold water

· Combine ingredients as directed for Flaky Pastry for 2-Crust Pie, traditional method. Shape 1 smooth ball of dough. (See "To Make Pie Shell.") Makes enough for one 10″ pie shell.

Pastry Made with Oil

The pastry dough is tender. Be sure to roll it between sheets of waxed paper. One advantage of using oil is that it's easy to measure.

PASTRY FOR 2-CRUST PIE

Crust has a smooth top and is tender

2 c. sifted flour
1 tsp. salt
½ c. salad oil
3 tblsp. cold water

· Sift flour and salt into mixing bowl. Add oil, mix well with fork. Sprinkle cold water over mixture and mix well.

• With hands press mixture into a smooth ball. (If mix is too dry, add 1 to 2 tblsp. more oil, a little at a time and then shape ball.) Divide ball in half and flatten both parts slightly. Makes one 8 or 9″ two-crust pie or two 8 or 9″ pie shells.

TO MAKE 2-CRUST PIE

Bottom Crust: Wipe countertop or board with a damp cloth so waxed paper will not slip. Roll out 1 dough ball to circle between two 12″ square sheets waxed paper to edge of paper. Peel off top sheet of paper and gently invert pastry over pie plate; peel off paper. (The pastry is tender. If it tears, press edges together or lightly press a patch over it.)

• Fit pastry carefully into pie pan, using care not to stretch. Trim evenly with edge of pan.

Top Crust: Roll out remaining dough ball between two sheets of waxed paper as directed for Bottom Crust. Peel off top paper. Add filling to pastry-lined pan. Arrange rolled pastry over filled pie and peel off paper. Cut vents for steam to escape. Trim crust ½″ beyond edge of pie pan; fold top crust under bottom crust. Flute edge. Bake as pie recipe directs.

PASTRY FOR 1-CRUST PIE

1⅓ c. sifted flour
½ tsp. salt
⅓ c. salad oil
2 tblsp. cold water

• Combine ingredients as directed for Pastry for 2-Crust Pie with salad oil. Make 1 smooth ball of dough. (If mixture is too dry, add 1 to 2 tblsp. more oil, a little at a time.) Makes one 8 or 9″ pie shell.

TO MAKE PIE SHELL

Unbaked Pie Shell: Wipe countertop or board with a damp cloth so paper will not slip. Roll out pastry between two 12″ sheets waxed paper to edge of paper. Peel off top sheet of paper and gently invert pastry over pie pan; peel off paper. Fit pastry into pie pan, pressing gently with finger tips toward center of pan.

• Trim crust ½″ beyond edge of pie pan, fold under edge of crust and crimp to make upright rim. Refrigerate until ready to fill and bake.

Baked Pie Shell: Make pie shell as directed for Unbaked Pie Shell, only prick entire surface evenly with 4-tined fork. Refrigerate ½ hour. Meanwhile, preheat oven. Bake pie shell in very hot oven (450°), 10 to 15 minutes, until browned. Cool before filling.

PASTRY TART SHELLS

Shells are crisp, tender and flaky

2 c. sifted flour
1 tsp. salt
¾ c. shortening or ⅔ c. lard
4 to 5 tblsp. cold water

• Combine flour and salt in mixing bowl. Cut in shortening with pastry blender or with two knives until mixture is the consistency of coarse cornmeal.

• Sprinkle on cold water, 1 tblsp. at a time, tossing mixture lightly and stirring with fork. Add water each time to the driest part of mixture. The dough should be just moist enough to hold together when pressed gently with a fork. It should not be sticky.

· Divide pastry into 6 parts. Shape into smooth balls and roll out each ball to make 4½ to 5″ circles.

· Fit pastry circles over back of inverted 3½″ muffin-pan cups. Make pleats so pastry will fit snugly. Prick entire surface with 4-tined fork. Or fit pastry over inverted custard cups, prick well and set on baking sheet. Refrigerate 30 minutes before baking.

· Preheat oven to very hot (450°). Bake tart shells 10 to 12 minutes, or until golden. Cool on racks. Then carefully remove from pans, or custard cups. Fill as desired. Makes about six 3″ tarts, depending on how thin the pastry was rolled.

Note: Regardless of the size of your muffin-pan cups, you can bake tart shells on them. With a string, measure one of the inverted cups up one side, across the bottom and down on the other side. Cut the string this length. Find a bowl, saucer or small plate in the kitchen that has the same diameter as the string. Or cut a cardboard this size. Use for a pattern to cut the rolled pastry in circles. Fit pastry rounds on alternate muffin cups—6 on a pan with 12 cups. Pleat pastry to fit snugly.

Crackly Meringue Pie Shells

Fill angel-white or light brown meringue pie shells with ice cream. Top with slightly sweetened strawberries, raspberries or sliced peaches, or with chocolate sauce. You'll have a praiseworthy dessert. Or make an Angel Pie (see recipes in this chapter) and you'll agree it deserves its name.

PERFECT MERINGUE FOR PIE AND TART SHELLS

Here are the rules to follow for success every time.

Choose a cool, dry day to make meringue shells, if possible. Humidity often softens meringues.

Be sure your tools are dry and clean. It takes only a tiny speck of fat to ruin meringues.

Use egg whites at room temperature. Take eggs from the refrigerator, separate and let whites stand at least 1 hour before beating.

Let your electric mixer do the work—save your arm. The beating takes from 25 to 30 minutes. The sugar must be completely dissolved or the meringue will weep. To test, rub a little of the meringue between the fingers. It should feel smooth. If grainy, continue beating until it feels smooth.

Cool before filling.

9″ MERINGUE PIE SHELL

Baked meringue pie shells almost always crack and fall in the center

3 egg whites (room temperature)
¼ tsp. cream of tartar
⅛ tsp. salt
¾ c. sugar

· Combine egg whites, cream of tartar and salt. Beat until frothy. (Do not underbeat.) Gradually add sugar and beat until stiff glossy peaks form. Meringue should be shiny and moist and all sugar dissolved.

· Spread over bottom and sides of a well greased 9″ pie pan. Build up sides. (You can make fancy edge with cake decorator, if desired.)

• Bake in very slow oven (275°) 1½ hours. Turn off oven heat; leave meringue in oven with closed door 1 hour. Complete cooling in pan away from drafts. Spoon in filling and chill.

Variation

MERINGUE TART SHELLS: Prepare ingredients as for Meringue Pie Shell, but drop spoonfuls of meringue onto baking sheet lined with brown paper. Make 8 mounds of even size; place them 3″ apart on baking sheet. With back of spoon hollow out each meringue mound to make a tart shell. Bake in very slow oven (275°) 1 hour. Turn off oven heat and leave meringue tart shells in oven with door closed 1½ hours longer. Complete cooling away from drafts.

• At serving time, fill with ice cream and top with berries, cut-up fruit or butterscotch, chocolate or other sauce. Or fill with fresh berries or fresh fruit and top with a scoop of ice cream or whipped cream (see photo).

• To store Meringue Tart Shells for a few days, loosely wrap them, when cool, in waxed paper. Keep in a cool, dry place, such as a cupboard. Do not put in airtight containers or meringues will soften. Makes 8.

10″ MERINGUE PIE SHELL

- 4 egg whites
- ¼ tsp. cream of tartar
- ¼ tsp. salt
- 1 c. sugar

• Combine ingredients as directed in recipe for 9″ Meringue Pie Shell.

Easy-to-make Crumb Crusts

GRAHAM CRACKER AND VANILLA WAFER CRUSTS

Graham cracker crumbs, finely rolled, are available in packages. Each 13¾-oz. package will make three 9″ pies. Or you can make the crumbs in a jiffy by blending the crackers in an electric blender. If you crush and roll the crackers, place them in a plastic bag or between sheets of waxed paper before rolling.

Baking gives a firmer and more crunchy crust, but the unbaked type is satisfactory for chiffon and other light and fluffy pie fillings.

Vanilla wafers also make fine pie crusts. Since they are sweetened, you need not add sugar to the crumbs.

BAKED GRAHAM CRACKER CRUMB CRUST

This crust is crunchy and firm

- 1⅓ c. graham cracker crumbs (16 to 18 crackers)
- ¼ c. sugar
- ¼ c. soft butter or regular margarine
- ¼ tsp. ground nutmeg or cinnamon (optional)

• In medium mixing bowl combine graham cracker crumbs, sugar, butter and nutmeg; blend until crumbly. Save out ⅓ c. crumbs to sprinkle on top of pie, if desired. Press remaining crumbs evenly on bottom and sides of 9″ pie pan, making a small rim.

• Bake in moderate oven (375°) 8

minutes, or until edges are lightly browned. Cool, then fill as pie recipe directs.

UNBAKED GRAHAM CRACKER CRUMB CRUST: Use the same ingredients as for the baked crust; do not make rim on pie shell. Chill about 1 hour, or until set before filling.

VANILLA WAFER CRUMB CRUST

1⅓ c. fine vanilla wafer crumbs (about 24 wafers)
¼ c. soft butter or regular margarine

· Mix vanilla wafer crumbs with butter until crumbly. Press on bottom and sides of 8 or 9″ pie pan, reserving 3 tblsp. mixture to sprinkle on top of pie, if desired. Bake in moderate oven (375°) 8 minutes, or until edge is lightly browned.

Specialty Pie Crusts

COUNTRY TEAROOM PASTRY

Favorite pastry in a Wisconsin farm woman's tearoom famous for its pies

4 c. sifted flour
1 tblsp. sugar
1½ tsp. salt
1½ c. lard
1 egg
1 tblsp. vinegar
½ c. cold water

· Blend flour, sugar and salt. Cut in lard until particles are the size of peas.
· Beat egg, blend in vinegar and water. Sprinkle over flour mixture, a tablespoonful at a time, tossing with fork to mix. Gather dough together with fingers so it cleans the bowl. Chill before rolling. Makes two (9″) two-crust pies and one (9″) pie shell.

CHOCONUT PIE SHELL

A chocolate-flavored pecan pastry

1 c. sifted flour
2 oz. sweet cooking chocolate, grated or ground
¼ tsp. salt
¼ c. shortening
3 tblsp. milk
½ tsp. vanilla
¼ c. finely chopped pecans

· Stir together flour, grated chocolate and salt. Cut in shortening with two knives or blend with pastry blender until mixture resembles coarse meal. Combine milk and vanilla; add gradually to dry mixture, tossing lightly with a fork. Form into ball.
· Roll out on lightly floured pastry cloth to ⅛″ thickness. Cut in circle 1½″ larger than inverted 9″ pie pan. Fit loosely in pan; pat out air bubbles; turn edge under and flute.
· Sprinkle with chopped pecans and press gently into pastry. Prick sides and bottom with a fork.
· Bake in hot oven (400°) 10 to 12 minutes. Makes one (9″) pie shell.

Coconut Pie Crusts

UNBAKED COCONUT CRUST

Crunchy-perfect for chiffon pies

1½ c. cookie coconut
½ c. confectioners sugar
3 tblsp. melted butter

• Combine coconut with confectioners sugar. Gradually stir in butter. Press evenly over bottom and sides of an oiled 8 or 9″ pie pan. Refrigerate until firm, about 1 hour.

TOASTED COCONUT CRUST

Fill at serving time with ice cream

2 c. flaked coconut
¼ c. butter or regular margarine

• Place coconut and butter, mixed together, in 9″ pie pan. Toast in moderate oven (300°) 15 to 20 minutes, stirring occasionally, until golden brown. Press over bottom and sides of pie pan. Cool before filling.

Gold-tipped Meringues

Meringues decorate more 1-crust pies than all other toppings put together. And they glorify more lemon pies than any other kind. That's partly because lemon meringue pies long have been farm favorites. But there are other reasons. Meringues are easy to make, too, and they glamorize pies that are lighter endings for hearty meals than 2-crust specials. Then, the practical cook makes meringues with the egg whites left over from fillings that call for yolks.

To be successful with meringue toppings all you need do is *follow the directions* in our recipes. Do pay special attention to dissolving the sugar in the egg whites and to spreading the meringue over the top of the filling so that it touches the edge of the crust around the pie. This prevents shrinkage. To keep the topping high and handsome, the way it comes from the oven, protect it from drafts. Home economists sometimes make a screen of stiff paper to stand up around the pie to divert wandering breezes. Let pie cool on rack at least 1 hour.

You can tint meringue before spreading it on pie, if you wish. We like delicate pink meringue on our Pink Party Pie (see Index). And you can put meringue in your pastry tube and press a fluffy collar around the edge of a pie and a design in the center. One farm homemaker says she sometimes makes a meringue lattice on fruit pies with colorful fillings. Here are her directions: Pipe four strips across pie one way (touching ends to crusts), four the other way, slantwise, so openings will be diamond-shaped. Broil 8 to 10″ from heat until delicately browned, 2 to 3 minutes.

PERFECT MERINGUE FOR TOPPING PIES

For 8″ Pie

2 egg whites
¼ tsp. cream of tartar
⅛ tsp. salt
¼ tsp. vanilla
¼ c. sugar

For 9″ Pie

3 egg whites
¼ tsp. cream of tartar
¼ tsp. salt
½ tsp. vanilla
6 tblsp. sugar

For 10″ Pie

4 egg whites
¼ tsp. cream of tartar
¼ tsp. salt
½ tsp. vanilla
½ c. sugar

· Have egg whites at room temperature to obtain greatest volume. Place them in a medium bowl with cream of tartar, salt and vanilla.

· Beat with electric or hand beater, at medium speed, until entire mixture is frothy. Do not beat until eggs stiffen.

· Add sugar, a little at a time, beating well after each addition. Do not underbeat. Beat until sugar dissolves to help prevent beading (those brown syrup drops on top). To test, rub some of the meringue between your fingers to see if it's still grainy. (The grains are undissolved sugar.) Continue to beat until stiff, pointed peaks form when you lift beater slowly.

· Place spoonfuls of meringue around edge of pie filling, spreading it so it touches inner edge of crust to seal all around. This prevents shrinkage. Pile remainder of meringue in center of pie and spread to meet meringue around edge. If the filling is not covered completely, the oven heat may cause it to weep. (Stirring the cooked filling may cause it to weep; water will collect under the meringue.) Lift up meringue over pie in points with back of teaspoon.

· Bake in moderate oven (350°) 12 to 15 minutes, or until meringue peaks are golden brown. Too long baking may cause weeping. Cool gradually away from drafts.

COUNTRY-STYLE MERINGUE: With egg whites plentiful in farm kitchens, many country pie bakers like to use 5 egg whites and 10 tblsp. sugar to make a high cover on their 9 and 10″ pies.

Note: You can substitute 1 tsp. lemon juice for cream of tartar when making meringues for lemon, lime and orange pies. The acid in the juice gives the same result—a wonderful meringue!

Treasury of Fruit Pies

The top pie crust is thin and crisp, golden at the center, shading to a more delicate brown around the edges. Thick, fragrant fruit juices bubble through the vents. Could any dessert be more tempting than freshly baked pie when you take it from the oven?

This section starts with the ABCs of fruit pies—apple (nine kinds!), blueberry and cherry. That's certainly a good beginning. Other special country pies are currant, elderberry, gooseberry, mulberry, strawberry/rhubarb, peach, pear, plum and prune.

A treasury of pies made with fresh, frozen and dried fruits awaits you in this section. They'll bring happiness to your family and friends.

FAVORITE APPLE PIE

A pie that lives up to its name—plain or caramelized. It's one of our best

Pastry for 2-crust pie
6 large tart apples
2 tblsp. flour
½ c. sugar
½ c. brown sugar, firmly packed
¾ tsp. ground cinnamon
¼ tsp. ground nutmeg
⅛ tsp. ground ginger
⅛ tsp. salt
1 tblsp. lemon juice
3 tblsp. butter or regular margarine

• Peel and quarter apples into saucepan (cut each quarter into about 4 slices). Add ¼ c. cold water; simmer until tender, about 5 minutes. Cool.
• Fill pastry-lined 9″ pie pan with apples.
• Combine remaining ingredients, except butter; sprinkle over apples; dot with butter. Moisten edges of undercrust.
• Adjust top crust; cut 6 vents (cut like chevrons–1 in each piece); flute edges.
• Bake in very hot oven (450°) 10 minutes; reduce heat to moderate (350°) and bake 45 minutes longer. Makes 6 servings.

Variation

CARAMEL APPLE PIE: Cover bottom pastry with ¼ c. melted butter or regular margarine; spread evenly with ½ c. brown sugar, firmly packed, then sprinkle with ½ c. pecans. Follow above recipe, using only ¼ c. brown sugar. This makes a luscious caramelized pie.

APPLE PIZZA PIE

Dramatic big pie, sensational in taste

1¼ c. flour
1 tsp. salt
½ c. shortening
1 c. shredded Cheddar cheese
¼ c. ice water
½ c. powdered non-dairy "cream"
½ c. brown sugar, firmly packed
½ c. sugar
⅓ c. sifted flour
¼ tsp. salt
1 tsp. ground cinnamon
½ tsp. ground nutmeg
¼ c. butter
6 c. peeled apple slices (½″ thick)
2 tblsp. lemon juice

• Mix 1¼ c. flour and 1 tsp. salt; cut in shortening until crumbly. Add cheese. Sprinkle water over mixture gradually; shape into ball. Roll pastry into 15″ circle on floured surface; place on baking sheet and turn up edge.
• Combine powdered non-dairy "cream," sugars, ⅓ c. flour, ¼ tsp. salt and spices. Sprinkle half of this mixture over pastry. Cut butter into remaining half until crumbly.
• Arrange apple slices, overlapping them in circles on crust. Sprinkle with lemon juice and remaining crumbs.
• Bake in very hot oven (450°) 30 minutes or until apples are tender. Serve warm. Makes 12 servings.

MAPLE-GLAZED APPLE PIE

Gingersnaps joined with maple syrup make this a special pie

Pastry for 2-crust pie
6 c. sliced peeled apples
½ c. sugar
¼ c. brown sugar, firmly packed
½ c. crushed gingersnaps
½ tsp. ground cinnamon
¼ tsp. salt
½ c. chopped walnuts
¼ c. melted butter
¼ c. maple syrup

• Arrange half the apples in pastry-lined 9″ pie pan.
• Combine remaining ingredients except syrup; mix well. Spread half of mixture over apples. Repeat with remaining fruit and mixture.
• Adjust top crust and flute edges; cut vents. Bake in moderate oven

(350°) 35 minutes. Heat maple syrup to boiling; brush over pie and return to oven 15 minutes longer.

DEEP-DISH APPLE PIE

Country pie to eat with a spoon—it's juicy, mellow and spiced just right

Pastry for 1-crust pie
1 c. sugar
¼ c. flour
½ tsp. ground cinnamon
⅛ tsp. ground nutmeg
⅛ tsp. salt
8 c. sliced peeled apples
1 tblsp. lemon juice
2 tblsp. butter or regular margarine

· Combine sugar (amount of sugar depends on tartness of apples, but you may need 1½ c.), flour, cinnamon, nutmeg and salt in 9″ square pan. Add apples and lemon juice. Stir to combine. Dot with butter and top with pastry, rolled 1″ larger than top of pan. Cut steam vents; trim and flute edge just inside edge of pan. Or pull points of fluting over outer rim of pan to fasten crust.
· Bake in hot oven (425°) about 50 minutes, until apples are tender and crust is browned. Serve warm or cool in bowls with light cream or topped with scoops of vanilla ice cream. Or top pie with whipped cream and drizzle with Cinnamon Syrup (recipe follows). Makes 8 servings.

CINNAMON SYRUP: In a small saucepan over heat stir constantly ¼ c. cinnamon candies (red hots) and ¼ c. water until candies dissolve. Partially cool at room temperature to drizzle over pie at serving time.

FROSTED APPLE/RAISIN PIE

One of the FARM JOURNAL *immortals—it's won many friends in every state*

Pastry for 2-crust pie
¾ c. sugar
2 tblsp. flour
⅛ tsp. salt
½ tsp. ground cinnamon
6 c. sliced peeled tart apples
½ c. seedless raisins
2 tblsp. orange juice
3 tblsp. butter or regular margarine
Orange Frosting

· Combine sugar, flour, salt and cinnamon; mix with apples and raisins; place in pastry-lined 9″ pie pan. Sprinkle with orange juice; dot with butter. Adjust top crust and flute edges; cut vents.
· Bake in hot oven (400°) about 40 minutes, or until crust is browned and apples are tender.
· Spread Orange Frosting over hot pie.

ORANGE FROSTING: Mix 1 c. confectioners sugar, 3 tblsp. strained orange juice and 1 tsp. grated orange peel.

FROSTED BIG APPLE PIE

Jumbo apple pie for treating a crowd—have a pot of coffee ready to pour

Egg Yolk Pastry
4 tsp. lemon juice
5 lbs. peeled, thinly sliced, tart apples (about 12 to 15 c.)
¾ c. sugar
¾ c. brown sugar, firmly packed
1 tsp. ground cinnamon
¼ tsp. salt
½ tsp. ground nutmeg
Confectioners sugar icing

• Roll out half the pastry into rectangle and use to line 15½″ × 10½″ × 1″ jelly-roll pan. Sprinkle lemon juice on apples. Place half the apples in bottom of pastry-lined pan.

• Combine remaining ingredients, except apples and frosting. Sprinkle half the mixture over apples in pan. Spread remaining apple slices on top and sprinkle with remaining sugar-spice mixture.

• Top with remaining pastry, rolled out; seal and crimp edges. Brush with milk and sprinkle with a little sugar. Cut vents or prick with fork as for all 2-crust fruit pies.

• Bake in hot oven (400°) 50 minutes. When cool, drizzle with confectioners sugar mixed with milk to make a thin icing. Cut in squares to serve. Makes 24 servings.

EGG YOLK PASTRY

5 c. sifted flour
4 tsp. sugar
½ tsp. salt
½ tsp. baking powder
1½ c. lard
2 egg yolks
Cold water

• Combine dry ingredients; cut in lard.

• Beat egg yolks slightly in measuring cup with fork and blend in enough cold water to make a scant cupful. Sprinkle over flour mixture, a little at a time, tossing with fork until mixture is moist enough to hold together.

• Roll out like any pastry. Makes pastry for 1 Frosted Big Apple Pie or 3 (2-crust) 9″ pies.

SPICY APPLE CRUNCH PIE

New, unusually delicious apple pie

Unbaked 9″ pie shell
3 egg yolks
1½ c. sugar
1 tblsp. flour
1 tsp. ground cinnamon
⅛ tsp. ground cloves
1 tblsp. melted butter
1 tblsp. vinegar
1 c. grated peeled apples (2 to 3 medium)
½ c. chopped pecans
3 egg whites

• Beat egg yolks until thick and lemon-colored.

• Combine sugar, flour and spices. Add to egg yolks alternately with butter and vinegar; mix well.

• Stir in apples and pecans.

• Beat egg whites until stiff peaks form. Fold into apple mixture, blending well.

• Pour into unbaked pie shell.

• Bake in moderate oven (350°) about 50 minutes, or until knife inserted 1″ from edge of pie comes out clean.

APPLE/CRANBERRY/MINCE PIE

Tasty, attractive, open-face pie

10″ Pie	9″ Pie
10″	Unbaked 9″ pie shell
1 (1 lb.) can	1⅓ c. whole cranberry sauce
1 c.	¾ c. prepared mincemeat
4 c.	2½ c. coarsely chopped tart apples
3 tblsp.	2 tblsp. melted butter
⅓ c.	¼ c. sugar
¼ c.	3 tblsp. cornstarch
½ tsp.	¼ tsp. salt

• Combine cranberry sauce, mincemeat, apples and butter.

· Combine dry ingredients; stir into fruit mixture. Spoon into pastry shell.

· Top with pastry cutouts in leaf shapes. Bake in hot oven (400°) 40 to 50 minutes. Larger pie, 8 servings; smaller pie, 6 servings.

PEANUT-CRUNCH APPLE PIE

Peanut butter adds good flavor

10″ Pie	9″ Pie
10″	Unbaked 9″ pie shell
¼ tsp.	¼ tsp. salt
1 c.	¾ c. sugar
3 tblsp.	2 tblsp. flour
½ tsp.	½ tsp. vanilla
1 tblsp.	2 tsp. lemon juice
7½ c.	5½ c. thinly sliced tart apples
¼ c.	3 tblsp. melted butter
¼ c.	3 tblsp. cold crunchy peanut butter
⅓ c.	¼ c. sugar
¾ c.	½ c. coarsely crushed corn flakes
⅛ tsp.	⅛ tsp. salt

· Combine ¼ tsp. salt, 1 c. sugar (¾ c. for a 9″ pie), flour, vanilla and lemon juice. Toss with apples. Spoon into pie shell. Drizzle on butter.

· Blend chilled peanut butter, ⅓ c. sugar (¼ c. for 9″ pie), corn flakes and ⅛ tsp. salt with pastry blender. Sprinkle over apple layer.

· Bake in moderate oven (350°) 50 to 60 minutes. Larger pie, 8 servings; smaller pie, 6 servings.

PUMPKIN/APPLE PIE

Combination of two pie favorites

10″ Pie	9″ Pie
10″	Unbaked 9″ pie shell
⅓ c.	⅓ c. brown sugar, firmly packed
1 tblsp.	1 tblsp. cornstarch
½ tsp.	½ tsp. ground cinnamon
¼ tsp.	¼ tsp. salt
⅓ c.	⅓ c. water
2 tblsp.	2 tblsp. butter
3 c.	3 c. sliced tart apples
2 eggs	1 egg
½ c.	⅓ c. sugar
1 c.	¾ c. canned or cooked, mashed pumpkin
¼ tsp.	¼ tsp. salt
½ tsp.	¼ tsp. ground ginger
¾ tsp.	½ tsp. ground cinnamon
¼ tsp.	⅛ tsp. ground cloves
1 c.	¾ c. evaporated milk

· Combine brown sugar, cornstarch, ½ tsp. cinnamon and ¼ tsp. salt in a large saucepan. Stir in water and butter. Bring to a boil; add apples and cook 4 minutes over medium heat. Set aside.

· Beat eggs in separate bowl. Add sugar, pumpkin, ¼ tsp. salt, ginger, ¾ tsp. cinnamon, (½ tsp. for 9″ pie), cloves and evaporated milk. Blend well.

· Spoon apple mixture into pie shell. Carefully spoon pumpkin layer over apples. Bake in moderate oven (375°) 50 to 55 minutes. Larger pie makes 8 servings; smaller pie makes 6 servings.

Note: If desired, you can garnish top with whipped cream and walnut halves.

ROSY CRAB APPLE PIE

Red, red apples make the prettiest pie

Pastry for 2-crust pie
1 c. sugar
1 tblsp. flour
¼ tsp. salt
6 c. finely chopped unpeeled crab apples

1 tsp. vanilla
1½ tblsp. lemon juice
⅓ c. water
1½ tblsp. butter

· Combine sugar, flour and salt; toss together with apples.
· Pour apple mixture into pastry-lined 9″ pie pan. Sprinkle with mixture of vanilla, lemon juice and water. Dot with butter. Cover with top pastry; flute edges and cut vents.
· Bake in hot oven (400°) 50 minutes, or until filling is tender and crust is browned.

Note: Before mixing filling, steam apple bits 1 to 2 minutes and cool quickly to preserve color.

NO-CRUST APPLE PIE

Calorie-counters vote for this pie

6 peeled medium tart apples, cut in eighths
½ c. sugar
1 tsp. ground cinnamon
½ c. water
3 tblsp. butter or regular margarine
¼ c. brown sugar, firmly packed
½ c. sifted flour
½ tsp. baking powder
½ tsp. salt

· Mix apple slices with ½ c. sugar, cinnamon and water in saucepan. Cook about 10 minutes or until apples are partially cooked. Turn into 9″ pie pan.
· Cream butter; gradually cream in brown sugar. Sift together flour, baking powder and salt. Add to creamed mixture and mix thoroughly with spoon. Sprinkle over the apples.
· Bake in moderate oven (350°) about 45 minutes, until apples are tender and top nicely browned. If desired, serve with whipped dessert topping.

COUNTRY BLUEBERRY PIE

Tastes as if you rushed berries from the blue thickets into the pie

Pastry for 2-crust pie
3 c. frozen blueberries
Blueberry juice
Water
¾ c. sugar
2 tblsp. quick-cooking tapioca
1½ tblsp. cornstarch
1 tsp. lemon juice

· Thaw berries until most of free ice has disappeared. Drain off juice, measure and add water to make ½ c. liquid; stir into mixture of sugar, tapioca and cornstarch in saucepan. Heat rapidly until thickening is complete. Boiling is not necessary. Set aside to cool.
· Add berries and lemon juice to cooled, thickened juice. Pour filling into pastry-lined 9″ pie pan. Cut vents in top crust; cover pie, seal and flute edge.
· Bake in hot oven (425°) 30 minutes, or until nicely browned. For a brown undercrust, bake on lowest oven shelf.

Note: Blueberries in this recipe are frozen without sugar.

BURGUNDY BERRY PIE

Blend of blueberries and cranberries taste like an exciting new fruit

Pastry for 2-crust pie
1 c. sugar
3 tblsp. cornstarch
Dash salt
2 c. frozen blueberries (without sugar)
1½ c. whole cranberries

· Combine sugar, cornstarch and salt. Stir into mixed berries. Spread into pastry-lined 9″ pie pan.
· Adjust top crust; flute edges and cut vents. Bake in hot oven (425°) 40 to 50 minutes, until pastry is lightly browned and juices bubble through vents.

CHERRY PIE SPECIAL

Top pie made with canned cherries widely available the year around

Pastry for 2-crust pie
2 (1 lb.) cans pitted tart red cherries (water pack)
2½ tblsp. quick-cooking tapioca
¼ tsp. salt
¼ tsp. almond extract
1 tsp. lemon juice
4 drops red food color
1¼ c. sugar
1 tblsp. butter or regular margarine

· Drain cherries. Measure ⅓ c. liquid into mixing bowl. Add tapioca, salt, almond extract, lemon juice and food color, then cherries and 1 c. sugar. Mix and let stand a few minutes.
· Fit pastry into bottom of 9″ pie pan. Trim ½″ beyond outer rim of pan. Fill with cherry mixture. Dot with butter. Sprinkle with remaining sugar. Moisten rim with water.
· To make crisscross top interlace 14 strips, pressing ends against moistened rim and folding lower crust up over them. Moisten rim again and circle it with remaining 4 strips. Press down firmly. Sprinkle top with sugar.
· To keep high rim from browning faster than crisscross strips, circle pie with a stand-up foil collar. Fold foil over rim and leave on during entire baking.
· Bake in hot oven (425°) 40 to 45 minutes. Serve warm.

PERFECT CHERRY PIE

Once they taste this pie, you'll buy frozen cherries just to make it

Pastry for 2-crust pie
3 c. pitted tart frozen cherries
1 c. tart cherry juice
3 tblsp. sugar
2 tblsp. quick-cooking tapioca
1⅔ tblsp. cornstarch (5 tsp.)
⅛ tsp. almond extract

· Thaw cherries until most of the free ice has disappeared. Drain off the juice; measure 1 c. juice and stir it into mixture of sugar, tapioca and cornstarch in saucepan. Heat rapidly until thickening is complete. Boiling is not necessary. Set aside to cool.
· Add cherries and almond extract to cooled, thickened juice. Pour filling into pastry-lined 9″ pie pan. Cut vents in top crust; cover pie, seal and flute edge.
· Bake in hot oven (425°) 30 to 35 minutes, or until nicely browned. For a brown undercrust, bake on lowest oven shelf.

Note: Proportions of sugar, tapioca and cornstarch are based on 5 parts cherries frozen with 1 part sugar.

CRANBERRY/RAISIN PIE

Colorful Cape Cod pie that's perfect with turkey, chicken or pork

Pastry for 2-crust pie
3 c. fresh cranberries
2 tblsp. flour

2 c. sugar
¼ tsp. salt
⅔ c. boiling water
1 c. seedless raisins
2 tsp. grated lemon peel
2 tblsp. butter or regular margarine

· Remove stems from cranberries.
· Combine flour, sugar and salt in saucepan. Stir in cranberries, water, raisins and lemon peel. Cover and cook until cranberries start to pop. Remove from heat and add butter. Cool until lukewarm.
· Pour filling into pastry-lined 9″ pie pan. Arrange lattice of pastry strips on top; fold lower crust up over them.
· Bake in hot oven (425°) 40 to 50 minutes, or until juices bubble in lattice openings and crust is browned.

FRESH CURRANT PIE

Just tart enough, very juicy; the filling has gorgeous bright color

Pastry for 2-crust pie
3 c. washed, stemmed currants
1½ c. sugar
3 tblsp. quick-cooking tapioca
½ tsp. salt
1 tblsp. butter or regular margarine

· Drain currants. Place in a bowl and crush lightly with spoon.
· Combine sugar, tapioca and salt. Add to currants and stir gently to mix.
· Turn into pastry-lined 9″ pie pan; dot with butter. Adjust top crust; flute edges and cut vents.
· Bake in hot oven (425°) until crust is golden and the juices are bubbly, 35 to 45 minutes.

GOOSEBERRY PIE

Gather berries at edge of the woods and make this old-fashioned special

Pastry for 2-crust pie
1½ c. sugar
½ c. flour
4 c. fresh gooseberries
2 tblsp. butter or regular margarine

· Stir sugar and flour together.
· Distribute half of gooseberries in pastry-lined 9″ pie pan. Sprinkle with half the sugar-flour mixture. Top with remaining gooseberries and then with remaining sugar-flour mixture. Dot with butter.
· Add top crust with vents cut in it; seal and flute edge. Cover edge of pie with 3″ strip of foil to prevent browning too much.
· Bake in hot oven (425°) 35 to 45 minutes, until juices start to bubble through vents; remove foil last 15 minutes of baking. Cool.

ELDERBERRY/APPLE PIE

A dessert that makes search for elderberries along fence rows pay off

Pastry for 2-crust pie
2 c. elderberries
1½ c. chopped peeled tart apples
1 c. sugar
⅛ tsp. salt
3 tblsp. quick-cooking tapioca
2 tblsp. butter

· Wash and stem elderberries. (Hold berries in palm of hand and pull stems off with wire egg beater, the kind shaped like tennis racquet.)

· Combine elderberries, apples, sugar, salt and tapioca, crushing berries with spoon.
· Spoon mixture into pastry-lined 9" pie pan; dot with butter; top with pastry lattice.
· Bake in hot oven (400°) 35 to 40 minutes, or until apples are tender and crust is golden.

STREUSEL CONCORD GRAPE PIE

You can bake filling between two crusts if you prefer pastry

Unbaked 9" pie shell
4½ c. Concord grapes
1 c. sugar
¼ c. flour
2 tsp. lemon juice
⅛ tsp. salt
Oat Streusel

· Wash grapes and remove skins by pinching at end opposite stem. Reserve skins.
· Place pulp in saucepan and bring to a boil; cook a few minutes until pulp is soft. Put through strainer or food mill, while pulp is hot, to remove seeds.
· Mix strained pulp with skins. Stir in sugar, flour, lemon juice and salt.
· Place grape mixture in pastry-lined pie pan. Sprinkle on Oat Streusel.
· Bake in hot oven (425°) 35 to 40 minutes.

OAT STREUSEL: Combine ½ c. quick-cooking rolled oats, ½ c. brown sugar, firmly packed, and ¼ c. flour. Cut in ¼ c. butter or regular margarine to distribute evenly. Sprinkle over pie.

Gather Mulberries for Pies

The recipe for mulberry pie properly starts: "Select a sunny summer day when the breezes are light. Stand on the shady side of the mulberry tree and fill your pail with the knobby, long, glistening berries." Or if you are of a different berry-picking school: "Spread a worn sheet on the emerald grass beneath the tree, shake the branches lightly and run from the shower of juicy, warm, sweet berries that plop down."

Certainly mulberries are one of the easiest berries to transfer directly from tree to pail. There's no stooping, kneeling or squatting the way there is when you are picking strawberries, raspberries and blackberries.

Bake a wonderful country pie that day—a pie most city people never are fortunate enough to see or taste. Combine the sweet mulberries with a tart fruit, like gooseberries, or rhubarb. The sweet-tart blend is extra-delicious. We give you a recipe for the berry-rhubarb team that makes one of the most economical farm fruit pies—and one of the best.

MULBERRY PIE

Enjoy this summer pie every month —freeze berries and rhubarb to make it

Pastry for 2-crust pie
2 c. mulberries
1 c. finely sliced rhubarb
1 c. sugar
¼ c. flour
2 tblsp. butter or regular margarine

· Combine mulberries and rhubarb in medium bowl.
· Combine sugar and flour. Sprinkle about ⅓ of mixture in bottom of pastry-lined 9″ pie pan. Turn mulberries and rhubarb into pie pan and add remaining sugar-flour mixture. Dot with butter. Adjust top crust, cut steam vents and flute edges.
· Bake in hot oven (425°) 40 to 50 minutes, or until crust is browned and juices bubble in vents.

DEEP-DISH PEACH PIE

Summer's golden special—make it of ripe fruit; serve fresh from oven

Pastry for 1-crust pie
2 c. sugar
½ c. flour
½ tsp. ground cinnamon
½ tsp. ground mace
8 c. sliced peeled fresh peaches
3 tblsp. butter

· Roll pastry into a 10″ square. (Invert pan, before adding filling, over pastry and cut crust in a straight line 1″ beyond edge of pan.)
· Combine sugar, flour, cinnamon and mace. Stir gently into ripe peaches. Pour into a 9″ square pan. Dot with butter.
· Place pastry over peaches. Fold edge of crust under and flute against inside of pan. Cut steam vents.
· Bake in hot oven (425°) until lightly browned, about 40 to 50 minutes. Serve warm with cream, whipped cream or vanilla ice cream. Serves 9.

ALL-SEASON PEACH PIE

Favorite of Maine church suppers

Unbaked 9″ pie shell
2 (1 lb.) cans peach halves, well drained
⅓ c. sugar
3 tblsp. cornstarch
¾ tsp. ground nutmeg
¼ tsp. salt
¾ c. heavy cream
¾ tsp. vanilla
Whipped cream

· Arrange peach halves, cut side up, in pie shell.
· Combine sugar, cornstarch, ½ tsp. nutmeg, salt, cream and vanilla. Pour over peaches in shell; sprinkle with remaining nutmeg.
· Bake in hot oven (400°) 40 minutes, or until peaches are tender. Serve with whipped cream.

Note: Extra-good made with fresh peaches. Use ½ c. instead of ⅓ c. sugar.

PEACHY PRALINE PIE

Pecans and brown sugar give this summer Dixie pie superb flavor

Unbaked 9″ pie shell
¾ c. sugar
3 tblsp. flour
4 c. sliced peeled peaches
1½ tsp. lemon juice
⅓ c. brown sugar, firmly packed
¼ c. flour
½ c. chopped pecans
3 tblsp. butter or regular margarine

· Combine ¾ c. sugar and 3 tblsp. flour in large bowl. Add peaches and the lemon juice.
· Combine brown sugar, ¼ c. flour and pecans in small bowl. Mix in butter until mixture is crumbly. Sprinkle one third of pecan mixture over bottom of pie shell; cover with the peach mixture and sprinkle with remaining pecan mixture.
· Bake in hot oven (400°) until

peaches are tender, about 40 minutes.

GOLDEN PEACH PIE

Winter pie—juicy and luscious with summer's fresh peach taste

Pastry for 2-crust pie
3 c. frozen sliced peaches
1 c. peach juice
1½ tblsp. brown sugar
1½ tblsp. sugar
2⅓ tblsp. quick-cooking tapioca
1½ tblsp. cornstarch
⅛ tsp. ground cinnamon
1 tsp. lemon juice

· Thaw peaches until most of free ice has disappeared. Drain off the juice, measure and stir it into mixture of sugars, tapioca, cornstarch and cinnamon in saucepan. Heat rapidly until thickening is complete. Boiling is not necessary. Set aside to cool.

· Add peaches and lemon juice to cooled, thickened juice. Pour filling into pastry-lined 9″ pie pan. Cut vents in top crust; cover pie, seal and flute edge.

· Bake in hot oven (425°) 30 minutes, or until nicely browned. For a brown undercrust, bake on lowest oven shelf.

Note: Proportions of sugar, tapioca and cornstarch are based on 5 parts peaches frozen with 1 part sugar.

PEACH/STRAWBERRY PIE

Tastes like pie made with fresh berries and peaches. Try it some winter day

Pastry for 2-crust pie
1½ c. frozen sliced peaches
1½ c. frozen strawberries
½ c. peach juice
½ c. strawberry juice
3 tblsp. sugar
2½ tblsp. quick-cooking tapioca
1½ tblsp. cornstarch
1 tsp. lemon juice

· Thaw fruit until most of free ice has disappeared. Drain off the juices and measure, then stir into mixture of sugar, tapioca and cornstarch in saucepan. Heat rapidly until thickening is complete. Boiling is not necessary. Set aside to cool.

· Add fruit and lemon juice to cooled, thickened juice. Pour filling into pastry-lined 9″ pie pan. Cut vents in top crust; cover pie, seal and flute edge.

· Bake in hot oven (425°) 30 to 35 minutes or until nicely browned. For a brown undercrust, bake on lowest oven shelf.

Note: Proportions of sugar, tapioca and cornstarch are based on 5 parts peaches frozen with 1 part sugar; 4 parts strawberries frozen with 1 part sugar.

Variation

PEACH/BLUEBERRY PIE: Substitute blueberries for strawberries. If blueberries were frozen unsweetened, use ⅓ c. sugar; add water to the combined fruit juices to make 1 c. liquid.

Winter Pear Pies

Now that juicy, meaty fresh pears are available the winter through, you can bake pear pies from late summer, when the Bartletts are ripe in many places, until May. Try using Bosc pears, the fruit with a rich russet exterior and tender, buttery, sugar-sweet flesh, or the Anjou variety, the pear shaped like a huge teardrop. The Anjou is green, but turns a creamy yellow when ripe, is fine-grained and has a delicate spicy flavor. It is available from October through April, the Bosc from September through January. Either kind will make a perfect Ginger/Pear Pie.

OPEN-FACE PEAR PIE

Use fully ripened Bartlett pears to make this interesting pie

Unbaked 9″ pastry shell
4 medium pears
Juice of ½ lemon
¼ c. butter or regular margarine
1 c. sugar
¼ c. flour
3 eggs
1 tsp. vanilla
⅛ tsp. salt
⅛ tsp. ground mace
Whipped cream (optional)

· Peel, halve and core pears. Brush with lemon juice. Place pears cut side down in pie shell with narrow ends toward center.

· Cream together butter and sugar. Beat in flour, eggs, vanilla and salt. Pour over pears. Sprinkle lightly with mace.

· Bake in moderate oven (350°) 45 minutes or until filling is set and lightly browned. Cool on rack 1 hour or longer before cutting. Top with whipped cream. Serve the same day you bake the pie—pear filling may darken if you keep pie overnight.

FRENCH PEAR PIE

Spices, orange and lemon flavors and ripe, juicy pears blend deliciously

Unbaked 9″ pie shell
5 large Bartlett pears
3 tblsp. frozen orange juice concentrate
½ tsp. grated lemon peel
¾ c. flour
½ c. sugar
⅛ tsp. salt
1 tsp. ground cinnamon
½ tsp. ground ginger
⅓ c. butter or regular margarine

· Peel, core and slice pears thinly. Toss lightly with undiluted orange juice concentrate and lemon peel. Arrange in pie shell.

· Mix together remaining ingredients until crumbly. Sprinkle evenly over pears, being careful to cover all.

· Bake in hot oven (400°) 40 minutes, or until fruit is tender.

PEAR/ANISE PIE

Serve thin Parmesan cheese slices with this delightful gourmet pie

Pastry for 2-crust pie
5 c. sliced peeled Anjou pears (6 medium)
⅔ c. sugar
4 tblsp. cornstarch
1½ tsp. whole anise seeds
2 tsp. grated lemon peel
Lemon juice
2 tblsp. butter or regular margarine
½ c. confectioners sugar

· Combine pears, ⅔ c. sugar, cornstarch, anise seeds and lemon peel. Mix gently. Place in pastry-lined 9″ pie pan.

· Sprinkle pie filling with 1½ tsp. lemon juice. Dot with butter. Adjust top crust and flute edges; cut vents.

· Bake in hot oven (400°) until pears are tender and crust is lightly browned, about 40 minutes.

· While pie is hot, brush with glaze made by mixing confectioners sugar with enough lemon juice for spreading consistency (about 2½ tsp.). Cool.

GINGER/PEAR PIE

Elegant! Lemon and ginger-flavored fresh pear slices enveloped in pastry

Unbaked 9″ pie shell
¾ c. sugar
2 tblsp. flour
¾ tsp. ground ginger
¼ tsp. salt
3 ripe winter pears
2 tblsp. soft butter
2 eggs, separated
1 tsp. grated lemon peel
3 tblsp. lemon juice
¾ c. milk

• Combine ¼ c. sugar, 1 tblsp. flour, ginger and salt. Sprinkle in pie shell.
• Peel and core pears, slice thinly and lay slices over sugar-flour mixture.
• Cream butter; add remaining ½ c. sugar and 1 tblsp. flour. Add egg yolks, lemon peel and juice. Beat thoroughly.
• Add milk and mix.
• Beat egg whites until stiff. Fold into lemon mixture. Pour over pears.
• Bake in hot oven (425°) 10 minutes; reduce heat to 350°; bake 30 minutes.

PEAR/PINEAPPLE PIE

Use pears that hold their shape. Anjou pears are a good choice

10″ Pie	9″ Pie
Pastry for 2-crust pie	
3 tblsp.	2 tblsp. flour
½ c.	⅓ c. sugar
¾ tsp.	½ tsp. salt
¾ tsp.	½ tsp. ground nutmeg
7 c.	5 c. thinly sliced pears
½ c.	⅓ c. crushed pineapple, well-drained
2 tblsp.	2 tblsp. raisins
3 tblsp.	2 tblsp. lemon juice

• Combine flour, sugar, salt and nutmeg. Toss with pears and remaining ingredients. Spoon into pie shell. Roll out top crust; make cutout in center. Place on filling; seal and crimp edges.
• Bake in moderate oven (375°) 50 to 60 minutes. Larger pie, 8 servings; smaller pie, 6 servings.

Plum-delicious Pie

By the time school bells ring in September, silver-dusted purple Italian plums, grown extensively in Idaho, appear on fruit counters. Pies made with "blue plums," as farm women commonly call them, end many autumn meals in fine fashion.

A spicy, buttery crumb topping complements the tart-sweet fruit flavor of this juicy Purple Plum Pie, the favorite recipe of an Iowa homemaker, who bakes it in a heavy paper bag from her grocery store. The bag catches any runaway juices that bubble over and prevents the edges and top of the pie from browning too much. Also, she doesn't have to watch it as it bakes.

PURPLE PLUM PIE

Best faintly warm with nippy cheese slices or scoops of ice cream

Unbaked 9″ pie shell
4 c. sliced, pitted purple plums
½ c. sugar
¼ c. flour

¼ tsp. salt
¼ tsp. ground cinnamon
1 tblsp. lemon juice
Spicy Topping

• Remove pits and cut plums in quarters. Combine with sugar, flour, salt and cinnamon. Turn into pie shell and sprinkle with lemon juice. Sprinkle Spicy Topping over plums, mounding crumbs up in center of pie.
• Place pie in heavy brown paper bag from supermarket. Be sure bag is large enough to cover pie loosely. Fold over open end twice to close, and fasten with paper clips. Set on baking sheet in hot oven (425°); bake 1 hour. Remove from oven, let rest a few minutes before removing pie from paper bag. Partially cool on rack. Serve warm.

SPICY TOPPING: Combine ½ c. flour, ½ c. sugar, ¼ tsp. ground cinnamon and ¼ tsp. ground nutmeg. Cut in ¼ c. butter or regular margarine until mixture resembles coarse crumbs.

RAISIN PIE

Pies made from seedless and seeded raisins taste different—try both

Pastry for 2-crust pie
2 c. raisins (seedless or seeded)
2 c. boiling water
⅓ c. sugar
⅓ c. brown sugar, firmly packed
2¼ tblsp. cornstarch
⅛ tsp. salt
2 tsp. grated lemon peel
½ tsp. grated orange peel
2 tblsp. lemon juice
1 tblsp. orange juice
2 tblsp. butter or regular margarine

• Add raisins to water; simmer until tender (3 to 5 minutes). Combine sugars, cornstarch and salt; stir into hot raisins. Cook slowly, stirring constantly, to full rolling boil; boil 1 minute. Remove from heat.
• Blend in fruit peel and juices. Pour hot filling into pastry-lined 9″ pie pan; dot top with butter. Adjust top crust; flute edges and cut vents.
• Bake in hot oven (425°) 30 to 40 minutes. Serve slightly warm, plain or with scoops of lemon sherbet.

Note: Use a lattice pastry top, or cook filling in saucepan until it thickens; partly cool and pour into a baked pie shell. Spread with meringue and bake in moderate oven (350°) until delicately browned, 12 to 15 minutes. Or omit meringue and at serving time spread on thin layer of whipped cream.

TIPS FROM GOOD COOKS: After rinsing in warm water, spread raisins in a flat pan. Cover and heat slowly in moderate oven (350°) until they become plump. To obtain full flavor, cut raisins in halves with your kitchen scissors.

CALIFORNIA PRUNE PIE

Four-seasons pie—as tempting and rewarding in June as in January

Baked 9″ pie shell
2 c. cooked prunes
1 orange, peeled and diced (⅓ c.)
½ c. brown sugar, firmly packed
¼ tsp. salt
2 tblsp. cornstarch
1 c. liquid from prunes
1 tblsp. grated orange peel
2 tblsp. butter
2 tblsp. sugar
1 c. heavy cream, whipped
Orange sections
Walnut halves

• Drain cooked prunes, reserving 1 c. liquid; pit and measure. Remove all white inner peel when peeling orange.

· Combine brown sugar, salt and cornstarch. Add prune liquid and bring to a boil, stirring constantly. Cook until thick. Add prunes, orange, orange peel and butter; cook 10 minutes, stirring occasionally. Cool.

· Pour into pie shell. Refrigerate until mealtime. To serve, add 2 tblsp. white sugar to whipped cream and spread on pie. To dress up pie, garnish with orange sections and a few walnut halves.

HONEYED RHUBARB PIE

Honey-lemon flavor enhances rhubarb

Pastry for 2-crust pie
4 c. (½″ pieces) rhubarb
1¼ c. sugar
6 tblsp. flour
¼ tsp. salt
2 tsp. grated lemon peel
⅓ c. strained honey
4 to 5 drops red food color
2 tblsp. butter or regular margarine

· Combine rhubarb, sugar, flour, salt and lemon peel; mix well. Blend in honey and food color. Let stand several minutes.

· Spoon rhubarb mixture into pastry-lined 9″ pie pan; dot with butter. Adjust top crust and flute edges; cut vents. (For sparkling top, brush with milk and sprinkle with sugar.)

· Bake in hot oven (400°) 50 to 60 minutes.

FRESH RHUBARB PIE

This rosy rhubarb pie has a fascinating, though subtle, orange taste

Pastry for 2-crust pie
1⅓ c. sugar
⅓ c. flour
½ tsp. grated orange peel
⅛ tsp. salt
4 c. (½″ pieces) rhubarb
2 tblsp. butter

· Combine sugar, flour, orange peel and salt. Add to pink rhubarb.

· Place in pastry-lined 9″ pie pan and dot with butter.

· Adjust top crust (lattice top is attractive) and flute edges to make high-standing rim; cut vents.

· Bake in hot oven (425°) 40 to 50 minutes, or until juice begins to bubble through vents and crust is golden brown. Partially cool.

Note: If your rhubarb is not the pink variety, add a few drops of red food color to filling. To eliminate peeling rhubarb, use tender, young stalks. The amount of sugar varies with the tartness of the rhubarb—from 1⅓ c. to 2 c. Usually rhubarb is less tart early in the season.

Variations

SPICED RHUBARB PIE: Omit the grated orange peel and add ¼ tsp. ground nutmeg.

PINEAPPLE/RHUBARB PIE: Substitute 1 c. drained crushed pineapple (canned) for 1 c. rhubarb.

GLAZED STRAWBERRY/ RHUBARB PIE

Luscious spring dessert. Serve pie warm with sour cream spread on top

Pastry for 2-crust pie
1¼ c. sugar
⅛ tsp. salt
⅓ c. flour
2 c. fresh strawberries
2 c. (1″ pieces) fresh rhubarb
2 tblsp. butter or regular margarine
1 tblsp. sugar

• Combine 1¼ c. sugar, salt and flour.
• Arrange half of strawberries and rhubarb in pastry-lined 9″ pie pan. Sprinkle with half of sugar mixture. Repeat with remaining fruit and sugar mixture; dot with butter.
• Adjust top crust and flute edges. Brush top of pie with cold water and sprinkle on 1 tblsp. sugar. Cut vents.
• Bake in hot oven (425°) 40 to 50 minutes or until rhubarb is tender and crust is browned.

Variation

LATTICED STRAWBERRY/RHUBARB PIE: Use a lattice top to show off the beauty of this spring pie.

WONDERFUL STRAWBERRY PIE

The best two-crust strawberry pie you'll ever make or taste

Pastry for 2-crust pie
2⅔ c. frozen strawberries
1⅓ c. strawberry juice
3 tblsp. sugar
2½ tblsp. quick-cooking tapioca
1½ tblsp. cornstarch
1 tsp. lemon juice

• Thaw berries until most of free ice has disappeared. Drain off the juice; measure and stir it into mixture of sugar, tapioca and cornstarch in saucepan. Heat rapidly until thickening is complete. Boiling is not necessary. Set aside to cool.
• Add berries and lemon juice to cooled, thickened juice. Pour filling into pastry-lined 9″ pie pan. Cut vents in top crust; cover pie, seal and flute edge.
• Bake in hot oven (425°) 30 minutes, or until nicely browned. For a brown undercrust, bake on lowest oven shelf.

Note: Proportions of sugar, tapioca and cornstarch are based on 4 parts strawberries frozen with 1 part sugar.

Custard and Meringue-topped Pies

Homespun pumpkin pie, deep and spicy, dominates autumn dessert plates in country homes. Along with apple pie, pumpkin has held its prestige from one generation to the next.

Another fabulous custard-filled pie is the majestic lemon meringue. The baked pie shell holds clear, buttercup-yellow custard with gold-tipped meringue. These two treats illustrate the wide diversity in custard pies. And how different they are from rich nut pies in which the custard usually combines with pecans, walnuts or peanuts.

Our recipes for custard pies come, for the most part, from cherished recipe files in ranch, farm and plantation homes across country.

TAWNY PUMPKIN PIE

Filling is a rich, mellow golden brown

Unbaked 9″ pie shell
2 eggs, slightly beaten
1 (1 lb.) can pumpkin (2 c.)
¾ c. sugar
½ tsp. salt
1 tsp. ground cinnamon
½ tsp. ground ginger
¼ tsp. ground cloves
1⅔ c. light cream or evaporated milk
Caramelized Pecan Topping (optional)

• Blend together eggs and pumpkin.

Stir in sugar, salt, cinnamon, ginger and cloves. Blend in cream.

· Turn into pie shell. Bake in hot oven (400°) 45 to 55 minutes or until knife inserted halfway between center and edge of pie comes out clean. Cool completely on rack.

· Gently drop Caramelized Pecan Topping by spoonfuls over cooled pie to cover top. Broil 5″ from heat until mixture begins to bubble, about 3 minutes. Watch carefully (if cooked too long, top will turn syrupy). Cool on rack.

CARAMELIZED PECAN TOPPING: Combine 3 tblsp. soft butter or regular margarine, ⅔ c. brown sugar, firmly packed, and ⅔ c. coarsely chopped pecans.

LEMON MERINGUE PIE SUPREME

Meringue billows top nippy, luscious, buttercup-yellow filling

Baked 9″ pie shell
7 tblsp. cornstarch
1½ c. sugar
¼ tsp. salt
1½ c. hot water
3 egg yolks, beaten
2 tblsp. butter or regular margarine
1 tsp. grated lemon peel
½ c. fresh lemon juice
3 egg whites (room temperature)
¼ tsp. cream of tartar
6 tblsp. sugar

· Mix cornstarch, 1 c. sugar and salt in saucepan; gradually stir in hot water. Cook over direct heat, stirring constantly, until thick and clear, about 10 minutes.

· Remove from heat. Stir ½ c. hot mixture into yolks; stir this back into hot mixture. Cook over low heat, stirring constantly, 2 to 3 minutes. Remove from heat; stir in butter. Add lemon peel and juice, stirring until smooth. Cool. Pour into baked pie shell.

· Beat egg whites with cream of tartar until frothy; gradually beat in 6 tblsp. sugar, a little at a time. Beat until meringue stands in firm, glossy peaks. Spread meringue on filling, making sure it touches inner edge of crust around pie.

· Bake in moderate oven (350°) 15 minutes or until delicately browned. Cool.

Note: You can freeze this pie. Put in freezer without wrapping. When frozen, slip into plastic bag or wrap in moisture-vapor-proof freezer material. Seal, label, date and return to freezer. Recommended storage time: up to 1 month. To serve, remove from freezer 2 to 3 hours before serving.

BLACK BOTTOM LEMON PIE

New taste thrill—chocolate in lemon meringue pie. It's a gourmet treat

Baked 9″ pie shell
2 squares semisweet chocolate
4 eggs, separated
¼ c. lemon juice
3 tblsp. water
1 tsp. lemon peel
1 c. sugar

· Melt chocolate over hot water. Spread evenly over bottom of cool pie shell.

· In top of double boiler, beat egg yolks until thick and lemon-colored. Add lemon juice and water, mixing well. Then stir in lemon peel and ½ c. sugar. Cook over hot (not boiling) water, stirring constantly, until thick, about 12 minutes. Remove from hot water.

· Beat egg whites until frothy. Add

remaining ½ c. sugar gradually, beating constantly until stiff, glossy peaks form. Fold half of this mixture into egg yolk mixture. Pour over chocolate in pie shell.

· Spoon remaining egg white mixture into pastry tube and make a lattice design on top of filling.

· Bake in slow oven (325°) 10 to 15 minutes, or until lightly browned. Cool.

KEY WEST LIME PIE

Tropical pie has refreshing, tangy taste; a cool, lime-green filling

Baked 9″ pie shell
⅓ c. cornstarch
1½ c. sugar
¼ tsp. salt
1½ c. water
3 egg yolks, beaten
¼ c. fresh lime juice
1 tblsp. grated lime peel
Few drops green food color
Meringue (3 egg whites)

· Combine cornstarch, sugar and salt in saucepan; gradually add water, stirring until smooth. Bring to a boil over medium heat, stirring, and boil 1 minute.

· Remove from heat and quickly add one half the hot mixture to the egg yolks, mixing well. Return to the hot mixture, blending thoroughly.

· Bring the mixture to a boil, stirring, over medium heat. Boil 1 minute longer.

· Remove from heat; stir in lime juice and peel and food color to make filling a delicate green. Pour into cool pie shell at once. Completely cover with meringue (see Perfect Meringue for Topping Pies in Index).

· Bake in moderate oven (350°) 12 to 15 minutes, or until meringue is golden. Cool on rack away from drafts, at least 1 hour before cutting.

GOLDEN RAISIN PIE

Sour cream-raisin meringue pie with medley of spices and orange undertone

Baked 8″ pie shell
¼ c. sugar
1½ tblsp. cornstarch
½ tsp. salt
½ tsp. ground ginger
½ tsp. ground cinnamon
⅛ tsp. ground cloves
⅛ tsp. ground nutmeg
½ c. light corn syrup
3 egg yolks, beaten
1 c. dairy sour cream
1 c. light raisins
1 tblsp. grated orange peel
Meringue (3 egg whites)

· Mix sugar, cornstarch, salt and spices in top of double boiler. Stir in corn syrup, egg yolks, sour cream, raisins and orange peel.

· Cook over hot water, stirring, until smooth and thick, about 15 to 18 minutes. Pour into cool pie shell.

· Top with meringue (see Perfect Meringue for Topping Pies in Index) while filling is hot.

· Bake in moderate oven (350°) until brown, 12 to 15 minutes.

BANANA MERINGUE PIE

Pie cuts best if refrigerated 4 hours

Baked 9″ pie shell
⅓ c. sifted flour
⅔ c. sugar
¼ tsp. salt
2 c. milk, scalded
3 eggs, separated
¼ c. butter or regular margarine
1 tsp. vanilla
Meringue (3 egg whites)
3 medium bananas

· Combine flour, sugar and salt in saucepan. Blend scalded milk in slowly. Cook, stirring constantly, over medium heat until mixture thickens and boils. Continue cooking and stirring 1 minute.
· Remove from heat and add a little hot mixture to beaten egg yolks. Quickly stir into mixture in saucepan. Return to medium heat and cook, stirring constantly, 3 minutes or until it thickens again and mounds slightly.
· Remove from heat and add butter and vanilla, stirring until butter is melted. Cool while you make meringue (see Perfect Meringue for Topping Pies in Index).
· Slice peeled firm bananas into pie shell, making an even layer. Pour lukewarm filling over bananas. Spoon meringue over filling and spread over top, making sure it touches inner edges of crust all around pie.
· Bake in moderate oven (350°) about 12 minutes, until peaks of meringue are golden brown.

BUTTERSCOTCH MERINGUE PIE

Good to the last forkful—tender, crisp pastry with buttery, brown sugar filling

Baked 9" pie shell
⅓ c. sifted flour
1 c. brown sugar, firmly packed
¼ tsp. salt
2 c. milk, scalded
3 egg yolks, beaten slightly
3 tblsp. butter or regular margarine
½ tsp. vanilla
Meringue (3 egg whites)

· Mix flour, sugar and salt; gradually add milk. Cook over moderate heat, stirring constantly, until mixture thickens and boils. Cook 2 minutes and remove from heat.
· Add small amount milk mixture to egg yolks, stir into remaining hot mixture; cook 1 minute, stirring constantly.
· Add butter and vanilla; cool slightly. Pour into pastry shell and cool.
· Top with meringue (see Perfect Meringue for Topping Pies in Index). Bake in moderate oven (350°) 12 to 15 minutes.

RHUBARB CUSTARD PIE

Tangy rhubarb in rich creamy custard is an early spring farm-style treat

Unbaked 9" pie shell

Filling:
1½ lbs. rhubarb (about 4 c.)
¾ c. sugar
2 tblsp. flour
1 tblsp. lemon juice
⅛ tsp. salt

Topping:
3 eggs
1 c. heavy cream
2 tblsp. melted butter or regular margarine
¼ tsp. ground nutmeg
2 tblsp. sugar

Filling: In bowl, combine rhubarb, cut in ¼" slices, sugar, flour, lemon juice and salt. Toss to mix and turn into pie shell. Bake in hot oven (400°) 20 minutes.
Topping: Beat eggs slightly in bowl; stir in cream, butter and nutmeg to blend. Pour over hot rhubarb in pie shell.

• Bake 10 minutes; sprinkle with sugar. Bake 10 minutes more, or until pie's top is browned. Cool before cutting.

PEACH CUSTARD PIE

Custard pie with a delicate peach flavor—filling has pumpkin pie texture

Unbaked 9″ pie shell
1 c. sugar
3 tblsp. flour
½ tsp. salt
½ tsp. ground ginger
½ tsp. ground cinnamon
½ tsp. ground nutmeg
1½ c. fresh Peach Purée
3 eggs, slightly beaten
1 c. milk
1 (6 oz.) can evaporated milk

• Combine sugar, flour, salt and spices. Add Peach Purée and stir well. Add eggs, milk and evaporated milk; blend.

• Pour part of mixture into unbaked pie shell. Place in oven and then carefully pour in the remaining mixture. Bake in very hot oven (450°) 10 minutes, then in slow oven (325°) about 45 minutes, or until knife comes out clean when inserted halfway between center and outer edge of pie. Cool to serve.

PEACH PURÉE: Peel soft, ripe peaches and put through a sieve, colander or food mill. Or use an electric blender.

SOUTHERN PECAN PIE

A young cousin of chess pie

Unbaked 9″ pie shell
1 c. pecan halves
3 eggs
1 c. light corn syrup
1 tblsp. melted butter or regular margarine
½ tsp. vanilla
1 c. sugar
1 tblsp. flour

• Arrange nuts in pie shell.

• Beat eggs; add and blend corn syrup, butter and vanilla.

• Combine sugar and flour. Blend with egg mixture and pour over nuts in pie shell. Let stand until nuts rise, so they'll get a nice glaze during baking.

• Bake in moderate oven (375°) 40 to 50 minutes, or until filling is set.

CHOCOLATE PECAN PIE

This pie sells fast at food bazaars

Unbaked 9″ pie shell
1 c. semisweet chocolate pieces
⅔ c. evaporated milk
2 tblsp. butter
2 eggs, beaten
1 c. sugar
2 tblsp. flour
¼ tsp. salt
1 tsp. vanilla
1 c. chopped pecans

• Combine chocolate pieces, evaporated milk and butter in a small saucepan. Cook over low heat until mixture is creamy and smooth.

• Combine remaining ingredients and gradually stir in the chocolate mixture.

• Pour into pie shell. Bake in moderate oven (375°) 40 minutes or until firm. Cool pie completely before serving.

DATE PECAN PIE

Sweet and rich—serve with coffee

Unbaked 9" pie shell
1 c. dairy sour cream
3 eggs, beaten
1 c. sugar
1 tsp. ground cinnamon
¼ tsp. salt
¾ c. dates, cut in pieces
½ c. chopped pecans
Whipped cream or ice cream

· Combine sour cream, eggs, sugar, cinnamon and salt in a bowl; mix well. Add dates and pecans. Blend well. Pour into pie shell.
· Bake in moderate oven (375°) 30 minutes, or until filling is set and browned. Serve spread with whipped cream.

RAISIN/BLACK WALNUT PIE

Best seller in a Home Demonstration Club's booth at a Virginia county fair

Unbaked 9" pie shell
3 eggs, beaten
¾ c. light brown sugar, firmly packed
¼ c. soft butter or regular margarine
1 c. dark corn syrup
½ c. crushed black walnuts
1 tsp. vanilla
1 c. seedless raisins

· Combine eggs, sugar, and butter, beating until thick and fluffy. Add corn syrup; beat until fluffy. Add walnuts and vanilla; add raisins, beating gently.
· Turn into pie shell. Bake in moderate oven (375°) 30 to 40 minutes, until firm in the center.

BLACK WALNUT PIE

So rich you can cut pie in 8 servings; so delicious no one will want you to

Unbaked 9" pie shell
½ c. sugar
½ c. brown sugar, firmly packed
1 c. light corn syrup
3 tblsp. butter or regular margarine
3 eggs, slightly beaten
1 c. chopped black walnuts
1 tblsp. sugar
1 tblsp. flour

· Combine ½ c. white sugar, brown sugar and corn syrup in saucepan. Heat just to boiling. Remove from heat and add butter. Stir until butter melts.
· Gradually stir hot mixture into eggs. Stir in black walnuts.
· Combine 1 tblsp. sugar and the flour. Sprinkle evenly over bottom of pastry-lined pie pan. Turn walnut mixture into pastry.
· Bake in moderate oven (375°) 40 to 50 minutes, or until filling is set.

PEANUT PIE

Selected from a recipe collection of a good North Carolina cook

Unbaked 8" pie shell
1 c. dark corn syrup
3 eggs
3 tblsp. flour
2 tblsp. melted butter
¼ tsp. salt
1 c. whole toasted peanuts

· Combine syrup, eggs, flour, butter and salt in mixing bowl. Beat with rotary beater 60 turns only.
· Spread toasted peanuts in bottom of unbaked pastry shell. Pour liquid mixture over top. Bake in moderate

oven (375°) 30 minutes, or until filling is firm.

TO TOAST PEANUTS: Place shelled nuts in shallow pan in moderate oven (350°) about 10 minutes, or until nuts are slightly brown.

OATMEAL PIE

Many who eat this think it's pecan pie; it's less expensive, but luscious

Unbaked 9″ pie shell
¼ c. butter or regular margarine
½ c. sugar
½ tsp. ground cinnamon
½ tsp. ground cloves
¼ tsp. salt
1 c. dark corn syrup
3 eggs
1 c. quick-cooking rolled oats

· Cream together butter and sugar. Add cinnamon, cloves and salt. Stir in syrup.
· Add eggs, one at a time, stirring after each addition until blended. Stir in oats.
· Pour into pie shell and bake in moderate oven (350°) about 1 hour, or until knife inserted in center comes out clean.

Note: During baking, the oatmeal forms a chewy, "nutty" crust on top —pie is rich, delicately spiced.

Refrigerator Pies

Some country pies taste best when chilled thoroughly. Safety demands that those containing egg-milk and cream cheese mixtures be kept in the refrigerator until serving time. Make these refreshing desserts in the morning and chill them for meals later in the day—especially in hot, humid weather when you won't want to hold them.

APRICOT ANGEL PIE

Golden, delectable, make-ahead dessert

10″ Meringue Pie Shell (see Index)
2 tblsp. water
1 tsp. unflavored gelatin
4 egg yolks
½ tsp. lemon peel
5 tblsp. lemon juice
⅔ c. sugar
1 c. dried apricots, cooked and puréed
1 c. heavy cream, whipped
⅓ c. slivered, toasted almonds

· Measure 2 tblsp. water into a small bowl. Sprinkle gelatin over surface and let stand until softened.
· Combine egg yolks, lemon peel and juice. Beat well. Add sugar; beat.
· Pour into top of double boiler. Place over boiling water. Cook until very thick, about 7 minutes, stirring constantly. Add softened gelatin and stir until dissolved. Add puréed apricots; cool.
· Fold whipped cream into apricot mixture. Fill meringue shell. Chill overnight. Sprinkle top with almonds.

CHOCOLATE ANGEL PIE

Lovers of chocolate rate this "tops"

9″ Meringue Pie Shell (see Index)
⅓ c. chopped pecans or walnuts
¾ c. semisweet chocolate pieces
¼ c. hot water
1 tsp. vanilla
⅛ tsp. salt
1 c. heavy cream, whipped

· Prepare Meringue Pie Shell as directed, but just before baking sprinkle pie shell with nuts.

· Melt chocolate pieces in double boiler over hot, not boiling, water. Add hot water, vanilla and salt. Cook and stir until smooth. Cool.
· Fold in whipped cream and pour into pie shell. Chill 4 hours or overnight. Spread thin layer of whipped cream over top when serving, if desired.

CHERRY ANGEL PIE

Elegant and fancy-looking dessert for special occasions—tastes scrumptious

10″ Meringue Pie Shell (see Index)
1 (1 lb. 4 oz.) can sweetened frozen cherries, thawed
1 envelope unflavored gelatin
¼ c. cold water
¼ c. confectioners sugar
½ tsp. vanilla
1 c. heavy cream, whipped
½ c. flaked coconut
¼ c. chopped pecans

· Simmer cherries 5 minutes. Drain, reserving juice. Cool cherries.
· Soften gelatin in cold water. Heat 1 c. cherry juice to boiling. Add softened gelatin and stir until it is dissolved. Remove from heat, cool and chill until mixture thickens to the consistency of syrup. Beat until fluffy.
· Beat confectioners sugar and vanilla into whipped cream. Fold into gelatin mixture. Fold in cherries, coconut and nuts. Spread into cooled Meringue Pie Shell. Chill several hours.

LEMON ANGEL PIE

Gay as a daisy—meringue holds white capped billows of lemon filling

9″ Meringue Pie Shell (see Index)
4 egg yolks
½ c. sugar
¼ c. lemon juice
1 tblsp. grated lemon peel
1 c. heavy cream, whipped

· Beat egg yolks until thick and lemon-colored. Gradually beat in sugar. Stir in lemon juice and peel. Cook over simmering water, stirring constantly, until mixture is thick, about 5 to 8 minutes. Mixture should be thick enough to mound slightly when dropped from spoon. Cool.
· Spread cool lemon mixture into Meringue Pie Shell. Top with whipped cream. Chill 12 hours or overnight.

LEMON CHIFFON PIE

Lemon fluff in crisp, spicy crust

9″ Unbaked Graham Cracker Crumb Crust (see Index)
1 envelope unflavored gelatin
¼ c. cold water
4 egg yolks, beaten
½ c. sugar
¼ tsp. salt
¼ c. lemon juice
¼ tsp. grated lemon peel
4 egg whites, beaten stiff
¼ c. sugar

· Soak gelatin in cold water.
· Combine egg yolks, ½ c. sugar and salt. Add lemon juice and peel. Cook over boiling water, stirring constantly, until thick.
· Stir in gelatin. Chill until thick and syrupy.
· Beat egg whites and ¼ c. sugar. Fold into egg yolk mixture. Turn into crust. Chill until firm, about 3 hours. If desired, serve with Frosted Grapes.

FROSTED GRAPES: Dip 1 lb. white or green grapes, broken into clusters, in 1 egg white, slightly beaten with

1 tblsp. water. Roll in sugar, spread on waxed paper. Chill in refrigerator at least 1 hour.

PEPPERMINT CHIFFON PIE

Chocolate crumb crust holds the pink and white candy-flecked filling

9″ Chocolate Cookie Crumb Crust (see Index)
1 envelope unflavored gelatin
¼ c. cold water
¾ c. milk
½ c. sugar
¼ tsp. salt
1 c. crushed peppermint stick candy
4 egg yolks, slightly beaten
4 egg whites, beaten stiff
Whipped cream

· Soak gelatin in cold water.
· Scald milk; stir in sugar, salt and peppermint candy.
· Add egg yolks to milk mixture; cook over boiling water until mixture coats spoon.
· Stir in gelatin; chill until syrupy.
· Fold egg whites into chilled mixture. Pour into crumb crust. Chill until firm, about 3 hours. Serve with whipped cream.

PEANUT BUTTER CHIFFON PIE

Favorite of a Georgia homemaker

9″ Unbaked Graham Cracker Crumb Crust (see Index)
1 envelope unflavored gelatin
1 c. cold water
3 egg yolks, well beaten
½ c. sugar or light corn syrup
½ tsp. salt
½ c. smooth peanut butter
½ tsp. vanilla
3 egg whites
½ c. heavy cream, whipped stiff (optional)
Peanut halves
Chocolate pieces

· Soften gelatin in ¼ c. water.
· Combine egg yolks, ¼ c. sugar, ¼ c. water and salt in top of double boiler; blend. Add gelatin.
· Place over boiling water; beat constantly with rotary beater until thick and fluffy (about 5 minutes). Cool.
· Place peanut butter in bowl; add remaining ½ c. water gradually; beat until smooth. Add vanilla and egg yolk mixture; blend. Chill until slightly thickened, but still syrupy (10 to 15 minutes).
· Beat egg whites until foamy; add remaining sugar gradually, beating until stiff. Fold into peanut butter mixture. Turn into crumb crust (you may use baked pastry shell). Chill until firm. Makes 6 servings.
· To serve, cover top with thin layer whipped cream if desired. (Cream is pretty but detracts from the peanut flavor.) Decorate with "daisies" of peanuts and chocolate pieces for centers.

PINK LEMONADE PIE

Pink of perfection—this delicious, unusual refrigerator cream pie

8″ Vanilla Wafer Crumb Crust (see Index)
1 (6 oz.) can frozen pink lemonade concentrate
¾ c. water
1 envelope unflavored gelatin
¼ c. sugar
1 c. heavy cream
Few drops of red food color
¼ c. vanilla wafer crumbs

· Chill crumb crust.
· Thaw lemonade concentrate and combine with ½ c. water.

• Soften gelatin in remaining ¼ c. water; dissolve over hot water.
• Add dissolved gelatin and sugar to lemonade; stir until sugar dissolves. Chill until mixture is thick but not set (about 1 hour).
• Whip thickened gelatin mixture until light and fluffy. Then whip cream and fold into gelatin mixture. Add food color to tint a delicate pink. Pour into chilled crust. Sprinkle with crumbs. Chill.

CHOCOLATE CHEESE PIE

Heavenly, but serve small portions to the dieters at your table

9″ Chocolate Graham Crust
1 (6 oz.) pkg. semisweet chocolate pieces
1 (8 oz.) pkg. cream cheese, softened
¾ c. light brown sugar, firmly packed
⅛ tsp. salt
1 tsp. vanilla
2 eggs, separated
1 c. heavy cream, whipped

• Melt chocolate over hot (not boiling) water; cool about 10 minutes.
• Blend cream cheese, ½ c. sugar, salt and vanilla. Beat in egg yolks, one at a time. Beat in cooled chocolate. Blend well.
• Beat egg whites until stiff but not dry. Gradually beat in ¼ c. sugar; beat until stiff and glossy.
• Fold chocolate mixture into beaten whites. Fold in whipped cream.
• Pour into chilled crust, reserving ¼ of mixture for decorating. Chill until filling sets slightly. With tapered spoon, drop reserved mixture in mounds over top of pie. Chill overnight.

CHOCOLATE GRAHAM CRUST: Mix thoroughly 1½ c. graham cracker crumbs, ¼ c. brown sugar, firmly packed, ⅛ tsp. ground nutmeg, ⅓ c. melted butter or margarine and 1 square unsweetened chocolate, melted. Press into 9″ pie pan. Chill until firm.

SHORT-CUT CHOCOLATE CHEESE PIE

This dieters' version of the preceding recipe has less filling, fewer calories

9″ Chocolate Graham Crust (see preceding recipe)
1 (6 oz.) pkg. semisweet chocolate pieces
1 (3 oz.) pkg. cream cheese, softened
¼ c. light brown sugar, firmly packed
1 envelope dessert topping mix

• Melt chocolate over hot (not boiling) water. Remove from heat. Stir in the cheese until it is blended. Stir in sugar.
• Prepare topping mix as directed on package; blend ½ c. into chocolate mixture. Fold in remaining topping.
• Spread filling in crust. Chill overnight.

SANTIAGO CHOCOLATE PIE

Cook's trick—fold nuts and raisins or dates into the whipped cream topping

Baked 9″ pie shell

Filling:
3 squares unsweetened chocolate
3½ c. milk
⅔ c. sifted cake flour
¾ c. sugar
¾ tsp. salt
1 egg or 2 egg yolks
2 tblsp. butter or regular margarine
1½ tsp. vanilla

Topping:

½ c. heavy cream
2 tblsp. sugar
¼ c. chopped raisins or dates
¼ c. broken nuts

· To make filling, combine chocolate and milk in top of double boiler. Cook over hot water until chocolate melts. Beat with a rotary beater until smoothly blended.

· Sift flour; measure; sift again with sugar and salt.

· Add a small amount of chocolate mixture, stirring until smooth. Return to double boiler and cook until thickened, stirring constantly. Then cook 10 minutes longer, stirring occasionally.

· Beat the whole egg or egg yolks. Add a little of hot mixture, stirring vigorously. Return to double boiler; cook 2 minutes, stirring constantly.

· Remove from boiling water. Add butter and vanilla. Cool slightly.

· Pour into pie shell. Chill.

· To make topping, whip cream until slightly thick. Add sugar and whip until just stiff. Fold in raisins or dates and nuts. Spread over top of filling.

FRENCH BLUEBERRY PIE

Whole blueberries and blueberry sauce make this a pie to remember

Baked 9″ pie shell
2 (3 oz.) pkgs. cream cheese
2 tblsp. milk
1 tsp. grated lemon peel
4 c. fresh or frozen unsweetened blueberries, thawed
1 tblsp. lemon juice
⅛ tsp. salt
Water
1 c. sugar
2 tblsp. cornstarch

· Soften cream cheese. Add milk and lemon peel; beat until smooth. Spread cheese mixture evenly in bottom of baked pie shell.

· Sprinkle 2 c. whole blueberries over cheese layer.

· Mash remainder of blueberries; spoon into a 1½ c. measure. Add lemon juice and salt and enough water to make 1½ c. of pulp and liquid. Place in a small saucepan.

· Mix sugar and cornstarch. Stir into the blueberry pulp. Bring to a boil, stirring constantly, and cook for about 2 minutes or until thickened. Cool mixture to lukewarm.

· Spoon the blueberry sauce over blueberries. Chill pie for several hours.

FRENCH STRAWBERRY PIE

Glossy glazed berries on top hide the surprise, a rich custard layer

Baked 9″ pie shell
⅓ c. sugar
3½ tblsp. cornstarch
6 egg yolks, slightly beaten
2 c. milk, scalded
1 tsp. vanilla
1 (12 oz.) jar currant jelly
2 c. fresh strawberries

· Combine sugar, cornstarch and egg yolks in saucepan. Gradually stir in the milk, while bringing to a boil. Cook, stirring constantly, 1 minute.

· Remove from heat and add vanilla. Cool and chill.

· Melt the currant jelly over heat. Cool until it is about ready to set. Brush the inside of pie shell with part of the jelly. Spoon in custard filling.

· Arrange stemmed, washed and drained strawberries, pointed ends up, on top of pie. Spoon remaining currant jelly over berries to glaze them. Chill a few hours before serving.

TWO-TIERED STRAWBERRY PIE

Another make-ahead dessert to chill until time to serve your guests

Baked 9″ pie shell
½ c. sifted confectioners sugar
½ tsp. vanilla
¼ tsp. almond extract
1 (3 oz.) pkg. cream cheese
½ c. heavy cream, whipped
⅓ c. sugar
2 tblsp. cornstarch
⅓ c. water
⅓ c. grenadine syrup
1 tblsp. lemon juice
2 c. fresh whole strawberries

· Add confectioners sugar, vanilla and almond extract to cheese and beat until smooth and creamy.
· Fold in whipped cream. Spread evenly over bottom of baked pie shell. Chill thoroughly several hours.
· Combine ⅓ c. sugar and cornstarch in saucepan. Add water slowly, stirring to make a smooth mixture. Add grenadine and lemon juice.
· Cook, stirring constantly, until thick and clear. Cool.
· Add to strawberries, stir to coat with glaze. Spread over top of chilled cheese layer. Chill before serving.

RASPBERRY GLACÉ PIE

"My company special," says the Minnesota woman who shares this

Baked 9″ pie shell
1 qt. red raspberries
1 c. water
1 c. sugar
3 tblsp. cornstarch
Few drops red food color
2 tsp. lemon juice
1 (3 oz.) pkg. cream cheese (room temperature)
1 tblsp. milk
Whipped cream (optional)

· Wash berries gently in cold water, lift out and spread on paper toweling to drain thoroughly.
· Place 1 c. berries and ⅔ c. water in saucepan; simmer 3 minutes. Run through strainer to remove seeds.
· Blend sugar, cornstarch and remaining ⅓ c. water. Add to cooked raspberries and cook until mixture is thick and translucent, stirring constantly. Remove from heat, add food color and lemon juice. Cool.
· Combine cream cheese with milk and spread evenly over bottom of pie shell. Pour remaining berries into pie shell, reserving a few of the prettiest ones for garnishing. Spread cooled, cooked berry mixture over berries. Chill until firm, at least 2 hours. Serve garnished with whipped cream and whole berries.

PINEAPPLE POSY PIE

Yellow flowers with cherry centers trim this pie that's gay as a festival

9″ Graham Cracker Crumb Crust (see Index)
1 (6 oz.) can frozen pineapple juice concentrate
1 envelope unflavored gelatin
¼ c. cold water
4 egg yolks, beaten until thick and creamy
½ c. sugar
¼ tsp. salt
2 tblsp. finely grated orange peel
4 egg whites
¼ c. sugar
⅔ c. heavy cream, whipped

· Thaw pineapple juice concentrate and simmer until it is reduced to ½ c. (or until the total is ⅓ less). Cool.
· Soften gelatin in water at least 5 minutes.
· Add egg yolks to pineapple juice; add gelatin and ½ c. sugar. Place in double boiler. Cook 10 minutes, stirring often. Remove from heat. Add salt and orange peel. Mix well and chill until mixture thickens, but do not let it set. It usually takes about 45 minutes.
· Beat egg whites until frothy, then gradually add ¼ c. sugar while continuing to beat. Beat until stiff peaks form. Fold in whipped cream. Fold egg white mixture into pineapple filling and spoon into cool pie shell.
· At serving time, garnish, if desired, with 6 pineapple flowers. To make flower, arrange 5 drained pineapple tidbits around a maraschino cherry.

Note: A coconut pie shell may be used instead of the crumb crust. See recipe for Toasted Coconut Crust in Index.

Creamiest Cream Pies in the Country

Farm women make the world's best cream pies. For two reasons: They almost always have the necessary ingredients on hand, and they have lots of practice—the pies taste so wonderful that they're favorites.

A Colorado ranch woman says she bakes cream pies for church sales because they are spoken for by the time she delivers them. Her husband sums up his regard for the dessert by saying: "My definition for good is different from Webster's. To me, good is the kind of cream pies my wife bakes."

VANILLA CREAM PIE

An all-time favorite with 7 variations

Baked 8″ pie shell
½ c. sugar
3 tblsp. flour
1 tblsp. cornstarch
¼ tsp. salt
1½ c. milk
3 egg yolks, slightly beaten
1 tblsp. butter or regular margarine
1 tsp. vanilla

· Combine sugar, flour, cornstarch and salt in top of double boiler. Mix with wooden spoon. Blend in milk gradually, then add egg yolks. Add butter.
· Place over rapidly boiling water so pan is touching water. Cook until thick and smooth, about 7 minutes, stirring constantly. Scrape down sides of pan frequently.
· Remove from heat. Add vanilla. Stir until smooth and blended, scraping sides of pan well. Pour hot filling into pie shell. Partially cool, then refrigerate until served.

Note: Quantities may be doubled and filling cooked for 2 (8″) pies at the same time.

Variations

CHOCOLATE CREAM PIE: Melt 1½ squares unsweetened chocolate in milk in top of double boiler. Set aside to cool. Then proceed as directed for Vanilla Cream Pie filling, using the chocolate-milk mixture and increasing sugar to ¾ c.

BUTTERSCOTCH CREAM PIE: Substitute ¾ c. brown sugar, firmly packed, for white sugar and increase butter to 2 tblsp. Proceed as for Vanilla Cream Pie.

BLACK BOTTOM PIE: Add 2 tsp. unflavored gelatin to dry ingredients. Cook filling as directed in recipe for Vanilla Cream Pie. Add ½ c. hot filling to ½ c. semisweet chocolate pieces; stir until they melt and mixture is smooth. Spread chocolate mixture in bottom of baked 9″ pie shell. Cover and set remaining filling aside. Add ¼ tsp. salt to 3 egg whites; beat until frothy. Gradually add 3 tblsp. sugar, beating until stiff peaks form. With beater, beat half of this meringue into cream filling until mixture is smooth. Fold remaining half of meringue into mixture. Spread on chocolate layer in pie shell. Chill pie several hours before serving.

CHERRY CREAM PIE: Add 2 tsp. unflavored gelatin to dry ingredients and cook filling as directed for Vanilla Cream Pie. Remove from heat; cover and set aside. Add ¼ tsp. salt to 3 egg whites; beat until frothy. Gradually add 3 tblsp. sugar, beating until stiff peaks form. Beat half of meringue into cream filling until mixture is smooth. Fold remaining half of meringue into mixture. Spread 1 c. commercially canned or homemade cherry pie filling on bottom of baked 9″ pie shell. Cover with cream filling. Chill several hours before serving.

STRAWBERRY SPONGE CREAM PIE: Drain 1 (10 oz.) pkg. partially thawed frozen strawberries. If necessary, add water to make ½ c. juice. Combine 2 tblsp. cornstarch and 1 tblsp. sugar in small saucepan; slowly add juice, stirring to make smooth paste. Cook over low heat, stirring constantly until mixture is thick and clear. Remove from heat and stir in strawberries. Set aside. Prepare filling for Vanilla Cream Pie, reducing flour to 2 tblsp. and egg yolks to 2. Pour into baked 9″ pie shell. Beat egg whites at high speed until frothy. Gradually add 3 tblsp. sugar, beating at high speed until very stiff peaks form. Fold thickened fruit into egg whites. Spread evenly on hot cream filling, sealing to crust all around. Bake in moderate oven (350°) about 30 minutes. Cool before serving.

RASPBERRY CREAM PIE: Follow directions for Strawberry Sponge Cream Pie, substituting raspberries for strawberries.

BLUEBERRY CREAM PIE: Follow directions for Strawberry Sponge Cream Pie, substituting blueberries for strawberries. Add 1 tsp. lemon juice to berries.

STRAWBERRY SATIN PIE

Taste-testers scored this pie 100%

Baked 9″ pie shell
½ c. sliced toasted almonds
Creamy Satin Filling
1½ c. fresh strawberries
Shiny Glaze

· Cover bottom of baked pie shell with almonds.
· Cover almonds with Creamy Satin Filling. Chill thoroughly at least 3 hours, or overnight.
· Slice strawberries in halves, reserving a few perfect berries for center of pie. Arrange on filling in layers, starting at outer edge. Place

25. BIG PIES—From top to bottom, Pear/Pineapple, Pumpkin/Apple and Apple/Cranberry/Mince Pies. Recipes for both 9″ and 10″ pies, pages 418, 410, 409.

26. ICE CREAM TOPKNOTS—Use them to glamorize Orange Tapioca Pudding, fruit-filled Meringues or your favorite applesauce cake. Recipes, pages 307, 402, 359.

27. STRAWBERRY PARFAIT RING—Make and freeze ring. To serve this company dessert, add ripe berries and sprinkle with coconut. Recipe, page 323.

28. REFRIGERATOR CAKE—Rich, make-ahead dessert pleases chocolate fans. Ideal for afternoon and evening dessert parties. Recipe, page 308.

some berries cut side up to make a pattern. Cover with Shiny Glaze. Refrigerate at least 1 hour.

CREAMY SATIN FILLING: Combine ½ c. sugar, 3 tblsp. cornstarch, 3 tblsp. flour and ½ tsp. salt in saucepan.

• Gradually add 2 c. milk, stirring until smooth. Cook, stirring constantly, until mixture is thick and bubbling.

• Stir a little of this hot mixture into 1 slightly beaten egg, then add to hot mixture and cook until just bubbling hot.

• Cool, then chill thoroughly. This mixture will be very thick. Beat with mixer or rotary beater until smooth.

• Fold in ½ c. heavy cream, whipped, and 1 tsp. vanilla.

SHINY GLAZE: Crush ½ c. fresh strawberries. Add ½ c. water and cook 2 minutes; strain through sieve. Combine ¼ c. sugar and 1 tblsp. cornstarch in small saucepan; stir in berry juice. Cook, stirring constantly, until thick and clear. Cool; spoon carefully over strawberries in the pie.

CREAM PIE FOR FREEZING

Makes three pie fillings—use one and freeze two. It saves time

2 tsp. unflavored gelatin
6 c. milk
2 c. sugar
9 tblsp. cornstarch
½ tsp. salt
6 egg yolks, beaten
6 tblsp. butter or regular margarine
3 tsp. vanilla

• Soften gelatin in ¼ c. milk.

• Scald remaining milk. Add the combined sugar, cornstarch and salt; continue heating rapidly until boiling, stirring constantly.

• Stir about ½ c. of the hot mixture into egg yolks; pour back into saucepan; simmer 5 minutes more.

• Stir in gelatin mixture; add butter and vanilla. Pour into three 8″ pie pans; freeze. (Frozen filling will be right diameter to fit 9″ shell.)

• Remove from pan, wrap in moisture-proof freezer material; return to freezer.

To Bake: Place unthawed filling in 9″ pastry shell. You may cover it with a fruit or coconut layer (see variations), then top with meringue, making sure it touches crust all around. Bake in moderate oven (375°) about 10 to 12 minutes. (For best results, avoid heating the filling completely through.) Cool.

MERINGUE: Beat 3 egg whites (fresh or thawed frozen) with ¼ tsp. cream of tartar until frothy; beat in 6 tblsp. sugar, a little at a time. Beat until meringue stands in firm peaks. Spread on frozen filling at once.

Variations

BANANA CREAM PIE: Slice 2 ripe bananas over frozen filling; sprinkle with 1 tblsp. confectioners sugar. Cover with meringue and bake.

STRAWBERRY OR PEACH CREAM PIE: Arrange 1½ c. sliced strawberries or peaches over frozen filling; sprinkle with 3 tblsp. confectioners sugar; cover with meringue and bake as directed.

COCONUT CREAM PIE: Sprinkle 1½ c. flaked coconut over frozen filling; cover with meringue and bake.

Mincemeat Pies, Warm and Fragrant

Christmas holidays and blustery, cold weather call for mincemeat pies with coffee. Many country families still make their own mincemeat, canning or freezing it. We give you three heirloom family recipes—Venison, Green Tomato, and Elegant Homemade Mincemeats. You'll have a difficult time deciding which kind you like best.

Busy women of course buy jars and packages of mincemeat at their supermarkets.

BASIC HOMEMADE MINCEMEAT PIE

• You will need 4 c. homemade mincemeat for a 9" pie pan lined with pastry. Dot the filling with 1 tblsp. butter, adjust top crust, cut vents and flute edges. Brush top with light cream, if desired. (It's a good idea to cover pie edges with 2 to 3" strip of aluminum foil the first half hour of baking to prevent excessive browning. Remove the last 15 minutes of baking.)

• Bake in hot oven (425°) 40 to 45 minutes, or until pastry is golden. Partially cool on rack before serving. Or cool completely and reheat in slow oven (325°) at serving time.

MINCE/CRANBERRY PIE

For social functions during holidays

Pastry for 2-crust pie
1⅔ c. prepared mincemeat
1 (7 oz.) can whole cranberry sauce (1 c.)
¼ c. honey
½ tsp. grated lemon peel
1 tsp. flour
⅛ tsp. salt

• Combine mincemeat, cranberry sauce (canned or home cooked), honey and peel. Add flour and salt; mix. Pour into pastry-lined 9" pie pan. Moisten pastry rim with water.

• Roll out top crust; cut design with knife or make lattice pastry top. Adjust top over filling; seal and crimp edges.

• Bake in hot oven (400°) 35 minutes, until lightly browned.

Note: You may use 1 pkg. mincemeat. Prepare according to directions.

MINCEMEAT/PUMPKIN PIE

Flatter your guests with pie that boasts of the flavors of two fillings

Unbaked 9" pie shell
1 c. cooked pumpkin
½ c. brown sugar, firmly packed
½ tsp. salt
¾ tsp. ground cinnamon
¾ tsp. ground nutmeg
3 eggs
½ c. heavy cream
1 c. prepared mincemeat

• Combine pumpkin, sugar, salt, spices, eggs and cream and beat only until blended. Stir in mincemeat. Pour into unbaked pie shell. Bake in hot oven (425°) about 35 minutes, until filling is set. Serve warm.

DEEP-DISH PEAR AND MINCEMEAT PIE

Cheese pastry tops mincemeat and pears in this unforgettable dessert

Cheese Pastry
4 large pears (3 c. sliced)

¼ c. sugar
1 tblsp. flour
¼ tsp. salt
1½ c. prepared mincemeat
1 tblsp. lemon juice
2 tblsp. butter

• Arrange pear slices in bottom of an 8″ square baking dish. Combine sugar, flour and salt; sprinkle over pears. Cover with mincemeat; sprinkle with lemon juice and dot with butter.
• Roll out Cheese Pastry to fit top of fruit in dish. Place on fruit. Crimp edges and cut vents for steam to escape. Bake in hot oven (425°) 35 to 40 minutes. Serve warm.

CHEESE PASTRY: Combine 1 c. sifted flour and ½ tsp. salt; cut in ⅓ c. shortening until mixture resembles coarse meal. Add ¼ c. grated Cheddar cheese and toss to blend. Add 2 tblsp. water gradually to form a dough that holds together.

GREEN TOMATO MINCEMEAT

Makes downright delicious pies—the best way to salvage green tomatoes

6 lbs. green tomatoes
2 lbs. tart apples
2 c. raisins
4 c. brown sugar, firmly packed
2 c. strong coffee
1 lemon (grated peel and juice)
2 tsp. grated orange peel
½ c. vinegar
1 tsp. salt
1 tsp. ground nutmeg
1 tsp. ground allspice

• Core and quarter tomatoes and apples; put through food chopper with raisins.
• Combine all ingredients in large saucepan. Simmer 2 hours, stirring frequently.
• Pack at once in hot pint jars. Adjust lids. Process in boiling water bath (212°) 25 minutes.
• Remove jars from canner and complete seals unless closures are self-sealing type. Makes about 10 pints.

VENISON MINCEMEAT

Team with pastry to make that famous Christmas pie of the Old West

4 lbs. venison "trim" meat with bones
Water
¾ lb. beef suet
3 lbs. apples, peeled and quartered
2 lbs. seedless raisins
1 (15 oz.) box seeded raisins
1 (12 oz.) box currants
1 tblsp. salt
1 tblsp. ground cinnamon
1 tblsp. ground ginger
1 tblsp. ground cloves
1 tblsp. ground nutmeg
1 tsp. ground allspice
1 tsp. ground mace (optional)
2 qts. apple cider, grape or other fruit juice
1 lb. brown sugar

• Trim fat from venison. Cover with water; simmer until meat is tender. Refrigerate venison in cooking liquid overnight. Remove all fat from top of liquid. Separate meat from bones and put meat through food chopper using coarse blade. (There should be enough ground venison to make at least 2 qts. ground meat.)
• Grind suet and apples.
• Combine all ingredients in large kettle. Simmer 2 hours to plump fruit and blend flavors. Stir often to prevent sticking.
• Pack at once in hot pint jars. Adjust lids. Process in pressure canner

at 10 pounds pressure (240°) 60 minutes.

• Remove jars from canner and complete seals unless closures are self-sealing type. Makes about 11 pints.

Note: You can freeze mincemeat. Recommended storage time is 3 months.

ELEGANT HOMEMADE MINCEMEAT

It takes time to make this mincemeat, but it's worth the effort

3 lbs. beef round
Water
½ lb. suet
2½ qts. apples, peeled and chopped
2 lb. seedless raisins
2 lb. dried currants
¼ lb. citron, diced
2 tblsp. candied orange peel, chopped
2 c. sugar
2 tsp. salt
4 tsp. ground cinnamon
2 tsp. ground nutmeg
2 tsp. ground allspice
2 tsp. ground ginger
1½ tsp. ground cloves
2 c. apple cider
2 c. pineapple juice
Grated peel of 1 lemon
Juice of 1 lemon
2 c. white corn syrup
¾ c. cider vinegar
¼ c. butter or regular margarine

• Simmer beef in small amount water until tender; remove, cool, discard bone or gristle and put meat through food chopper (medium blade). Cook down stock until ¾ c. remains.

• Grind suet fine. Combine meat, suet and apples in 2-gal. crock. Add raisins, currants, citron and orange peel.

• Combine in saucepan sugar, salt, spices, cider, pineapple juice, lemon peel and juice and corn syrup. Heat to boiling point. Add vinegar and butter; mix well. Add to ingredients in crock. Store, covered, in very cold place 3 to 4 weeks, stirring every few days. Or package in desired amounts and freeze. Makes enough filling for 8 pies.

Pink Party Ice Cream Pie

Glamorous Pink Party Pie is queen of all ice cream pies that made their debut in our Countryside Test Kitchens. Its popularity continues more than a decade after we created it.

PINK PARTY PIE

FARM JOURNAL'S *famous ice cream pie*

1 recipe Pink Pastry
1 qt. strawberry ice cream
1 (10 oz.) pkg. frozen strawberries, thawed and drained
2 egg whites
¼ tsp. cream of tartar
¼ c. sugar
Few drops red food color

• Line a 9" pie pan with Pink Pastry (see recipe which follows).

• Pile softened ice cream into baked pie shell and spread; freeze overnight.

• To serve, heat oven to extremely hot (500°). Arrange strawberries on ice cream.

• Make meringue with egg whites,

cream of tartar and sugar. Tint a delicate pink. Spread meringue over pie, covering edges so ice cream will not melt.

· *Set pie on wooden bread board* in oven and bake about 5 minutes, or until lightly browned. Serve at once.

Variation

PINK AND WHITE PARTY PIE: Put 2 c. fresh strawberries in baked pie shell, top with 1 pt. vanilla ice cream, 1 c. berries and meringue. Brown as directed.

PINK PASTRY

Good standard pastry recipe—you can of course omit the food color

1 c. sifted flour
½ tsp. salt
⅓ c. lard
3 to 4 drops red food color
2 tblsp. water

· Mix sifted flour and salt; cut in lard with pastry blender. Add food color to water. Sprinkle on the water and mix with a fork until all the flour is moistened. Gather the dough together and press firmly into a ball. Line pie pan with pastry; flute edges and prick pastry. Bake in hot oven (425°) 8 to 10 minutes. Cool. Makes enough pastry for 1 (8 or 9″) pie shell.

Note: You can substitute ⅓ c. plus 1 tblsp. shortening for the lard.

Miniature Pies or Tarts

Individual servings of any food flatter guests, who rightly think: "This miniature was made especially for me." Pies are no exception; tarts appear special, with each person having his own little pie. The hostess has her own reasons—tarts are easy to serve and there's no last-minute cutting. Cherry and Pecan Tarts, tiny pies, are finger food.

CHERRY TARTS

Pick-up tarts to eat like cookies—they're colorful and delicious

1 c. flour
½ c. butter or regular margarine
1 (3 oz.) pkg. cream cheese
1 (1 lb. 5 oz.) can cherry pie filling

· Mix flour, butter and cream cheese to make dough. Wrap in waxed paper and refrigerate at least 2 hours, or overnight. (If overnight, let stand at room temperature ½ hour before rolling.)

· Roll to ¼″ thickness and cut in 12 circles (about 2½″) and 24 rings the same size, using doughnut cutter. Moisten edge of a circle with water and lay one ring on it. Moisten edge of ring and place second ring on top of it. Press edge of tart with a sharp fork. Repeat until all pastry is used.

· Place on baking sheet and bake in very hot oven (450°) 7 minutes. Cool.

· Fill tarts with prepared cherry pie filling. For added appeal, top each tart, just before serving, with 1 tsp. sweetened whipped cream. Makes 12 tarts.

Variation

MINCEMEAT TARTS: Fill cooled tart shells with mincemeat pie filling instead of cherry. Garnish with whipped cream.

PECAN TARTLETS

Delicious—eat them like cookies

1 c. butter or regular margarine
2 (3 oz.) pkgs. cream cheese
2½ c. flour
¾ tsp. salt
1½ c. chopped pecans
1 c. brown sugar, firmly packed
2 eggs, slightly beaten
2 tblsp. melted butter or regular margarine
½ tsp. vanilla
½ c. light corn syrup

· Soften 1 c. butter and cheese. Blend in half the flour at a time and ½ tsp. salt; shape pastry into two 2″ diameter rolls; wrap and chill overnight.
· Slice pastry into 36 portions; press into 2″ muffin-cup pans. Line cups; do not make rims.
· Place half the nuts in lined cups.
· Using a rotary beater, gradually add sugar to eggs. Add melted butter, remaining ¼ tsp. salt and vanilla. Stir in syrup. Pour into tart shells.
· Sprinkle with remaining nuts. Bake in moderate oven (350°) about 20 minutes. Makes 3 dozen.

Note: For tiny bite-size tarts, bake in paper bonbon cups. Have pastry at room temperature when you line cups.

CHOCOLATE CREAM TART FILLING

Strong chocolate flavor—delightful with a snowy drift of flaked coconut

½ c. Cocoa Paste
1 envelope dessert topping mix

· Thaw Cocoa Paste.
· Prepare topping mix according to package directions. Add Cocoa Paste; continue beating until creamy and smooth. Chill in refrigerator several hours before serving. Makes filling for 6 (3″) tarts.

COCOA PASTE

1⅓ c. cocoa
1 c. sugar
2 c. boiling water

· Combine cocoa and sugar in heavy saucepan. Add water slowly, stirring to make a smooth mixture.
· Cook and stir over high heat until mixture boils. Reduce heat to low and continue cooking for 15 minutes, stirring occasionally.
· Pour into bowl; cool. Package in ½ c. portions; freeze, or store in refrigerator. (May be stored up to 4 weeks in refrigerator or freezer.) Makes 2 cups.

PUMPKIN CREAM TART FILLING

True pumpkin flavor—spicy! Garnish filled tarts with toasted pecans

1⅓ c. Pumpkin Paste
1 envelope dessert topping mix

· Thaw Pumpkin Paste.
· Prepare topping mix according to package directions. Add Pumpkin Paste; continue beating until creamy and smooth. Chill in refrigerator several hours before serving. Makes filling for 6 (3″) tarts.

PUMPKIN PASTE

1 c. sugar
½ c. brown sugar, firmly packed
⅓ c. sifted flour
1½ tsp. ground cinnamon
1½ tsp. ground nutmeg
¾ tsp. salt
3 c. canned pumpkin
¾ c. water

• Combine sugars, flour, spices and salt. Add to pumpkin in heavy saucepan; mix thoroughly. Add water.
• Cook 15 minutes over low heat, stirring occasionally.
• Pour into bowl; cool. Package in 1⅓ c. portions; freeze. (May be stored up to 4 weeks in freezer.) Makes 4 cups.

LEMON CREAM TART FILLING

Light and lemony—and so good when topped with sliced strawberries

½ c. Lemon Paste
1 envelope dessert topping mix
Few drops yellow food color

• Thaw Lemon Paste; keep cold.
• Prepare topping mix according to package directions. Add Lemon Paste; continue beating until creamy and smooth. Add more milk for thinner mixture, if desired. Add food color.
• Chill in refrigerator several hours. Makes filling for 6 (3″) tarts.

LEMON PASTE

½ c. butter
⅓ c. sifted flour
1 c. sugar
1 c. boiling water
½ c. lemon juice
1 tblsp. grated lemon peel

• Melt butter in heavy saucepan. Add flour and stir to make smooth paste. Mix in ¼ c. sugar. Add water slowly, stirring to make a smooth mixture. Add remaining sugar, lemon juice and peel.
• Cook and stir over high heat until mixture boils. Reduce heat to low and continue cooking for 15 minutes, stirring occasionally.
• Pour into bowl; cool. Package in ½ c. portions; freeze, or store in refrigerator. (May be stored up to 4 weeks in refrigerator or freezer.) Makes 2 cups.

STRAWBERRY CHIFFON TARTS

Fresh as spring—and luscious

Tart shells (pastry for 2-crust pie)
2 c. fresh strawberries
¾ c. sugar
1 envelope unflavored gelatin
¼ c. cold water
½ c. hot water
1 tblsp. lemon juice
⅛ tsp. salt
1 c. heavy cream
2 egg whites
12 strawberries

• Crush 2 c. berries; cover with ½ c. sugar and let stand 30 minutes.
• Soften gelatin in cold water; dissolve in hot water. Cool. Add crushed berries, lemon juice and salt. Chill until mixture mounds when dropped from spoon. Test frequently while chilling.
• Fold in ½ c. cream, whipped. Beat egg whites until frothy; gradually add remaining ¼ c. sugar, beating until glossy, firm peaks form. Fold into strawberry mixture. Spoon into tart shells and chill until firm.
• To serve, garnish with remaining ½ c. cream, whipped, and whole berries. Makes about 12 (3″) tarts.

Variation

STRAWBERRY CHIFFON PIE: Spoon filling into 9″ Graham Cracker Crumb Crust.

PUMPKIN CHIFFON TARTS

Sweet and spicy holiday dessert

Tart shells (pastry for 2-crust pie)
1 envelope unflavored gelatin
¾ c. light brown sugar, firmly packed
½ tsp. salt
1 tsp. pumpkin pie spice
3 eggs, separated
¾ c. milk
1¼ c. canned pumpkin
⅓ c. sugar
Whipped cream
Amber Caramel Sauce

· Combine gelatin, brown sugar, salt and spice in saucepan. Combine egg yolks and milk; stir into gelatin mixture. Cook, stirring constantly, until mixture comes to a boil. Remove from heat; add pumpkin. Chill mixture until it mounds slightly when dropped from spoon. Test frequently for mounding stage.

· Beat egg whites until frothy; add ⅓ c. sugar and beat until glossy, stiff peaks form.

· Fold pumpkin mixture into egg whites. Spoon into tart shells. Chill until firm. Serve topped with whipped cream; pass Amber Caramel Sauce to pour over. Makes about 12 (3″) tarts.

AMBER CARAMEL SAUCE: Combine 1 c. brown sugar, firmly packed, ½ c. light corn syrup and ½ c. water in small saucepan and bring to a boil. Cook, uncovered, 5 minutes.

· Remove from heat; stir in 1 tsp. vanilla. Serve warm or cold. Makes about 1⅓ cups.

Variation

PUMPKIN CHIFFON PIE: Spoon filling into a 9″ Graham Cracker Crumb Crust.

chapter 14

The Cookie Jar

IF YOU HAD A DOLLAR for every batch of cookies baked last year in farm kitchens across the country, you'd be rich. Of all types of baking, cookie-making is most popular. For a good reason; once the cookies are baked and put away, you can serve them on a moment's notice.

Many cookies are good keepers, too, although you may have to hide them or lock them in the freezer! And they come in "portions" which can be multiplied easily. Little children manage them well–fewer crumbs to sweep up than with cake. And cookies encourage milk-drinking, for cookies and milk go together like peaches and cream. Husbands and youngsters are the lovable incentives that turn many a woman into a talented cookie-baker.

There is almost no end to variety in cookies. In the roundup of FARM JOURNAL recipes assembled through the years, even our food staff was amazed at the size of our collection. As we culled, there were constant comments like: We *must* include Lemon/Coconut Squares–so many readers have asked for the recipe. And please put in the molasses cookies –they're so good. So this chapter is one of our big "cookie jars." (An even larger source, is our big cookbook, *Homemade Cookies*.)

Pointers on Freezing Cookies

To Freeze Baked Cookies: Arrange baked, cooled cookies in a box or container lined with aluminum foil or plastic wrap, separating layers with wrap. Seal the foil or wrap, close the box.

• To thaw, let stand in container at room temperature a short time, about 10 minutes.

To Freeze Unbaked Cookies: Package dough for drop cookies in airtight containers or wrap in aluminum foil or plastic wrap. Shape dough for refrigerator cookies in rolls, wrap in aluminum foil or plastic wrap. Package unbaked rolled, cut-out or sliced cookies in frozen food containers, separating layers with double thickness of waxed paper. Keep the number of layers at a minimum to avoid crushing. Freeze dough for bar cookies in the pan in which you will bake it; cover pan. Or freeze in airtight containers.

· To thaw, let dough for drop cookies stand at room temperature until it is soft enough to spoon onto baking sheet. Thaw refrigerator cookie dough enough so that you can slice it. Place frozen rolled, cut-out and sliced cookies on baking sheet without thawing. Slip pan of bar cookie dough into preheated oven without thawing, or if frozen in container, thaw just enough at room temperature to spread dough in pan.

Maximum Storage Time: Baked cookies and cookie dough may be stored 9 to 12 months.

Adaptable Bar Cookies

Bar cookies are the easiest of all to make—bake the dough in a pan and cut it in bars. Almost like a sleight-of-hand performance, you come up with rich, moist cookies. You can serve them plain, snowy with confectioners sugar or frosted and decorated. They serve equally well for dessert, snacks and party refreshments.

Brownies are king in this cookie class. We give you two superior recipes—Candy-top Brownies and Brownies for a Crowd. Many country women prize a few recipes for big-pan cookies that speed the baking. Try our new Almond Brittle Bars, which look like candy and taste twice as good, and our own version of old-fashioned Chocolate Chip Bars.

Success with bar cookies depends to no small extent on using the pan size designated in the recipe. Here are other pointers: Spread or press dough evenly in the pan for uniform baking. To avoid overbaking, test for doneness by inserting a wood pick in the center as you do for a cake. If it comes out clean, the cookies are done. Fudge-type cookies are done when the top looks dull. Partially cool pan of cookies before cutting in bars, unless recipe directs otherwise.

BROWNIES FOR A CROWD

Cookies are moist and they keep well

½ c. regular margarine
1 c. sugar
4 eggs
1 tsp. vanilla
1 (1 lb.) can chocolate syrup (1½ c.)
1 c. plus 1 tblsp. sifted flour
½ tsp. baking powder
¼ tsp. salt
½ c. chopped walnuts
6 tblsp. regular margarine
6 tblsp. milk
1 c. sugar
½ c. semisweet chocolate pieces
1 tsp. vanilla

· Beat ½ c. margarine with 1 c. sugar until light and fluffy. Beat in eggs, two at a time, and 1 tsp. vanilla.

Mix well. Stir in chocolate syrup.
• Sift together flour, baking powder and salt. Stir into chocolate mixture. Add nuts. Pour into well-greased 15½ × 10½ × 1″ jelly roll pan and spread evenly.
• Bake in moderate oven (350°) 22 to 25 minutes, or until slight imprint remains when touched lightly with finger. Remove pan to rack, and let cookies cool.
• Meanwhile, combine 6 tblsp. margarine, milk and 1 c. sugar in saucepan; stir to mix. Bring to a boil and boil 30 seconds. Add chocolate pieces; stir until mixture thickens slightly and cools. Stir in 1 tsp. vanilla. Spread over cooled cookies, then cut in 2½ × 1″ bars. Makes 5 dozen.

CANDY-TOP BROWNIES

These candy-like cookies always win compliments. They're good travelers

2 c. sugar
2 eggs
4 squares unsweetened chocolate
½ c. butter or regular margarine
½ c. flour
2 tsp. vanilla
½ c. chopped walnuts
1 egg, beaten
2 tblsp. light cream
2 tblsp. butter or regular margarine

• Combine 1 c. sugar and 2 eggs; beat.
• Melt 2 squares chocolate with ½ c. butter; add to egg mixture. Blend in flour, 1 tsp. vanilla and nuts. Spread in greased 8″ square pan.
• Bake in moderate oven (350°) 25 to 35 minutes; cool on rack.
• Combine remaining 1 c. sugar, beaten egg, cream, 2 squares chocolate, 2 tblsp. butter and 1 tsp. vanilla. Bring to a boil, stirring constantly. Remove from heat and stir until of spreading consistency. Spread over cooled brownies. Cut in 2″ squares. Makes 16.

LEMON/COCONUT SQUARES

Cookies have fresh lemon-coconut flavor—an all-time favorite

Cookie Dough:
1½ c. sifted flour
½ c. brown sugar, firmly packed
½ c. butter or regular margarine

Filling:
2 eggs, beaten
1 c. brown sugar, firmly packed
1½ c. flaked or shredded coconut
1 c. chopped nuts
2 tblsp. flour
½ tsp. baking powder
¼ tsp. salt
½ tsp. vanilla

Frosting:
1 c. confectioners sugar
1 tblsp. melted butter or regular margarine
Juice of 1 lemon

• Mix together ingredients for cookie dough; pat down well in buttered 13 × 9 × 2″ pan. Bake in very slow oven (275°) 10 minutes.
• To make filling, combine eggs, sugar, coconut, nuts, flour, baking powder, salt and vanilla. Spread on top of baked mixture. Bake in moderate oven (350°) 20 minutes.
• While still warm, spread with frosting made by combining confectioners sugar, melted butter and lemon juice. Cool slightly; cut in 2″ squares. Complete cooling on racks. Makes about 24.

FRUIT BARS

Good keepers—if you hide them

2 c. seedless raisins
1½ c. chopped mixed candied fruit
1 c. chopped walnuts
½ c. orange or pineapple juice
2 tsp. vanilla
1 c. butter or regular margarine
1 c. sugar
1 c. brown sugar, firmly packed
2 eggs, beaten
4½ c. sifted flour
2 tsp. ground cinnamon
2 tsp. baking powder
1 tsp. baking soda

· Rinse raisins in hot water, drain; dry on towel.

· Combine raisins, candied fruit, nuts, juice and vanilla; let stand.

· Cream together butter, sugars and eggs. Sift together dry ingredients and add in thirds to creamed mixture; mix until smooth. Add fruit mixture; blend well. Let stand 1½ hours in refrigerator, or overnight.

· When ready to bake, spread dough in greased 15½ × 10½ × 1″ jelly roll pan. Bake in hot oven (400°) 15 to 20 minutes, until lightly browned. Cool in pan set on rack. When cool, cut in bars about 3 × 1″. Makes about 4 dozen.

NUT AND FRUIT BARS

These cookies are cash catchers at Christmas food sales—they sell fast

3 eggs
1 tsp. vanilla
1 c. sugar
1 c. sifted flour
½ tsp. salt
1 tsp. baking powder
1 c. chopped walnuts
1 (8 oz.) pkg. pitted dates
1 (6 oz.) jar maraschino cherries, drained
Confectioners sugar

· Combine eggs and vanilla. Beat well. Add sugar and flour sifted with salt and baking powder; blend well. Stir in nuts and fruits.

· Bake in greased 15½ × 10½ × 1″ jelly roll pan in moderate oven (350°) 30 minutes. Cool in pan on rack. Cut in 2″ squares. Sprinkle with sugar. Store in airtight box. Makes 3 dozen.

APPLESAUCE FUDGIES

Cookies retain moisture and freshness longer than many brownies

2 squares unsweetened chocolate
½ c. butter
½ c. sweetened applesauce
2 eggs, beaten
1 c. brown sugar, firmly packed
1 tsp. vanilla
1 c. sifted flour
½ tsp. baking powder
¼ tsp. baking soda
¼ tsp. salt
½ c. chopped walnuts

· Melt chocolate and butter together.

· Mix applesauce, eggs, sugar and vanilla. Sift dry ingredients into applesauce mixture. Stir until blended; add chocolate and stir well.

· Pour into greased 9″ square pan. Sprinkle with walnuts. Bake in moderate oven (350°) 30 minutes. Cut in 2¼″ squares; cool in pan on racks. Makes 16.

ALMOND BRITTLE BARS

Break these crisp cookies in irregular pieces—they'll look like candy

1 c. butter or regular margarine
2 tsp. instant coffee powder

1 tsp. salt
¾ tsp. almond extract
1 c. sugar
2 c. sifted flour
1 (6 oz.) pkg. semisweet chocolate pieces
½ c. finely chopped almonds

• Beat together butter, coffee powder, salt and almond extract. Gradually beat in sugar; beat until light and fluffy.
• Stir in flour and chocolate pieces. Press batter into ungreased 15½ × 10½ × 1″ jelly roll pan. Sprinkle almonds over top.
• Bake in moderate oven (375°) 23 to 25 minutes, or until golden brown. Set pan on rack; cut in 2½ × 1½″ bars while warm. When cool, remove from pan. Makes 40.

Note: If you want to break the cookies in irregular pieces, cool baked cookie dough in pan on rack, then break it in pieces with your fingers.

CHOCOLATE CHIP BARS

You bake these cookies in a big pan

1 c. butter or regular margarine
1 c. light brown sugar, firmly packed
1 tsp. vanilla
⅛ tsp. salt
2 c. sifted flour
1 (6 oz.) pkg. semisweet chocolate pieces
1 c. chopped pecans or walnuts

• Beat butter with sugar until mixture is light and fluffy. Beat in vanilla.
• Blend salt with flour and stir into beaten mixture, mixing well. Fold in chocolate pieces and nuts. Press into ungreased 15½ × 10½ × 1″ jelly roll pan.
• Bake in moderate oven (350°) 20 minutes. While warm, cut in 2½ × 1½″ bars. Cool in pan on rack. Makes 3 dozen.

LEBKUCHEN

Spiced cookies with glazed tops

¾ c. honey
¾ c. sugar
1 large egg
1 tsp. grated lemon peel
1 tblsp. milk
2¾ c. sifted flour
½ tsp. salt
1 tsp. ground cinnamon
1 tsp. ground allspice
¼ tsp. ground cloves
⅓ c. chopped citron
½ c. chopped blanched almonds
1 c. sifted confectioners sugar
4 tsp. water (about)

• In large saucepan heat honey slightly, but do not boil. Remove from heat and stir in sugar. Beat in egg, then add lemon peel and milk.
• Sift together flour, salt, cinnamon, allspice and cloves. Stir, a little at a time, into honey mixture. Stir in citron and almonds. Form dough into a ball; wrap in waxed paper and chill several hours or overnight.
• Divide dough in half and let stand 15 to 20 minutes to warm slightly to make spreading in pans easier. Spread each half in a greased 13 × 9 × 2″ pan (use a metal spoon moistened in water to spread dough).
• Bake pans of dough separately in hot oven (400°) about 15 minutes, or until lightly browned. (Or test for doneness by touching lightly with fingertip. If no imprint remains, cookies are done.)

· Place pans on cooling racks and brush cookie tops at once with confectioners sugar mixed with enough water to make a smooth icing. While still warm, cut in 3 × 1″ bars or diamond shapes; remove from pans to cool on racks. When cool, store cookies in airtight containers. They will keep several weeks. Four or five days before serving, a cut apple or orange placed in canisters mellows and improves flavor of cookies. Makes about 6 dozen.

ENGLISH TEA SQUARES

Strawberry jam fills these cookies

¾ c. butter or regular margarine
1 c. sugar
1 egg
1 tsp. vanilla
2 c. sifted flour
¼ tsp. ground allspice
1 c. chopped almonds or walnuts
½ c. strawberry jam
3 tblsp. confectioners sugar

· Beat butter until light; add sugar and beat until light and fluffy. Beat in egg and vanilla to blend well. Stir in flour, allspice and almonds.

· Spoon about half of mixture into lightly greased 9″ square pan. Carefully spread strawberry jam over top. Top with remaining dough.

· Bake in moderate oven (350°) 40 to 45 minutes, or until delicately browned. Remove to cooling rack and sift confectioners sugar over top. When cool, cut in 1½″ squares. Makes 3 dozen.

CHEESECAKE BARS

They taste luscious like cheesecake

⅓ c. butter or regular margarine
⅓ c. brown sugar, firmly packed
1 c. sifted flour
½ c. chopped walnuts
¼ c. sugar
1 (8 oz.) pkg. cream cheese
1 egg, beaten
2 tblsp. milk
1 tblsp. lemon juice
½ tsp. vanilla

· Cream butter and brown sugar until light; add flour and chopped walnuts. Cream with spoon until mixture forms crumbs. Set aside 1 c. mixture for topping. Press remaining crumb mixture into ungreased 8″ square pan.

· Bake in moderate oven (350°) 12 to 15 minutes. Set pan on rack to cool.

· Combine white sugar and cream cheese; beat until smooth. Add egg, milk, lemon juice and vanilla. Beat thoroughly to mix. Spread evenly in pan over baked crumbs. Sprinkle reserved 1 c. crumbs over top.

· Bake in moderate oven (350°) 25 to 30 minutes. Set pan on rack to cool. Cut in 2 × 1″ bars and store in refrigerator. (Cookies are perishable and must be kept in refrigerator until eaten.) Makes 32.

FROSTED CARROT BARS

Cookies are wonderfully moist

4 eggs
2 c. sugar
1½ c. salad oil
2 c. sifted flour
2 tsp. baking soda
2 tsp. ground cinnamon
1 tsp. salt
3 c. finely grated carrots (9 medium)
1½ c. flaked coconut
1½ c. chopped walnuts
Cream Cheese Frosting

• Beat eggs until light; gradually beat in sugar. Alternately add salad oil and flour sifted with soda, cinnamon and salt. Mix well.

• Fold in carrots, coconut and walnuts. Spread evenly in two greased 13 × 9 × 2″ pans.

• Bake in moderate oven (350°) 25 to 30 minutes. Set pans on racks and cool. Spread with Cream Cheese Frosting, then cut in 3 × 1″ bars. Remove from pans and place in covered container. Store in refrigerator or freezer. Makes 6½ dozen.

CREAM CHEESE FROSTING: Blend 1 (3 oz.) pkg. cream cheese with 1 tblsp. dairy half-and-half or whole milk. Add 2½ c. sifted confectioners sugar, 3 tblsp. dairy half-and-half or whole milk (or enough to make a frosting of spreading consistency), 1 tsp. vanilla and ⅛ tsp. salt. Beat to mix.

PENUCHE DREAM BARS

Also try the chocolate variation

Bottom Layer:

½ c. shortening
½ c. brown sugar, firmly packed
1 c. sifted flour
½ tsp. salt
2 tblsp. milk

Top Layer:

2 eggs
1 c. brown sugar, firmly packed
1 tsp. vanilla
½ tsp. salt
2 tblsp. flour
½ tsp. baking powder
1 (3½ oz.) can flaked coconut (1⅓ c.)
1 c. chopped pecans

• For bottom layer, cream shortening and brown sugar until light and fluffy. Mix together flour and salt; add to creamed mixture. Stir in milk. Pat evenly in greased 9″ square pan.

• Bake in slow oven (325°) about 20 minutes, until light brown. Remove from oven.

• To make top layer, combine eggs, brown sugar and vanilla; beat until mixture thickens.

• Sift together salt, flour and baking powder; add to egg mixture. Mix well; stir in coconut and pecans. Spread evenly over baked bottom layer.

• Bake in slow oven (325°) about 20 minutes, until golden brown. Set pan on rack and let cool, then cut in 2¼ × 1″ bars. Makes 3 dozen.

Variation

CHOCOLATE DREAM BARS: Make and bake bottom layer as for Penuche Dream Bars, but use ⅓ c. butter or regular margarine instead of ½ c. shortening. Make top layer, substituting 1 (6 oz.) pkg. semisweet chocolate pieces for the coconut. Spread on baked layer and bake 15 to 20 minutes. Cool in pan on rack. Spread Easy Chocolate Icing on top and cut in 2¼ × 1″ bars.

EASY CHOCOLATE ICING: Melt 1 tsp. butter with 1 square unsweetened chocolate over warm, not boiling, water. Remove from heat and stir in 1½ to 2 tblsp. hot water. Add enough sifted confectioners sugar (about 1 c.) to make icing that spreads easily. Beat until smooth. Makes enough to ice from 3 to 4 dozen cookies, depending on size, or a 9″ square pan of cookies.

DATE SANDWICH BARS

Easy to tote when you're asked to bring cookies. They'll win praise

- ¼ c. sugar
- 3 c. cut-up dates
- 1½ c. water
- ¾ c. soft butter or regular margarine
- 1 c. brown sugar, firmly packed
- 1¾ c. sifted flour
- ½ tsp. baking soda
- 1 tsp. salt
- 1½ c. quick-cooking rolled oats

· Mix sugar, dates and water, and cook over low heat until mixture thickens. Stir to prevent scorching. Set aside to cool.

· Thoroughly mix butter and brown sugar. Beat until fluffy.

· Stir flour, baking soda and salt together. Stir into the brown sugar-butter mixture. Add rolled oats and mix well. Divide in half and spread one part into greased 13 × 9 × 2″ pan. Flatten and press it down with hands so the mixture will cover the bottom of the pan.

· Spread the cooled date mixture on top. Sprinkle evenly with the second half of the rolled oat mixture. Pat it down lightly with hands.

· Bake in hot oven (400°) 25 to 30 minutes, or until a delicate brown. Remove from oven; while warm, cut in 2 × 1½″ bars. Remove bars at once from pan to racks to cool. Makes about 30.

SEA FOAM COOKIES

You sprinkle peanuts on meringue top

- ½ c. shortening
- ½ c. sugar
- ½ c. brown sugar, firmly packed
- 2 eggs, separated
- 1 tsp. vanilla
- 2 c. sifted flour
- 2 tsp. baking powder
- 1 tsp. baking soda
- ½ tsp. salt
- 3 tblsp. milk
- 1 (6 oz.) pkg. semisweet chocolate pieces
- 1 c. brown sugar, firmly packed
- ¾ c. chopped salted peanuts

· Cream shortening with sugar and ½ c. brown sugar until light and fluffy. Beat in egg yolks and vanilla.

· Sift together flour, baking powder, soda and salt; stir into creamed mixture alternately with milk. (The dough will be stiff.) Press dough into greased 13 × 9 × 2″ pan. Sprinkle evenly with chocolate pieces.

· Beat egg whites until soft peaks form; gradually add remaining 1 c. brown sugar and beat until very stiff and glossy. Spread over dough in pan. Scatter peanuts evenly over top.

· Bake in slow oven (325°) 30 to 35 minutes. Cool in pan set on rack, then cut in 3 × 1″ bars. Makes 39.

FROSTED MOLASSES CREAMS

Coffee flavors these molasses cookies

- ½ c. shortening
- ½ c. sugar
- 1 egg, beaten
- ½ c. molasses
- ⅓ c. strong, hot coffee
- 1½ c. sifted flour
- 1½ tsp. baking powder
- ¾ tsp. salt
- ¼ tsp. baking soda
- 1 tsp. ground cinnamon
- ½ tsp. ground cloves
- Creamy Coffee Icing

· Cream together shortening and

sugar; blend in egg, molasses and coffee.

• Sift together dry ingredients; add to creamed mixture and blend well. Pour into greased and waxed paper-lined 13 × 9 × 2″ pan.

• Bake in moderate oven (350°) 25 minutes. While warm, frost with Creamy Coffee Icing. Cool in pan on rack, then cut in 3 × 1″ bars. Makes about 39.

CREAMY COFFEE ICING: Cream ¼ c. butter or margarine with 2 c. confectioners sugar. Add about 2 tblsp. cold coffee, enough to make an icing of spreading consistency; mix until smooth.

CHOCOLATE/WALNUT COOKIES

Country kitchen favorite, rich with the taste of chocolate and black walnuts

1 c. sugar
2 eggs, well beaten
2 squares unsweetened chocolate
½ c. butter or regular margarine
1 c. sifted flour
1 tsp. baking powder
¼ tsp. salt
1 c. finely chopped black walnuts
1 tsp. vanilla
Sifted confectioners sugar

• Gradually add sugar to eggs. Melt chocolate with butter; stir into eggs.

• Sift together flour, baking powder and salt. Add to first mixture with nuts and vanilla.

• Bake in greased 15½ × 10½ × 1″ jelly roll pan in moderate oven (350°) 12 to 15 minutes. Cool slightly in pan; dust with confectioners sugar. Cool completely in pan on rack; cut in diamonds, triangles or 1¾″ bars. Makes about 7 dozen.

Family-favorite Drop Cookies

Most cookie jars or freezers in country homes store drop cookies, first choice of all cookies in many a family. Some drop cookies are hearty, such as Chocolate Hermits, California Fig Cookies, and Hampshire Hermits with a delightful faint blend of lemon and citron flavors.

The Kansas City homemaker who introduced FARM JOURNAL food editors to Chocolate Hermits makes small cookies when she entertains women guests; she frosts them and decorates each top with a chocolate curl. But they can be adapted to the occasion. When men are among the guests, she makes man-size cookies spread with a thick layer of frosting.

BEST-EVER BUTTERSCOTCH COOKIES

Taste-testers gave these blue ribbons

1 tblsp. vinegar
1 c. evaporated milk (about)
½ c. butter or regular margarine
1½ c. brown sugar, firmly packed
2 eggs
1 tsp. vanilla
2½ c. sifted flour
1 tsp. baking soda
½ tsp. baking powder
½ tsp. salt
⅔ c. chopped walnuts or pecans
Brown Butter Frosting
Walnut or pecan halves

• Put vinegar in a 1-cup measure;

add evaporated milk and set aside.

· Beat butter until light; add brown sugar and beat until mixture is light and fluffy. Beat in eggs and vanilla to blend thoroughly.

· Sift together flour, baking soda, baking powder and salt.

· Stir evaporated milk and add alternately with dry ingredients to creamed mixture. Stir in chopped nuts. Drop rounded tablespoonfuls of dough about 2½″ apart onto lightly greased baking sheet.

· Bake in moderate oven (350°) 10 to 12 minutes, or until lightly browned and barely firm to touch. Remove cookies and cool on racks. When cool, spread with Brown Butter Frosting and press a walnut or pecan half in each cookie. Makes about 5 dozen.

BROWN BUTTER FROSTING: Melt ½ c. butter in small saucepan and cook over medium heat, stirring constantly, until butter stops bubbling and is nut-brown in color (do not scorch). Combine with 2 c. sifted confectioners sugar and 2 to 4 tblsp. boiling water; beat until smooth and of spreading consistency. Makes enough to frost about 5 dozen cookies.

CREAM CHEESE DROP COOKIES

Lemon and cheese flavors blend tastily

¾ c. butter
1 (3 oz.) pkg. cream cheese
1 c. sifted confectioners sugar
1 tblsp. lemon juice
1 tsp. vanilla
2 tsp. grated lemon peel
2 c. sifted cake flour
1 c. chopped pecans
Sifted confectioners sugar (for rolling)

· Cream butter and cream cheese until light and fluffy. Gradually add 1 c. confectioners sugar, beating thoroughly. Stir in lemon juice, vanilla and lemon peel. Add flour and mix well. Stir in nuts.

· Drop by scant teaspoonfuls about 2″ apart onto ungreased baking sheet. Bake in slow oven (300°) about 25 minutes, until set but not brown. While hot roll in sifted confectioners sugar. Cool on racks. Makes 4 dozen.

GUESS-AGAIN COOKIES

Crisp bits in these are potato chips!

1 c. butter or regular margarine
½ c. sugar
1 tsp. vanilla
2 c. sifted flour
½ c. crushed potato chips
½ c. chopped pecans

· Beat butter, sugar and vanilla until light and fluffy. Add flour, potato chips and nuts; mix well.

· Drop by scant teaspoonfuls 2″ apart onto ungreased baking sheet. Flatten by pressing with bottom of drinking glass, greased and dipped in sugar (grease and sugar glass as needed).

· Bake in moderate oven (350°) 10 to 11 minutes. Remove to racks to cool. Makes about 5 dozen.

FLORENTINES

Lacy cookies for special occasions

¾ c. heavy cream
¼ c. sugar

¼ c. sifted flour
½ c. very finely chopped slivered blanched almonds
¾ c. very finely chopped candied orange peel (4 oz. pkg.)
2 (4 oz.) bars sweet cooking chocolate

• Stir cream and sugar together to blend well. Stir in flour, almonds and orange peel. Drop by scant teaspoonfuls about 1¼″ apart onto heavily greased and floured baking sheet. *Flatten cookies with spatula;* they will be about ½ to ¾″ apart after flattening.
• Bake in moderate oven (350°) about 10 to 12 minutes, until cookies brown lightly around edges. (Centers of cookies will be bubbling when you remove them from oven.) Let stand 2 or 3 minutes or until they become firmer. Place on wire rack or waxed paper to cool.
• Meanwhile, melt chocolate over hot, not boiling, water. When cookies are cool, turn upside down and brush with melted chocolate. Let dry several hours or overnight at room temperature to give chocolate time to set. (In hot, humid weather, use chocolate confection coating, melted, instead of sweet cooking chocolate.) Store in covered container in refrigerator or freezer. Makes about 4 dozen.

PUMPKIN COOKIES

Mother's choice—children eat these soft cookies without making crumbs

½ c. shortening
1¼ c. brown sugar, firmly packed
2 eggs
1 tsp. vanilla
1½ c. mashed cooked or canned pumpkin
2½ c. sifted flour
4 tsp. baking powder
½ tsp. salt
½ tsp. ground cinnamon
½ tsp. ground nutmeg
1 c. raisins
1 c. chopped nuts

• Cream together shortening and brown sugar. Add eggs; beat thoroughly. Mix in vanilla and pumpkin.
• Sift together dry ingredients. Blend into creamed mixture. Stir in raisins and chopped nuts.
• Drop dough by heaping teaspoonfuls about 2″ apart onto greased baking sheet. Bake in a moderate oven (375°) about 15 minutes until lightly browned. Remove cookies and cool on racks. Makes 5 dozen.

WALNUT LACE COOKIES

Crisp, thin, fragile and very delicious

⅓ c. sifted flour
½ tsp. baking powder
⅛ tsp. salt
¼ c. butter or regular margarine
1 c. brown sugar, firmly packed
1 egg, slightly beaten
1 c. chopped walnuts

• Sift together dry ingredients.
• Blend butter, brown sugar and sifted dry ingredients with pastry blender as for pie crust. Add egg and mix thoroughly. Stir in walnuts.
• Drop thin batter by half teaspoonfuls about 2″ apart onto heavily greased baking sheet. (Cookies spread during baking.) Bake in moderate oven (375°) 5 to 6 minutes. Remove from baking sheet at once and cool on racks. Makes about 5½ dozen.

CALIFORNIA FIG COOKIES

Favorite of California ranchers—bake them and you'll understand why

- 1 c. chopped golden or black figs (½ lb.)
- ⅓ c. water
- 1 c. butter or regular margarine
- ½ c. sugar
- ½ c. brown sugar, firmly packed
- 1 egg
- 1 tsp. vanilla
- 2 c. sifted flour
- 2 tsp. baking powder
- ½ tsp. salt
- Walnut or pecan halves (optional)

• Cook figs with water, stirring frequently, until thickened, about 5 minutes. Set aside to cool.

• Beat butter with both sugars until light and fluffy; beat in egg and vanilla to blend well.

• Sift together flour, baking powder and salt. Mix into creamed mixture. Then stir in cooled figs.

• Drop by teaspoonfuls about 2″ apart onto lightly greased baking sheet. Press a walnut half on top of each cookie. Bake in moderate oven (375°) 10 to 12 minutes, until lightly browned. Remove cookies and cool. Makes 4 dozen.

HAMPSHIRE HERMITS

Lemon Glaze complements the citron flavor in these hearty cookies

- ⅔ c. butter or regular margarine
- 1 c. light brown sugar, firmly packed
- 2 eggs
- 2 tblsp. dairy sour cream or buttermilk
- 1¾ c. sifted flour
- 1¾ tsp. ground cinnamon
- ¼ tsp. ground ginger
- ¼ tsp. cloves
- ¼ tsp. baking soda
- ⅛ tsp. salt
- 1 c. chopped nuts
- ½ c. chopped raisins or currants
- ½ c. finely chopped citron
- Lemon Glaze

• Beat butter until light. Gradually add brown sugar and beat after each addition until light and fluffy. Beat in eggs, one at a time, beating to mix thoroughly. Stir in sour cream.

• Sift together flour, spices, baking soda and salt. Add to creamed mixture and beat until batter is smooth. Gradually add nuts, raisins and citron.

• Drop batter from tablespoon 2″ apart onto greased baking sheet. Bake in moderate oven (350°) about 12 to 15 minutes, until cookies are golden brown. Remove cookies to racks and while warm, brush with Lemon Glaze. Makes about 3 dozen.

LEMON GLAZE: Add 2 tblsp. lemon juice to 1 c. sifted confectioners sugar. Stir until smooth; brush over warm cookies (glaze is thin and tart).

POWDERED SUGAR COOKIES

The rich, dainty cookies please guests

- ½ c. shortening
- ½ c. butter
- 1½ c. confectioners sugar
- 1 egg
- 1 tsp. vanilla
- ¼ tsp. almond extract
- 2½ c. sifted flour
- 1 tsp. baking soda
- 1 tsp. cream of tartar
- ¼ tsp. salt
- 1 c. chopped pecans
- ¾ c. confectioners sugar (for coating)

• Beat shortening and butter until

light; gradually add 1½ c. confectioners sugar, beating constantly. Beat in egg, vanilla and almond extract to mix well.

• Sift together flour, baking soda, cream of tartar and salt. Add to creamed mixture. Stir in nuts.

• Drop by teaspoonfuls 1″ apart onto ungreased baking sheet. (Or shape in 1″ balls.) Bake in hot oven (400°) 8 to 10 minutes. Remove to cooling racks, and while still warm, roll in confectioners sugar. When cool, roll in confectioners sugar again for snowy white coating. Makes about 6 dozen.

SOFT MOLASSES COOKIES

Family-style cookies like Grandma used to make—we updated the recipe

1 c. butter or regular margarine
1 c. sugar
1 large egg
1 c. light molasses
4¾ c. sifted flour
3 tsp. baking soda
½ tsp. salt
1 tsp. instant coffee powder
2 tsp. ground cinnamon
1 tsp. ground ginger
½ tsp. ground cloves
¾ c. milk
Raisins or walnut halves

• Beat butter until light; gradually add sugar and beat until fluffy. Beat in egg to blend thoroughly; then beat in molasses.

• Sift together flour, baking soda, salt, coffee powder and spices. Add to first mixture alternately with milk. Beat about 30 seconds.

• Drop dough by heaping teaspoonfuls about 2″ apart onto lightly greased baking sheet, using care to keep cookies round. Press a raisin in center of each cookie.

• Bake in moderate oven (375°) about 12 to 15 minutes, or until done. Place cookies on racks to cool. Makes about 5½ dozen.

BLACK WALNUT COOKIES

Tastes like sour cream cookies Grandma served with applesauce

½ c. shortening
¾ c. sugar
1 egg
½ tsp. vanilla
2 c. sifted flour
1 tsp. baking powder
1 tsp. ground cinnamon
½ tsp. salt
¼ tsp. baking soda
½ c. dairy sour cream
½ c. chopped black walnuts

• Cream shortening and sugar until light and fluffy. Beat in egg and vanilla.

• Sift together dry ingredients. Add to creamed mixture alternately with sour cream. Stir in walnuts.

• Drop by teaspoonfuls about 2″ apart onto greased baking sheet. Press flat with bottom of drinking glass, dipping glass into sugar before pressing each cookie.

• Bake in moderate oven (375°) 9 to 12 minutes. Remove cookies and cool on racks. Makes 4½ dozen.

CORN FLAKE COOKIES

Coconut makes these cookies special

2 c. sifted flour
1 tsp. baking soda
½ tsp. salt
½ tsp. baking powder
1¼ c. shortening
1 c. sugar
1 c. brown sugar, firmly packed
2 eggs, well beaten
1 tsp. vanilla
2 c. flaked or shredded coconut
2 c. corn flakes

· Sift together flour, soda, salt and baking powder.

· Cream shortening; gradually add sugars; beat until light. Add eggs and vanilla.

· Combine dry ingredients and creamed mixture; add coconut and corn flakes.

· Drop small teaspoonfuls 1½" apart onto greased baking sheet.

· Bake in moderate oven (350°) 8 to 10 minutes, or until delicately browned. Spread on racks to cool. Makes 8 dozen.

CHOCOLATE HERMITS

Make dainty, tea-size or man-size cookies according to your needs. Top with a chocolate confectioners sugar frosting (see Index)*—a decorative curl for dainty, tea-size, a generous covering for the man-size cookies*

1⅓ c. sifted flour
2 tsp. baking powder
½ tsp. salt
1 tsp. ground cinnamon
½ c. shortening
1 c. sugar
1 egg, well beaten
3 squares unsweetened chocolate, melted
1 tsp. vanilla
⅓ c. milk
1 c. chopped raisins
1 c. chopped nuts

· Sift together flour, baking powder, salt and cinnamon.

· Cream shortening; add sugar gradually; cream until fluffy.

· Add egg to creamed mixture with chocolate; blend well. Add vanilla and milk. Stir in dry ingredients, raisins and nuts. Mix well; chill 30 minutes.

· Drop by teaspoonfuls about 2" apart onto greased baking sheet. Bake in moderate oven (350°) 15 minutes. Remove cookies and cool. Makes 2 dozen.

TWO-WAY COOKIES

As easy to bake chocolate/orange and coconut cookies as one kind

4 c. sifted flour
1 tsp. salt
1 tsp. baking soda
1 c. regular margarine
1 c. sugar
1¼ c. light brown sugar, firmly packed
3 eggs
1 tsp. vanilla
½ tsp. orange extract
1 (6 oz.) pkg. semisweet chocolate pieces
1 (3½ oz.) can flaked coconut

· Sift together flour, salt and baking soda.

· Cream margarine until fluffy; gradually add sugars. Add eggs, one at a time, beating thoroughly after each addition. Add vanilla; blend.

· Add sifted dry ingredients. Mix well. Divide batter in half.

· Add orange extract and chocolate pieces to one half dough and coconut to other half. Drop by rounded teaspoonfuls about 2" apart onto greased baking sheet.

· Bake in a moderate oven (350°) 12 to 15 minutes. Remove cookies and cool on racks. Makes about 6 dozen.

CARAMEL APPLE COOKIES

You can frost the cookies before freezing or just before serving

½ c. shortening
1⅓ c. brown sugar, firmly packed
1 egg
2¼ c. sifted flour

1 tsp. baking soda
½ tsp. salt
1 tsp. ground cinnamon
1 tsp. ground cloves
½ tsp. ground nutmeg
1 c. grated peeled apples
1 c. light raisins
½ c. apple juice
1 c. chopped walnuts
Caramel Icing

· Cream shortening, sugar and egg until light and fluffy. Sift together dry ingredients and add to creamed mixture. When well blended, stir in remaining ingredients, except icing.
· Drop by level tablespoonfuls 3″ apart onto greased baking sheet. Bake in moderate oven (350°) about 12 minutes, or until lightly browned.
· Remove cookies and cool on racks. When cool, spread with Caramel Icing. Makes about 4 dozen.

CARAMEL ICING: Combine ¼ c. butter and ¼ c. brown sugar, firmly packed, in saucepan; cook until sugar dissolves, about 3 minutes. Add 1½ c. sifted confectioners sugar, ¼ tsp. salt and 2½ tblsp. dairy half-and-half or light cream; beat until smooth. (If frosting becomes too thick when spreading on cookies, thin it by adding a little more cream.)

FRUITY GUMDROP COOKIES

Apples, gumdrops and raisins—no wonder the cookies are so tasty

2 c. sifted flour
½ tsp. salt
2 tsp. baking powder
½ tsp. ground cinnamon
½ c. shortening
½ c. sugar
1 egg, beaten
¾ c. thick applesauce
1 c. gumdrops, cut in small pieces (no black candies)
1 c. raisins

· Sift together flour, salt, baking powder and cinnamon.
· Cream shortening and sugar; add egg and applesauce; mix well.
· Add flour mixture; stir until well blended; stir in gumdrops and raisins.
· Drop by teaspoonfuls about 2″ apart onto lightly greased baking sheet. Bake in hot oven (400°) 10 to 15 minutes, until lightly browned. Transfer to cooling rack. Makes 4 dozen.

ORANGE/CARROT COOKIES

Cheerful as a Kansas sunflower—kind to the budget, attractive and tasty

1 c. shortening
¾ c. sugar
1 c. mashed cooked carrots
1 egg
1 tsp. vanilla
2 c. sifted flour
2 tsp. baking powder
½ tsp. salt
Golden Glow Topping

· Cream shortening and sugar until fluffy. Add carrots, egg and vanilla; mix well.
· Sift together flour, baking powder and salt; add to carrot mixture; mix well. Drop batter by teaspoonfuls about 2″ apart onto greased baking sheet.
· Bake in moderate oven (350°) about 20 minutes. Place cookies on racks to cool. While warm, spread with Golden Glow Topping. Makes 5 dozen.

GOLDEN GLOW TOPPING: Combine juice of ½ orange, grated peel of 1 orange, 1 tblsp. butter or regular margarine and 1 c. sifted confectioners sugar. Blend until smooth.

ORANGE-GLAZED PRUNE COOKIES

Brown cookies with yellow topknots

- **2 c. brown sugar, firmly packed**
- **1 c. butter or shortening**
- **2 eggs, beaten**
- **½ c. milk**
- **3½ c. sifted flour**
- **1 tsp. baking powder**
- **1 tsp. baking soda**
- **1 tsp. ground cinnamon**
- **½ tsp. salt**
- **2 c. chopped cooked prunes**
- **1 c. chopped walnuts**
- **1 tsp. vanilla**
- **Orange Glaze**

· Cream together sugar and butter; stir in eggs and milk.

· Sift together flour, baking powder, soda, cinnamon and salt; stir into creamed mixture. Add prunes, nuts and vanilla.

· Drop by teaspoonfuls about 2″ apart onto greased baking sheet. Bake in moderate oven (350°) 15 to 20 minutes, until lightly browned. Remove cookies and cool on racks.

· Spread tops of cooled cookies with a thin layer of Orange Glaze. Makes 8½ dozen.

ORANGE GLAZE: Combine 3 c. confectioners sugar, grated peel of 1 orange and ¼ c. orange juice. Blend thoroughly until smooth.

OATMEAL/COCONUT CRISPS

You can keep dough tightly covered in refrigerator several days to bake as needed. A big recipe—a great cookie

- **2 c. butter or regular margarine**
- **2 c. brown sugar, firmly packed**
- **2 c. sugar**
- **2 tsp. vanilla**
- **4 eggs**
- **3 c. sifted flour**
- **2 tsp. salt**
- **2 tsp. baking soda**
- **6 c. quick-cooking rolled oats**
- **1½ c. flaked coconut**

· Cream together butter and brown and white sugars until fluffy. Stir in vanilla; then add eggs, one at a time, beating after each addition.

· Sift together flour, salt and baking soda. Add to creamed mixture. Stir in rolled oats and coconut. Drop by teaspoonfuls about 2″ apart onto well-greased baking sheet.

· Bake in moderate oven (350°) 10 to 15 minutes. Cool cookies on racks. Makes 14 dozen.

Note: You can omit the 1½ c. coconut and divide dough into thirds. Add ⅓ c. flaked coconut to one part, ⅓ c. raisins to second part and ⅓ c. chopped walnuts to the third part.

Variations

OATMEAL/RAISIN COOKIES: Use 1½ c. raisins instead of the coconut.

OATMEAL/NUT COOKIES: Use 1½ c. chopped walnuts instead of the coconut.

OATMEAL/BUTTER CRISPS: Omit the flaked coconut.

SALTED PEANUT COOKIES

Discovered by a food scout in Maine —cookies always get favorable reception

- **2 eggs**
- **2 c. brown sugar, firmly packed**
- **1½ c. melted butter or regular margarine**
- **1½ c. chopped salted peanuts**

2½ c. sifted flour
1 tsp. baking soda
1 tsp. baking powder
½ tsp. salt
3 c. rolled oats
1 c. corn flakes

· Beat eggs; add sugar and mix well. Stir in butter, then peanuts and mix.
· Sift together flour, soda, baking powder and salt. Combine with rolled oats and corn flakes. Combine with egg mixture and stir well to mix.
· Drop by tablespoonfuls about 2″ apart onto greased baking sheet. Bake in hot oven (400°) 8 to 10 minutes. Makes 6 dozen.

Note: You can drop the dough from a teaspoon for dainty tea- or coffee-time treats, instead of the family-size cookies.

Rolled Cookies for All Occasions

You can cut rolled cookies in shapes to fit the season or theme—they're most versatile. Arrange Easter Lamb Cookies on a plate or tray spread with green cellophane grass for a charming centerpiece. Serve Wild Rose Cookies at your late spring party to suggest the lovely pink blooms along the roadside. Bake Sugar Cookies cut in fancy shapes, and decorate them to tie with ribbons and hang on the Christmas tree. If you can't find cutters the shapes you want, cut your design from heavy cardboard. Grease it on one side, lay greased side down on rolled dough and cut around the pattern with a knife dipped in flour.

When making rolled cookies, rub flour into the stockinet cover on the rolling pin and lightly into the pastry cloth. This helps to keep dough from sticking. If dough is too soft to roll easily, chill it.

Roll dough lightly to even thickness so the cookies will bake uniformly. (The thinner the dough, the crisper the cookies). Dip cutter in flour and shake off excess; then cut cookies close together. Lift cutouts with broad spatula onto baking sheet to avoid stretching them out of shape. Remove from baking sheets and spread on cooling racks as soon as they come from the oven.

HARD-COOKED EGG COOKIES

Nuts and cinnamon decorate tops of these rich, yellow cookies

1 c. butter or regular margarine
1 c. sugar
1 egg
5 sieved hard-cooked egg yolks (about 1 c.)
1 tblsp. finely grated lemon peel
3 c. sifted flour
1 egg, slightly beaten
1 tsp. sugar
2 tsp. ground cinnamon
½ c. chopped nuts

· Beat butter, 1 c. sugar and 1 egg to blend thoroughly. Add hard-cooked egg yolks and lemon peel. Stir in flour.
· Roll dough about ¼″ thick on lightly floured surface; cut with 2″ round cutter. Place ½″ apart on ungreased baking sheet. Brush tops of cookies with slightly beaten egg.
· Combine 1 tsp. sugar and cinnamon; sprinkle sugar-cinnamon mixture and nuts over cookies.
· Bake in slow oven (325°) 20 to 25 minutes, or until delicately browned. Remove cookies and cool

on racks. Store in container with loose-fitting lid to retain crispness. Makes about 52.

Variation

MOLDED HARD-COOKED EGG COOKIES: Instead of rolling dough, shape in 1″ balls. Place 2″ apart on ungreased baking sheet. Flatten by pressing with lightly greased bottom of juice glass. Brush tops with slightly beaten egg, sprinkle with sugar-cinnamon mixture and nuts, and bake like rolled cookies. Makes about 68 molded cookies.

GINGER COOKIES FOR A CROWD

A big recipe to make when you wish to put cookies in the freezer

5½ c. sifted flour
1 tblsp. baking soda
2 tsp. baking powder
1 tsp. salt
¾ tsp. ground ginger
1 tsp. ground cinnamon
1 c. shortening
1 c. sugar
1 egg, beaten
½ tsp. vanilla
1 c. dark molasses
½ c. strong coffee

· Sift together flour, soda, baking powder, salt, ginger and cinnamon.
· Cream shortening; add sugar gradually; beat until light; add egg and vanilla.
· Add molasses and coffee, then sifted dry ingredients; mix well; chill.
· Roll out on lightly floured board ¼″ thick; cut with round 2″ cutter.
· Place about 2″ apart on greased baking sheet. Bake in hot oven (400°) 8 to 10 minutes. Spread on racks to cool. Makes 12 dozen.

COUNTRY MOLASSES COOKIES

Cutouts as varied as the shape and size of your cookie cutters

1 c. sugar
1 c. shortening
1 c. light molasses
1 tblsp. vinegar
6 c. sifted flour
½ tsp. salt
1 tsp. baking soda
½ tsp. baking powder
1 tsp. ground ginger
1 tsp. ground cinnamon
2 eggs, beaten

· Combine sugar, shortening, molasses and vinegar in saucepan; bring to boil and cook 2 minutes. Cool.
· Sift together flour, salt, soda, baking powder and spices.
· Add eggs to cooled molasses mixture. Add dry ingredients and mix well. Chill.
· Roll out dough on lightly floured board, about ⅛ to ¼″ thick. Cut with cookie cutters of desired shapes; place 1″ apart on greased baking sheet.
· Bake in moderate oven (375°) 8 to 10 minutes, or until done. Transfer cookies to racks to cool. Makes about 12 dozen.

HONEY WAFERS

Crisp, dainty bran cookies—superior

½ c. butter
½ c. honey
2 c. sifted flour
1 tsp. baking soda
½ tsp. ground cinnamon
¼ tsp. ground cloves
¼ tsp. ground allspice
¼ c. crushed bran flakes

· Cream together butter and honey.

· Sift together flour, baking soda, cinnamon, cloves and allspice. Mix with bran flakes.
· Combine dry ingredients with honey and butter. Chill 1 hour, or until firm enough to roll easily.
· Roll ⅛″ thick on lightly floured board. Cut with floured cookie cutter. Place about 2″ apart on greased baking sheet; bake in moderate oven (350°) 8 to 10 minutes. Remove cookies and cool on racks. Makes 3 dozen.

WILD ROSE COOKIES

These party cookies look like flowers

1 c. butter or regular margarine
½ c. very fine granulated sugar (super fine)
¼ tsp. vanilla
2¼ c. sifted flour
Pink decorating sugar
Yellow decorating sugar, or tiny yellow candies

· Cream butter with sugar until light and fluffy; beat in vanilla.
· Divide flour in thirds. Stir first third into creamed mixture and blend well. Repeat with second third and then with last third. Knead gently until smooth, about 5 minutes. Shape in ball, wrap in clear plastic wrap or waxed paper and chill several hours, or overnight.
· Divide dough in fourths. Pat one portion at a time ¼″ thick on lightly floured surface. Cut with 2½″ round scalloped cutter. Place dough cutouts ½ to 1″ apart on ungreased baking sheet. Sprinkle liberally with pink sugar, leaving ¾″ circle in center uncovered.
· Cut a circle of stiff paper about the same size of cookies and cut out a ¾″ circle in center. Lay on cookie and carefully spoon yellow sugar into hole in paper; lift off paper. Or, if you can find small yellow candies, use them.
· Bake in slow oven (325°) 12 to 15 minutes, until firm, but do not brown. Transfer cookies to racks and cool. Makes 5 dozen.

Note: You can bake the cookies after adding pink sugar, cool them and add dots of frosting, tinted yellow, to make the centers. Use ½ recipe for Ornamental Icing. For dainty teatime cookies, use a 1″ round, scalloped cookie cutter.

ORNAMENTAL COOKIE ICING: Combine 1½ to 2 c. confectioners sugar with enough slightly beaten egg white (1 to 2 tblsp.) to make an icing you can put through decorating tube or small plastic bag with small hole cut in one corner, but which will have enough consistency to hold its shape on cookies. Write and draw on cookies with this icing to give them a festive look. A second batch of icing can be made easily if needed.

RAISIN GRIDDLE COOKIES

Keep packages of dough in your freezer to bake on short notice

3½ c. sifted flour
1 c. sugar
1½ tsp. baking powder
1 tsp. salt
½ tsp. baking soda
1 tsp. ground nutmeg
1 c. shortening
1 egg
½ c. milk
1¼ c. raisins

· Sift dry ingredients together into

bowl. Cut in shortening until mixture is mealy.

• Beat egg, add milk and blend. Add egg mixture and raisins to flour mixture. Stir until all the ingredients are moistened and dough holds together.

• Roll on lightly floured board to ¼″ thickness. Cut with 2″ round cutter.

• Heat griddle until a few drops of water dance on it. (Do not overheat griddle.) Oil griddle lightly and place cookies on it. As the bottoms brown, the tops become puffy. Then turn and brown on other side. Serve warm. Makes about 4 dozen.

Variation

LEMON GRIDDLE COOKIES: Make dough for Raisin Griddle Cookies, but omit raisins and add 1 tsp. grated lemon peel. Bake as directed.

PEPPERNUTS

Store these spicy, hard cookies in airtight containers. You can add a slice of apple to mellow them

3 eggs, beaten
3½ c. brown sugar, firmly packed
4 c. sifted flour
1 tsp. baking powder
2 tblsp. ground cinnamon
1 tblsp. ground cloves
Ornamental Cookie Icing (see Index)
Red cinnamon candies (optional)

• Combine eggs and sugar; beat well.

• Sift together dry ingredients; add gradually to egg-sugar mixture (dough will be very stiff).

• Divide dough. Roll with hands on lightly floured board into rolls the thickness of your middle finger. Cut in ½″ slices. Place 1 to 1½″ apart on greased baking sheet.

• Bake in slow oven (300°) 30 minutes. Remove cookies and cool on racks.

• Shortly before serving you can top each peppernut with a dab of Ornamental Cookie Icing and a red cinnamon candy (red hots), if you like. Makes 27 dozen.

FROSTED GINGER CREAMS

Soft cookies iced in white—delicious

1 c. shortening
1 c. brown sugar, firmly packed
2 eggs
1 c. dark molasses
2 tblsp. vinegar
5 c. sifted flour (about)
1 tblsp. ground ginger
1 tblsp. baking soda
½ tsp. baking powder
1 tsp. salt
2 tblsp. butter or regular margarine
2 c. sifted confectioners sugar
1 tsp. vanilla
3 tblsp. milk or cream

• Cream together shortening and brown sugar until light; beat in eggs, one at a time, beating well to blend. Add molasses and vinegar.

• Sift together 4 c. flour, ginger, soda, baking powder and salt; stir into batter. Add additional flour to make a soft dough easy to roll.

• Roll dough on lightly floured surface; cut in 2 or 3″ circles. Place about 1″ apart on lightly greased baking sheet.

• Bake in moderate oven (375°) 10 to 15 minutes. Remove cookies and cool on wire racks.

• Meanwhile, blend butter and confectioners sugar together, add vanilla and milk and beat until smooth. Spread over tops of cooled cookies, leaving a ¼″ rim of brown cookie around the white frosting. Store in airtight containers. Makes 5½ dozen.

EASTER LAMB COOKIES

Stand lambs in green cellophane grass on tray for centerpiece

- **1 c. regular margarine**
- **⅔ c. sugar**
- **1 egg**
- **1 tsp. vanilla**
- **2½ c. sifted flour**
- **½ tsp. baking powder**
- **1 egg, separated**
- **1 c. cookie coconut**
- **¼ tsp. water**
- **2 drops red or blue food color**

• Beat together margarine and sugar until light and fluffy. Beat in 1 egg and vanilla to blend thoroughly.

• Sift together flour and baking powder. Add to creamed mixture. Divide dough in half; wrap each half in waxed paper and chill.

• On lightly floured surface, roll half of dough very thin, less than ⅛″ if possible. Cut with lamb cookie cutter or pattern.

• Beat white from separated egg until foamy. Brush onto unbaked cookies. Sprinkle with half of cookie coconut. Place 1″ apart on greased baking sheet.

• Bake in moderate oven (350°) 7 to 10 minutes. Cool cookies on racks.

• Meanwhile, roll second half of dough; cut in same way, but decorate before baking with egg yolk paint: Beat yolk from separated egg with water; add food color. Paint on unbaked cookies; sprinkle with coconut and bake as for first half of cookies. Makes about 76 (38 from each half of dough).

CHEESE/JAM COOKIE TARTS

Use several kinds of jam for color variation—festive party cookies

- **1 c. butter**
- **1 (8 oz.) pkg. cream cheese**
- **2 c. sifted flour**
- **½ c. jam (grape, apricot, peach or berry)**

• Beat together butter and cream cheese until light and fluffy. Blend in flour. Chill overnight.

• Roll dough about ⅛″ thick and cut with 2″ round cutter. Spread tops with jam; arrange ½″ apart on ungreased baking sheet. (Cookies shrink during baking.)

• Bake in moderate oven (350°) 10 to 12 minutes. Remove cookies and cool on racks. Makes about 6 dozen.

Note: Store cookies in container with loose lid in a cool place, or package and freeze them. To use if frozen, thaw in wrapper at room temperature about 15 minutes. To restore crispness to stored cookies, spread them on baking sheets and heat in slow oven (300°) about 5 minutes.

OATMEAL/MOLASSES COOKIES

A big recipe for big cookies

- **8½ c. sifted flour**
- **1 tblsp. salt**
- **2 tblsp. baking soda**
- **8 c. quick-cooking rolled oats**
- **2½ c. sugar**
- **1 tblsp. ground ginger**
- **2 c. melted shortening**
- **2 c. light molasses**
- **4 eggs, beaten**
- **¼ c. hot water**
- **3 c. seedless raisins**
- **2 c. ground black walnuts or English walnuts**
- **Sugar (for tops)**

· Reserve ½ c. flour. Sift together 8 c. flour, salt and baking soda.

· In a very large bowl or dishpan, mix rolled oats, sugar and ginger. Stir in shortening, molasses, eggs, hot water, sifted dry ingredients, raisins and nuts. Work dough with hands until well mixed. Add the reserved ½ c. flour if needed to make dough workable.

· Roll dough to ¼″ thickness; cut with 3½″ round cutter. Place 2 to 3″ apart on lightly greased baking sheet. Brush with water and sprinkle with sugar.

· Bake in moderate oven (375°) 8 to 10 minutes. Remove cookies to racks to cool. Makes 6 dozen.

MINCEMEAT/CHEESE COOKIES

Perfect non-sweet addition to cookie tray—taste like mincemeat pie!

1 c. butter or regular margarine
2 c. grated Cheddar cheese (½ lb.)
2 c. sifted flour
1 (9 oz.) pkg. prepared mincemeat
½ c. water

· Cream butter until light; add cheese (at room temperature) and cream until well blended. Stir in flour; mix well and chill.

· Meanwhile, cook mincemeat and water until slightly thickened. Set aside to cool.

· Roll dough ⅛″ thick on lightly floured surface; cut in 2″ circles. Put half of circles about 1″ apart on lightly greased baking sheet. Place 1 tsp. cooled mincemeat mixture in center of each cookie on baking sheet. Top each with another circle of dough; press edges with fork to seal. Prick cookie tops in several places with tines of kitchen fork.

· Bake in moderate oven (350°) 15 minutes, or until lightly browned. Remove cookies to racks to cool. Makes 3½ dozen.

CHRISTMAS SUGAR COOKIES

FARM JOURNAL *readers say this is their favorite cookie for Christmas tree*

1¼ c. soft butter
2 c. sugar
2 eggs
5 c. flour
1 tsp. salt
4 tsp. baking powder
1 tsp. ground nutmeg
½ c. milk

· Cream butter and sugar. Add eggs and beat until fluffy.

· Stir together dry ingredients and add alternately with milk to creamed mixture. If dough is sticky, add flour to handle.

· Roll ¼″ thick on well-floured pastry cloth; cut. Place bake-on decorations on cookies. Bake on ungreased baking sheet in moderate oven (375°) 8 minutes. Cool on racks. Makes about 100 cookies, depending on size.

CHOCOLATE SUGAR COOKIES

Pretty sprinkled with tiny multicolored candies before baking

¾ c. shortening
1 c. sugar
1 egg
¼ c. light corn syrup
2 squares unsweetened chocolate, melted
2 c. flour
1 tsp. baking soda

¼ tsp. salt
1 tsp. ground cinnamon

• Cream shortening, sugar and egg. Stir in syrup and chocolate.
• Sift dry ingredients; add to creamed mixture. Chill 1 hour.
• Roll ⅛″ thick on well-floured pastry cloth. Cut into shapes. Bake on ungreased baking sheet in moderate oven (350°) 10 to 12 minutes. Cool on racks. Frost and decorate, if desired. Makes about 30, using 3″ cookie cutters.

Note: To make a Christmas cookie tree, cut paper drinking straws into 1″ lengths. Push one into each unbaked cookie. Bake cookies. Remove straws by gently twisting them out while cookies are still warm. Anchor a 2½- to 3-foot evergreen tree in wet sand in an 8″ flower pot. (Keep sand wet.) Decorate cookies; pull narrow, brightly colored ribbons through holes in cookies; tie to tree.

Ever-ready Refrigerator Cookies

With rolls of cookie dough in the refrigerator or freezer, you're ready to serve warm-from-the-oven cookies with tea or coffee when friends or business callers drop by. And you can perk up family meals with fresh, warm cookies on short notice. As a starter, serve our Lemon Thins with tea. Bake Mincemeat Refrigerator Cookies to serve with coffee—the big recipe makes nine dozen cookies but you can bake them as needed if you keep the dough in the freezer.

Shape the dough firmly into smooth rolls for attractive cookies. Wrap snugly in plastic wrap or aluminum foil, twisting ends. Place in refrigerator if you want to bake the cookies within three days. Otherwise place dough in freezer where it will keep from 9 months to a year.

Use a knife with a thin, sharp blade to slice the cookies. Keep the slices even in thickness and shape. And do watch them while baking—they brown quickly. Remove cookies from oven when they are a light brown.

The fresh baking fragrance signals everyone within smelling distance that something good is happening—be ready to welcome visitors!

OATMEAL REFRIGERATOR COOKIES

Bake at serving time—nothing is better than cookies warm from oven

1½ c. sifted flour
1 tsp. baking soda
1½ tsp. salt
1 c. shortening
1 c. sugar
1 c. brown sugar, firmly packed
2 eggs, well beaten
1 tsp. vanilla
3 c. quick-cooking rolled oats

• Sift together flour, soda and salt.
• Cream shortening; add sugars gradually; beat until light; add eggs and vanilla.
• Combine sifted dry ingredients and creamed mixture; blend thoroughly. Add oats.
• Shape dough into rolls 2″ in diameter. Wrap tightly in waxed paper and chill thoroughly.
• Cut into ⅛″ slices; bake 1½″ apart on ungreased baking sheet in hot oven (400°) 6 to 8 minutes. Remove cookies and cool on racks. Makes 6 dozen.

BUTTERSCOTCH REFRIGERATOR COOKIES

Keep a few cans of dough on hand to bake on short notice—flavor is rich

3½ c. sifted flour
1 tsp. salt
1 tsp. ground cinnamon
1 tsp. baking soda
½ c. shortening
½ c. butter
2 c. brown sugar, firmly packed
2 eggs, well beaten
2 tblsp. warm water
1 tsp. vanilla
1 c. chopped nuts

· Sift together flour, salt, cinnamon and soda.
· Cream shortening and butter; gradually add sugar; beat until light. Add eggs, water and vanilla; mix well.
· Combine dry ingredients and creamed mixture; blend well. Add nuts.
· Shape dough into rolls 2″ in diameter. Wrap tightly in waxed paper and chill thoroughly—overnight for best results. (Or pack into frozen fruit juice cans and chill thoroughly. Detach bottom of can; use to push dough out to slice.)
· Bake 1½″ apart on ungreased baking sheet in hot oven (400°) 10 to 12 minutes. Spread on racks to cool. Makes 6 dozen.

LEMON THINS

Crisp, thin, delicately browned cookies

1 c. butter or regular margarine
½ c. sugar
1 egg, beaten
2 c. sifted flour
½ tsp. baking powder
⅛ tsp. salt
1 tblsp. lemon juice
½ tsp. grated lemon peel

· Cream together butter and sugar; add egg; mix well.
· Sift together flour, baking powder and salt; combine with sugar mixture. Add lemon juice and peel.
· Form into rolls 1½ to 2″ in diameter; wrap tightly in waxed paper and chill.
· Slice very thin. Bake 1½″ apart on ungreased baking sheet in moderate oven (375°) 8 to 10 minutes. Remove cookies and cool on racks. Makes 5 to 6 dozen.

BLACK WALNUT COOKIES

A cousin of the old-fashioned Pennsylvania Dutch slapjacks—extra-good tasting

6 c. sifted flour
1 tsp. salt
½ tsp. baking soda
1 tsp. cream of tartar
1¾ c. butter or regular margarine
2¼ c. brown sugar, firmly packed
½ c. sugar
2 eggs, beaten
2 tsp. vanilla
1½ c. black walnuts
1½ c. flaked or shredded coconut

· Sift together flour, salt, soda and cream of tartar.
· Cream butter; add brown and white sugars gradually and beat until fluffy. Add eggs and vanilla; mix well.
· Grind nuts and coconut together in food chopper using medium blade, or use blender. Add to creamed mixture. Add sifted dry ingredients and blend well. Chill.
· Shape dough in four rolls about 2″ in diameter. Wrap tightly in

waxed paper and chill thoroughly.
• Cut rolls in 1/8" slices; place about 1" apart on ungreased baking sheet. Bake in moderate oven (350°) 10 to 12 minutes. Remove cookies and cool on racks. Makes 8 to 9 dozen.

MINCEMEAT REFRIGERATOR COOKIES

Excellent companion for ice cream

3/4 c. butter
1 c. sugar
1 egg
1/2 tsp. vanilla
1 tsp. finely grated lemon peel
3/4 c. prepared mincemeat
3 c. sifted flour
1/2 tsp. baking soda
1/2 tsp. salt
1 tsp. ground cinnamon
1/2 c. chopped walnuts

• Cream together butter and sugar until light and fluffy. Beat in egg, vanilla and lemon peel. Stir in mincemeat.

• Sift together flour, baking soda, salt and cinnamon; gradually add to creamed mixture; mix well. Stir in nuts.

• Divide dough in half. Place each part on a lightly floured sheet of waxed paper and form in a roll 1 1/2" in diameter, about 12" long. (Sprinkling waxed paper with a little flour helps you to shape smooth rolls.) Wrap rolls in waxed paper and refrigerate several hours, overnight or 2 or 3 days.

• With sharp knife, cut dough in 1/8" slices; place 1 1/2" apart on ungreased baking sheet. Bake in moderate oven (375°) about 10 minutes. Remove cookies to cooling racks. Makes 9 dozen.

EASY DATE FILL-UPS

For very crisp cookies, chill filling and add shortly before serving

1/2 c. butter
1/2 c. lard
1/2 c. dairy sour cream
3/4 c. brown sugar, firmly packed
2 tsp. baking soda
1 tsp. salt
1 tsp. vanilla
2 1/2 c. sifted flour
2 c. quick-cooking rolled oats
1 1/4 c. halved dates (8 oz.)
1/2 c. sugar
1/4 c. water

• Blend together butter, lard, dairy sour cream, brown sugar, baking soda, salt and vanilla. Add flour and oats and mix well.

• Divide dough in half. Shape each part in a roll 2" in diameter. Wrap in foil or waxed paper and refrigerate overnight, or at least 8 hours. (For faster chilling place in freezer.)

• To bake, cut dough in 1/8" slices; place about 1" apart on ungreased baking sheet. Bake in moderate oven (350°) 8 to 12 minutes, or until light golden brown. Remove and cool on racks.

• To make filling, combine dates, white sugar and water in saucepan. Cook over medium heat until thick and smooth, stirring constantly. Cool until lukewarm.

• At serving time, spread half of cooled cookies on top sides with date filling; top with remaining cookies. Makes about 4 dozen.

Variation

AUSTRIAN COOKIE ROUNDS: Omit the date filling. Melt together in custard cup, set in hot water, 1/2 c. semi-sweet chocolate pieces and 1 tblsp.

shortening. Spread on half of cookies while still slightly warm to coat them with a glaze. Let harden. Before serving, spread a thin layer of currant or other red jelly on the unglazed cookies and top with a glazed cookie, glazed side up.

ALMOND REFRIGERATOR COOKIES

Easy version of Chinese almond cookies—and just as delicious

1 c. butter or regular margarine
2 c. sifted flour
¾ tsp. salt
¾ c. sugar
½ tsp. vanilla
½ tsp. almond extract
1 egg yolk
1 tblsp. water
½ c. blanched almonds, cut in halves (see Index)

· Cut butter into flour with pastry blender as for pie crust. Work in salt, sugar, vanilla and almond extract with hands. Shape in two long rolls 1 to 1½" in diameter. Wrap tightly in plastic wrap or waxed paper and refrigerate 1 hour, or until firm.

· Cut rolls in ¼" slices and place 1" apart on lightly greased baking sheet. Brush top of each cookie sparingly with egg yolk mixed with water. Press an almond half in center of each.

· Bake in hot oven (400°) 8 to 10 minutes, or until lightly browned. Cool slightly on baking sheet before removing to cooling rack. (If you do not cool them a little on baking sheet, they will crumble.) Makes about 6½ dozen.

CHOCOLATE COOKIE SANDWICHES

Fill with pastel pink and green frosting for a lovely tea-party cookie tray

½ c. shortening
½ c. sugar
1 egg
3 tblsp. milk
2 squares unsweetened chocolate, melted and cooled
1¾ c. sifted flour
1 tsp. salt
½ tsp. baking powder
Peppermint Frosting

· Cream shortening and sugar until fluffy; beat in egg, milk and chocolate.

· Sift together flour, salt and baking powder. Stir into creamed mixture. Shape dough in two smooth rolls about 2" in diameter, 6" long. Wrap each in waxed paper and chill several hours until firm, or overnight.

· Slice rolls thin, about ⅛", with sharp knife. Place 1½" apart on lightly greased baking sheet. Bake in moderate oven (375°) 7 to 10 minutes (watch carefully). Remove cookies and cool on racks. Spread half the cookies with Peppermint Frosting. Top with remaining cookies. Makes 2½ dozen.

PEPPERMINT FROSTING: Combine 2 c. sifted confectioners sugar, 1½ tblsp. butter and 2½ tblsp. dairy half-and-half or light cream. Beat until smooth. Add 3 to 4 drops peppermint extract. Divide in half; to one part add 3 drops red food color, to the other, 2 drops green food color.

Tempting Molded Cookies

Some of the cookies that are the most fun to make are the kind you shape with your hands. Roll the dough between your palms to make balls, such as our Chocolate Bonbon Cookies with red Peppermint Glaze. Cookie canes are a popular shape for the Christmas season. The important rule in shaping is to make smooth surfaces.

If you're a beginner with molded cookies, do not try to hurry. This is a baking art in which practice leads to perfection. Be sure the cookies are uniform in shape and thickness to insure even baking. Chill the dough if it seems too soft to work with.

When you want to treat your family and friends, bake a batch of old-time Snickerdoodles with our new-time recipe. These crinkly cookies have sugar-cinnamon tops and taste wonderful.

EASY CANE COOKIES

Tie red and green ribbons on canes to dress them up for Christmas

1 c. butter or regular margarine
1 c. confectioners sugar
1 egg
1 tsp. vanilla
¼ tsp. peppermint extract
2½ c. sifted flour
½ tsp. salt
½ c. crushed red and white peppermint candy
2 tblsp. sugar

• Beat together butter and confectioners sugar until light and fluffy. Beat in egg, vanilla and peppermint extract to blend well.

• Combine flour and salt and stir into creamed mixture. Wrap dough in waxed paper and chill at least 1 hour.

• When ready to shape, mix crushed candy with white sugar. Roll 1 level measuring tablespoonful of dough on surface sprinkled with small amount of crushed candy mixture to make a 6" rope. Place on greased baking sheet. Curve one end down to form handle of cane. Repeat until all the crushed candy and dough have been used.

• Bake in moderate oven (375°) about 12 minutes, until lightly browned. Remove at once from baking sheet and cool on racks. Makes about 3½ dozen.

Note: You can use stick candy of different colors and different extracts instead of the peppermint candy.

CHOCOLATE BONBON COOKIES

Red glaze makes tiny cookies shine

2 c. sifted flour
½ tsp. baking powder
½ tsp. salt
½ c. butter or regular margarine
½ c. sugar
1 egg
1 square unsweetened chocolate, melted
1 tsp. vanilla
Peppermint Glaze
Silver dragées, nuts or canned frostings (for decorations)

• Sift together flour, baking powder and salt.

• Cream butter and sugar together until light and fluffy. Beat in egg, melted chocolate and vanilla. Stir in flour mixture, a third at a time, blending well. The dough will be stiff.

· Roll rounded teaspoonfuls of dough, one at a time, into balls between hands. Place balls about 2″ apart on lightly greased baking sheet.

· Bake in moderate oven (350°) about 12 minutes, until firm. Remove from baking sheet to wire racks. Repeat until all dough is baked. Cool thoroughly.

· To glaze cookies, arrange at least 1″ apart on racks over waxed paper. Spoon Peppermint Glaze over to cover cookies completely (scrape glaze that drips onto waxed paper back into bowl). Spoon a second coating of glaze over the cookies; let cool. Trim with silver dragées, nuts or frostings from pressurized cans. Makes about 31.

Note: For Christmas holidays, use green frosting to make holly leaves, dots of red frosting for holly berries.

PEPPERMINT GLAZE

Perfect for decorating chocolate cookies

3 c. sifted confectioners sugar
2 to 3 tblsp. water
¼ tsp. red food color (optional)
¼ tsp. peppermint extract

· Combine all ingredients and beat until smooth. The glaze should be thin enough to pour from a spoon. If it gets too thick while working with it, add a few drops of water and beat until smooth. Makes about 1 cup.

Variation

VANILLA GLAZE: Omit peppermint extract and red food color; add ½ tsp. vanilla and make glaze as directed.

EASY CHOCOLATE CRACKLES

These cookies made with cake mix have a moist, fudge-like center

1 (1 lb. 2½ oz.) pkg. devil's food cake mix
2 eggs, slightly beaten
1 tblsp. water
½ c. shortening
Confectioners sugar (for coating)

· Combine cake mix, eggs, water and shortening. Mix with a spoon until well blended.

· Shape dough into balls the size of walnuts. Roll in confectioners sugar.

· Place 1½″ apart on greased baking sheet. Bake in moderate oven (375°) 8 to 10 minutes. Remove cookies and cool on racks. Makes 4 dozen.

PECAN BONBONS AND LOGS

For variety bake part of dough in logs—bonbons are very pretty

2 c. sifted flour
¼ c. sugar
½ tsp. salt
1 c. butter or regular margarine
2 tsp. vanilla
2½ c. finely chopped pecans
Confectioners sugar (for coating)

· Sift flour, sugar and salt into mixing bowl. Blend in butter and vanilla with pastry blender. Add 2 c. nuts.

· Shape half the dough into ½″ balls. Roll in remaining nuts. Place about 1½″ apart on greased bak-

ing sheet and bake in moderate oven (350°) 15 to 20 minutes. Cool cookies on racks.
• Roll remaining dough into logs; bake. While warm, roll in confectioners sugar. Makes 4 dozen.

PEPPARKAKOR

Swedish gingersnaps with a "bite"

1 c. sugar
1 c. butter or lard
1 c. light molasses
1 tsp. baking soda
1 tsp. salt
1 tblsp. ground ginger
½ tsp. pepper
3½ c. sifted flour
Sugar (for dipping)

• Cream sugar and butter until light and fluffy. Beat in molasses.
• Sift together baking soda, salt, ginger, pepper and flour; add to creamed mixture and beat to mix well. Chill dough until easy to handle.
• Shape dough with hands into balls the size of large marbles. Dip in sugar before baking. Place 1½" apart on lightly greased baking sheet.
• Bake in moderate oven (350°) 12 to 15 minutes, or until lightly browned. Cool on baking sheet 1 minute, then transfer to rack to cool completely. Makes about 7 dozen.

SNICKERDOODLES

Crisp cookies have sugar-cinnamon tops

½ c. butter or regular margarine
½ c. lard
1½ c. sugar
2 eggs
1 tsp. vanilla
2⅔ c. sifted flour
2 tsp. cream of tartar
1 tsp. baking soda
¼ tsp. salt
2 tblsp. sugar
1 tsp. ground cinnamon

• Beat butter and lard until light; add 1½ c. sugar and beat until fluffy. Beat in eggs and vanilla.
• Sift together flour, cream of tartar, baking soda and salt; add to beaten mixture.
• Combine 2 tblsp. sugar and cinnamon.
• Shape dough in small balls, about 1", and roll in sugar-cinnamon mixture. Place 2" apart on ungreased baking sheet. Bake in hot oven (400°) 8 to 10 minutes. (Cookies flatten during baking.) Remove cookies and cool on racks. Makes about 6 dozen.

MEXICAN FIESTA BALLS

Gala cookies have chocolate, coffee and maraschino flavor blend

1 c. butter
½ c. sugar
2 tsp. vanilla
2 c. sifted flour
¼ c. cocoa
1 tblsp. instant coffee powder
½ tsp. salt
1 c. finely chopped nuts
½ c. chopped drained maraschino cherries
1 c. confectioners sugar (for coating)

• Beat butter until light; gradually add sugar. Beat until light and fluffy. Add vanilla and beat to blend well.
• Sift together flour, cocoa, coffee powder and salt; gradually add to creamed mixture. Blend in nuts and

cherries; chill until easy to handle.
· Shape dough into balls 1″ in diameter and place 1″ apart on ungreased baking sheet. Bake in slow oven (325°) 20 minutes. Remove cookies to cooling racks and, while warm, roll in confectioners sugar. Makes 5 dozen.

MOLASSES BUTTERBALLS

Superior unspiced molasses cookies

1 c. butter or regular margarine
¼ c. molasses
2 c. sifted flour
½ tsp. salt
2 c. finely chopped walnuts
Confectioners sugar (for coating)

· Cream butter; add molasses.
· Sift flour and salt; stir in nuts.
· Add flour mixture to creamed mixture; blend well. Shape dough into small balls, about 1″ in diameter.
· Place about 1″ apart on ungreased baking sheet. Bake in moderate oven (350°) 25 minutes, or until lightly browned. Roll in confectioners sugar while warm. Cool cookies on racks. Makes about 4 dozen.

JUMBO SUGAR COOKIES

Crisp, big, thin cookies with crinkly tops sell fast at food bazaars

2 c. sugar
1 c. shortening
2 eggs
2 c. sifted flour
2 tsp. cream of tartar
1 tsp. baking soda
1 tsp. salt
1 tsp. ground cinnamon (for tops)
2 tblsp. sugar (for tops)

· Beat together 2 c. sugar and shortening until light and fluffy. Beat in eggs to mix thoroughly.
· Sift together flour, cream of tartar, baking soda and salt. Stir into creamed mixture. On lightly floured waxed paper, form dough into four rolls, each about 12″ long and 1 to 1¼″ in diameter. Cut in 1″ slices. Dip tops of cookies in mixture of cinnamon and 2 tblsp. sugar. Place 3″ apart, cinnamon-sugar sides up, on greased baking sheet.
· Bake in moderate oven (375°) about 12 minutes. Let stand on baking sheet 1 minute before removing to cooling racks. Makes 4 dozen.

MOLDED SUGAR COOKIES

Baking contest blue ribbon winners —they're crisp outside, soft within

2½ c. sifted flour
2 tsp. cream of tartar
1 tsp. baking soda
½ tsp. salt
1 c. butter
1 tsp. vanilla
1 c. sugar
2 eggs, beaten

· Sift together flour, cream of tartar, baking soda and salt.
· Cream butter, vanilla and sugar until light and fluffy. Add eggs and beat well. Add sifted dry ingredients, a fourth at a time, stirring to mix thoroughly. Chill 1 hour.
· Shape dough in 1″ balls and place 2½″ apart on greased baking sheet. Flatten by pressing with bottom of drinking glass coated with sugar. (Dip bottom of glass in sugar before flattening each cookie.)
· Bake in moderate oven (375°) 8 minutes, or until golden. Remove cookies to racks to cool. Makes about 5½ dozen.

GINGER BLOSSOM COOKIES

They look like pretty brown flowers with creamy almonds making centers

- **¾ c. shortening**
- **1 c. brown sugar, firmly packed**
- **¼ c. light molasses**
- **1 egg, beaten**
- **2¼ c. sifted flour**
- **1 tsp. ground ginger**
- **1 tsp. ground cinnamon**
- **½ tsp. ground cloves**
- **2 tsp. baking soda**
- **¼ tsp. salt**
- **25 blanched almonds**

· Cream shortening and sugar; add molasses and egg; blend well.

· Sift dry ingredients; add to creamed mixture; mix well.

· Roll into balls about 1½" in diameter; place 2½" apart on greased baking sheet. Flatten slightly; press almond in center of each.

· Bake in moderate oven (350°) 12 to 15 minutes. Remove cookies and cool on racks. Makes 25.

EIGHT-IN-ONE SUGAR COOKIES

Country women like to serve cookies warm from oven. This mix helps

- **2 c. butter or regular margarine**
- **2 c. sugar**
- **1 c. brown sugar, firmly packed**
- **4 eggs**
- **6½ c. sifted flour**
- **1 tblsp. cream of tartar**
- **2 tsp. baking soda**
- **¼ c. milk**

· Cream together butter and sugars until smooth and fluffy. Stir in unbeaten eggs, one at a time.

· Sift together dry ingredients; add to creamed mixture alternately with milk. Mix thoroughly.

· Divide dough in eight 1-cup lots. Wrap each tightly in foil or plastic wrap; freeze. Then place in plastic bag. To use, thaw dough just enough that you can shape or drop it. (This dough, tightly wrapped, will keep several days in refrigerator.) Place about 2" apart on greased baking sheet and bake in moderate oven (375°) 10 to 15 minutes. Spread cookies on racks to cool. Mix makes 8 cups dough; each cup makes 2 to 3 dozen cookies, depending on the kind you bake.

CHOCOLATE CHIP BALLS: Knead into 1 c. cookie dough, 1 tblsp. cocoa and ⅓ c. semisweet chocolate pieces. Shape into about 24 round balls; flatten slightly with spatula. Bake as directed.

COCONUT/ALMOND COOKIES: Knead into 1 c. cookie dough, 1 c. flaked coconut and ¼ to ½ tsp. almond extract. Shape into about 24 balls; place on greased baking sheet and press flat with spatula. Top each with a piece of candied cherry. Bake as directed.

PECAN BALLS: Knead into 1 c. cookie dough, ½ c. finely chopped pecans and ¼ tsp. vanilla. Shape into 24 round balls. Bake as directed.

GINGER COOKIE BALLS: Stir into 1 c. cookie dough, 1 tblsp. dark molasses and ¼ tsp. ground ginger. Shape into about 24 balls (dip fingers occasionally in water so dough doesn't stick to hands). Bake as directed.

GUMDROP COOKIE BALLS: Mix into 1 c. cookie dough, ½ c. finely cut gumdrops (cut with scissors). Shape into 24 balls; crisscross with a fork. Bake as directed.

FRUIT 'N' SPICE DROP COOKIES: Stir into 1 c. cookie dough, ½ c. cooked and drained, chopped dried fruit, 2 tblsp. brown sugar, ¼ tsp. ground cinnamon and ⅛ tsp. ground cloves. Drop by teaspoonfuls 2″ apart onto greased baking sheet. Bake as directed. Makes 30.

ORANGE WAFERS: Stir into 1 c. cookie dough, ¼ tsp. grated orange peel and ¼ c. sugar mixed with 4 tsp. orange juice. Drop by teaspoonfuls 2″ apart onto greased baking sheet. Bake as directed. Makes 24 thin cookies.

BANANA/LEMON DROPS: Stir into 1 c. cookie dough, ¼ c. mashed ripe banana, ½ tsp. grated lemon peel and ¼ tsp. lemon juice. Drop 1 teaspoonful at a time into finely rolled corn flakes. Coat by turning gently with spoon. (Dough is very soft.) Place 2″ apart on greased baking sheet and bake as directed. Watch carefully so cookies do not scorch. Makes 2 dozen.

COOKIE STARTER

Notice variety of cookies to make with this—all are exceptionally good

2¼ c. sifted flour
¾ tsp. salt
1 c. butter or regular margarine

· Sift flour and salt into bowl.
· Cut in butter until mixture resembles coarse bread crumbs.
· Store in clean jar with tight-fitting lid. Keep in refrigerator or freezer. Makes 3 to 4 cups.

Tips on using mix:
· Let the crumbs reach room temperature before adding other ingredients. Loosen with a fork if mix is too compact. Your electric mixer can help you make cookie dough from the mix.
· To short-cut cookie-making, shape dough into roll; wrap and chill thoroughly. Slice and bake cookies as desired. When dough is cold, allow more time for baking. To get a thicker cookie, shape teaspoonfuls of dough with fingers and roll in palms of hands into balls; stamp with flat-bottomed glass and bake.
· When you bake and then freeze, wrap cookies in foil or plastic wrap, or store them in freezer containers.

OLD ENGLISH GINGER CONES

1 c. Cookie Starter
¼ tsp. baking soda
1½ tsp. ground ginger
¼ tsp. ground nutmeg
¼ tsp. ground cinnamon
¼ c. dark brown sugar, firmly packed
1 tblsp. dark molasses
1 tblsp. buttermilk
Sifted confectioners sugar

· Combine all ingredients, except confectioners sugar, and mix well. Form dough into ball; chill 2 hours.
· Shape in 1″ balls. Roll in confectioners sugar, then pat very thin with glass dipped in confectioners sugar. Place 3″ apart on greased baking sheet.
· Bake in moderate oven (350°) 4 minutes, until lightly browned.
· Remove cookies while still hot. Twist over wooden spoon handle and sprinkle with sugar. Cool on racks. Makes 1½ dozen.

BLIND DATES

1 (3 oz.) pkg. cream cheese (room temperature)
1 c. Cookie Starter
½ tsp. vanilla
2 tblsp. confectioners sugar
24 pitted dates
Sifted confectioners sugar

• Combine first 4 ingredients. Form into four balls. Chill dough 2 hours.
• Work with one ball at a time, and roll ⅛″ thick on board dusted with confectioners sugar. Cut in rounds with 2½″ cutter.
• Place date in center of each round. (Date may be stuffed with nut, or use ½ date and 1 nut.) Fold edges over and pinch ends to points.
• Place 1″ apart on lightly greased baking sheet, seam side down. Bake in moderate oven (350°) 10 to 12 minutes.
• Sprinkle with confectioners sugar. Remove cookies and cool on racks. Makes 2 dozen.

ICE CREAM WAFERS

1 c. Cookie Starter
½ tsp. vanilla
1 egg yolk
⅓ c. sugar
½ tsp. baking powder
Sifted confectioners sugar

• Mix all ingredients, except confectioners sugar.
• Chill dough thoroughly.
• Sprinkle board and rolling pin with confectioners sugar. Roll small amount of dough ⅛″ thick.
• Cut with small cookie cutter and place 1″ apart on greased baking sheet. Bake in moderate oven (350°) about 6 minutes, until cookies are lightly browned.
• Dust with confectioners sugar. Remove and cool on racks. Makes 3 dozen.

Variations

ORIENTAL ALMOND COOKIES: Make up Ice Cream Wafers recipe, substituting ½ tsp. almond extract for the vanilla. Chill dough until firm enough to handle, about 1 hour. Shape into balls about 1″ in diameter. Flatten with glass dipped in confectioners sugar. Place cookies 3″ apart on lightly greased baking sheet. Beat egg white with fork. Brush a little on each cookie. Decorate each cookie with slivered, blanched almonds to make flower. Bake in moderate oven (350°) about 12 minutes. Remove cookies and cool on racks. Makes 2 dozen.

ORANGE AND LEMON WAFERS: Make up Ice Cream Wafers recipe omitting vanilla and adding grated peel of 1 orange and grated peel of ½ lemon. Roll out and cut cookies into different shapes. Place 1″ apart on lightly greased baking sheet. (Or roll into balls, using 1 teaspoon dough for each cookie. Dip fork into confectioners sugar and make waffle design by crisscrossing with fork. Don't mash cookies too flat.) Bake in moderate oven (350°) 10 minutes. Decorate with strips of orange peel. Remove cookies and cool on racks. Makes 1½ dozen.

SESAME COOKIES: Make Ice Cream Wafers recipe, substituting ¼ tsp. baking soda and ½ tsp. cream of tartar for baking powder. Add ½ c. toasted coconut and ¼ c. sesame seeds (if unavailable add another ¼ c. toasted coconut). Mix ingredients well. Shape dough into roll. Chill 15 minutes. Slice ⅛″ thick and place 1″ apart on greased baking sheet. Bake in moderate oven (350°) 15 minutes, or until lightly browned. Remove and cool on racks. Makes 2½ dozen.

Note: In Charleston, South Carolina, and elsewhere in the South they're called Benne Cookies—benne is the Southern name for sesame seeds.

VICTORIAN SPICE COOKIES: Make up Ice Cream Wafers recipe using brown sugar instead of white, and ¼ tsp. baking soda instead of baking powder. Add ½ c. chopped walnuts, 1 tsp. cocoa, ⅛ tsp. ground nutmeg, ½ tsp. ground cinnamon and ¼ tsp. ground allspice. Mix together all ingredients. Form into balls using 1 tsp. dough for each. Put 1″ apart on greased baking sheet. Make hole in centers of cookies with fingertip. Place ¼ tsp. firm jelly in each hole. Bake in moderate oven (350°) about 10 minutes, or until cookies are firm. Remove cookies and cool on racks. Makes 2½ dozen.

Tender Pressed Cookies

Rich and tender Spritz—a Swedish cookie, is perhaps the most popular pressed cookie in America; at least farm women make it most frequently. By using the different plates of the cookie press, you can bake cookies in several exciting shapes. Our recipe for Spritz is made with butter in the original way. Orange/Cheese Cookies are a true delight. Here are a few tips from our Countryside Test Kitchens for making pressed cookies:

If the dough is very warm, chill it briefly, but if the dough is too cold, it crumbles. If it seems too soft, work in 1 to 2 tblsp. of flour; if too stiff, add 1 egg yolk. Be sure to use cold baking sheets; if they're warm, the fat in the dough melts and it pulls away from the baking sheet when you lift up the press.

SPRITZ

Change shape of these tender cookies by using different press plates

1 c. butter
⅔ c. confectioners sugar
1 egg
1 egg yolk
1 tsp. almond extract, vanilla or ¼ c. grated almonds
2½ c. sifted flour

· Combine butter, sugar, egg, egg yolk and almond extract. Work in flour.

· Use a fourth of the dough at a time; force it through cookie press 1″ apart onto ungreased baking sheet in desired shapes. Bake in hot oven (400°) 7 to 10 minutes, or until set but not browned. Remove cookies and cool on racks. Makes 4 to 6 dozen, depending on size.

PEANUT BUTTER PRESSED COOKIES

Glamorized peanut butter cookies

¾ c. butter or regular margarine
3 tblsp. peanut butter
½ c. sugar
1 egg yolk
½ tsp. vanilla or almond extract
1¾ c. sifted flour
¼ tsp. salt

· Beat together butter and peanut butter until light. Gradually beat in sugar, beating until light and fluffy. Beat in egg yolk and vanilla to blend thoroughly.

• Sift together flour and salt. Add to creamed mixture; mix to a smooth dough.

• Fit desired plate into cookie press. Put one fourth of the dough in cookie press at a time. Force cookies 1″ apart onto ungreased baking sheet. Bake in moderate oven (375°) 8 to 10 minutes, or until delicately browned. Remove cookies and cool on racks. Makes about 3 dozen.

ORANGE/CHEESE COOKIES

They look like little washboards—taste rich and luscious

1 c. butter or regular margarine
1 (3 oz.) pkg. cream cheese
1 c. sugar
1 egg
1 tblsp. grated orange peel
1 tblsp. orange juice
2½ c. sifted flour
1 tsp. baking powder
Dash of salt

• Combine butter and cream cheese; beat until light. Gradually add sugar, beating until mixture is fluffy. Beat in egg, orange peel and juice to blend thoroughly.

• Sift together flour, baking powder and salt. Add to creamed mixture, blending well.

• Put plate with narrow slit in cookie press. Put a fourth of dough into press at a time and press rows of strips of dough about 1″ apart onto ungreased baking sheet. With knife, mark strips in 2″ lengths.

• Bake in moderate oven (375°) 8 to 10 minutes, until very delicately browned. Immediately cut strips into pieces on knife marks. Remove cookies and cool on racks. Makes about 12½ dozen.

Note: Sprinkle some of the cookies before baking with chocolate shot (jimmies) for a tasty, interesting touch.

Country Kisses

These dainty cookies are also called meringues, but people in the country still prefer their original name, "kisses." And clever hostesses know that they provide the world's best way to utilize leftover egg whites. The light and airy cookies are good party fare.

The surprise in Meringues à la Belle is the delicate salty taste from the crushed crackers in the cookies. Try Coconut Kisses, the perfect escort for iced lemonade on warm afternoons.

COCONUT KISSES

Chewy, moist, macaroon-like cookies

¼ tsp. salt
½ c. egg whites (4 medium)
1¾ c. sugar
½ tsp. vanilla or almond extract
2½ c. shredded coconut

• Add salt to egg whites and beat until foamy. Gradually beat in sugar. Continue beating until mixture stands in stiff peaks and is glossy. Fold in vanilla and coconut.

• Drop by heaping teaspoonfuls 2″ apart onto greased baking sheet. Bake in slow oven (325°) 20 minutes, or until delicately browned and set. Remove from baking sheet and cool on racks. Makes about 3 dozen.

Variations

WALNUT KISSES: Substitute finely chopped walnuts for the coconut in recipe for Coconut Kisses.

CHOCOLATE/COCONUT KISSES: Follow directions for making Coconut Kisses, but stir in 1 square unsweetened chocolate, melted and cooled until lukewarm, before folding in coconut.

CORN FLAKE KISSES

These cookies stretch food budgets

¼ tsp. salt
2 egg whites
1 c. sugar
1 tsp. grated orange peel or vanilla
3 c. corn flakes

· Add salt to egg whites and beat until foamy. Gradually beat in sugar. Continue beating until mixture stands in peaks and is glossy. Fold in orange peel and corn flakes.

· Drop by teaspoonfuls 2″ apart onto greased baking sheet. Bake in moderate oven (350°) 15 to 18 minutes, or until set and delicately browned. Remove from baking sheet and cool on racks. Makes about 3 dozen.

MERINGUES À LA BELLE

Crackers add crunch, good salty taste

3 egg whites
¾ c. sugar
½ tsp. baking powder
1 tsp. vanilla
⅔ c. crushed saltine crackers
½ c. chopped nuts

· Beat egg whites until frothy. Gradually add sugar, beating until meringue stands in soft peaks; scrape bottom and sides of bowl occasionally with rubber spatula. Blend in baking powder and vanilla. Fold in crackers and nuts.

· Drop mixture by rounded teaspoonfuls 1″ apart onto two lightly greased baking sheets. Bake one sheet at a time in slow oven (300°) about 20 minutes. Remove from baking sheets at once and cool on racks. Makes about 3 dozen.

chapter 15

Refreshing Beverages

SIPPING BEVERAGES with friends is an old farm custom. The coffee break started in pioneer kitchens; it never has gone out of style. Afternoon tea is firmly established in some country homes. And today's children, like those of previous generations, head for the kitchen and glasses of milk when they return home from school. Country people of all ages drink milk for a pickup.

Many kinds of drinks have an enthusiastic following, as recipes in this chapter indicate. Hot and cold chocolate and cocoa specials and festive fruit punches are typical examples. Fruit drinks often serve diverse purposes; they appear at gala parties and receptions but like hot coffee and iced tea, also may go to the field to sustain the men on sultry afternoons.

You'll find recipes in this chapter for iced and chilled drinks to take in vacuum bottles on motor trips for roadside enjoyment and to serve at picnics and community meals. Tomato juice, regardless of whether you consider it a drink or an appetizer (it's both), has a loyal following. Did you ever serve it in a punch bowl? Directions in this chapter tell how to make a lovely ice ring to decorate and chill the juice.

Be sure to try Sparkling Strawberry Punch when juicy, ripe berries are in season. Serve our Orange Ginger Punch in a punch bowl decorated with clusters of green grapes and purple asters at your autumn church or club party. And get ready for yuletide entertaining by making and refrigerating Basic Cranberry Syrup to mix with other fruit juices.

No collection of revered FARM JOURNAL fruit beverage recipes omits Hot Apple Punch, a recipe that came to us from a Utah hostess. Its fragrance permeates the house, setting the stage for pleasant conversation and sipping. It's a favorite of children as well as grownups.

Old-fashioned Lemonade

Cool off on a hot day with Old-fashioned Lemonade. It has stood the test of time as a thirst quencher. This is different from most lemonades because you slice lemons thin, add sugar and press out the juices. If you grow mint in your garden, stick perky, big sprigs in every glass —looks cool, smells cool and tastes cool.

Or keep the mix in your freezer for Limelight Banana Crush, a favorite of Utah hostesses. You'll be ready to fix the fruity drink for an afternoon party or evening refreshment on short notice. You need no accompaniment, but if you can forget calories, little chocolate brownies taste wonderful with this drink.

OLD-FASHIONED LEMONADE

Press lemon slices to extract juices

4 lemons
¾ c. sugar
1 qt. water
1 tray ice cubes

• Wash fruit. Cut into thin slices; remove seeds. Place lemon slices in a large bowl. Cover fruit with sugar. Let stand 10 minutes, then press firmly with potato masher to extract juice. Add water, continue to press fruit with masher until liquid is well flavored. Add ice cubes.

• Taste lemonade for sweetness when it's chilled. If you wish, add more sugar and stir to dissolve. Pour over two ice cubes in tall glasses; add lemon slices to each glass. Makes about 7 servings.

Variations

LEMON/LIMEADE: Use 2 limes and 2 lemons. Increase sugar to 1 c. Prepare according to directions for Old-fashioned Lemonade.

LEMON/ORANGEADE: Use 2 oranges and 3 lemons. Decrease sugar to ½ c. Prepare according to directions for Old-fashioned Lemonade.

LIMELIGHT BANANA CRUSH

Easy mix-in-the-glasses drink will take spotlight when you serve it

4 c. sugar
6 c. water
1 (46 oz.) can pineapple juice
2 (12 oz.) cans frozen orange juice concentrate, thawed
1 (12 oz.) can frozen lemonade concentrate, thawed
5 bananas
Lemon-lime carbonated beverage
Sliced strawberries (optional)

• Dissolve sugar in water. Add juices. Peel and mash bananas; put through food mill. Stir into juice. Ladle into wide-topped freezer containers, leaving 1" head space. Cover tightly; freeze. Makes 6 quarts. Recommended storage time, up to 1 month.

• To serve, thaw Banana Crush in refrigerator to mush consistency, about 4 hours; half fill glasses with mixture. Fill with chilled carbonated beverage; stir. Pretty garnished with fresh strawberry slices. You will get 8 (12 oz.) glasses from 1½ qts. Banana Crush.

STARLIGHT THREE-FRUIT PUNCH

Make it ahead and store in freezer

2 (6 oz.) cans frozen orange juice concentrate, thawed
2 (6 oz.) cans frozen lemon juice concentrate, thawed
6 c. water
1 (46 oz.) can pineapple juice
1 c. sugar
2 (12 oz.) bottles ginger ale, chilled

· Combine concentrates, add water and pineapple juice; stir in sugar. Makes 4 quarts.
· Ladle into wide-topped freezer containers, leaving 1″ head space. Cover tightly and freeze. Recommended storage time, up to 1 month.
· To serve, partially thaw juice mixture at room temperature, about 5 hours. Place in punch bowl. Stir with fork to break up chunks of ice. Add ginger ale. Makes about 30 servings in punch cups.

Punch Bowl Favorites

The rhubarb in your garden gives Good Luck Punch a lovely pink color and refreshing taste. One of our teenage readers who gave a graduation party with purple iris for the decoration, successfully substituted grape juice for the rhubarb. To make punch that packs some punch, add ginger ale or sparkling water just before serving.

Wreathe the punch bowl with ivy from the yard for a festive effect and float garden blossoms on orange or lemon slices. You can fasten a daisy, rosebud or freesia to the citrus "boat" by pulling the stem through the center. If you coat flowers with paraffin before floating them they will not wilt so fast. Freezing maraschino cherries or mint leaves in the ice cubes also provides a gala touch.

Another hostess trick is to make rainbow-hued ice cubes for lemonade, orange, or other drinks. Just add a few drops of food color to the water for the different ice cube trays. When the cubes are frozen, put them in the punch cups, one color in each cup, just before pouring.

GOOD LUCK PUNCH

Pretty pink party punch

1 qt. rhubarb (about 2 doz. stalks)
Water
3 c. sugar
2 c. water
Juice of 6 lemons
1 c. pineapple juice
Rhubarb juice
1 qt. ginger ale

· Cut rhubarb in 1″ pieces; add water to cover. Cook until soft, about 10 minutes. Drain through cheesecloth bag or sugar sack. Measure—should be 3 qts. juice.
· Dissolve sugar in 2 c. water; cook 10 minutes to make a syrup.
· Add lemon, pineapple and rhubarb juices. Pour over chunk of ice in punch bowl.
· Just before serving, add ginger ale. Makes 1 gallon punch or 24 servings.

FRUIT PUNCH

Decorated ice ring adds eye appeal

1 (6 oz.) can frozen orange juice concentrate
2 (6 oz.) cans frozen limeade concentrate
1 (6 oz.) can frozen lemonade concentrate
1 (1 lb. 14 oz.) can pineapple juice
1 pt. cranberry juice cocktail
2 to 4 c. cold water
2 qts. ginger ale, chilled
1 qt. plain soda water, chilled
Fruit Ice Ring
Mint

• Empty frozen juice concentrates, pineapple and cranberry juice and water into large container or bowl. Thaw; stir well.

• Pour mixture into punch bowl. Add ice cubes. Just before serving, gently pour in ginger ale and soda water. Top with Fruit Ice Ring; garnish with sprigs of mint or fresh strawberry slices. Makes 30 servings.

FRUIT ICE RING: Use any combination of lime, lemon or orange slices. Arrange in a pattern in the bottom of the 8″ ring mold. Add only enough water to cover fruit; freeze. When frozen, fill mold with water and freeze. To unmold, loosen ring by dipping bottom of mold into warm water. Float on top of punch.

Christmas Cranberry Drinks

Tulip-red cranberries make the perfect base for hospitable chilled drinks during the yuletide season. Here's a recipe for Basic Cranberry Syrup which our food editors developed. You can keep this in the refrigerator handy for making pretty punches quickly. Here are the directions:

BASIC CRANBERRY SYRUP

With this on hand, you'll always be ready to serve stop-in guests

3 lbs. whole cranberries
5 c. sugar
2 qts. water
5 sticks cinnamon

• Combine ingredients in a large kettle; bring to a boil. Mash cranberries with potato masher; simmer 15 minutes. Strain through several layers of cheesecloth or muslin. Stir in enough water to make 2½ quarts syrup. Store in refrigerator. Serve iced or very cold, mixed with other fruit juices, ginger ale or iced tea, as desired. We give you a few suggestions.

Variations

ZIPPY CRANBERRY COOLER: Mix 1 part Basic Cranberry Syrup with 2 parts chilled ginger ale.

CRANBERRY/APPLE DRINK: Mix equal portions of Basic Cranberry Syrup, apple juice and carbonated water.

CRANBERRY/LEMON SPARKLE: Combine 2 (6 oz.) cans frozen lemonade concentrate and 1 qt. Basic Cranberry Syrup. Add 1½ qts. water and 1½ qts. ginger ale. Makes about 18 cups.

CRANBERRY TEA: Mix equal portions of Basic Cranberry Syrup, carbonated water and iced tea.

CHRISTMAS PUNCH

Festive red two-fruit holiday drink. Add ginger ale if you like the bubbles

1 qt. apple juice
1 (1 qt.) bottle cranberry juice cocktail
½ c. lemon juice
Canned pineapple chunks, drained (for garnish)

• Mix juices. Chill. Garnish with pineapple chunks. Makes 12 servings.

CARDINAL PUNCH

Tea and fruit juices join in this—float a thin lemon slice in each glass

2½ c. boiling water
2 tblsp. black tea
¼ tsp. ground allspice
¼ tsp. ground cinnamon
⅛ tsp. ground nutmeg
¾ c. sugar
1 (1 pt.) bottle cranberry juice cocktail
½ c. orange juice
⅓ c. lemon juice
1½ c. cold water

• Pour the rapidly boiling water over tea; add spices. Cover and let steep 5 minutes. Strain and stir in sugar.
• Add cranberry, orange and lemon juices and cold water. Cover; chill thoroughly. Makes 8 servings.

CRANBERRY SPIKE

Be ready for company. Keep ingredients in cupboard and refrigerator

1 (1 pt.) bottle cranberry juice cocktail
1 (12 oz.) can apricot nectar
2 tblsp. lemon juice

• Combine chilled juices. Serve over ice cubes. Makes 1 quart.

RASPBERRY FLOAT

Punch sparkles and invites—it's colorful and tastes like berries

3 (3 oz.) pkgs. raspberry flavor gelatin
4 c. boiling water
1½ c. sugar
4 c. cold water
½ c. lime juice
2¼ c. orange juice
1¼ c. lemon juice
1 qt. ginger ale
2 (10 oz.) pkgs. frozen raspberries

• Dissolve gelatin in boiling water; add sugar, cold water and juices; cool, but do not chill or gelatin will congeal. (If you let it congeal, heat just enough to bring back to liquid state.)
• When time to serve, pour punch into punch bowl. Add ginger ale and frozen raspberries. Stir until raspberries break apart and are partially thawed. Makes about 4 quarts.

Easy-to-fix Orange Ginger Punch

It's important always to chill the punch bowl itself in advance. Since space in refrigerators is seldom adequate for a big punch bowl, it's a good idea to fill the bowl with cracked ice. Remove it just before you pour in the punch.

When you add the bottles of chilled ginger ale to this special punch, hold them high above the bowl, pouring in a steady stream on the sherbet. The force of the liquid sloughs off the frozen sherbet to give the drink an interesting appearance.

Fruit and flower decorations on the punch bowl entrance guests. This punch, which is orange in color, is perfect for autumn parties. Fasten tiny clusters of little purple asters and green grapes (use small grapes and only a few in a cluster) here and there on the outside of the punch bowl with transparent tape. Then you omit garnishes in the bowl. If fresh flowers are unavailable, artificial may be used, but be sure they're tiny ones.

For the Christmas season, use cranberry sherbet instead of orange and decorate the outside of the bowl with sprigs of holly and mistletoe.

ORANGE GINGER PUNCH

Refreshing easy-to-fix party punch

3 qts. orange ice (or sherbet)
5 qts. chilled ginger ale

· Place large chunks of orange ice in chilled punch bowl.
· Pour ginger ale over, holding the bottles some little distance above the punch bowl. Garnish with fresh mint leaves and maraschino cherries, if desired, or with seedless green grapes when in season. Makes 55 punch cup servings.

Note: Use different kinds of sherbet instead of the orange if you prefer a different color and flavor.

Coolers Men Like

Drown a parching outdoor thirst with one of these three light summer drinks. Men like them, whether they're riding a tractor or playing golf on a hot day.

Recipes are big enough for several tall-glass servings. Fix the coolers ahead and refrigerate; freeze enough to fill two ice cube trays. Combine frozen cubes with chilled drink–they won't water it down like plain ice.

CHERRY/APPLE DRINK

The tanginess soothes a dry throat

2 envelopes unsweetened cherry flavor instant soft drink mix
½ c. sugar
1 (6 oz.) can frozen lemonade concentrate, thawed
1½ qts. apple juice or cider
2¼ qts. ice water

· Combine ingredients; stir until sugar dissolves. Makes 1 gallon.

CITRUS REFRESHER

Not too sweet–not too tart. It's just right to quench thirst

2 (6 oz.) cans frozen lemonade concentrate, thawed
1 (6 oz.) can frozen orange juice concentrate, thawed
2 c. pineapple juice
3½ qts. ice water
5 tblsp. instant tea (optional)

· Combine ingredients in order given. Makes 4½ quarts.

HARVEST COOLER

Looks so cool and hits the spot in hot, humid weather–refreshing

1 (3 oz.) pkg. lime flavor gelatin
1 c. boiling water
1 qt. pineapple juice
Juice of 3 lemons
1¼ qts. ice water

• Dissolve lime gelatin (adds body) in boiling water. Stir in remaining ingredients; chill thoroughly. Shake before serving. Makes 2¾ quarts.

THIRST-QUENCHER

Tote this hot-weather cider-fruit juice drink to the men in the field

1 (32 oz.) can or bottle apple cider
1 (18 oz.) can grapefruit juice
1 (18 oz.) can orange juice
Ice water
Sugar to taste

• Pour cider, grapefruit juice and orange juice in 10-qt. pail. Fill with ice water. Add sugar sparingly. Makes 10 quarts.

HALF-AND-HALF COOLER

Quick refreshment for a hot afternoon—in the house or outdoors

1 (6 oz.) can frozen limeade concentrate
4 cans cold water
1 qt. chilled ginger ale
1 lemon or lime, thinly sliced

• Combine concentrate with water according to can directions. When ready to serve, add ginger ale and lemon. Makes 8 (8 oz.) servings.

Variation

GINGERED HALF-AND-HALF COOLER: Use any flavor frozen or canned juice instead of limeade. Combine with equal amount chilled ginger ale.

TUTTI-FRUTTI PUNCH: Add water as directed on cans to 1 (6 oz.) can frozen orange concentrate and 1 (6 oz.) can frozen lemonade concentrate.
• Combine with 1 (12 oz.) can apricot nectar and 1 (1 pt. 2 oz.) can pineapple juice. Chill. Serve iced. Makes about 3 quarts.

3-CITRUS FRUIT DRINK

Cool-looking lime sherbet adds appeal

1 (6 oz.) can frozen orange juice concentrate
1 (6 oz.) can frozen lemonade concentrate
1 qt. cold water
2 (7 oz.) bottles carbonated water
1 pt. lime sherbet

• Blend together orange and lemonade concentrates and 1 qt. water. Pour over ice cubes in pitcher. Carefully pour in carbonated water; stir gently. When ice thoroughly chills mixture, fill glasses ¾ full. Top with spoonfuls of lime sherbet. Makes 6 servings.

Note: You may substitute 2 c. plain cold water for carbonated water.

SPARKLING STRAWBERRY PUNCH

A festive drink—really perfect for showers and school parties

4 c. strawberries
½ c. sugar
3 c. orange juice
¾ c. lemon juice
1½ qts. ginger ale, chilled
½ c. sugar
1 c. strawberries, sliced

• Mash 4 c. strawberries with ½ c. sugar. Let stand 1 hour. Force through strainer. Add orange and lemon juices, ginger ale and ½ c. sugar to strained strawberry juice. Pour into large punch bowl. Add sliced strawberries. Makes about 3 quarts.

Hot and Fragrant Punches

Some people prefer hot to iced fruit punches on cold, blustery days. We first found that out by serving Hot Apple Punch when entertaining in our Countryside Test Kitchens. Its inviting aroma forecasts something special on the way. The drink lives up to its fragrant promise.

HOT APPLE PUNCH

An all-time Farm Journal *favorite*

2¼ c. sugar
4 c. water
2 (2½") sticks cinnamon
8 whole allspice berries
10 whole cloves
1 whole piece ginger root (about size of quarter)
4 c. orange juice (fresh, canned or reconstituted frozen)
2 c. lemon juice
2 qts. apple cider or juice

· Combine sugar and water and boil 5 minutes. Remove from heat; add spices. Let beverage stand, covered, 1 hour. Strain.
· Just before serving, combine syrup, fruit juices and cider; bring quickly to boiling. Remove from heat; serve at once. Makes 4½ quarts.

SPICY HOT GRAPE PUNCH

Guest-pleasing on a cold evening

2 c. grape juice
½ c. sugar
1 stick cinnamon
1 tsp. whole cloves
1 tblsp. lemon juice
1 (6 oz.) can frozen orange juice concentrate, reconstituted

· Combine all ingredients. Bring to a boil. Strain and serve hot in teacups. Makes 8 servings.

SPICY PERK-A-PUNCH

This is easy to make for a crowd

2 qts. cranberry juice cocktail
2 qts. pineapple juice
1 qt. water
⅔ c. brown sugar, firmly packed
1 tblsp. whole cloves
1 tblsp. whole allspice
4 (2") sticks cinnamon
2 lemons, sliced and quartered

· Combine fruit juices and water in a 30-cup electric percolator. Place remaining ingredients in basket. Percolate about 30 minutes; serve from percolator. Makes 5 quarts, or 28 servings.

Note: Use your 30-cup coffeemaker for serving hot and cold drinks to a large crowd. With the coffee basket removed, there's plenty of room for ice. Turning the spigot is easier than dipping from a punch bowl or pouring from a pitcher.

HOT SPICY PUNCH

Refreshing for winter parties

½ c. tea leaves
4 sticks cinnamon
6 whole cloves
2 qts. boiling water
½ c. sugar
1 c. lemon juice
1 c. orange juice
1 qt. pineapple juice
2 c. cranberry juice cocktail
2 qts. apple cider (full-flavored, sweet cider)
2 qts. ginger ale

• Tie together in cheesecloth tea leaves, cinnamon and cloves. Submerge in boiling water; then remove from heat and steep 10 minutes. Remove bag.
• Add sugar, fruit juices and cider. Heat just to boiling, stirring.
• Pour ginger ale into 2-gal. punch bowl; then pour in hot punch. (A metal spoon in punch bowl will keep hot liquid from breaking it.) Makes about 2 gallons.

MULLED APRICOT NECTAR

Heat this spicy treat after guests arrive—they'll enjoy its aroma and taste

1 (46 oz.) can apricot nectar
½ lemon, sliced
2 (2½") sticks cinnamon
15 whole cloves
8 whole allspice berries

• Combine all ingredients in heavy saucepan and bring to boiling point. Simmer gently 5 minutes.
• Remove from heat; cover; allow to stand 30 minutes.
• Strain. If you wish, sweeten to taste with honey or sugar. Heat before serving. Makes about 5 cups.

Delightful Dairy Drinks

Milk shakes started out in country kitchens with cold milk poured into a glass fruit jar, lightly sweetened and flavored delicately with vanilla. The children watched while Mother screwed the lid on the jar, shook vigorously until the mixture foamed, ready to pour. Sometimes a weary grownup fixed the invigorating, build-up drink; country people always have had great faith in the good nutrition milk provides.

Electric blenders and mixers now take the place of shaking the glass fruit jar. And many exciting flavorings and sweetenings are added to modern shakes—ice cream, bananas, pineapple, peaches, strawberries, peppermint candy and honey—you name it!

BANANA MILK SHAKES

Banana flavor makes milk drinking more inviting to children

2 c. milk
2 ripe bananas
2 tblsp. sugar or molasses

• Combine all ingredients in blender. Mix at high speed for 1 minute. Mixture should be smooth and foamy.
• Pour into glasses. Serve immediately.
• For a tasty variation use 2 tblsp. chocolate syrup in place of the sugar or molasses. Makes 3 servings.

Note: You can mash bananas, add the other ingredients and blend them in the electric mixer instead of the blender.

PEPPERMINT MILK SHAKES

Pretty, pink, rich—a tasty way to salvage broken Christmas candy canes

½ c. crushed peppermint candy
2 c. milk
1½ pts. vanilla ice cream

• Add candy to milk and beat to blend (electric blender works best).
• Add ice cream and beat until smooth. Serve at once. Makes 6 (6 oz.) glasses.

PINEAPPLE MILK SHAKE

A drink that will pinch-hit for dessert if passed with chocolate cookies

1 c. milk
½ c. crushed pineapple, undrained
1 tsp. sugar
1 tblsp. lemon juice

· Combine all ingredients in blender. Mix at high speed for 1 minute. Mixture should be smooth and foamy.

· Pour into serving glasses. For a thicker drink add a small scoop of ice cream during mixing. Makes 1 large serving.

Note: Reconstituted dry milk may be used instead of whole milk.

STRAWBERRY MILK SHAKES

A hit at children's birthday parties

½ (10 oz.) pkg. frozen strawberries or 1 pt. cleaned fresh strawberries and ¼ c. sugar
1½ c. cold milk
½ pt. vanilla ice cream

· Blend all ingredients well. Makes 2 large glasses.

Note: Add ¼ c. plain malted milk or use raspberries in place of strawberries.

FRESH PEACH SHAKES

New way to serve juicy peaches and ice cream—a luscious summer treat

1 c. diced fresh peaches
1 to 2 tblsp. sugar
2 tblsp. lemon juice
1 c. cold milk
½ pt. vanilla ice cream

· Mix all ingredients until thick and fluffy. Makes 2 large glasses.

HONEYED PEACH MILK SHAKES

They're both a drink and dessert. Try ice cream of other flavors

1 c. diced fresh peaches
¼ c. honey
½ tsp. vanilla
1½ c. milk
1 pt. vanilla ice cream

· Mix peaches and honey. (Honey keeps peaches from darkening as well as sweetening them.) Add remaining ingredients and mix in blender to a smooth cream. Serve in tall glasses. Makes 4 servings.

Note: Never keep honey in refrigerator; cold temperatures encourage it to crystallize. When crystallized, set the container of it in warm water to liquefy it. Honey must be at room temperature to blend with milk.

Milk Steamers and Coolers

Serve them hot in mugs or cups or serve them frosty cold in glasses. These good-for-you drinks are refreshing either way. The weather often decides for the cook which one will have the greatest appeal at the moment.

SPICED STEAMER

Keep some of the syrup on hand in refrigerator to speed up the making

2 qts. milk
1 c. Spiced Syrup
⅛ tsp. salt
Marshmallows or whipped cream

· Heat milk in double boiler, covering to prevent film from forming. Stir hot milk into syrup. Add salt. Serve hot in mugs, topped with marshmallows. Makes 8 servings.

SPICED SYRUP: Mix in saucepan 2 c. water, ¼ c. whole cloves, ½ c. red cinnamon candies and ½ c. sugar. Simmer 15 minutes, stirring occasionally. Strain. Use 2 tblsp. for a cup of milk.

Variations

· Omit Spiced Syrup, salt and marshmallows for the following:

COFFEE/COCOA: Mix 3 tblsp. instant coffee, 3 tblsp. instant cocoa and 1 tblsp. sugar. Stir into hot milk. Pour into mugs; top with whipped cream. Serve at once.

BUTTERSCOTCH: Add ¼ c. butter and ½ c. dark brown sugar, firmly packed, to hot milk. Blend; serve at once, sprinkled with ground cinnamon.

Note: You may use dry milk in steamers. Either reconstitute it and heat or slowly stir dry milk into hot water. If you prefer a sweeter drink, use whole milk with extra dry milk added.

CHOCOLATE/BANANA MILK

Children and grownups alike enjoy this substantial luncheon or supper drink

3 c. milk
3 medium, ripe bananas
½ c. instant chocolate mix

· Blend half of ingredients in blender 1 minute. Pour into pitcher. Blend second half of ingredients 1 minute. Add to pitcher. Makes 4 servings.

Note: For a South-of-the-border touch, add ½ tsp. ground cinnamon to chocolate.

HONEY/PEANUT FOAM

Add coffee for a grownup's treat

1 tblsp. honey
2 tblsp. peanut butter
1 c. milk
2 tblsp. dry milk
Frozen Milk Cubes

· Whip ingredients, except cubes, in drink mixer or blender until well blended and foamy. Pour over Frozen Milk Cubes. Makes 1 big (10 oz.) glass.

FROZEN MILK CUBES: Pour reconstituted dry milk into ice cube tray and freeze.

Variation

COFFEE/HONEY/PEANUT FOAM: Blend ¼ c. honey and ½ c. peanut butter in your electric mixer. Slowly add 1 qt. milk, continuing to beat; scrape mixer bowl often. Add ½ c. dry milk and (for adults) 1 tsp. instant coffee; whip until foamy. Pour over frozen milk cubes. Makes 4 (10 oz.) glasses.

ORANGE EGGNOG

Pretty enough for the punch bowl at a hot-weather party

3 c. water
1½ c. dry milk
6 eggs, separated
½ c. sugar
1 tsp. vanilla
1 pt. orange sherbet
Red and yellow food colors (optional)
Ground nutmeg

· Mix water and dry milk. Chill thoroughly.

· Beat egg whites until stiff; gradually add ¼ c. sugar, continuing to beat.

· Beat egg yolks until very light; add remaining sugar and vanilla. Fold in egg whites.

· When well blended, gradually pour into milk mixture, folding as you pour.

· Add sherbet and whip until foamy. If desired, add red and yellow food colors to tint a deeper orange. Pour into punch bowl or glasses. Sprinkle with nutmeg. Makes 2½ quarts.

Variation

QUICK ORANGE EGGNOG: To make eggnog in electric drink mixer, blender or mixer, combine and blend ¾ c. water and ⅓ c. dry milk. Add 1 egg, ⅛ tsp. vanilla and ½ c. orange sherbet; whip until foamy. Pour into glass. Sprinkle lightly with nutmeg. Makes 2 (8 oz.) glasses.

PEPPERMINT FLUFF

Perfect summer twosome: pretty pink drink and chocolate cookies

- **3 c. milk**
- **¾ c. crushed peppermint candy**
- **¼ c. cold water**
- **1½ tsp. lemon juice**
- **½ tsp. vanilla**
- **¼ c. dry milk**
- **1 tblsp. sugar**

· Scald milk in double boiler. Add candy and stir until dissolved. Chill.

· Combine water, lemon juice, vanilla and dry milk in deep bowl. Beat with electric beater about 6 minutes or until stiff. Gradually add sugar. Beat 1 minute or until blended. Chill.

· When ready to serve, whip peppermint mixture until foamy. Fold in half of whipped dry-milk mixture. Pour into glasses.

· Use remaining whipped dry milk to top each drink, about ¼ c. per glass. Sprinkle with bits of crushed peppermint candy. Makes 4 (10 oz.) glasses.

STRAWBERRY FROST

Tempting and rewarding

- **1 qt. milk**
- **3 tblsp. strawberry instant soft-drink mix**
- **½ c. strawberry ice cream**

· Combine ingredients; beat until foamy. Makes 4 (10 oz.) glasses.

Chocolate-flavored Milk Drinks

Among the popular milk drinks are those that contain chocolate or cocoa. Rich and luscious French Chocolate appears at many tea parties. With a pot of it at one end of the table and tea on the other end, you always please guests.

FRENCH CHOCOLATE

Serve in your prettiest teacups

- **½ c. semisweet chocolate pieces**
- **½ c. light corn syrup**
- **¼ c. water**
- **1 tsp. vanilla**
- **1 pt. heavy cream**
- **2 qts. milk**

· In saucepan over low heat, stir

chocolate pieces, corn syrup and water together until chocolate is melted. Pour into a small pitcher or cup, cover and chill until cool. Add vanilla.

· In a large bowl, beat the cream, while gradually adding the chocolate mixture. (Using electric mixer at medium speed.) Continue beating until mixture just mounds; spoon fluffy chocolate whipped cream into a crystal serving bowl and refrigerate. (You can fix this in the morning for the afternoon tea, or an hour ahead.)

· Just before serving, scald the milk and pour into a warmed serving pot. Place on tray with cups and saucers and crystal bowl of chocolate whipped cream.

· To serve, spoon some of the whipped cream mixture into each cup; fill cups with hot milk. Let guests stir the two together before sipping. Makes 16 servings in teacups, about 35 servings in chocolate cups.

INSTANT COCOA

Keep this on hand for teens after the game—float marshmallows in cups

1 (1 lb.) pkg. dry milk
1 c. sugar
¾ c. cocoa
¼ tsp. salt

· Sift all ingredients together three times; place in a tightly covered container. Store in a cool place. Makes 27 to 30 servings with hot water added.

TO USE INSTANT COCOA: Combine ⅓ c. of the mix with hot water in serving cup and stir to mix. Or combine 1⅓ c. of mix with 1 qt. hot water.

COCOA SYRUP

Handy for youngsters' entertaining

½ c. sifted cocoa
1 c. sugar
⅛ tsp. salt
1 c. boiling water
1 tsp. vanilla

· Combine cocoa, sugar and salt in saucepan. Add the water gradually, stirring until mixture is smooth.

· Cook over medium heat, stirring until mixture comes to a boil. Boil 1 minute without stirring.

· Remove from heat and cool. When cool, stir in vanilla. Pour into jar or other container, cover and refrigerate until needed. Makes 1¼ cups.

HOT COCOA, PARTY-STYLE

After ice skating or sledding, warm up the youngsters with this hot drink

6 c. milk
¾ c. Cocoa Syrup
Pink whipped cream
Peppermint candy sticks

· Heat milk until bubbles form around edge of saucepan. Add Cocoa Syrup, stirring until well mixed with milk.

· Pour into mugs or cups and top with whipped cream, tinted a delicate pink with a drop or two of red food color. Put a stick of candy in each serving for a stirrer. Makes 6 servings.

Variation

ICED COCOA: Beat cold milk with Cocoa Syrup to combine. Pour over ice cubes in tall glasses. To make 1 glass, use 2 tblsp. Cocoa Syrup to 1 c. milk.

CHOCOLATE MALTED MILK

Just the health drink for folks who are a little underweight

½ c. malted milk powder
3 c. milk
4 egg yolks, beaten
¾ c. chocolate syrup
1½ tblsp. sugar
4 egg whites, stiffly beaten
Ground nutmeg

· Mix malted powder with ¼ c. milk to form a smooth paste. Stir in beaten egg yolks. Add remaining milk and chocolate syrup.

· Add sugar to beaten egg whites. Add half of whites to chocolate mixture; beat with rotary beater, or shake until foamy. Pour over crushed ice in tall glasses.

· Pile remaining egg white meringue on top of each glass. Sprinkle with nutmeg. Makes 4 to 6 servings.

Children's Specials

COCOA FLOAT: Make 4 c. hot cocoa with instant cocoa mix as directed on label. Serve in cups, topping each with a scoop of vanilla ice cream. Dust with cinnamon if desired. Serve at once. Very refreshing on a cold day. Serves 8 to 10.

CHILDREN'S ROOT BEER: Pour ¾ c. chilled, liquefied dry milk in each tall glass. Stir in ¼ c. chilled root beer. Add a big spoonful of vanilla ice cream to each.

STRAWBERRY SODAS

These country-good sodas contain jam from fruit closet or refrigerator

1½ qts. strawberry ice cream
½ c. strawberry jam
3 (7 oz.) bottles ginger ale

· Divide the ice cream between 8 tall (10 oz.) glasses. Add 1 tblsp. strawberry jam to each glass. Fill with ginger ale. Stir with a long spoon to mix. Makes 8 servings.

Tomato Juice—A Prime Favorite—Hot or Cold

When it comes to vegetable appetizers that you sip, tomato juice leads all the rest. This is a perennial favorite of people in all age groups —especially of men. It has almost everything desirable in an appetizer, such as lovely color, stimulating flavor, wide availability and congeniality with most of the dips and vegetable nibbles. Stuffed celery and crisp crackers are ideal accompaniments.

Tomato juice brightens country meals the year round, but it's especially welcome when winter comes. Try cups of piping hot Spiced Tomato Juice with toasted cheese sandwiches and buttered succotash, the kind made with yellow corn. Serve this on a chilly, stormy evening and your supper will be a success.

TOMATO JUICE IN PUNCH BOWL

A country hostess who likes to entertain many friends at a time often serves tomato juice in her punch bowl. "It keeps everyone in the living room out of the way while I arrange the food on the buffet," she says, adding, "I usually freeze a ring of ice for a garnish."

Here is how she fixes it a few days before her party. She uses a ring mold that fits into the punch bowl. On the bottom of it she arranges thin lemon, cucumber and radish slices, pours on ¾″ cold water and puts it in the freezer. When frozen, she fills the mold about three fourths full of water and returns it to the freezer.

To turn out the decorative ring in the punch bowl, she quickly dips the bottom of the mold in warm water. She pours on the chilled tomato juice, seasoned as the spirit moves. The gala ring floats in the red juice, festive side up.

TOMATO JUICE COMBINATIONS

TOMATO/CLAM: Combine 2 parts tomato juice with 1 part clam juice. Serve heated or cold with lemon wedges, carrot sticks or celery. You can give it a gourmet touch by adding 1 or 2 tblsp. sherry to 1 qt. of this mixture.

TOMATO/SAUERKRAUT: Combine 2 parts tomato juice with 1 part sauerkraut juice; chill thoroughly.

HOT BUTTERED: Serve hot tomato juice in cups or mugs, stirring in 1 tsp. butter for each cup.

TOMATO/LEMON: Combine 1 qt. tomato juice and ⅓ c. lemon juice; add 1½ tsp. Worcestershire sauce, ¼ tsp. celery salt and ¼ tsp. dill weed.

TOMATO/CREAM: Float 1 tblsp. whipped cream on top each serving of tomato juice.

TOMATO/PINEAPPLE: Fill a glass half full with chilled pineapple juice; tip glass and slowly pour tomato juice down the side of glass until nearly full. Serve at once.

SEASONINGS AND GARNISHES FOR TOMATO JUICE

HERB SEASONINGS: To 1 qt. tomato juice add ¼ tsp. of one of the following dried herbs: basil leaves, thyme leaves, dill weed, parsley flakes, or ½ bay leaf. Heat juice slowly 15 minutes. Serve either hot or cold with a thin slice of lemon or lime sprinkled with paprika. (Remove bay leaf after heating.)

SPICY SEASONINGS: To 1 qt. tomato juice add ¼ tsp. of one of the following: chili powder, celery salt, onion salt or seasoned salt. Or, add ½ tsp. ground cloves or 6 whole cloves. Heat slowly 15 minutes and serve hot or cold. (Remove whole cloves.)

HOT SEASONINGS: To 1 qt. tomato juice add 1 to 3 tsp. red or green taco sauce, 4 drops Tabasco sauce or ½ tsp. prepared horse-radish. Any of these hot-flavored seasonings may be added to ½ c. heavy cream, whipped; float a dollop on each serving of cold or hot tomato juice.

GARNISHES: Decorate your servings of tomato juice with any of the following: thin lemon slices—add a sprinkle of paprika for red or a dash of dill weed for green; thin slices of small frankfurters or precooked sausages in hot tomato juice; or sprigs of fresh herbs such as basil, thyme, marjoram or parsley. For something different, use leaves of either lemon verbena or rose geranium, or any of the minty geraniums in the Pelargonium line.

SPICED TOMATO JUICE

Hostess success tip: Serve this hot cheery drink and delight your friends

- **1 (46 oz.) can tomato juice**
- **6 tblsp. brown sugar**
- **6 whole cloves**
- **2 (2½″) sticks cinnamon**
- **½ lemon, sliced**

· Combine all ingredients in heavy saucepan. Bring to boil; simmer 5 minutes. Strain; serve hot. Makes about 5 cups.

Coffee and Tea Drinks

COFFEE/BUTTERSCOTCH FOAM

End a meal with this filling drink

- **4 tsp. instant coffee powder**
- **½ c. boiling water**
- **1½ c. cold water**
- **¼ c. butterscotch topping**
- **½ pt. vanilla ice cream**

· Dissolve coffee in hot water; add cold water. Combine with remaining ingredients in blender or large bowl of electric mixer. Blend or beat until frothy. Pour into tall glasses. Sprinkle with cinnamon if desired. Makes 3 servings.

SWEDISH COFFEE

Superb for a crowd—make it in a big kettle and pour it from pitchers

- **2 eggs**
- **2½ lbs. regular grind coffee**
- **2 c. cold water**
- **18 qts. cold water**

· Mix eggs and broken shells with coffee. Add 2 c. water. Divide in two equal parts; place each part in a cheesecloth bag and tie securely. Allow space for the coffee to swell.
· Measure 9 qts. water into each of two large coffeepots or kettles. Immerse a cheesecloth bag of coffee in water in each container. Bring to a boil. Stir and then remove from heat.
· Leave bags in pots at least 3 to 4 minutes, up to 10 minutes if you like a beverage of greater strength. Makes about 96 (6 oz.) cups.

Note: Usually about half the guests (48) like sugar and cream in coffee; you will need 3 c. cream and 50 cubes of sugar.

HOT SPICED TEA

Fruited, spiced and fragrant

- **6 c. water**
- **1 tsp. whole cloves**
- **1 (1″) stick cinnamon**
- **2½ tblsp. black tea**
- **¾ c. orange juice**
- **2 tblsp. lemon juice**
- **½ c. sugar**

· Place water in saucepan; add cloves and cinnamon. Bring to a boil and remove from heat. Add the tea at once, stir to distribute and immerse leaves. Cover and steep 5 minutes. Strain.

• While tea steeps, heat orange and lemon juices, with sugar added, to a boil. Stir into the hot tea and serve at once in teacups. Makes 7 or 8 servings.

LEMON ICED TEA

Easy and quick and so good

12 tea bags
1 qt. boiling water
2 qts. cold water
1 (6 oz.) can frozen lemonade concentrate

• Steep tea in boiling water 5 minutes. Remove tea bags. Stir in cold water and lemonade concentrate. Serve in ice-filled glasses. Makes 12 servings.

HOT TEA FOR 30 TO 35

• You have to alter your regular system of tea making when you wish to make a larger quantity than your pot will hold. First, you make a Tea Concentrate, then you add hot water:

• Bring 6 c. (1½ qts.) freshly drawn cold water to a full boil; remove from heat and add ¼ lb. loose tea. Stir to distribute and immerse leaves; cover.

• Let steep 5 minutes exactly. Strain into a warmed teapot or pitcher. You will have about 1 quart Tea Concentrate.

• To serve, have ready a pot of very hot water. Add about ¼ c. Tea Concentrate to each teacup and fill with hot water. (Or put the same proportions in teapot.)

HOT TEA FOR 200

• Make the Tea Concentrate as for Tea for 30 to 35, but use 1 lb. loose tea and 1½ gallons freshly boiling water. Steep 10 minutes instead of 5 minutes.

• While you can use either loose tea or tea bags, most women believe it is economical and less messy to use loose tea for making the brew for a crowd.

• Instant teas also are available. Follow package directions when using them. Some of these quick teas are the dried extract of freshly brewed tea, while others contain equal parts of the dried extract and carbohydrates, which protect the flavors. Read the label.

Additions to Hot Tea in Brewing: Add a little grated orange peel to the pot when steeping tea. Or add a rose geranium leaf, a few whole cloves or sprigs of fresh mint.

What to Serve with Hot Tea: Lump sugar, thin lemon slices and a pitcher of light cream or milk are the traditional accompaniments. (Some tea experts, especially the English, say that milk does not mask the tea taste the way cream does.) Some people like the flavor of whole cloves stuck in the lemon slices.

• Among other excellent accompaniments to hot tea are a small pitcher of orange juice or pineapple juice to add to the poured tea; sugar-dusted fresh mint leaves; clove-studded thin lime or orange slices; and stick cinnamon to use for stirrers.

ICED TEA FOR 200

• Make the Tea Concentrate as for Hot Tea for 200. Add 1 c. of Concentrate to every 6 c. cold water.

Note: Sometimes iced tea has a

cloudy look. Cloudiness does not affect the taste, but you can restore the clarity by stirring a little boiling water into the tea just before pouring it into the glasses. Cloudiness usually develops if you chill hot tea in the refrigerator.

chapter 16

Friendly Appetizers and Snacks

APPETIZERS ARE A PROMISE of good food to come. Their mission is not to appease hunger but to please the eye and promote sociability. Snacks, on the other hand satisfy hunger. In many hospitable homes at least a few snacks are always ready in the freezer. Our Snack Packs (designed for the holidays but appropriate for any season) are of two types: ready to serve cold or run through the oven. And with our Countryside Test Kitchen Basic Red Sauce in the refrigerator, you can quickly set out a bowl of Nippy Cheese Dip to serve with crackers.

Today's country hostess likes to invite the family and dinner guests to sip tomato or fruit juice in the living room while she puts the finishing touches on the meal. Dips are popular, too—we give you recipes.

If you like to serve a first-course appetizer at the dinner table, try our Spiced Fruit Cocktail, which you can make one day and chill for use the next. Fruit and Sherbet Cocktail or the summer beauty, Melon-boat Cocktail, are refreshing and color-bright.

Nibblers frequently favor confections, such as popcorn, cereal and nut treats. You will want to try our Spicy Crunch and Peanut Chews.

Use the appetizers and snacks in this chapter to make people happy—to keep country hospitality alive in these frustrating times. Good food and good talk are country companions of long standing.

Versatile Fruit Cocktails

If you like to serve a first course at the table in your company meals, the next three recipes make gorgeous meal starters that taste as good as they look. Melon-boat, Spiced Fruit and Fruit and Sherbet Cocktails also are exquisite, light desserts. Try them and see if you don't agree that they start and end meals with equal appeal and distinction.

MELON-BOAT COCKTAIL

Refreshing in summer when melons reach their flavor peak

- 1 large cantaloupe
- ½ c. Fresh Mint Syrup
- 1½ to 2 c. pineapple chunks and sliced strawberries

· Cut cantaloupe into sixths; make a crisscross pattern in wedges. Spoon about 1 tblsp. Fresh Mint Syrup over each. Heap fruit in center. Makes 6 servings.

Note: Use honeydew melon instead of cantaloupe, or pour Fresh Mint Syrup over servings of melon cubes; a combination of fresh and frozen fruits like pineapple, orange and grapefruit; strawberries, raspberries or blueberries; drained, canned fruit cocktail or other fruits. To step up color and flavor, add scoops of lime, orange, lemon or raspberry sherbet.

FRESH MINT SYRUP

Good to keep in refrigerator to serve over melons and fresh fruits

- 1 c. sugar
- ⅔ c. water
- ½ c. chopped mint leaves
- ¼ c. lemon juice
- ½ c. orange juice

· Combine sugar and water in small saucepan; boil 3 minutes. Add mint; cool. Strain.
· Add juices; chill. Makes 1½ cups.

SPICED FRUIT COCKTAIL

Surprise flavor delight. You can make it a day ahead and refrigerate

- 2 (1 lb. 1 oz.) cans fruit for salad or fruit cocktail
- 1 (1 lb. 1 oz.) can light cherries
- 2 tblsp. lemon juice
- 1 (6″) stick cinnamon
- 1 tsp. whole cloves
- ⅛ tsp. salt

· Drain syrup from fruit into saucepan. Add lemon juice, spices (tied in cheesecloth bag) and salt. Boil 5 minutes. Remove spices. Pour over fruit. Chill several hours or overnight.
· Serve in sherbet glasses. Garnish each serving with a sprig of mint, if you like. Makes 6 servings.

FRUIT AND SHERBET COCKTAIL

Bright color contrasts make appetizers pretty as nosegays at each place

- 1 (1 lb. 14 oz.) can pineapple chunks, chilled
- 1 (10 or 11 oz.) can mandarin oranges, chilled
- 1 pt. lime sherbet

· Drain fruits. Half fill glasses with pineapple chunks; top with scoop of sherbet. Fill around sherbet with orange sections. Makes 6 servings.

3-in-1 Fruit Juice Cocktails

Small glasses of chilled fruit juice stimulate the appetite when they start a meal, either in the living room or at the table. The trio of treats that follow are three times as good as most juice appetizers—three kinds of fruit juices blend their charms in each cocktail. The resulting ambrosial flavors intrigue; everyone who sips tries to figure out what they are. The garnishes provide a festive look.

29. LEMON CHEESE CAKE—A special-occasion Southern cake. Its name comes from the curd-like filling. Cake contains no cheese. Recipe, page 382.

30. PEANUT BUTTER CHIFFON PIE—Tasty pie wears whipped cream topping. Omit cream for a more pronounced peanut flavor. Extra-good. Recipe, page 429.

31. RAISIN GRIDDLE COOKIES—Store the cut-out dough circles in freezer to bake on electric or other griddle later. Special treats. Recipe, page 461.

32. OATMEAL/MOLASSES COOKIES–These farmer-size, chewy cookies make friends whenever they appear. Recipe makes 6 dozen cookies. Recipe, page 463.

3-IN-1 FRUIT JUICE COCKTAILS

RUBY PUNCH: Combine 4 c. cranberry juice cocktail, 1 c. pineapple juice and 1 c. orange juice. Garnish each drink with a quarter of thin slice of orange. Makes 8 (6 oz.) glasses.

PINEAPPLE GLOW: Combine 3 c. apple juice, 3 c. pineapple juice, ¼ c. maraschino cherry juice and ¼ tsp. almond extract. Garnish each drink with a maraschino cherry and a sprig of mint. Makes 8 (6 oz.) glasses.

ROYAL ADE: Combine 3 c. apple juice, 3 c. grape juice, 2 tblsp. lime juice and ¼ tsp. ground nutmeg. Garnish with lime slices. Makes 8 (6 oz.) glasses.

Friendly Dips and Dippers

Provide your guests with something crisp and crunchy to scoop up the dips you set before them. Fresh vegetable pickups, assorted crackers, and corn and potato chips make fine dippers. Hostesses appreciate dips because they can fix most of them ahead and chill. It's a good idea to take them out of the refrigerator long enough before serving to soften a little.

Serve your dips in pretty little bowls. The number of guests often determines how many dips to offer, but usually plenty of two or three kinds admirably fill the bill. One of them might be hot—especially if you have a chafing dish. People always gather around Hot Crab Dip. It's a winner.

TEXAS CHILI DIP

Watch men and boys dip into this —they'll like that hot chili taste

1 (15½ oz.) can chili with beans
1 c. creamed cottage cheese
2 tblsp. chopped chili peppers, fresh or canned, or bottled hot-pepper sauce
2 tblsp. lemon juice

• Turn chili, cottage cheese and peppers into mixer bowl; beat together at low speed until blended, adding lemon juice. (If you use hot-pepper sauce, sometimes called taco sauce, omit chopped peppers and add sauce with lemon juice.)

• Chill about 4 hours. Serve as a dip for cucumber slices, cauliflowerets, celery and carrot sticks, or with toasted wedges of cornmeal tortillas, slices of party rye bread, crackers or corn and potato chips. Makes 2⅔ cups.

GARBANZO DIP

Our taste-testers all voted this a top-notch dip—it is an adaptation of a favorite Middle Eastern dish

1 (15 oz.) can garbanzos (chick-peas)
1½ tsp. salt
⅛ tsp. pepper
3 cloves garlic, chopped
½ c. salad oil
¼ c. lemon juice
2 tblsp. chopped parsley

• Drain chick-peas through sieve and wash under cold running water until water runs clear. Place in blender with salt, pepper, garlic, salad oil and lemon juice. Blend until smooth. You may need to add 1 extra tblsp. oil to make mixture liquid enough.

• Remove from blender container and combine with parsley. Chill thoroughly. Garnish with extra parsley sprigs, and serve as a dip for crisp fresh vegetables or with sesame seed crackers. Makes about 2 cups.

SMOKY COTTAGE CHEESE DIP

Serve this with carrot, celery and cucumber sticks and cauliflowerets

1 c. creamed cottage cheese
1 (3 oz.) pkg. cream cheese
2 tblsp. light cream or milk
1 tsp. minced onion
½ tsp. liquid smoke
¼ tsp. garlic salt
½ c. minced ripe olives

• Beat together cottage cheese, cream cheese and cream. Blend in remaining ingredients. Makes 1⅔ cups.

CREAM CHEESE AND CLAM DIP

A snack folks rave about. Serve corn or potato chips alongside

2 (3 oz.) pkgs. cream cheese
1 (7½ oz.) can minced clams
2 drops Tabasco sauce
¼ tsp. salt
Dash of pepper
1 tsp. minced onion
1 tsp. lemon juice

• Soften cream cheese. Drain clams and add 2 tblsp. clam juice to cheese. Blend until smooth.
• Add minced clams, Tabasco sauce, seasonings, onion and lemon juice. Mix well and chill. Makes 1⅓ cups.

CURRIED EGG DIP FOR VEGETABLES

Good with almost every vegetable —especially chilled cucumber strips

¼ tsp. Tabasco sauce
½ tsp. curry powder
¼ tsp. dry mustard
½ tsp. salt
½ c. mayonnaise
1½ tblsp. finely chopped onion
½ c. finely chopped celery
1 tsp. minced parsley
4 hard-cooked eggs, finely chopped

• Combine Tabasco, curry powder, dry mustard and salt. Stir into mayonnaise.
• Combine onion, celery and parsley; stir into mayonnaise mixture. Fold in eggs. Chill until ready to serve. Makes 2 cups.

NIPPY CHEESE DIP

Set a bowl of this out for guests who like to dunk and nibble

1 (8 oz.) pkg. cream cheese
¼ c. Basic Red Sauce (see Index)

• Soften cream cheese at room temperature.
• Whip cheese with electric mixer or wooden spoon. Add Red Sauce gradually, beating after each addition, until light and fluffy.
• Serve with snack-style crackers, potato chips, corn chips or vegetable dippers. Makes about 2 cups.

HOT CRAB DIP

Quick and easy, guest approved

1 (5 oz.) jar sharp process cheese spread
1 (8 oz.) pkg. cream cheese
1 (7½ oz.) can crabmeat, flaked
2 tblsp. light cream
½ tsp. Worcestershire sauce

• Combine ingredients in top of double boiler. Cook, stirring occasionally, until mixture is blended and hot.

• Serve hot in chafing dish or other heated casserole with potato chips or crackers. Makes 2½ cups.

Pick-up Vegetable Appetizers

Bring in an assortment of crisp, icy-cold raw vegetables, arranged attractively on a tray, platter or big plate. Or put them in big bowls of crushed ice. Then carry in tempting, go-with dips, chilled thoroughly. You'll not need to coax people to gather round and eat.

Bright vegetable nibblers appeal to almost everyone, but especially to calorie counters. You'll even encounter a few braves who eat the dippers and resist the dips. Pamper them by providing a shaker of salt or a small bowl of seasoned salt.

Hostesses like to serve raw vegetable appetizers for several reasons. They have eye and taste appeal and require no cooking. And they don't dull appetites for the meal to follow. (Incidentally, many of the appetizers make pretty salad garnishes.)

Here is a list of attractive vegetable appetizers. Select any of them you like, but remember to consider color and shape contrasts.

Cut all vegetable strips about 3″ long and ½″ wide. Soak all the vegetables in ice water 1 hour and dry. If you aren't ready to serve them, put each vegetable in a jar, cover tightly and refrigerate for a few hours.

Asparagus stalks, 2 to 3″ tip ends
Broccoli buds, bite-size
Carrots, scraped and cut in sticks
Cauliflower flowerets, bite-size
Celery, cut in 3″ lengths, or celery fans
Cucumbers, peeled and cut in sticks
Green onions or scallions, small
Peppers, sweet green and red, cut in strips
Radishes, small red (if fresh from garden, leave tufts of leaves on top end, or make radish roses or accordions)
Sweet onions, large (slice crosswise, remove outer skin and separate in rings)
Turnips, young, peeled and cut in slender strips.
Zucchini and other summer squash, young, cut in strips without peeling

CELERY FANS: Cut each celery branch or rib in 3″ lengths. Make 3 to 6 parallel cuts close together almost to the other end. Or cut from both ends almost to the center. Put in ice water about 1 hour so strips will curl.

RADISH ROSES: Use a small sharp knife with a thin blade. Cut off root, then cut 4 or 5 petals from root end almost to stem end, leaving a thin uncut strip between petals. Put in ice water for at least an hour.

RADISH ACCORDIONS: Cut long, red radishes crosswise in 10 to 12 thin strips, but not quite through to the opposite side. Chill in ice water so slices will spread.

• Add some of these chilled raw vegetables to your arrangement:

Cherry tomatoes, tiny
Yellow tomatoes, small
Firm, ripe tomatoes, peeled and cut in quarters

Whole mushrooms, small
Watercress, small sprigs

Vegetables on Picks

Impale bite-size pieces of crisp, raw vegetables on one end of toothpicks or cocktail picks; stick toothpicks into a big satiny, purple eggplant. Use vegetables of contrasting colors and set the eggplant holding appetizers on small pine branches or a leaf-covered plate. You can substitute a well-shaped, firm, green cabbage head for the eggplant. Here are some vegetables appropriate to serve this way:

Cherry tomatoes
Yellow tomatoes, small
Celery fans
Red radishes or radish roses
Green peppers cut in squares
Chinese cabbage, cut in bite-size chunks
Canned whole mushrooms, drained
Fresh mushroom caps, filled with blue or other cheese spread
Small green pepper squares centered on carrot slices, one end of pick holding pepper in place (pepper looks like center of carrot "flower")
Artichoke hearts, frozen, cooked by package directions, drained and chilled

Party Appetizers Guests Like

Set out an attractive tray of before-dinner tidbits to put your guests in a sociable mood. They'll enjoy nibbling while they chat, until dinner is ready to serve. A tart fruit drink or chilled tomato juice tastes good with these snacks. Or, with hot broth, tea or coffee, they're fine for light refreshments during a winter evening.

You won't want to serve more than two or three kinds at a time. So take your pick of the recipes that follow.

LITTLE PIZZAS: Bake 1 can ready-to-bake refrigerator biscuits according to package directions. Cool and split each in half. Spread each half with a little tomato paste. Sprinkle with a little orégano. Top with a thin slice of mozzarella or natural sharp American cheese; add a drop or two of salad oil. Sprinkle with Parmesan cheese. Bake in hot oven (450°) 6 to 8 minutes. Top each with a piece of anchovy. Serve whole or cut in half, but serve hot. Makes 20 whole pizzas.

CURRIED EGG CANAPÉ: Chop 2 hard-cooked eggs finely. Add 1 tblsp. mayonnaise, ¼ tsp. salt and ¼ tsp. curry powder. To serve, cut bread into rounds or desired shapes. Butter lightly. Spread with egg mixture. Decorate some with carrot wedges and a slice of green olive; top others with ripe olive slices. Makes about ½ cup spread.

ROQUEFORT OR BLUE CHEESE MOLD: Place 1 (8 oz.) pkg. cream cheese in a mixing bowl. Let it come to room temperature. Add 6 oz. Roquefort or blue cheese, ½ tsp. vinegar, ½ tsp. prepared mustard and ⅛ tsp. Worcestershire sauce. Cream or beat until smooth. Chill; form into a ball. Roll in ¼ c. chopped salted peanuts. Refrigerate. Serve as a spread for crackers. Makes 1½ cups.

• Another attractive way to mold the cheese mixture is in a small roll as for refrigerator cookies. Wrap in foil, waxed paper or plastic film. Chill.

If you make the roll the right size, the slices will fit top of crackers.

· Or pass a wooden tray of fragrant cheese and assorted crackers for dessert or evening refreshments. Lay individual servings of cheese of different kinds and crackers on tray. Bring in pot of steaming hot coffee. And watch the men's enthusiasm!

EASY BLUE CHEESE SNACKS: Spread blue cheese on thin apple slices that have been dipped in lemon juice. Put together sandwich-style.

PEPPY ONION DIP: Combine 1 (1½ oz.) pkg. onion soup mix, 1 c. dairy sour cream, ¼ c. milk and 1 tsp. prepared mustard in a bowl. Cover and let stand in refrigerator 1 hour or more to thicken, overnight if you wish. Makes 1 cup.

FRANKS IN HOT SAUCE: Combine 1 (8 oz.) can tomato sauce, ½ c. chili sauce, ½ c. chopped onion, 1 beef bouillon cube and 2 tblsp. chopped celery leaves. Cook 10 minutes. Cut ½ lb. frankfurters into pieces about 1″ long. Add to sauce. Simmer 5 to 10 minutes. Serve hot. Makes 1 cup sauce. You can double recipe and serve in electric skillet or chafing dish.

CHICKEN BITS: Remove skin and bone from 4 whole chicken breasts. Cut into bite-size pieces. Dip in 2 beaten eggs, then in 1 c. prepared flavored bread crumbs (or use crushed herb-seasoned croutons). Fry in hot salad oil until lightly browned. Serve hot with dips. If you wish, make several hours ahead, refrigerate, then reheat 10 minutes in a moderate oven (350°). Good dipped in hot ketchup or tartar sauce. Makes about 4 dozen chicken bits.

Freeze Snack Packs for the Holidays

Tasty nibbles give a lift to any gathering, and freezable Party Snack Packs also give the busy hostess a lift. If you prepare several packs with a variety of festive treats before the party or holiday rush, you'll be all set when the guests arrive.

Snacks with tomato juice or hot consommé can start off your holiday or other buffet or open house, provide a light supper for television watchers, or refreshments for hungry teens after the game or caroling. They're handy to take to card parties or club meetings.

Your guests and family, during the yuletide, will appreciate this appetizing change from the usual sweet holiday fare, and you'll know that snackers are getting needed protein. Try dressing a Party Pack with a holiday ribbon to extend Christmas good wishes to a busy neighbor or friend.

HOT SNACK PACKS

· Select 2 to 4 of the following snacks per tray: Cornmeal/Bean Tarts, Pizza Franks, Chicken Turnovers and Deviled Ham Twists. Prepare according to recipe directions which follow.

· Place assorted unbaked snacks close together in an 11¼ × 7¼″ disposable aluminum foil pan or pizza pan. Freeze until firm; cover tightly with plastic wrap, then with aluminum foil. Seal foil to edges of each tray securely with freezer tape. Then tape all the snack trays in a neat stack for convenient storage in your freezer.

• To serve hot snack assortments, remove foil and plastic wrap and bake unthawed in a preheated hot oven (400°) 15 to 20 minutes, until the snacks are nicely browned and puffed.

CORNMEAL/BEAN TARTS

South-of-the-border flavor excitement in bite-sized tarts

Pastry:

2 c. sifted flour
1 tsp. salt
1 c. cornmeal
⅔ c. shortening
⅔ c. grated Cheddar cheese
⅔ c. water

Filling:

1 (15½ oz.) can refried beans
¾ c. grated Provolone cheese (or other sharp cheese)
2 tsp. garlic salt
2 tblsp. red chili sauce
1½ tsp. crushed dried red pepper
¼ tsp. chili powder
2 tblsp. butter

• To make pastry shells, sift together flour and salt; stir in cornmeal. Cut in shortening until mixture resembles fine crumbs. Stir in grated cheese. Sprinkle water over mixture, tossing lightly with a fork until pastry is uniformly dampened.

• Roll to about ⅛″ thickness on lightly floured surface. Cut with 2″ biscuit cutter. Press pastry circles into tiny tart cups, ruffling edges. For larger bean tarts, use small muffin-pan cups. Bake in hot oven (400°) 13 minutes.

• Combine filling ingredients in top of double boiler; heat until cheese melts. Spoon into cornmeal tarts. Makes 2½ dozen.

PIZZA FRANKS

Bits of wieners wear biscuit jackets

2¼ c. sifted flour
4 tsp. baking powder
½ tsp. cream of tartar
¼ tsp. garlic salt
¼ tsp. onion salt
1 tblsp. sugar
¼ c. Parmesan cheese
¼ tsp. basil leaves
½ tsp. orégano leaves
⅓ c. shortening
⅓ c. milk
⅓ c. tomato paste
1 egg
1 lb. wieners, cut in ½″ pieces

• Sift together dry ingredients. Stir in cheese, basil and orégano. Cut in shortening to make coarse crumbs. Add milk, tomato paste and egg; stir with fork until dough follows fork around the bowl.

• Knead on floured board five or six times. Roll dough ½″ thick. Cut in 1″ rounds (we used a doughnut hole cutter). Press dough around franks to form cups. Makes 8 dozen.

CHICKEN TURNOVERS

These have a delicate hint of curry

1 tblsp. chopped onion
¼ c. diced green olives
1 (3 oz.) can mushroom pieces (reserve liquid)
1 tblsp. butter
1 tsp. flour
1 tsp. curry powder
¼ tsp. salt
1½ c. ground cooked chicken
1 (9½ oz.) pkg. pie crust mix

• Sauté onion, olives and mushroom pieces in butter. Stir in flour, curry powder and salt, then mushroom broth. Simmer 1 minute; add chicken. Prepare pastry according to package directions. Roll out and cut in 3″ circles.

• Place 1 tsp. chicken mixture in center of each pastry circle. Fold pastry over, dampen edges and seal with a fork or handle-end of a table knife. Makes 2½ dozen.

DEVILED HAM TWISTS

Biscuit "butterflies," ham-filled

3 (4½ oz.) cans deviled ham
3 tblsp. chopped walnuts
3 tblsp. minced onion
¼ c. minced, pimiento-stuffed olives
½ tsp. ground red pepper
6 finely crushed saltines
¾ c. milk
2¾ c. all-purpose buttermilk biscuit mix
Paprika

• Combine ham, walnuts, onion, olives, red pepper and saltines, stirring until well-blended and smooth.

• Stir milk into biscuit mix to make soft dough; beat 20 strokes until stiff. Divide dough in half. Roll each portion into a 12″ square; spread 1 c. ham mixture on half of square. Fold uncovered half over ham mixture to form a 12 × 6″ rectangle. With a sharp knife or pastry wheel cut in 36 (2 × 1″) rectangles. Twist each gently to form a bow and sprinkle with paprika. Repeat with remaining dough and ham mixture. Makes 6 dozen.

COLD SNACK PACKS

• Cream butter, spread it to the edges of frozen bread slices. Stack several slices and trim off all crusts with a sharp knife.

• Spread filling on bread slices and cut in triangles, squares or bars. Garnish open-face sandwiches and freeze according to directions given for Hot Snack Packs.

• At serving time, uncover snack trays, thaw 30 minutes at room temperature.

TUNA TOPPERS

Mustard, pimiento-stuffed olives and sour cream add special zing

1 (7 oz.) can tuna, drained and flaked
¼ c. diced pimiento-stuffed olives
1 tblsp. prepared mustard
2 tblsp. dairy sour cream
⅛ tsp. pepper

• Combine ingredients. Flake finely with a fork. Spread mixture evenly on 4 slices buttered white bread. Cut each slice in quarters. If desired, garnish with sliced pimiento-stuffed olives. Makes 16 snacks.

SAVORY HAM

Small sandwich triangles with two fillings—ham and cheese mix

1 (3 oz.) pkg. cream cheese, softened
1 tblsp. chili sauce
1 tsp. chili powder
1 tsp. Worcestershire sauce
4 to 5 drops Tabasco sauce
1 tsp. capers and juice (optional)
1 clove garlic, crushed
1 tblsp. pickle relish
⅛ tsp. salt
4 oz. sliced, fully cooked ham
Cream cheese (for garnish)

• Combine all ingredients, except ham. Spread mixture on 6 slices white bread and top with a ham slice. Cut each bread slice in 4 triangles. To garnish, pipe ribbons of cream cheese on top in a decorative design. Makes 24.

CHEESE AND BEEF POTPOURRI

Dainty open-face sandwich fingers are bright with vivid colors

1 (8 oz.) pkg. cream cheese, softened
2 tblsp. blue cheese, crumbled
⅓ c. chopped walnuts
¼ c. crumbled dried beef
2 tsp. minced green onion tops
4 to 5 drops Tabasco sauce
⅛ tsp. ground red pepper
Dried beef (for garnish)

• Whip cream cheese. Add remaining ingredients and spread on 6 slices buttered whole wheat bread. Cut each slice in 3 fingers. Garnish with additional chopped dried beef. Makes 18.

Shrimp Appetizers

First-course shrimp appetizers get meals off to a good start because they're almost everyone's favorite. This means you'd better plan for seconds. We give you recipes for two excellent shrimp meal beginners. Spiced Shrimp is a do-ahead dish. You fix it one day and chill it until the next—almost to the time your guests will arrive. Set a bowl of the appetizer on the buffet table and provide picks so everyone can spear his shrimp. Or, at the sit-down dinner, serve the appetizer in individual cocktail sherbet glasses lined with lettuce.

Creole Fried Shrimp is what its name implies, a treat from Cajun country in southwest Louisiana. A visitor from that area brought it to our Countryside Test Kitchens. It's so tasty that several of our editors not only use it for an appetizer, but also for a main dish (making the balls somewhat larger).

CREOLE FRIED SHRIMP

Serve these tasty tidbits on picks for easy dipping in the sauce

2 tblsp. shortening
2 tblsp. flour
2 tblsp. finely chopped onion
1 tblsp. finely chopped green pepper
1 tblsp. finely chopped celery
¾ c. water
2½ c. shrimp, cleaned and finely chopped or ground
2 tsp. salt
1 tsp. ground red pepper
1½ c. soft moistened bread crumbs
2 tblsp. minced parsley
Fine bread crumbs (for coating)
Shrimp Sauce Erath

• Heat shortening; add flour and stir constantly until golden brown. Add onion, green pepper and celery; stir until soft.

• Add water, shrimp and seasonings; simmer 15 minutes. Remove from heat and cool slightly. Add 1½ c. bread crumbs and parsley. Shape mixture into small balls and roll in fine bread crumbs.

• Fry in deep hot fat (350°) about 2 minutes, or until golden brown. Drain on paper towels. Serve with Shrimp Sauce Erath. Makes 5 dozen small balls.

SHRIMP SAUCE ERATH: Combine ¼ c. mayonnaise, ¼ c. Worcestershire sauce, ¼ c. ketchup, 1 tsp. horseradish, ¼ tsp. garlic juice, ½ tsp. salt and ⅛ tsp. pepper; chill thoroughly. Sprinkle grated hard-cooked egg yolk on top just before serving. Makes about ¾ cup.

Note: Make the shrimp balls larger

for a main dish. Pass a bowl of the sauce to ladle over them.

SPICED SHRIMP

Fix this the day before entertaining

1 lb. cooked, peeled and deveined shrimp (4 c.)
3 medium onions, thinly sliced
1 lemon, sliced
½ c. white vinegar
¼ c. water
2 tsp. salt
1 tsp. sugar
½ tsp. dry mustard
¼ tsp. ground ginger
½ tsp. peppercorns
1 bay leaf
⅛ tsp. Tabasco sauce
¼ c. lemon juice
½ c. salad oil

· Fill a bowl with alternating layers of shrimp, sliced onions and lemon.
· Combine vinegar, water, salt, sugar, dry mustard, ginger, pepper, bay leaf and Tabasco sauce in a saucepan. Bring to a boil; cover, simmer 5 minutes. Cool.
· Strain; add lemon juice and oil. Pour over shrimp. Cover, and refrigerate 24 hours. Stir occasionally. Drain before serving. Have wooden picks for spearing. Makes 1 quart.

Fruit Nibbles

Nibbles featuring dried fruits are a part of Christmas in the country. They travel in gift-wrapped packages from one home to another in many neighborhoods. Bowls of these confections get plenty of attention at holiday open houses. Among the universal favorites are Chocolate Raisin Clusters—really good!

CHOCOLATE RAISIN CLUSTERS

Easy to fix and a joy to eat

1 (6 oz.) pkg. semisweet chocolate pieces
¼ c. light corn syrup
1½ tsp. vanilla
2 tblsp. confectioners sugar
2 c. seedless raisins

· Combine chocolate pieces and syrup in top of double boiler over hot water. Set over low heat. Stir until chocolate is melted. Remove from heat.
· Add vanilla, confectioners sugar and raisins. Stir to coat with chocolate.
· Drop from teaspoon onto buttered baking sheet. Chill. Store in a cool place, in a covered container. Makes 30 pieces, about 1¼ pounds.

APRICOT STICKS

Fruits make this confection special

20 large dried apricot halves
½ c. flaked or shredded coconut
¼ c. candied pineapple, chopped fine
Sugar

· Wash apricots. Cover with boiling water; let stand 5 minutes, or until softened. Drain; dry on paper toweling.
· Combine coconut and pineapple; mix thoroughly.
· Flatten each apricot half, skin side down. Spread portion of coconut-pineapple mixture over surface. Roll, jelly roll fashion. Place on tray to dry at room temperature.
· Roll in sugar. Store in loosely covered container at room temperature. Makes 20 apricot confections.

PRUNE CRYSTAL BALLS

Lemon, orange and prune flavors blend

1¾ c. sugar
2 c. water
2 thin slices of lemon
2 c. dried prunes
Salted peanuts, walnuts or Brazil nuts
2 tsp. grated orange peel

· Combine 1½ c. sugar, water and lemon slices in saucepan. Place over medium heat; bring to boil.
· Add prunes, and simmer gently over low heat, uncovered, 20 minutes. Cool; drain well. With sharp paring knife, slit prunes open and carefully remove pits.
· Fill centers with two or three salted peanuts, a walnut half or a piece of Brazil nut. (For variation, stuff a miniature marshmallow into prune with nuts.)
· Blend orange peel with remaining ¼ c. sugar. Roll stuffed prunes in mixture. Makes about 3 dozen.

PEAR PINWHEELS

They add interest to holiday sweets

¾ lb. dried pears
⅓ c. chopped dates
2 tblsp. honey
2 tblsp. chopped Brazil nuts, pecans or walnuts

· Pour boiling water over pears. Let stand 5 minutes, until softened. Drain; remove excess moisture with paper toweling. Pears should not be mushy, but soft and pliable.
· Arrange half of pears, skin side down, as rectangle on waxed paper. Overlap edges slightly so there are no spaces between pears. Cover with waxed paper and, with rolling pin, flatten into one smooth sheet. Repeat with remaining pears.
· Combine dates (should be moist and soft) and honey. Blend smooth; add nuts, and mix well.
· Spread half of mixture on each pear sheet. Roll, jelly roll fashion, into a log. Smooth down any rough spots with knife or small spatula. If surface seems too moist, let stand overnight at room temperature.
· Cut each log into 16 pieces. Makes 32.

BOLOGNA CANDY

Looks like summer sausage, tastes like elegant candy—rich and luscious

2 c. sugar
1 c. milk
1 lb. dates (2½ c.)
1 c. flaked coconut
½ c. chopped nuts

· Combine sugar and milk in 2-qt. heavy saucepan. Cook over medium heat to soft ball stage (234°), stirring occasionally.
· Add dates and cook, stirring constantly until mixture is very thick and leaves the side of pan when stirred.
· Remove from heat. Stir in coconut and nuts. Cool slightly. Turn out on wet towel. When cool enough to handle and hold shape, roll up in towel. Place in refrigerator and chill.
· Make a roll 2″ in diameter about 18″ long like rolls of cookie dough. Cut in slices to serve. Makes 2¼ pounds.

Nut Nibbles

Pick-up nut nibbles please at any season, but they're indispensable during the Christmas holidays. They answer for gifts, sell at bazaars and contribute interest to the dessert table. And they are equally at home in party refreshments—the bridge club's supper, coffee party, afternoon tea and the wedding or other receptions. We recommend our nut confections. They are delicious, different and distinctive.

WALNUT MINTS

Nuts have a peppermint candy taste

1 c. sugar
½ c. water
1 tblsp. light corn syrup
½ tsp. salt
6 large marshmallows
5 drops oil of peppermint or ½ tsp. peppermint extract
3 c. walnut halves or pieces

• Combine sugar, water, corn syrup and salt in a 2-qt. heavy saucepan. Place over low to medium heat and stir until sugar is dissolved, then cook to the soft ball stage (234 to 236°).

• Remove from heat; add marshmallows and stir until melted. Add flavoring and nuts, stirring only until well combined.

• Drop by teaspoonfuls onto waxed paper. If mixture starts to set, return to heat for a minute and add a few drops of boiling water. Store in covered container, in refrigerator or freezer. Makes about 36 patties or 1¼ pounds.

ALMOND ACORNS

Truly delicious party confections

¼ c. semisweet chocolate pieces
⅔ c. blanched almonds
1 (2½ oz.) jar chocolate shot (jimmies)

• Place chocolate pieces in pan over hot water. Let stand until soft, then stir to smooth paste.

• Spread almonds in shallow pan; heat in moderate oven (350°) about 20 minutes. Or deep-fat fry at 265° about 1 minute until light brown.

• Dip one end of each almond into melted chocolate, then into chocolate jimmies. Place on waxed paper until firm. Makes about 5 dozen.

ORANGE WALNUTS

Flavor secret is fresh orange juice

1½ c. sugar
½ c. orange juice
Few drops yellow food color (optional)
1 tsp. grated orange peel
½ tsp. vanilla
3 c. walnut halves

• Combine sugar and orange juice in 2-qt. heavy saucepan. Cook to soft ball stage (240°). Add a little food color to tint a delicate orange.

• Remove from heat, add orange peel, vanilla and walnut halves. Stir until syrup begins to look cloudy. Before it hardens, spread mixture on a waxed paper-lined baking sheet so nuts do not overlap. When cool, break in bite-size pieces. Store in covered container, in refrigerator or freezer. Makes about 1 pound.

FROSTED PECANS

Sweet-tasting sour cream frosting coats nuts and adds rich flavor

½ c. dairy sour cream
1½ c. sugar
1½ tsp. vanilla
3 c. pecan halves

• Combine sour cream, sugar and vanilla in 2-qt. heavy saucepan. Cook to soft ball stage (234°), stirring frequently to prevent scorching.

· Add pecans and stir to coat. Turn onto buttered baking sheet and separate with 2 forks. Package and freeze in airtight containers, if you like. Makes about 1¼ pounds.

Variation

FROSTED SOUR CREAM WALNUTS: Substitute walnut halves for the pecans.

SPICY MIXED NUTS

Salted nuts sugared and spiced—good with colas and other soft drinks

1 c. sugar
½ tsp. ground cinnamon
¼ c. evaporated milk
2 tsp. water
1½ c. salted mixed nuts
½ tsp. vanilla

· Combine sugar, cinnamon, evaporated milk and water in a 2-qt. heavy saucepan. Place over medium or medium-low heat and cook to the soft ball stage (236 to 238°), stirring constantly to prevent curdling.

· Remove from heat; mix in nuts and vanilla. Let stand 15 minutes, then stir with a wooden spoon until mixture thickens. Pour at once onto waxed paper-lined baking sheet, spreading as thinly as possible. When cool, break in bite-size pieces. Store in covered container, in refrigerator or freezer. Makes 1 pound.

Note: If mixed nuts contain Brazil nuts, cut them in 2 or 3 pieces.

Variation

SPICY PEANUTS: Instead of the salted mixed nuts, use red-skinned salted Spanish peanuts.

SUGARED PEANUTS

Sugary peanuts with glint of gold

1½ c. sugar
1 c. water
1 c. raw Spanish peanuts, crushed slightly

· Combine 1 c. sugar and ½ c. water in 1½-qt. heavy saucepan. Bring to a boil stirring constantly. If sugar crystals form on sides of pan, wipe them off. Add peanuts; cook and stir over low heat until syrup becomes grainy.

· Remove from heat and pour into coarse sieve, reserving the loose sugar. Keep peanuts warm in oven that has been heated to 250° then turned off.

· Place sugar removed in sieving with remaining ½ c. sugar and ½ c. water back into saucepan. Cook to the firm ball stage (245°).

· Add peanuts to hot syrup and stir until syrup grains. Pour onto unbuttered baking sheet or marble slab and separate. When cool, store in covered container, in refrigerator or freezer. Makes about 1 pound.

Note: When syrup reaches the firm ball stage, you can color and flavor it, if you like, with 3 drops yellow food color and ½ tsp. vanilla.

Country Ways with Peanuts

CRISP PEANUTS

· Heat salted peanuts in moderate oven (350°) before serving. Cool to crisp. Toss with raisins if you like. Unshelled peanuts also may be heated to crisp.

Peanut Pointers:

• Blend ½ c. ground peanuts into 2 c. of tangy cheese sauce for baked macaroni and cheese.
• Blend together ¾ c. applesauce, ½ c. peanut butter, and ½ c. marshmallow creme for a yummy filling between cake layers. Frost whole cake with plain white icing.
• Add ½ c. peanut butter to your regular graham cracker pie crust recipe–it's different and delicious!
• Cover your favorite coffee cake batter with this Peanut Crunch Topping: Combine and blend together until fine like crumbs, ¾ c. flour, ½ c. sugar, 3 tblsp. butter and 1 c. finely ground peanuts.
• Add 2 c. coarsely ground peanuts to ½ gallon vanilla ice cream recipe for peanut ice cream.

PEANUT/CHOCOLATE SAUCE

Great to ladle over vanilla ice cream

1 (4 oz.) pkg. chocolate pudding and pie filling
¾ c. water
¾ c. light corn syrup
¼ tsp. salt
1 tblsp. butter or regular margarine
⅓ c. peanut butter
½ tsp. vanilla

• Empty pudding contents into saucepan. Gradually add water, mixing until smooth. Add corn syrup and salt; mix.
• Cook over medium heat, stirring constantly until mixture comes to a boil.
• Remove from heat and add butter, peanut butter and vanilla; stir until melted. Serve warm or cold over ice cream. Makes 1¾ cups.

PEANUT/SOUR CREAM CANDY

Recipe from a peanut grower's wife

2 c. sugar
⅛ tsp. salt
1 c. dairy sour cream
⅛ tsp. ground cinnamon
½ tsp. vanilla
3 drops almond extract
1 c. peanuts

• Mix sugar, salt and cream in 2-qt. heavy saucepan; boil gently, without stirring, to firm ball stage (245°). Cool to lukewarm (110°); add flavorings and beat until creamy.
• Fold in peanuts. Pour into buttered 8" square pan. When cool, cut in squares. Makes 36 squares.

SKILLET TOASTED PEANUTS

• Sauté 1 c. raw, shelled peanuts in 2 tblsp. butter or regular margarine about 5 minutes. Drain on paper toweling, and sprinkle with salt.

Finger-food Nibbles

Among the most casual refreshments to share with guests of all ages are nibbles or snacks eaten with the fingers. They should never be messy, but be a thoughtful hostess and keep a stack of paper napkins nearby just in case they're needed. The variety of these friendly snacks is almost endless. Those you make with breakfast cereals–Spicy Crunch, for instance–especially delight the younger crowd.

Popcorn may be old-fashioned, but it's popular as ever. We give you some new ways to fix it: Oven-made Caramel Corn for example. Set out mugs of cider or apple juice to accompany popped corn and you'll not need to coax family or guests to help themselves.

End an evening of visiting or bridge with candy—pass a plate of Prize-winning Fudge, Pioneer Potato Candy or Virginia Peanut Brittle and refill the coffee cups. You'll send your guests out in a happy frame of mind.

PEANUT CHEWS

Peanut butter fans will like these crunchy snacks, cousins of cookies

- 9 c. corn flakes
- 1½ c. sugar
- ¼ tsp. salt
- ¾ c. light corn syrup
- ¼ c. butter or regular margarine
- ¾ c. water
- 2 tsp. vanilla
- ½ c. crunchy peanut butter

· Place corn flakes in a bowl.
· Combine sugar, salt, syrup, butter and water. Bring to a boil and reduce heat. Cook to hard ball stage (250°), using care not to overcook.
· Remove from heat and stir in vanilla and peanut butter. Pour over corn flakes. Toss with fork to completely cover corn flakes with syrup. Work quickly.
· Drop mixture in clusters onto waxed paper. Makes about 40 (2½″) clusters.

SPICY CRUNCH

Raisins and nuts make this a real treat

- 3 c. oat puffs (cereal circles)
- 2 c. bite-size shredded rice biscuits
- 2 c. bite-size shredded corn biscuits
- 2 c. bite-size shredded wheat biscuits
- 1 c. raisins
- 1 c. pecan halves
- ½ c. butter or regular margarine
- 1⅓ c. brown sugar, firmly packed
- ¼ c. light corn syrup
- 2 tsp. ground cinnamon
- ½ tsp. salt

· Butter a large bowl; toss cereals, raisins and pecans in it to mix.
· Combine butter, brown sugar, corn syrup, cinnamon and salt in a heavy skillet. Stir constantly over medium heat until boiling. Boil 3 minutes.
· Pour hot syrup over cereal mixture; stir to coat thoroughly.
· Spread on two buttered baking sheets. Cool. When firm, break into pieces. Makes about 2½ quarts.

COCONUT CRISPS

Cookie-like bars, luscious with dates, nuts and snowy coconut topknots

- 6 c. oven-toasted rice cereal
- 1 c. chopped walnuts
- ¾ c. butter or regular margarine
- 1¼ c. sugar
- 2 tblsp. milk
- ¼ tsp. salt
- 1 c. chopped dates
- 1 tblsp. vanilla
- 2 tblsp. lemon juice
- 1 (3½ oz.) can flaked coconut

· Combine cereal and walnuts in greased 13 × 9 × 2″ pan.
· Combine butter, sugar, milk, salt and dates. Cook to the soft ball stage (240°); stir occasionally. Remove from heat; add vanilla and lemon juice.
· Pour hot syrup over cereal mixture and stir lightly to coat cereal. Spread mixture evenly in pan. Sprinkle coconut over top and press mixture firmly into pan.

• Let set 4 hours or longer. When firm, cut in 3 × 1¼″ bars. Makes 30.

STRAWBERRY DIVINITY

Color is pretty, berry flavor is good

- **3 c. sugar**
- **¾ c. light corn syrup**
- **¾ c. water**
- **2 egg whites**
- **1 (3 oz.) pkg. strawberry flavor gelatin**
- **1 c. broken or cut-up nuts**

• Combine sugar, corn syrup and water in 3-qt. heavy saucepan. Cook over medium heat, stirring constantly until sugar dissolves. If sugar crystals form on sides of pan, wipe them off. Continue cooking to the hard ball stage (252°).

• Meanwhile, beat egg whites until stiff, but not dry; blend in gelatin.

• When syrup reaches 252°, pour in a thin stream over egg whites, beating constantly with electric mixer on medium speed. Beat as long as possible, using wooden spoon if mixture becomes too stiff for mixer.

• Add nuts and pour into lightly buttered 9″ square pan. When cool and firm, cut in 36 pieces. Makes about 2 pounds.

CHOCOLATE RIPPLE DIVINITY

White candy marbled with chocolate

- **2 c. sugar**
- **½ c. water**
- **½ c. light corn syrup**
- **⅛ tsp. salt**
- **2 egg whites**
- **1 tsp. vanilla**
- **1 (6 oz.) pkg. semisweet chocolate pieces**

• Combine sugar, water, corn syrup and salt in a 2-qt. heavy saucepan. Cook over low heat, stirring constantly until sugar is dissolved. If sugar crystals form on sides of pan, wipe them off. Cook to hard ball stage (252°) without stirring.

• Beat egg whites until stiff. Pour hot syrup slowly over egg whites, beating constantly. Add vanilla. Continue beating by hand or with electric mixer on medium speed until mixture begins to lose its gloss and a small amount dropped from a spoon holds soft peaks. (If the candy gets too stiff for the mixer, complete the beating with a wooden spoon.)

• Fold in chocolate pieces quickly and drop from teaspoon onto buttered waxed paper. Makes 24 pieces, or about 1 pound.

SEA FOAM

Walnuts glorify this creamy candy

- **1¾ c. light brown sugar, firmly packed**
- **¾ c. sugar**
- **½ c. hot water**
- **¼ c. light corn syrup**
- **¼ tsp. salt**
- **2 egg whites**
- **1 tsp. vanilla**
- **½ c. broken walnuts (optional)**

• Combine sugars, water, corn syrup and salt in 2-qt. heavy saucepan. Cook, stirring constantly, until sugars dissolve and mixture reaches a boil. If sugar crystals form on sides of pan, wipe them off. Continue cooking, without stirring, at a fairly low boil to the hard ball stage (260°). Remove from heat.

• At once beat egg whites until stiff. Pour hot syrup in thin stream over egg whites, beating constantly with electric mixer on high speed. Add vanilla; continue beating until candy forms soft peaks and starts to lose its gloss (this will take about 10 minutes).

• Stir in nuts. Drop rounded teaspoonfuls onto waxed paper, swirling candy to make peaks. Makes 30 to 36 pieces, or about 1 pound.

FRUITED SEA FOAM

Mixed fruits sparkle in snowy candy

3 c. sugar
⅔ c. water
½ c. light corn syrup
2 egg whites
⅛ tsp. salt
½ tsp. vanilla
1 c. candied mixed fruits

• Combine sugar, water and syrup in a 2-qt. heavy saucepan. Cook, stirring constantly, until sugar dissolves and mixture reaches a boil. If sugar crystals form on sides of pan, wipe them off. Boil to the hard ball stage (252°).

• Combine egg whites and salt, beat until stiff. Pour hot syrup over egg whites, beating constantly until mixture loses gloss.

• Add vanilla and beat until mixture forms peaks. Fold in candied mixed fruit, reserving 2 tblsp. for topping. Pour into buttered 8″ square pan. Scatter reserved mixed fruit on top. When cool and firm, cut in squares. Makes about 36 pieces or 1½ pounds.

VIRGINIA PEANUT BRITTLE

Boys' favorite—mothers who find it at church sales take some home

2 c. sugar
1 c. light corn syrup
1 c. water
2 c. unroasted peanuts, cut in pieces
¼ tsp. salt
1 tsp. butter or regular margarine
¼ tsp. baking soda

• Combine sugar, corn syrup and water in a 12″ heavy skillet. Cook slowly over medium heat, stirring constantly until sugar is dissolved. Continue cooking until mixture reaches the soft ball stage (236°).

• Add peanuts and salt; cook to just beyond the soft crack stage (290 to 300°). Add butter and soda, stirring to blend (mixture will foam).

• Pour onto 2 large buttered baking sheets or 2 inverted buttered large pans. Lift candy around edges with spatula and run spatula under candy to cool it partially and keep it from sticking. While candy is still warm, but firm, turn it over and pull edges to make the brittle thinner in the center. When cold, break into pieces with knife handle. Makes about 2¼ pounds.

CONFECTIONERS SUGAR FUDGE

Clock tells you when candy is done

2 (1 lb.) pkgs. confectioners sugar
2 (6 oz.) cans evaporated milk (1⅓ c.)
2 tblsp. butter
2 (6 oz.) pkgs. semisweet chocolate pieces
6 tblsp. marshmallow creme
1 c. chopped nuts

• Combine sugar, milk and butter in 3-qt. heavy saucepan. Bring to a boil, stirring constantly. Boil 4 minutes.

• Add chocolate pieces and marshmallow creme. Beat until chocolate melts and fudge thickens. Add nuts.

• Turn into buttered 8″ square pan.

When cool and firm, cut in 36 or 49 pieces. Makes about 3 pounds.

CARAMEL WALNUT ROLL

Crunchy walnuts coat buttery candy

- **1¼ c. light brown sugar, firmly packed**
- **½ c. sugar**
- **1⅓ c. dark corn syrup**
- **6 tblsp. butter**
- **1 c. evaporated milk**
- **½ tsp. vanilla**
- **⅛ tsp. salt**
- **2 c. walnut halves**

· Combine sugars and syrup in 3-qt. heavy saucepan. Bring to a boil over medium heat, stirring constantly. Cook until syrup reaches firm ball stage (245°) and is thick.

· Add butter, stirring to melt. Slowly add evaporated milk so mixture continues to boil, stirring constantly. Continue cooking until mixture again reaches 245°. Remove from heat, add vanilla and salt.

· Pour into buttered 13 × 9 × 2″ pan. Cool until candy is firm enough to handle easily.

· Spread walnut halves on waxed paper measuring the same size as pan. Turn candy out on top of walnuts and roll as for jelly roll, pressing nuts into caramel.

· Divide roll into thirds and make 3 small rolls. Wrap rolls in waxed paper or slice and wrap pieces individually in waxed paper. Makes 3 small rolls or 3 dozen pieces.

BEST-EVER CHOCOLATE FUDGE

Milk chocolate gives this big batch of moist fudge its special taste

- **1 c. butter or regular margarine (2 sticks)**
- **4½ c. sugar**
- **1 (7 oz.) jar marshmallow creme (about 2 c.)**
- **1 (14½ oz.) can evaporated milk (1⅔ c.)**
- **8 (1½ oz.) milk chocolate bars, broken in pieces**
- **1 (12 oz.) pkg. semisweet chocolate pieces**
- **2 c. chopped walnuts**

· Combine butter, sugar, marshmallow creme and evaporated milk in 3-qt. heavy saucepan. Bring to a boil over medium to low heat, stirring constantly until sugar dissolves. Boil steadily over low heat 7 minutes, stirring occasionally. Keep mixture at a fairly low boil all the time. The saucepan will be almost full of the cooking mixture.

· Remove from heat. Add milk chocolate bars, chocolate pieces and nuts; stir until chocolate is melted and blended into mixture.

· Pour at once into two lightly buttered 9″ square pans. While warm, mark candy in each pan in 64 pieces, or pieces the size you like; when cool and firm, cut. Makes about 5½ pounds.

PRIZE-WINNING FUDGE

Creamy with a rich chocolate flavor

- **1 (12 oz.) pkg. semisweet chocolate pieces**
- **3 (4 oz.) bars sweet cooking chocolate**
- **1 (7 oz.) jar marshmallow creme (about 2 c.)**
- **4½ c. sugar**
- **⅛ tsp. salt**
- **2 tblsp. butter or regular margarine**
- **1 (14½ oz.) can evaporated milk (1⅔ c.)**
- **2 c. chopped walnuts**

· Put chocolate pieces, cooking

chocolate and marshmallow creme in bowl.

· Combine sugar, salt, butter and evaporated milk in 3-qt. heavy saucepan. Bring to a boil, stirring until sugar dissolves. Boil steadily over medium heat 6 minutes (keep boiling all the time). Stir constantly to prevent scorching.

· Pour boiling syrup over chocolate and marshmallow creme in bowl; beat until chocolate is melted. Stir in walnuts.

· Pour into a lightly buttered 13 × 9 × 2″ pan. Let cool until firm. Cut in 77 or the desired number of pieces. When cold, pack in airtight containers and store in a cold place. Makes about 5 pounds.

AMERICAN-STYLE NOUGAT

Simply delicious—everyone asks for another piece of this favorite

Part 1:

1½ c. sugar
1¼ c. light corn syrup
¼ c. water
3 small egg whites

Part 2:

3 c. sugar
3 c. light corn syrup
4 tsp. vanilla
½ c. melted butter
1 tsp. salt
3 c. blanched, delicately toasted and slivered almonds

· To make Part 1, combine sugar, corn syrup and water in a 3-qt. heavy saucepan. Cook over medium heat, stirring until sugar dissolves. Continue to cook at a low boil to the soft ball stage (238°).

· When syrup reaches 230°, beat egg whites until they stand in peaks.

· When syrup reaches 238°, add it in a fine stream to egg whites, beating constantly with electric mixer on medium speed, or with a wooden spoon, until mixture becomes thick and is lukewarm. It will keep several days if well covered with waxed paper and stored in the refrigerator.

· To make Part 2, combine sugar and corn syrup in 4-qt. heavy saucepan. Cook over medium heat, stirring constantly, to the soft crack stage (275°).

· Meanwhile, place Part 1 in lightly buttered large bowl. Pour hot candy (Part 2) over it all at one time. Mix with heavy wooden spoon. Slowly add vanilla and butter, continuing to mix with heavy wooden spoon.

· Add salt and nuts, mix again. Turn into two well-buttered 9″ square pans, flattening top of candy with buttered hands. Let stand several hours.

· Turn onto cutting board and cut each pan of candy into 81 squares, or the desired number of pieces, and wrap with waxed paper. Makes about 5 pounds.

Pioneer Potato Candy

Potato candy is an "I remember" sweet—there was bustling excitement in grandmothers' kitchens when this treat was made for the Christmas holidays. Grandchildren of those days haven't forgotten how wonderful it tasted.

A FARM JOURNAL reader recently wrote from Iowa: "Last year the kids came from Grandma's with the recipe for potato candy and a sample of it. I hardly could believe you could make such wonderful candy with potatoes. I tried the recipe and had success with it."

Our recipe for Pioneer Potato Candy, contributed by a Wisconsin homemaker, gives the measurement of cooked, unseasoned, mashed potatoes. Potatoes have a high water content, which depends on the climate (dry or wet season), the time of year (new potatoes contain more water than old ones), and the variety. The amount of water in the potatoes affects the quantity of confectioners sugar you need to add.

The trick is to add enough sugar to produce a candy mixture with the consistency of a stiff dough so that you can knead it. The result is a type of fondant that you can dip in melted chocolate and roll in chopped nuts or coconut. Or you can omit the dipping and decorate the candy pieces with nuts. This, like all other potato candies, is at its best when eaten fresh. This is a big recipe; you may wish to make half of it the first time.

PIONEER POTATO CANDY

For true pioneer candy, omit peanuts and chocolate, more recent additions

1 c. warm unseasoned mashed potatoes
½ tsp. salt
2 tsp. vanilla
2 lbs. confectioners sugar
1 lb. chocolate confection coating or chocolate for dipping
⅔ c. ground salted peanuts, or 1 c. shredded coconut

• Combine potatoes, salt and vanilla in a 4-qt. mixing bowl. Sift confectioners sugar over potatoes, stirring and adding about 1 c. at a time. Mixture will liquefy when first sugar is added, then gradually begin to thicken. When it becomes the consistency of stiff dough, knead it even though all the sugar has not been added (likewise, add more sugar if needed).

• After kneading, cover with a damp cloth; chill until a small spoonful can be rolled into a ball.

• Shape in small (½") balls. Dip balls in melted chocolate, then roll in peanuts or coconut. Makes about 8 dozen ½" balls, or 2 pounds.

Note: Chocolate confection coatings look like chocolate, but are a blend of such ingredients as sugar, hard vegetable shortening, cocoa, chocolate flavoring, salt and vanilla. They are marketed by the pound in both dark and milk chocolate flavors. You can find them in candy supply stores, in some supermarkets around the holidays and in catalogues of reliable mail order houses. Because they are less sensitive to heat than other chocolates for dipping, candy-makers consider them an especially good choice for summer use. *Dipping chocolate* comes in large chunks and is sold by the pound in candy stores and supply houses, in some supermarkets and at candy counters in variety stores (once known as dime stores). *Semisweet chocolate* comes in 8-ounce packages and is available in practically every food store. It is more expensive than regular dipping chocolate, but many candy-makers find it more convenient when they dip only a pound or two of candy.

Famous Partners–Crackers and Cheese

CHEESE CRACKERS

The cheese is in the crisp crackers

- 1½ c. sifted flour
- ½ tsp. salt
- 1 tblsp. chopped chives
- ½ c. butter or regular margarine
- ½ lb. sharp process cheese, grated (2 c.)

· Combine flour, salt and chives.

· Cream together butter and cheese. Add flour and mix well.

· Roll into 1″ balls; place on ungreased baking sheet. Flatten to about ¼″ thickness (bottom of glass tumbler good for this). Prick top with a fork.

· Bake in moderate oven (350°) 12 to 15 minutes. Good with dips. Makes 5 dozen crackers.

CHEESE BONBONS

Great with coffee or tea–a welcome change from sweet accompaniments

- ¾ c. shortening (part butter)
- 1½ c. shredded sharp cheese
- ¼ c. grated Parmesan cheese
- 1½ c. sifted flour
- 1 tsp. salt
- 1 tsp. paprika
- Small pecan halves

· Cream shortening until light and fluffy; add cheese.

· Sift together dry ingredients; add to creamed mixture and mix well.

· Form dough into small balls about 1″ in diameter; put on ungreased baking sheet about 1″ apart. Place pecan half on each. Bake in moderate oven (350°) 15 minutes. Makes about 6 dozen.

Corn's Popping

Popcorn and winter evenings go together in the country. Muffled sounds of kernels bursting inside the popper are tantalizing music. Popcorn balls make ideal party food for youngsters. The following recipes for fun-time popcorn come from country kitchens.

POPCORN BALLS

Packages of the white balls go from home to youngsters away at school

- 5 qts. popped corn
- 4 c. sugar
- 2 tsp. salt
- 1 c. water
- 2 tblsp. butter or regular margarine
- ¼ tsp. cream of tartar

· Turn popped corn into bowl. Cook other ingredients to firm ball stage (245°). Pour syrup over corn, stirring gently to coat kernels.

· Butter hands and quickly shape corn into 3″ balls. Makes 20 balls.

CHOCOLATE POPCORN BALLS

Here's just the snack for nibblers with a sweet tooth who like chocolate

- 5 c. popped corn
- 1 c. sugar
- ½ c. water
- ⅓ c. light corn syrup
- 3 tblsp. butter or regular margarine
- 3 squares unsweetened chocolate, melted

· Place popped corn in large bowl.
· Bring remaining ingredients to a boil and cook to the hard ball stage (254°). Pour slowly over popped corn. Mix quickly. Butter hands and shape into 2″ balls. Makes 12 balls.

MOLASSES POPCORN BALLS

Molasses provides the old-time flavor

1¾ c. light molasses
2 c. sugar
⅔ c. water
2 tsp. vinegar
½ tsp. baking soda
3½ qts. popped corn, salted

· Combine molasses, sugar, water and vinegar. Cook to hard ball stage (250°). Remove from heat; wipe crystals off pan.
· Add soda; stir to mix thoroughly. Pour over corn, mixing well. Shape into 2½″ balls. Makes 10 balls.

TRICKS WITH POPPED CORN

CHEESE: Add ⅓ c. dry, grated sharp cheese to ¼ c. melted butter. Pour over freshly popped, salted corn; toss lightly and serve at once.

PEANUT: When melting butter to pour over hot popped corn, add a spoonful of peanut butter. It blends with the butter and gives a pleasing flavor.

POPCORN VALENTINE: Press popped corn, coated with syrup, into heart-shaped mold or molds while it is warm and pliable. Allow to cool. Turn out on plate. Slice to serve. Syrup may be tinted pink before it is poured over corn.

QUICK CARAMEL CORN: Melt ½ lb. light caramel candy with 2 tblsp. water over boiling water; stir to make smooth sauce. Pour mixture over 2 qts. salted popcorn to coat kernels; spread on lightly greased baking sheet. Cool; break apart.

POPCORN-ON-STICKS: Grease hands lightly; then form popcorn cylinders to put on sticks. You can make cylinders by lightly pressing syrup-coated corn into small, greased juice cans. Remove can bottoms to push out cylinders. Insert a wooden skewer into every cylinder.

MARSHMALLOW POPCORN BALLS

No candy thermometer needed

1 c. popcorn (unpopped)
1 tsp. salt
¼ c. butter or regular margarine
½ lb. marshmallows

· Pop corn; sprinkle with salt.
· Melt butter in skillet. Cut marshmallows in quarters. Alternate layers of popcorn and marshmallows in skillet.
· Cover; heat slowly until marshmallows are partially melted. Mix well; form into 2″ balls. Makes 9 balls.

POPCORN NIBBLE-ONS

Great to nibble on when sipping fruit or tomato juice or eating apples

3 qts. popped corn
2 c. cheese snack crackers or nibblers
2 c. salted Spanish peanuts
2 c. pretzel sticks
⅓ c. melted butter
½ tsp. bottled steak sauce
½ tsp. garlic salt
½ tsp. onion salt
½ tsp. curry powder
½ tsp. salt

· Combine popped corn, crackers, peanuts and pretzels in large roasting pan.
· Combine remaining ingredients and add to first mixture. Toss to mix.
· Heat in very slow oven (250°) about 1 hour, stirring every 15 minutes. Cool. Store in airtight container. Makes about 4½ quarts.

Note: These Popcorn Nibble-ons can be made ahead, packed in airtight containers and stored in the freezer. They will keep for several months, and are good to have on hand to serve guests.

OVEN-MADE CARAMEL CORN

Be ready for evening callers–make this inexpensive snack the new way

5 qts. popped corn
1 c. butter or regular margarine (2 sticks)
2 c. brown sugar, firmly packed
½ c. light corn syrup
1 tsp. salt
½ tsp. baking soda

· Spread freshly popped corn in a large, shallow sheet pan. Put it in a very slow oven (250°) to keep warm and crisp.
· Combine butter, brown sugar, corn syrup and salt in 2-qt. heavy saucepan. Place over medium heat, stirring until sugar dissolves. Continue to boil to the firm ball stage (248°), about 5 minutes.
· Remove from heat and stir in baking soda. Syrup will foam.
· Take popped corn from oven and pour hot caramel mixture over it in a fine stream. Stir to mix well. Return to oven for 45 to 50 minutes, stirring every 15 minutes. Cool and serve, or store.
· To store, pour into airtight containers and set in a cold place. Makes about 5 quarts, or almost 2 pounds.

HONEYED POPCORN BALLS

Brown sugar and honey make them good

1½ qts. unbuttered popped corn, salted
½ c. brown sugar, firmly packed
½ c. sugar
¼ c. honey or light or dark corn syrup
⅓ c. water
1 tblsp. butter

· Put popped corn in a large bowl or metal dishpan; place in warm oven (225°).
· Combine sugars, honey and water in 2-qt. heavy saucepan. Heat slowly, stirring until sugar is dissolved. Cook to firm ball stage (242°). Add butter and stir only enough to mix. Slowly pour the hot syrup over warm popped corn; mix thoroughly.
· With buttered palms and fingers, shape immediately into balls slightly larger than a baseball, using as little pressure as possible. Makes twelve 2″ popcorn balls.

chapter 17

Praise-winning Food for All Occasions

THIS COOKBOOK contains recipes for dishes to fit many situations. As you leaf through the pages, you will discover many you'll want to try for dishes to serve at social gatherings, take to food sales and bazaars, prepare for the holidays and other events as well as for your ordinary family dinners. Here are lists of some of the specialties tailored to meet different occasions exceptionally well. These are samplers, or suggestions—there are many others. To locate the recipes, see the Index.

Dishes to Tote

Country foods are good travelers. Foods you carry need to be sturdy enough to hold up during their journeys, attractive enough to get favorable attention when set out before the crowd and so tasty that you'll be asked again to bring them to other suppers. Here are favorites you'll want to try:

Western Baked Beans
Spanish Limas
Winter Take-along Casserole
Green Rice
Potato/Cheese Scallop
Eggplant Parmigiana
Scalloped Sweet Potatoes and Apples
Homey Scalloped Corn
Cinnamon/Chocolate Cake
Polka Dot Picnic Cake
Chocolate Angel Food Cake
Ambrosia Chiffon Cake
Chocolate Cherry Cake
Grand Champion Sponge Cake
Rocky Mountain Cake
Date/Oatmeal Cake
Oatmeal Pie
Frosted Big Apple Pie
Tawny Pumpkin Pie
Veal Loaf
Easy-serve Baked Ham
Harvest Ham Balls
Stuffed Meat Loaf
Meat Ball Stew
Mazetti
Macaroni Meat Ball Soufflé
Lasagne Casserole
Spring Asparagus and Egg Bake
Cashew Tuna Luncheon

Apple/Cranberry Crisp
Peanut Butter Chiffon Pie
Fresh Fruit Cobblers
Concord Grape Cobblers
Stay-crisp Cabbage Salad
Golden Macaroni Salad
Cabbage/Onion Salad
Sauerkraut Salad
Glazed Fruit Salad
Homemade Noodles
Brown Potato Soup
Floating Vegetable Salad
Fermented Dill Pickles
Mulberry Pie
Rosy Crab Apple Pie
Elderberry Apple Pie
Raisin Griddle Cookies
Homemade Mixer-Butter
Homemade Cottage Cheese

Old-fashioned Country Specials

A revival of interest in many old-time specials is sweeping the countryside. These are foods that taste so good no one wants to forget them. Home economists in our Countryside Test Kitchens updated recipes for the old-fashioned treats that appear in this cookbook, but they retained the memorable flavors. These dishes will give your meals the true country taste. You'll find a fine assortment of them all through this book, but here is a sampling.

Old-fashioned Lemonade
Pressed Chicken
Country-fried Green Tomatoes
Green Tomato Mincemeat
Venison Mincemeat
Glass-jar Sauerkraut
Stone-jar Sauerkraut
Oven Apple Butter
Apple/Geranium Jelly
Twentieth-century Hominy
Buckwheat Cakes
Yeast Waffles
Sour Dough Biscuits
Silver Dollar Hotcakes
Pioneer Potato Candy
Pumpkin Cake
Sweet Cream Cake
Potato Chocolate Cake
Lemon Cheese Cake

Money Makers

Homemade food sells well in many communities and brings in cash to help support churches and many worthy causes. It often earns money for good home cooks who find a market for their specialties. Many recipes in this cookbook produce food with sales appeal. The list that follows is for some of those that proved their earning capacity at food bazaars and sales.

Chicken Tamales
Pineapple/Carrot Marmalade
Lemon/Carrot Marmalade
American-style Nougat
Strawberry Divinity
Virginia Peanut Brittle
Confectioners Sugar Fudge
Sea Foam
Fruited Sea Foam
Orange Walnuts
Peanut Chews
Chocolate/Nut Loaf
Applesauce Fruitcake
Date/Nut Cake
Two-tone Pound Cake
Brown Sugar Pound Cake
Jeweled Pound Cake
Fruitcake Bonbons
Cinnamon/Chocolate Cake
Holiday Cranberry Cake
Carrot/Pecan Spice Cake

Date/Oatmeal Cake
Date/Pecan Pie
Chocolate/Pecan Pie
Maple-glazed Apple Pie
Jumbo Sugar Cookies
Pineapple/Date Loaf
Carrot Sandwich Bread
Swedish Rye Bread Supreme
Orange/Nut-glazed Raisin Bread
Old-fashioned Oatmeal Bread
Honey Whole Wheat Bread
Oatmeal/Molasses Cookies

For Women's Luncheons

Bring on beautiful salads and piping hot, buttered rolls. This is the type of food most women rate tops for luncheon parties. You will observe that many of the following recipe suggestions are for hearty salads. That's because they take the main-dish role. Some hostesses like to serve a dessert. To decide for or against providing a sweet ending, consider how serious your guests are about cutting down on their calorie intake.

Avocado/Strawberry Ring
Mint Julepeach Salad
Salad Niçoise
Regal Chicken Salad
Jellied Egg Salad
Pea/Shrimp Salad
Fruit Salad Plate
Garden Loaf Salad
Jellied Beef Mold
Frozen Fruit Salad-Dessert
Baked Asparagus/Cheese Sandwich
Pink Party Pie
Strawberry Parfait Ring
Lemon Mist
Lemon Daffodil Dessert
Pears Cardinale
Fresh Fruit Compote
Coconut/Honey Ice Cream
Ice Cream in Orange Shells
Strawberry/Buttermilk Sherbet

Having Dinner Guests?

When guests come to dinner or supper in the country, the hostess sets before them what she considers her best food. Select recipes from the following suggestions and you can be confident of their success.

Country-style Beef Wellington
Beef and Rigatoni Stew
Glazed Pork Roast
Fresh Pork Pot Roast with Dumplings
Rosy Ham Ring
Cranberry/Orange-glazed Ham
Marinated Lamb Roast
Roast Veal with Sweet Onions
Pork Chops with Apples
Salmon Loaf with Shrimp Sauce
Shrimp Marengo
Smoky Cottage Cheese Dip
Nippy Cheese Dip
Cream Cheese and Clam Dip
Vegetables on Picks
Curried Egg Dip for Vegetables
Texas Chili Dip
Hot Snack Packs
Crusty Fried Chicken
Roast Ducklings in Lemon/Carrot Sauce
Chicken-stuffed Pancakes
Roast Young Chickens
Nippy Cheese Loaf
Ribbon Sandwich Loaf
Catalina Tossed Salad
Sherbet Salad Dressing

Farmhouse Green Salad with
  Cheese/Garlic Dressing
Sour Cream Dressing
Hot Slaw with Apples
Stay-crisp Cabbage Salad
Sweepstakes Potato Salad
Baked German Salad
Corn-stuffed Tomatoes
Walnut Carrots
Italian Eggplant
American-Chinese Asparagus
Fresh Broccoli with Orange Sauce
Corn Curry
New Peas in Cream
Peas and Cabbage
Pineapple Beets
Potato Roses
Refrigerator Mashed Potatoes
Sunshine Potato Balls
Golden Rutabaga Ring
Twice-baked Rolls
Sweet Potato Biscuits
Refrigerator Bran Muffins
Molded Rhubarb Swirl
Favorite Fudge Cake
Poppy Seed Layer Cake
14-Carat Cake
Fudge/Lemon Cake
Melon-boat Cocktail
Fruit and Sherbet Cocktail
Ruby Punch
Pineapple Glow
Royal Ade
Cucumber Cool Soup
Frosty Spanish Vegetable Soup
Potato Soup with Dumplings
Vichyssoise
Golden Raisin Pie
Strawberry Satin Pie
Burgundy Berry Pie
Chocolate/Orange Torte
  Gingerbread
Strawberry Shortcake Royale
Crispy Sundae Crunch
Ice Cream in Orange Shells
Buffet Party Dessert
Ice Cream Birthday Cake

The Coffee Break

It's the custom in many country homes to serve coffee at mid-morning and also often sometime during the afternoon. The two-piece refreshments consist of coffee and one go-with, usually homemade bread or cookies, either freshly baked or taken from the freezer. (Some people choose tea or milk, or a cool drink in hot weather.) Here are some excellent accompaniments, whatever the beverage:

Finnish Coffee Bread
Brioche
Hot Cross Buns
Potato Doughnuts
German Blueberry Kuchen
Election Day Cake
Caramel Twists
Cinnamon/Pecan Rolls
Marmalade Coffee Cake
Sugar-top Coffee Cake
Cinnamon Leaf Ring
Candy-top Brownies
Lemon/Coconut Squares
Fruit Bars
Mincemeat/Cheese Cookies
Orange/Carrot Cookies
Frosted Ginger Creams
Molasses Butterballs
California Fig Cookies
Hampshire Hermits
Thirst-quencher
Half-and-half Cooler

Tea-Party Treats

No one has invented a more charming way to entertain friends than to invite them to come for tea.

Here are some of the recipes that will serve this occasion well:

Hot Tea for 30 to 35
Hot Tea for 200
Iced Tea for 200
Hot Spiced Tea
Hot Apple Punch
Spicy Hot Grape Punch
Spicy Perk-a-Punch
Sparkling Strawberry Punch
Mulled Apricot Nectar
Basic Cranberry Syrup
Tomato Juice in Punch Bowl
Starlight Three-fruit Punch
Limelight Banana Crush
French Chocolate
Teatime Open-face Sandwiches
Cucumber Sandwiches
Pecan Tartlets
Strawberry Chiffon Tarts
Pumpkin Chiffon Tarts
Florentines
Walnut Lace Cookies
Wild Rose Cookies
Chocolate Bonbon Cookies

Cooking for a Crowd

You don't have to live in Hawaii to entertain your friends at a luau (pig roast), but living in the country helps. There's plenty of space for guests to gather around the pit with the light of a full moon adding atmosphere. Other occasions call for country entertaining. Some of the food specials for them appear on the following list. Notice, too, that several hearty soups receive a mention. Country women like to use big recipes and to freeze the surplus soup ready to heat on cold rainy or snowy evenings for their families and guests. Country people are weather conscious; they plan meals with it in mind.

Whole Pit-roasted Pig
Big Community Barbecue
Barbecue Sauce for a Crowd
Brunswick Stew
Roast Raccoon
Bean Soup
Vegetable/Beef Soup
Minestrone
Split Pea/Vegetable Soup
Idaho Lentil Soup
French Onion Soup
Corn Chowder
Herbed Potato Soup
Creamy Cauliflower Soup
Garden Row Soup
Orange Ginger Punch
Raspberry Float
Good Luck Punch
Fruit Punch
Hot Spicy Punch
Hot Apple Punch
Tender Brown Beef Cubes
Banana Splits
Marshmallow Sauce

index